49.95

Jews and the German State

JEWISH SOCIETY AND CULTURE

General Editor DAVID SORKIN

David Bankier *The Germans and the Final Solution*
Edited by David Cesarani *The Making of Modern Anglo-Jewry*
Artur Eisenbach *The Emancipation of the Jews in Poland (1780–1870)*
Ben-Cion Pinchuk *Shtetl Jews under Soviet Rule*
Peter Pulzer *Jews and the German State*
Simon Schwarzfuchs *A History of the Rabbinate*

FORTHCOMING

Tony Kushner *The Jews in Post-War Britain*
Frances Malino *Zalkind Hourwitz: A Jew in the French Revolution*

Jewish Communities of the Modern World

Esther Benbassa & Aron Rodrigue *The Jews of Turkey*
Todd Endelman *The Jews of England*
Paula Hyman *The Jews of France*
Hillel Kieval & Michael Silber *The Jews of the Habsburg Empire*
David Sorkin *The Jews of Germany*
Norman Stillman *The Jews of North Africa*
Jack Wertheimer *The Jews of the United States*
Steven J. Zipperstein *The Jews of Russia*

Jews and the German State

The Political History of a Minority, 1848–1933

Peter Pulzer

BLACKWELL
Oxford UK & Cambridge USA

Copyright © Peter Pulzer 1992

Peter Pulzer is hereby identified as author of this work in accordance with Section 77 of the Copyright, Designs and Patents Act 1988.

First published 1992
Reprinted 1994

Blackwell Publishers
108 Cowley Road, Oxford, OX4 1JF, UK

238 Main Street
Cambridge, Massachusetts 02142, USA

British Library Cataloguing in Publication Data
A CIP catalogue record for this book is available from the British Library.

Library of Congress Cataloging in Publication Data
Pulzer, Peter G. J.
Jews and the German state: the political history of a minority,
1848–1933 / Peter Pulzer.
p.   cm.
Includes bibliographical references and index.
ISBN 0–631–17282–3
1. Jews—Germany—History—1800–1933.   2. Jews in public life—
Germany.   3. Jews—Germany—Politics and government.   4. Political
parties—Germany.   5. Germany—Politics and government—19th
century.   6. Germany—Politics and government—20th century.
7. Germany—Ethnic relations.   I. Title.
DS135.G33P85   1992
943′.004924—dc20
91–31477
CIP

Typeset in 10 on 12 pt Ehrhardt by Graphicraft Typesetters Ltd, Hong Kong
Printed in Great Britain by T.J. Press (Padstow) Ltd, Padstow, Cornwall.

This book is printed on acid-free paper.

For
Matthew and Patrick
in the hope that they
will not need its lessons

Contents

Maps

Tables

Abbreviations

ADGB	*Allgemeiner Deutscher Gewerkschaftsbund*
AfA	*Arbeitsgemeinschaft freier Angestelltenverbände*
AZJ	*Allgemeine Zeitung des Judentums*
BAK	Bundesarchiv Koblenz
BBB	*Bayerischer Bauernbund*
BdI	*Bund der Industriellen*
BdL	*Bund der Landwirte*
BLBI	*Bulletin des Leo Baeck Instituts*
BT	*Berliner Tageblatt*
BVP	*Bayerische Volkspartei*
CEH	*Central European History*
CSVD	*Christlich-Sozialer Volksdienst*
C.V.	*Centralverein deutscher Staatsbürger jüdischen Glaubens*
CVDI	*Centralverband Deutscher Industrieller*
CVZ	*C.V. – Zeitung*
DDP	*Deutsche Demokratische Partei*
DIGB	*Deutsch-Israelitischer Gemeindebund*
DIZ	*Deutsche Israelitische Zeitung*
DNHV	*Deutschnationaler Handlungsgehilfenverband*
DNVP	*Deutschnationale Volkspartei*
DStP	*Deutsche Staatspartei*
DT	*Deutsche Tageszeitung*
DVP	*Deutsche Volkspartei*
FVg	*Freisinnige Vereinigung*
FVP	*Fortschrittliche Volkspartei*
FVp	*Freisinnige Volkspartei*

FZ	*Frankfurter Zeitung*
GJR	*Geheimer Justizrat*
GKR	*Geheimer Kommerzienrat*
G St Dahlem	Geheimes Staatsarchiv Dahlem
[H]	Information given to Dr. Ernest Hamburger, New York
IdR	*Im deutschen Reich*
IGB	*Israelitisches Gemeindeblatt*
IJB	*Internationaler Jugendbund*
ISFAM	*Israelitisches Familienblatt*
ISK	*Internationaler Sozialistischer Kampfbund*
JIDG	*Jahrbuch des Instituts für Deutsche Geschichte/Jahrbuch für Deutsche Geschichte*
JM	*Jüdische Monatshefte*
JR	*Jüdische Rundschau*
JR	*Justizrat*
JSS	*Jewish Social Studies*
JVP	*Jüdische Volkspartei*
KC	*Kartell-Convent jüdischer Corporationen*
KfdO	*Komitee für den Osten*
KPD	*Kommunistische Partei Deutschlands*
KPO	*Kommunistische Partei Deutschlands-Opposition*
KR	*Kommerzienrat*
KRA	*Kriegsrohstoffabteilung*
KVZ	*Kölnische Volkszeitung*
KZ	*Kreuz-Zeitung*
JSS	*Jewish Social Studies*
LBYB	*Year Book of the Leo Baeck Institute*
MVA	*Mitteilungen des Vereins zur Abwehr des Antisemitismus*
NDAZ	*Norddeutsche Allgemeine Zeitung*
NJM	*Neue Jüdische Monatshefte*
NSDAP	*Nationalsozialistische Deutsche Arbeiterpartei*
NZ	*Die Neue Zeit*
PJ	*Preußische Jahrbücher*
PLV	*Preußischer Landesverband jüdischer Gemeinden*
RjF	*Reichsbund jüdischer Frontsoldaten*
SAG	*Sozialdemokratische Arbeitsgemeinschaft*
SAP	*Sozialistische Arbeiterpartei Deutschlands*
SPD	*Sozialdemokratische Partei Deutschlands*
SPW	*Sozialistische Politik und Wirtschaft*
StAP	Staatsarchiv Potsdam-Orangerie
StBR	*Stenographische Berichte über die Verhandlungen des deutschen Reichstages*

StBRNB	*Stenographische Berichte über die Verhandlungen des Reichstages des Norddeutschen Bundes*
StPrA	*Stenographische Berichte des Preussischen Abgeordnetenhauses*
USPD	*Unabhängige Sozialdemokratische Partei Deutschlands*
VdDJ	*Verband der Deutschen Juden*
VDSt	*Verein deutscher Studenten*
VfZ	*Vierteljahrshefte für Zeitgeschichte*
VIOD	*Vereinigung jüdischer Organisationen Deutschlands zur Wahrung der Rechte der Juden des Ostens*
V.n.J.	*Verband nationaldeutscher Juden*
VNR	*Volksnationale Reichsvereinigung*
VZ	*Vossische Zeitung*
ZEG	*Zentraleinkaufsgesellschaft*
ZfG	*Zeitschrift für Geschichtswissenschaft*
ZfP	*Zeitschrift für Politik*
ZStM	Zentrales Staatsarchiv Merseburg
ZStP	Zentrales Staatsarchiv Potsdam

Entscheidungsjahr 1932 – Werner Mosse and Arnold Paucker (eds), *Entscheidungsjahr 1932. Zur Judenfrage in der Endphase der Weimarer Republik.*

KuR – Werner Mosse and Arnold Paucker (eds), *Deutsches Judentum in Krieg und Revolution, 1916–1923.*

KuS – Karl Heinrich Rengstorf and Siegfried von Kortzfleisch (eds), *Kirche und Synagoge. Handbuch zur Geschichte von Christen und Juden.*

WD – Werner Mosse and Arnold Paucker (eds), *Juden im wilhelminischen Deutschland, 1890–1914.*

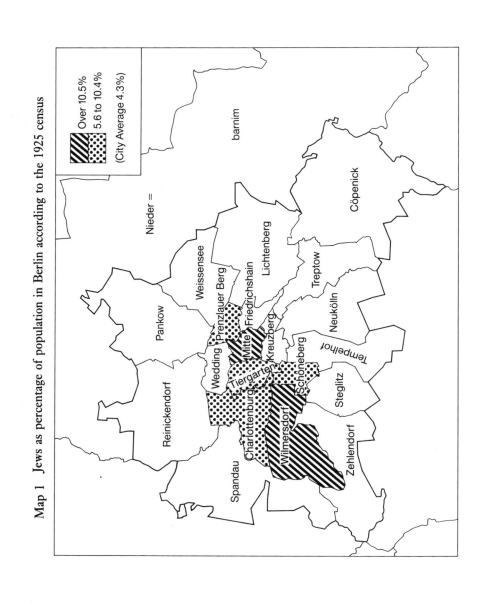

Map 1 Jews as percentage of population in Berlin according to the 1925 census

Over 10.5%

5.6 to 10.4%

(City Average 4.3%)

Nieder =

barnim

Cöpenick

Reinickendorf

Pankow

Weissensee

Wedding

Prenzlauer Berg

Friedrichshain

Lichtenberg

Mitte

Kreuzberg

Treptow

Tiergarten

Charlottenburg

Schöneberg

Neukölln

Tempelhof

Spandau

Wilmersdorf

Steglitz

Zehlendorf

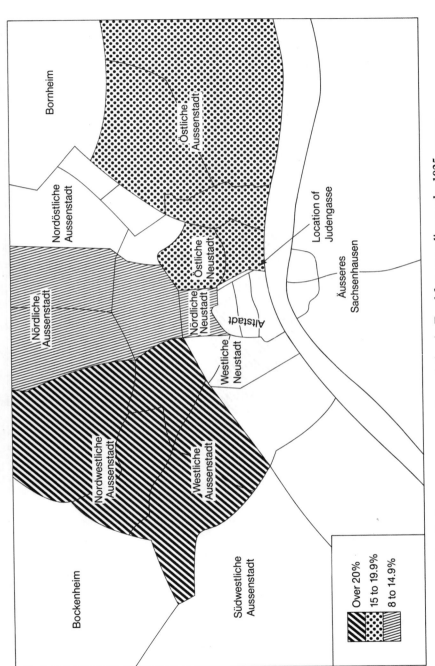

Map 2 Jews as percentage of population in Frankfurt according to the 1925 census

Bornheim

Östliche Aussenstadt

Nordöstliche Aussenstadt

Östliche Neustadt

Location of Judengasse

Äusseres Sachsenhausen

Nördliche Aussenstadt

Nördliche Neustadt

Altstadt

Westliche Neustadt

Nordwestliche Aussenstadt

Westliche Aussenstadt

Bockenheim

Südwestliche Aussenstadt

Over 20%

15 to 19.9%

8 to 14.9%

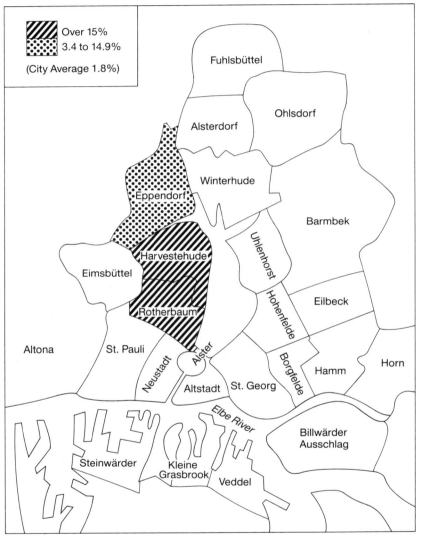

Map 3   Jews as percentage of population in Hamburg according to the 1925 census

Introduction

This is a book about a minority, one whose history is marked by peculiar achievements and peculiar vicissitudes. At the beginning of the First World War the economist Gustav von Schmoller reassured his countrymen: 'We have ... no occasion to regard the existence of 615,021 Israelites among the sixty million inhabitants of Germany as undesirable, let alone harmful.'[1] It was a sentiment of which many Jews had inwardly tried to convince themselves and which they had tried to preach to others. Had it met with general assent, this book would have no subject. The essays presented here are not, except incidentally, about the internal organization of the Jewish community or the intellectual and theological currents within it in the nineteenth and twentieth centuries, fascinating and important though those topics are. Nor are they primarily about anti-Semitism, concerning which there is now a substantial literature, except in so far as this is relevant to my main subject. What the book is about is the 'Jewish Question'; the first of the essays printed here deals with it in some detail. The Jewish Question in Germany has the same three aspects that Ralf Dahrendorf detected in the German Question: a question put by the Germans to other people, a question put by other people to the Germans and one they might well put to themselves.[2] Competing answers to the questions emerged within twelve months of each other at the beginning of the reign of the Emperor William II. On

---

1 Gustav von Schmoller, 'Die heutige Judenfrage' in *idem.*, *Zwanzig Jahre deutscher Politik, 1897–1917*, Munich and Leipzig: Duncker & Humblot, 1920, p. 179.
2 Ralf Dahrendorf, *Society and Democracy in Germany*, London: Weidenfeld and Nicolson, 1967, p. 3.

8 December 1892, the German Conservative Party, adopting its new programme in the Tivoli Hall in Berlin, proclaimed: 'We combat the widely
obtruding and decomposing Jewish influence on our popular life.'[3] In the
following March a Jewish response emerged in the form of the Central
Association of German Citizens of the Jewish Faith (*Centralverein deutscher
Staatsbürger jüdischen Glaubens*, C.V.). The first saw the Jews as a coherent,
homogeneous group, with common interests and aims, anomalous in and
harmful to the German Christian nation. The second saw them as citizens
who, though sharing a special religious and cultural heritage, in all other
respects resembled the Gentile Germans of their day in the variety of their
activities and allegiances. In this respect, therefore, the kernel of the Jewish
Question was the same in 1914 as in 1812: how far could – and should – Jews
become assimilated in (or, in the words of some of the participants in the
controversy, amalgamated with) German society? The answers varied and
divided Jewish as much as non-Jewish opinion. They were followed with
interest in much of the rest of the civilized world, since the German-Jewish
community enjoyed a leading, even dominant, intellectual position among
other Jewries. But the answers also evolved, as the structure of German Jewry
changed in ways that few had expected or were prepared for.

The principal characteristic of German Jewry in the nineteenth and early
twentieth centuries was its modernization. It emerged as one of the main
examples of what Ezra Mendelsohn has defined as the 'West European' type
of Jewish community. This is characterised by

a high degree of acculturation and aspirations to assimilation, a general tendency
to abandon both Yiddish and Orthodoxy. ... Such Jewish communities tended to be
middle class [and] highly urbanized, though they rarely constituted a remarkably high
proportion within the general urban population. The typical Western European Jewry
possessed a low birth-rate and high rate of intermarriage; its sense of Jewish identification was usually religious, not national secular.

The 'Eastern European' type, in contrast, displayed

a relative weakness of acculturation and assimilation, the preservation of Yiddish
speech and religious Orthodoxy ... and a lower middle-class and proletarian socio-
economic structure ..., a high birth-rate and a low rate of intermarriage, and, while it
was largely urban in nature, many of its members still lived in the old-style *shtetl*
(small Jewish town). ... A certain degree of acculturation and secularization had
occurred, but ... most typically led not to assimilation, but to modern Jewish nationalism of one form or another. There existed in this type of community two legitimate

3   Wolfgang Treue (ed.), *Deutsche Parteiprogramme seit 1861*, 4th edn, Göttingen:
Musterschmidt, 1968, p. 88.

forms of identity – religious (meaning almost always Orthodox ...) and national (usually secular national).[4]

Though Mendelssohn is deliberately dealing in typologies, not exact description, and though no two 'Western European' Jewish communities are alike, it is evident that German Jewry fell into the Western category, in some respects archetypally, paradigmatically and self-consciously so. This had two consequences for German-Jewish history.

The first was that the Western, 'modern' aspect of the German-Jewish community became an essential part of its identity, both in answering the question posed by others and in answering the question posed by itself. To proclaim that they had left the ghetto, that they had entered civilization, that they were not like their 'Eastern' neighbours or 'Eastern' immigrants, was a dominant theme among German Jews for much of the nineteenth century, though a more sympathetic understanding of 'Eastern' ways did emerge towards the end of our period.[5] This claim to 'Western' allegiance was frequently taken up by anti-Semites in a number of ways. There were those for whom successful Jewish assimilation was simply one aspect – in extreme cases, the single most undesirable aspect – of liberal, enlightened secularism. The successfully Westernized Jew was precisely what they disliked most about the way the world was going. Then there were those for whom Westernization had not gone far enough: those for whom the ultimate logic of emancipation and assimilation was the disappearance of the Jew as Jew, if necessary by conversion. In so far as that had not happened by the last decades of the nineteenth century, they argued that the Jews had failed to honour their part of the bargain entailed by legal emancipation. Lastly there were those who simply regarded the Westernization of the Jews as fraudulent. Behind the mask of the 'German citizen of the Jewish faith' there lurked the real, unchanged ghetto Jew, incapable of civilized behaviour either for reasons of tribal morality, as imparted, for instance, by the alleged teachings of the *Talmud*, or for reasons of racial inferiority.

The second consequence was even more problematical. If the tendency of a Western-type Jewish community was indeed to acculturate to the dominant

4   Ezra Mendelssohn, *The Jews of East Central Europe Between the World Wars*, Bloomington Ind.: Indiana University Press, 1983, pp. 6–7.
5   Steven E. Aschheim, *Brothers and Strangers. The East European Jew in German and German Jewish Consciousness, 1800–1923*, Madison, Wis.: University of Wisconsin Press, 1982, ch. 6–8; Jack Wertheimer, *Unwelcome Strangers. East European Jews in Imperial Germany*, New York and Oxford: Oxford University Press, 1987, ch. 9; Trude Maurer, *Ostjuden in Deutschland 1918–1933*, Hamburg: Hans Christians, 1986, ch. XII, XIII.

society, to abandon distinctive forms of public and private behaviour, to practise family limitation and exogamy, then sooner or later that community would disappear. It would cease to be a minority within the majority, because all the characteristics that distinguish the one from the other would have become blurred. Yet this did not happen. The Jews of Germany were still in 1914, indeed in 1933, indisputably a distinctive minority; different from what it had been, no doubt, in 1848 or 1815, but not so totally different as to be unrecognizable as its successor.

True, there were prophets of doom within the German-Jewish community who claimed that disappearance was indeed its long-term fate. They pointed to the diminishing birth-rate and the increasing rate of apostasy, conversion and inter-marriage as irrefutable evidence.[6] That all these factors caused German Jewry to fray at the edges is undeniable. The number of Jews, as defined by religious affiliation, did slowly decline both absolutely and relatively. But what projections based on these trends failed to take into account was the adaptability of German Jewry. As religious observance declined, or became more varied, other forms of identity increased in importance. This means that we have to try to resolve a paradox. How did it come about that a religious minority so strongly subjected to modernizing and secularizing pressures succeeded in preserving so much of its identity over more than a century?

The cohesion of pre-modern Jewry, in Germany as elsewhere, was not difficult to explain. Nationality, religion and economic function overlapped almost completely. That was due only in part to externally imposed restrictions. Ghettoization and exclusion from guilds, landownership and many occupations reinforced the cohesion, but did not cause it; it was but one example, admittedly in an extreme form, of the rigidities and fragmentation of European society. Religious affiliation defined everyone's identity, not just the Jew's. Gradations of privilege and subordination determined the social status and occupation of most of the population. Those who were born as peasants died as peasants.

From the second half of the eighteenth century onwards a number of developments, some external to the German-Jewish community and some originating within it, combined to break up this cohesion. The first and most important was economic change: the growth of a mercantile-industrial economy out of a predominantly 'natural' agricultural-artisan economy. The role of the Jews in this was both active and passive. Given the predominance of Jews in financial services, especially as court bankers in the 300-odd secular

6   E.g. Felix A. Theilhaber, *Der Untergang der deutschen Juden. Eine volkswirtschaftliche Studie*, Berlin: Jüdischer Verlag, 1921; Stefan Behr, *Der Bevölkerungsrückgang der deutschen Juden*, Frankfurt-am-Main: J. Kaufmann, 1932.

and ecclesiastical states, as military purveyors and administrators of monopolies, they were in an excellent position to initiate and lubricate the economic expansion of the nineteenth century and in some instances to influence
its direction.

However, the number of Jews involved in court and private banking from
the middle of the eighteenth to the middle of the nineteenth century was
small: probably not more than one thousand in all at a time when the total
Jewish population of the German states was about a quarter of a million. But
in the course of time almost all of Germany's Jews were affected by the surge
of economic modernization. Whatever their occupation, they were inexorably
sucked into general society. Inter-action with non-Jews, which had been the
exception, often deliberately avoided, now became the inescapable norm.
With this development one of the chief defences against the dilution of
Jewishness was weakened.

Increased inter-action was determined not only by economic change, but
by migration. Modernization meant urbanization. In the course of the nineteenth century the Jews of Germany all but deserted the villages and small
towns that had been their homes and flocked to the major cities, especially the
capital, Berlin. By 1910 a quarter of Germany's Jews lived in Berlin, by 1933
three out of ten lived there and seven out of ten in cities of over 100,000
inhabitants. The movement of population was from places with strong Jewish
cohesion to places with weak cohesion.

A further development that accompanied the change in the social structure
of German Jews and which threatened Jewish cohesion was the Enlightenment and particularly its Jewish form, the *Haskalah*, and the consequent
emergence of Reform Judaism. The *Haskalah* and Reform Judaism arose out
of increasing inter-action, but were also designed to encourage it. Both were
symptoms of dissatisfaction with existing Jewish religious and intellectual life,
heavily influenced by the unfavourable view of the Jewish religion held by the
leading philosophers of the day, including Kant and Hegel.[7] They challenged
two of the strongest traditional sources of authority within European Judaism,

---

7 Immanuel Kant, *Die Religion innerhalb der Grenzen der bloßen Vernunft* (1793),
in *Werke* (ed. Ernst Cassirer), Berlin: de Gruyter 1923, vol. VI, pp. 139–353, esp.
pp. 272–8; *idem, Religion within the Limits of Reason Alone* (trans. and ed. Theodore
M. Greene and Hoyt H. Hudson), New York: Harper, 1960, pp. 116–21; Georg
Friedrich Wilhelm Hegel, *Die Positivität der christlichen Religion* (1796), in *Hegels
Theologische Jugendschriften* (ed. Harmann Nohl), Tübingen: J. C. B. Mohr, 1907, pp.
148–51, 244–60; *idem, Early Theological Writings* (trans. T. M. Knox), Chicago:
University of Chicago Press, 1948, pp. 177–205; Hans Liebeschütz, *Das Judentum
im deutschen Geschichtsbild von Hegel bis Max Weber*, Tübingen: J. C. B. Mohr, 1967,
pp. 24–42.

the *Talmud* and the rabbis, by claiming a place for the secular scholar and by borrowing from non-Jewish thinkers:

> The new outlook necessitated a re-evaluation of the culture of the surrounding non-Jewish society which was no longer seen as an alien religious and national tradition, but rather as the fruit of human creative powers and thus part of a common universal heritage. ... The belief that humanism had become the guiding principle of the political leadership and educated classes of European society led to the conclusion that there could be a new basis for the relationship between Jews and their surroundings. Jewish cultural, political and social involvement in their surroundings now appeared to be a desirable and feasible goal.[8]

The culmination of these developments was the creation in 1818 of the *Wissenschaft des Judentums* ('Scholarship of Judaism') by a number of leading reform theologians. Under one name or another the institutions of the *Wissenschaft* were the leading academies of Judaism in Germany until their closure in 1938.[9]

The effect of these teachings and their increasing acceptance by German Jews was to break one of the main links that had bound together pre-modern Jewry, that between nationality and religion, between Judaism and Jewishness. The ideal of the enlightened Reform Jew was to become a German citizen of the Jewish faith, to take his place in the German nation on the basis of religious pluralism.

Parallel with this narrowing of the definition of Jewishness, and the move into surrounding society – surrounding urban, middle-class society, to be more precise – went the decline of a major force in Jewish socialization, the Jewish school. The most spectacular symptom of this was the well-documented surge of Jews into secondary and higher education, which began as early as the 1840s and which was a most conspicuous aspect of the entry of the Jews into the secular world.[10] But this affected only a minority of the

8   Emanuel Etkes, 'Immanent Factors and External Influences in the Development of the Haskalah Movement in Russia', in Jacob Katz (ed.), *Toward Modernity. The European Jewish Model*, New Brunswick, NJ and Oxford: Transaction Books, 1978, p. 15.

9   Michael A. Meyer, 'Jewish Religious Reform and Wissenschaft des Judentums – The Positions of Zunz, Geiger and Frankel', *LBYB* XVI (1971), pp. 19–41. Nahum Glatzer, 'The Beginnings of Modern Jewish Studies', in Alexander Altmann (ed.), *Studies in Nineteenth-Century Jewish Intellectual History*, Cambridge, Mass.: Harvard University Press, 1964, pp. 27–45.

10   Monika Richarz, *Der Eintritt der Juden in die akademischen Berufe. Jüdische Studenten und Akademiker in Deutschland, 1678–1848*, Tübingen: J. C. B. Mohr, 1974; Steven M. Lowenstein, 'The Pace of Modernization of German Jewry in the Nineteenth Century', *LBYB* XXI (1976), pp. 43–4.

Jewish population, though a large and influential minority. Even greater in its impact on the community as a whole was the move of Jewish children into Christian or state schools. By the middle of the nineteenth century not more than half the Jewish children of Prussia attended Jewish schools; by 1931 this had become a mere 16 per cent. The bigger the city, the faster the rate of secularization. In Berlin, as early as 1850, the figure for attendance at Jewish schools was 29 per cent.[11]

Given all these pressures, the effect of which was to weaken Jewry internally, it is not surprising that the community lost members through indifference, apostasy and inter-marriage. Precise figures for the whole of Germany are difficult to come by for this period in its entirety. For the nineteenth century some 22,500 conversions have been estimated; for the first third of the twentieth century at least 10,000. The career or status advantages to be derived from baptism diminished in the course of the twentieth century; on the other hand the decline of religious belief led to an increase in resignations from Judaism, as from the various Christian denominations, especially after the First World War. The rate of inter-marriage also increased, accelerating, as might be expected, in the course of the twentieth century, and rising with the degree of urbanization. In the years 1875–9 96 per cent of Prussian Jews married endogamously, in 1930–3 76 per cent. In Berlin 27 per cent of Jews entered mixed marriages in the latter period, in Hamburg 39 per cent.[12]

It is evident that on the eve of the Nazi take-over the German-Jewish community had undergone quantitative diminution through modernization, whether this took the form of urbanization, secularization, political and theological fragmentation, low fertility or conversion. Given this history of attenuation, what was remarkable was the degree of cohesion that the Jews of Germany still retained. It was remarkable, given all these forces that tended to diminish the strength of Jewish identity, not that one Jew in four should marry 'out', but that three in four should continue to marry 'in'.

What we have to explain, therefore, is the survival, in many respects the very vigorous survival, of Germany's Jews as a group until the politically-inspired assault on their existence under the Third Reich. There are two main reasons for this, which are separate yet interconnected. The first is external: anti-Semitism, continued discrimination, whether social or governmental, and therefore continuing isolation, whether psychological, political or social. The second is internal: the persistence into the modern world of what, for want of a better term, may be called ethnicity.

What one might call the liberal paradigm of Jewish assimilation turned out to have miscalculated the future. What many liberals assumed, and many

11   Richarz, *Der Eintritt*, p. 145.
12   Usiel O. Schmelz, 'Die demographische Entwicklung der Juden in Deutschland von der Mitte des 19. Jahrhunderts bis 1933', *BLBI* 83 (1989), pp. 39–41.

traditionalists feared, was that as society modernized and secularized, so the features that divide one group from another would lose weight and distinctiveness, that status would increasingly depend on achievement rather than ascription and that inherited differences would be levelled by common systems of education.[13]

It would be idle to deny that that is the direction in which things have developed; equally idle to deny that they have developed far more slowly and far less completely than the liberal paradigm suggested. As Glazer and Moynihan commented, when they discovered in the 1960s that New York was anything but the melting-pot of official American ideology:

If something expected keeps on failing to happen, there may be more reasons than accident that explain [it]. Beyond the accidents of history, one suspects, is the reality that human groups endure, that they provide some satisfaction to their members, and that the adoption of a totally new ethnic identity, by dropping whatever one is to become simply American is inhibited by ... a subtle system of identifying, which ranges from brutal discrimination and prejudice to merely naming.[14]

And though twentieth-century America is not nineteenth-century Germany, and some of the reasons for the perpetuation of ethnicity in America have to do with its peculiar character as a country of immigration, 'the reality that human groups endure [and] provide some satisfaction to their members' is not restricted to one nation or period. It helps to explain a great many minority–majority and inter-minority relationships throughout the world. Ethnic links are a two-fold phenomenon: sociological, in providing group membership, and psychological, in providing an identity. Ethnicity can also combine interest with an affective tie, as Daniel Bell has argued, becoming 'a strategic choice by individuals who, in other circumstances, would choose other group memberships as a means of gaining some power or privilege.[15] This function of ethnicity is illustrated in chapter 2, which deals with the triangular dispute between Protestants, Catholics and Jews over judicial appointments.

The concept of ethnicity, then, provides a possible explanation for the place of Jews in German society in modern times. There is, however, more than one variable to be considered. All minorities are abnormal, as Simon

13   Nathan Glazer and Daniel P. Moynihan, (eds), *Ethnicity. Theory and Experience*, Cambridge, Mass.: Harvard University Press, 1975, pp. 6–7.
14   Nathan Glazer and Daniel P. Moynihan, *Beyond the Melting Pot. The Negroes, Puerto Ricans, Jews, Italians and Irish of New York City*, 2nd edn, Cambridge, Mass.: MIT Press, 1970, p. xxxiii.
15   Daniel Bell, 'Ethnicity and Social Change', in Glazer and Moynihan, *Ethnicity*, p. 169.

Kuznets pointed out in his seminal study of Jewish economic behaviour; otherwise they would not be minorities. Their abnormality may be observed in their economic structure or their political behaviour, but what defines them is their culture.[16] It is the possible connection between milieu and behaviour that has fascinated scholars for two centuries; and while they have been principally concerned with the religious roots of economic behaviour, the questions they raise are of wider relevance. These questions fall into three categories:

1 Do the 'abnormal' behaviours of all minorities show any similarities?
2 Do we distinguish between religious and other minorities?
3 Do members of the same denomination behave similarly, irrespective of whether they are in a minority or a majority?

In other words: is mere minority status a causal factor, or is the individual nature of the particular minority significant?

That excluded religious minorities show a tendency 'to be more useful to their country' than those who belong to majorities, because they are required to compensate for lack of status by effort, was first pointed out by Montesquieu.[17] For him mere minority status was conclusive. Subsequent experience has shown that life is more complicated than that. We can all think of minorities that have flourished and of others that have not. Minority status may be a necessary condition for exceptional material success; it is evidently not a sufficient one.

Two German scholars who showed special interest in Jewish minority behaviour were Werner Sombart and Max Weber. For Sombart the causal connection between Jews and the rise of modern economies is direct and demonstrable: 'It is essentially they who impregnate economic life with a modern spirit, because it is they who first bring the innermost idea of capitalism to its full development. ... Israel passes like a sun over Europe: wherever it gets to, sees new life sprouting forth, where it departs from, all that has flourished decays.'[18] The special qualification that the Jews have for this pioneering role is derived from the teachings of their religion, which enables them to view the world through rational eyes.[19] While much of the evidence

16 Simon Kuznets, 'Economic Structure and Life of the Jews', in Louis Finkelstein (ed.), *The Jews. Their History, Culture and Religion*, New York: Harper Bros, 1961, pp. 1600–1, 1658.
17 Charles Louis de Secondat, Baron de Montesquieu, *Lettres Persanes*, LXXXV.
18 Werner Sombart, *Die Juden und das Wirtschaftsleben*, Leipzig: Duncker & Humblot, 1911, pp. 24, 15.
19 Ibid., pp. 225–95; cf. Max Weber, *Economy and Society. An Outline of Interpretive Sociology* (ed. Guenther Roth and Claus Wittich), New York: Bedminster Press, 1968, pp. 615–33.

that Sombart adduces for his thesis has not withstood critical examination, his general proposition remains useful: that the particular way a minority behaves is to be explained by a cultural predisposition.

A more sophisticated approach along these lines is that of Max Weber. His starting point, in seeking to explain the special character of the Jewish people, and indeed its remarkable survival in nearly two thousand years of diaspora, appears similar to that of Montesquieu. Beginning with the period of the Babylonian captivity, he argues, 'toward the outside world Jewry increasingly assumed the type of a ritualistically segregated guest people (pariah people)',[20] and finds parallels with the Jews in such other 'pariah groups' as the Jains and Parsees of India.[21] A 'pariah people' he defines as 'a distinctive hereditary group lacking autonomous political organization and characterised by internal prohibitions against commensality and intermarriage. ... Two additional traits are political and social disprivilege and a far-reaching distinctiveness in economic functioning.'[22]

But once he embarked on his celebrated investigation of the differential economic behaviour of different Christian denominations, Weber realized that minority status had little explanatory value. The general observation that in any religiously-mixed state, Protestants, whether in a minority or a majority, were better represented in the most advanced sectors of the economy than Catholics led him to seek an explanation 'in the permanent intrinsic character of their beliefs, and not only in their temporary external historico-political situations'.[23] Otherwise one could not account for the failure of the Catholic minorities of the German Empire or Britain or America to behave like the Huguenot or Mennonite or Quaker minorities in those countries. Moreover, even if there is a correlation between Protestantism – or particular Protestant sects – and capitalist economic development, it is by no means self-evident which is cause and which effect. It is perfectly possible that a religion of personal responsibility and divine election was attractive to individuals, cities or provinces that were already economically well-developed and that the newly-chosen religion favoured the transmission of an established advantage.[24]

There are two ways in which these hypotheses can help to elucidate the initial entry of Jews into commercial occupations and their continued predilection for them long after the peculiar circumstances that gave rise to it had

20 Max Weber, *Ancient Judaism*, ed. by Hans H. Gerth and Don Martindale, Glencoe, Ill.: Free Press, 1952, p. 417; also pp. 336, 363, 376.
21 *Idem, The Protestant Ethic and the Spirit of Capitalism*, London Allen & Unwin 1930, p. 191.
22 *Idem, Economy and Society*, p. 493.
23 *Idem, The Protestant Ethic*, p. 40.
24 Ibid., pp. 35–6.

ceased to apply. Few scholars would now accept the direct link between religious belief and economic behaviour asserted by both Sombart and Weber, at least as far as European Jews are concerned. The separate social spheres occupied by Jews and Christians during the Christian era no doubt owe much to the Jews' status as a 'pariah nation'. But the particular forms of Jewish economic activity were determined more by external factors than internal choice. The 'intrinsic character' of Judaism is therefore not much help in explaining Jewish economic behaviour. What is of rather more use is Weber's notion of the group's role in the transmission of values that the group has made its own. For what is readily observable is that the 'abnormal' economic structure of German Jews, acquired during the pre-industrial period, survives after the functional need for this has ceased to operate. Though Jews show rapid upward mobility once greater opportunities are open to them, and though they enter certain professions, such as law, medicine or journalism, in large numbers and also become industrial entrepreneurs, again unevenly distributed among different sectors, most Jews stay in trade of one kind or another and cling stubbornly to self-employment. It is difficult to dissent from the conclusion of Avraham Barkai, a leading Israeli expert on German-Jewish economic history, which he based on an examination of the Rhenish-Westphalian industrial area, the largest and most dynamic in the whole of Germany:

The stagnation of the Jewish occupational structure, despite all the diversification within the commercial sector itself, cannot be sufficiently emphasized. Even in the region considered here, in which fast industrialization provided a maximum of opportunities for mobility and new forms of economic success, Jews held fast to their traditional callings, above all in retail trade and a number of preferred 'Jewish' economic sectors. ... In general the Jewish occupational and social profile remained, almost without change, closer to that of the Jews of Germany as a whole than of those economically active in Rhineland-Westphalia. This can only mean that the decisive impulse came from group-specific factors and not from local economic developments, a significant conclusion for any research on minorities.[25]

I have concentrated on the question of group continuity in Jewish economic behaviour because this has been the subject of the most intense research and is where the evidence is most readily available. If Barkai is right and post-emancipation German Jews stuck to habits for which there was no longer an obvious economic rationality, which may indeed have run counter

25 Avraham Barkai, 'Die sozio-ökonomischen Entwicklung der Juden in Rheinland-Westfalen in der Industrialisierung (1850–1910)', *BLBI* 66 (1983), pp. 66–7; see also Werner E. Mosse, *Jews in the German Economy. The German Jewish Economic Elite, 1820–1935*, Oxford: Oxford University Press, 1987, pp. 15–31.

to economic rationality, then 'ethnicity' is the only satisfactory explanation for such behaviour. However, the group that behaved in this 'ethnic' way underwent significant internal changes. The most important was that Jewishness could no longer be equated with Judaism. German Jewry ceased to be a purely religious minority and became a socio-cultural minority defined by its religious affiliation. And even that was an unsatisfactory defining criterion, for ethnicity, i.e. the influence of the socio-cultural environment, could survive the loss of faith, secession, inter-marriage or conversion, for 'as long as historical memory serves'.[26] The last unbaptized member of the Mendelssohn banking family died in 1888,[27] but that did not stop that banking house from being considered Jewish, or its members from being aware of their Jewish heritage. Indeed, there was a curious caste within the baptized Jewish *haute banque*, consisting of such families as the Mendelssohns, Warschauers, Simsons and Oppenheims who inter-married over more than one generation.[28] The extent to which a 'non-Jewish Jew' could sense an ethnic affinity is illustrated by Sigmund Freud's letter to the *B'nai B'rith* lodge of Vienna on the occasion of his seventieth birthday:

I am a Jew myself, and it has always appeared to me not only undignified, but outright foolish to deny it. What tied me to Jewry was – I have to admit it – not faith, not even national pride, for I was always an unbeliever, having been brought up without religion, but not without respect for the so-called 'ethical' demands of human civilization. Whenever I have experienced feelings of national exaltation, I have tried to suppress them as disastrous and unfair, frightened by the warning example of those nations among which we Jews live. But there remained enough to make the attraction of Judaism and the Jews irresistible, many dark emotional powers, all the stronger the less they could be expressed in words, as well as the clear consciousness of an inner identity, the familiarity of the same psychological structure, and before long there followed the realization that it was only to my Jewish nature that I owed the two qualities that have become indispensable to me throughout my difficult life. Because I was a Jew, I found myself free of many prejudices which restrict others in the use of the intellect: as a Jew I was prepared to be in the opposition and to renounce agreement with the 'compact majority'.[29]

Other factors also helped to maintain Jewish ethnicity under rapidly changing conditions, or at least to compensate for the disintegrative influences that

26 Sombart, *Die Juden und das Wirtschaftsleben*, p. 9.
27 Felix Gilbert (ed.), *Bankiers, Künstler und Gelehrte. Unveröffentlichte Briefe der Familie Mendelssohn aus dem 19. Jahrhundert*, Tübingen: J. C. B. Mohr, 1975, p. xvi.
28 Mosse, *Jews in the German Economy*, p. 37, fn. 8.
29 Ernst L. Freud (ed.), *Letters of Sigmund Freud, 1879–1939*, London: Hogarth Press, 1961, pp. 367–8.

we have noted. Jewish migration to the cities, the majority of which had little tradition of tightly-knit communal organization, did not have quite the fragmenting effect one might have expected. Like most immigrant groups Jews clustered in their new places of residence. In Frankfurt 64 per cent of the city's Jews lived in four of the fourteen districts in 1900; in 1925 the proportions had scarcely altered, though the districts were not the same. In Hamburg in 1885 48 per cent lived in two of the twenty districts, 64 per cent in three districts; here, too, the degree of concentration was the same in 1925, though the districts were not. Seventy per cent of Berlin's Jews lived in five Western or central districts in 1925 (Mitte, Charlottenburg, Prenzlauer Berg, Wilmersdorf, Schöneberg), which meant that a quarter of Germany's Jewish population was concentrated in an area of a few square miles.[30] Half the Jews of Germany lived in five cities in 1925.

Jews also found a substitute in secular organization for a civic structure that was decreasingly based on the synagogue. The *Centralverein*, founded in 1893, had a membership of 40,000 by 1914 and 60,000 by 1932, which suggests that it represented between one-third and one-half of Jewish families.[31] The Jewish women's organization, the *Jüdischer Frauenbund*, founded in 1904, had 32,000 members in 1913 and some 50,000 in the 1920s.[32] Youth, student and sporting organizations flourished to an equal extent. Some of these had a specific programme – Zionist or Orthodox – but the majority were concerned with representing Jewish interests and maintaining a Jewish identity within general society. They were open equally to the religiously observant and non-observant. The effect of this was felt externally as well as internally. The new organizations 'provided new ways of being Jewish'; they also maintained, and indeed increased, the visibility of Jews as a group, not merely as individuals.[33]

It could be argued that this Jewish organizational renaissance was not a spontaneous development, but a response to anti-Semitism. That anti-Semitism contributed to continued Jewish cohesion, and helped to define the enduring minority character of German Jews, is undeniable. But was it a

30 Based on data in Steven M. Lowenstein, 'Jewish Residential Concentration in Post-Emancipation Germany', *LBYB* XXVIII (1983), pp. 471–95.

31 Arnold Paucker, 'Zur Problematik einer jüdischen Abwehrstrategie in der deutschen Gesellschaft', *WD*, pp. 489–90; Arnold Paucker, *Der jüdische Abwehrkampf gegen Antisemitismus und Nationalsozialismus in den letzten Jahren der Weimarer Republik*, 2nd edn, Hamburg: Leibniz, 1969, p. 27.

32 Marion A. Kaplan, *The Jewish Feminist Movement in Germany. The Campaigns of the Jüdischer Frauenbund, 1904–1938*, Westport, Conn.: Greenwood, 1979, pp. 89, 10–11.

33 Calvin Goldscheider and Alan S. Zuckerman, *The Transformation of the Jews*, Chicago: University of Chicago Press, 1984, p. 135.

major, even a decisive, factor? There is a danger in reading German history backwards, especially the history of anti-Jewish sentiments and activities in Germany, so that all events and developments point to a culmination in the Third Reich. Shulamit Volkov, for instance, has argued that while there is undeniable continuity in the rhetoric of the Nazis and of nineteenth-century anti-Semites, the genocidal terror of Nazism was *sui generis*:

If the earlier German anti-Semitism did indeed bring forth the National Socialists, it must have differed in its essentials from all earlier forms of anti-Semitism and been unique for its place and time.

On the contrary:

It had little significance for later events, and if one compares it with its contemporaneous French example, then even its characteristic traits lose much of their uniqueness. German anti-Semitism of those days was, even when all its peculiarities are taken into account, closer to the French version of that time than to later National Socialist positions.[34]

Indeed, at the time of the Dreyfus Affair French anti-Semitism reached a degree of intensity for which there was no parallel in Germany before 1933.[35]

There is much to be said for this warning against over-estimating ninet-eenth-century German anti-Semitism, at least in its agitational form. It is for this reason that I distinguish, when it comes to identifying continuities, between anti-Semitism and the Jewish Question and devote the first chapter in this book to this distinction. Although there was no absence of anti-Semitism, i.e. politically articulated prejudice or social discrimination, in Germany's Western neighbours, these countries witnessed the early and fairly painless disappearance of the debate on Jewish rights from the constitutional agenda. In France the revolutionary emancipation measures were not rescinded when the monarchy was restored in 1815 and Jewish disabilities were quietly removed in Belgium, the Netherlands and to a large extent Switzerland in the first half of the nineteenth century. In Britain the last political disability disappeared in 1858 when Jews were enabled to take their seats in the House of Commons. In the United States there had never been a Jewish Question, since Article VI of the constitution forbade all religious discrimination, though a handful of individual states retained some restrictions. In Germany, in contrast, there was a continuing debate throughout

34 Shulamit Volkov, 'Kontinuität und Diskontinuität im deutschen Antisemitismus 1878–1945', *VfZ*, 1985, Heft 2, p. 224; also pp. 232, 243.
35 Ibid., p. 236.

the nineteenth century as to whether Jews, either as non-Christians or as non-Germans, could ever qualify as full citizens. Neither the Basic Rights of the German People, as adopted by the Frankfurt Parliament in 1848, nor the Law on the Equality of All Confessions passed by the parliament of the North German Confederation in 1869, stilled this debate.

As is almost always the case, a debate about the Jews is not only a debate about the Jews. It was primarily a debate about the character of the German nation in response to the challenge of the French Revolution and the Napoleonic invasions. The events in France had sent two messages across Europe: that of the one and indivisible nation and that of the Rights of Man. Though there were Jacobins and revolutionaries in Germany both during the period of the Revolution and after its defeat, and though their ideas seemed briefly to have triumphed in 1848, they were far from ever attaining an ideological hegemony.

The two principal forms that the German response took were both hostile to an elimination of the Jewish Question. The first was counter-revolutionary conservatism, that resisted all attacks on the unity of throne and altar and re-emphasized the Christian character of the state as a rampart against the assaults of liberalism and secularism. The second was integral nationalism, defined by hostility to all alien elements, whether originating beyond the frontiers of the German states or within them. The basis of the nation was not citizenship, as in France in 1789, but the *Volk*, defined by common culture and descent, united by ties that were sacramental, not contractual. These two currents combined in what the Jewish publicist Saul Ascher termed 'Germanomanie'.[36]

For the Bavarian Catholic historian Joseph von Görres the ties of nationality were 'not accidental, transitory and therefore capable of being destroyed': 'it is the national baptism that everyone has received who really belongs to his *Volk*'.[37] At the other end of the political spectrum, the founder of the nationalist gymnast movement, Friedrich Ludwig Jahn, insisted that a genuine *Volk* was a '*Volk* of deeds', not a 'mere *Volk* in name; its outward community of state will maintain itself through the force of internal links, it will not lose its way in escapism in the manner of gypsies and Jews'.[38] His battle-cry was against all enemies of the people, 'Frenchmen, *Junker*, priests and Jews'. So, too, for the great prophet of the anti-Napoleonic national

---

36   Saul Ascher, *Die Germanomanie. Skizze zu einem Zeitgemälde*, Berlin: Achenwall, 1815.
37   Joseph von Görres, *Gesammelte Schriften, 1. Abteilung: Politische Schriften*, Munich: Literarisch-artistische Anstalt, 1854, vol. I, p. 184.
38   Friedrich Ludwig Jahn, *Deutsches Volkstum. Werke*, (ed. C. Euler), Hof: Lion, 1886, vol. I, p. 234.

uprising, Johann Gottlieb Fichte, a true *Volk* ('*Urvolk*') like the German had to subsist 'without the interference and ruination by anything foreign'.[39]

Rejection of Jews as fellow-nationals or fellow-citizens was not merely consistent with such a view of state and nation; it was explicitly emphasized. As Saul Ascher put it as early as 1815:

> It cannot surprise us that according to the views of these enthusiastic idealists, through which Germandom and Christendom are to be so fused that the one could not exclude the other, the Jews emerged in the first instance as the antithesis of this doctrine. ... To maintain the fire of enthusiasm, fuel had to be gathered, and our Germanomaniacs wished to find, in the small Jewish population, the kindling for spreading the flame of fanaticism.[40]

Nor was this ideology restricted, as in France or Britain, to propagandists or agitators who were outsiders in political society, such as Adolphe Toussenel, Edouard Drumont or Hilaire Belloc. It was shared by academics, ministers and highly-placed civil servants.

A common charge laid against Jews was that they constituted 'a state within the state', a phrase first used by Fichte,[41] repeated by his fellow-nationalist prophet Ernst Moritz Arndt, and then the conservative Protestant historian Christian Friedrich Rühs,[42] to be followed by many others. A condition for the ending of second-class citizenship, therefore, was that Jews should cease to be Jews, either by conversion or by unconditional assimilation, a demand summarized by Heinrich von Treitschke in 1879: 'Let them become Germans, let them feel simply and properly as Germans.'[43] But in proclaiming this absolute demand, he was merely echoing a familiar argument. For Rühs: 'Every people [*Volk*], that wishes to assert and develop its individuality and dignity, must seek to remove and exclude all alien components, which it cannot absorb ardently and completely. This is the case with

39 Johann Gottlieb Fichte, *Reden an die deutsche Nation. Sämtliche Werke*, Berlin: Veit, 1846, vol. VII, p. 383.
40 Ascher, *Die Germanomanie*, pp. 14, 16.
41 Fichte, *Beiträge zur Berichtigung der Urtheile des Publikums über die Französische Revolution. Sämtliche Werke*, vol. VI, pp. 148, 153.
42 Ernst Moritz Arndt, *Blick aus der Zeit auf die Zeit*, Frankfurt-am-Main: Eichenberg, 1814, p. 201; Christian Friedrich Rühs, *Über die Ansprüche der Juden an das Bürgerrecht*, 2nd edn, Berlin: Realschulverlag, 1816, p. 5; H. Naudh (i.e. J. Nordmann et al.), *Die Juden und der deutsche Staat*, 5th edn, Hamburg: Otto Meißner, 1962, p. 8. For a discussion of the origins and spread of the phrase see Jakob Katz, 'A State within a State, the History of an anti-Semitic Slogan', in *idem*, *Emancipation and Assimilation. Studies in Modern Jewish History*, Farnborough: Gregg International 1972, pp. 47–76.
43 Heinrich von Treitschke, 'Unsere Aussichten', *PJ*, 15 November 1879, p. 573.

the Jews.' While it would be inhumane to expel or suppress them completely, he proposed that: 'Everything must be done in the way of mercy to persuade them towards Christianity and thus to true allegiance to the individuality of the German people [*deutsche Volkseigenthümlichkeit*], in order thus to bring about the demise of the Jewish people in the course of time.'[44] Jakob Friedrich Fries, the Jena philosopher who was one of the main patrons of the nationalist student corporations, *Burschenschaften*, claimed in defence of his anti-emancipation pamphlet of 1816 that he merely wanted to see 'the Jewish community reformed and abolished as a commercial caste, so that Jews might enter the state as citizens with full rights';[45] what he had actually written was that 'this caste must be exterminated root and branch'. 'To improve the civic situation of the Jews means exterminating Jewry.'[46]

The demand for unconditional assimilation would have been more convincing, had the same authors not described Jews in such unfavourable terms that sudden conversion seemed the least likely outcome. Everything that Treitschke retrospectively disliked about the German radical movement of the 1840s, cosmopolitanism and hatred of Christianity, he attributed to the 'oriental ancestry' of the agitators.[47] And it was he who gave currency, ostensibly by quoting others, to the slogan, 'The Jews are our misfortune.' Rühs had denied that the defects of the Jewish character were attributable to external factors such as discrimination and persecution: Jews had shown the same undesirable qualities in Spain and Poland, despite their privileged status there.[48] For Fries they were 'a class of metics, who have the peculiar fancy of raising physical segregation from the native population into a principle.'[49] Jews therefore become acceptable as citizens only if they perform the near-impossible.

Such widespread views would have mattered less if they had been restricted to intellectuals and propagandists. What differentiated the German states from France, Britain or America is that they were shared by many policymakers. Ludwig von Vincke, the Governor (*Oberpräsident*) of the Prussian province of Westphalia, proposed to the Minister of the Interior in 1826 that 'all Jews in the kingdom of Prussia be given the choice either to accept

44 Rühs, *Über die Ansprüche der Juden*, pp. 32, 39.
45 Ernst Ludwig Theodor Henke, *Jakob Friedrich Fries (1773–1843). Aus seinem handschriftlichen Nachlaße dargestellt*, Leipzig: Brockhaus, 1867, pp. 147–8.
46 Jakob Friedrich Fries, *Über die Gefährdung des Wohlstandes und Charakters der Deutschen durch die Juden*, Heidelberg: Mohr & Winter, 1816, pp. 18, 10.
47 Heinrich von Treitschke, *Deutsche Geschichte im Neunzehnten Jahrhundert*, Leipzig: S. Hirzel, 1878–94, vol. III, pp. 704–5, vol. IV, p. 434, vol. V, p. 139.
48 Rühs, *Über die Ansprüche der Juden*, pp. 20–2.
49 Fries, *Über die Gefährdung*, p. 12.

baptism within the next ten years or to leave the state unconditionally.'[50] His subordinate, *Regierungsrat* J. J. Esser, who shared the view that Jews were 'a state within the state', concluded that a 'non-Christian could never be a good citizen'.[51] Frederick Wilhelm IV's minister, Ludwig von Thile, told the United Prussian Diet of 1847 that it was 'inconsistent with Christianity to grant rights of political authority to Jews', since their fatherland was Zion, not Prussia[52] – a view that coincided with that of the King. In Baden, State Councillor Johann Ludwig Kübler asserted that Jews were 'a fully closed, hereditarily conspiratorial society for specific political principles and commandments ... which excludes any gradual progress towards higher culture'.[53]

It was the exception rather than the rule for a public servant to write, as did the Governor of the Province of Posen in 1842:

> We can only wish that the attitude would gradually disappear among the Christian population that the Jews were an alien nation, imposed upon the state and only to be tolerated as a necessary evil, and that one should become accustomed to regard the Jews as a component of the people, distinguished only by their religion, but in all other respects fellow-citizens and fellow-subjects similar to the Christians.[54]

Once the question of emancipation was finally settled in 1869, the Jewish Question as a component of the constitutional debate disappeared from the agenda. Agitation to rescind equal rights was now restricted to oppositional anti-Semites. When General Konstantin von Gebsattel of the Pan-German League sent a confidential memorandum to the Crown Prince in 1913, through whom it reached highly-placed politicians and other members of the Imperial family, recommending anti-parliamentary and anti-Jewish measures, both Chancellor Bethmann-Hollweg and the Emperor replied coolly. While neither was completely out of sympathy with Gebsattel's prejudices, the Emperor thought his proposals 'downright childish'; the Chancellor that it was impossible to take them seriously.[55]

50   'Darstellung der Juden in der Provinz Westfalen', quoted in Arno Herzig, *Judentum und Emanzipation in Westfalen*, Münster: Aschendorffsche Verlagsbuchhandlung, 1973, p. 35.

51   Ibid., p. 25.

52   Eleonore Sterling, 'Der Kampf um die Emanzipation der Juden im Rheinland vom Zeitalter der Aufklärung bis zur Gründung des deutschen Reiches', in Konrad Schilling (ed.) *Monumenta Judaica. 2000 Jahre Geschichte und Kultur der Juden am Rhein*, Cologne: Stadt Köln, 1963, p. 304.

53   Quoted in Helmut Berding, *Moderner Antisemitismus in Deutschland*, Frankfurt-am-Main: Suhrkamp, 1988, p. 63.

54   ZStM Rep. 77, xxx, ad 117, vol. II, p. 20.

55   Hartmut Pogge von Strandmann and Immanuel Geiss, *Die Erforderlichkeit des Unmöglichen. Deutschland am Vorabend des ersten Weltkrieges*, Frankfurt-am-Main: Europäische Verlags-Anstalt, 1965, pp. 34–8.

That did not mean, however, that the Jewish Question disappeared. It transferred, instead, to the unofficial sphere. While Jews could no longer be excluded from full citizenship, they could still be excluded from important areas of civil society and *de facto* from many sections of the public service. The most important arena of social discrimination was the student body. Active anti-Semitism in the universities began in the late 1870s, culminating in the foundation of the *Verein deutscher Studenten* in 1881. Twenty years later VDSt could claim that 'the social isolation of the Jewish student has in the main been achieved',[56] largely by putting pressure on the great majority of student corporations (*Corps* and *Burschenschaften*) not to admit Jewish members. Although these corporations enrolled only a minority of students, their well-known role in providing the future political and academic elite gave them a disproportionate influence, so that the VDSt's claim was not without validity.

From the 1880s onwards it was virtually impossible for an unbaptized Jew to get a commission or reserve commission in the Prussian army or to gain a diplomatic appointment. The number of Jewish civil servants or teachers in state schools was negligible in relation to the level of qualified persons and it was by no means easy for a suitably qualified unbaptized Jew to gain a full university professorship or high judicial appointment.[57] Social and political organizations with a strong nationalist ideology, such as the Agrarian League, the Pan-German League or the gymnasts, tried periodically to bar Jews from membership, not always successfully.[58] What mattered, however, was that in universities, in the public services and in the purely social sphere, the question whether the Jew was fully recognized as an equal was never allowed to rest. It was raised in the press, in the Reichstag and in state parliaments. It was certainly present in the mind of any Jew planning a career. Franz Oppenheimer, later to become a distinguished economist, recalled of his student days:

It was made almost impossible for us to behave 'normally'. We were forced to drive ourselves to peak performance. Indeed, we had to legitimate ourselves again and again as properly belonging, whether we were conscious of it or not (and most of the time

56 Norbert Kampe, *Studenten und 'Judenfrage' im Deutschen Kaiserreich. Die Entstehung einer akademischen Trägerschicht des Antisemitismus*, Göttingen: Vandenhoeck & Ruprecht, 1988, p. 140.
57 Werner T. Angress, 'Prussia's Army and the Jewish Reserve Officer Controversy Before World War I', *LBYB* XVII (1972), pp. 19–42; Norbert Kampe, 'Jüdische Professoren im deutschen Kaiserreich' in Rainer Erb and Michael Schmidt (eds), *Antisemitismus und jüdische Geschichte. Studien zu Ehren von Herbert A. Strauss*, Berlin: Wissenschaftlicher Autoren-Verlag, 1987, pp. 185–211; and below, pp. 108–14
58 Roger Chickering, *We Men Who Feel Most German. A Cultural Study of the Pan-German League, 1886–1914*, London: Allen & Unwin, 1984, p. 233.

we were conscious of it), while the non-Jew was legitimated without further ado in the absence of evidence to the contrary.[59]

Anti-Semitism, discrimination and permanent consciousness that the 'Jewish Question' had not gone away undoubtedly helped to determine the political attitudes of most Jews after the foundation of the Empire, just as the struggle for emancipation had increasingly determined them in the preceding decades. That applied all the more so since anti-Semitism and opposition to emancipation were, as I have argued, not isolated phenomena, but part of a general reaction to the ideology of the Enlightenment and the French Revolution. For Fries it was French influence that 'burst the beneficial ties and began to corrode our whole civic life. ... May heaven avert that a false semblance of enlightenment and humanity inoculate the constitution awaiting a new formulation with its defects.'[60] H. E. Marcard, a Prussian military official who organized an anti-emancipation petition in Westphalia in 1843, warned against 'un-German Liberalism' which, with democracy, was 'the enemy of the historically created spirit of the people'.[61] Diederich Hahn, later a leading figure in the Agrarian League, called on 'Christian-Germanic youth' at the founding congress of the VDSt to 'exterminate ... the defects of the new *Reich*: Jewry and Francomania [*Judentum, Franzosentum*]'.[62] Treitschke, too, thought that Jewish cosmopolitanism had an inner affinity with the French.[63] Such sentiments became even more commonplace after 1918, when Germany acquired a constitution based on Western democratic principles, which its opponents were only too ready to denounce on the grounds of both its foreign origins and Jewish inspiration.

All these, however, are local factors that reinforced the political identity of German Jews. As we have seen, ethnicity survives and indeed flourishes in environments much more hospitable to minorities than that of modern Germany. The character of the German-Jewish minority, in its relations with state authorities and in the political attitudes that predominated within it, was determined as much by its internal dynamics and by the need to adapt to a rapidly changing external world, as by the undeniable hostile pressures.

It is this last proposition that the main chapter in this volume, chapter 3, is devoted to. The political postures of German Jews showed a distinctive and

59   Franz Oppenheimer, *Erlebtes, Erstrebtes, Erreichtes. Erinnerungen*, 2nd edn, Düsseldorf: Melzer, 1964, p. 80.

60   Fries, *Über die Gefährdung*, pp. 20–4.

61   H. E. Marcard, *Über die Möglichkeit der Juden-Emanzipation im christlich-germanischen Staat*, Minden: Eßmann, 1843, p. 43.

62   Karl Maßmann and R. P. Oßwald, *VDSter. Fünfzig Jahre Arbeit für Volkstum und Staat*, Berlin: Liebheit & Thiesen, 1931, p. 7.

63   Treitschke, *Deutsche Geschichte*, vol. III, p. 704.

recognizable pattern in the century or so before 1933. These postures did not lack variety: Jews – or persons of Jewish descent – could be found supporting almost every political party or ideological organization, from racialist pan-Germanism to revolutionary Socialism. But there was also a persistent clustering and that was to the left of centre, however defined: either in the various Progressive or Left-Liberal parties or the left wing of the National Liberal Party or in the Social Democratic Party, or in related non-party pressure groups and leagues, such as the *Hansa-Bund* or (after 1918) the *Reichsbanner Schwarz–Rot–Gold*, or in the newspapers and journals that articulated that range of viewpoints. In their political stance the Jews of Germany were as 'asymmetrical' as in their economic activities.[64] The question therefore arises whether, and how far, the two were related; why that stance differed so notably from that of the non-Jewish middle class in Germany; and whether the explanation, as for the economic asymmetry, is to be found in reasons internal to the German-Jewish existence or external to it.

It would be tempting to explain the predilection for constitutionalism, international conciliation and social concern by reference to Jewish religious or intellectual tradition, and both anti-Semites and apologists for the Jews have tried to do so. The right-wing Catholic publicist Martin Spahn spoke for many when he attributed the victory of the Left in the 1912 Reichstag elections to the activities of 'Jewish fellow-citizens': 'For the Jew, more than any other civilized human beings [*Kulturmenschen*], is an element inclined to migration and especially frequently involved in migration. In consequence of this he is, in political life, an element with a special fondness for leftward inclination and radical activity.'[65] This was little more than an echo of the doctrines popularized for much of the nineteenth century. Treitschke, writing in the 1870s and 1880s, held that Jewish cosmopolitanism was incapable of understanding occidental nations: the Germans 'innocently accepted as German enlightenment and German progressivism what in truth was Jewish hatred of Christianity and Jewish cosmopolitanism'.[66] Wolfgang Menzel, the scourge of the 'Young Germany' literary movement of the 1830s, attributed to 'Judaism' 'all the loathsomeness that lies in the boundless insolence, in the pandering to French fashion, in the malicious but impotent hatred of all things German and Christian'.[67] Among prominent Jews Eduard Bernstein

---

64   The adjective is Fritz Stern's. Fritz Stern, 'The Burden of Success: Reflections on German Jewry' in *idem. Dreams and Delusions. The Drama of German History*, New York: Random House, 1987, p. 105.

65   Martin Spahn, 'Die radikale Krise im Reich', *Hochland*, March 1912, p. 705.

66   Treitschke, *Deutsche Geschichte*, vol. III., pp. 704–5.

67   Wolfgang Menzel, 'Unmoralische Schriften' (1835), in Heinrich H. Houben, *Gutzkow-Funde. Beiträge zur Litteratur- und Kulturgeschichte des 19. Jahrhunderts*, Berlin: L. A. Wolff, 1901, p. 203.

talked of the Jews' 'vocation for mediation': 'to stress at all times that which unites peoples, to help the voice of reason gain its rights in periods of conflict'.[68] Others, especially during and after the First World War, spoke of a specifically Jewish social conscience or duty to adopt pacifism.[69]

The trouble with these propositions, whether favourable or unfavourable towards Jews, is that they are not really verifiable. Other religions also teach the renunciation of nationalism; and the social or philanthropic ethic of Christianity or Islam is no weaker than that of Judaism. The political views of Jews are no more to be explained by the 'intrinsic character' of their religion than are their economic activities. Nor can the left-of-centre stance be explained solely in terms of economic interest. It is true that the Jews of Germany were an overwhelmingly urban and increasingly metropolitan population, dealing predominantly in financial services or the consumer goods sector, and that this would incline them towards supporting a competitive, non-corporatist domestic economy and an open international economy; that those of them who were in the professions had reasons to favour careers open to talents; and that a high proportion of them were self-employed. But that, by itself, does not explain their politics. Most Jews, though no longer poverty-stricken by the time the German Empire was founded, were in fairly humdrum occupations. They were small shopkeepers or artisans or in routine white-collar work. Such a social position would not necessarily lead to left-wing liberalism, let alone Social Democracy. It is in any case rather *simpliste* to assume that all – or most – political opinions are primarily an expression of material interest, the more so as the German-Jewish left-of-centre stance was time-bound. It is essentially a feature of the mid-to-late nineteenth and early twentieth centuries, when it had its parallels in other European countries.

In view of all of this it might be more fruitful to look for explanations in the political environment and to regard emancipation as the key independent variable. The agenda for civic equality was set for Europe by the French Revolution and for Germany by the Revolution of 1848. More than any other events these two politicized the Jews of Europe and of Germany. The process was gradual and uneven, but by the middle of the nineteenth century the majority of German Jews had acquired a commitment to a constitutional nation-state, while no doubt differing among themselves on the degree of constitutionalism and the extent of the nation-state's boundaries. The 1869 law of the North German Confederation, guaranteeing religious equality and

68 Eduard Bernstein, 'Vom Mittlerberuf des Juden', *NJM* I, 25 April 1917, pp. 397 ff.
69 See Eva G. Reichmann, 'Der Bewußtseinswandel der deutschen Juden', *KuR*, pp. 520–5.

adopted by the newly-created Empire in 1871, was the culmination of this process. Or so it seemed. Had the chapter of emancipation been closed by this law, as it had earlier in the century by similar provisions in Western Europe and North America, the issue might have died away as a matter of dominant concern to the Jewish population. That it did not was due to the survival of what I have termed the Jewish Question, i.e. the continuing debate about the appropriate place of the Jew in society. At no stage in German history between 1871 and 1933 was there a consensus that the Jew was a citizen like any other. There were certainly influential Gentiles who supported that proposition and others who were indifferent to it. But there were, at any one time, enough opponents of it, from members of the Imperial family downwards, for the issue to be present in the minds of most Jews.

The perpetuation of anti-Semitism, the Jewish Question and occupational asymmetry constituted a vicious circle from which escape was difficult and which is the best single explanation for the political asymmetry. Anti-Semitism, i.e. the continuing articulation of a prejudice, however unpleasant, was the least of the obstacles to the successful integration the German-Jewish community. Its loudest and most persistent practitioners were, with few exceptions, persons of low political status. Optimists among German Jews could console themselves with the thought that Imperial Germany had no Dreyfus Case, no Russian-style pogroms and no publicly-elected anti-Semitic mayors as in Austria. They could conclude from this that anti-Semitism was 'a curable disease';[70] even German Zionists were prepared to dismiss it as 'irksome, but by no means dangerous'.[71]

Whether the occupational asymmetry was purely the outcome of past or present discrimination, or also reflected an endogenous pattern of preferences, has already been discussed. What concerns us here is its effect on both Jews and non-Jews. Many of the more highly-educated Jews resented the restrictions on their career opportunities; perhaps not many of them would have chosen to become regular soldiers or career civil servants, but they wanted to be free to choose. Many of their compatriots were aware of the strong Jewish presence in banking and large-scale commerce, in journalism and publishing, in medicine and the law. They may have exaggerated the degree of concentration, either out of prejudice or because the conspicuous Jewish presence in Berlin and other major centres made it seem larger than it was; but that it existed, and was frequently commented on, helped to perpetuate the Jewish Question. One symptom of this, already mentioned,

70 Cit. Ismar Elbogen and Eleonore Sterling, *Die Geschichte der Juden in Deutschland*, Wiesbaden: Fourier, 1982, p. 275.
71 'lästig ..., aber keineswegs gefährlich.' Richard Lichtheim, *Die Geschichte des deutschen Zionismus*, Jerusalem: Rubin Mass, 1954, p. 143.

was the exclusion of Jews from reserve commissions and student corporations, the intention and effect of which was to close certain high-status career opportunities to them.

There was an added reason for this occupational concentration that turned out to be more short-term than many of the commentators at the time appreciated. For a limited period Jews formed the avant-garde of the German bourgeoisie. By the middle of the nineteenth century, and certainly by its end, Jews were more urban, better educated and richer than their Protestant or Catholic compatriots. That was not, however, destined to be a permanent state of affairs. As first Protestants and then Catholics began to catch up, the Jewish advantage disappeared, to an extent that was certainly noticeable by 1933. This development, or its likelihood, escaped most critics of Jewish occupational asymmetry. Some of these critics were Jews, like the Zionist Moritz Goldstein, who caused a stir with his 1912 article on the 'German-Jewish Parnassus', advising Jews to vacate their prominent place in German letters.[72] Those who were Gentiles were not necessarily ill-intentioned. Werner Sombart, whose broad brush-strokes often got things right even if the detail was sloppy, was perceptive enough to see that assimilation, far from being a cure for anti-Semitism, was part of the problem. The more Jews succeeded in seizing the opportunities offered by emancipation, the greater the tensions between Jews and non-Jews would be; it followed that anti-Semitism would, if anything, increase.[73] His own prescription was Jewish self-restraint: 'States grant their citizens full legal equality and the Jews will possess the intelligence and tact not to take advantage of this legal equality everywhere and to the full extent.'[74] This, too, was a familiar message, a moderate version of deputy Duport's words to the French Constituent Assembly: 'The law will say that Jews may be elected; habit will perhaps oppose itself to their election'.[75]

The Jewish balance-sheet at the end of the Imperial period was therefore mixed. To quote Fritz Stern again, 'German Jews throve visibly – and suffered invisibly.'[76] It was the second item in this ledger, even more than

72 Moritz Goldstein, 'Deutsch-jüdischer Parnass', *Der Kunstwart* XXV/11, March 1912; see also *idem*, 'German Jewry's Dilemma Before 1914. The Story of a Provocative Essay', *LB YB* II (1957), pp. 236–54.

73 Werner Sombart, *Die Zukunft der Juden*, Leipzig: Duncker & Humblot, 1912, p. 43.

74 Ibid., p. 87.

75 Assemblée Nationale, 23 December 1789. 'La loi dira que les juifs soient éligibles; les moeurs s'opposent peut-être à ce qu'ils soient élus'. Achille-Edmond Halphen, *Recueil des lois ... concernant les Israélites depuis la Révolution de 1789*, Paris: Bureaux des Archives Israélites, 1854, p. 190.

76 Stern, 'The Burden of Success', p. 100.

the first, that ensured their continuing political asymmetry. What defined German Jewry in the early twentieth century was common experience rather than organization; political rather than economic interest; and a feeling that, however well they might have done for themselves, certain prizes to which they thought themselves entitled had been denied them. All this pointed in the direction of the politics of 'formal rationality', in favour of a society, whether domestic or international, in which equitable law prevailed. Societies in which this formal rationality, as defined by Weber,[77] is strongly embedded can cope relatively easily with non-conforming minorities and can ride out conflicts between the demands of this rationality and communitarian ethical codes. Germany in our period did not fulfil this condition. Hence the failure of communication between even the most assimilating Jew and the most benevolently conciliatory non-Jew. The recognition of this led Talcott Parsons to conclude during the Second World War that 'many Jews are typical "intellectuals" ... they are unaware of the extent to which they offend the non-rational sentiments of others.'[78] Sigmund Freud's claim that his minority status freed him 'of many prejudices which restrict others in the use of the intellect'[79] merely confirms this thesis. To it may be added one more hypothesis, advanced by David Vital, that Jewish exclusion from power, and therefore from the realities of the practice of politics, helped to perpetuate naïveté and utopianism, especially in international affairs. Hence,

it is not surprising that until quite recent times most Jews (in common, be it said, with many other men of good will) wanted to believe that the well-known dilemmas of *raison d'état* and ends and means were largely, if not entirely, capable of resolution. In international politics, at any rate, most Jews tended to be distant if unconscious followers of Woodrow Wilson.[80]

There is a further factor that helped to stabilize Jewish political loyalties, and that is that political values and partisan orientations, once established, tend to be transmitted from one generation to the next; the family is – or was in the period we are concerned with – the most powerful socializer. Thus

77 Weber applied this concept primarily to economic activity, but also used it in a legal-constitutional context. *Economy and Society*, vol. II, pp. 657–8; see also Wolfgang J. Mommsen, *The Political and Social Theory of Max Weber. Collected Essays*, Oxford: Blackwell, 1989, pp. 161–4.
78 Talcott Parsons, 'The Sociology of Modern Anti-Semitism', in Isacque Graeber and Stuart Henderson Britt (eds), *Jews in a Gentile World*, New York: Macmillan, 1972, p. 116; see also, ibid., p. 106;
79 See fn. 29.
80 David Vital, *The Future of the Jews*, Cambridge, Mass. and London: Harvard University Press, 1990, pp. 35–6.

German-Jewish political habits, like economic habits, once acquired, tended to perpetuate themselves, even if the circumstances that had given rise to them no longer applied. Which of these hypotheses are confirmed by the chapters in this book is for the reader to judge. The conflict between formal rationality and the communitarian ethical code comes out most clearly in the second chapter, which deals with religion and judicial appointments under the Empire. The more direct political consequences for Jews as citizens and for the Jewish relationship with the ideology of liberalism form the subject-matter of the third and fourth chapters. The last is an attempt to draw conclusions from the failure of all these undertakings.

Earlier versions of these chapters have appeared in various volumes published over the last fifteen years. Chapter 1, 'Why Was There a Jewish Question in Imperial Germany?', was first read as a paper at an Oxford-Bonn colloquium at the University of Bonn in 1979 and was then published in an expanded form in Year Book XXV of the Leo Baeck Institute. Chapter 2, 'Religion and Judicial Appointments in Imperial Germany', first appeared in Year Book XXVIII of the Leo Baeck Institute. Both have been revised for publication here. The main chapter, 'Jews in German Politics', has a more complicated origin. The first nine sections are based on my German-language contribution 'Die jüdische Beteiligung an der Politik' in the symposium *Juden im Wilhelminischen Deutschland, 1890–1914* (Schriftenreihe wissenschaftlicher Abhandlungen des Leo Baeck Instituts 33), edited by Werner E. Mosse and Arnold Paucker (Tübingen: J. C. B. Mohr, 1976). The remainder started life as an edited version of a German-language draft chapter by Dr Ernest Hamburger, who had planned to write an account of Jews in the politics of the Weimar Republic – a successor volume to his classic *Juden im öffentlichen Leben Deutschlands. Regierungsmitglieder, Beamte und Parlamentarier in der monarchischen Zeit, 1848–1918* (No. 19 in the same *Schriftenreihe*). This was cut short by his death in 1980. That edited chapter was published in Year Book XXX of the Leo Baeck Institute as: Ernest Hamburger and Peter Pulzer, 'Jews as Voters in the Weimar Republic'. For the present book I have conflated the two essays, completely revised them and greatly expanded them in the light of new scholarly publications and my own further research. Chapter 4 was originally presented at a joint seminar of the Leo Baeck Institute and the Friedrich-Naumann-Stiftung in 1985. It was published in German in *liberal* 1986, Heft 4, and in a slightly different form in English in *Das deutsche Judentum und der Liberalismus – German Jewry and Liberalism* (Liberale Texte. Schriften der Friedrich-Naumann-Stiftung, St Augustin: Comdok, 1986). The final chapter was written as an Introduction to *Die Juden im Nationalsozialistischen Deutschland – The Jews in Nazi Germany* (Schriftenreihe wissenschaftlicher Abhandlungen des Leo Baeck Instituts 45), edited by Arnold Paucker (Tübingen: J. C. B. Mohr, 1987), where it appeared in both English and German. It, too, has been revised.

I am most grateful to Dr Arnold Paucker, the Director of the London Leo Baeck Institute and Editor of the Institute's Year Book, for permission to use material that originally appeared in publications for which he is responsible. I also owe a debt to the Leverhulme Foundation and the Historische Kommission zu Berlin for financial support in my researches; and to the staffs of the following institutions for their help and advice: The Bodleian Library, Oxford; the University Library, Cambridge; the British Library, the British Library of Political and Economic Science, the Wiener Library and the German Historical Institute in London; the Library of the Free University and the two branches (East and West) of the Deutsche Staatsbibliothek, Berlin; the Senatsbibliothek, Berlin; the University Library and the Library of the Bundestag, Bonn; the Bayerische Staatsbibliothek and the libraries of the Institut für Zeitgeschichte and the Geschwister-Scholl-Institut für Politische Wissenschaft, Munich; the Leo Baeck Institute, New York; the Zentrales Staatsarchiv, Merseburg and Potsdam, the Staatsarchiv Potsdam and the Geheimes Staatsarchiv, Berlin-Dahlem; the Central Archives of the History of the Jewish People, the Jewish National and University Library and the Library of the Leo Baeck Institute, Jerusalem. I have benefited from the advice and help of so many persons that it would be invidious to list them. Some of them are thanked individually in footnotes. Above all I want to thank my family for putting up with the anti-social habits without which this book could not have been completed; and Mrs Michèle Jacottet who coped with a manuscript that would have driven others to despair.

1
Why Was There a Jewish Question in Imperial Germany?

Despite Leopold von Ranke's famous warning, we are liable to assess the importance of historical questions with hindsight. Indeed, we cannot help doing so: part of our knowledge of an epoch is our knowledge of what came next. If an observer at the turn of the century had been asked where in Europe anti-Semitism was at its strongest, he would probably have answered Russia, the homeland of pogroms and the Black Hundreds, possibly France where the Dreyfus Case was at its climax, conceivably Austria where Karl Lueger had just been elected mayor of the capital city. It is unlikely that he would have answered Germany. On the other hand, there is little doubt that more has been written about the pre-1914 anti-Semitism of Germany than of all other countries combined. The reasons for this are to be found in post-1933 experience.

The same applies to the slightly different problem of why there was a Jewish Question in Imperial Germany. Here the trend in the volume of writing has been reversed. The first publications bearing the title 'die jüdische Frage' appeared in 1838; in 1842 no fewer than five articles or pamphlets (including Bruno Bauer's) appeared bearing the word 'Judenfrage' in their title.[1] For the next century or so a vast literature was published, claiming to

1 Although this particular expression was used sporadically in English and French from the middle of the eighteenth century onwards, the instances cited are those of the first usage in German. On this whole question see Jacob Toury, ' "The Jewish Question": A Semantic Approach', *LBYB* XI (1966), esp. pp. 85–93; also Ulrich Eichstätt, *Bibliographie zur Geschichte der Judenfrage*, Hamburg, 1938, nos 1033, 1035, 1259, 1825, 1843, 1846.

deal with this topic. Since the Second World War the notion that the mere existence of Jews might be the cause of a problem has been considered tasteless or even embarrassing; but historical treatment of the phenomenon, again with an emphasis on Germany, has flourished.

Consideration of the Jewish Question is not, of course, entirely separate from that of anti-Semitism. Both phenomena illustrate not merely aspects of Jewish life and Jewish–Gentile group relations; they also illuminate aspects of state, society and nationality in general, in this case in Imperial Germany. But the Jewish Question is sufficiently distinct to warrant separate treatment and to divide consideration of it into a number of components:

1 Are Jews a race, a nation or a religious community?
2 What, if any, are the terms on which Jews should have rights of citizenship?
3 What, if anything, should be done about the peculiar occupational distribution of Jews?
4 Does the international scattering of Jews make them peculiar as a race, nation or religious community?
5 Would it help anyone, including Jews, if they were encouraged to settle somewhere else?

In the light of these criteria, one can see why there was a 'Jewish Question' in some countries, but not in others. Its existence is not surprising in states with large and distinctive Jewish populations, such as pre-1914 Russia and Austria-Hungary, or inter-war Poland and Romania. In these regions the first three of our questions remained largely unresolved, with the result that an increasing number of Jews and Gentiles were attracted to an affirmative answer to question 5. Equally, one can see why, despite the Dreyfus Case and the agitation against Jewish immigration in Britain[2] at the beginning of the twentieth century, there was no Jewish Question in Western Europe. It was not a question of numbers – the Jews of Germany amounted, after all, to 1 per cent of the population – rather that the problems raised by the relationship between nationality and citizenship and the citizen's rights *vis-à-vis* the state had (at any rate for the time being) been solved in the developed countries of Western Europe. Barriers of birth and religion to the enjoyment of political rights and social facilities had been removed not only *de jure* but to a large extent *de facto*. These problems had not been settled in Germany

2 On the latter question, see Lloyd P. Gartner, *The Jewish Immigrant in England 1870–1914*, London: Allen and Unwin, 1960; Bernard Gainer, *The Alien Invasion. The Origins of the Aliens Act of 1905*, London: Heinemann, 1972; John A. Garrard, *The English and Immigration: A Comparative Study of the Jewish Influx, 1880–1910*, Oxford: Oxford University Press, 1971.

and the barriers not removed. That is why the Jewish Question had not disappeared.

The Jewish Question in Germany was a function of the German concepts of the nation and of political rule. The particular roles that Jews played in German society and the development of the German economy certainly caused tensions. They are central to any consideration of anti-Semitism and the existence of anti-Semitism made the Jewish Question more important than it would otherwise have been. But these socio-economic factors were at most secondary, aggravating elements in the Jewish Question as we have defined it. They were not the causes of its existence.

The concept of nationality in Germany is central to our whole subject, for the nineteenth century was characterized by the struggle to create and define a German national consciousness. The modern origins of this consciousness are to be found in the wars of liberation against Napoleon, and the nature of this political mass experience was decisive in the German people's sense of common identity.[3] It would be wrong to deduce from this that German nationalism was inherently hostile to Jews: the relationship was more complex. One can, of course, make a catalogue of early German nationalists and their anti-Semitic utterances; nothing is easier and it has been frequently done. But one can equally point to the part Jewish writers played in 'Jung Deutschland' and to the anti-Semitism of such diverse opponents of the nationalist movement as Ludwig von der Marwitz and Wolfgang Menzel. The role of nationalist ideology in defining the position of the Jew is different. Nationalism was a defensive creed – in Professor Bracher's phrase an *Abwehrideologie*.[4] It preached unity directed at a common enemy, an enemy who was Western and identified with beliefs in the rights of man, individualism and political rationalism. It coincided with the romantic movement, with its emphasis on the cultural component of nationality and the sanctity of unique traditions. Because it was defensive and romantic, German nationalism was exclusive; the need to ensure the internal cohesion of the tribe put a high premium on internal loyalty; it also put a high premium on rigorously defining the outsider. The debate in the *Burschenschaften*, which began as early as 1817, as to whether a Jewish student could belong to them, illustrates

---

3   For recent scholarly treatment of this topic, see Gerhard Schulz, 'Der späte Nationalismus im politischen Denken des neunzehnten Jahrhunderts', in Hans Liebeschütz and Arnold Paucker (eds), *Das Judentum in der deutschen Umwelt, 1800–1850. Studien zur Frühgeschichte der Emanzipation*, Tübingen: J. C. B. Mohr, 1977.
4   Karl Dietrich Bracher, *Die Auflösung der Weimarer Republik. Eine Studie zum Problem des Machtverfalls in der Demokratie*, 4th edn, Villingen-Schwarzwald: Ring-Verlag, 1964, p. 4.

the strength of this obsession.[5] What the ideology of nationalism contributed to the German 'Jewish Question', therefore, was not some congenital anti-Semitism, but the search for all-embracing definitions, for all-or-nothing criteria of what, or who, was German.

Doctrines concerning the state, though different in content, were similar in their impact. Early German nationalism had been the ideology of a people that lacked a state; contemporaneous theories of the state did not define citizens or territory in ethnic terms. Only extreme nationalists, like Friedrich Ludwig Jahn, insisted that *Volk* and *Staat* should be co-terminous. For the moment, therefore, it will suffice for our purpose if we concentrate on those doctrines current in the first half of the nineteenth century that bore directly on administrative practice; in other words, on theories of citizenship.

Just as political nationalism in Germany had its origins in French doctrines of national self-determination, so the modernization of the state followed French enlightenment models. Both, however, developed hostility to the French and, indeed, Western European emphasis on the rights and value of the individual. What characterized the orthodoxy of the Prussian and later of the German bureaucracy was a dogmatic enlightenment, which saw super-stition, ignorance, prejudice and all local peculiarities as obstacles to good citizenship. The ideal was a direct relationship between the individual and the state, unimpeded by the pluralism of autonomous groups or the retention of traditionalist practices.

The implications of these attitudes came out clearly in the debate on Jewish emancipation which lasted from the end of the eighteenth century until the 1860s. Both Christian Wilhelm von Dohm and Wilhelm von Humboldt saw as the ultimate aim of any policy of emancipation the abandonment by Jews of their religion. A change in the situation of the Jews was for them inseparable from the reform of society in general: '[The government] will have realized its great intention', wrote Dohm, 'when the nobleman, the peasant, the scholar, the artisan, the Christian and the Jew is, more than all of this, a citizen.'[6] For Humboldt, Minister for Education and Religious Affairs at the time of the Prussian government's emancipation proposals in 1809, equal citizenship would remove the stigma of opportunism from conversions. The Jews' embracing of Christianity would then become 'desirable, pleasing

5 Oscar Scheuer, *Burschenschaft und Judenfrage. Der Rassenantisemitismus in der deutschen Studentenschaft*, Berlin: Verlag Berlin-Wien, 1927; also Monika Richarz, *Der Eintritt der Juden in die akademischen Berufe. Jüdische Studenten und Akademiker in Deutschland, 1678–1848*, Tübingen: J. C. B. Mohr, 1974, pp. 150–7.
6 Christian Wilhelm von Dohm, *Über die bürgerliche Verbesserung der Juden*, Berlin and Stettin: Nicolai, 1781–3, vol. I, p. 26.

and beneficial'.[7] For State Councillor Koehler, who shared Humboldt's sentiments, 'the final purpose of our legislation must surely remain to banish totally all differences in civil rights between Christians and Jews', so as 'to assimilate the Jews totally to us'.[8]

The same sentiments characterized the majority of the reports that the heads of provincial governments submitted to the Prussian Ministry of the Interior in 1842. The governor (*Regierungspräsident*) of Breslau commented that military service for Jews 'must inevitably contribute materially to [their] most desirable general fusion with the rest of the nation'.[9] The Silesian *Regierungspräsidenten* jointly acknowledged that 'since 1812 it has been the task of the state to neutralize the separatist peculiarities of the Jewish character'.[10] Their colleague in Posen echoed this interpretation:

It is most desirable that the Christian population should progressively lose its concept of the Jews as a foreign nation, imposed on the state and only to be tolerated as a necessary evil, and that we should rather accustom ourselves to considering the Jews as a section of the population distinguished only by their religion, but in all other respects as fellow-citizens and fellow-subjects similar to the Christians.[11]

The culmination of this philosophy found expression in the North German Confederation's law of 3 July 1869 on the freedom and equality of religion.

In its generosity, its optimism, its faith in the highest standards of human behaviour, this philosophy seems at first sight to be the opposite of the integral, exclusive nationalism of the Romantics. But the two attitudes shared certain characteristics, as the more wide-awake Jewish advocates of emancipation noticed. Gabriel Riesser was aware that there were some who 'wished to lay the foundations of German nationality, instead of on the fundamentals of common liberty, common rights and common welfare, on large-scale hatred of the French, and small-scale hatred of the Jews'.[12] And Abraham Geiger dissociated himself from those who, in sympathy with the wishes of

---

7   Gutachten der Sektion des Cultus zum Schroetter'schen Entwurf, 17.7.1809. Ismar Freund, *Die Emanzipation der Juden in Preußen unter besonderer Berücksichtigung des Gesetzes vom 11. März 1812. Ein Beitrag zur Rechtsgeschichte der Juden in Preußen*, Berlin: M. Poppelauer, 1912, vol. II, p. 276.

8   Gutachten des Staatsrats Koehler zum Schroetter'schen Entwurf, 13.5.1809, *ibid.*, p. 253.

9   Berichte über das Judenwesen. ZStM, Rep. 77, XXX, ad 117, vol. II, 10–11 (27.7.1842).

10   Ibid., vol. I, 232 (8.10.1842).

11   Ibid., vol. II, 20 (1.4.1842).

12   Gabriel Riesser, 'Betrachtungen über die Verhandlungen der zweiten Kammer des Großherzogtums Baden über die Emanzipation der Juden', in *Gesammelte Schriften*, Frankfurt: Verlag der Riesser-Stiftung, 1867–8, vol. II, p. 361.

the enlightened dogmatists, 'would like to give up everything in order to gain only one thing'.[13] These doubts illustrate that the law of 3 July 1869, far from settling the Jewish Question, in some respects helped to exacerbate it. There are a number of reasons for supposing this to be so.

Firstly, with the creation of the Empire, *Volk*, as defined in the earlier decades of the century, merged with *Staat*, as defined in these decades. Ethnic and civic criteria now coincided. Nationality could no longer be defined without citizenship, nor citizenship without nationality. In the non-national state, the citizen had been defined by his loyalty: there was therefore a strong incentive to minimize the number of outsiders and to integrate Jews into the state. That had indeed been the aim of the enlightened dogmatists in the bureaucracy. In the national state there was a temptation to define loyalty by nationality: this created an incentive to maintain a distinction with outsiders and therefore to exclude Jews, or at least treat them with suspicion. The effect of this was to strengthen the barriers to social pluralism and cultural heterogeneity and to weaken the element of enlightenment in the principles on which the state was run.

Secondly, the law of 3 July 1869 constituted some kind of bargain between the state and the existing nation, on the one hand, and the Jews, on the other. But since the terms of the bargain were never clarified, accusations never ceased that both sides were failing to honour it. As far as governments were concerned, the aims of 'fusion', 'assimilation' and 'neutralization' remained unchanged and unqualified. But what would constitute assimilation? The abandonment of peculiar forms of speech and dress? Renunciation of special dietary laws, festivals and days of worship? An occupational distribution indistinguishable from the rest of the population? The abandonment of the Jewish religion altogether? All of these criteria found their advocates. To be fair, there were those on the Jewish side who did not disagree, sometimes in terms that now strike us as ridiculous and even pathetic. On the other hand, beside the undoubted Jewish success in some of the occupations associated with the triumph of Liberalism, there were the equally undoubted obstacles to the pursuit of other careers, especially in education and public service. As a consequence, there ensued a dialogue of the deaf: as long as Jews were not prepared to abandon all forms of separate culture, said some, they could not demand complete acceptance. As long as they were not offered complete acceptance, said others, they could scarcely be expected to renounce their traditions.

Thirdly, the question of entry to the public service raised, in turn, that of interpreting the 1869 law which, in due course, became an Imperial law. The law presupposed a secular, liberal political order and the constitution of the

13   Abraham Geiger, 'Das Judentum unserer Zeit und die Bestrebungen in ihm' (1835), in Ludwig Geiger (ed.), *Nachgelassene Schriften*, Breslau: Jacobsohn, 1875–8, vol. I, p. 454.

Reich was an entirely secular document. It contained no mention of God or religion. It also declared, in Article 2, that *Reich* legislation had precedence over that of the states. Against that, most of the states had constitutions dating from the 1850s, and even where these underwent amendment after 1871 their assimilation to the *Reich* constitution tended to be incomplete. In matters relevant to the rights of Jewish citizens they were apt to be ambiguous. Two examples: while Article 12 of the Prussian constitution guaranteed freedom of religion and outlawed discrimination, Article 14 emphasized the Christian character of state schools. Similarly the 'oath of a Christian' required in courts of law made the courts to some extent Christian institutions. The Christian character of the states was further emphasized by the episcopal roles of Protestant crowned heads. Since the most sensitive areas in Jewish public employment, namely education and the judiciary, remained the province of the states, and since others, such as the military, remained largely under royal prerogative, the contradiction between the secular Empire and the Christian member-states was an important contributor to the perpetuation of the Jewish Question after 1871.

The difficulties created by the 1869 law need to be seen in a wider context. Our hypothesis has been that while anti-Semitism cannot be understood without the socio-economic factors, the Jewish Question was largely a constitutional one. But, of course, the two do not inhabit separate worlds. We need to ask why the German Empire was a less secularized state than were contemporary France or Belgium *de jure*, or Britain *de facto*. The answer is to be found in the manner of German unification, which in turn is to be explained by the balance of forces during the 1860s within and between the German states. The creation of a German nation-state was an aspiration of the middle class, but the Empire was a creation of the Prussian army. The wars of the 1860s brought victories not only by Prussia against Austria and France but by the dynasty over parliament, by the army over the middle class, by autocracy over self-government. This is so well-known that one hesitates to mention it at all; nevertheless its relevance is obvious. One reason why there was a Jewish Question after 1871 is that the process of unification scarcely affected the constitutions of the states. The other is that the social structure of the Empire affected the expectations of the Jewish community and their response to it.

As Reinhard Rürup has emphasized, the slow progress of emancipation in Germany, accompanied by a public debate lasting almost ninety years, made the 'Jewish Question' an apparently permanent feature of political life.[14]

14   Reinhard Rürup, 'Kontinuität und Diskontinuität der "Judenfrage" im 19. Jahrhundert', in Hans-Ulrich Wehler (ed.), *Sozialgeschichte Heute. Festschrift für Hans Rosenberg zum 70. Geburtstag*, Göttingen: Vandenhoeck und Ruprecht, 1974, p. 398; also *idem*, 'Emancipation and Bourgeois Society', *LBYB* XIV (1969), pp. 86–8.

Contemporary observers were fully aware of this. Ludwig Philippson, replying in the middle of the 'Liberal decade' to the Catholic publicist Freiherr von Loë, remarked:

> If the author rests his case on the writings by Christian authors in favour of emancipation, we are entitled to catalogue ten against emancipation for every one of the former. Indeed, precisely the fact that so much has been written and said demonstrates that it took the Germans an extraordinary effort to acknowledge equality of rights, which even today has been completely achieved in only a few states. In North America, France, Holland, Belgium, England, Denmark and Italy there have been few written exchanges on the subject, but it was carried out in the briefest time.[15]

But progress was further retarded by the kind of Germany that emerged from the wars of unification. This explains what happened to the twin Jewish aspirations of emancipation and assimilation. For most Jews, emancipation was negatively defined: it consisted of the removal of legal barriers to equal citizenship. So, too, assimilation was predominantly negative – the abandonment of peculiarities as a prerequisite for social and intellectual, as opposed to merely commercial or professional, intercourse with Christian citizens. But the satisfaction of these aspirations also presupposed a change in the structure of Gentile society. What Jews wanted, though they did not always make this clear, was assimilation not to the German nation but to the German middle class. A necessary condition for success, therefore, was the domination of German society by the middle class. In so far as this did not happen at any time before 1914 – in contrast with the states of Western Europe – the desire to assimilate was bound to meet frustration.

In this respect the revival of anti-Semitism within a decade of the emancipation law becomes relevant. It has been argued that this in turn breathed new life into the Jewish Question and prevented it from expiring, as mid-century Liberals might reasonably have expected it to.[16] But it could equally be argued that the opposite was true – that it was the survival of the Jewish Question which stimulated the resurgence of anti-Semitism. In so far as anti-Semitism in Imperial Germany had economic causes and in so far as the Jew, in his capacity as the successful capitalist, became the hate-object of the discontented, this demonstrated the continuation of pre-emancipation roles. Because the change-over from a feudal-absolutist to a bourgeois-capitalist order had been incomplete, Jews continued to perform economic

15 Ludwig Philippson, 'Judentum und Deutschtum', in *Gesammelte Abhandlungen,* Leipzig: G. Fock, 1911, vol. I, p. 162.
16 E.g. Rürup, 'Kontinuität und Diskontinuität', p. 403. The terms of the debate were further confused by the insistence of many anti-Semites that what they were discussing was the 'Jewish Question'.

tasks that were both distinctive and widely disliked. Because in the society of Imperial Germany Jews continued to form a 'quasi-estate',[17] they could evoke the jealousy of other estates. Because the civil equality, proclaimed by the 1869 law, did not correspond with the constitutional theory and political reality of the majority of the individual states, it was easy to agitate, not merely for the revocation of emancipation, but against its practical implementation. That anti-Semitism in Imperial Germany was as much the consequence as the cause of a continuing Jewish Question is shown by the experience of Germany's more bourgeois Western neighbours. There, too, there were epidemics of anti-Semitism, but they did not lead to a revival of the Jewish Question. It was because Germans failed to solve the Jewish Question in the period of emancipation that anti-Semitism there could become politically dangerous.

How did Jews react to the obstacles to assimilation in the German Empire? For the initial period, Jews sought refuge in the formula of the German citizen of the Jewish faith ('deutscher Staatsbürger jüdischen Glaubens'), the public German and private Jew. Nowhere was this formulation propagated more fervently than in the principal organ of Liberal Judaism, the *Allgemeine Zeitung des Judentums*. In 1878, at the height of the first wave of anti-Semitism, it claimed: 'In vain have Jews demonstrated, theoretically and practically, that apart from their worship and their charitable institutions, they have no special and common concerns.'[18] Thirty years later it could still speak in the same vein: 'Jewish citizens may believe or not believe what they wish in their synagogues, in political life they are German citizens and not Jews.'[19] Nor was this version of the place of the Jew in modern society restricted to Jews. Hermann Oncken in many ways spoke for the academic generation of his day in a message to Jewish youth in 1911:

The process of growing together into one organism has taken longer than idealists in both camps had expected. Amalgamation is more difficult and ... it is perhaps to be considered complete only after a number of generations. It remains the ideal from the point of view of German culture and the German nation, and therefore also of those Jews who have roots in both.[20]

By the end of the First World War, such sentiments had an old-fashioned ring to them. But in the 1870s and 1880s, most Jews and most liberal

17   As argued by Lawrence Schofer, 'Emancipation and Population Change', in Werner Mosse, Arnold Paucker and Reinhard Rürup (eds), *Revolution and Evolution. 1848 in German-Jewish History*, Tübingen: J. C. B. Mohr, 1981, p. 64.
18   *AZJ*, 11 July 1878, p. 371.
19   Ibid., 13 December 1907, p. 589.
20   'An den Verband jüdischer Jugend', cit *Berliner Börsen-Courier*, 10 April 1911.

supporters of civic equality would insist that in fighting discrimination or prejudice they were concerned not with a Jewish question but with a constitutional question. This explains in particular the reluctance of Jews to organize to defend their interests in the early decades of the Empire and their slow response to the revival of anti-Semitism.[21] The anti-Semitic campaign of the late 1870s raised, among other questions, the one that Jews were most sensitive to – were they really Germans, could they ever really become Germans? The overwhelming pressure on Jews was to abjure all distinctiveness: on this point anti-Semites and Liberals agreed. Treitschke's demand, 'Let them become Germans, let them feel simply and properly as Germans',[22] was echoed by the Liberal Alfred Dove: 'Remain what you are, but not as you are! … Be Germans with us.'[23]

The response to this from Jewish assimilationist spokesmen was entirely defensive. It denied not the premise: that Jews ought indeed to be complete Germans, but the conclusion: that they had failed to fulfil their part of the emancipation bargain. Such organizations as existed within the Jewish community, e.g. the *Deutsch-Israelitischer Gemeindebund*, issued advice to Jews: to be modest in their public bearing, diligent in their work and restrained in public controversy. Yet to argue like this was to concede that the terms of equality were to be defined by the emancipator alone. It evaded the hypothesis that equal rights also meant equal rights to agitate, to litigate and to offend against good taste. It acknowledged, in the words of Maximilian Horwitz, a later Jewish community leader, that 'step-children must be doubly well-behaved'.[24] The same unwillingness to attract attention informed the reaction of Jewish leaders and journals to the revival of anti-Semitism. The general tendency was to play it down, to let it blow over. The reason for this was not merely the hope, perhaps reasonable in the 1870s, that Stoecker and Treitschke were the terminal symptom of a dying prejudice and not the first indication of a new wave. It was also the conscious decision not to appear as an organized group with special interests to defend. To have done so would

21 On this topic see in particular Michael A. Meyer, 'The Great Debate on Anti-semitism: Jewish Reaction to New Hostility in Germany 1879–1881', *LBYB* XI (1966), and Ismar Schorsch, *Jewish Reactions to German Anti-Semitism, 1870–1914*, New York: Columbia University Press, 1972, ch. 2.
22 Heinrich von Treitschke, 'Unsere Aussichten', *PJ*, 15 November 1879, p. 573.
23 Alfred Dove, 'Humboldt als Judengenoss', *Im Neuen Reich*, vol. I, 1 (1871), p. 390.
24 'An unsere Glaubensgenossen', *Mitteilungen des deutsch-israelitischen Gemeindebundes*, Oct. 1880, cit. Jehuda Reinharz, *Fatherland or Promised Land. The Dilemma of the German Jew, 1893–1914*, Ann Arbor, Mich.: University of Michigan Press, 1975, p. 27; Arnold Paucker, 'Zur Problematik einer jüdischen Abwehrstrategie in der deutschen Gesellschaft', *WD*, p. 529, esp. fn. 139.

have cast doubt on the efficacy of emancipation and the reality of assimilation. Such attitudes were based on self-deception. To accept the all-inclusive definitions of nationality common to liberal and illiberal advocates of national unification, to accept the all-inclusive definitions of citizenship common to monarchist conservatives and enlightened bureaucrats, was to ignore that belonging to a religious denomination had its social implications, and that belonging to a social group with a long history and distinctive culture was bound to influence the personal and spiritual characteristics of its members.

By the 1890s this particular self-deception was beginning to become more difficult to maintain, though it was replaced by others, just as unhelpful. By the 1890s it was obvious that the advance of civilization would not, by itself, consign anti-Semitism to oblivion, nor would the mere passage of legislation end discrimination. Not only was publicly-proclaimed anti-Semitism flourishing, but state authorities failed to prosecute even the most extreme agitators. With the exception of the SPD, political parties were reluctant to adopt Jews as parliamentary candidates. Perhaps most seriously, it was more difficult in 1893 than in 1873 for a Jew to gain public appointment on his merits. All this forced a revision of the principle that Jews should not organize. This change of policy, which resulted in the formation of the *Centralverein deutscher Staatsbürger jüdischen Glaubens*,[25] was helped by a general evolution in political activism and the multiplication of interest organizations. The *Centralverein* was created in 1893, the same year as the Agrarian League and the Pan-German League. One of its founders, Eugen Fuchs, commented that in an age of interest groups Jews would have to form their own lobby.[26]

But there were also reasons specific to the situation of Jews for a change of policy. The first was the renewal of anti-Semitism. Although there had been a Gentile counter-attack to this, in the form of the *Verein zur Abwehr des Antisemitismus*, Jews increasingly deviated from the view, current since the days of Moses Mendelssohn, that the Jewish case should be pleaded by disinterested Gentiles. The second was the continuation of discrimination. Here, too, Jewish leaders felt that they had to take on governments and the courts themselves and to shed any embarrassment at doing so. Rather more controversially, they pressed for Jews to be nominated as parliamentary candidates by non-Socialist parties in districts with good prospects, with the Jews so elected to act in a representative capacity: the Jewish commu-

25 For the origins and evolution of the *Centralverein*, see Schorsch, *Jewish Reactions*, ch. 4 and 5, and Paucker, 'Zur Problematik', *WD*, pp. 479–548.

26 *IdR*, March 1896, p. 170, cit. Marjorie Lamberti, *Jewish Activism in Imperial Germany. The Struggle for Civil Equality*, New Haven, Conn., and London: Yale University Press, 1978, p. 15.

nity, it was argued, needed Jews to speak out against anti-Semitism and discrimination.[27]

In the course of time the *Centralverein* went further; slowly and perhaps unconsciously it redefined, through its activities, the terms of assimilation. It took up a campaign against apostasy, to the extent of branding converts as deserters. It encouraged the study of Jewish religion and history, especially among Jewish children. In other words by 1914 it was emphasizing the value of precisely those attributes that had in 1870 been regarded as obstacles to German Jews becoming Jewish Germans. Where, then, did the self-deception lie? It was revealed by the name that the *Centralverein* chose for itself. Though its activities, indeed its very existence, implied a break with the unqualified assimilationism of the 1870s, its vocabulary did not adapt to this break. Its leaders hovered uneasily between the earlier orthodoxy of 'we are Germans like everyone else' and a frank recognition that there could and should not be only one kind of German. It would be unfair to blame them too strongly for this. The failure of their self-definition reflected the failure of the German nation at large to arrive at a satisfactory relationship between nationality and citizenship. This dual failure was illustrated by the constant battle that Jewish representative organizations fought with the governments over the legal status of Jews. This battle was fought along many sectors: the appointment of Jews as judges and the Prussian educational reform of 1905–6 will serve as well as any.

Of all the public positions that Jews aspired to, of all the denials of equal opportunity that they most resented, those in the judiciary loomed largest. In the twenty years before 1914 the states' policies in judicial appointments and promotion were constantly debated. Policies varied from state to state, although all acknowledged that they were bound by the law of 1869. Baden and Hamburg were the most liberal, Saxony the least so. Prussia, Bavaria and the Grand Duchy of Hesse occupied intermediate positions.[28]

The position of critics of the state governments was straightforward. It was obvious that Jewish candidates were not being treated on their merits. Jewish lobbyists and their allies and government officials performing a tightrope act were not alone in feeling the frustrations of a constitution that proclaimed norms widely evaded and objectionable to many. One anti-Semitic paper said of Prussian ministers:

These gentlemen are subject to the constitution. ... The constitution requires them to turn their hearts into a murderer's den. ... It is a sign of our own weakness that

27 E.g. *AZJ*, 17 October 1893, p. 505.
28 See below, pp. 57–61.

ministers may no longer say openly what they feel in their hearts. ... The constitution is the enemy, because it contains the emancipation of the Hebrews.[29]

For some years after the 1901 debate in the Prussian parliament, officials were required to comment whether local conditions made the nomination of a Jewish judge advisable.[30] This exercise may have been an empty formality, but nothing points more convincingly to the existence of a Jewish Question than the mere fact that these debates took place so frequently and that ministers and their officials were required to have policies on a matter that the 1869 law would have settled long ago if that law had been the only criterion for action.

The debate on the Prussian School Bill of 1905 illustrated these dilemmas even more graphically. The existing law dated from 1847. It provided for Christian, but not Jewish, religious instruction in state schools and made it optional for local authorities to subsidize Jewish denominational schools and Jewish religious teachers in state schools. It is evident that though most Jewish pupils attended denominational or inter-denominational Christian schools, virtually no Jewish teachers were employed in them. Even before the introduction of the 1905 Bill, Jewish leaders faced dilemmas of both principle and practice. Should they, along with the Liberal parties, demand completely inter-confessional schools without religious instruction, or should they demand equal status for Jewish denominational schools and for Jewish religious instruction in state schools? Should they risk offending their political allies in the Progressive parties, whose policy was to demand secular education, or acknowledge that, given the electoral system in Prussia, there was no prospect of a majority for such a demand? Yet to make the best of generally confessionalized educational systems seemed to most of them a bad bargain: it was the first step towards re-segregation and away from assimilation. In the end the attitude of the Catholic *Zentrum* was crucial to the shape in which the bill finally passed. The *Zentrum* was not in favour of discrimination against Jews, but neither was it in favour of driving Christianity out of the schools. It therefore supported amendments that made subsidies to Jewish religious instruction mandatory and under certain circumstances entitled a rabbi to sit on the school board.[31]

What the debates on the judiciary and education illustrated – and one could choose plenty of other examples – was that in matters of everyday

29   *Deutsche Hochwacht*, 11 February 1905.
30   Ernennung von Land- und Amtsrichtern und Staatsanwälten, ZStM, 2.2.1., 17031, *passim*.
31   For a full account of these debates, see Lamberti, *Jewish Activism*, ch. 7.

importance Germany after 1871 was still governed by the member-states, not the Imperial government.

The attitude of the *Zentrum* to the Prussian School Bill showed not that it was anti-Semitic (though some of its members and journals were), but that its political universe was bounded by the assumptions of the 1850 Prussian constitution. It was based on the notion that an individual's religious faith was a matter of public policy and that churches had a right and duty to participate in the formulation of that policy. The evasions of the various ministers of justice showed not that they were anti-Semitic (though some of them, and quite a few of their officials, were), but that their evaluation of the rights of religious denominations was based in the pre-Liberal era. For the most part they served states in which Christians collectively had legitimate claims and Jews collectively did not. It is the states, more than the Empire, that support the often-made contention that though Germany underwent a revolutionary economic change between 1871 and 1914 this was not accompanied by the changes in social and political attitudes normally associated with urbanization and industrialization. Hence the 1869 law, which presupposed an open, bourgeois society, remained, if not a dead letter, then an inadequate guide.

There is a further reason why the 1869 law proved contentious, namely the German predilection for legal positivism, the tendency to take essentially normative legislation literally and to litigate on that basis, to demand of the due process of law that it should solve human relationships. That the spirit and the letter of the law on religious equality were systematically broken in Imperial Germany is undeniable. Whether all such breaches were best dealt with by the same type of formal protest is an open question. In Britain, too, for instance, there were no Jewish members of the Foreign Office[32] before 1914, and being a Jew was undoubtedly an obstacle to gaining an Oxford or Cambridge college fellowship.[33] Yet there is no record of parliamentary questions on the subject, although there was no shortage of Jewish MPs or Gentile sympathizers with Jewish civic aspirations. One can offer only tentative explanations for this. One is that unwritten rules and conventions covered areas of social life that were larger in Britain than in Germany. Another is that social mobility was at this period greater in Britain and this opened other, compensatory avenues to the ambitious Jew. The suggestion

---

32 Zara S. Steiner, *The Foreign Office and British Foreign Policy, 1898–1914*, Cambridge: Cambridge University Press, 1969, p. 19.
33 Cf. A. F. Pollard's letter after L. B. Namier failed to be elected to a fellowship at All Souls College in 1911: 'The Warden and the majority of Fellows shied at his race, and eventually we elected the two next best.' J. Namier, *Lewis Namier. A Biography*, Oxford: Oxford University Press, 1971, p. 101.

of one recent historian of English anti-Semitism that 'Anglo-Jewry's ... lay
leadership provided a catching example of successful integration into Gentile
society'[34] is seductive but valid only because the barriers to integration were
in any case weak. English Jews were never subject to special legislation. They
were excluded from certain privileges as non-Protestants or aliens; therefore
their legal emancipation was a less traumatic experience for the host society.

In Germany the Jewish Question remained on the agenda but some aspects
were more salient than others. Those who held that Jews were a separate,
unassimilable race were a small, though growing, and noisy minority. So, too,
were those who felt that emigration was the only solution to the dilemma
of German–Jewish co-existence. The question had a narrower scope: it arose
out of the unfulfillable and contradictory prescriptions for the conditions of
post-emancipation Jewish life. Most Germans, Gentile and Jewish, agreed
that Jews had ceased to be a nation but remained a religious denomination.
Some argued that they should cease to be the latter as well; others that as
long as they remained a religious denomination they could not escape the
disadvantages of living in a predominantly Christian state. As for the occupational distribution of Jews, which worried Jewish reformers as much as
anti-Semites, this was a problem only if one wanted it to be one. It is not
self-evident that every religious or ethnic minority should in this respect be a
microcosm of the larger unit. The problem arises only if the minority
concerned is especially associated with socio-economic transformations that
arouse suspicion and fear, and associated with interests on whose merits there
is no consensus.

There were, then, two aspects of the Jewish Question in Imperial Germany
that ensured its survival. The first was constitutional. As long as articles like
No. 14 of the Prussian constitution existed side by side with the 1869 law the
very norms of public policy were in doubt. It has become fashionable to
downgrade the importance of constitutions and statutes in ordering relations
within society. Of course, such documents are not drafted in vacuums. They
reflect the real relations of forces in societies as well as their intellectual and
legal traditions. But because they tend to change more slowly than economic
or social relations, because they possess a normative force, because a great
deal of public conflict is about their interpretation, there is much to be gained
from occasionally looking at the super-structures that govern men's lives.

The second aspect was social and ideological. It deals with the relationship
between the emergence of bourgeois society and the evolution of secular
notions of citizenship. Imperial Germany corresponded neither with the
fully-developed bourgeois societies of Western Europe, nor with the semi-

34   Gisela C. Lebzelter, *Political Anti-Semitism in England 1918–1939*, London:
Macmillan, 1978, p. 179, fn. 11 and pp. 6–7.

patriarchal societies of Eastern Europe, where the bourgeoisie was still a subordinate force. The peculiar way in which the Empire was created led to a mixture of conservative, non-secular notions of citizenship that equated non-conformity with disloyalty, and revolutionary notions of nationality inclined to be intolerant of awkward and anomalous categories. The demands which this made on a non-Christian minority, whose political ideal had to be one of libertarian Enlightenment and what Max Weber called 'formal rationality' in administration, could not be satisfied. Those who governed Germany, and those who increasingly influenced its public opinion, could not decide between the insistence that Jews should assimilate more and the conviction that they were incapable of ever doing so. If Nietzsche was right in observing that the question 'What is German?' never dies out among Germans,[35] it is easy to see why the question 'Can a Jew be a German?' never received a satisfactory answer. Comprehensive definitions of nationality and citizenship, designed to solve all problems of allegiance, invariably intensify them, by drawing attention to the outsider. This conclusion is as valid today as in 1879.

Each country's history is unique, and so is the history of each religious or ethnic minority within it. But such histories are not self-contained. 'Germany's Jews', a recent contributor to the unending debate has written, 'indignantly rejected all talk of a "Jewish Question" as a survival of primitive politics. In retrospect we know that in a sense, and a sense they did not intend, they were right: the so-called Jewish Question had no reality in isolation. It was part of, and a clue to, the larger question: the German Question.' To which he wisely added: 'German questions ... are not German questions alone'.[36]

35 Friedrich Nietzsche, *Jenseits von Gut und Böse*, [Kröners Taschenbuchausgabe] Stuttgart: Kröner, 1976, p. 175.
36 Peter Gay, *Freud, Jews and Other Germans. Masters and Victims in Modernist Culture*, New York: Oxford University Press, 1978, pp. 19, 28.

2

Religion and Judicial Appointments in Imperial Germany

The German Empire of 1871–1918 was a land of opportunity, not least for its Jews. Many who were gifted with enterprise or intellect reached wealth and eminence. But it was a land of unequal opportunity, with most branches of the public services, whether military or civil, virtually barred to the unbaptized Jew. Of all the public service careers the one in which Jews most resented discrimination, and most frequently complained of it, was the judiciary. Their case was summarized in the well-known pamphlet by Bernhard Breslauer, *Die Zurücksetzung der Juden im Justizdienst*, published in 1907 by the *Verband der Deutschen Juden*. His conclusion, after having compared the appointment and promotion of Jewish and Christian candidates and that of unbaptized and baptized Jews in Prussia, was that Jews were

set back *deliberately* in every respect and, as the comparison with baptized [Jews] shows, solely by virtue of their religious denomination. ... If the guardians of justice knowingly infringe the law and the constitution to the detriment of a part of the population, if they favour by promotion precisely those whose behaviour betrays what is as a rule a low level of moral fibre, how can justice flourish, how can the public summon the confidence indispensable for the maintenance of justice?[1] ... Everywhere in Germany the picture is the same, everywhere Jews are either entirely excluded from

---

1 *Die Zurücksetzung der Juden im Justizdienst. Denkschrift im Auftrage des Verbandes der Deutschen Juden, gefertigt von seinem ersten Schriftführer, Justizrat Bernhard Breslauer*, Berlin: Verband der Deutschen Juden, 1907, p. 6.

Table 2.1 Religious composition of Prussian judiciary, 1880–1904

| | *1880* | | | | *1904* | | |
	Prot. %	*RC* %	*Jewish* %	*Prot.* %	*RC* %	*Jewish* %
Grade V (magistrates, state attorneys)	72.6	23.6	3.7	71.5	24.2	4.3
Grade IV (presiding magistrates, associate high court judges, superior state attorneys)	78.7	21.3		78.6	21.0	0.3
Grade III (presiding high court judges, senior state attorneys)	81.3	18.7		79.0	21.0	
Grade II (chief justices)	84.6	15.4		84.6	15.4	
Grade I (ministerial under and chief secretaries)	–	–		81.8	18.2	

Source: G St Dahlem, Rep. 84a, 11944: 54, 171–2

the judiciary, or discriminated against and excluded from the rank of the higher judiciary.[2]

The statistical evidence was irrefutable. Although the number of Prussian judicial posts had increased by almost 50 per cent between the mid-1870s and mid-1890s, the number of Jewish judges had almost halved: from 46 out of 680 (or 6.8 per cent) to 29 out of 1,004 (2.9 per cent).[3] A comparison of the denominational composition of the various ranks of the judiciary tells the same story (see table 2.1).

Yet a closer look at table 2.1 shows that the story was not as straightforward as Breslauer's analysis in terms of Jews and Christians suggested. Imperial Germany had a heavily segmented society, divided not only into Christians and Jews, but into Catholics and Protestants, believers and non-believers, Conservatives, Liberals and Socialists. All these allegiances

2 Ibid., p. 7.
3 Ibid., p. 6.

determined status and access to the public service, and their multiplicity explained why the problem of religion and judicial appointments proved so intractable. In addition, political and judicial authority was decentralized. Though there was from 1879 onwards an Imperial Supreme Court (*Reichsgerichtshof*), the vast majority of cases, civil and criminal, were heard by state courts, and the judges who presided over them owed their appointments to twenty-five different ministers of justice. This meant that the petitions and debates relating to discrimination also took place in the individual states.

The most important of these debates, and the one that attracted the greatest attention, was that in the Prussian Chamber of Deputies in 1901. It was opened by Martin Peltasohn, one of the Jewish members of the Progressive Union (FVg), whose specific complaint was the differential treatment of Jewish and Christian solicitors in appointments as public notaries. According to Peltasohn it took the average Christian lawyer eight years to become a notary, the average Jewish lawyer eighteen years: in the Posen judicial district only one Jewish notary had been appointed in twenty years, in the neighbouring district of Bromberg quite junior Christian lawyers had been appointed over the heads of Jews who held the title of *Justizrat*.[4] The difficulty in securing this highly coveted appointment was particularly keenly resented by Jewish lawyers, since many of them embarked on a private legal practice only because they despaired of becoming judges.

What caused the public stir, however, was not Peltasohn's complaint, familiar enough as it was, but the reply of the Minister of Justice, Karl Heinrich von Schönstedt. It made three main points. The first was that when making appointments he had to consider the interests of the population rather than of the candidates. The second was that clients frequently turned to notaries for advice in sensitive and confidential matters: there was a widespread preference among the population, 'the justification for which could not be denied', for officials who shared the client's confession. The third argument was the most sensational of all: 'I should not have expected that in this respect deputy Peltasohn would direct his reproaches against the Department of Justice, given that it is the only one in the entire monarchy that employs any Jewish court clearks [*Assessoren*] at all.'[5]

The reactions to these assertions were only in part predictable. Progressive deputies questioned how many citizens genuinely minded what their officials' religion was[6] and pointed out that the interests or wishes of the population

4   *StPrA*, 31 Jan. 1901, 927.
5   Ibid., 928–30.
6   Theodor Barth (FVg), ibid., 932.

could not be satisfied by breaching the law or the constitution.[7] (The relevant sections of the Prussian constitution were Article 4 – equality before the law – and Article 12 – equality of rights and duties irrespective of religious allegiance.) The National Liberal press also commented unfavourably on the minister's declaration. For the *Kölnische Zeitung*, 'it would contradict the constitution if the other departments were to adopt the principle of not appointing any Jews'[8] and the *National-Zeitung*, normally loyal to the government, spoke of 'a confession of permanent breaches of the constitution in Prussia'.[9] The National Liberal deputies of the Prussian chamber took a more ambiguous line, as will be seen below.

For the Conservative and anti-Semitic press the episode provided a field-day. The Conservative *Kreuz-Zeitung* gave general support to the minister,[10] the radical anti-Semitic *Staatsbürger-Zeitung* demanded that no Jews at all should be appointed,[11] the Agrarian *Deutsche Tageszeitung* that they should be appointed only in proportion to their share of the population.[12] For the *Deutsche Zeitung* the constitution was irrelevant, since the Jews were a race, not a religious denomination.[13] *Die Post* claimed that the insensitive appointment of Jewish judges had led to the election of Hermann Ahlwardt, the radical anti-Semitic Reichstag deputy for Arnswalde-Friedeberg, and to the anti-Jewish riots at Konitz in Pomerania.[14] All this unsolicited approval, not to mention the letters and telegrams of support that flowed into the ministry,[15] was a matter of embarrassment to Schönstedt, who did not aspire to the reputation of being an anti-Semite: 'If the anti-Semitic party wished to make the attempt to become my champion in the light of my remarks in the recent sitting, I should be obliged gratefully to decline'.[16]

Crucial to the outcome of this debate was the attitude of the *Zentrum*. Ever since the 1870s the Catholic party had, out of a mixture of principle and expediency, been an enemy of exceptional legislation and discrimination. On this occasion, however, its deputies and its press supported the minister. There are a number of reasons for this and they explain the often uneasy and

7   Hans Crüger (FVp), ibid., 8 Feb. 1901, 1281.
8   *Kölnische Zeitung*, 1 Feb. 1901, a.m.
9   *National-Zeitung*, 1 Feb. 1901, p.m.; also 9 Feb. 1901, a.m.
10 *KZ*, 1 Feb. 1901, p.m., 2 Feb. 1901, p.m.; also 31 May 1905.
11 *Staatsbürger-Zeitung*, 1 Feb. 1901, p.m.
12 *DT*, 1 Feb. 1901, p.m., 2 Feb. 1901, p.m.
13 *Deutsche Zeitung*, 15 Feb. 1901, p.m.
14 *Die Post*, 2 Feb. 1901, p.m.
15 G St Dahlem, Rep. 84a, 11944: 99ff; 3259: 65, 76, 99, 112.
16 *StPrA*, 8 Feb. 1901, 1228.

sometimes tense relationship between Jews and Catholics in the *Reich*, which existed side by side with their periodic alliances.

The first had to do with church and state. The *Reich* was a secular state; its constitution was silent on the question of religion, though the *Zentrum* would have liked a bill of rights included. But this was not true of the individual states. Notwithstanding the freedom of religion guaranteed by Article 12 of the Prussian constitution, Article 14 guaranteed the Christian character of those institutions that were 'connected with the exercise of religious functions'. Exactly what this category covered was a matter of dispute: education and marriage most obviously; other candidates were the military and the prison service, because of the chaplains attached to them, and all state ceremonies. The judiciary mattered because of the status of the oath. Throughout the 1850s and 1860s ministers of justice insisted that Jews could not be admitted to any office that involved the taking of oaths, though they were, from 1851, appointed law clerks (*Referendare*) and court clerks (*Assessoren*) with the proviso that they could not administer oaths. In 1859 the Minister of Justice, Louis Simons, justified this policy on the grounds not only that the constitution had not superseded Article 2 of the *Judengesetz* of 1847, which specifically barred judicial office to Jews, but that 'the country's Christian population agreed in its overwhelming majority' with the government's line.[17] Though the government suspended Article 2 of the *Judengesetz* the next year it was only in 1870 that the Liberal minister August Leonhardt, in response to the Emancipation Law of 1869, appointed the first three Jewish magistrates.[18]

In addition the Prussian *Konvention* of 1841, guaranteeing the equal treatment of the two principal Christian churches, remained in force until 1918, although breached by the *Kulturkampf* legislation of the 1870s. Attempts by Jewish organizations to gain equality of representation remained uniformly unsuccessful.[19]

Hence Catholic spokesmen felt justified in starting from the premise, one that they shared with the Conservatives, that Prussia was *de facto* a Christian state:

Admittedly the constitution does not say that we live in a Christian state [one *Zentrum* deputy declared]. But the greater part of our population does not abandon its belief

17   *StPrA*, 23 March 1859, 493.
18   Sievert Lorenzen, *Die Juden in der Justiz*, 2nd edn, Berlin: Deckert, 1943, pp. 75–6, 87–8, 104, 109.
19   For details of this campaign see Marjorie Lamberti, 'The Prussian Government and the Jews: Official Behaviour and Policy-Making in the Wilhelminian Era', *LBYB* XVII (1972), pp. 5–17.

in a Christian state. The great majority of the population takes the view that there is, after all, a partition between Christian and Jewish *Weltanschauung*. ... Religious sentiment is a power of elemental force and it is a mark of great wisdom if the royal state government, within decent limits, of course, tries to show it appropriate consideration.[20]

The Conservative spokesman put it even more bluntly:

The Conservative Party is united in expressing its thanks for the fact that the judicial administration takes account of the place that the Christian religion has amongst us ... and that we may therefore well speak of the actual existence of a Christian state (Very good! on the right and *Zentrum*).[21]

The second reason for the *Zentrum*'s support for Schönstedt had to do with the isolated and vulnerable position of the Catholic community in the *Reich* and in particular in Prussia. This was a complex phenomenon. Some of its causes were socio-economic. The Catholic population of the German states was disproportionately occupied in agriculture; it was under-represented in institutes of selective and higher education, in the more profitable commercial and professional occupations and in the higher reaches of public administration. For every 100,000 males in Prussia between 1887 and 1897 there were 33 Catholic university students, 58 Protestant and 519 Jewish in the three secular faculties. In the law faculty, which provided the necessary qualification for entry into the public service, the ratios were 9:17:104.[22] This is not the place to go into the well-known controversy on the role of the 'Protestant ethic' in stimulating ambition, enterprise and social mobility, merely to state that few contemporary observers would have dissented from the judgement of the Catholic commentator Johannes Rost: 'The fact that in material matters the German Catholics have been left behind is beyond dispute.'[23] This Catholic disadvantage in fields where Jews were conspicuously successful was a major cause of tension between the two communities.

But the 'ghetto' status of the Catholics also had political causes. Most Catholics had been unhappy about the creation of a *kleindeutsch* Empire, to the exclusion of Austria; most ardent German nationalists, in particular the

20   Anton Schmitz (*Zentrum*), *StPrA*, 9 Feb. 1901, 1330.
21   Bernhard Irmer (Conservative), *StPrA*, 8 Feb. 1901, 1282.
22   Wilhelm Lossen, *Der Anteil der Katholiken am akademischen Lehramte in Preußen. Nach statistischen Untersuchungen*, Cologne: J. P. Bachem, 1901, pp. 114–17; 'Die Parität an den deutschen Universitäten', *Historisch-politische Blätter für das katholische Deutschland* CXXI (1898), pp. 275–81.
23   Johannes Rost, *Die wirtschaftliche und kulturelle Lage der deutschen Katholiken*, Cologne: J. P. Bachem, 1911, p. 2.

National Liberals, shared the anti-clericalism and anti-Romanism that was probably at its peak in Europe in the decades following the promulgation of the Syllabus of Errors (1864) and the Infallibility decree (1870). The Kulturkampf legislation of the 1870s, designed in form to strengthen the state *vis-à-vis* the churches but implemented in practice to discriminate against Catholic institutions, was accompanied by an intensive purge of Catholic officials.[24] And while the *Zentrum* thereafter pursued the long-term aim of repealing all the discriminatory legislation, it concentrated in particular on improving its share in public appointments.

It did so in the name of the principle of *Parität*, as enshrined in the 1841 *Konvention*. The practical implementation of this, as interpreted by the *Zentrum*, meant a share of official posts, at all levels, proportionate to the Catholic share of the population (33.6 per cent in Prussia in 1871, 36.3 per cent in 1910), a level that was far from being achieved even before the decimations of the *Kulturkampf*. Occasional protests against the Prussian government's personnel policies also raised the grievances of the Jews. Ludwig Windthorst (significantly), speaking at the time that the Anti-Semitic Petition was circulating, insisted: 'In Germany *Parität* is constitutionally in force. ... I shall also plead the right that I claim for the Catholics and the Catholic Church and its servants on behalf of the Protestants and no less for the Jews'.[25] But in general this was a Catholic–Protestant quarrel, for it was a Protestant-dominated administration that failed to appoint Catholics. The Catholic catalogue of grievances, laid out in Julius Bachem's pamphlet *Die Parität in Preußen*, concluded: 'It is therefore high time that we should work our way out of our second-class political, economic and social status with all the powers at our disposal, that we ... should achieve a place equal to that of the Protestants at the table of public life.'[26] Similarly Bernhard von Bülow, Chancellor and Prussian Prime Minister from 1900 to 1909, assured the *Zentrum* politician Matthias Erzberger in 1916: 'During the whole of my term of office I regarded the practice of full parity of the two Christian confessions

24 Margaret L. Anderson and Kenneth Barkin, 'The Myth of the Puttkamer Purge and the Reality of the Kulturkampf: Some Reflections on the Historiography of Imperial Germany', *Journal of Modern History* (December 1982), pp. 647–86; Manfred Scholle, *Die preußische Strafjustiz im Kulturkampf 1873–1888*, Marburg: Elwert, 1974; Karl Bachem, *Vorgeschichte, Geschichte und Politik der deutschen Zentrumspartei*, Cologne: J. P. Bachem, 1927–32, vol. III, pp. 301–2, vol. IV, pp. 283–4, vol. IX, pp. 65–84, esp. pp. 74–6 for the judiciary.
25 *StBR*, 16 April 1880.
26 [Julius Bachem], *Die Parität in Preußen. Eine Denkschrift*, Berlin: J. P. Bachem, 1897, pp. 152–3; see also Andreas Grunenberg, *Das Religionsbekenntnis der höheren Beamten in Preußen*, vol. I: *Die höheren staatlichen Beamten*, Berlin: Puttkammer & Mühlbrecht, 1914, p. 408.

as a fundamental principle of my domestic political activity and, as a result of the experiences of the war, I see this parity more than ever as the pre-condition of a happy future of our German people'.[27] The *Zentrum's* third reason had to do with its concept of the public service. It did not see this in Weberian terms, which stress the segregation of official activity from the sphere of private life. For Weber, 'it is decisive for the specific nature of modern loyalty to an office that, in the pure type, it does not establish a relationship to a person.' This is designed to lead to the 'objective' discharge of business, i.e. 'a discharge of business according to *calculable rules*' and 'without regard for persons'.[28] Instead its view was closer to the modern American notion of representative bureaucracy, 'responsive to the demands and needs of the community. ... It is not neutral. Its procedures and decisions are not subject to scientific formulation by administrative experts acting alone.'[29]

The *Kölnische Volkszeitung* spelt this out as follows: 'Officials are there for the sake of the people, therefore the composition of the people should guide the structure of the public service. Then every sector of the population that is at all numerous will receive justice, and will see its desire satisfied to find members of its own confession among those in office and authority',[30] a point of view it would be happy to share with 'all just Protestants and impartial Jews'. Karl Bachem, one of the *Zentrum's* chief spokesmen, put his party's demands even more specifically: 'What a state as mixed in its religious proportions as Prussia needs is complete confidence between government and people, and this confidence can only be built by Catholics in the higher and highest administrative posts who, in addition, completely merit the confidence of the Catholic Church.'[31] In other words, Catholic officials and judges were there to ensure justice for Catholic citizens; and they had to be not merely nominal Catholics (like the Minister of Justice, Schönstedt) but what their opponents would have dubbed 'clericals' or 'ultramontanes'. Given this equation of equality before the law with parity and the insistence that equality meant quotas, one can see why for most of the time Catholics concentrated their fire on Protestants and ignored the status of Jews in the public service. *Die Parität in Preußen* did not mention Jews at all. But one can also see why,

27 Matthias Erzberger, *Erlebnisse im Weltkrieg*, Stuttgart: Deutsche Verlags-Anstalt, 1920, p. 22.
28 Max Weber, *Economy and Society. An Outline of Interpretive Sociology* (ed. Guenther Roth and Claus Wittich), New York: Bedminster Press, 1968, pp. 959, 975.
29 Peter Woll, *American Bureaucracy*, 2nd edn, New York: W. W. Norton, 1977, pp. 249–51. Also Samuel Krislov and David H. Rosenbloom, *Representative Bureaucracy and the American Political System*, Englewood Cliffs: Prentice-Hall, 1981.
30 *KVZ*, 11 Feb. 1902.
31 *StPrA*, 1 March 1894, 760; also K. Bachem, *Vorgeschichte*, vol. IV, p. 284.

Table 2.2   Religious distribution of lawyers in Prussia, 1887–1904

	1887	*%*	*1904*	*%*
Protestant	1,529	53.3	2,181	46.5
Catholic	755	26.3	1,230	26.2
Jewish	586	20.4	1,281	27.1

Source: G St Dahlem, Rep. 84a, 11944: 54, 171–2

once the question of Jewish notaries and judges was raised, the *Zentrum* should have reacted as it did. For a glance at the appointment and promotion statistics would show that figures did not – as they so rarely do – speak for themselves.

There were a lot of Jewish lawyers in the German Empire. The denominational breakdown for Prussia of accredited solicitors (including notaries) was as shown in table 2.2. From the early 1890s onwards, the number of Jewish lawyers actually exceeded that of Catholics. In Berlin, according to Schönstedt, 526 out of 851 (62 per cent) lawyers were Jewish in 1901, as were 65 out of 176 (37 per cent) notaries.[32] As table 2.1 shows, in the lower reaches of the judicature the ratio of Jews to Catholics at the turn of the century was 1:6, whereas the ratio in the population was 1:30. Since neither Jews nor the appointment of Jews to judicial office was evenly spread geographically there were some conspicuous concentrations of Jewish magistrates, notaries and court clerks (see table 2.3).

Zentrum spokesmen therefore claimed to wonder what the Jews and their Liberal allies were complaining about. Had not Liberals tolerated the *Kulturkampf* purges? Was their press not studiously silent, if not hostile, when Catholics demanded parity? 'The debate has publicly revealed with what double standards the Progressive orators on tolerance and equality measure, depending on whether it is a case of Catholics or Jews',[33] wrote the *Kölnische Volkszeitung*.

Yet this complaint, too, missed a number of points. The first is that the appointment of Jews, however numerous, was almost entirely restricted to the lower ranks of the judicial service: very few unbaptized Jews became high court judges and none became public prosecutors. Catholics did penetrate the higher ranks, even if Protestant dominance was never overthrown. (As late as 1910, of 373 Prussian public prosecutors (*Staatsanwälte*) 66, or 18 per cent,

32 *StPrA*, 31 Jan. 1901, 929.
33 *KVZ*, 9 February 1901, p.m.; also ibid., 6 March 1894, a.m., in reply to *FZ*, 3 March 1894; *Westfälischer Merkur*, 4 Feb. 1901, p.m.

Table 2.3 Percentage of Jews among magistrates, notaries and court clerks in Prussia

Court district	Magistrates (1894)	(1905)	Notaries (1896)	Court clerks (1880)
Berlin	6.2	6.0	24.7	21.2
Breslau	7.9	6.3	19.9	23.6
Kassel	0	1.5	2.2	3.3
Celle	1.1	0.6	3.6	3.9
Cologne	2.4	4.1	0	3.3
Frankfurt	1.8	5.3	7.3	12.3
Hamm	1.9	2.5	4.9	2.4
Kiel	3.1	3.1	5.6	4.2
Königsberg	8.1	8.5	7.0	9.4
Marienwerder	12.4	10.2	11.0	17.5
Naumburg	2.0	1.5	4.8	1.1
Posen	6.4	4.5	24.2	26.8
Stettin	4.2	2.9	5.9	9.1

Source: G St Dahlem, Rep. 84a, 11944: 22, 63, 98, 173

were Catholics; none was Jewish.)[34] More importantly, it was not so much double standards as incompatible standards that Jews and Catholics operated. For the Jew religious equality meant a career open to talents, for the Catholic a career open to quotas. This contrast between an individualist-competitive and a protectionist-corporatist social ethos admitted of little compromise and demonstrated the lack of consensus on public values in the German Empire. Above all, this straightforward denominational analysis of the problem over-simplified the social reality of Germany just as much as Breslauer's Jewish–Christian dichotomy had done. Religious discrimination in the German Empire was also political discrimination, but it was not the only form of political discrimination. As the Liberal *Vossische Zeitung* pointed out: 'A member of the *Zentrum* stands a much better chance than a Protestant member of the Progressive party',[35] and infinitely better, one might add, than a Social Democrat of any or no religious affiliation.

The cross-purposes at which the various parties to this dispute were talking accounted for the outcome of the debate. Theodor Barth of the Progressive Union (FVg), a future president of the *Verein zur Abwehr des Antisemitismus*, moved: 'The Chamber of Deputies resolves to express its expectation that in

34 Grunenberg, *Das Religionsbekenntnis*, p. 187.
35 *VZ*, 31 August 1893, p.m.

the appointment of notaries the interests of the whole population will be taken into account in accordance with Articles 4 and 12 of the constitution.' However, a Conservative amendment to add 'as hitherto' after 'notaries' passed the House against the votes of only the two Progressive parties. The chamber thereupon passed, again against the votes of the Progressive parties, a motion moved by Irmer of the Conservatives and Oktavio von Zedlitz-Neukirch of the more moderate Free Conservatives, supporting the Minister of Justice's policy of 'consideration for the needs of the Christian population'.[36]

This line-up was slightly unusual, since the governmental majority contained not only, as might be expected, the Conservatives and, for the reasons given, the *Zentrum*, but the Free Conservatives and the National Liberals as well. The Free Conservatives were not an anti-Semitic party and their strong links with industry would have made overt anti-Semitism an embarrassment. Given their position on the political spectrum, however, they had no compunction about electoral agreements with those that were. Their principal instinct was support for the authority of the government and this no doubt helped to explain both their electoral strategy and their stance in the 1901 debate. Their leader, von Zedlitz-Neukirch, certainly did not count as an anti-Semite; indeed, on other occasions he was prepared to speak up on behalf of Jewish grievances, e.g. the exclusion of Jews from regular and reserve commissions in the army.[37] Like most German nationalists and imperialists of his generation, he had stronger anti-Catholic than anti-Jewish feelings: in an earlier debate on religious discrimination he had accused the *Zentrum* of raising the parity question 'in order to revive the temporal power of the Church'.[38] Similar political priorities applied to the National Liberals, at any rate in the Prussian chamber, where liberal pressures were weaker than they were on the Reichstag delegation. Their speakers declared themselves satisfied that the government did not practise the exclusion of Jews from the judiciary on principle and expressed themselves equally opposed to the *Zentrum*'s insistence on numerical justice.[39]

The 1901 debate was neither the first nor the last on religious discrimination in the public service, but in Prussia at least it seems to have been the most crucial. As so often happened in the German Empire, a public insistence that the government's prerogatives were not to be influenced by parliamentary or journalistic agitation concealed considerable anxiety on the

36   *StPrA*, 9 Feb. 1901, 1295.
37   Cit. *AZJ*, 5 January 1911, p. 3.
38   *StPrA*, 2 March 1894, 792.
39   Hermann Reichardt (National Liberal), *StPrA*, 8 Feb. 1901, 1238–40; Karl Heinrich Sattler (do.), 9 Feb. 1901, 1331–4.

part of the authorities not to let discontent get out of hand. Throughout the Imperial period, Prussian ministers of justice requested detailed breakdowns of the confession of judicial employees,[40] sometimes, as the context makes clear, in response to Catholic or Jewish pressures, sometimes out of concern for Conservative or anti-Semitic fears. On occasion there were also enquiries about policies elsewhere, e.g. in the Imperial Department of Justice or in Alsace-Lorraine.[41] The replies were generally defensive; the State Secretary for Alsace-Lorraine reported, for instance, that while there was no policy of discrimination, no occasion had recently arisen for the appointment of Jews.[42] Schönstedt's predecessor, von Schelling, who had instigated many of these enquiries, in turn felt obliged to reassure the head of the Emperor's civil cabinet, Heinrich von Lucanus, that he was appointing Jewish magistrates in Berlin 'only in the most limited degree'.[43]

Quite often a detailed internal correspondence related to complaints in the press about alleged discrimination in some particular High Court district. For instance, it was alleged that in the Frankfurt district Jewish court clerks were admitted only if they signed a declaration renouncing a career in the judiciary.[44] The Chief Justice concerned, Dr Hagens, publicly explained that there was 'exceedingly great pressure' ('äußerst großer Andrang') from Jewish candidates for a judicial career[45] – in his confidential report to Schönstedt he called it excessive ('übergroß')[46] –, that the renunciation had been required of only a minority of the Jewish applicants and had also been demanded of some Christians.

In fact, it would have been difficult to sustain a charge of systematic anti-Semitism against Hagens. Between 1894 and 1905 the number of Jewish magistrates in the Frankfurt court district rose from three to ten, a higher rate of increase than in any other district.[47] Hagens wrote numerous testimonials for Jewish candidates; the closest one can get to an adverse comment was that on the unfortunate Dr Rawitscher, who was commended for his tact, complaisance, dignity and patience 'despite his unimpressive appearance' ('trotz seines nicht bestechenden Äußeren').[48] If one were really looking for blatant anti-Semitism in the higher judiciary one needed to go no further

40 E.g. G St Dahlem, Rep. 84a, 3528: 35, 110–17.
41 G St Dahlem, Rep. 84a, 11948: 99–101.
42 G St Dahlem, Rep. 84a, 11948: 103–4. For full text see Appendix II, p. 67.
43 G St Dahlem, Rep. 84a, 11948: 105–7. For full text see Appendix III, p. 68.
44 *BT*, 3 September 1901.
45 *FZ*, 9 September 1901
46 G St Dahlem, Rep. 84a, 11944: 141.
47 See table 2.3 above.
48 26 Feburary 1892. G St Dahlem, Rep. 84a, 11932.

than Hagens's colleague in Breslau, who in 1911 recommended 'a significant curtailment in the utilization of Jewish judges' since 'the average Jew is not endowed with a sense of justice'.[49]

Another consequence of the 1901 debate – this time one that showed sensitivity to anti-Semitic rather than Jewish pressures – was a closer ministerial check on individual Jewish appointments. It was a common claim by ministers of justice (as will be seen below in the discussion on Hesse and Bavaria) that, whatever laws and constitutions might say, there were certain localities, generally rural and small-town, where Jewish magistrates were simply not acceptable. The evidence for this assumption is sketchy. There were occasional petitions against the appointment of a Jewish magistrate,[50] but it does not follow that these were a genuine reflection of popular opinion. In any case there seems to have been little system in the criteria adopted by the ministry: Jewish candidates were considered just as suitable ('unbedenklich', 'angängig', 'kann ... Verwendung finden') in rural Silesia and East Prussia as in Berlin or Frankfurt.[51]

Though this meticulous monitoring continued until 1914, systematic discrimination in Prussia ceased with the departure of Schönstedt in 1905. The anti-Semitic press, which honoured him for having to some extent resisted and delayed the 'threatening strangulation of our judicial estate through the Jewish element',[52] would have even greater cause to regret him under the regime of his successor, Max von Beseler.

Although two unbaptized Jews had earlier been appointed high court judges under special circumstances, it was Beseler who, influenced by Breslauer's memorandum, secured William II's agreement in 1907 to a policy of promoting Jews to the rank of Associate High Court Justice (*Oberlandesgerichtsrat*), but not to that of Presiding High Court Justice. Four such promotions occurred during his term of office, as did an acceleration of Jewish appointments as notaries, so that by 1909 an official Jewish publication felt able to declare that discrimination had 'been mitigated within the realm of the practicable'.[53] In 1917 Beseler's successor, Peter Spahn, secured William's approval to the promotion of Jews to the highest ranks 'in exceptional cases' and the first Jewish *Landesgerichtsdirektor* was appointed in 1918.[54]

49   G St Dahlem, Rep. 84a, 2941: 187–9. Full text in Appendix I.
50   E.g. in Celle, Lower Saxony. *DT*, 24 March 1901.
51   ZStM, 2.2.1, 17031.
52   *DT*, 23 October 1905.
53   *Jahrbuch für jüdische Geschichte und Literatur*, 1909, p. 5.
54   Lorenzen, *Die Juden in der Justiz*, p. 144; Ernest Hamburger, *Juden im öffentlichen Leben Deutschlands. Regierungsmitglieder, Beamte und Parlamentarier in der monarchischen Zeit, 1848–1918*, Tübingen: J. C. B. Mohr, 1968, pp. 44–8.

Prussia was not the only state in which the government's judicial appointments policy was contentious. While a few – Hamburg, Baden and, after the introduction of constitutional government in 1911, Alsace-Lorraine – pursued relatively non-discriminatory policies, even where High Court posts were concerned, the majority tried to keep their judiciary *judenfrei*. In some instances, e.g. Württemberg and Braunschweig, this seemed to raise little protest.[55] In Saxony, which had one of the most consistently anti-Jewish administrations of the Imperial epoch, one Jewish high court judge, Selig Ornstein, was appointed in 1879 and none thereafter.[56] A few Jewish court clerks were also nominated but with the proviso – even after 1869 – that they were to administer no oaths, which led at least one of them to refuse the appointment.[57] A Social Democratic interpellation about discrimination in 1890 was dismissed on grounds of prerogative and explained by the Prussian ambassador in Dresden in terms of the SPD's desire to tap Jewish financial support.[58] The government of Saxony made no bones about its discriminatory policy, which it claimed was 'universally known' and which even extended to the exclusion of Jews from juries.[59] But the greatest controversies were caused by debates in the Grand Duchy of Hesse and in Bavaria.

Hesse was one of the strongholds of the popular anti-Semitic movement – in 1893 three of its nine Reichstag deputies were anti-Semites – and the government strongly opposed its spread.[60] But it equally adamantly refused to employ any Jews in any part of its public service above the most subordinate grades. Nor were these attitudes as inconsistent as might appear. The government's primary concern was to inhibit agitation, from whatever direction. Its sensitivity to public criticism is shown by the prosecution it initiated in 1899 against the *Frankfurter Zeitung*, which had published a detailed investigation of the Hessian government's policy and concluded that this was in breach of the constitution.[61]

The court decided against the newspaper and sent one of its editors,

55 Hamburger, *Juden im öffentlichen Leben Deutschlands*.
56 Lorenzen, *Die Juden in der Justiz*, pp. 106–7. Ernest Hamburger's statement that there were no Jewish judges at all in Saxony (*Juden im öffentlichen Leben Deutschlands*, p. 51) is therefore in need of revision.
57 Dr Friedrich Wachtel. ZStM, Rep. 120, A XII 5, Nr 1, Bd 7: 81–2.
58 ZStP, 15.01, 16792: 29–30.
59 Lorenzen, *Die Juden in der Justiz*, p. 140.
60 Richard S. Levy, *The Downfall of the Anti-Semitic Political Parties in Imperial Germany*, New Haven, Conn., and London: Yale University Press, 1975, pp. 139–40; Werner Jochmann, 'Struktur und Funktion des deutschen Antisemitismus', *WD*, p. 428, n. 138.
61 *Geschichte der Frankfurter Zeitung 1856–1906*, Frankfurt Verlag der Frankfurter Zeitung, 1906, pp. 720–2.

Alexander Giesen, to prison for six months, principally on the grounds that discrimination had not been proved. In his defence the Minister of Justice, Dittmar, had used the same arguments that Schönstedt was to use two years later. The first was to deny systematic discrimination:

The government had never arrived at a decision not to appoint Jews as judges. ... [He did not] consider a Jewish judge as being on principle out of the question. If someone were not appointed because he is a Jew then that amounted, in his opinion, to a breach of the constitution. But if someone were not appointed because he appeared, for some reason, to be unsuitable for the office, that could not be objected to, however inconvenient that might be for the person concerned.[62]

The second was to assert that in so far as there was unsystematic discrimination, this was dictated by the public interest. In that respect he echoed the words of his predecessor, Jakob Finger, whose response to criticism by a *Zentrum* deputy had been:

I am no opponent of the nomination of Jews to a court ... but there are certain snags in using these gentlemen everywhere and in every position. In the countryside we should, it is my firm conviction from my knowledge of the countryside, cause great offence if we posted Jewish judges there. I have no objection at all to a Jewish judge every now and again becoming a member of a multi-judge court; but out of regard to public opinion and the popular voice this can happen only in moderation.[63]

In fact, Dittmar went slightly further and specified a particular vacancy for which he had regarded a Jewish as candidate unsuitable, even though he had the appropriate seniority:

The mayor there was at the head of the anti-Semitic movement in Germany, moreover the town had a garrison, a Jewish judge was not possible there without doing damage to himself and his office.

He also sympathized with an off-the-record confession by Finger who

had once privately commented that other states envied Hesse its *judenrein* judiciary. The prejudices against the Jews were spread far beyond the anti-Semitic circles themselves. He did not share these but could not simply make them disappear. Because of the mood of the population, the doubts and difficulties that stood in the way of the appointment of Jewish judges existed to a far larger degree than elsewhere.[64]

62 *FZ*, 13 October 1899.
63 *2. Kammer Hesse*, 7 April 1894, p. 7.
64 *FZ*, 13 October 1899.

The court was convinced by the minister's evidence:

There is no constitutional right or claim to a particular office on the part of a Jew or Christian. To be sure it is to be admitted that the sense and spirit of our new legislation point in the direction of ironing out confessional differences in the conditions of employment. ... But it is to be admitted, and is recognized throughout the *Reich*, that this equalization has not in fact taken place, despite all existing laws. Therefore the practice adopted by the Hessian government of deciding each case as it arises, out of regard for the office and the person, is to be seen as correct. Appointment is a political act, therefore the prudent considerations of the political authorities have to be decisive. It has been proved that Jews are not excluded on principle.[65]

This was not quite the end of this affair. Two years later the Jews of Hesse presented a petition, complaining of the failure to observe the constitutionally-guaranteed equality of religions.[66] The petition was debated in the Justice Committee of the Second Chamber and in the whole House; Dittmar again assured the Jews that they enjoyed equality in achieving public office with all other denominations and the chamber passed a resolution *nem. con.* in favour of the principle of religious equality.[67] Only the anti-Semitic deputy Phillip Köhler caused some embarrassment by blurting out that 'the great majority of deputies sitting here embrace anti-Semitic views, are, strictly speaking, anti-Semites.'[68] But life went on as before. Everyone concerned indignantly denied Köhler's charge, but acted as if it were true. A small number of Jewish notaries continued to be appointed, but it was not until 1910 that the first (and, until 1918, the only) Jewish judge in Hesse achieved office.

In Bavaria pressures on the government were equally ineffective, though with opposite results. Under the restricted and indirect franchise that operated in Bavaria until 1906 the mass of the Catholic population (71 per cent of the total) was under-represented and the government was in Liberal or secularly-inclined aristocratic hands. This permitted a relatively free policy in public appointments. In the course of the 1890s, and gaining momentum after the turn of the century, a campaign got under way to democratize the constitution, especially in favour of the overwhelmingly Catholic rural population (only 21.5 per cent of the Bavarian Catholic population lived in towns, compared with 31.8 per cent of the Protestant).[69] The rival leaders of this movement were the anti-clerical Bavarian Peasant League (*Bayerischer*

65   *FZ*, 14 October 1899.
66   *2. Kammer Hesse*, 31. Landtag, Drucksachen, 4. Band, Nr. 675.
67   Ibid., pp. 1–2; *2. Kammer Hesse*, 20 November 1901, 1805–6.
68   *2. Kammer Hesse*, 20 November 1901, 1798.
69   Rost, *Die wirtschaftliche und kulturelle Lage*, p. 179.

Bauernbund) and the peasant wing of the *Zentrum*, organized in the *Bayerischer Christlicher Bauernverein*, who for this purpose formed a tactical alliance with the Social Democrats.

The principal spokesman of the *Bauernverein* was Dr Georg Heim, who also led the assault on Jews in the judiciary.[70] Directly inspired by the Prussian Landtag debate of early 1901, he introduced a motion in the finance committee of the Bavarian Landtag to restrict the appointment of Jewish judges, where it was defeated. He then raised the matter in the Chamber, proposing that 'Israelites should be admitted to the judiciary as far as possible only in the proportion of the Israelite population to the whole population'.[71] He justified this not on the grounds of parity but because 'the Christians have the community of race and homeland; the Jews constitute in every respect a state within the state; Jews participate disproportionately in crimes against property; Jews have a hand in all new, generally underhand business that turns up; ... if things develop as they have been, half the judges will soon be Jews.'[72]

Heim's motion was opposed by the Liberals and Social Democrats, as well as by the government. The minister of justice, Freiherr von Leonrod, pointed out that the number of Jewish judges could not be considered excessive. Though 152 of Bavaria's 845 lawyers (18 per cent) were Jewish, this was true only of 2.1 per cent of the judges and notaries; in contrast with Prussia, however, this number did include three high court judges and ten public prosecutors. He also echoed the misgivings of his Hessian and Prussian colleagues: 'I also acknowledge that in some districts a judge of the Jewish confession may have the exercise of his office prejudiced by popular attitudes. For that reason it has hitherto been my endeavour to avoid the employment of Jewish judges in such districts.' But to adopt denominational proportions would be unconstitutional.[73] The strongest support for Heim came from the Protestant Conservatives and Agrarians of Northern Bavaria. The *Zentrum* itself was divided – a minority, like the government, emphasizing the principle of equal rights[74] – with the result that Heim's motion was passed fairly narrowly, by 77 votes to 51. Since it was then rejected by the Upper House, it remained a dead letter. The government continued to appoint Jewish judges much as before, including two to the high rank of *Senatspräsident*, although in

70   The most recent biography of this folk-hero, while detailing his struggle for the rights of peasants, makes no mention of his anti-Jewish campaign. Hermann Renner, *Georg Heim, der Bauerndoktor. Lebensbild eines ungekrönten Königs*, Munich: Bayerischer Landwirtschafts-Verlag, 1960.
71   *Verhandlungen der Kammer der Abgeordneten des bayerischen Landtages*, Stenographische Berichte, 29 November 1901, 928.
72   Ibid., 929.
73   Ibid., 938.
74   E.g. Pfarrer Anton Köhl, ibid., 953.

other branches of the public service the growing influence of the *Zentrum* led to a diminution of Jewish appointments.[75]

That so much of the public discussion on the religious composition of the judiciary should have occurred in 1901 was not accidental. The debate in Prussia in January and February, and Schönstedt's justification of his policy, had a nation-wide impact. The Jewish petition in Hesse, Heim's motion in Bavaria and the greater vigilance in the press, as instanced by the *Frankfurter Zeitung*'s campaign against *Oberlandesgerichtspräsident* Hagens, are directly attributable to this. Yet the controversy was never dead from the first day of the Empire to the last, and that this was so reveals a great deal not just about anti-Semitism, the 'Jewish Question' – and, for that matter, the 'Catholic Question' –, but about the political and social structure of the Empire.

Though discrimination in public service appointments was occasionally aired in the Reichstag, the issue was essentially one for the state governments, since the greater part of the administration and the overwhelming share of law enforcement was in their hands. All state governments were bound by the *Reich* law of 3 July 1869 which ended all discrimination on religious grounds. Most post-1848 state constitutions contained some declaration of religious equality, though some, like that of Prussia, were sufficiently ambiguous to permit of endless exegesis. The great majority of the states were, in the matter of public appointments, in breach of both the 1869 law and their own constitutions. Some, like Saxony, gloried in this with impunity. Others, like Hesse, wriggled and got away with denying the patently obvious. Jewish spokesmen and their allies among the Liberal and Social Democratic parties frequently pointed this out, but in a way that did not do full justice to the complex social evolution that Germany was undergoing.

Their argument was a simple one: the letter of the law should apply and the law said that religious affiliation was an irrelevance in public appointments. It was an argument based on secular individualism, on the notion of personal rights and the subordination of church interests to the public good. But was religion an irrelevance in the public life of the Empire? Clearly Imperial Germany was not a patriarchal society where the unity of throne and altar, or squire and parson, went unquestioned. But in most German states it was socially inconvenient or procedurally very difficult not to belong to a religious denomination. Religious observance, though it declined between 1871 and 1918, was still high and public ceremonies were often also ecclesiastical.[76] In most states churches enjoyed established status and

75 Hamburger, *Juden im öffentlichen Leben Deutschlands*, pp. 50–1, 63.
76 The literature on 'secularization' is enormous. For the process in Germany during this period, see the valuable contributions by Ismar Schorsch, Vernon Lidtke, Geoffrey G. Field and Fritz Stern in the section 'Religion and Secularization', *LBYB* XXV (1980), pp. 3–77.

received subsidies, arrangements that sometimes included Jewish congregations as well. Imperial Germany, then, could not be described as a secular society either, if by that we mean one in which religious belief and affiliation are relegated to the private sphere, with no impact on public policy, moral standards or the status of the individual.

This intermingling of the religious and the secular in German public life is one explanation for the divergence between Jews and Catholics in the dispute on judicial posts. The divergence, it should be said, was not complete. In Hesse, as we have seen, the *Zentrum* supported Jewish claims, as did a section of the Bavarian *Zentrum*. It was less than just of an influential Jewish publication to claim: 'The *Zentrum* has never cared whether justice is to be accorded to Jews in those branches of the state service from which they are still excluded. On the contrary, it has recently always approved of discrimination against the Jews. It remembers the principle of parity only when it can be used against the Jews.'[77]

But the issue of parity is nevertheless the key to the divergence. What the *Zentrum* wanted was not secularism but ecclesiastical pluralism; equality of rights not for individuals but for religious corporations. If this meant raising Jewish congregations to the same privileged status that the Christian churches enjoyed, that was acceptable, as the debate on the Prussian School Bill of 1905 showed.[78] The Jewish claim that individual merit should be the sole criterion for preferment was part of that secularizing pressure that the *Zentrum* was bound to resist, especially since it was being pressed in a sphere where partial concessions to merit had already enabled Jews to out-compete Catholics. What made the antagonism even greater was that the Catholic interpretation of religious equality was clearly contrary to the 1869 law. This stipulated that the holding of public office should *not* be dependent on religious affiliation: the demand for parity, on the contrary, would make religious affiliation the principal criterion.

The attitudes of the governments, too, revealed the uncertain stage Germany had reached in the journey from 'traditional' to 'rational' forms of authority (to revert to Weber's categorization). Ministers and bureaucrats had two primary concerns: to avoid trouble and maintain, as far as possible, the existing structure of power and influence. Governments desired to ignore public opinion, but on occasion also feared it.[79] The governments of Saxony

---

77   *Jahrbuch für jüdische Geschichte und Literatur*, 1903, p. 3.

78   Marjorie Lamberti, *Jewish Activism in Imperial Germany. The Struggle for Civil Equality*, New Haven, Conn., and London: Yale University Press, 1978, ch. 7.

79   For a further discussion of this point, see Michael A. Riff, 'The Government of Baden Against Antisemitism: Political Expediency or Principle?', *LBYB* XXXII (1987), esp. pp. 119–21, 133–4.

and Hesse were unmoved by liberal pressures; that of Bavaria took no overt notice of Heim's illiberal Landtag majority. But the Prussian government's obsessive collection of religious statistics and local opinion showed that it needed to be prepared to answer awkward questions.

A good illustration of the ambivalent attitude to public opinion is policy on organized anti-Semitism. Most state governments – Saxony being the principal exception – opposed the anti-Semitic political parties: some took quite vehement administrative steps to minimize their influence, especially when this threatened public order. At the same time they were convinced that anti-Jewish prejudices were widespread among their populations, especially in rural areas, and that to post Jewish magistrates there was to invite problems that added unnecessarily to the burdens of office. As the strength of anti-Semitic parties declined, and Jewish lobbying became more persistent in the decade before the First World War, there was some liberalization of appointment and promotion policies. German governments, whether of the *Reich* or of the states, were subject to pressure from below, but in a haphazard way and to a far from predictable degree.

The same criteria of maintaining authority determined the question of 'discrimination'. That Jewish applicants failed to get posts in the judiciary for which they were qualified because they were Jews is undeniable. They were discriminated against. That the same happened to Catholics, especially if they had 'clerical' sympathies, is also undeniable. They, too, were discriminated against. Both categories were non-conformist, potentially subversive. But there were many other categories of Germans who also failed to conform in one way or another and who were therefore also victims of discrimination to some degree.

Ceteris paribus, a Protestant stood a better chance of a government job than a Catholic, but an observant Catholic stood a much better chance than an atheist. A Conservative or National Liberal Protestant stood a better chance than a conservative Catholic; but how good were the chances of a Left-Liberal Protestant compared with those of a conservative Catholic? A Social Democrat – a sizeable minority by 1914, when the party had over a million members – had no chance at all in most states and only a minimal one in the Southern states. The most spectacular evidence of the premium on conformity was the professional success of the baptized Jews. According to Breslauer's figures, from 1875 to 1895 155 unbaptized Jews and 105 baptized Jews were appointed to the judiciary. Of the latter no fewer than 27.8 per cent were promoted to High Court or presiding judges, compared with 18.3 per cent of all appointees.[80] On this narrow criterion it could be argued that baptized Jews – a small proportion of the totality of Jews and a minute proportion of

80 *Die Zurücksetzung der Juden im Justizdienst*, pp. 5, 9.

the whole population – were the most highly-privileged confessional category in the Empire.

There were, of course, other forms of discrimination in German society that affected many more individuals than those discussed here. Rivalry for entry into the public service was, by definition, restricted to the educated middle class, a stratum to which most members of the working class and peasantry had no entry. The obstacles they faced were financial and psychological rather than administrative, and therefore in a different category from those we have been considering. They nevertheless entered into the argument, since those who pointed to the disproportionate Jewish presence in higher education and the middle-class professions did so in order to argue that Jews as a group were the holders of privilege rather than the victims of discrimination.

The position of both Jews and Catholics in the judicial services of Imperial Germany must be seen in the context of a segmented, semi-secularized society, in which legal norms pointed in the direction of 'formal rationality', as defined by Weber,[81] but many social attitudes remained rooted in older concepts of estates and corporatism, and many social relations were determined by status, not contract. None of this is to deny the injustice that many individuals suffered; it is, rather, an attempt to explain what was at stake for the many participants in these disputes, and why it was so difficult to formulate commonly acceptable criteria for resolving them.

81   See above p. 25.

APPENDIX I

Breslau, 30 April 1911

The President of the Provincial Supreme Court
    to the
Minister of Justice in Berlin

General report for the years 1905 to 1910. Part 26: the state of the administration of justice and public administration, as they concern general business.

6) The Jewish Question

The Jewish question, too, constitutes an extraordinarily difficult question in the province of Silesia in its application to the administration of justice.

The deep aversion of the inhabitants of Silesia of Christian descent to Jews – baptized Jews are not here distinguished from them – is still on the increase. There can be no doubt that this is a question not of a religious difference but of a racial antithesis. But this antithesis is much more intense here in the East than in Western Germany, where a gradual process of assimilation of Jews to Christians is taking place. Silesian Jewry receives constant reinforcements from the lands of Slav tongue, especially Russia. The Jews, who in their home country live in strict segregation, have a way of life, moral concepts, feelings, attitudes and outward customs that contrast with German culture to a degree that cannot be underestimated. They do not aspire towards adopting this culture, but seek to impose their ways of thinking on to the Germans. In any case, they strictly preserve for themselves their own peculiarities.

Especially when it comes to the process of law, on the one hand the utilization, or rather the misuse, of legal institutions for commercial purposes is the order of the day, on the other it is impossible to find any understanding for the proposition that the means do *not* justify the end. The high intellectual endowments of the race lead to hair-splitting legalistic abstractions that often result in extraordinary ingenuities on the part of trainees at the provincial Supreme Court. Here, too, attempts to secure understanding for a different approach are often in vain. It is our conviction that the average Jew is not endowed with a sense of justice; altruism, from which this is derived, is incomprehensible to the self-centred Jew.

Now the Jew is tough and ambitious and possesses a spirit of enterprise that is in many cases to be warmly commended. Hence the unquestioned superiority of the Jews in law examinations.

The following figures illuminate the requirements for the judiciary arising out of this state of affairs.

In the years 1908 to 1910, 386 trainees were appointed articled court clerks in the district of Breslau,

	Evangelical	Catholic	Jewish
passes			
a) total	198	104	84
b) 'good' passes	22	8	20
as % of a)	11.1	7.7	23.8

that is to say with quite conspicuously better examination results among the Jews. In part this may be explained by the current form of the examination. In any case it is a strong warning against formal over-estimation of examination results. Exclusive consideration of them would have the inescapable consequence of a large increase of the Jewish element.

In Silesia the Jew is held in low esteem. The better classes of society avoid him. Where there are friendly informal relations among the judiciary, the military or other officials, these threaten to be disturbed as soon as a Jewish judge appears in the ranks of the judiciary. Only recently it required the personal intervention of the undersigned to secure the participation of a socially unexceptionable Jewish judge at a communal luncheon in Rybnik. In Silesia officials enjoy exceptionally high respect. The only branch of the public service that contains Jews in its higher ranks is the judiciary. For these reasons it is regarded by the populace as a low-grade organization. In the small towns a Jewish judge succeeds only rarely in acquiring the public standing that a magistrate needs for the beneficial exercise of his duties.

One may think as one pleases about the Jewish question, to strive against the aversion – psychologically not unjustified – to Jewry can result only in damage to the administration of law and the standing of the courts. In every nomination of a Jewish judge one will therefore have to examine very carefully whether the location permits his employment and whether he possesses that measure of adaptability to Christian-Germanic *Weltanschauung* without which a judge in Silesia cannot – let us face it – discharge his official duties. The result will be, to be sure, a significant curtailment in the utilization of Jewish judges.

Vierhaus Müller

[G St Dahlem, Rep. 84a, 2941: 187–9]

APPENDIX II

Strasbourg, 5 January 1893

Ministry for Alsace-Lorraine
The State Secretary
  to the
Royal Prussian Minister of Justice,
Berlin

In reply to your esteemed communication of the 30th ult., I 6033, I have the honour respectfully to inform your Excellency that no Israelites are employed by the judicial administration of Alsace-Lorraine among the higher judiciary (chief justices, presiding high court judges, high court judges and senior state attorneys). In the rural magistrates' courts [*Landgerichte*] four judges of the Jewish persuasion have been appointed and one in a magistrates' court [*Amtsgericht*]. If the non-appointment of Israelites as a matter of principle has been avoided, then the decline in the migration of applicants from the other German states since the appointment of the most recent of the above-mentioned five judges, who was nominated as judge with seniority dated 17 December 1881, has provided no further occasion for the appointment of persons of the Jewish persuasion. In making the nominations that have already occurred, care was taken, wherever practicable, to avoid filling vacancies in single-magistrate's courts by Israelites. The Imperial law of 3 July 1869 has not been introduced in Alsace-Lorraine. As a result the existing legal provisions have remained in force, by virtue of which the employment of adherents of the Jewish religion was not excluded, and in fact practised.

[G St Dahlem, Rep. 84a, 11948: 103–4]

APPENDIX III

Berlin, 26 April 1893

To the Royal Privy Councillor and Privy
   Cabinet Councillor of His Majesty
   the Emperor and King,
   Excellency Dr. von Lucanus

A newspaper published in Berlin[1] has connected the announcement of appointments to the newly-created judicial posts by the local court authorities with the comment that among the judges nominated to these positions a disproportionately large number of Jewish names was to be found. I feel myself prompted by this to inform your Excellency most respectfully of the following:

Arising out of the increase in the number of judicial posts in the Budget of 1893/94, as well as in consequence of the promotion of several judges, there were, in April of this year, 53 vacancies in local magistrates' courts. These were filled by 51 Christian and 2 exceptionally competent Jewish judges. The President of the Supreme Court had proposed the transfer to Berlin of Jewish candidates other than the two appointed, also in the light of their competence. Since, however, I regarded an increase in the Jewish element among the judges here as objectionable in the interest of the maintenance of justice, I thought myself obliged to implement the transfer of Jewish judges to Berlin only in the most limited degree.

[v. Schelling]

[G St Dahlem, Rep. 84a, 11948: 105–7]

1   The reference is to the *Kreuz-Zeitung*, 18 April 1893, p.m.

3

Jews in German Politics

By the third quarter of the nineteenth century the achievement of a constitutional nation-state had become the political ideal of most German Jews, even more than of their Gentile fellow-citizens; the events of the 1860s and 1870s, and of the decades that followed, show how heavily the fate of this particular minority depended on the strengths and weaknesses of German Liberalism, and how intimately its morale fluctuated with Liberal break-throughs and disappointments. But Jews had entered the general society of the German states by stages, and these stages determined not only the extent of their identification with German political life, but their differing associations with conservatism, liberalism and radicalism.

Up to the end of the eighteenth century the great majority of the Jews of the German states lived lives that were marginal to the economy and the rest of society, engaged in peddling or begging at near-destitution level.[1] Above them was a smaller stratum of small-scale merchants, cattle-dealers, tavern-keepers, rabbis, teachers and doctors whose condition ranged from genteel poverty to modest affluence and who were the antecedents of the Jewish lower

---

1 Jacob Toury, 'Der Eintritt der Juden ins deutsche Bürgertum', in Hans Liebeschütz and Arnold Paucker (eds), *Das Judentum in der deutschen Umwelt 1800–1850. Studien zur Frühgeschichte der Emanzipation*, Tübingen: J. C. B. Mohr, 1977, pp. 142–50; Rudolf Glanz, *Geschichte des niederen jüdischen Volkes in Deutschland. Eine Studie über historisches Gaunertum, Bettelwesen und Vagantentum*, New York, esp. pp. 128–71.

middle class, bourgeoisie and intelligentsia that expanded so rapidly in the course of the nineteenth century. Above them again was a minute stratum of 'court Jews' – bankers, administrators of state monopolies, military provisioners, wholesale merchants and scholars. They were the only Jews who could be said to be integrated in general society or who articulated any demands for civic equality. That the first stage of the debate on emancipation took place in the context of monarchical rule, a stratified social structure and within the assumptions of German absolutism explains the form that Jewish aspirations took. Enlightenment in the German states tended to mean a common body of values and mentalities rather than a political or intellectual programme. Widespread admiration for Montesquieu and Locke and for the balanced British constitution was combined with a consensus that there were adequate safeguards against the abuse of monarchical power. Though Montesquieu was widely known and widely admired in eighteenth-century Germany and *De l'Esprit des Lois* was translated within five years of its publication in France, this was not primarily for his advocacy of the separation of powers as a guarantee of political liberties. His German commentators, beginning with his translator Abraham Gotthelf Kästner, accepted his emphasis on the quality of legislation for ensuring the welfare of the state, but thought this equally guaranteed by the virtue of the ruler. Johann Heinrich Gottlob von Justi doubted whether 'any single people can convincingly prove that it has gained anything through the restriction of royal power'.[2] Instead, with few exceptions, they seized upon his emphasis on the 'spirit' of laws, i.e. the primacy of local traditions and national characteristics, in determining their best form.

'Every country has its own form of government', wrote Johann Jakob Moser, 'England must be governed in the English way, Germany in the German way, Württemberg in accordance with its traditional constitution'.[3] Even admirers of the British constitution, like Justi or Justus Möser, were sceptical of the practical benefits it brought, thinking the English were 'slaves to liberty' and suffered from an excessive *esprit de commerce*.[4] Moreover, a high proportion of the German educated elite were state employees, whether as bureaucrats, academics or clergy; they were participants, even if critical participants, in the existing system of government. Nor were their rulers, even if absolute or semi-absolute, tyrants. The experience of life under the

2   Rudolf Vierhaus, 'Montesquieu in Deutschland. Zur Geschichte seiner Wirkung als politischer Schriftsteller im 18. Jahrhundert', in *idem, Deutschland im 18. Jahrhundert. Politische Verfassung, soziales Gefüge, geistige Bewegungen*, Göttingen: Vandenhoeck & Ruprecht, 1987, p. 28.
3   Ibid., p. 24.
4   Michael Maurer, *Aufklärung und Anglophilie in Deutschland*, Göttingen: Vandenhoeck & Ruprecht, 1987, pp. 119–21.

Emperor Joseph II, or Frederick William I and Frederick the Great of Prussia or the numerous rulers of the smaller states did not suggest that radical constitutional change, or resort to the principles of natural rights, were a prerequisite for tolerable political conditions.

The bourgeoisie of education were still the dominant segment of the middle stratum of society at the end of the eighteenth century and, in contrast with England and the Netherlands, certainly more influential than the bourgeoisie of commerce. It was therefore not surprising that they should elevate their principal attribute, intellectual self-cultivation, *Bildung*, into a social ideal, 'a new secular form of individual salvation'.[5] Where the English and French Enlightenment gave priority to the political liberty of the individual, the *Gebildeten* of Germany tended to look to the state to emancipate them from the privileges of landowners, guilds and estates. Of Locke's works it was not the *Treatises on Civil Government* that made the greatest impact, nor even the *Letter Concerning Toleration*, but *Some Thoughts on Education*.[6] They therefore attributed to the state, as the guarantor of liberty and educated values, a tutelary role in raising as many citizens as possible to a civilized level. Though the ideal of *Bildung* was emancipatory, it was not necessarily egalitarian. Some of its adherents believed that all human beings could and should benefit from education, others did not. Dohm, for instance, proposed education for all 'in accordance with their station in life'.[7] *Bildung*, therefore, was both a weapon against privilege and a defence against the masses.

This climate of opinion had a number of important implications for the question of Jewish civic rights. The first was that, on the grounds of both humanity and *raison d'état*, discrimination against Jews appeared reprehensible. Joseph II granted his first Patent of Toleration in 1781, 'convinced on the one hand of the perniciousness of all religious intolerance, and on the other hand of the great advantage of a true Christian tolerance to religion and the state'.[8]

---

5 David Sorkin, *The Transformation of German Jewry, 1780–1840*, Oxford: Oxford University Press, 1987, p. 17.

6 Vierhaus, 'Aufklärung als Lernprozess', in *idem, Deutschland im 18. Jahrhundert*, p. 86.

7 Christian Wilhelm von Dohm, 'Über Volkskalender und Volksschriften überhaupt', in Wilhelm Gronau, *Christian Wilhelm Dohm nach seinem Wollen und Handeln. Ein biographischer Versuch*, Lemgo: Meyer, 1822, pp. 572–90, esp. 574–5.

8 Ferdinand Maass, *Der Josephinismus. Quellen zu seiner Geschichte in Österreich 1760–1790*, vol. II, *Fontes Rerum Austriacarum*, 2. Abt., 72. Band, Vienna: Herold, 1953, pp. 278–9. The 1781 Patent applied to non-Catholic Christians only. For the edict relating to the Jews of Lower Austria, including Vienna, see Alfred Francis Pribram, *Urkunden und Akten zur Geschichte der Juden in Wien*, Vienna and Leipzig: Braumüller, vol. I, pp. 494–500.

Nearly forty years earlier, in 1745, the Prussian bureaucrat, *Geheimer Finanzrat* Adolf Gebhart Manitius, had dismissed all restrictions on Jews as a 'false *praejudicium politicum*'. In the then climate of opinion he thought nobody would find it easy to be so simple-minded 'as to approve the *inveteratum odium religionis* on account of different thoughts and opinions in religious matters, and for that reason deny a whole nation tolerance, protection and *officia humanitatis*'. He was impressed by 'the example of those republics, where trade flourishes most, [which showed] that Jews do no harm to commerce, but support and encourage it to a notable extent'.[9] Three-quarters of a century before that the Great Elector of Brandenburg-Prussia, Frederick William I, had bluntly told the estates of Brandenburg that 'the Jews and their businesses seem not harmful but rather useful to us and the country.'[10] Frederick William was indeed the initiator of inviting persecuted religious minorities, whether Jews, Huguenots or – at a later stage – Protestants from the Habsburg realms, in order to reconstruct his state after the devastations of the Thirty Years' War.[11]

The second implication arose out of the first. If the prejudice against Jews appeared not only outdated but counter-productive, it did not follow automatically that all Jews should be emancipated. Centuries of persecution and enforced concentration on trade had lowered their moral and cultural standing. Emancipation was therefore to be a regenerative process, though cause and effect could take more than one form. Christian Wilhelm von Dohm, also a Prussian civil servant, whose pro-emancipation book of 1781 launched the public debate not only in Germany but in France, argued that emancipation must come first: only then, in the general framework of a reform of society that removed all barriers of status, would it be possible 'to turn the Jews into useful and contented members of society'.[12] Would they thereby cease to be 'real Jews'? 'What difference would that make to the state, which demands nothing further from them than that they should become good citizens and could hold any religious opinions that they pleased?'[13] But it was equally possible, also in the name of enlightenment, to reverse Dohm's argument and insist on what became known as the 'emancipation contract': equal rights

9   2 December 1745. Selma Stern, *Der preußische Staat und die Juden*, Berlin: Akademie-Verlag, vol. III/2, 1925, pp. 173–6.

10   8/18 December 1672. Ibid., vol. I/1, p. 49.

11   Stefi Jersch-Wenzel, *Juden und 'Franzosen' in der Wirtschaft des Raumes Berlin/Brandenburg zur Zeit des Merkantilismus*, Berlin: Colloquium-Verlag, 1978, pp. 25–42, 113–44.

12   Christian Wilhelm Dohm, *Über die bürgerliche Verbesserung der Juden*, I. Theil, Berlin and Stettin: Nicolai, 1781, p. 111.

13   Ibid., II. Theil, 1783, p. 174.

would come once the Jews had shown good will and reformed themselves. The 1809 emancipation edict of the Grand Duchy of Baden specified: 'This legal equality can become fully operative when they in general exert themselves to match the Christians in political and moral formation.'[14] But whatever the terms of the contract, there was agreement on two propositions: that the Jews were in need of improvement, and that reform of their civic status and of their cultural condition were inter-dependent.

The third implication was the conclusion that articulate Jews drew from this debate. We are talking here of a small group of intellectuals and cultured merchants who did not necessarily form a consensus on all points. But in the main they accepted the terms of the argument as formulated by the Christian representatives of the Enlightenment. Jews, they agreed, needed to be raised to a higher moral and cultural level. Improved political status would impose reciprocal obligations. Understandably they argued that political freedom had to come first: 'One must begin with the release from burdens in order to produce utility', as David Friedländer, one of the leaders of the *Haskalah* put it.[15] But beyond that the *Haskalah* did not have a revolutionary, or even a radical, political philosophy. Its ideals were those of the Christian Enlightenment and therefore compatible with loyalty to state and monarch. Indeed, Jewish life had developed rather more favourably since the end of the Thirty Years' War under princely rule, where Jews could play a well-defined economic role, than in free cities, where they were unwelcome competitors to burghers and were frequently expelled. No praise could be too high for the enlightened monarch. For Friedländer, King Frederick William I of Prussia was an 'illustrious philanthropist' under whom 'our humbled spirit will be lifted up'.[16] His contemporary, Naphtali Herz Wessely, prayed that Joseph II's 'house of wisdom … be a model of wisdom for all rulers of the earth'.[17] For Moses Mendelssohn, Frederick the Great was 'crowned by God, the wonder of the nations'.[18]

There were important exceptions to this contractual view of emancipation among both Jews and Christians. Moses Mendelssohn, the father of the *Haskalah*, insisted that emancipation rested on natural rights, not

---

14   Adolf Lewin, *Geschichte der badischen Juden seit der Regierung Karl Friedrichs 1738–1909*, Karlsruhe: G. Braun, 1909, p. 91.
15   David Friedländer, *Akten-Stücke, die Reform der Jüdischen Kolonieen in den Preußischen Staaten betreffend*, Berlin: Voss, 1793, p. 28.
16   Ibid. pp. 54–5, cit. Sorkin, *The Transformation of German Jewry*, p. 74.
17   Cit. Sorkin, *The Transformation of German Jewry*, p. 66.
18   Felix Gilbert (ed.), *Bankiers, Fürsten und Gelehrte. Unveröffentlichte Briefe der Familie Mendelssohn aus dem 19. Jahrhundert*, Tübingen: J. C. B. Mohr, 1975, p. xxxviii.

conditions.[19] Equally Wilhelm von Humboldt, the most important Christian advocate of emancipation after Dohm, insisted in his 1809 memorandum that only immediate and total legal equality was consistent with justice.[20] But Mendelssohn and Humboldt, for all their eminence, were in a minority and their views did not prevail.

Given that most Jewish intellectuals accepted the doctrine of the tutelary state and that the bankers and merchants of the princely courts held a specific and privileged position, it is not surprising that the earliest Jews to take part in public life did so as supporters of the existing order. The outstanding example of this during the Napoleonic wars was the Rothschild family, by now established in its five centres. The armies of the anti-Napoleonic coalition could hardly have been raised and supplied without their efforts, even though it was the French troops that had broken down the walls of the Frankfurt ghetto. The Rothschilds, indeed, remained consistently conservative. Mayer Karl von Rothschild, Amschel Mayer's grandson, was a member of both North German parliaments in 1867 and from then until his death in 1886 served in the Upper House of the Prussian parliament. Though belonging to no party, he was close to the Free Conservatives.[21]

The Rothschilds were not unique in bankers' conservatism. Abraham Oppenheim had become a Conservative member of Cologne city council in 1846, though he switched to moderate liberalism after the outbreak of the Revolution. During the revolutionary upheavals, the loyalist *Vaterländischer Verein* in Baden counted representatives of such leading banking and manufacturing families as Moritz Lenel and Joseph Hohenemser among its members. Its secretary was Dr Leopold Ladenburg, a lawyer and member of the Supreme Council (*Oberrat*) of Baden Jews and brother of the banker Seligmann Ladenburg. In Berlin Abraham Mendelssohn acted as economic adviser to the government and the Crown Prince was able to flee the capital through the good offices of the silk merchant Joel Wolff Meyer, a city councillor, and the Anhalt banker Moritz Cohn.[22]

19 Alexander Altmann, *Moses Mendelssohn. A Biographical Study*, London: Routledge & Kegan Paul, 1973, pp. 514–52; idem, *Trostvolle Aufklärung. Studien zur Metaphysik und politischen Theorie Moses Mendelssohns*, Stuttgart: Frommann-Holzborg, 1982, p. 167.
20 Wilhelm von Humboldt, 'Gutachten der Sektion des Cultus zum Schroetter'-schen Entwurf', in Ismar Freund, *Die Emanzipation der Juden unter besonderer Berücksichtigung des Gesetzes vom 11. März 1812. Ein Beitrag zur Rechtsgeschichte der Juden in Preußen*, Berlin: M. Poppelauer, 1912, vol. I, pp. 270–1.
21 Jakob Toury, *Die politischen Orientierungen der Juden in Deutschland. Von Jena bis Weimar*, Tübingen: J. C. B. Mohr, 1966, pp. 125, 353.
22 Ibid., pp. 16–17, 51, 57; Lenel, Ladenburg: *Allgemeine Deutsche Biographie*, Berlin: Duncker & Humblot, 1953–, vol. XIII, pp. 386–92, vol. XIV, pp. 203–5. Lewin, *Geschichte der badischen Juden*, p. 281.

The formal entry of Jews into public politics was made possible by the Prussian municipal reform of Freiherr vom Stein in 1808. This introduced a limited franchise, and the right to vote and be elected were specifically independent of religious denomination. The Prussian emancipation edict of 1812 was partial only. It realized one half of Dohm's programme by making Jews economic but not political citizens. Moreover, it did not apply to the territories Prussia acquired after the defeat of Napoleon in 1815 which nearly doubled the Jewish population of Prussia, so that nineteen different codes applied to Jews in Prussia alone until they were finally unified in 1847. Other states slowly enacted piecemeal reforms, in some cases retaining a separate municipal organization for Jews. The only one to adopt anything approaching complete equality of rights was Hesse-Kassel in 1833.[23]

Even after the Stein reform, however, local politics retained a strong corporatist element and in those towns where Jews were numerous or well-to-do they constituted an interest with a title to representation. This was illustrated in Berlin in 1806 when the stock exchange corporation created a deputation of seven members on which three seats were reserved for Jews.[24] When the new-style municipalities came into being in Prussia, prominent Jews quickly acquired office in the major cities. In Berlin the banker Salomon Veit was elected in 1809 and the ex-banker David Friedländer was appointed honorary alderman (*unbesoldeter Stadtrat*), as was the baptized Ferdinand Moses Levy (Baron Delmar). In Königsberg David Friedländer's nephew, Samuel Wulff, occupied the same position.[25] It is significant that all of these also held leading positions in the Jewish communal organization; indeed in Berlin there grew up a convention that the community president should become an honorary alderman, a convention that also initially applied to the Secretary of the (Huguenot) French Colony.[26]

The Conservative mood of the 1820s and 1830s did not favour the election of further Jews in the bigger cities, unless they were baptized. A revival began in Königsberg, where between 1838 and 1840 five Jews were elected to the city council and the banker Robert Warschauer was appointed *Stadtrat*.[27]

23 Gerhard Hentsch, *Gewerbeordnung und Emanzipation der Juden im Kurfürstentum Hessen*, Wiesbaden: Kommission für die Geschichte der Juden in Hessen, 1979, pp. 75–84; Jacob Toury, 'Types of Municipal Rights in German Townships – The Problem of Local Emancipation', *LBYB* XXII (1977).

24 Hugo Rachel and Paul Wallich, *Berliner Großkaufleute und Kapitalisten*, new edn, Berlin: de Gruyter, 1967, vol. III, p. 10.

25 Stefi Wenzel, *Jüdische Bürger und kommunale Selbstverwaltung in preußischen Städten, 1808–1848*, Berlin: Colloquium-Verlag, 1967, pp. 34, 35–6, 38.

26 Ibid., pp. 40, 67–8.

27 Jacob Toury, 'Der Anteil der Juden an der städtischen Selbstverwaltung im vormärzlichen Deutschland', *BLBI* 23 (1963), p. 278.

In Breslau, where opposition to Jewish advancement was strong among the Christian business community, fewer Jews secured election. One of them, the merchant Heymann Lassal, elected in 1846, is perhaps best known as the father of Ferdinand. He was joined by Löbel Milch, the member of a well-known philanthropic family, as *Stadtrat* in 1846, a position Milch combined with membership of the Jewish community's executive – to be followed in both posts by his son Hugo – , and by the money broker Moses Pappenheim, also prominent in community affairs.[28] In Berlin seven Jews were elected during the 1840s, four of them prominent businessmen.

The political affiliation of these pre-1848 politicians is not always easy to determine. Some, especially bankers, were, as we have seen, conservatively inclined. In cities like Königsberg and Berlin, where Liberalism was on the rise from the late 1830s onwards, Jews reflected that trend. The rentier David Alexander Benda, a member of the Berlin *Kaufmannschaft*, elected in 1838, was described as 'an enthusiastic democrat'; the iron merchant Louis Wollheim became an adjutant of the civic guard during the revolution in Breslau.[29]

The predominantly corporatist character of pre-1848 politics meant that direct commercial organization was at least as attractive for articulating the predominantly economic interests of middle-class Jews. There was more to be achieved in merchants' corporations and chambers of commerce than in town halls. When the Berlin *Kaufmannschaft* was founded in 1820 Joseph Mendelssohn, Moses' eldest son, became its deputy chairman, becoming chairman in 1834. His son Franz was chairman in the 1880s. Also in 1834 Simon Oppenheim, the younger son of the founder of the Salomon Oppenheim bank, became president of the Cologne Chamber of Commerce.

Outside the major cities Jewish political activity was on a different scale. In all there were some 300 Jewish municipal politicians in the various states between 1815 and 1848. Biographical details about them are sketchy. Of those whose occupations can be identified, some 70 per cent were businessmen of some kind, while 19 per cent belonged to the professions.[30] These figures are plausible, given the absence at this stage of a highly-developed Jewish intelligentsia or professional class in the smaller towns; the great majority of these businessmen-councillors were concentrated in the areas of heaviest Jewish population in the Eastern provinces of Prussia. Here, in Posen, West Prussia and Silesia, Jews frequently dominated commerce, even if their businesses were mostly on a small scale. That in turn meant that under the

28 Aaron Heppner, *Jüdische Persönlichkeiten in und aus Breslau*, Breslau: Schatzky, 1931, pp. 35, 69.
29 Wenzel, *Jüdische Bürger*, pp. 46, 90–1.
30 Toury, *BLBI* 23, p. 285.

graduated, three-class franchise they occupied the higher electoral classes and could in some cases have dominated the entire council. When Jews were entitled to naturalization in the province of Posen after 1833, the officials of the Ministry of the Interior stressed the 'disadvantageous effects' of giving Jews political power in accordance with their wealth.[31] The government decided to limit the number of Jews who could serve on a council to between two-ninths and one-third.[32] The Jews of Posen were slow to take advantage of this right. Not until 1843 were the first two Jewish deputy councillors (*Stadtverordnetenstellvertreter*) elected in the city of Posen and the first two full councillors did not follow until 1846. Except in the Eastern parts of the province, these public figures tended to side with the Germans in the nationality conflicts with the Poles; that had been one of the Prussian government's motives in the naturalization measure. Indeed, the election of Jews to the Posen city council had the effect of breaking the Polish majority.[33]

In Silesia, which was economically more developed and where Jews had been enfranchised by the 1808 legislation, their public participation emerged much more quickly. They were successful in the first elections in Beuthen and Groß-Strehlitz; in Glogau, which at that time had a Jewish community of 1,500, eleven municipal office-holders of varying kinds were elected between 1809 and 1811 and the election of Jews, and their appointment as local officials, such as small-town mayors (*Schulzen*) and municipal treasurers (*Stadtkämmerer*), continued throughout the 1820s.[34] The majority of those whose occupation is verifiable were, as is to be expected, businessmen. Even more than in the bigger cities those who served in municipal office in the Eastern provinces tended also to be office-holders within the Jewish community.[35]

The general resumption of political activity in the decade before the 1848

---

31 'da nun ein zu großer Einfluß der Juden auf die Beschlüße der Stadtverordneten-Versammlung ... höchst nachteilig seyn würde'. *Ober-Präsident* Flottwell to Minister of Interior von Rochow, 4 July 1841, ZStM 2.2.1.23699 (33); similarly 19 June 1847.

32 Two out of nine councillors in eight towns, one-quarter in six, one-third in seven, four out of fifteen in two. In one town, Kempen, in which Jews made up 3,709 inhabitants out of 6,503, they were originally allocated half the seats, but eventually only one-third. ZStM, 2.2.1, 23699 (121).

33 Aron Heppner and Isaak Herzberg, *Aus Vergangenheit und Gegenwart der Juden in Posen (Stadt)*, Koschmin: J. Tuch, 1914, p. 155; Toury, *BLBI* 23, p. 283.

34 R. Berndt, *Geschichte der Juden in Groß-Glogau*, Glogau, 1873, pp. 109–11; Wenzel, *Jüdische Bürger*, p. 117; Toury, *BLBI* 23, pp. 267–70.

35 Wenzel, *Jüdische Bürger*, pp. 96–132, 168–85; Aron Heppner and Isaak Herzberg, *Aus Vergangenheit und Gegenwart der Juden und der jüdischen Gemeinden in den Posener Landen*, Koschmin and Breslau: J. Tuch, 1904–29, *passim*.

Revolution also saw the spread of Jewish political participation to other regions of Germany. The gradual southward and westward move of Jewish political awakening was most noticeable in the Rhineland, where Jews were elected in twelve cities and towns from the late 1830s onwards, a development that reflected the economic dynamism of the region as well as the accompanying acceptance of Jews as equal members of society. The provincial assembly of the Rhineland was the only one in Prussia to advocate equal rights for Jews before 1848.[36] Elsewhere in Prussia progress was patchy. Most of those elected belonged to local economic elites, like the banker Louis Levison in Minden (Westphalia), Joseph Hirsch, a member of the metal-processing dynasty of Halberstadt, and A. E. Max of Magdeburg. The last two both held the title of *Kommerzienrat*, then rare among Jews. Hirsch was also president of the local Jewish community.[37]

In the non-Prussian states progress was equally partial. A number of Jews were elected in Hesse-Kassel after the emancipation of 1833, including the banker Philipp Feidel in Kassel; in Braunschweig the banker Ludwig Helfft, who was also president of the Jewish community, was elected; Jews were also successful in the Grand Duchy of Hesse-Darmstadt. In Bavaria, where permanently resident Jews were enfranchised in 1813, practical obstacles to entry into politics remained formidable. Only in the Bavarian Palatinate, where Napoleonic influence remained, did a number of Jews gain public office. Elected Jews were also rare in Baden and Württemberg. Little is known of those elected in the smaller communes. Those in Stuttgart, Mannheim and Karlsruhe reflected the general trend in bigger cities by being professional men and, in at least one case, committed Liberals.[38]

None of this altered the contrast, which lasted until the 1860s, between Jews who were active in public life in the Eastern provinces of Prussia and those active elsewhere. In Western and Southern Germany they were the exception rather than the rule; they acted as individuals even when they were, as was often the case, also office-holders in their communities. In the Eastern provinces and especially in Silesia, it was increasingly taken for granted that Jews *qua* Jews, and economically prominent Jews in particular, constituted an interest to be represented. This resulted in the emergence of a number of

---

36   Eleonore Sterling, 'Der Kampf um die Emanzipation der Juden im Rheinland vom Zeitalter der Aufklärung bis zur Gründung des deutschen Reiches', in Konrad Schilling (ed.), *Monumenta Judaica. 2000 Jahre Geschichte und Kultur der Juden am Rhein*, Cologne: Stadt Köln, 1963, pp. 299–301.

37   Levison: Arno Herzig, *Judentum und Emanzipation in Westfalen*, Münster: Aschendorffsche Verlagsbuchhandlung, 1973, pp. 79–81; Max: Toury, *BLBI* 23, p. 275; Hirsch: W. E. Mosse, *The German-Jewish Economic Elite, 1820–1935. A Socio-Cultural Profile*, Oxford: Oxford University Press, 1989, pp. 67–70, 166.

38   Toury, *BLBI* 23, pp. 273–4.

local Jewish dynasties, such as the Behrend family in Cöslin and Neustettin (Pomerania), the Apolant and Borchardt families in Jastrow (Brandenburg), the Sorauer and Guttmann families in Beuthen (Upper Silesia), not to mention the Friedländers of Königsberg and the Freund–Milch families of Breslau.[39]

The predominance of apolitical or conservatively-inclined businessmen among representative Jewish public figures should not distract from a change in the terms of the emancipation debate in the first half of the nineteenth century. The French Revolution, the proclamation of the Declaration of the Rights of Man and of the Citizen and the unconditional granting of equal rights to Jews in 1791 had radicalized advocates of emancipation in Germany, who began looking beyond the tutelary state to natural rights. The partial and selective emancipations in Prussia, Baden, Württemberg and Bavaria were the high-water mark of the 'Enlightenment' achievement. Disappointment over their terms and the further retraction of these limited rights, by legislative or administrative means, after 1815 further diminished faith in the enlightened state. But what shifted the ground most was the change in the dominant political ideology of the German states. The struggle against Napoleon and the ideas of the Revolution, crowned with triumph in 1815, had produced the doctrine of the Christian-German state, hostile to religious equality, ethnic pluralism or anything that smacked of 1789.[40] Under eighteenth-century absolutism, loyalty had been the main political virtue. Hence a German, Frenchman or Jew could be equally welcome to an enlightened ruler, provided he was useful and obedient. Under nineteenth-century nationalism, as defined in Germany, nationality and citizenship depended on each other. It became increasingly clear that while individual Jews, as economic citizens, could prosper, the collective condition of Jews could not be changed within the existing political system.

There thus arose, in the period between 1815 and 1848, a new generation of Jewish intellectuals who sought salvation for their co-religionists in the emergent liberal and democratic movements. 'We can have no expectation of princes', Johann Jacoby wrote in 1847: 'It is quite different with regard to the party of the people. "Extermination of every prejudice, war against useless restriction on freedom" is its watchword. Under its banner we have to line up, in order to extirpate together the prejudices and restrictions that weigh on us.'[41] For Heinrich Heine, 'the Jews will be truly emancipated when the

---

39   Ibid., pp. 278–81; Kurt Schwerin, 'Die Juden in Schlesien. Aus ihrer Geschichte und ihrem Beitrag zu Wirtschaft und Kultur', *BLBI* 56/7 (1980), pp. 50, 64; Marcus Kopfstein, *Geschichte der Synagogen-Gemeinde in Beuthen, O-S.*, Beuthen: M. Nothmann, 1909, pp. 23–4, 61.

40   See Introduction above, pp. 15–8.

41   Letter to Dr E. J. Waldeck, 10 March 1847, cit. Gustav Mayer, 'Liberales Judentum im Vormärz', *Der Jude* I/10, January 1917, p. 675.

emancipation of the Christians has been completely won and secured. ...
They must not, as Jews, aspire to what they have long been entitled to as
Germans.'[42] Ludwig Börne echoed this theme of common servitude: 'Is not
Germany the ghetto of Europe? Do not all Germans have a yellow patch on
their hats?'[43]

The almost universal autocracy, the denial of national self-determination,
the arbitrary variations of legal status from one town or province to another
were, after all, the common conditions of Germans before 1848. The civic
restrictions on Jews were greater than those on Gentiles, but not unique. It
was therefore not suprising that the similar frustrations among Jews and
non-Jews should evoke similar responses; that among politically aware Jews
and non-Jews Liberalism should seem the obvious way out. Liberalism
offered national self-determination and representative government; the potential contradictions between these two aspirations were not yet widely evident.
True, there were constitutionalists who did not care strongly for the national
cause, and there were nationalists who rated civil liberties rather low, but
among most reformers, among the public in general and in government
circles the two causes passed for synonymous. The double appeal of Liberalism to dissatisfied Jews was particularly strong. They assumed that
discrimination was inherent in the autocratic state and that there could therefore be no emancipation without the end of autocracy. It followed that only
with the coming of the rule of law would the Jew cease to be a special and
inferior kind of citizen. Just as the constitutional state, treating everyone alike
on the basis of individual citizenship, would provide the Jew with a new
framework for his existence, so, even more strongly, would the nation-state.
Particularism was, after all, the basis of autocracy and discrimination; a new
polity, based on cultural affinity, would supersede the distinction between
Jew and non-Jew. 'The name of our fatherland is not Prussia, Hanover,
Hamburg, but Germany',[44] asserted the Hamburg educator and later member
of the Reichstag, Anton Rée. Gabriel Riesser, the intellectual father of the
emancipation movement, expressed himself even more passionately: 'If you
offer me with one hand emancipation, the object of my most intense desires,
with the other the realization of the beautiful dream of the political unity of
Germany, conjoined with its political freedom, I should without hesitation

---

42   Heinrich Heine, 'Ludwig Marcus: Spätere Note' (1854), in *Sämtliche Werke*,
Leipzig: Insel-Verlag, 1910, vol. IX, p. 474.
43   Ludwig Börne, 'Menzel der Franzosenfresser' (1844), in *Sämtliche Schriften*,
Düsseldorf: Joseph Melzer, 1964, vol. III, p. 889.
44   Anton Rée, *Die Sprachverhältniße der heutigen Juden im Interesse der Gegenwart
und mit besonderer Rücksicht auf Volkserziehung besprochen*, Hamburg: Gobert, 1844,
p. 58, cit. Toury, *Orientierungen*, p. 34.

choose the latter: for I have the firmest, most profound conviction that the former is contained within it.'[45] This identification of the cause of Jewish emancipation with that of German national self-determination reached its climax in the often quoted words of Rabbi Leopold Stein in 1848: 'From now on we do not recognize our cause as being special. ... We are Germans and want to be nothing else! We have no other fatherland than the German fatherland and we wish for no other! Only by our *faith* are we Israelites, in every other respect we belong with devotion to the state in which we live.'[46] Indeed the assumption that the liberation of any one part of mankind depended on that of mankind as a whole was probably more widely held in 1848 than before or since, though few Jews at this stage went so far as to see the ultimate emancipation of Jew and Gentile in Socialism.

Jewish political activity in the pre-1848 years follows a pattern that was to re-emerge in the Wilhelmine period and to a limited extent in the Weimar Republic. Almost all writers and publicists were on the side of change, so much so that the cause of progress and reform could be portrayed by those hostile to it as Jewish-dominated. As early as 1821 Ludolf Holst discerned a Jewish 'attempt ... to gain complete dominance over the world of ideas'.[47] For Wolfgang Menzel, the chief literary antagonist of 'Young Germany', the whole of that movement was 'Young Palestine',[48] a phrase that anticipated Treitschke's reference to the 'Oriental chorus-masters of subversion'.[49] Thus, as early as the 1830s the problematical relationship between Jews and radicalism had become a factor of political life. Problematical because not all radicals were Jews and not all politically active Jews were radicals or even Liberals, but at the same time what Karl Rotteck called the 'party of movement' would not have been the same without its Jewish component. Consider what the *Rheinische Zeitung*, the most important radical organ of the 1840s, would have been without Marx, Heine, Moses Hess, Dagobert Oppenheim or Andreas Gottschalk. The Jewish reputation for radicalism was thus firmly established.

Secondly, however, there was within the Jewish community a distinct

45 Gabriel Riesser, 'Bemerkungen zu den Verhandlungen der Badischen Ständever-sammlung über die Emancipation der Juden im Jahre 1833' (1835), in *Gesammelte Schriften*, Frankfurt: Verlag der Riesser-Stiftung, 1867–8, vol. II, p. 672.
46 *AZJ*, 27 March 1848, p. 210.
47 Cit. Toury, *Orientierungen*, p. 6.
48 Wolfgang Menzel, 'Unmoralische Schriften' (1835), in Heinrich H. Houben, *Gutzkow-Funde. Beiträge zur Litteratur- und Kulturgeschichte des 19. Jahrhunderts*, Berlin: L. A. Wolff, 1901, p. 200.
49 'Wohl war die Zahl der orientalischen Chorführer nicht groß, aber der Jude besitzt bekanntlich die Gabe sich zu vervielfältigen', in Heinrich von Treitschke, *Deutsche Geschichte im Neunzehnten. Jahrhundert*, Leipzig: S. Hirzel, 1889, vol. IV, p. 434.

dissonance between the activists, many of whom did not even claim to speak for Jewry or had severed formal links with it, and the bulk of the population – a dissonance that was to re-appear in the 1890s. Most Jews were at this time Orthodox in religion and passive and loyalist in politics, so much so that Gabriel Riesser felt bound to defend Jews against the charge, not only of 'ultra-liberal convictions', but of 'shameful servility'.[50] Religious instinct taught them to respect civil authority, the instinct of survival to prefer that authority, however repressive, to the mob. Not least there was the fear that too secular a society, too strong an emphasis on the German-ness of the Jew, would involve the sacrifice of communal, traditional values. As the ultra-orthodox *Treue Zionswächter* put it: 'Above all emancipation emancipates the Jews from Judaism.'[51] Years later, after legal emancipation was complete, the ultra-Orthodox *Israelit* echoed this sentiment by declaring: 'There may be rights of which the Orthodox Jew cannot take advantage.'[52]

The greater conservatism of the majority of those Jews who actually held political office, as opposed to the publicists and agitators, led to a division within the Jewish elite. Beside the local notables there grew up a secular Jewish intelligentsia of doctors, lawyers and teachers, as well as the journalists already referred to, who were, as a group, more liberal in outlook. They entered municipal politics in increasing numbers from the late 1830s onwards, predominantly in the larger cities. One occupational group that straddled the worlds of business and of the intellect was that of booksellers, publishers and newspaper proprietors. They included two Berlin city councillors, Carl Heymann and Moritz Veit, and many of the activists of 1848. Veit was in later years to become a prominent figure in Berlin politics. He was a member of the Frankfurt Parliament and of the Prussian Chamber of Deputies; in 1853 he became chairman of the Berlin Jewish representative council and in 1863 deputy chairman of the Berlin City Council.[53] One politically active publishing family was that of the Levysohns in Silesia. The printer Heymann Levysohn was, in a way that was typical of the Eastern provinces, president of the Jewish community in Glogau and deputy chairman of the city council. His son Friedrich Wilhelm, for some time the publisher of Bettina and Achim von Arnim, was elected to the Frankfurt Parliament. Of his sons in turn, Ulrich became director of the *Berliner Börsen-Courier* and Arthur became chief editor of the leading Berlin Liberal

50   Riesser, 'Bemerkungen', p. 665.
51   *Der Treue Zionswächter*, 1849, p. 20.
52   *Der Israelit* XV, 1874, p. 772, cit. Mordechai Breuer, *Jüdische Orthodoxie im Deutschen Reich, 1871–1918. Sozialgeschichte einer religiösen Minderheit*, Frankfurt: Athenäum-Jüdischer Verlag, 1986, p. 264.
53   Wenzel, *Jüdische Bürger*, pp. 61–2.

newspaper, the *Berliner Tageblatt*.[54] Another radical publishing house was that of Zacharias Loewenthal of Mannheim, later of Frankfurt, where he published Marx's and Engels' *The Holy Family*. He was co-founder of the publishing house of Rütten and Loening, having changed his name upon baptism. Doctors, lawyers and other learned persons were also reported as elected in Königsberg, Erfurt, Posen, Minden, Kolberg, Karlsruhe, Mannheim and Stuttgart. At least some of these are identifiable as Liberals.[55]

While the public campaign for Jewish emancipation was increasingly in the hands of intellectuals, it would not be right to assume that bankers or merchants were indifferent. Many of the petitions in the 1830s and 1840s came from Jewish communities, within which men of business were more often than not the most prominent members. Above all, the Cologne bankers Simon and Abraham Oppenheim initiated the campaign in the province of Rhineland in 1841 with their petition to the King, published in the form of a pamphlet.[56] The best-known of the plutocratic democrats was the youngest Oppenheim brother, Dagobert, the principal financier of the *Rheinische Zeitung*, edited for most of its short career by Dr Marx, as the Prussian censor was in the habit of referring to him.[57]

2   1848–1859: REVOLUTION AND REACTION

What propelled the Jews of Germany into permanent political awareness and commitment was the Revolution of 1848. This was not primarily due to the ostentatious part that many Jews played in armed insurrection, radical journalism and the organization of clubs and elections.[1] Like their predecessors, these men were untypical, and by no means all Jews were delighted at this further public association between Judaism and radicalism: there was resentment among the ultra-Orthodox at those 'who constantly ... wish to impose themselves on us as spokesmen and are forever ready with their unsolicited advice',[2] and general caution among those who saw the anti-Jewish riots of early 1848 as a warning.

54   Schwerin, *BLBI* 56/7, p. 56.
55   Toury, *BLBI* 23, pp. 273–4, 278, 280, 283.
56   *Unterthänigste Immediat-Eingabe der zu Cöln wohnenden Banquiers Abraham und Simon Oppenheim, Die Rechtsverhältnisse der Juden in der Monarchie, insbesondere in den Rheinprovinzen betreffend*, Cologne, 1841.
57   Michael Stürmer, Gabriele Teichmann and Wilhelm Treue, *Wägen und Wagen. Sal. Oppenheim jr. & Cie. Geschichte einer Bank und einer Familie*, Munich: Piper, 1989, p. 106.

1   Toury calculates their number at about 640. *Orientierungen*, p. 66, fn. 81.
2   *Der Treue Zionswächter*, 1849, p. 1.

More decisive was the general association of liberalism, parliamentarism and national unification with the cause of Jewish emancipation. The Basic Rights of the German People, proclaimed by the National Parliament in Frankfurt, specified in paragraph 13 that 'the enjoyment of civic and citizens' rights is neither conditioned nor restricted by religious belief.' Even before that Jews had become generally entitled to political equality and to participate in the elections to the National Parliament and the parliaments of the various states. Five Jews, plus six baptized, became members of the Pre-Parliament, seven, plus seven baptized, were elected as full or substitute members to the National Parliament. They included such distinguished names as Gabriel Riesser, Moritz Veit, Ludwig Bamberger and Johann Jacoby. Riesser became Second Vice-President, the baptized Eduard Simson Vice-President and then President.

The political affiliations of the leading politicians spanned a wide spectrum, but in essence foreshadowed later patterns. A small number, in Frankfurt, Berlin and the parliaments of the smaller states, belonged to the Right. Most of these were baptized, including Friedrich Julius Stahl, their most distinguished representative, who sat in the Prussian Upper House. In fact, the most important Jewish loyalists, like the banker Moritz Cohn of Dessau, who financed the Crown Prince Wilhelm's flight to England,[3] were to be found outside the legislatures. A rather larger number, including Johann Jacoby, Ludwig Bamberger and Heinrich Simon, belonged to the Left. Here, too, some of the most important men, like Karl Marx and Stephan Born, were active outside the parliaments. But the majority, including Riesser and Simson, Moritz Veit and Raphael Kosch, were constitutionalists and men of the liberal centre, a category that embraced monarchists and republicans, Greater German federalists and pro-Prussian Lesser Germans.[4]

Even more significant than this burst of activity and the ultimately unproductive 'speeches and majority resolutions', as Bismarck was later to dismiss them, were the decisions of most of the individual states to grant complete equality. Bavaria was the major exception. These new rights were not, in general, revoked during the Reaction, but were widely evaded by administrative means. However, the circumstances under which they were first enacted made a deep impression on the Jewish community and contributed more than any other factor to the lasting alliance between Jews and Liberalism. In this

---

3   See above, p. 74.
4   For comprehensive surveys of Jewish politicians during the Revolution see Ernest Hamburger, *Juden im öffentlichen Leben Deutschlands. Regierungsmitglieder, Beamte und Parlamentarier in der monarchischen Zeit, 1848–1918*, Tübingen, J. C. B. Mohr, 1968, pp. 170–209; Toury, *Orientierungen*, pp. 47–99; Margarita Pazi, 'Die Juden in der ersten deutschen Nationalversammlung (1848/49)', *JIDG* V (1976), pp. 199–209.

sense, the Frankfurt Parliament may have left a different legacy to them than to most Germans. The experience of Frankfurt generally discredited parliamentarism, politicians and parties; a discredit from which, arguably, German public consciousness has never fully recovered.[5] It did not discredit it for Jews.

Equally, it helped to strengthen the identification of national unity with civil rights. The individual states may have enacted emancipation, but they had also failed to implement it. German national unity would provide not only a moral basis for a new, dignified existence, but a legal one. This realization explains the form that Jewish political activity took in the decades following 1849.

In the aftermath of the Revolution Jews adopted a low profile politically and were in general anxious to live down the reputation they had gained as radicals in 1848. As Julius Fürst, the radical editor of *Orient*, had prophesied: 'Emancipation is in our country a legacy of the Revolution, and, along with the latter, this emancipation will probably be vanquished, too.'[6] That attitude came to an end with the onset of the 'new Era' – the accession of William I to the throne of Prussia in 1858, marked by a cautious liberalization of domestic politics and a revived interest in German unification under Prussian leadership.

3 THE LIBERAL EPOCH

In the period 1858–66 almost twice as many Jews served in state parliaments and municipalities as in the preceding decade.[1] State legislators were without exception Liberals and some of them, e.g. Fischel Arnheim of Bavaria and Rudolf Kusel of Baden, were directly instrumental in the removal of Jewish disabilities.[2] But this was no longer the major concern of Jewish politicians, hence their increasing adherence not merely to the cause of unity, but to the *kleindeutsch* version under Prussian leadership that seemed more and more the only practicable one.

Public politics in Germany revived with the creation of a *kleindeutsch*

---

5   The historian Gerhard A. Ritter has spoken in this context of 'the trauma of the helplessness of parliament'. Ritter, 'Entwicklungsprobleme des deutschen Parlamentarismus', *idem* (ed.), *Gesellschaft, Parlament und Regierung. Zur Geschichte des Parlamentarismus in Deutschland*, Düsseldorf: Droste, 1974, p. 18.
6   *Der Orient*, 25 November 1848, p. 374.

1   Toury, *Orientierungen*, p. 114.
2   Hamburger, *Juden im öffentlichen Leben Deutschlands*, pp. 211, 235–6.

umbrella body, the *Deutscher Nationalverein*, in 1859, its party political twin, the *Deutsche Fortschrittspartei*, in 1861 and the federalist, *großdeutsch* rival to these, the *Deutscher Reformverein*. Estimates of the number of Jews involved in the foundation of the *Nationalverein* vary slightly: thirteen have been identified among the signatories of the founding appeal and sixteen among the delegates to the first general meeting at Coburg. The executive elected at Coburg included Gabriel Riesser and Moritz Veit, as well as the baptized lawyer August Metz.[3] Rather more significant was the way in which the creation of the *Nationalverein* ushered in a convergence of the interests and attitudes of the Jewish and Gentile middle class. The *Nationalverein*'s programme was in essence that of the 1848 Lesser Germans. It proclaimed 'equal rights for all religious denominations';[4] in its assumption that individual equality was the best solution to political and social problems it appealed to the secularized Jew and Christian alike. It did not devote much time to the Jewish Question, but it attracted leading advocates of emancipation like Moritz Wiggers, the (Gentile) Liberal who was the proponent of the 1869 law that finally granted full legal equality. As was common throughout the nineteenth and twentieth centuries, Jews were most active in the association's publicity: the *Deutsche Jahrbücher für Politik und Literatur* were edited by Heinrich Bernhard Oppenheim and Ludwig Bamberger, the *Demokratische Studien* by the baptized Ludwig Walesrode. A leading organizer in Frankfurt was Leopold Sonnemann, the banker and industrialist who in 1856 founded the *Frankfurter Zeitung*, the mouthpiece of South German democratic Liberalism.

What reinforced the inter-denominational liberal alliance was the anti-Semitic tone of much of the opposition, occasionally from the radical Left (e.g. the *Mitteldeutsche Volkszeitung*), more generally from the Right. 'We thought', the ultra-Conservative *Kreuz-Zeitung* said of the election of Riesser and Veit to the executive, 'that they belonged to another nation'.[5] The *Berliner Revue*, edited by Hermann Wagener, saw in the revival of Liberalism the typical Jewish attempt to extend economic power to the political sphere:

---

3   Shlomo Na'aman, 'Jüdische Aspekte des Nationalvereins (1859–1867)', *JIDG* XV (1986), pp. 285–308; Richard le Mang, *Der deutsche Nationalverein*, Berlin: Verlag der Buchhandlung der nationalliberalen Partei, 1909, p. 26.
4   Le Mang, *Der deutsche Nationalverein*, p. 95.
5   'Bisher dachten wir, sie gehörten zu einer anderen Nation', *KZ*, 21 September 1859; similarly *KZ*, 27 March, 25 May, 1 October 1859. See also Joseph Edmund Jörg, *Die neue Ära in Preußen*, Regensburg: Manz, 1860; Anon (i.e. Johannes Nordmann, possibly in conjunction with Lothar Bucher and Hermann Wagener), *Die Juden und der deutsche Staat*, Hamburg: Otto Meißner, 1860.

The share of the Jews in the creation and oppressive domination of the power of money ... shows how the Jews have succeeded in almost transforming all the freedoms of modern liberalism, especially freedom of manufacture, trade and the press and the free division and alienation of landed property into Jew monopolies.

To hand management of social and parliamentary affairs to the Jews ... after they have raised themselves up as the dominant money power in the cities ... would be a betrayal of our past and our future.[6]

Jews were less prominent in the conservative *Reformverein*, though the continuing popularity of monarchical legitimacy among the older banking families led to support from the Frankfurt Ladenburgs and the Bavarian Eichtals.[7]

For many doubters the Prussian victory over Austria at Königgrätz in 1866 was decisive. The *Allgemeine Zeitung des Judentums*, recalling the 'equal participation of Jewish citizens', concluded that the new 'unity before the law' would have to lead to their 'complete legal equality'.[8] Of the Jewish politicians active in the various parliaments only Johann Jacoby persevered in opposition to the constitution of the North German Confederation, created after the defeat of Austria; of those in the parliaments of the Southern states all actively favoured the treaties of adherence to the Confederation.[9]

It would be a mistake to assume that Jewish support for the liberal cause was occasioned exclusively by narrow concern for legal rights, though specifically Jewish journals were bound to emphasize that aspect, or for economic interests. The aspirations of the Jewish community coincided at this time with that of the professional and commercial middle class in general, and the legislative achievements of the decade 1867–77 seemed to confirm the wisdom of the tactical alliance. It was the Parliament of the North German Confederation that passed the Law on Religious Equality; it and the Reichstag of the Empire, created in 1871, passed the laws that facilitated business enterprise, freedom of movement, uniform legal codes and coinage. But much as these reforms benefited individuals, what was significant about them was the change in political atmosphere that they brought about. When

6 'Judenverfolgungen und Emancipation von Juden', *Berliner Revue* XXVI, 1861, p. 416; 'Der Talmud und die jüdische Reform', ibid., vol. XXII, 1860, p. 10; see also 'Die politische Judenschule', satirizing the *Demokratische Studien*, ibid., vol. XXII, pp. 214–18, vol. XXIII, pp. 64–6; 'Das Handwerk und seine jüdischen Widersacher', ibid., vol. XXIII, pp. 509–12.
7 Toury, *Orientierungen*, pp. 111–12.
8 'Was haben wir zu thun?', *AZJ*, 18 September 1866, p. 595.
9 Hamburger, *Juden im öffentlichen Leben Deutschlands*, pp. 248–50.

Levin Goldschmidt, who had reached higher public office than almost any other Jew in Imperial Germany, looked back on his political career with the words:

> Long before party programmes of that kind existed, I was active ... on behalf of the independence of the judiciary, the freedom of advocates, the removal of guild restrictions and the economically damaging investment tax ... against the need to license joint-stock companies, for a unitary gold-based currency, for trial by jury and commercial courts staffed by businessmen, for a German supreme court, for the introduction of a German commercial legal code and a German civil code,[10]

he summarized those guarantees of an open society that were important even to those who did not have the personal ambition of becoming a member of parliament or judge, a company director or professor. It was this change of atmosphere that led the Jewish historian Simon Dubnow to say: 'In the mood of celebration that gripped Germany it was as if the spectre of the Jewish Question had completely vanished.'[11]

This sense of identification with the new political order went had in hand with the increased level of Jewish political activity. A total of twenty-two persons of Jewish descent sat in the Reichstag between 1867 and 1878, almost all of them Liberal (see table 3.1). The 1874 Reichstag contained eleven Jews, a number not exceeded again until 1912. The thirty-nine deputies in state parliaments (Landtage) showed a similar distribution (see table 3.2).

What the figures in tables 3.1 and 3.2 illustrate is a convergence – temporary, as it turned out – of the typical Jewish political stance and the status quo. The sheer numbers indicate a degree of political integration qualitatively different even from the revolutionary years and the Liberal revival of the early 1860s, let alone the pre-1848 period and the decade of Reaction. The partisan allegiance shows overwhelming support for the *klein-deutsch* nation-state, but a strong minority favouring further constitutional development. Within the *Reichspartei* – the less particularist of the two right-wing parties, known as Free Conservatives in Prussia – and even the Conservatives, Jews were tolerated as long as they were baptized, and baptized Jews were on balance more right-wing than the unbaptized. Support for the Social Democrats was at this stage still low. As far as one can tell, Jewish politicians during these years represented the opinions of the bulk of the Jewish population, in contrast with the dissonance of earlier and later periods.

10 Levin Goldschmidt, *Zur Reichstagswahl vom 21.2. und 2.3.1887*, Berlin: Puttkammer & Mühlbrecht, 1887, p. 9.
11 Simon Dubnow, *Die neueste Geschichte des jüdischen Volkes*, Berlin: Jüdischer Verlag, 1920, vol. II, p. 333.

Table 3.1 Jewish members of the Reichstag, 1867–1878

	Professing Jews	Baptized	Total
Social Democrat	2	–	2
Left Liberal	6	1	7
National Liberal	7	3	10
Reichspartei	1	1	2
Conservative	–	1	1
	16	6	22

Source: Based on data in Ernest Hamburger, *Juden im öffentlichen Leben Deutschlands. Regierungsmitglieder, Beamte und Parlamentarier in der monarchischen Zeit, 1848–1918*, Tübingen: J. C. B. Mohr, 1968, pp. 252–3, 301. The figures for the Social Democrats include Johann Jacoby, who was elected in 1874 but declined to take his seat.

Table 3.2 Jewish members of the Landtage, 1867–1878

	Professing Jews	Baptized	Total
Left Liberal	·11	1	12
'Liberal'	2	–	2
National Liberal	15	5	20
Free Conservative	–	1	1
Conservative	–	1	1
Uncertain	2	1	3
	30	9	39

Source: Based on data in Jakob Toury, *Die politischen Orientierungen der Juden in Deutschland. Von Jena bis Weimar*, Tübingen: J. C. B. Mohr, 1966, pp. 341–54

The occupations of these politicians illustrated the degree to which intellectuals and professional men were replacing businessmen in the Jewish political elite. Here, too, there was a convergence between Jews and Gentiles. Relatively few German entrepreneurs took a leading role in national politics, even in those movements, like the *Nationalverein*, whose success would bring them obvious economic benefits. Leonor Reichenheim was the only Jewish industrialist to feature among the founders of the *Deutsche Fortschrittspartei*. Of the 1867–78 group of Jewish Reichstag deputies, only two were entrepreneurs –

Reichenheim of Berlin and the Hamburg merchant Marcus Wolf Hinrichsen, both National Liberals. In addition to them the conservatively-inclined Mayer Karl von Rothschild and the eccentric railway speculator and land-owner Henry Bethel von Strousberg of the Free Conservative Party were briefly members of the North German Reichstag; one could, at a pinch, count Ludwig Bamberger as a banker and include the Socialist Julius Motteler, a rentier. As might be expected, the proportion of businessmen was higher in the Landtage during this period: 14 out of 39. They were without exception Liberal and in the majority of cases National Liberal, though not all Landtage had separate Liberal party groups at this stage.

Another characteristic of Jewish politicians in this period, at least at the *Reich* level, was their relatively weak links with the Jewish community. Lasker, Bamberger and Heinrich Bernhard Oppenheim, the parliamentary leaders of the National Liberals, Max Hirsch, the co-founder of the Liberal trade unions, Leopold Sonnemann, the editor of the *Frankfurter Zeitung* and the lone anti-Bismarckian Democrat in the House, all considered themselves fully emancipated individuals, Jews at best in their private lives or not at all. The less eminent deputies and the state and local politicians had stronger organizational links.

However, even in this period of near-consensus on Liberalism, one should not ignore personal idiosyncrasy or idealism as determinants of political outlook. Only this would explain the attachment of Jewish industrialists to Socialism, like Ludwig Loewe, who was a Lassallean in the 1860s, and Paul Singer, who switched from Liberalism in 1869 and ended a distinguished political career as co-chairman of the SPD. Equally, conservative or loyalist sentiments continued, as monitored by Prussian Provincial Governors when recommending candidates for the coveted titles of *Kommerzienrat* or *Geheimer Kommerzienrat* or other honours. Candidates were praised for their 'patriotic convictions', 'loyal and correct attitudes' and 'strict conservatism'.[12] An interesting stereotype occurs in the report of the police president of Brandenburg, who praises a possible nominee for his 'good political convic-tion, which is notoriously rare among Jews'.[13] It could be argued that those in line for such awards were older men, with the attitudes of an earlier period, and that those who sought such titles, which brought commercial as well as social advantages, were likely to be conformist and that was, indeed, one of the purposes of this system. But in general oppositional behaviour delayed, rather than prevented, awards. Between 1819 and 1900 89 Jews were appointed *Kommerzienrat* (14.8 per cent of the total) and 21 appointed

12 ZStM, Rep. 120, AIV5, 13d15 (101).
13 W. E. Mosse, *Jews in the German Economy. The German-Jewish Economic Elite, 1820–1935*, Oxford: Oxford University Press, 1987, p. 82, fn. 35.

Geheimer Kommerzienrat (17.6 per cent of the total).[14] Several of these were prominent Left Liberals or opposed the government's tariff policies, such as Wilhelm Herz.

An even more significant symptom of integration was the modest opening of public appointments to Jews. Moritz Elstätter, Minister of Finance in Baden from 1868 to 1893 and delegate to the Bundesrat, the Upper House of the new *Reich*, was the first and, as it turned out, only unbaptized Jew before 1918 to become a cabinet minister. Two baptized Jews became Prussian ministers in this period: Karl Rudolf Friedenthal, Minister of Agriculture from 1874 to 1879, and Heinrich von Friedberg, Minister of Justice from 1879 to 1889, having previously been State Secretary of the *Reich* Office of Justice. No unbaptized Jew could become an officer in the Prussian army, nor in the Prussian-dominated regiments of the other states of the Empire; in Bavaria, which retained autonomy in these matters, they could.[15] Until the mid-1880s it was possible, however, for a Jew to become a reserve officer. Nor could practising Jews become members of the administrative civil service of Prussia and the *Reich* or – with one notable exception – of the foreign service. They could, however, now become judges in Prussia, though not rising above the rank of *Landesgerichtsrat* (District Court Justice), and continuing to be excluded from the public prosecuting service. Of the other states, some were even more restrictive, Saxony, Braunschweig and the Grand Duchy of Hesse continuing to exclude them from all public appointments. The first state to appoint a Jewish judge had been Hamburg, where Gabriel Riesser became a High Court Justice (*Obergerichtsrat*) in 1860. The most liberal state in all respects was Baden, followed by Hamburg and Bavaria. The Imperial judiciary contained two distinguished Jews: Levin Goldschmidt was appointed a Justice of the Supreme Commercial Court (*Bundeshandelsobergericht*) in Leipzig in 1869 and Jakob Friedrich Behrend a Justice of the Imperial Supreme Court (*Reichsgericht*) in 1887.[16] In addition the baptized Eduard Simson was appointed President of the *Reichsgericht* in 1879, having been President not only of the Frankfurt Parliament in 1849, but also of the Prussian Chamber of Deputies, of the North German Reichstag and of the Imperial Reichstag.

Small as this breakthrough was, it was important for two reasons. The appointment of practising Jews to such offices was without precedent and represented a change of public policy. Baptized Jews had had access to public appointments since the beginning of the century, the grounds for

14 Ibid., pp. 74, 83.
15 Hermann Rumschöttel, *Das bayerische Offizierskorps, 1866–1914*, Berlin: Duncker & Humblot, 1973, p. 245.
16 See above, p. 57.

discrimination having been religious, not racial, but the increase in their number suggested that the social stigma of Jewish descent now counted for less. The academic profession was one in which the ritual requirement of baptism had been particularly resented. Before 1848 seventeen professing Jews had managed to become *Privatdozenten* (non-stipendiary lecturers), mostly in the central and Southern states – three at Göttingen (then in the Kingdom of Hanover), three at Marburg, six at Heidelberg and one at Tübingen. Prussia accounted for only four, Bavaria for none. Four of these seventeen nevertheless yielded to the pressure to convert to Christianity after being appointed. Article 8 of the Prussian Emancipation Edict of 1812 admitted Jews to academic positions, but this right was suspended in 1822 after the legal philosopher Eduard Gans had applied for a Chair at Berlin; he secured the Chair in 1828, having converted in 1825. Of the three who subsequently became full Professors (*Ordinarien*) before 1848, all first underwent baptism and only two had become Associate Professors (*Extraordinarien*) without baptism – the orientalist Gustav Weil of Heidelberg, who gained the title without the stipend in 1845 and became an *Ordinarius* in 1861; and the lawyer Samuel Marum Meyer of Tübingen in 1831, baptized in 1834, becoming *Ordinarius* in 1837 and then Rector in 1849–50. Not until the 1847 law on the status of Jews had suspended the 'lex Gans' was a professing Jew appointed *Privatdozent* at a Prussian university, the physiologist Robert Remak, who had previously applied unsuccessfully. Five years earlier the physicist Peter Theophil Riess was the first unbaptized Jew to become a member of the Prussian Academy of Sciences, the election of Moses Mendelssohn in 1771 not having been confirmed by Frederick II. The first Jew to become a full professor in a German state was the mathematician Moritz Abraham Stern at Göttingen in 1859. The first to achieve this in Berlin was Ludwig Traube, who was made a *Privatdozent* a year after Remak, also in the faculty of medicine, and became an *Ordinarius* in 1872.[17] Appointments as *Privatdozent* became more common from the late 1860s onwards, as did those as Associate Professors (*außerordentliche Professoren*). By the end of the 1870s

17   Gans: Hans Günther Reissner, *Eduard Gans. Ein Leben im Vormärz*, Tübingen: J. C. B. Mohr, 1965, pp. 55–8, 91–3; Riess: Peter Honigmann, 'Peter Theophil Riess, der erste Jude in der preußischen Akademie der Wissenschaften', *JIDG* XIV (1985), pp. 181–90; Remak: Norbert Kampe and Heinz-Peter Schmiedebach, 'Robert Remak (1815–1865). A Case Study in Jewish Emancipation in the Mid-Nineteenth Century German Scientific Community', *LBYB* XXXIV (1989), pp. 95–129. See also Monika Richarz, *Der Eintritt der Juden in die akademischen Berufe. Jüdische Studenten und Akademiker in Deutschland, 1678–1848*, Tübingen: J. C. B. Mohr, 1974; David L. Preston, 'The German Jews in Secular Education, University Teaching, and Science: A Preliminary Enquiry, *JSS* XXXVIII (1976), pp. 99–116.

there were about twenty Jewish *Ordinarien*.[18] Most of the appointments were in ideologically neutral subjects, such as the natural sciences and medicine, not in culturally or politically sensitive ones such as Classical Philology, German Literature, History or Law. Two of the most significant appointments, therefore, were made by the Liberal Prussian Minister of Education, Adalbert Falk: that of Levin Goldschmidt to the Chair of Commercial Law at Berlin and that of the leading neo-Kantian, Hermann Cohen, to the Chair of Philosophy at Marburg, the latter having failed to get the support of the University Senate on an earlier occasion.[19] To list these individual instances of Jewish entry into hitherto closed domains is not to suggest that there was an increase in collective influence. Measured by his practical impact on public affairs, the single most effective Jew of this period was Ludwig Bamberger. Thanks to his expertise in currency and banking matters he played a leading role in the creation of a gold-based *Reichsmark* and an Imperial central bank, the Reichsbank. His centralization of the new Empire's financial institutions was, in the judgement of Professor Werner Mosse, 'among the rare instances in which a Jewish politician or public figure demonstrably influenced major political decisions'.[20]

What explains this brief golden age of the public acceptance of Jews was simply the convergence of their values and aspirations with those of the majority of the German middle class. Hence Jewish enthusiasm for the new *Reich* was no mere power-worship – though in some individual cases it was also that. But there was an element of wishful thinking in the uncritical acceptance of the pre-1848 orthodoxy that German national unification would bring Jewish salvation; there was a general unwillingness to recognize the dark side of all – not only German – nationalism, the intolerant, authoritarian, xenophobic and aggressive potential in the nationalist mentality. True, Börne and Heine had feared no good would come of the triumph of German nationalism and even Riesser, who in general went along with the orthodoxy, was aware that there were those who 'want to found German nationality ... as on large-scale hatred of the French, so on small-scale hatred of the Jews'.[21] But there were relatively few who, in the year of the victory over France, saw,

18 Hamburger, *Juden im öffentlichen Leben Deutschlands*, p. 55.
19 Julius Ebbinghaus, 'Die Berufung Cohens auf den Marburger Lehrstuhl', *Archiv für Philosophe* IX (1959), pp. 90–2.
20 W. E. Mosse, *Economic Elite*, p. 240; see also a less favourable assessment in Marie-Lise Weber, *Ludwig Bamberger, Ideologie statt Realpolitik*, Stuttgart: Steiner, 1987, pp. 139–59.
21 Gabriel Riesser, 'Betrachtungen über die Verhandlungen der zweiten Kammer des Großherzogtums Baden über die Emancipation der Juden', in *Gesammelte Schriften*, vol. II, p. 361.

as did Sonnemann's collaborator Guido Weiss, the seeds that the Empire contained: 'Don't you think [he wrote to Jacoby] that after the triumph of battle, the whole would be worthily crowned with a bit of Jew-baiting, and would we not deep down wish it on the Oppenheims, the Bambergers etc?'[22]

In time most of the Jewish Bismarckians were woken from their wishful thinking. Bamberger recalled that on his return to Germany from Paris in 1863

the whole matter [i.e. anti-Semitism] was so alien to me, that I related quite naïvely to it. ... Only after the middle of the seventies, as the wind from above turned in the direction of reaction ... did I become aware of the beginning of the movement within the bosom of my own party, and I began to emerge from my naïveté. ... If anyone had said to me then [in 1863] that the time would come when I should be accused of representing French interests, or personal advantage or most of all Jewish assumptions in German matters![23]

In the meantime there were relatively many who supported one aspect or another of Bismarck's illiberalism during the Liberal era. Important sections of Jewish opinion supported the *Kulturkampf*,[24] as did some of the Liberal papers often referred to as the 'Judenpresse', particularly the *National-Zeitung*. But of the Jewish members of the Reichstag both Lasker and Bamberger voted against the Anti-Jesuit Law and Wolffson abstained; the baptized Friedenthal also voted against. They were the only National Liberal and *Reichspartei* deputies to do so. Bamberger did, however, vote for the 'pulpit paragraph', which banned political activity by the clergy, and he, Oppenheim and Lasker toed the party line on the Anti-Socialist Law – the one action in his career that Lasker sincerely regretted.[25] Sonnemann and the *Frankfurter Zeitung*, on the other hand, consistently opposed all discriminatory legislation.

One Jew of this period, prominent and influential, though not a politician or in the conventional sense a public figure, was the banker Gerson Bleichröder, Bismarck's personal financial adviser and closely involved in the policies of Prussia in the crucial period of its emergence as the agent of

22 'Und gönnten wir's den Oppenheim', Bamberger usw. nicht ganz im Stillen?', 29 August 1870. Cit. Toury, *Orientierungen*, p. 157.
23 Ludwig Bamberger, *Erinnerungen* (ed. Paul Nathan), Berlin: Georg Reimer, 1899, pp. 258, 520.
24 Werner E. Mosse, 'The Conflict of Liberalism and Nationalism and its Effect on German Jewry', *LBYB* XV, 1970, pp. 136–8; Uriel Tal, *Christians and Jews in Germany. Religion, Politics and Ideology in the Second Reich, 1870–1914*, Ithaca: Cornell University Press, 1975, pp. 97–120.
25 James F. Harris, *A Study in the Theory and Practice of German Liberalism. Eduard Lasker, 1829–1884*, Lanham, MD: University Press of America, 1984, p. 51.

German unification. Without his skills it would have been difficult for Prussia to finance the war against Austria, or negotiate the indemnity with France or the accession of Bavaria to the new Empire.[26] Though his close association with Bismarck was well-known at the time, the details of his operations could only be guessed at, and therefore became the subject of speculation, rumour and libel. Those who hated Bismarck hated his banker; those who wished to get at Bismarck could do so by getting at his banker; those who disapproved of the Liberal legislation and the swift rise of capitalism under Bismarck's aegis in the 1870s could blame Bleichröder for it. There is scarcely an anti-Bismarckian pamphleteer or orator of the period – Konstantin Frantz, Rudolf Meyer, Otto von Diest-Daber, 'Ottoman Beta', F. F. Perrot in the *Kreuz-Zeitung*, Adolf Stoecker – for whom Bleichröder was not a stick for beating Bismarck with.[27]

In retrospect this seems paradoxical. Bleichröder was undoubtedly rich and undoubtedly favourable to capitalism. He donated much money to charities, some of them Jewish, but used his influence only once to promote a Jewish political cause, namely the campaign to ensure equal rights for Jews in Romania in the Treaty of Berlin in 1878.[28] But he was also, in his political views and the policies he advocated, far from typical of the Jew-in-politics of the Liberal epoch. He did not support the gold standard for the *Reichsmark*; he came to favour protective tariffs, like other conservatively-inclined bankers, such as Rothschild and Abraham von Oppenheim; he supported railway nationalization, a corporatist parliament and the anti-Socialist laws.[29] Anti-Semites saw in him the typical money-Jew who was taking over the world. But in the manner of his dealings, his rescue of the fortunes of more than one imprudent or dishonest aristocrat, his deference to the monarchy, his identification with state authority, he was a throw-back to the older type of 'court Jew', the last of his kind. He was ennobled in 1872, only the second professing Jew in Prussian history to be so honoured and the

26 Fritz Stern, *Gold and Iron. Bismarck, Bleichröder and the Building of the German Empire*, London: Allen and Unwin, 1977, pp. 81–156.
27 Konstantin Frantz, *Die Religion des Nationalliberalismus*, Berlin and Munich: M. Hutter, 1872; *idem, Der Nationalliberalismus und die Judenherrschaft*, Leipzig: Roßberg, 1874; *idem, Der Untergang der alten Parteien und die Parteien der Zukunft*, Berlin: F. Graf Behr, 1878; Rudolf Meyer, *Politische Gründer und die Korruption in Deutschland*, Leipzig: Bidder 1877; Otto von Diest-Daber, *Bismarck und Bleichröder. Deutsches Rechtsbewußtsein und die Gleichheit vor dem Gesetze*, Munich: Verlag des deutschen Volksblattes, 1897; Ottoman Beta (i.e. O. H. Bettziech), *Der Geist Bleichröders und der Geist Friedrichs des Großen*, Berlin, 1890; *KZ*, 29 June 1875.
28 Stern, *Gold and Iron*, pp. 369–93; N. M. Gelber, 'The Intervention of German Jews at the Berlin Congress, 1878', *LBYB* V (1960), esp. pp. 228–48.
29 Stern, *Gold and Iron*, pp. 179–80, 189–92, 199–200, 219.

first with male heirs (his predecessor, Abraham von Oppenheim, being child-less). Anti-Semites were interested in the appearance – Bleichröder as the millionaire and the conspicuous *parvenu*; Bismarck in the reality – Bleich-röder as the discreet, conservative loyalist. In the words of his biographer: 'If he had not existed, the anti-Semites could not have invented him.'[30]

4 BISMARCK'S CHANGE OF COURSE AND THE RISE OF ANTI-SEMITISM

The identification of Jewish aspirations and the German nation-state did not last long. It was challenged by two inter-connected developments: the revival of anti-Semitism and Bismarck's breach with the National Liberals. Anti-Semitism had never disappeared entirely, even during the Liberal apogee of the 1860s,[1] and the stirrings had become louder after the stock-market crash of 1873. But the articles in the *Kreuz-Zeitung*, the Catholic *Zentrum's Germania* and the popular weekly *Die Gartenlaube*, as well as the books and pamphlets of Konstantin Frantz, Rudolf Meyer and Wilhelm Marr, could all be written off as the grumblings of disgruntled *Reichsfeinde* (enemies of the state).[2] By linking the Jews with Liberalism and portraying Bismarck as the servant of both, they merely reinforced Jewish loyalty towards, and dependence on, the *Reich*. The situation changed when such propaganda came from intellectually respectable sources such as Heinrich von Treitschke's articles in the *Preußische Jahrbücher*[3] – as his antagonist Theodor Mommsen put it, 'What *he* said was thereby made respectable'[4] – or from sources such as Court

---

30 Ibid., p. 531.

1 See above, pp. 86–7.

2 *KZ*, 29 June–3 July 1875; *Germania*, 1875: nos. 174, 185, 189, 190, 201, 203, 207, 228; 28 March 1876, 7 September 1877; Peter Pulzer, *The Rise of Political Anti-Semitism in Germany and Austria*, rev. edn, London: Peter Halban, 1988, pp. 72–97.

3 Heinrich von Treitschke, 'Unsere Aussichten', *Preußische Jahrbücher*, vol. XLIV, November 1879, pp. 572–6; 'Herr Graetz und sein Judentum', ibid., December 1879, pp. 660–70; 'Noch einige Bemerkungen zur Judenfrage', ibid., vol. XLV, January 1880, pp. 85–95; 'Zur inneren Lage am Jahresschlusse', ibid., vol. XLVI, December 1880, pp. 643–5; 'Erwiderung an Herrn Th. Mommsen', ibid., pp. 661–3; 'Die jüdische Einwanderung in Deutschland', ibid., vol. XLVII, January 1881, pp. 109–10.

4 'Was *er* sagte, war damit anständig gemacht', Theodor Mommsen, 'Auch ein Wort über unser Judenthum', Berlin: Weidmann, 1881: reprinted in Walter Boehlich (ed.), *Der Berliner Antisemitismusstreit*, Frankfurt: Insel-Verlag, 1964, p. 221.

Preacher Adolf Stoecker, who appeared to have at least the indirect support of authority and of whose conduct the Emperor 'was of the opinion that [it] would all come to nothing, and considers the row as useful, in order to cut the Jews down to size somewhat.'[5] The Anti-Semitic Petition which circulated in 1880, demanding a reversal of Jewish legal equality, evoked no direct disavowal from the Prussian government, merely the statement from the Vice-President of the State Ministry that 'the government had no intention of bringing about a change in the law'.[6]

At the same time, for reasons that were only indirectly related, Bismarck had concluded his re-alignment with the Christian-conservative forces of the Conservative Party and the *Zentrum*, at the expense of a weakened and divided National Liberal Party, on the basis of protective tariffs and an end to further constitutional evolution. Stoecker and Treitschke on the one hand, Bismarck on the other, were concerned with the extent to which Liberalism had infiltrated society and the administration. Stoecker and Treitschke explicitly linked the Jews with this development, Bismarck only by implication. Pragmatist as always, he distinguished between 'moneyed Jewry', whose 'interests [are] on balance inter-connected with the maintenance of the institutions of our state and whom we cannot do without', and propertyless Jewry in the press and in parliament, 'which ... attaches itself to all political opposition'.[7] Having, in the earlier 1870s, publicly praised the Jewish contribution to the state, and occasionally even paid private tribute,[8] he now intended to proceed 'in the hope that the silly Jew-boy Lasker and his following, these theoretical speech-makers', would be displaced.[9]

But for a perceptive Jew the revival of anti-Semitism and the government's turn to the Right reinforced each other. Their significance lay not so much in the immediate legislative consequences, which could, after all, be reversed, but in their symbolic content. Just as the protectionists had demanded

5   29 September 1880. Friedrich Curtius (ed.), *Denkwüdigkeiten des Fürsten Chlodwig von Hohenlohe-Schillingfürst*, Stuttgart and Leipzig: Deutsche Verlags-Anstalt, 1906–7, vol. II, p. 307.

6   *StPrA*, 22 November 1880.

7   16 November 1880 to the Minister of Religious Affairs, Robert von Puttkamer, cit. Walter Frank, *Hofprediger Adolf Stoecker und die christlichsoziale Bewegung*, 2nd edn, Hamburg: Hanseatische Verlagsanstalt, 1935, p. 91; see also Moritz Busch, *Tagebuchblätter*, Leipzig: Grunow, 1888–9, pp. 12–13: 'Die Reichgewordenen sind nicht gefährlich. Die gehen nicht auf die Barrikade und zahlen pünktlich ihre Steuern.'

8   *StPrA*, 30 January 1872; Bismarck, *Die gesammelten Werke*, Berlin: Stollberg, 1929, vol. XI, p. 227.

9   'der dumme Judenjunge Lasker und sein Anhang, diese theoretischen Redner', 10 March 1878: Erich Foerster, *Adalbert Falk. Sein Wesen und Wirken als preußischer Kultusminister*, Gotha: Klotz, 1927, p. 485.

'economic legislation which will re-awaken in the people the spirit of love and sense for authority'[10] and declared that 'the state based on the rule of law [*Rechtsstaat*] has outlived itself. We shall have to return to the so-called patrimonial and patriarchal state',[11] so Ludwig Bamberger was aware that 'it is not a question of a few marks' worth of import duties in the dispute over economic principles ... but of life and death in the arena of free, peaceful, modern development'.[12]

That anti-Semitism was a weapon to be used against Liberalism was obvious to most of them; indeed, many underestimated the genuine force of the new political direction by seeing it only as an anti-Liberal manoeuvre.[13] Jews could react in one of two ways: by following the Catholic example and creating organizations specifically designed to defend sectional rights, or by reinforcing those Liberal forces that would ensure their survival as free and equal members of the German nation. They overwhelmingly chose the second. The Berlin Jewish Community did appeal to the Prussian Minister of the Interior against the Stoecker agitation, but wrung an evasive reply out of him only after their fourth *démarche*. A proposal by the editor of the *Allgemeine Zeitung des Judentums*, Ludwig Philippson, to launch a public meeting, went unanswered.[14] The *Deutsch-Israelitischer Gemeindebund* (DIGB), founded in 1872, though growing slowly, still represented only a small proportion of communities.[15] A committee of notables, headed by Professor Moritz Lazarus, organized two public meetings in late 1880, and was heard of no more.[16]

10   Cit. Helmut Böhme, *Deutschlands Weg zur Großmacht. Studien zum Verhältnis von Wirtschaft und Staat während der Reichsgrüdungszeit*, Cologne: Kiepenheuer & Wietsch, 1966, p. 401.

11   Ibid., p. 561.

12   Ludwig Bamberger, 'Die Sezession', Berlin: Springer, 1880: reprinted in *Gesammelte Schriften*, Berlin: Rosenbaum & Hart, 1894–8, vol. V, p. 132.

13   E.g. *AZJ*, 16 July 1878, p. 455; also 'Das Geheul der Reactionäre', ibid., 20 August 1878, pp. 529–30; Ludwig Bamberger, *Deutschtum und Judentum*, Leipzig: F. A. Brockhaus, 1880, pp. 9–10; Eduard Lasker to Hermann Baerwald, 12 September 1881, in Julius Heyderhoff and Paul Wentzke (eds), *Deutscher Liberalismus im Zeitalter Bismarcks. Eine politische Briefsammlung*, Bonn: K. Schroeder, 1925–6, vol. II, p. 383.

14   'Berliner Zustände', *AZJ*, 16 November 1880, pp. 721–3.

15   Jacob Toury, *Soziale und politische Geschichte der Juden in Deutschland 1847–1871. Zwischen Revolution, Reaktion und Emanzipation*, Düsseldorf: Droste Verlag, 1977, pp. 269–76; Bernhard Jacobsohn, *Der deutsch-israelitische Gemeindebund nach Ablauf des ersten Decenniums seit seiner Begründung*, Leipzig, 1879, pp. 10, 31, 69–70.

16   Michael A. Meyer, 'The Great Debate on Antisemitism. Jewish Reaction to New Hostility in Germany, 1879–1881', *LBYB* XI (1966), p. 169.

As a tactical decision the abstention from public agitation may have been sound: given the political structure of Imperial Germany, success was much more likely to come from private moves, like the approach by Bleichröder that evoked a reluctant rebuke from the Emperor for the Court Preacher.[17] But there was a stronger reason for this low-profile strategy. What those who had taken such pride in their integration and assimilation resented most was this gratuitous reminder that their efforts were unappreciated:

We of the younger generation might have hoped that we should gradually succeed in acclimatizing ourselves to the 'nation of Kant' [wrote Hermann Cohen], that existing differences would be levelled out through the principled help of moral politics and a historical consciousness urged on each of us. ... This confidence has been broken: the old unease is being re-awakened.[18]

Moritz Lazarus echoed this sentiment:

The worst thing for us Jews, especially for those who work within German culture is this: our pride is broken, in our innermost being we are injured more as Germans than as Jews.[19]

And Bamberger, writing to Lasker, abroad at the time, saw Stoecker's agitation as doing more damage to Germany than to the Jews: 'One can understand why the Germans are hated among all nations.'[20] The whole logic of their attitude and aspiration had been that Jewishness was a private matter. Nothing offended them more than the suggestion that they had, as Jews, separate, collective interests. 'In face of all common interests we Jews are all individuals', claimed Moritz Lazarus; only the revival of anti-Semitism had again given the Jews a common cause.[21] Moreover, though assimilationist Jews would not react defensively against racialist propaganda – a marginal phenomenon at this time – they were exceedingly sensitive to the kind of charge Treitschke had made, that Jews had failed to integrate themselves into German culture. Many Jews acknowledged that they owed what Emil

17 Frank, *Hofprediger Adolf Stoecker*, p. 86.
18 Hermann Cohen, 'Ein Bekenntniß in der Judenfrage', Berlin: Ferd. Dümmler, 1880: reprinted in Boehlich, *Der Berliner Antisemitismusstreit*, pp. 124–5; and in Bruno Strauss (ed.), *Hermann Cohens Jüdische Schriften*, Berlin: C. A. Schwetschke, 1924, vol. II, p. 73.
19 Moritz Lazarus, *Unser Standpunkt. Zwei Reden an seine Religionsgenossen am 1. und 16. Dezember 1880*, Berlin: Stuhr'sche Buchhandlung, 1881, p. 7.
20 15 November 1880. Heyderhoff and Wentzke, *Deutscher Liberalismus*, vol. II, p. 371.
21 Lazarus, *Unser Standpunkt*, p. 5.

Lehmann, one of the founders of the *Deutsch-Israelitischer Gemeindebund*, termed the 'reciprocal obligation' ('Gegenleistung') for emancipation;[22] they complained of the injustice of Treitschke's accusation, but not of his demands. Harry Breßlau, one of his chief antagonists, agreed that: 'The demand itself, that you make in that sentence, is one ... that I support completely and utterly', adding only: 'If you were furthermore to specify the means whereby this process of transforming Jews into Teutons could be accelerated, you would earn the gratitude of every impartial and unprejudiced Jew.'[23] Hermann Cohen, in words he was later to regret, asserted: 'We all wish that we simply had the German, Teutonic appearance of which we now wear only the climatic side-effects.' As for the temporary survival of 'peculiarities' ('Absonderlichkeiten'), 'we must continue to show our commitment to ridding ourselves of them'.[24]

Given these premises, Jews were, in the words of the *Allgemeine Zeitung*, 'bound and tied more than ever to Liberalism',[25] though from now on this tended not to mean the National Liberal Party. Though the National Liberal split in 1880 was not caused by the Jewish Question, the growing conservatism of the government, of which the toleration of anti-Semitism was a symptom, meant that most National Liberal Jewish parliamentarians joined the *Sezession* which amalgamated in 1884 with the old *Fortschrittspartei* to form the new *Freisinnige Partei*. Lasker, for one, was under no illusion that the *Sezession* required Jewish patronage: 'The idea has arisen among a number of Jews simultaneously that Jews are on this occasion under an obligation to give special help', he wrote, explaining: 'The intention is to damage the liberal cause by describing it as "Jewish". It would be a suitable antidote, if the liberal cause were to be strengthened with vigorous support by the Jews.'[26] He had travelled a long way since 1868, when he declared in the North German Reichstag that he would abstain on principle on any matters relating to Jewish interests.[27]

Among those who met to appeal for Jewish funds were Bleichröder's brother Julius and the industrialist and progressive deputy Ludwig Loewe,

---

22 Emil Lehmann, 'Höre, Israel. Aufruf an die deutschen Glaubensgenossen' (1869), in *Gesammelte Schriften*, Dresden: C. Weiske, 1899, p. 62.
23 Harry Breßlau, *Zur Judenfrage*: reprinted in *Der Berliner Antisemitismusstreit*, Boehlich p. 62.
24 Cohen, 'Ein Bekenntniß': reprinted in Boehlich, *Der Berliner Antisemitismusstreit*, p. 140; Strauss, *Cohens Jüdische Schriften*, vol. II, p. 85.
25 *AZJ*, 16 July 1878, p. 455.
26 12 September 1881, Heyderhoff and Wentzke, *Deutscher Liberalismus*, vol. III, p. 383.
27 StBRNB 16 June 1868, vol. I, p. 496.

who had featured in Lazarus's committee of the previous year. Bamberger was much more cautious: he had objected to Lasker that a list of free-trade speakers at a meeting of the parliamentary party looked too 'semitic'.[28] In any case the new political developments sharply reduced the number of Jewish legislators. The kind of urban, metropolitan constituencies where Jews were most easily adopted were gradually being conquered by Social Democracy. The swing to the Right swept nine of the thirteen Jewish deputies out of the Prussian Landtag in the 1879 elections. The remainder were, with the exception of the baptized Conservative Oscar Hahn, Left Liberals. Lasker failed to get renominated; Friedenthal, feeling increasingly out of place among the Free Conservatives, retired. The Reichstag elections of 1881 had a similar effect, reducing Jewish numbers from nine to six, all unbaptized and all Left Liberals – either Progressives or 'Secessionists'. During the 1870s, four Jews, Lasker, Bamberger, Wolffson and the baptized Friedrich Dernburg, had sat in the parliamentary executive of the National Liberal Party. After 1881, there were none; even before leaving the party, Lasker and Bamberger had suffered a loss of support in the voting for the party Executive in 1879.[29] Left-Liberal opponents of the National Liberals had sometimes to suffer anti-Semitic campaign slogans.[30] Only in Southern Germany did National Liberal Jews continue to sit in state parliaments. Even among Left Liberals, no new Jews were re-adopted to replace those that died or retired, with the exception of Josef Stern, the son-in-law of Guido Weiss, the editor of the *Frankfurter Zeitung* and thus a member of the peculiar radical-democratic oligarchy of Frankfurt. As a consequence, the Prussian Landtag was without Jewish members, at any rate in the confessional sense, from 1886 until 1898. With the retirement of Bamberger in 1893 only Social Democrats sat in the Reichstag as unbaptized Jews until 1912.

The fruitful and in many instances happy alliance between the Jewish and Gentile middle classes of Germany lasted a bare two decades. It was beginning to fray even before 1878, as the left wing of the National Liberal Party became increasingly critical of Bismarck's authoritarianism, though it did not – as we shall see – come to a sudden end when Bismarck turned to a tariff policy and the National Liberal Party split. But 1878 was nevertheless a symbolic date. From that year onwards it looked as though the liberalization of the state had come to a halt; that the kind of open society, in which merit, not status, earned rewards, half-achieved by the late 1870s, would remain

---

28   Stanley Zucker, 'Ludwig Bamberger and the Rise of Anti-Semitism in Germany, 1848–1893', *CEH* III/4, December 1970, p. 345.
29   Thomas Nipperdey, *Die Organisation der deutschen Parteien vor 1918*, Düsseldorf: Droste, 1961, p. 165.
30   Zucker, *CEH* III/4, pp. 345, 349, 351.

Table 3.3 Jewish members of the Reichstag, 1881–1893

	Professing Jews	Baptized	Total
Social Democrat	5	–	5
Left Liberal	6	2	8
National Liberal	–	–	–
Reichspartei	–	1	1
	11	3	14

Sources: Ernest Hamburger, *Juden im öffentlichen Leben Deutschlands. Regierungsmitglieder, Beamte und Parlamentarier in der monarchischen Zeit, 1848–1918*, Tübingen: J. C. B. Mohr, 1968, pp. 252–3, 406

Table 3.4 Jewish members of the Landtage, 1879–1893

	Professing Jews	Baptized	Total
Social Democrat	1	–	1
Left Liberal	7	2	9
National Liberal	3	2	5
Free Conservative	–	1	1
Conservative	–	1	1
Uncertain	1	–	1
	12	6	18

Source: Toury, *Orientierungen*, pp. 351–4

as distant a goal as it was then. The effect of that disillusionment was that Jewish politicians, Jewish publicists and the greater part of the Jewish population, though loyal and patriotic, were concentrated in oppositional groupings and the politically unreliable Jew became a common stereotype. Police reports on Left-Liberal meetings in Berlin make this clear. Sometimes the observation is matter-of-fact: a meeting in Neukölln in 1882 was 'attended by some forty to fifty persons, mostly Jewish gentlemen'; the memorial meeting for Eduard Lasker was 'in its composition, Progressive-Jewish'. At other times, as of a meeting of the Halle'sches Tor branch, 'the objective observer of these events was bound to register that especially the extreme tendency [within the branch] was represented by Semitic elements', including Dr Josef Loewenthal, 'a notorious reporter for Jew-papers [*Judenblätter*]', i.e. the Ullstein-owned *Berliner Zeitung*.[31]

Given these unmistakeable trends, it remains to be asked why the Jewish reaction to growing political isolation and officially tolerated anti-Semitism was so hesitant and weak. There are a number of possible explanations, in addition to those given above. In the first place it was by no means obvious that the change of course of 1879 was definitive. Bamberger, embittered by his defeat, may have despaired of 'the German middle classes, over whom, following the end of the *Kulturkampf*, the hereditary rulers, *Junker* and clerics, have once more become masters. German parliamentarism was an episode and I was a partner in this episode. Never mind'.[32] Others may well have reflected that Bismarck and William I were mortal, and that long-term factors would work in favour of the middle classes and liberal reforms. Working within the system therefore continued to be attractive. Above all, the loyalty to the *Reich* and to its external security must not be under-estimated. The last two factors operated in particular in the *Kartell* elections of 1887, called by Bismarck on the issue of renewing the military budget, when a vote for Bismarck's policies might imply a vote, either at the first or the second ballot, for Conservatives or others with specifically anti-Semitic views. For Levin Goldschmidt it was a question of priorities: 'What Herr Wolff [the Conservative candidate in his constituency] thinks ... about the erroneously so-called 'Jewish Question' I neither know nor care ... especially when the battle is about quite different matters, namely the most important interests of state and *Reich*.'[33] Moritz Lazarus reflected Jewish vulnerability to the charge of oppositionism: 'It was necessary for something to happen to refute by a deed the assertion, cultivated unanimously by friend and foe, that Jew and Progressive are necessarily one and the same thing, that every Jew must, as a Jew, belong to the opposition.'[34]

These defensive claims seemed all the more urgent, given the way that the pro-government publicity machine implied, from 1878 onwards, that Jewish money, influence and ambition were behind the bourgeois opposition. Bismarck was quite prepared to play this game, though selectively and only through intermediaries. In 1879 he told Lucius von Ballhausen that his wish was 'to separate the right wing of the National Liberals ... from "the Semites"',

31 StAP, Pr.Br. Rep. 30, Berlin C, Pol. Präs., Tit. W., Nr. 536a, vol. I (118, 353, 110); Lasker meeting: ibid., Tit. L. Nr. 465 (34).

32 Ernst Feder (ed.), *Bismarcks großes Spiel. Die geheimen Tagebücher Ludwig Bambergers*, Frankfurt: Societäts-Verlag, 1933, p. 339 (6 June 1887).

33 Goldschmidt, *Zur Reichstagswahl*, p. 27. Originally published in *NZ*, 27 February 1887.

34 Moritz Lazarus, *An die deutschen Juden*, Berlin: Walther & Apolant, 1887, p. 7.

though he distinguished, as always, between rich (i.e. useful and loyal) Jews and the rootless agitators of the Left.[35] The *Norddeutsche Allgemeine Zeitung* which, under the editorship of Emil Pindter, generally reflected Bismarck's views, defended the government's intimate relationship with banking houses in raising loans, but was quite prepared to draw attention to the Jewish surnames – Sonnemann, May, Horix, Holdheim – of those elected to the executive of the Frankfurt-based *Deutsche Volkspartei.*[36] Bismarck himself was under dual pressure: from Bleichröder to take a public position against anti-Semitism and from his new political allies to side with Stoecker against the Left Liberals. He therefore decided to tone down his attacks on Stoecker so as 'to do nothing that could be construed as agreeing with the worst enemies of the government'.[37] According to Herbert von Bismarck, who needed no urging in these matters, his father wanted the press to emphasize that 'Jewish money' had been the paymaster of the 'progressive Republicans' in the 1881 Reichstag elections.[38] Before the 1884 elections he instructed the Prussian Minister of the Interior Puttkamer that the popular masses would be alienated by open opposition to anti-Semitism, but that open support for it would 'drive a lot of Jewish money [*Judengeld*] into the Progressive electoral chest';[39] Bleichröder echoed this warning to the Emperor.[40]

In the 1887 election Bismarck's *Kartell* enjoyed the support of some prominent National Liberal Jews,[41] but the relationship was not without its tensions. At the previous election, just after the government had proposed a stock exchange tax, strongly supported by Conservatives and anti-Semites, Bismarck felt obliged to complain to Franz Mendelssohn, a senior member (*Ältester*) of the Berlin Merchant Corporation, that the brokers of Berlin were subsidizing his enemies, to which Mendelssohn replied that one could hardly expect *die Finanzwelt* to vote for Stoecker – leaving it open whether the objection to Stoecker was his anti-Semitism or his anti-capitalism.[42] Bleichröder, too, for all his unreciprocated loyalty to his master, found

---

35 Robert Freiherr Lucius von Ballhausen, *Bismarck-Erinnerungen des Staatsministers Freiherrn Lucius von Ballhausen*, Stuttgart and Berlin: J. G. Cotta, 1920, pp. 163–4, 216, 236–7; Bismarck, *Gesammelte Werke*, vol. VI (3), p. 199.

36 *NDAZ*, 26 October 1880, p.m.; 21 May 1880, p.m.

37 To Tiedemann, 29 November 1880. Cit. Stern, *Gold and Iron*, p. 524.

38 Hans-Ulrich Wehler, *Bismarck und der Imperialismus*, Cologne: Westdeutscher Verlag, 1969, p. 472.

39 *Idem, Das deutsche Kaiserreich*, Göttingen: Vandenhoeck & Ruprecht, 1973, pp. 112–13.

40 Stern, *Gold and Iron*, p. 526.

41 See above, p. 103.

42 Feder, *Bismarcks großes Spiel*, pp. 338–9.

himself increasingly in a dilemma. In 1878 he had generously supported the election campaign of the protectionist *Centralverband Deutscher Industrieller* and of Herbert von Bismarck. In 1881, when government-encouraged anti-Semitism was at its height, he had, as he afterwards claimed, abstained from voting, having been forced to choose between an anti-Semite and a Progressive.[43] In the *Kartell* election he was again prevailed upon to dig into his pocket, but this time on condition that Joseph Cremer, a Catholic journalist and author of the *Germania*'s anti-Semitic articles during the 1870s, was dropped as a *Kartell* candidate.[44]

If the first wave of anti-Semitism subsided quickly and frightened few, the second, which began with the election of Otto Böckel in 1887 and culminated in the election of sixteen anti-Semites to the Reichstag in 1893, had a quite different effect, for here was an autonomous movement with a genuine popular base. In addition, the prospects of a change in government policy had diminished. The death of the Emperor Frederick III in 1888, after a reign of only ninety-nine days, whether or not he had called anti-Semitism 'the shame of the century', was the first blow. The new Emperor, William II, after a number of hesitations, made it clear that he did not intend to pursue a more liberal course, a decision confirmed by the resignation of Count Leo Caprivi as Imperial Chancellor in 1894. By this time the Conservative party had adopted its anti-Semitic programme and two organizations had been formed to oppose this trend: the *Verein zur Abwehr des Antisemitismus* and the *Centralverein deutscher Staatsbürger jüdischen Glaubens*. The *Deutsch-Israelitischer Gemeindebund*, after its slow start, now comprised 500 affiliated communities, about a quarter of the total, but covering some two-thirds of the Jewish population of the Empire.[45]

For a quarter of a century most Jews and most Liberals had denied the anti-Semites' claim that there was a Jewish Question, or that Jews *qua* Jews had any claims or interests in society beyond a guaranteed equality of rights. By 1893 hopes based on the liberal citizen-theory began to appear illusory. The 1890s saw the slow revival of something scarcely heard since the 1850s: an open discussion, from the Jewish side, of the role of the Jew in politics. There was, in the words of a recent historian, 'a beginning of a Jewish revision of the terms of emancipation'.[46]

43 Stern, *Gold and Iron*, pp. 197–8, 529.

44 Erich Ekkehard (ed.), *Sigilla Veri. Lexikon der Juden-Genossen und -Gegner aller Zeiten und Zonen, insbesondere Deutschlands ...*, 2nd edn, Erfurt: Bodung, 1929, vol. I, p. 648.

45 Ismar Schorsch, *Jewish Reactions to German Anti-Semitism, 1870–1914*, New York, London and Philadelphia: Columbia University Press, 1972, p. 222.

46 Ibid., p. 12.

5 JEWS AND THE STATE, 1893–1914

By 1893 spokesmen for the Jewish community and their Gentile well-wishers were aware that they had to overcome two distinct, though connected, obstacles to civic equality: the anti-Semitism of public opinion and political parties, and the discriminatory policies of the *Reich* and state governments; and that both obstacles had become established features of the Empire. The need to counter-act public anti-Semitic propaganda was made urgent by the success of anti-Semitic candidates in the 1890 Reichstag elections and the Conservatives' adoption of the Tivoli Programme; it was reinforced by the further anti-Semitic gains of 1893 and the ritual murder accusation in Xanten in 1891. The lead was taken by a group of intellectuals and politicians, including Max von Forckenbeck, Theodor Mommsen, Albrecht Weber and Gustav Freytag, who were grouped round Theodor Barth's periodical, *Die Nation*. Many of them had been associated with the Declaration of the Notables of 1881, drawn up to counter-act the Anti-Semitic Petition and Treitschke's *Preußische Jahrbücher* articles.[1] At the founding assembly of the *Verein zur Abwehr des Antisemitismus* (*Abwehr-Verein* for short) in 1890 the historian Rudolf von Gneist, a National Liberal, was elected president, though old age and ill-health prevented him from taking an active part. He was succeeded on his death in 1895 by Heinrich Rickert, who in turn was succeeded by Theodor Barth in 1902. Both were prominent members of the *Freisinnige Vereinigung*, the more moderate of the two wings into which the Left Liberals had split in 1893.

The policy of the *Verein* was simply to implement the spirit and the letter of the constitution: 'We stand here above all as citizens [Rickert declared] irrespective of religious denomination, as citizens who have the duty and the right to defend and protect the fundamentals of our constitution.'[2] The predominance of Gentiles among the leaders and, initially, among subscribing members emphasized the view that anti-Semitism was a German problem. The *Verein* was specifically not an organization for the defence of Jewish interests, nor even for the perpetuation of the Jewish community. Its supporters clung to the liberal-citizen view of the Jew's rights and duties, with assimilation as the ideal. They respected genuinely devout Judaism, but saw more hope in conversion and inter-marriage.[3] Above all, they opposed the founding of specifically Jewish societies or organizations as 'separatist

---

1 See above pp. 96–7.
2 *MVA*, May 1901, p. 37.
3 Theodor Mommsen, 'Auch ein Wort': Boehlich, *Der Berliner Antisemitismusstreit*, p. 228. Albrecht Weber, *MVA* III/53, 31 December 1893, pp. 471–3.

games' (*Abschließungsspielerei*)[4] and 'after-effects of protected status' (*Nachwirkung der Schutzjudenheit*).[5]

Many Jews valued the *Verein*'s political fight, if only out of assent with Moses Mendelssohn's dictum that the Jewish cause was best defended by non-Jews.[6] The leadership consisted of professional and business notables, overwhelmingly Protestant. Within a year it claimed 12,000 members; thereafter membership stabilized at between 8,000 and 9,000.[7] Though the public image of the *Verein* was, at any rate in its early stages, Gentile, Jews were heavily involved from the start. The initiators of the idea of a defence body against anti-Semitism included the Progressive Berlin city councillor Edmund Friedemann and Barth's assistant editor, Paul Nathan. Financially the *Verein* was at all times dependent on Jewish largesse, especially through the Frankfurt banker Charles L. Hallgarten. In the course of time Jews became more openly associated with the *Verein*'s activities; indeed some local branches, for instance that of Cologne, were almost exclusively Jewish in membership and 'equal Christian and Jewish participation' became a formal principle in 1904.[8]

For all its inter-denominationalism, there was one thing the *Verein* could not do, and that was to promote specifically Jewish participation in public life. That could be achieved only by self-consciously Jewish organizations. The Stoecker–Treitschke campaign had, as we have seen, relatively little impact on Jews. But in the political atmosphere of 1893 neither the steady growth of the DIGB nor the foundation of the *Abwehr-Verein* sufficed for some of them. Of the sudden flood of books and pamphlets dealing with the anti-Semitic assault, the most influential publication was Raphael Loewenfeld's initially anonymous *Schutzjude oder Staatsbürger?* (*Citizen or Protected Jew?*) which led within a short interval to the foundation of the *Centralverein deutscher Staatsbürger jüdischen Glaubens* (C.V.). Like the *Abwehr-Verein*, it gave priority to countering anti-Semitism; also like the *Abwehr-Verein*, and unlike the incipient Jewish student movement which combined in 1896 into the *Kartell-Convent jüdischer Corporationen*, it abjured separatism. It emphasized not only the Jew's political allegiance to the 'dearly

---

4 *MVA*, X/51, 19 December 1900, pp. 401–3; XIII/36, 9 September 1903, pp. 281–2.
5 Mommsen, 'Auch ein Wort': Boehlich, *Der Berliner Antisemitismusstreit*, p. 226.
6 Moses Mendelssohn, 'An den Baron Hirschen in Dresen', 18 October 1775, in *Gesammelte Schriften. Nach den Originaldrucken und Handschriften* (ed. G. B. Mendelssohn), Leipzig: Brockhaus, 1843–5, vol. V, pp. 639–40.
7 Barbara Suchy, 'The Verein zur Abwehr des Antisemitismus (I) – From its Beginnings to the First World War', *LBYB* XXVIII (1983), pp. 209–10.
8 Ibid., pp. 213–14, 219.

beloved fatherland [*teurem Vaterland*]',[9] but his cultural allegiance, through the 'cultivation of German convictions [*Pflege deutscher Gesinnung*]'.[10] Nevertheless, its very existence implied that, given the German political situation, the Jew *qua* Jew had an obligation to participate politically, and to press Jewish claims to equal citizenship when the appropriate authorities failed to do so.

The C.V. was founded, like the *Abwehr-Verein*, by middle-class notables most of whom were closely associated with one or other of the Liberal parties. And though initially its principal aim was to defend Jewish rights it soon developed in other directions. In the first place it became a mass movement, with a membership of some 40,000 in 1914, thus affecting one Jewish family in three. In the second place it laid a claim, by 1913, to 'embracing *all* Jews, without distinction regarding their religious tendency or party political position'.[11] It did not quite succeed in this: it failed to attract the Orthodox and Zionist minorities; and workers and white-collar and rural strata were under-represented within it.[12] It did, however, in the course of time cultivate a new, positive Jewish identity by anathematizing converts and reviving interest in Jewish culture. The second generation of leaders, exemplified by Eugen Fuchs, chairman from 1917 to 1919, and Ludwig Holländer, executive secretary (*Syndikus*) from 1908 onwards, had come up through the Jewish student corporations. They symbolized the revival of a more confident Jewish consciousness characteristic of the years before the First World War, which found expression in a number of activities to be discussed below.

The scope of the C.V. was at all times greater than that of the *Abwehr-Verein*. It was concerned not only with counter-propaganda, but with countering all forms of discrimination, of which the most important were the failure of state and *Reich* authorities to appoint qualified Jews to official posts; their reluctance to prosecute anti-Semitism under the penal code; and the decline in Jewish candidatures for political office.

Hopes that the increasing appointment of Jews to academic and state offices during the 1860s and 1870s would ultimately lead to equality of opportunity were soon disappointed. In fact, from the 1880s onwards there was a decline which was not arrested until just before the First World War, a trend

---

9   [Raphael Loewenfeld], *Schutzjude oder Staatsbürger? Von einem jüdischen Staatsbürger*, Berlin: R. Loewenfeld, 1893, p. 3.

10   'Unsere Stellung', *IdR*, I/1, July 1895, p. 6.

11   'An die deutschen Staatsbürger jüdischen Glaubens', Berlin, 1913, cit. Evyatar Friesel, 'The Political and Ideological Development of the Centralverein before 1914', *LBYB* XXXI (1986), p. 141.

12   Arnold Paucker, 'Zur Problematik einer jüdischen Abwehrstrategie in der deutschen Gesellschaft', *WD*, p. 490.

directly connected with the governmental switch from Liberalism to Conservatism in Prussia and the *Reich*. This was not merely because Jews were associated (however incorrectly in individual cases) with Liberalism, but because the switch in the political balance of power reinforced the patrimonial attitudes and encouraged the exercise of prerogatives on the part of established institutions. The discriminations to which this led were varied: since the state was a Christian-monarchical one, unbaptized Jews were excluded more rigorously than the baptized. But Catholics also suffered discrimination; no Social Democrat could hope for public preferment; and even a nonconformist bourgeois, i.e. one who did not aim at a reserve commission in the army or had been refused one, was at a disadvantage. In general, the more a particular career was open to the middle classes, the better a Jew's chance of entry.

University teaching and the judiciary, requiring the most stringent professional qualifications, therefore emerge as the least unfavourable in this respect; the extent of Jewish penetration indicates their maximum opportunities under the Empire. After the free professions of law, medicine and journalism it was teaching that attracted educated Jews, though the public status of the teaching profession made entry difficult and promotion almost out of the question for the unbaptized. Education was a politically sensitive matter, whether for the Christian or for the Germanic state. The transmission of cultural goods was not to be lightly entrusted. This theme runs continuously from the objections of the Inner Academic Senate of Heidelberg in 1815: 'The status of an academic teacher must be considered as too honourable to be desecrated by a Jewish member's spirit of intrigue, selfishness and importunity',[13] to the views of the educationist Friedrich Paulsen in 1902 on Jewish pressure to enter the learned world: 'There can be no doubt that no European state can tolerate such a state of affairs, that it would consider it as foreign domination and would throw it off violently.'[14] As in the earlier part of the century, therefore, entry was easiest in relatively value-free disciplines such as mathematics, medicine and the physical sciences and most difficult in those touching most closely on the national ideology – German Literature, Classics and Constitutional Law. In the first two areas no professing Jew gained a Chair before the end of the Empire, whereas in Constitutional Law two Chairs were granted, both outside Prussia, namely to Heinrich Rosin, *Ordinarius* (1886) and Rector (1904–5) at Freiburg, and Eduard Rosenthal, *Ordinarius* (1896) at Jena. That baptism was a key to advancement was shown both by the eminence achieved by such legal scholars as Paul Laband,

---

13   Richarz, *Der Eintritt der Juden*, p. 171.
14   Friedrich Paulsen, *Die deutschen Universitäten und das Universitätsstudium*, Berlin: A. Asher & Co., 1902, pp. 199–200.

Ordinarius at Königsberg (1866) and Strasbourg (1879), Georg Jellinek, *Ordinarius* at Heidelberg (1891), Heinrich Dernburg, *Ordinarius* at Halle (1862) and Berlin (1873), and Edgar Loening, *Ordinarius* at Rostock (1883) and Halle (1886);[15] and by the differing fates of the Nobel prize winners. Up to 1918 seven Germans of Jewish origin were Nobel laureates. The poet Paul Heyse (Literature Prize) and the journalist Alfred Fried, who gained the Peace Prize, stood outside academic life. The remaining five were natural scientists. Adolf von Baeyer (Chemistry, 1905) was Jewish on his mother's side only and had held Chairs since 1872, first at Strasbourg, then at Munich. Otto Wallach (Chemistry, 1910), a Jew by religion, had held a Chair since 1889. Richard Willstätter (Chemistry, 1915), already a director at the Kaiser-Wilhelm-Institut in Berlin, became Baeyer's successor at Munich in the same year, though not without difficulty: 'This is the last time I give you my signature for a Jew', Ludwig III told his Minister of Education.[16] Ten years later, faced with repeated discrimination in appointments to Chairs – 'We have to take the times and the street into consideration', the zoologist Richard von Herting told him[17] – he ostentatiously resigned. Fritz Haber (Chemistry, 1918), *Ordinarius* at the Technische Hochschule, Berlin, since 1906 and also a director at the Kaiser-Wilhelm-Institut, was one of the relatively small group of German-Jewish academics who underwent baptism in the genuine conviction that this was the proper course for a secularized patriot and one in which he was directly influenced by Theodor Mommsen.[18]

The missing name among the Nobel laureates is that of Paul Ehrlich (Medicine, 1908) whose world-wide fame as the developer of salvarsan was insufficient to gain him a Chair in Prussia. Though he became honorary Professor at Göttingen and, at an advanced age, *Ordinarius* at the privately-founded University of Frankfurt, the highest state post he held was that of director of the Institute for Experimental Therapy at Frankfurt. Ehrlich's career demonstrated what those of Samuel Marum Meyer and Hermann Cohen had already shown, that monarchs and bureaucrats could be more enlightened than academics in rewarding talent. Appointments to the Kaiser-Wilhelm-Institut, the predecessor of the present-day Max-Planck-Gesellschaft, were by Imperial favour. In 1907 Ehrlich was honoured twice – a highly unusual proceeding[19] – by being made both Privy Medical Council-

15   Hamburger, *Jüden im Öffentlichen Leben Deutschlands*, pp. 56, 387.
16   'Das ist aber das letzte Mal, daß ich Ihnen einen Juden unterschreibe', Richard Willstätter, *Aus meinem Leben. Von Arbeit, Muße und Freunden*, 2nd edn., Weinheim/ Bergstrasse: Verlag Chemie, 1958, p. 235.
17   'Wir müßen doch auf die Zeit und die Straße Rücksicht nehmen', ibid., p. 341.
18   Rudolf A. Stern, 'Fritz Haber. Personal Recollections', *LBYB* VIII (1963), p. 88.
19   G St Dahlem, Rep. 90, 1767, 17.

lor (*Geheimer Medizinalrat*) and state councillor (*Rang der Räte*), Second Class; in 1911 he became a Privy Councillor (*Wirklicher Geheimrat*), which carried with it the title of 'Exzellenz'.

As the Liberal era declined, so did appointments of Jews. In 1917 there was a total of 13 Jewish *Ordinarien* at German universities, compared with 25 in 1909 and 22 in 1889. Given the general expansion of higher education, the Jewish share showed a relative decline from 2.8 per cent in 1889 to 2.5 per cent in 1909 and 1.2 per cent in 1917. In 1889 16 per cent of Jewish academics were *Ordinarien*, compared with 48 per cent of Christians; in 1909 11 per cent, compared with 39 per cent of Christians. Professing Jews were also likely to be older than their Christian colleagues: 38 per cent were over the age of sixty in 1909, compared with 24 per cent among Christians. Nor did the pressure to embrace Christianity diminish during this period. Indeed the ratio of baptized to professing Jews moved in favour of the baptized throughout the Imperial period at all levels of academic life, so much so that baptized Jews provided proportionately more *Ordinarien* than Christians.[20] Nevertheless, Jews had other opportunities. One of the most important were the Commercial Academies, private or municipal institutions that were often eager to recruit Jewish talent: the constitutional lawyer Hugo Preuß taught at Berlin, becoming Rector in 1906, the economist Julius Hirsch at Cologne, the economist Moritz Julius Bonn was Director of the Munich Commercial Academy. The lawyer Berthold Freudenthal taught at Frankfurt where he, too, became Rector. Even more significant in illustrating the relationship between the Jewish community, education and the state is the history of the University of Frankfurt.

Frankfurt University, inaugurated in 1914, was unique in Imperial Germany. It was an attempt to tap the municipal pride of a wealthy city, its considerable philanthropic tradition (heavily, but by no means exclusively, Jewish) and its existing academic assets, principally in medicine, for a university that would come under local rather than Prussian state control. This involved a conflict of principle: what was the justification for such an anomaly? And it entailed a conflict of interest: what kind of institution would this be and should it be tolerated in Prussia? The two foundations that formed the financial pillars of the project were the *Institut für Gemeinwohl* (Institute for the Common Weal) founded in 1891 by Wilhelm Merton and

20 Bernhard Breslauer, *Die Zurücksetzung der Juden an den Universitäten Deutschlands*, Berlin: Verband der deutschen Juden, 1911; Norbert Kampe, 'Jüdische Professoren im deutschen Kaiserreich', in Rainer Erb and Michael Schmidt (eds), *Antisemitismus und Jüdische Geschichte. Studien zu Ehren von Herbert A. Strauss*, Berlin: Wissenschaftlicher Autoren-Verlag, 1987, pp. 185–211. Figures exclude the theological faculties and the University of Frankfurt.

the *Georg und Franziska Speyersche Studienstiftung.* Merton was a native of Frankfurt, but was brought up in England; he reverted to German from British citizenship in 1900 and was baptized at the same time. Part of the fortune he made from Metallgesellschaft AG went into the *Institut*, which in 1896 became a limited liability company with an initial capital of over 500,000 RM. Among the projects it financed was the Academy of Commercial and Social Sciences set up under city auspices in 1901.[21] After the deaths of first the banker Georg Speyer and then his widow, the Speyer Foundation had a capital of 3 million RM. This endowed, among others, three Chairs at the Academy and also the Georg-Speyer-Haus, which accommodated the various medical institutes, amalgamated into the *Akademie für praktische Medizin* (Academy of Applied Medicine). Like the Commercial Academy, this was in turn subsumed into the university. In all, Jewish benefactors provided nearly three-quarters of the university's endowment.

The political lead for the process of founding the university came from the Lord Mayor, Franz Adickes, already closely involved in the city's academic endeavours as administrator of the Speyer Foundation, who formed a committee of five. Adickes had to fight on three fronts. Within the City Council the Left, including the Social Democrats and a section of the Progressives, opposed a scheme that would favour mainly the upper income groups. In Berlin there was hostility from the majority of the Prussian Parliament – Conservatives, *Zentrum* and National Liberals – out of a mixture of motives: jealousy by the neighbouring University of Marburg, sentimental attachment to the traditional university (which weighed especially with the National Liberals) and ideological suspicion. The *Kreuz-Zeitung* asked: 'Can the state renounce its vigilance over appointments to professorships? In that event no economist would be appointed at Frankfurt, where the spirit of Leopold Sonnemann exercises such strong influence, who did not belong to the school of Brentano or was [not] a follower of the *Frankfurter Zeitung.*'[22] Adickes felt constrained to write to Eugen Schiffer, himself a baptized Jew, who led the National Liberal opposition, 'not to lend support to parochial, anti-Semitic or anti-liberal motivations'.[23]

Equally strong were the pressures from Jewish supporters of the university scheme. Not that Frankfurt Jewish opinion was unanimous: there were numerous Jews in the dissident Liberal group.[24] But the voices of those deter-

21   Paul Kluke, *Die Stiftungsuniversität Frankfurt-am-Main, 1914–1932*, Frankfurt: Kramer, 1972, pp. 33, 91; Hans Achinger, *Wilhelm Merton in seiner Zeit*, Frankfurt: Kramer, 1965, pp. 112, 218; Mosse, *Economic Elite*, pp. 81–4, 318–20.
22   *KZ*, 14 January 1910; *Staatsbürger-Zeitung*, 9 July 1912.
23   8 March 1912, cit. Kluke, *Die Stiftungsuniversität Frankfurt-am-Main*, pp. 97, 109, fn. 104.
24   Ibid., pp. 66, 72, 83, 101.

Jews in German Politics 113

mined to ensure an open appointments policy in the new university were irresistible. The first annual report of the *Institut für Gemeinwohl* had already stressed the need 'to act free from any party or denominational position';[25] the Speyer Foundation's legacy to the Academy laid down a similar condition.[26] Moreover, there were two Jews on Adickes' committee, Freudenthal, the Rector of the Academy, and Ludwig Darmstädter, an industrial research chemist and pupil of Bunsen. Ludwig Heilbrunn, the rapporteur of the City Council's committee, was also Jewish: he had secured, in the draft of the contract for the foundation of the university: 'Art.4. No condition regarding the religious denomination of any nominee for a professorship shall be attached to any of the Chairs and, in accordance with that, religious or confessional status shall not in any instance be grounds for exclusion in filling a Chair or a position in the research institutes.'[27]

Numerous benefactions, including those of the Rothschild family and the banker Jacob Schiff (related by marriage to Heilbrunn), were conditional on the observance of this paragraph.[28] Another major Jewish benefactor was Charles Hallgarten, one of the forces behind the *Abwehr-Verein*. More than once the organ of the C.V. urged its readers 'to learn to close the all too ready Jewish helping hand' unless there was a guarantee of 'a university genuinely based on parity'.[29] That these conditions were satisfied in their essentials was shown by the appointment of Berthold Freudenthal to the Chair of Public Law, Ludwig Edinger (whose institute the university absorbed) to the Chair of Neurology, Josef Horowitz to that of Oriental Philology and, in the year of his death, Paul Ehrlich to that of Experimental Therapy. It was a victory for the spirit and letter of the constitution achieved on a narrow front and in uniquely favourable circumstances.

The obstacles that Jews faced in universities were negligible compared with those they faced in schools. Except in Baden, where primary education was inter-denominational, governments tacitly enforced the demands of anti-Semites for 'Christian teachers for Christian pupils'. Except during the Falk period Jewish teachers in Prussia were rarely found outside Jewish schools; the battle that Liberal-dominated municipalities, like Berlin, fought to appoint according to merit met with little success.[30]

Like education, law enforcement was a matter for the individual states; the

25 Ibid., p. 34.
26 Ludwig Heilbrunn, *Die Gründung der Universität Frankfurt-am-Main*, Frankfurt: J. Baer & Co., 1915, p. 15.
27 Ibid., p. 137; ZStM, 2.2.1. 21593.
28 Kluke, *Die Stiftungsuniversität Frankfurt-am-Main*, pp. 130, 139.
29 Henriette Fürth, 'Ein offener Brief', *IdR*, XVII/7-8, July–August 1911, p. 404; also ibid., XVII/9, September 1911, p. 485.
30 Hamburger, *Juden im Öffentlichen Leben Deutschlands*, pp. 61-2.

Imperial courts dealt only with a limited number of civil and constitutional issues. Judicial advancement therefore depended on the policies of the state governments. In Prussia this was openly discriminatory. By the time the Prussian Parliament debated the matter in 1901, two Jews had become High Court Judges, in each case through special patronage: Albert Mosse, with the support of Theodor von Holleben, German Ambassador in Tokyo, where Mosse had acted as constitutional adviser; and Siegfried Sommer, with the support of the Emperor himself.[31] Following that debate, and the memorandum by Bernhard Breslauer on behalf of the *Verband der Deutschen Juden*, Prussian policy relaxed. Baden, Bavaria and Hamburg had notably more liberal policies; in all of them Jews reached the rank of presiding high court judge, which happened in Prussia only just before the end of the World War. With the exception of Behrend no Jew served on the Imperial Supreme Court before 1918, but the Imperial government felt it expedient to appoint relatively generously in Alsace-Lorraine, up to the rank of presiding judge (*Senätspräsident*). Saxony, in contrast, refused Jewish appointments on principle and Hesse-Darmstadt and Württemberg made only minimal exceptions.[32]

Within the civil service administration, whether of the *Reich* or of the individual states, professing Jews were so rare, even during the Liberal era, that they could almost be listed individually. The only two to rise to positions of any eminence were Leo Lippmann, who became a *Regierungsrat* in Hamburg (and a *Staatsrat* during the Weimar Republic), and David Hugo Mayer, who entered the Baden Ministry of the Interior in 1879 and rose to *Geheimer Oberregierungsrat*. In the diplomatic service, exclusion was even more rigorous. Philip Eulenburg spoke for many when he urged the rejection of a Jewish applicant, because 'it is not a question of just *one* Semite, but before long several others of his kind will push through the breach created by him. ... Once one of them is inside, there will be a hullabaloo if others are turned down'.[33]

The armed services were equally exclusive. That this should have been so in the army, with its close connection with the Prussian crown and nobility, is unsurprising. True, by 1914 the aristocratic preponderance had vanished, except from the foot-guard and cavalry regiments and the General Staff.[34] But the remaining units were anxious to emulate the values and attitudes of

31   Ibid., p. 44; Werner E. Mosse, 'Albert Mosse: A Jewish Judge in Imperial Germany', *LBYB* XXVIII (1983) pp. 169–84.
32   See above, pp. 56–7.
33   'Ist aber einer reingekommen, so wird ein Zetergeschrei entstehen, wenn man andere ablehnt', cit. Lamar Cecil, 'Wilhelm II. und die Juden', *WD*, p. 323.
34   Karl Demeter, *The German Officer-Corps in Society and State, 1650–1945*, London: Weidenfeld & Nicolson, 1965, pp. 20–32.

the most favoured regiments; the bourgeois who had made good by securing commissions felt little solidarity with those who had failed, and they used the privilege of unanimity to keep all Jewish applicants out of their regiments, even as reserve officers. That Jews had fought with distinction and gained commissions during the wars of liberation and unification (and would again do so in the First World War) was irrelevant, since the army in peace-time served a political and social rather than a military function. This was true in particular of the reserve officer's status, widely regarded as a token of acceptability and reliability, which therefore affected the holder's chances of promotion in many civilian occupations.[35] During the Liberal decades Jews continued to obtain reserve commissions, but with the 1879 change of course, and the 1883 Prussian administrative change that removed personnel matters from the War Minister to the Chief of the Military Cabinet, such appointments became rarer and ceased altogether in 1885.

Precisely because the Prussian army was seen by so many as the heart of the Imperial power structure, its discriminatory practices were criticized inside and outside parliament, not only by Jewish and Liberal politicians, but by those of the *Zentrum*, Social Democrats and even the Free Conservatives,[36] with a frequency that rivalled only the question of judicial appointments. The reactions of the government were ambivalent. Its spokesmen could, with some justice, point out that officer selection lay within the autonomy of individual regiments. Even *Reich* Chancellor Bülow failed to get a commission for his protégé Albert von Goldschmidt-Rothschild, who was anything but a brash parvenu ('The young man was certain to be well received in all salons and clubs in Paris and even more so in London').[37] In public there was regret at any prejudice – 'inadmissible' (Minister of War von Einem)[38] and 'absolutely not justified' (his successor von Heeringen)[39] – and the highly conservative former Minister of Education Robert von Zedlitz-Trützschler, who had resigned from the Conservative Party over the Tivoli Programme, could not 'avoid considering that we deal with these matters

35 Eckhart Kehr 'Zur Genesis des Königlich Preußischen Reserveoffiziers', in *idem*, *Der Primat der Innenpolitik. Gesammelte Aufsätze zur preußisch-deutschen Sozialgeschichte im 19. und 20. Jahrhundert* (ed. Hans-Ulrich Wehler), Berlin: de Gruyter, 1965, pp. 53–63; Gerhard Ritter, *The Sword and the Sceptre. The Problem of Militarism in Germany*, London: Allen Lane, The Penguin Press, 1972, vol. II, pp. 93–104.
36 Werner T. Angress, 'Prussia's Army and the Jewish Reserve Officer Controversy Before World War I', *LB YB* XVII (1972), pp. 19–42.
37 Bernhard Fürst von Bülow, *Denkwürdigkeiten*, Berlin: Ullstein, 1930, vol. I, p. 405; see also Rudolf Vierhaus (ed.), *Das Tagebuch der Baronin Spitzemberg*, Göttingen: Vandenhoeck & Ruprecht, 1961, pp. 446–7 (2 April 1905).
38 *StBR*, 19 March 1909, vol. 235, p. 7622.
39 Ibid., 10 February 1910, vol. 259, p. 1105.

these days in a way that is not only one-sided and unjust ... but that we also do ourselves harm.'[40] But the status quo also had its highly-placed sympathizers, like the *Armeeinspekteur* von der Goltz: 'as if the salvation of the fatherland depended on whether we accepted a few dozen useless Isidors, Manasses and Abrahams as token Semites into the officer corps.'[41] The large number of Jewish officers in the Austrian and French armies, cited by the advocates of more enlightened policies,[42] was seen by their opponents as a cause of these countries' inferior military qualities.[43]

Bavaria had, by contrast, a not altogether deserved reputation for more liberal practices. Certainly Jews continued to get reserve commissions, though only in a minority of regiments and in modest numbers – some three per year between 1907 and 1913, just over 2.5 per cent of the total.[44] In the regular army the situation was less favourable. In the whole of the nineteenth century only six professing Jews were commissioned, of whom three subsequently converted.[45] None passed beyond the rank of major; the ablest of them, Captain Maximilian Hollerbaum, strongly recommended by his regimental commander, was denied promotion by his divisional commander, since he was 'by virtue of his religious denomination not suitable for the rank of battalion commander, that is, with responsibility for training an officer corps'.[46] The Bavarian military plenipotentiary in Berlin after 1905, General Ludwig von Gebsattel, was in complete sympathy with Prussian policy and reported von Einem's view that – whatever he may have pretended in the Reichstag – the aversion to Jewish officers was 'completely justified, ... considering that the whole Jewish character, the individual's whole manner of thinking and acting, like that of the tribe, is so fundamentally different from the mentality that is fortunately still prevalent in the German officer corps, so that infiltration by Jewish elements is to be considered not only harmful, but directly pernicious'.[47]

40   Graf Robert von Zedlitz-Trützschler, *Zwölf Jahre am deutschen Kaiserhof,* Stuttgart: Deutsche Verlags-Anstalt, 1924, pp. 187–8.
41   Generalfeldmarschall Colmar Freiherr von der Goltz, *Denkwürdigkeiten,* Berlin: E. S. Mittler, 1929, pp. 334–5.
42   *AZJ,* 24 September 1909.
43   *KZ,* 5 February 1913; General [Hermann] von Stein, *Erlebnisse und Betrachtungen aus der Zeit des Weltkrieges,* Leipzig: K. F. Köhler, 1919, p. 165.
44   Rumschöttel, *Das bayerische Offizierskorps,* pp. 250–1.
45   Ibid., p. 245.
46   Ibid., p. 248.
47   'Geheimbericht des bayer. Militärbevollmächtigten in Berlin, Oberst Ludwig Frhr. von Gebsattel an den General der Infanterie und bayer. Kriegsminister, Frhr. von Horn, betr. Juden als Mitglieder des Offizierskorps (14. Januar 1907), Hermann Rumschöttel, *Militärgeschichtliche Mitteilungen,* 1970/II, pp. 127–8.

That the situation should be similar in the navy was rather more surprising. The navy lacked the older service's aristocratic and royal traditions. It was intended, with some success, to appeal to the middle classes and to nationalist rather than Prussian sentiment; a navy had, after all, been a Liberal dream since 1848. It was certainly more bourgeois in its recruitment,[48] but that did not make it more liberal. Before 1918 it did not contain a single active officer of the Jewish faith. Even in 1915 an application from a Jewish candidate was passed on for Admiral Tirpitz's (unfortunately unrecorded) advice. Here, too, the discrimination was part of a wider search for reliability and conformity: an officer who, in 1909, married Albert Ballin's adopted (Protestant) daughter was persuaded to resign. Catholicism, even by marriage, was equally suspect: a naval surgeon who wished to marry a Catholic in 1912 was threatened with dismissal unless he promised to bring his children up as Protestants. The notion that Jewish political activity was at least unpatriotic, if not downright subversive, was widespread in the naval command: in April 1917, for instance, the 1st Marine Battalion was forbidden to read papers 'of Social Democratic and Jewish tendency'.[49]

The discrimination against Jews in all branches of the public service must be seen as part of the general pressure to ensure conformity in the Wilhelmine *Reich*. Certainly the personal anti-Semitism of some highly-placed officials, whether civilian or military, played a part in this. But an equally strong influence was the knowledge that to apply the spirit of the constitution would alter the nature of the Empire and, *a fortiori*, of the individual states. For instance, most opportunities that were closed to professing Jews were open, however unequally, to the baptized. There was a logic in this: to accept baptism was to accept citizenship on the state's terms, to insist on special status implied willingness to go along with its liabilities. Thus the running argument about reserve officers was not primarily about the frustrations of a handful of ambitious snobs, but about the rule of law. This was appreciated by the Jews involved – anyone who wanted the commission that badly could get himself baptized –, by the Catholic, Liberal and Social Democratic deputies who kept up a barrage of questions and, not least, by Walther Rathenau, who both yearned for acceptance and had his pride: 'I do not fight for the Jewish reserve lieutenant ... I fight against the injustice committed in Germany against German Jewry and, in part, against the German middle classes'.[50]

48   Holger H. Herwig, *The German Naval Officer Corps. A Social and Political History, 1890–1918*, Oxford: Oxford University Press, 1973, p. 40.
49   Ibid., p. 97, where the comments of Admirals Paul Behnke, Gustav Bachmann and Wilhelm Suchen are cited.
50   Walther Rathenau, 'Staat und Judentum. Eine Polemik', *Gesammelte Schriften*, Berlin: S. Fischer, 1918, vol. I, pp. 206–7.

The reluctance of the authorities to counteract anti-Semitic agitation was another major grievance of the Jewish defence organizations. Although several clauses of the 1879 Imperial Judicial Law (*Reichsjustizgesetz*) covered acts of which Jews complained, e.g. Articles 130, 166, 185–200, 311, 360,[51] it was difficult during the 1880s and 1890s to persuade the public prosecutors to act and almost impossible to secure convictions with anything more than nominal sentences. Despite the uniformity of the law, application varied, as might be expected, from state to state. Saxony, where the government excluded all Jews from the public service and placed public announcements in anti-Semitic newspapers,[52] and which was the only state to prohibit ritual slaughtering, was also the least sympathetic to Jewish litigation. An attempt by the DIGB to prosecute the local anti-Semitic leader, Alexander Pinkert, on the basis of his pamphlet[53] evoked a verdict from the Dresden District Court which, citing August Rohling and Treitschke as authorities, claimed that Jewish teachings 'cannot be criticised sufficiently harshly and must, on grounds of the maintenance of sound morality, be resisted with the greatest force by everyone'.[54]

In Baden, in contrast, the philo-Semitic Grand Duke Frederick I took a personal interest in opposing anti-Semitism, so much so that he received anonymous abusive letters.[55] Teachers or other civil servants who 'disturbed the harmony between different classes of the population' were threatened with dismissal, and the editor of the *Badischer Volksbote* was imprisoned for publishing 'inflammatory' articles.[56] The Baden government's motives were mixed: it reacted to anti-Semitism with disgust, but also saw in it a threat to the political hegemony of the National Liberal Party. Indeed the instinct of most governments was to discourage all expressions of public opinion and repress all agitation as a challenge to authority. The Prussian government treated the Anti-Semitic Petition of 1880 with the same contempt as it treated Jewish and Liberal protests against it. However, as soon as public order was threatened, it stepped in energetically. Following the riots in 1881 after the

51   Maximilian Parmod (i.e. Dr Max Apt), *Antisemitismus und Strafrechtspflege. Zur Auslegung und Anwendung der §§ 130, 166, 185, 193, 360/1 des Straf-Gesetzbuchs in höchstrichterlicher und erstinstanzlicher Praxis*, Berlin: S. Cronbach, 1894.
52   Richard S. Levy, *The Downfall of the Anti-Semitic Political Parties in Imperial Germany*, New Haven, Conn., and London: Yale University Press, 1975, pp. 95–6.
53   'Egon Waldegg' (i.e. Alexander Pinkert), *Die Judenfrage gegenüber dem deutschen Handel und Gewerbe. Ein Manifest an die deutsche Nation*, Dresden: Grumbkow, 1879.
54   Alfred Diamant, *Chronik der Juden in Dresden. Von den ersten Juden bis zur Blüte der Gemeinde und deren Ausrottung*, Darmstadt: Agora, 1973, p. 38.
55   Michael Riff, 'The Government of Baden against Antisemitism. Political Expediency or Principle?', *LBYB* XXXII (1987), p. 133.
56   Ibid., pp. 121–2, 124, 134.

synagogue fire at Neustettin, the Ministry of the Interior banned anti-Semitic speeches in Pomerania and West Prussia, the rioters were arrested and sentenced, and some municipalities were even directed to compensate Jews who had lost property.[57] When, several years later, the agitation reached Hesse-Nassau, the *Kasseler Reichsanzeiger* saw fit to warn teachers against any discriminatory practices.[58] In the neighbouring Grand Duchy of Hesse, where personnel policies were scarcely more enlightened than in Saxony, Grand Duke Ernst Ludwig denounced anti-Semitic agitation as 'reprehensible'.[59] A decree of 1892 barred civil servants from participating in anti-Semitic parties and the official *Gießener Anzeiger* was ordered not to accept notices of anti-Semitic meetings.[60] Yet the same government prosecuted the *Frankfurter Zeitung* when it drew attention to the Grand Duchy's own discriminatory practices.[61] Most states were concerned more with public order than with justice.

The covert practice of discrimination combined with the public denunciation of its advocacy may appear hypocritical; it was, in fact, consistent. So, too, in instances where states rejected claims for improved Jewish representation, it is difficult to distinguish prejudice from bureaucratic inertia. Thus the Chief of the Berlin police, Ludwig von Windheim, objected in 1901 to the *Centralverein* on the grounds that it would 'strengthen Jewish influences'.[62] The petition of 1900, designed to secure for the Jewish community the same unitary organization and official status that the law gave to the Protestant and Catholic churches in Prussia, was rejected by the Ministry of Interior on the grounds that it would 'add the weight of a political Jewish organization to the real power which Jewish citizens have disproportionately attained through money and property'.[63] Hypocrisy, or *raison d'état*, comes out more clearly in the reactions of Chancellor Bethmann-Hollweg and the Kaiser to the memorandum that General Konstantin von Gebsattel of the Pan-German League, had submitted to the Crown Prince in 1913 and which advocated, in addition to declaring a state of siege, depriving Jews of German citizenship, preventing them from publishing newspapers and owning real property, and encouraging

57 Martin Philippson, *Neueste Geschichte des jüdischen Volkes*, Frankfurt: J. Kauffmann, 1922, vol. II, p. 29.
58 Pulzer, *The Rise of Political Anti-Semitism*, p. 249.
59 *MVA* II/14, 3 April 1892, p. 124.
60 Levy, *The Downfall of the Anti-Semitic Political Parties*, pp. 139–40.
61 Hamburger, *Juden in öffentlichen Leben Deutschlands*, pp. 51–2.
62 Marjorie Lamberti, 'The Prussian Government and the Jews. Official Behaviour and Policy-Making in the Wilhelminian Era', *LBYB* XVII (1972), p. 15.
63 Minister of Religious Affairs Konradt Studt to Minister of Interior Hans Freiherr von Hammerstein, 8 August, 1901, cit. Lamberti, 'The Prussian Government', p. 11.

emigration. 'Downright childish', the Emperor observed; nevertheless, 'Jewish influence in the press ... is increasing steadily ... In it Jewry has found its most dangerous scene of action. ... Our efforts must indeed be directed towards excluding Jewish influence from the army with the greatest firmness, and restricting it as far as possible in artistic and literary activities'. Bethmann agreed 'that the Jewish spirit had contributed especially to the degeneration of the freedom of the press'.[64]

Against this widespread unwillingness to welcome – as opposed to tolerate – the Jew as a fellow-citizen, the C.V.'s attempts to use the penal code against anti-Semites seemed doomed. The insistence of the C.V.'s leaders, especially Raphael Loewenfeld, Eugen Fuchs and Martin Mendelsohn, that Jews must persevere in this eventually bore fruit.[65] By 1902 the C.V. was handling 100 cases annually and the public prosecutors gradually accepted that Articles 130 and 166 were applicable to anti-Semitic propaganda.[66] Between 1893 and 1915 at least 537 persons of anti-Semitic affiliation stood trial, earning prison sentences totalling 135 years.[67] Considering that in the everyday life of the average German Jew the attitudes and decisions of the government mattered more than the outpourings of minor demagogues, this was a considerable achievement. To refute anti-Semitic propaganda in open debate was an increasingly hopeless undertaking; to get the state apparatus to disapprove of it publicly gave moral reassurance as well as physical security. In its modest way it was a significant piece of collective Jewish political activity. It was, however, necessarily unspectacular compared with the activities of Jewish organizations and, even more, Jewish individuals in parliaments, political parties, elections and the press.

Parliaments did not, of course, offer the only platform for the exercise of political influence nor, arguably, the main platform in Imperial Germany. Certainly those who most resented the real or imagined influence of real or imagined Jews tended to draw attention to their activities in the press, in commerce and in banking. Those fields are, however, reserved for another section.

64   'Gedanken über einen notwendigen Fortschritt in der inneren Entwicklung Deutschlands'. Hartmut Pogge von Strandmann and Immanuel Geiss, *Die Erforderlichkeit des Unmöglichen. Deutschland am Vorabend des ersten Weltkrieges*, Frankfurt: Europäische Verlags-Anstalt, 1965, pp. 38, 34.
65   Arnold Paucker, 'Zur Problematik', *WD*, pp. 509–11; Schorsch, *Jewish Reactions*, pp. 123–32; Paul Rieger, *Ein Vierteljahrhundert im Kampf um das Recht und die Zukunft der deutschen Juden. Rückblick auf die Geschichte des Centralvereins deutscher Staatsbürger jüdischen Glaubens in den Jahren 1893–1918*, Berlin: Centralverein deutscher Staatsbürger jüdischen Glaubens, 1918, pp. 23, 26–34.
66   See regular reports in *MVA* and *IdR*.
67   Levy, *The Downfall of the Anti-Semitic Political Parties*, p. 159.

6 JEWS AND THE BOURGEOIS POLITICAL PARTIES

Bismarck's rupture with the Liberals, the revival of organized anti-Semitism, the state's neutrality in the face of this and its continued discrimination in public appointments had all ensured that Jewish membership of the national political consensus would be short-lived. The characteristic of Jewish political activity during the 1860s and 1870s had been loyalty to the 'Lesser German' solution of a Germany without Austria, active participation in the creation of the new state, a low degree of radicalism, little overlap with Jewish communal affairs and a studious desire not to appear as the spokesmen of Jewish sectional interest. The decline of the Liberal parties during the 1880s and their reluctance to put forward Jewish candidates was a double blow to Jews, not merely because it indicated a long-term, unfavourable shift in the balance of power, but because it showed the need for some other form of representation. In this respect the split in the Progressive Party over the military budget of 1893, though not in itself fatal, illustrated the exposed position of those dependent on Liberalism for political protection. It was the proximate cause of Bamberger's retirement from politics: 'This last revolting episode in the party grouping [i.e. the party split] was the last straw. ... And it is the anti-Semitism that makes me leave ... disgust and abhorrence, not at the Böckels and Liebermanns, but the three-quarters of the colleagues who are not in the least disturbed by this.'[1]

With Bamberger's retirement the last of the great Jewish consensus politicians left politics. From then on the pattern of activity began to resemble, in principle, if not in detail, that of the period before 1848. An increasing proportion of Jewish politicians and journalists belonged to the Left, inside or outside the Social Democratic Party. An increasing proportion of the others were closely connected with Jewish organizations, religious or secular, and were prepared to raise matters of Jewish concern. There was an increasing concentration on municipal politics, where interest representation could be carried out more easily.

These trends in turn caused strains within the Jewish population. As before 1848, the conspicuous identification of the most articulate Jews with radicalism embarrassed and disturbed the majority who, whatever their discontents, were not inclined towards revolution. Nor was there broad agreement on whether the Jew, as voter or elected representative, should 'think Jewish'. In particular, the reluctance of the Liberal parties to nominate Jewish candidates and, on occasion, to pursue Jewish grievances, put added strains on a relationship that had been taken for granted a generation earlier.

1 Letter to Otto Hartwig, 9 April 1893. Otto Hartwig, *Ludwig Bamberger. Eine biographische Skizze*, Marburg: Pfeil, 1900, p. 75.

Table 3.5   Jewish members of the Reichstag, 1893–1918

	Professing Jews	Baptized	Total
Social Democrat	15	2	17
Left Liberal	2	2	4
National Liberal	–	4	4
Reichspartei	–	1	1
	17	9	26

Source: Hamburger, *Juden im öffentlichen Leben Deutschlands*, pp. 252–3, 406

Table 3.6   Jewish members of Landtage, 1893–1918

	Professing Jews	Baptized	Total
Social Democrat	13	–	13
Left Liberal	19	4	23
'Liberal'	1	–	1
National Liberal	9	5	14
Uncertain	1	–	1
	43	9	52

Sources: Hamburger, *Juden im öffentlichen Leben Deutschlands*, pp. 380–98; Toury, *Orientierungen*, pp. 351–4

Bamberger's aggrieved departure from politics in 1893, like his break with the National Liberals thirteen years earlier, symbolized the narrowing political base available to the predominantly bourgeois Jewish population of Germany. The last professing Jew had disappeared from the Prussian Landtag in 1886; only in South Germany did Jewish deputies survive in state assemblies, two of them, significantly, National Liberals: the banker Karl Ladenburg in Baden, a veteran of the *Nationalverein* and father-in-law of the National Liberal leader Ernst Bassermann; the banker Otto Wolfskehl, father of the poet, in the Grand Duchy of Hesse; and the Progressive merchant Carl Maison in Bavaria.

The absence of Jews from the Prussian Landtag was a matter of particular concern to Jewish bodies at a time of rising anti-Semitism. As in the 1850s, so in both 1893 and 1898 – elections were quinquennial – the lack of Jewish candidates was deplored,[2] not merely because such a state of affairs was a tacit

2   *AZJ*, 1858, p. 298; 'Zu den Landtagswahlen', *AZJ*, 27 October 1893, p. 505; *AZJ*, 1 July 1898, p. 302; *IdR* IV/9, September 1898, p. 424.

tribute to the power of anti-Semitism, but because, as Eugen Fuchs of the C.V. put it, it was in the general interest 'if defence against anti-Semitic attacks is mounted by the attacked themselves'.[3]

To the question which parties should sponsor such candidates, and whether Jewish voters should give priority to normal party loyalty or to confessional duty, Jewish organs gave ambiguous answers. The C.V. claimed to be non-partisan and opposed only to anti-Semitism – 'party colours and the life of groupings do not concern us.'[4] But if anti-Semitism was the enemy, Jews were excluded from voting for the Conservative Party or for the Free Conservatives/*Reichspartei* which, though lacking an anti-Semitic programme, was frequently its electoral ally. In any case, neither was likely to adopt a professing Jew – though the baptized Otto Arendt sat in the Prussian Landtag for the Free Conservatives throughout this period and in the Reichstag from 1898 onwards. Nor were the National Liberals, predominantly right wing in Prussia, likely to be sympathetic. In contrast with the Southern states, there had been no Jewish deputy for that party since 1879, though by 1913 there would again be two. The National Liberals did, however, welcome notable baptized Jews, including Robert Friedberg, chairman of the parliamentary group from 1913 onwards, chairman of the party's executive and, in November 1917, Vice-President of the Prussian State Ministry (i.e. Deputy Prime Minister); Eugen Schiffer, who sat in both the party and the parliamentary executive, becoming State Under-Secretary in the *Reich* Treasury Office in 1917; and Felix Schwabach, also a member of the parliamentary executive.

On the other hand, official Jewish bodies were slow to recognize the possibility of closer relations with the Social Democratic Party, a problem discussed in more detail in the following section. What they sought for the moment was representation 'within the state-supporting parties'.[5] By a process of elimination that meant the parties of the Liberal Left. From 1893 to 1910 these were split between the *Freisinnige Vereinigung* (FVg), which was prepared to support the military budget and was in general more sympathetic towards imperialism, and the *Freisinnige Volkspartei* (FVp), led by the veteran oppositionist Eugen Richter. In its leadership, the FVg was distinctly the more plutocratic – of its thirteen Reichstag members in 1893, five (Karl Schrader, Hermann Frese, Heinrich Rickert, Theodor Barth and Georg von Siemens) either belonged to the Deutsche Bank or were close to it.[6] This, and the predominantly lower-middle-class clientele of the FVp, led many

3 Eugen Fuchs, 'Konfessionelle Kandidaturen', *IdR* IV/12, December 1898, p. 612.
4 *IdR*, III/10, October 1897, p. 500.
5 'Zu den Wahlen', *AZJ*, 3 June 1898, p. 254.
6 Hans Jäger, *Unternehmer in der deutschen Politik (1890–1918)*, Bonn: Röhrscheid, 1967, p. 122.

commentators to assume that the FVg must be the Jewish party *par excellence*. Maximilian Harden even dubbed it 'the Jewish *Zentrum*',[7] in an analogy with the Catholic party, and George Hallgarten made a similar deduction from the close relationship between the *Vereinigung*'s leaders (Barth, Rickert) and the *Abwehr-Verein*.[8]

There is little hard evidence in favour of this schematic allocation. It presupposes a rigidity of programme and organization that the bourgeois parties simply did not have: the character of their following depended too much on individual personalities and local circumstances. In many of the principal commercial centres with large Jewish populations – Berlin, Hamburg, Frankfurt, Breslau – the FVg scarcely existed. It was a predominantly North coast party, but its electorate in West Prussia, Pomerania, Mecklenburg, Schleswig-Holstein and the estuaries of the Ems and Weser was at least as rural as it was mercantile-urban. Also, whatever the party affiliation of the *Abwehr-Verein* leaders, those of the C.V., especially Eugen Fuchs and Maximilian Horwitz, were predominantly with the FVp and there is considerable evidence that Jewish voters preferred the more pronouncedly Liberal of the two parties, even when offered Jewish candidates with other labels. Thus in 1893 Jewish electors in the Tiergartenviertel of Berlin failed to support the Jewish notable nominated by the FVg[9] and in 1898 most Jews in Posen preferred the non-Jewish candidate of the FVp to the National Liberal Lewinski who was put up by a coalition that also included Conservatives and the FVg.[10]

In 1898 the C.V.'s ambition 'to have at least *one* deputy in the Prussian Landtag'[11] was satisfied with the election of the former Reichstag deputy Max Hirsch (the founder of Hirsch–Duncker trade unions) in Berlin I, the district on which the C.V. had had its eye, and that of Martin Peltasohn in the complicated and peculiar conditions of the province of Posen. In 1903 two further Jewish deputies were elected for Berlin, Oskar Cassel and Leopold Rosenow, and Hugo Gerschel replaced Max Hirsch on his death in 1905. In addition Louis Aronsohn and Eduard Wolff (the latter already returned at a by-election) became the second and third representatives of Posen, and Otto Münsterberg of Danzig the first from outside either Berlin or Posen. From then on Jewish membership of the Landtag fluctuated at around nine or ten,

7 'Ein jüdisches Centrum', *Die Zukunft*, 28 January 1893, esp. pp. 148–9.
8 George W. F. Hallgarten, *Imperialismus vor 1914. Die soziologischen Grundlagen der Außenpolitik europäischer Großmächte vor dem ersten Weltkrieg*, 2nd edn, Munich: C. H. Beck, 1963, vol. I, pp. 273, 339, vol. II, p. 39.
9 According to *Die Zukunft*, 4 November 1893, p. 240.
10 *IdR* IV/12, December 1898, p. 162; *AZJ*, 11 November 1898, p. 530.
11 'Zu den Landtagswahlen', *AZJ*, 25 October 1893, p. 505.

a number that the entry of the Social Democrats in 1908 helped to maintain. By 1913 there were also two National Liberals, Leopold Levy of Hohensalza (Inowroclaw) and Paul Liepmann of Charlottenburg, the latter having been only narrowly defeated in 1908. Thus in the last three Landtage before 1918, the Left Liberal groupings had sizeable Jewish memberships: 7 out of 33 in 1903, 7 out of 38 in 1908; 6 out of 37 in 1913. In addition there were four baptized Jews: Julius Lippmann (first elected in 1903), Otto Mugdan (1912), Oscar Meyer (1915) and Max Lewin (1916). Of the nine professing Jews elected before the reunification of the Left Liberals in 1910, three (Münsterberg, Wolff and Peltasohn) belonged to the FVg, the remainder, including all the Berlin representatives, to the FVp (see table 3.7).

Given that the Conservatives, as an anti-Semitic party, and the *Zentrum*, as a confessional party, could not be expected to nominate Jewish candidates, Jews could not reasonably complain of their representation in the Prussian parliament in the last ten years of the Empire. As overt and aggressive anti-Semitism declined, membership rose from the nadir of the years 1886–98 to a level which approximated that of 1867–78. In fact, by the end of the Imperial period, Jewish membership of legislative bodies, and its distribution by parties, clearly reflected the prevailing franchise.

The universal franchise for the Reichstag was least calculated to bring out the moral courage of the Liberal parties. The medium and large cities, where their strength had lain in the 1870s and 1880s, were being taken over by the Social Democrats; in small-town or rural constituencies they had to – or at any rate thought they had to – take account of anti-Semitic sentiments among their potential electors. Moreover, lacking a mass or regionally-defined electoral base, they had to rely, more than the other parties, on support at run-offs. In 1903 and 1912 no Progressive was elected in the first round and only five National Liberals were returned in the first round in 1903 and four in 1912. The consequence was that the Reichstag elections of the 1890s – those of 1893 and 1898 – were even less favourable to Jewish candidates than those for the Prussian Landtag.

By 1903 the situation had improved slightly. Jewish candidates were nominated by the FVp in Frankfurt-on-Main (Ludwig Bruck) and Breslau West (Adolf Heilberg), both held by the Social Democrats, but won in 1907 by non-Jewish Progressives; similarly Dr. Hollstein at Zittau (Saxony), which had been Liberal until 1898 and was also regained by the FVp in 1907. The FVg nominated Dr. Lewitt at Zabern (Alsace), which was lost by only 440 votes. The 1907 elections, called the Block elections, after the alliance that Chancellor Bülow had assembled and in which the Liberal and Conservative parties fought in alliance against Social Democracy and the *Zentrum*, improved the prospects of the Liberal parties in the big cities, but paradoxically reduced the chances of Jewish candidates, since it was necessary to conciliate the parties of the

Table 3.7 Party affiliation of Jewish deputies in the Prussian Landtag, 1903–1917

	1903				1908				1913				1917			
	Professing Jews	Baptized	Total Jews	Total party strength	Professing Jews	Baptized	Total Jews	Total party strength	Professing Jews	Baptized	Total	Total party strength	Professing Jews	Baptized	Total	Total party strength
Free Conservatives	–	1	1	64	–	1	1	60	–	1	1	53	–	1	1	53
National Liberals	–	1	1	76	–	3	3	65	2	2	4	73	2	2	4	73
Freisinnige Vereinigung (FVg)*	3	–	3	9	2	1	3	10	6	2	8	37	6	4	10	37
Freisinnige Volkspartei (FVp)*	4	–	4	24	5	–	5	28	1	–	1	10	1	–	1	10
Social Democrats	–	–	–	–	2	–	2	7	1	–	1		9	7	16	
Total	7	2	9		9	5	14		9	5	14		9	7	16	

* Merged in the *Fortschrittliche Volkspartei* (FVP) in 1910.

Source: Toury, *Orientierungen*, pp. 351–4.

Right.[12] On the other hand in Baden, where the Conservatives counted for little, Friedrich Weill narrowly failed to gain election for Karlsruhe. It was not until 1912 that unbaptized Jews reappeared in the Reichstag as deputies for the non-Socialist parties, both as Progressives: Ludwig Haas for Karlsruhe and, rather more improbably, Felix Waldstein for rural Schleswig-Eckernförde. In addition Hugo Preuß narrowly failed to qualify for the run-off in Dessau and the Prussian Landtag deputy Wolff was promised Conservative support in Fraustadt-Lissa (Posen), but the intervention of an independent Agrarian, who drew off Conservative votes, handed the seat to the *Zentrum*.[13]

The National Liberals, too, began to consider Jews as candidates after 1907. One, *Justizrat* Bernhard Falk, was selected for a by-election in 1910 at Mülheim and for Cologne in 1912, and two prominent Jews were approached in 1912: the Zionist Alfred Klee[14] and Walther Rathenau. Both declined, Rathenau after months of hesitation and in spite of personal appeals from Bassermann, Ballin and Theodor Wolff. The seat he was offered, Frankfurt-on-Oder, was National Liberal (temporarily lost to the SPD at a by-election), so the approach was a serious one. According to Count Harry Kessler, Rathenau felt his name would act 'as a red rag', in part because he was a Jew; but there were other factors at work, not least his wish for a supra-party candidature.[15]

As in Prussia, the National Liberal Reichstag grouping contained prominent baptized Jews: Friedberg (1893–8), Schiffer (1912–17) and Schwabach (1907–18) were joined at a by-election in 1916 by Jakob Riesser, the president of the *Hansa-Bund* and a member of the party's executive. Jewish descent was obviously no obstacle to high office in the National Liberal Party. The party leader, Ernst Bassermann, and his successor, Gustav Stresemann, both had Jewish wives and the leading positions of Friedberg and Schiffer have already been mentioned. But the small number of professing Jews among political candidates was reflected in the equally small representation in the party's 217-member executive: the two Prussian parliamentarians Liepmann and Levy, Bernhard Falk and the bankers Ludwig Max Goldberger and Paul von Schwabach. Curiously enough, though Jews appeared more

---

12 For detailed treatment of the complexities of this election, see below pp. 185–9.
13 Jürgen Bertram, *Die Wahlen zum deutschen Reichstag vom Jahre 1912*, Düsseldorf: Droste, 1964, pp. 90–1.
14 Toury, *Orientierungen*, p. 244, n. 81.
15 Harry Graf Kessler, *Walther Rathenau. Sein Leben und sein Werk*, Berlin: H. Klemm, 1928, p. 152; Walther Rathenau, *Tagebuch 1907–1922* (ed. Hartmut Pogge von Strandmann), Düsseldorf: Droste, 1967, pp. 127 (6 February 1911), 145 (22, 26 June 1911).

frequently as Left-Liberal deputies whether in the Reichstag or the states, they did not penetrate into leadership positions. Only the baptized Julius Lippmann advanced to deputy group chairman in the Prussian Landtag,[16] and Oskar Cassel was in the executive of the re-united party.

In contrast with the Reichstag franchise, the three-class system in Prussia favoured the well-off and middle classes against artisans, peasants and workers, and in particular enabled the Liberal parties to continue commanding the representation of urban and industrial areas. It also meant that they could restrict their appeal to the better-off and better-educated, since the votes of the lower middle classes, most prone to anti-Semitism, counted least. It was therefore rather less necessary 'to offer a sacrifice of the intellect to the moloch of anti-Semitism' – the C.V.'s description of the Liberals' reluctance to nominate Jews in the 1890s.[17] Other forms of unequal suffrage helped to elect Jews in a number of the smaller states: Braunschweig, Anhalt, Sachsen-Weimar and Sachsen-Meiningen.

In the Southern states, where universal suffrage was introduced after the turn of the century, the situation varied. In Baden and Württemberg, where the liberal parties had a solid popular following, where industrialization was moderate and political Catholicism in a minority, the change of electoral system did not seriously weaken them. As a consequence, Jewish candidates continued to be elected for the National Liberals in Baden (Robert Goldschmidt and Emil Mayer) and for the democratic *Volkspartei* in Württemberg (Albert Mayer and Hugo Elsas). In Bavaria, where Liberalism rested on a much narrower basis, the coming of universal suffrage provided an absolute majority for the *Zentrum* and strengthened Social Democracy. Under these circumstances only one baptized Jew entered the Landtag as a National Liberal and none for the Progressives.

The Jews elected under these greatly varying auspices shared a number of features that distinguished them significantly, even if not absolutely, from the earlier generation of parliamentarians. Certainly most of the Jewish parliamentarians of the 1870s and 1880s had sat for metropolitan areas, but the exceptions were numerous enough to matter: Lasker represented the small Thuringian state of Sachsen-Meiningen, Bamberger Bingen-Alzey in Hesse, H.B. Oppenheim Reuß ältere Linie, another Thuringian state, Max Hirsch a variety of seats including Plauen in Saxony and Delitzsch-Bitterfeld in Prussia, while Leonor Reichenheim represented Waldenburg in Silesia. After 1893, those of them who were not baptized sat almost exclusively for the major cities of the Empire or the individual states: Berlin, Hamburg-Altona,

16 Hans-Peter Reiss (ed.), *Von Bassermann zu Stresemann. Die Sitzungen des nationalliberalen Zentralvorstandes 1912–1917*, Düsseldorf: Droste, 1967, pp. 66–80.
17 *IdR* IV/11, November 1898, p. 124.

Frankfurt, Danzig, Darmstadt, Mannheim, Karlsruhe. This was due not so much to the concentration of Jewish electors in these places, for even when concentrated they tended to be in a minority; possibly it was because Jews were here most likely to be active professionally and therefore politically; but most probably it was because, despite the noise created by the Stoecker movement in Berlin, the large cities were the most resistant to anti-Semitism.

The other main difference, which applied to politicians at all levels, was a much greater degree of involvement in Jewish affairs, whether communal or secular. Again, the difference with the Liberal era was not absolute. Even at that time many of the deputies either held posts within the Jewish community – Isaac Wolffson and Marcus Wolf Hinrichsen in Hamburg, Ludwig Loewe in Berlin, Wolf Frankenburger in Nuremberg, Emil Lehmann in Dresden, Otto Wolfskehl in Darmstadt – or were active in Jewish welfare, like Anton Rée, Levin Goldschmidt and Emanuel Mendel. But some of the most prominent had no ties with Jewish organizations, though this did not inhibit them in fighting anti-Semitism or, like Lasker and Moritz Warburg, in being closely involved in legislation on Jewish affairs.[18]

In the Wilhelmine period this had changed. The dream of total absorption in German society had become less realizable, to some less attractive; in response to this fading dream, membership of lay organizations, with direct or indirect political aims – the C.V., the *Verband der Deutschen Juden*, the *Kartell-Convent* of Jewish student corporations – grew. Only survivors of an earlier period, like Max Hirsch, combined major public activity with indifference to Jewish affairs. The great majority of those who entered politics after 1893 were active, in some cases prominent, in one or another Jewish defence organization.

This was true in particular of Ludwig Haas, who had been one of the founders of Jewish student corporations, became active in the *Vereinigung badischer Israeliten* (the equivalent of the C.V. in Baden) and, after 1918, joined the executive of the C.V.; of Hermann Cohn, another member of the C.V. executive, active in the Left-Liberal politics of Anhalt, where he became president of the city council in the capital, Dessau, and a leading member of the Landtag; and of Felix Waldstein, Oskar Cassel, Martin Peltasohn and Wilhelm Langenbach, a member of the Hessian Landtag.[19] There was considerable overlap in membership of the C.V. and the *Verband der Deutschen Juden*, founded in 1904 for the more specific purpose of representing Jewish interests in negotiation with state authorities. Active participants included the

---

18   See above, p. 100.
19   Judith Schrag-Haas, 'Erinnerungen an meinen Vater', *BLBI* 12 (1961), pp. 73–93; Hamburger, *Juden im öffentlichen Leben Deutschlands*, pp. 112–13; Toury, *Orientierungen*, p. 244.

Table 3.8   Jewish population of the province of Posen

		Share of total population (%)
1816	51,971	6.3
1849	76,757	5.7
1871	61,982	3.9
1910	26,512	1.3

Source: Jakob Lestschinsky, *Das wirtschaftliche Schicksal des deutschen Judentums*, 1932, p. 56

Prussian Landtag deputies Leopold Levy, Eduard Wolff and Oskar Cassel, who became its chairman in 1917.[20] The outstanding example of Jewish interest-representation through elected politicians was the delegation of Jewish deputies to the Prussian Landtag from the province of Posen, a permanent feature from 1898 onwards. This arose less out of a sudden recognition of the justice of Jewish claims than out of the exacerbation of the German–Polish nationality struggle in which it was necessary to enlist the Jewish community as state-sustaining allies. The growth of a Polish boycott campaign against German and Jewish businesses helped to cement this alliance.[21] Although the Jewish population here was much reduced compared with the first half of the century (see table 3.8), and now a mere fraction of that of Greater Berlin (144,007 in 1910), it was the only part of the *Reich* in which Jews were sufficiently concentrated and their communal cohesion sufficiently rooted for them to act as a group. The constituencies with Jewish representatives all returned either two or three deputies each and cartels of the Conservative and Liberal parties faced Polish candidates, sometimes allied with the *Zentrum*.[22] All five of the deputies returned under this system, which required considerable sacrifice of principle by both Jews and anti-Semites, were men with impressive careers as notables: all were members either of their community executive (*Gemeindevorstand*) or of the executive of the community council (*Repräsentantenversammlung*); two (Wolff and Levy) were city council chairmen; three (Baerwald, Aronsohn and Levy) were aldermen;

20   Hamburger, *Juden im öffentlichen Leben Deutschlands*, p. 374; Walter Breslauer, 'Der Verband der Deutschen Juden (1904–1922)', *BLBI* 28 (1964), pp. 355, 358.
21   William H. Hagen, *Germans, Poles and Jews. The Nationality Conflict in the Prussian East, 1772–1914*, Chicago: University of Chicago Press, 1980, pp. 302, 371 fn. 106.
22   For details of these agreements see Alexander Plate, *Handbuch für das preußische Abgeordnetenhaus*, Berlin: W. Moser, 1908, pp. 281–5; 1913, pp. 276–81.

two (Aronsohn and Levy) were members of a provincial diet; Baerwald was prominent in the Chamber of Advocates in Posen, Aronsohn president of the Chamber of Commerce in Bromberg.[23]

The close inter-linking of communal, municipal and parliamentary office-holding, which was common to all the Jewish politicians from the Eastern provinces, was indicative of the new style of political participation, at any rate outside the increasingly important number of Social Democrats. Only a handful of the baptized now trod the centre of the political stage: by 1914 only Friedberg, Riesser and Dernburg were household names among political office-holders. Some businessmen and journalists were also well-known and widely thought to be personally influential – not always with justification.[24] If one adds prominence in professional and commercial organizations to elected office one begins to get a picture of Jewish elites, mainly of local significance and not very different in character from that of the first half of the century, except that they were much more numerous and much more likely to have a clear party identification. The number of Jewish municipal councillors in the Wilhelmine period has been calculated at over 1,500, twice the figure for the Liberal period,[25] the greatest concentration, as in earlier periods, being in the Eastern provinces.

In the province of Posen, thanks to the special regulations on Jewish municipal representation dating from the time of the naturalization decree,[26] this participation continued to be overtly communal, not simply the sum of individual contributions. Though the intention of these regulations had been to restrict Jewish influence they had, with the acceleration of westward migration, the opposite effect. In Grätz, for instance, the Jewish population declined from 1620 (45 per cent) in 1840 to 366 (9 per cent) in 1895, in Birnbaum from 790 (28 per cent) to 218 (7 per cent) during the same period, but the Jewish share of councillors remained unchanged. In the first decade of the twentieth century members of the community executive served as councillors in at least twelve of the smaller towns[27] of the province and as aldermen in at least six;[28] members of the executive of the community council served in at least four towns.[29] During the same time Jewish members served

23 Heppner and Herzberg, *Posener Landen*, pp. 348–50, 374; Hamburger, *Juden im öffentlichen Leben Deutschlands*, pp. 372–5; Jäger, *Unternehmer*, p. 84.
24 See below, p. 168.
25 Toury, *Orientierungen*, p. 324.
26 See above, p. 77.
27 Adelnau, Bomst, Krone, Czarnikau, Czempin, Gembitz, Gostin, Koschmin, Kruschwitz, Kurnitz, Nakel, Pleschen.
28 Jarotschin, Jutroschin, Kempen, Koschmin, Schwersenz, Usch.
29 Czarnikau, Gnesen, Koschmin, Tirschtiegel.

as city council chairmen in Bojanowo, Jarotschin, Kobylin, Koschmin, Mogilno (twice), Nakel and Ostrowo. In the larger towns the inter-relationship can be observed in even greater detail. In 1905 alone in Bromberg the three chairmen of the communal executive were respectively Alderman and Landtag deputy Louis Aronsohn, Alderman and later Landtag deputy Moritz Baerwald and city councillor Albin Cohnfeld; the three chairmen of the community council were Landtag deputy Martin Peltasohn, and city councillors Wolfen and Friedländer. In the same year in Hohensalza, the seven-man community executive included city council chairman and later Landtag deputy Dr Leopold Levy, the banker Alderman S. Salomonsohn and two city councillors; the fifteen members of the community council included Alderman *Justizrat* Latte and four city councillors.[30]

Salaried executive office was a good deal rarer than honorary elective office, but deputy mayors (*Beigeordnete*) were to be found in Krone a.d. Brahe, Kolmar, Pleschen and Zirke, a city treasurer in Schwersenz and a mayor in Jarotschin; the last two were to be extremely long-serving. The highest municipal office-holder of Jewish descent in the province was Richard Witting (the brother of Maximilian Harden) who was Lord Mayor of Posen from 1891–1902, in which capacity he was also a member of the Prussian Upper House. Posen, indeed, was an outstanding example of a city with an inter-connected network of Jewish notables. The first Jewish chairman of the city council, the iron merchant *Geheimer Kommerzienrat* Bernhard Jaffé, a National Liberal elected in the 1870s, was simultaneously president of the Chamber of Commerce and chairman of the communal council.[31] Two other Jews followed Jaffé in the presidency until 1918: GKR Michael Herz, who was also chairman of the communal council, and GKR Nazary Kantorowicz, also a member of the provincial diet, whose deputy Israel Friedländer was president of the Jewish community. The five Jews who succeeded Jaffé as city council chairman were all lawyers or doctors, indicating the extent to which the professions were displacing businessmen in local leadership; at least one of them, *Justizrat* Julius Salz, was also a member of the community execu-tive.[32] Posen also illustrated Jewish involvement in Left-Liberal party organ-isation. In 1910 the city council chairman *Justizrat* Michael Placzek was also one of the three chairmen of the city's *Freisinniger Verein* (the other two being a Protestant and a Catholic) and five of the sixteen members of the *Verein's* executive were also active in communal politics.[33]

30 Heppner and Herzberg, *Posener Land*, pp. 348–50, 487–8. Isaak Herzberg, *Geschichte der Juden in Bromberg. Zugleich ein Beitrag zur Geschichte der Juden des Landes Posen*, Frankfurt: Kauffmann, 1903, p. 87.
31 Heppner and Herzberg, *Posener Land*, pp. 865–6, 870–1; Wenzel, *Jüdische Bürger*, p. 196.
32 Ibid., pp. 870–1.
33 Hagen, *Germans, Poles and Jews*, p. 293.

A similar pattern applied to a lesser extent to neighbouring West Prussia and to Silesia and East Prussia, where fixed Jewish representation was not the rule. In Silesia, moreover, industrialization helped to stabilize the Jewish population (1871: 46,619; 1910: 44,985) and growth in the larger cities – not only Breslau, but Kattowitz, Beuthen and Gleiwitz – compensated for rural emigration. In Kattowitz Jews predominated among both city councillors and honorary aldermen from the mid-1870s to the mid-1890s.[34] In Breslau successive city council chairmen were Jewish almost without exception for seven decades: Max Simon (baptized) from 1868 to 1872; Wilhelm Salomon Freund, who had briefly belonged to the Prussian Landtag and the Reichstag and was, in addition, chairman both of the Silesian Chamber of Advocates and of the community council, from 1887 to 1915; his successor, *Justizrat* Adolf Heilberg, repeatedly Reichstag candidate, vice-chairman of the Silesian Chamber of Advocates and on the executive of the German advocates' association; to be followed in the Weimar Republic by the Social Democrat Eugen Bandmann.[35] The presidency of the Breslau Chamber of Commerce also became something of a Jewish monopoly. *Geheimer Kommerzienrat* Isidor Friedenthal, uncle of the Prussian minister,[36] was president from 1869 to 1886, while simultaneously president of the Jewish community; David Mugdan, the banker GKR Heinrich Heimann and the textile manufacturer Salomon Kaufmann were later vice-presidents. In Lower Silesia GKR Louis Grünfeld and Max Pinkus (the brother-in-law of Paul Ehrlich) were respectively vice-president and president of the Oppeln chamber of commerce and of their Jewish communities (Beuthen and Neustadt).[37]

Elsewhere in Germany similar patterns could be observed, though with less regional concentration and fewer dynasties. In Danzig Leyser Goldschmidt, brother of Levin Goldschmidt, presided over the merchant corporation (*Kaufmannschaft*), as did Konsul Rudolf Oppenheim and GKR M. Simon in Königsberg. Gustav Davidsohn, Martin Kadisch and *Justizrat* Behrendt all combined leading offices within the community with membership of the Danzig city council; Alderman Samter, a long-serving city father, was chairman of the community representative council.[38] In Königsberg, too, Jewish community notables were active in Left-Liberal politics. Max Arendt,

34 Wenzel, *Jüdische Bürger*, pp. 128–9.
35 Monika Richarz (ed.), *Jüdisches Leben in Deutschland. Selbstzeugnisse zur Sozialgeschichte des Kaiserreichs*, Stuttgart: Deutsche Verlags-Anstalt, 1979, Vol. II, pp. 289–309; Schwerin, *BLBI* 56/7, pp. 64–5.
36 See above, p. 91.
37 Schwerin, *BLBI* 56/7, pp. 39, 44, 48; Grünfeld: Richarz, *Jüdisches Leben*, vol. II, pp. 266–73.
38 Samuel Echt, *Die Geschichte der Juden in Danzig*, Leer: Rauterberg, 1972, pp. 56, 58, 72.

chairman of the community representative council from 1910 to 1930, was also president of the city council and the industrialist Max Magnus, president of the community executive from 1899 to 1908, was a city alderman. The most prominent Left Liberal in Königsberg during the Wilhelmine period was Max Lichtenstein, the brother-in-law of the SPD leader Hugo Haase. He was a member of the community executive, president of the local *B'nai B'rith* lodge, chairman of the Left-Liberal party organization, the *Verein 'Waldeck'*, and for a short period president of the city council.[39] He was also a member of the Prussian Landtag from 1912 to 1913, but failed to be re-nominated for the 1913 election, through a combination of denominational and ideological conflicts in the Königsberg FVP.[40] In Hamburg Gabriel Riesser was vice-president of the Bürgerschaft in 1860; Dr Isaak Wolffson presided over the Bürgerschaft in 1861–3 and later over the Chamber of Advocates; and Siegmund Hinrichsen was president of the Chamber of Commerce from 1889 to 1891 and of the Bürgerschaft for ten years after that.[41] His brother Marcus Wolf, who sat on the community executive and was active in the *Alliance Israélite Universelle*, was briefly a National Liberal Reichstag deputy and in the Bürgerschaft for thirty years. Both belonged to the *Fraktion Linkes Zentrum*. Isaak Wolffson's son Albert, who had less strong ties with the Jewish community, became leader of the *Fraktion der Rechten* (approximately National Liberal) and was three times elected to the city council executive (*Bürgerausschuß*); Max Warburg, the *de facto* head of the family banking house, served in the same grouping from 1903. Neither qualified for the city state's highest honour, membership of the Senate, Warburg being rejected as late as 1917. That baptism would have removed the obstacle was shown by the precedent of Gustav Ferdinand Hertz, elected in 1887.

In Bavaria, where Jewish society retained its traditional character more than in Berlin or Western and South-Western Germany, the same overlap between communal and public political activity occurred as in the Eastern provinces of Prussia. In Nuremberg the National Liberal JR Gustav Josephtal, president of the Jewish community from 1869 to 1909 and his successor in this office, Sigmund Held, were both presidents of the Chamber of Advocates (Josephtal from 1896, Held from 1903). Josephtal was one of the founders of the DIGB, a member of the executive of the C.V. and became a

---

39 Yoram K. Jacoby, *Jüdisches Leben in Königsberg/Pr. im 20. Jahrhundert*, Würzburg: Holzner, 1983, pp. 13, 24, 27, 40; Fritz Gause, *Geschichte der Stadt Königsberg in Preußen*, Cologne: Böhlau, 1965–71, vol. II, p. 618.

40 H. Hoppe, 'Der Fall Lichtenstein', *JR*, 5 September 1913, pp. 374–6.

41 Helga Krohn, *Die Juden in Hamburg. Die politische, soziale und kulturelle Entwicklung einer jüdischen Großstadtgemeinde*, Hamburg: Christians, 1974, pp. 79, 92, 93.

privy councillor (*geheimer Hofrat*) in 1900. His son Emil succeeded him as president of the Nuremberg branch of the C.V. and also became a member of the city council and the community council. The hop merchant Stephan Hopf, whose family married into the Josephtal family, was on the community executive, the city executive (*Magistratsrat*) and in the provincial diet.[42] In Würzburg, too, the lawyer Otto Stern and the mill-owner Adolf Schwabach, respectively president and treasurer of the community council, served as city councillors, as did the president of the wine merchants' association of Franconia, Bernhard Hellmann.[43] The 'complete notable', as one historian describes him, was GKR Karl Ladenburg of the Mannheim banking family. One of the first Jews to be a lay member of a commercial court (*Handelsrichter*), he was elected to the city council and the Baden Landtag as a National Liberal and ultimately became an honorary citizen of his native city.[44]

It was in small and medium cities and in regional capitals with an established Jewish population that these networks of notables, often inter-related, survived until 1918. Their composition and political affiliation reflected the changing environment. For the first two generations, up to the 1860s, they were predominantly businessmen and kept aloof from party politics. With the growth of a Jewish intelligentsia they were joined by lawyers, doctors and journalists; in politics they were predominantly Liberal, more often than not Progressive, but also National Liberal, especially in South-Western Germany. The fourth generation included some Socialists, like Siegfried Marck, grandson of the first Jewish alderman of Breslau, and Max Süßheim, member of the Bavarian Landtag from 1907 to 1920 and grandson of the Democrat Wolf Frankenburger who had belonged to the Bavarian Landtag from 1849 to 1859. The greater the metropolis – Hamburg, Cologne, Frankfurt and Berlin, for example – the greater the separation between communal, political and associational activity.

In Berlin Jews continued to be prominent in the merchant corporation (*Kaufmannschaft*), as they had been from its foundation in 1820. From the 1870s until 1918 the proportion of Jews (including baptized) among the senior members (*Ältesten*) rarely fell below one-third and at times exceeded one-half.[45] Benjamin Liebermann became its vice-president in 1872, Franz

42 Arnd Müller, *Geschichte der Juden in Nürnberg, 1146–1945*, Nuremberg: Stadtbibliothek, 1968, pp. 175–7; Max Freudenthal, *Die israelitische Kultusgemeinde Nürnberg, 1874–1924*, Nuremberg: J. Bulka, 1925, pp. 50, 56, 59, 124, 153.
43 Roland Flade, *Die Würzburger Juden. Ihre Geschichte vom Mittelalter bis zur Gegenwart*, Würzburg: Stürtz, 1987, pp. 159–60.
44 Mosse, *Economic Elite*, p. 235.
45 G St Dahlem, Rep. 84a, 9247, Berliner Kaufmannschaft.

(von) Mendelssohn its president in the 1880s, to be followed by GKR Wilhelm Herz. When the Berlin Chamber of Commerce was established in 1902, Herz became its president as well; he was succeeded on his death by his deputy, the younger Franz von Mendelssohn. Jews were as prominent in the municipal government of the capital as in its commercial representation. Wolf Straßmann had been city council chairman in the Liberal period (1875–85) and in the Wilhelmine period the number of Jewish councillors went into three figures.[46] The two major Liberal groupings both had Jewish leaders, *Justizrat* Oskar Cassel of the *Fraktion der Linken* and Leopold Rosenow of the *Fraktion der Neuen Linken*. Since the leaders of the Social Democratic grouping were also Jewish – Paul Singer from 1887 to 1911, followed by Hugo Heimann – one understands why even a moderate observer like Gustav von Schmoller was tempted to comment that 'one gains the impression that a city like Berlin is in essence characterized by Jews in its administration'.[47] Jews, some of them bearing eminent names, were certainly prominent among councillors, but they were not a homogeneous group: among businessmen there were the industrialist Ludwig Loewe, the newspaper proprietor Leopold Ullstein, Benjamin Liebermann and the silk manufacturer Magnus Meyer, like Liebermann a senior member of the *Kaufmannschaft*; among professional men Hugo Preuß, who became an honorary alderman in 1910, and Paul Nathan, as well as Oskar Cassel. But of the businessmen only Meyer and Loewe – as well as Wilhelm Herz – played an active part in the community, whereas the professional men were significantly involved only in the new lay organizations, such as the C.V., and in the charity for migrant Jews, the *Hilfsverein deutscher Juden*, founded by Nathan. In the rapidly-growing Berlin suburb of Charlottenburg, then a separate borough, 20 of the 72 councillors were Jews in 1912.[48] In addition to the baptized Oscar Meyer, the *Syndikus* of the Berlin Chamber of Commerce, they included such distinguished Liberal names as GJR Paul Liepmann and Georg Bernhard, later to be editor of the *Vossische Zeitung*, and among Social Democrats, Paul Hirsch and Ernst Heilmann, who were to be Prussian Prime Minister and SPD Landtag leader respectively in the Weimar Republic.[49]

Jewish participation in the government of major cities was facilitated not only by urbanization and occupational concentration, but by the electoral

---

46   'Well above 100' according to Hamburger, *Juden im öffentlichen Leben Deutschlands*, p. 549; Toury specifies 146, *Orientierungen*, p. 324.

47   Gustav von Schmoller, 'Die heutige Judenfrage', *Zwanzig Jahre deutscher Politik, 1897–1917*, Munich and Leipzig: Duncker & Humblot, 1920, p. 180.

48   *IdR* XVIII/6, June 1912, p. 293.

49   Oscar Meyer, *Von Bismarck zu Hitler. Erinnerungen und Betrachtungen*, 2nd edn, Offenbach: Bollwerk-Verlag, 1948, p. 68.

Table 3.9   Jewish tax liability in selected cities

	Jewish percentage of population (a)	*Jewish share of total taxation* (b)	(a) : (b)
Beuthen (Silesia)	4.0	26.9	1 : 6.7
Bromberg (Posen)	2.8	13.7	1 : 4.9
Gleiwitz (Silesia)	3.2	32.9	1 : 10.3
Posen	4.2	21.0	1 : 5.0
Bruchsal (Baden)	1.6	17.6	1 : 11.0
Karlsruhe (Baden)	1.9	11.7	1 : 6.2
Mannheim (Baden)	3.2	28.7	1 : 9.0
Greater Berlin	5.1	30.7	1 : 6.0
Breslau (Silesia)	4.3	20.3	1 : 4.7
Frankfurt	7.0	20.8	1 : 3.0
Krefeld (Rhineland)	1.7	6.6	1 : 3.9
Düsseldorf (Rhineland)	1.2	3.6	1 : 3.0
Koblenz (Rhineland)	1.2	0.4	1 : 0.3
Wiesbaden (Hesse)	2.6	8.2	1 : 3.1

Source: Werner Sombart, *Die Juden und das Wirtschaftsleben*, Leipzig: Duncker & Humblot, 1911, pp. 219–21

system. Urban local government was the last remaining stronghold of Liberalism in Imperial Germany, since the franchise frequently favoured the well-to-do in an even more extreme way than for the Landtage. In Prussia, despite a bewildering range of local variations, the proportion of the population who could vote in municipal elections was always lower, and the proportion allocated to the third electoral class frequently higher, than at Landtag elections.[50] Since, moreover, Jewish incomes, and therefore taxation liability, were well above the average, this further increased the advantage to Jewish electors where they were numerous. The disproportion was greatest in areas where traditional forms of Jewish economic activity survived longest – Silesia, Posen, West Prussia and the South-West – and was least in the Rhineland (See table 3.9). The net effect of these circumstances was that at the beginning of the twentieth century, as at the beginning of the nineteenth, the one arena where Jews as a group might hope to exert tangible political influence was in municipal government, though now mainly through the

50   Helmut Croon, *Die gesellschaftlichen Auswirkungen des Gemeindewahlrechts in den Gemeinden und Kreisen des Rheinlands und Westfalens im 19. Jahrhundert*, Cologne and Opladen: Westdeutscher Verlag, 1960, pp. 49–56.

groupings known collectively and not very precisely as 'municipal Liberalism' (*Kommunalfreisinn*).

The close association of so many Jews, many of them active in secular or religious organizations, with the varying shades of 'municipal Liberalism' raises the question of how representative these activists were of Jewish political opinion generally. A number of *a priori* assumptions suggest that they were. In the first place the links between electors and elected are closer in local than in national politics. In the second place political developments since the 1880s made all other bourgeois parties – leaving the Social Democrats on one side for the moment – decreasingly attractive. Most Jews identified with the Left Liberals not because that party paid special attention to Jewish claims – it did not, and it would have been contrary to its liberal-citizen view of political allegiance to do so, – nor because it specifically opposed anti-Semitism, which it sometimes did conscientiously and sometimes negligently, but simply because its advocacy of the rule of law, of careers open to talents and of economic liberty corresponded with the kind of society which Jews had most reason to confide in.

What further ideological implications this had, and how it affected Jewish support for, or dissent from, individual policies of the *Reich* government, will be discussed below.[51] The more immediate question is how far the equation of Jews and Left Liberalism, which is taken for granted by both contemporaries and later historians, was, or could be, translated into votes at elections. As far as the Reichstag was concerned, it is the numerical insignificance of the Jewish vote which most springs to mind. In 1910 Jews numbered 0.95 per cent of the total German population, though, thanks to their different age structure, they contributed 1.04 per cent of all electors.[52] The Jewish population was not, of course, evenly distributed. Of the total German-Jewish population, 23 per cent lived in Greater Berlin, and 38 per cent in the six largest conurbations (Berlin, Hamburg-Altona, Frankfurt, Breslau, Cologne, Munich). In the first four of these the Left-Liberal parties fought regularly. The same was true of other major centres, e.g. Nuremberg (Jewish population 1910: 7,815, 2.3 per cent of total population), Posen (5,611, 3.6 per cent), Königsberg (4,565, 1.9 per cent), Karlsruhe (3,058, 2.3 per cent), Wiesbaden (2,744, 2.5 per cent), Fürth (2,826, 4.2 per cent). On the other hand, there were cities with sizeable Jewish populations where only the National Liberals were represented. These included Cologne (12,393, 2.1 per cent), Leipzig (9,434, 1.6 per cent), Mannheim (7,402, 3.8 per cent), Hanover

---

51 See below, pp. 173–189.
52 Arthur Blaustein and Hermann Hillger (eds), *Hillgers Wegweiser für die Reichstagswahl 1912*, Berlin and Leipzig: H. Hillger, 1911, p. 74.

(5,386, 1.4 per cent), Düsseldorf (3,985, 1.1 per cent), Stuttgart (4,921, 1.7 per cent) and Mainz (2,926, 2.7 per cent).

Even these concentrations did not necessarily give the Jewish voter much sway, even assuming he wanted it. Many of the big cities listed were firmly in Social Democratic hands from the 1890s. Most of the relevant constituencies in Posen or Upper Silesia had heavy majorities for the *Zentrum* or the Polish Party. The constituencies in which Jews conceivably held the balance were: Berlin I, always closely fought between Progressives and Social Democrats; Frankfurt and Breslau West, which Progressives temporarily recaptured from the Social Democrats in the Block elections of 1907; and Cologne and Düsseldorf, where the National Liberals arbitrated in closely fought contests between *Zentrum* and Social Democrats. This may explain why it was in the major cities of the Rhine and Ruhr that National Liberal candidates tended to make the most specific disavowals of anti-Semitism.[53]

It is thus evident that a Jew whose primary loyalty was towards Left Liberalism could in very few cases cast an effective vote for that party and his choice at a run-off might well be between parties both of which were distasteful to him. The C.V.'s often repeated principle 'that wherever an anti-Semite is a candidate we support his opponent … and in particular the one with the best chances',[54] was in many cases simply not enforceable. It assumed that for every Jewish voter the defeat of an anti-Semite stood above all other considerations. But this assumption was unrealistic. It could in many cases mean voting for a Social Democrat or a *Zentrum* candidate. Before 1914 the majority of Jews were not yet prepared to vote Socialist – or if they did so, as in the framework of the agreement on run-off ballots between the *Fortschrittliche Volkspartei* and the SPD in 1912, it was for reasons not primarily connected with anti-Semitism. Indeed the Jewish press carried periodic complaints that Jewish electors had preferred an anti-Semitic candidate to a Socialist one, or had abstained in such a contest.[55] In the 1903 Prussian Landtag election, when Theodor Barth proposed a run-off agreement with the Social Democrats, he was opposed by prominent Jews in the FVg, including Oskar Cassel and Martin Philippson.[56] However, the growing intensity of the party battle after the turn of the century did give Jewish

---

53 E.g. Franz Moldenhauer in Cologne, *AZJ*, 12 June 1903, p. 278; and Alexander Hilbck in Dortmund, *IdR* IX/6–7, June–July 1903, p. 420.
54 Hugo Sonnenfeld, 'Der Centralverein und die politischen Wahlen', *IdR* IX/11, November 1903, p. 620.
55 E.g. in Kassel, *AZJ*, 10 July 1903, p. 326; *IdR* IX/11, November 1903, p. 620.
56 Marjorie Lamberti, *Jewish Activism in Imperial Germany. The Struggle for Civil Equality*, New Haven, Conn., and London: Yale University Press, 1978, p. 52.

voters and their mentors greater flexibility, which is discussed in more detail in the following section. This applied to approaches not only to the SPD but, especially in the Eastern provinces, to the *Zentrum* or Poles.

The relationship between German Jews and the *Zentrum* had always been ambiguous, even schizophrenic. It was burdened by the historic antagonism between the Catholic Church and European Jewry and the particular antagonism between the Church and Liberalism in the middle of the nineteenth century, at precisely the most intense phase of Jewish-Liberal symbiosis. Opposition to the secularizing tendencies of liberalism were frequently expressed in anti-Semitic terms, not merely by unofficial propagandists, but by leading prelates, such as Bishop Ketteler of Mainz[57] and Bishop Keppler of Rottenburg,[58] established theologians like Albert Maria Weiss OP, Georg Ratzinger and Franz Hettinger, and prominent journalists like Hans Rost, who edited the academic supplement (*Wissenschaftliche Beilage*) of the *Augsburger Post-Zeitung*.[59] Perhaps most offensive of all to Jews was the revival of 'anti-Talmudic' writings, which were exclusively Catholic in origin and purported to show that Jewish religious teachings permitted and legitimated immoral dealings with non-Jews: offensive, because though only the minority of traditionalist Jews accepted – or were even familiar with – Talmudic teachings by the 1870s, the message was explicitly counter-emancipatory. August Rohling's *Der Talmudjude* went through six printings between 1871 and 1877; 38,000 copies of the sixth edition were distributed gratis in Westphalia by the *Bonifatius-Verein*.[60] He had by this time secured a professorship in Old Testament Studies at Prague. The year 1876 also saw the re-publication by Bishop Konrad Martin of Paderborn of Joseph Rebbert's *Blicke in's Talmudische Judenthum*, which dated from 1848, another year of political upheaval. Rebbert's pamphlet was specifically issued as a

---

57   E.g. Wilhelm Emmanuel Freiherr von Ketteler, 'Die Centrums-Fraktion auf dem ersten deutschen Reichstage' (1872), in *Schriften, Aufsätze und Reden. Sämtliche Werke und Briefe* (ed. Erwin Iserloh), Mainz: von Hase & Koehler, 1971–, Abt. I, Bd. 4, pp. 72, 164; 'Der Culturkampf gegen die katholische Kirche und die neuen Kirchengesetzentwürfe für Hessen' (1874), in ibid., pp. 438–9; 'Der Bruch des Religionsfriedens und der einzige Weg zu seiner Wiederherstellung' (1875), in ibid., p. 515.

58   Rudolf Lill, 'Katholizismus nach 1848. B – Die deutschen Katholiken und die Juden in der Zeit von 1850 bis zur Machtübernahme Hitlers', in Karl Heinrich Rengstorf and Siegfried von Kortzfleisch (eds.), *Kirche und Synagoge. Handbuch zur Geschichte von Christen und Juden*, Stuttgart: Ernst Klett, 1970, vol. II, p. 379.

59   Hermann Greive, 'Die gesellschaftliche Bedeutung der christlich-jüdischen Differenz', *WD*, pp. 359–62.

60   Isaak Arie Hellwing, *Der konfessionelle Antisemitismus im 19. Jahrhundert in Österreich*, Vienna, Freiburg and Basle: Herder, 1972, pp. 76, 90.

campaign publication (*Wahlbroschüre*) for the 1876 Prussian Landtag election 'in order to draw attention to the Jewish Question, glaringly important in the social context'.[61]

The *Zentrum* press, in particular its chief organ *Germania*, was especially anti-Semitic at the height of the *Kulturkampf*, and again at the time of Bismarck's change of course, when it hoped, by routing the Liberal parties, to reverse anti-Church legislation.[62] It returned to such themes whenever tempers were heated by ritual murder accusations, as at Tisza-Eszlar in Hungary in 1883[63] and at Xanten and Konitz in Germany. Defending the overwhelmingly Catholic population of Xanten against charges of fanaticism, *Germania* felt itself honour-bound 'not to sacrifice without further ado a Christian population for the sake of the Jews'.[64] 'Fear and solicitude for the life of our children' led it to ask at the time of Konitz: 'Can we, after the established outcome at Skurz and Xanten and after today's expected outcome at Konitz, still have confidence that murders of Christian children will be punished and expiated?'[65]

While such outbursts from on high were episodic, there was an endemic undertone of anti-Semitism in the local Catholic press, in popular literature such as peasant almanacs and even in sermons.[66] As the *Zentrum* became increasingly dependent on rural and artisan voters, and its protectionist economic policies brought it more and more in line with those of the Conservative and even the anti-Semitic parties, local electoral agreements between them to fend off Liberal or Social Democratic challenges became not uncommon.[67] Nor did the *Zentrum*'s pre-occupation with the maintenance of denominational schools and its support for censorship in the arts, e.g. by its vote for the

---

61 Joseph Rebbert, *Blicke in's Talmudische Judenthum. Nach den Forschungen von Dr Konrad Martin, Bischof von Paderborn, dem christlichen Volke enthüllt. Nebst einer Beleuchtigung der neuesten Judenvertheidigung*, Paderborn: Bonifacius-Druckerei, 1876, p. 3.

62 *Germania*, 5 August 1879, p. 1, 9 August 1879, p. 1, 12 August 1879, p. 1, 2 September 1897, p. 1, 10 September 1879, p. 1, 26 September 1879, p. 3, 3 October 1879, p.1, 7 October 1879, pp. 1–2, 10 October 1879, pp. 1–2, 11 October 1879, pp. 1–2, 16 October 1879, pp. 1–2; also 26, 29 October 1879.

63 Ibid., 4 August 1883, II. Blatt, p. 2; 8 August 1883, II. Blatt, p. 1.

64 Ibid., 15 July 1892, III. Blatt, p. 1.

65 Ibid., 16 January 1900.

66 See in particular David Blackbourn, 'Roman Catholics, the Centre Party and Anti-Semitism in Imperial Germany', in Paul Kennedy and Anthony Nicholls (eds), *Nationalist and Racialist Movements in Britain and Germany Before 1914*, London: Macmillan, 1981, pp. 106–29.

67 Riff, *LBYB* (1987), pp. 127, 129.

government's *Lex Heinze* in 1895, make it attractive to a predominantly metropolitan Jewish public. That was one side of it. There were, however, two factors that counted in the *Zentrum*'s favour in the eyes of some Jewish voters. The first was that, notwithstanding the low-level populist rhetoric of some scribblers or rabble-rousers, the parliamentary leadership of the *Zentrum* was adamant in standing for the strict maintenance of civil equality. That was the line proclaimed by the first leader of the *Zentrum*, Ludwig Windthorst, and continued by his successor, Ernst Lieber.[68] At least some members of the hierarchy echoed this principle, including Archbishops Krementz and Fischer of Cologne and Kopp of Breslau, who denounced the blood libel, i.e. the superstition that Jews needed the blood of Christians for ritual purposes.[69] Some Catholic spokesmen went further and actively supported Jewish complaints against discrimination. How willing they were to do this depended on the context. Where Jews and Catholics were in competition, as in judicial appointments, Catholic support was not forthcoming.[70] But there were no such obstacles when it came to military appointments. Adolf Gröber, Count Hertling and Matthias Erzberger raised the matter on different occasions.[71] Gröber also spoke against measures to ban ritual slaughter, generally initiated by anti-Semitic deputies.[72]

In addition there was a small section of the Jewish population, rural and Orthodox, that had traditionally preferred the *Zentrum* to the secularism of the Liberal parties.[73] To these were now added the voices of C.V. and other spokesmen who wished to loosen the often unreciprocated affection of Jews for Left Liberalism and were especially disturbed by the alliance between the Liberal and Conservative parties in 1907. There is little evidence that many Jews followed their advice, which in any case was sometimes patronizingly expressed, in presenting the *Zentrum* as 'the lesser evil',[74] or as 'a little bridge, however weak and unsteady, into the land of liberty and equality'.[75]

---

68   Greive, 'Die gesellschaftliche Bedeutung', pp. 383–4; Lieber: Reichstag speech on 6 March 1895, *StBR*, vol. 139, pp. 1286–7; Pulzer, *The Rise of Political Anti-Semitism*, pp. 264–71.
69   Lill, 'Katholizismus nach 1848' in *KuS*, pp. 378, 379, 397.
70   See above, pp. 52–3, 62.
71   *StBR*, 25 February 1911, vol. 264, pp. 4985–6; 20 June 1913, vol. 290, p. 5655; Angress, *LBYB* XVII, (1972), p. 38.
72   *StBR*, 12 January 1911, vol. 263, pp. 3807ff; see also Ernst Lieber, ibid., 6 March 1895, vol. 139, p. 1286.
73   Toury, *Orientierungen*, pp. 246–54.
74   'Die Reichstagswahlen und die Juden', *AZJ*, 4 January 1907, p. 1.
75   Werner T. Angress, 'The Impact of the "Judenwahlen" of 1912 on the Jewish Question – A Synthesis', *LBYB* XXVIII (1983), p. 374.

The same ambiguity governed Jewish relations with the Polish community (with whom the *Zentrum* was generally allied in Posen, but not in Silesia or West Prussia). Though relations between Jewish and Polish communities were frequently good at the local level, in the nationalities conflict Jews identified, now as in 1848, with the German interest. This applied in particular at the level of Landtag and Reichstag elections, the two being inseparable, since the complicated compromises between the Conservatives, Progressives and, at a later stage, National Liberals dealt with both.[76] The price of these compromises was to require Jews to vote for Conservative candidates, though it was no doubt equally distasteful for many Protestants to protect German *Volkstum* by voting for a Jewish Liberal. The voting figures make it clear that, in Landtag elections at any rate, both sides stuck rigorously to their bargain. The climax for this test of Jewish conscience came in the 1908 by-election for the marginal Reichstag seat of Meseritz-Bomst. There was a straight fight between the Conservative, Count Kuno von Westarp, and a Polish-supported *Zentrum* candidate. Westarp assured the Jewish community that he 'completely accepted' their equality,[77] a declaration that contradictated both his party's Tivoli Programme and his record as a leader of the DNVP in the Weimar Republic. His victory by 1,265 votes was widely attributed to Jewish support and his later bad faith regarded as an object-lesson. Whether he really owed his election to his forked tongue is now difficult to establish. One would need to know how unanimously the 600–700 Jewish electors cast their votes, how they would have cast them in the absence of Westarp's declaration and how they would have cast them faced with a different candidate. There were, however, later echoes of this episode. When an agreement between the Progressives and National Liberals was being drawn up for the 1913 Landtag elections in the constituency of Posen-Land, one correspondent warned National Liberal headquarters that 'in the event of a gentleman standing very far to the Right [being adopted], some self-willed persons might abstain'.[78] At a Reichstag by-election in 1910, the Governor of the province of Posen warned the Minister of the Interior that if, through a split in the Liberal vote, an anti-Semite faced a Pole in the run-off, the Pole 'might gain votes, for instance, from the ranks of the Progressives'.[79]

In Silesia Jewish support for Polish or *Zentrum* candidates was more

76 Details in Bertram, *Die Wahlen zum deutschen Reichstag*, pp. 84–94.
77 'Die "Judenfrage" und die Konservativen', *AZJ*, 11 December 1908, pp. 593–4; Graf Kuno von Westarp, *Konservative Politik im letzten Jahrzent des Kaiserreichs*, Berlin: Deutsche Verlags-Gesellschaft, 1935, vol. I, p. 29.
78 Dr Hugo Ehrlich to National Liberal *Provinzialvorstand*, ZStP, 60 Vo3, 33, 90.
79 *Oberpräsident* von Waldow to Minister of Interior, 29 January 1910, ZStP, Rk 07.01, 1394 (40).

common, and not restricted to the Orthodox. This development became more important during the Weimar Republic. The same applied to rural Bavaria and parts of the Rhineland, where the *Zentrum* on occasion reciprocated by sponsoring Jewish candidates.[80] A few Jews became active supporters of the *Zentrum*, e.g. the Bavarian Dr Ludwig Wassermann, and the Westphalian Emil Schüler,[81] and the party counted converted Jews in its ranks, such as the Silesian coal magnate Dr Fritz von Friedländer-Fuld, a member of the Prussian Upper House, and the Cologne banker and industrialist Louis Hagen, who joined the party in 1919. But such phenomena were interesting rather than statistically significant.

The number of Jews who supported the *Deutschkonservative Partei* must have been even more insignificant after the adoption of the Tivoli Programme than before, though there were some among the Orthodox or among intellectuals who would have welcomed a political home for their conservatism. The most notable advocate of this was Adolf Grabowsky, a convert to Protestantism, the founder and editor of the *Zeitschrift für Politik*.[82] He had a number of followers, including the Breslau professor Arthur Sachs, the publicist Friedrich Blach and the Zionist Gustav Witkowsky.[83] The last two of these commended the more moderate *Reichspartei*, which neither preached nor condemned anti-Semitism. It was nevertheless linked in its membership with many propaganda organizations that had a strong anti-Semitic content, such as the Pan-German League, *Verein deutscher Studenten* and *Reichsverband gegen die Sozialdemokratie*,[84] and was prepared to accept members of the anti-Semitic *Deutsche Reformpartei* in its Reichstag grouping. It counted one convert, Otto Arendt, among its deputies and some of its members from time to time took up position against discrimination in the army, or the banning of ritual slaughter.[85] It may have attracted more votes than the *Deutschkonservative*, though presumably fewer than when it had counted Heinrich von Friedberg among its leading members. Outside the peculiar conditions of the

---

80 Toury, *Orientierungen*, pp. 243, 256, 259, 260.

81 Ibid., p. 259; *Germania*, 23 May 1909.

82 Dietrich Mende, 'Kulturkonservatismus und konservative Erneuerungsbestrebungen', in Hans Thierach (ed.), *Adolf Grabowsky. Leben und Werk. Dem Altmeister der Politischen Wissenschaft als Fest-und Dankesgabe gewidmet*, Berlin: Heymann, 1963, pp. 87–128; Adolf Grabowsky, 'Kulturkonservatismus und Antisemitismus', *Die Zeitschrift*, 26 August 1911; Richard Schmidt and Adolf Grabowsky (eds), *Die Parteien. Urkunden und Bibliographie der Parteienkunde*, Berlin and Leipzig: F. Meiner, 1912, vol. I, pp. 9–13.

83 Toury, *Orientierungen*, pp. 265–7.

84 See below pp. 174–6.

85 Army discrimination: Freiherr Octavio von Zedlitz-Neukirch in *Der Tag*, cit. *AZJ*, 5 January 1911, p. 3; Friedrich Linz, *StBR*, 25 February 1911, vol. 264, p. 4971; ritual slaughter: Wagner, *StBR*, 12 January 1911.

Eastern provinces it is doubtful whether either party had a significant Jewish following.

That leaves the various Liberal parties. The usually accepted estimates – that some 60–70 per cent of Jewish voters supported Left Liberalism during the Wilhelmine period and some 10–15 per cent the National Liberals[86] – may well under-estimate the strength of National Liberal support, if only because they ignore the absence of Left-Liberal organization in large parts of the country. Often the party constellation varied according to whether the election was for the Reichstag, Landtag or city council and in numerous constituencies or states there were organizations or groupings that united all wings of Liberalism, but were under the effective dominance of one of these wings.[87]

Two smaller, short-lived organizations are worthy of mention here. The first was the National Social Union, founded in 1896 by Friedrich Naumann, a former follower of Pastor Stoecker, who favoured a combination of colonial expansion, democratization and social reform that might have appealed to critical sections of the bourgeoisie. He himself had by then disavowed anti-Semitism and Article 3 of the party's constitution committed it to 'the undiminished maintenance of the civic equality of all citizens' – a commitment opposed, ironically enough by Hellmuth von Gerlach,[88] who in later years became one of the most determined enemies of anti-Semitism. On the other hand the party's insistence that 'we see Christianity as occupying the centre of our people's spiritual and moral life'[89] limited its attractiveness to Jews. In 1903 the National Social Union amalgamated with the *Freisinnige Vereinigung*, thereby finally breaking with its Christian-Social past. The second organization was the *Demokratische Vereinigung*, founded in 1908 by dissidents of the *Freisinnige Vereinigung*, led by Theodor Barth and including some former Naumannites, such as Hellmuth von Gerlach and Dr Rudolf Breitscheid, the later Social Democrat. Its unambiguous advocacy of democracy, secularism, free trade and internationalism, stopping short of economic collectivism,[90] was much more in line with sections of Jewish opinion. Its most prominent Jewish member was Paul Nathan; others included Julius

---

86 Hamburger, *Juden im öffentlichen Leben Deutschlands*, p. 163; Toury, *Orientierungen*, p. 275.

87 E.g. in Bavaria between 1899 and 1910. See Nipperdey, *Organisation*, pp. 24–36, esp. p. 33.

88 *Die Zeit*, 25 September, 26 September 1896; Theodor Heuss, *Friedrich Naumann. Der Mann, das Werk, die Zeit*, 2nd edn, Stuttgart: Wunderlich, 1949, p. 312.

89 Wolfgang Treue (ed.), *Deutsche Parteiprogramme seit 1861*, 4th edn, Göttingen: Musterschmidt, 1968, pp. 94–5.

90 'Programm beschlossen auf dem Parteitage in Köln, 1910', in Blaustein and Hillger, *Hillgers Wegweiser*, pp. 172–4.

Moses, who was to become prominent in SPD politics in the Weimar Republic, and Simon Bernfeld, a journalist with the *Israelitisches Gemeindeblatt*. Barth's periodical *Die Nation*, which had been a notable godfather of the *Abwehr-Verein*, was a meeting-point for many Jewish intellectual contributors and readers. Following its electoral failure in 1912 the *Demokratische Vereinigung* dissolved itself; it was too short-lived for a balanced judgement of its following to be possible.

Despite the continuing public debate on anti-Semitism and the impressive growth in the membership of Jewish organizations, the conclusion must be that neither for the bourgeois political parties, nor for the average Jewish voter, did Jewish considerations have high priority. Where the numbers or wealth of the local Jewish population encouraged it, the Progressives and, to a much smaller extent, the other parties were prepared to nominate Jews for municipal or Landtag seats, especially once the 'Böckel wave' had subsided. Had they listened to Jewish advice on these matters, they would in any case have received contradictory counsels. Against the view that Jews *qua* Jews were entitled to representation – the official line of the C.V. – there was the rejection of proportional 'ghetto candidatures',[91] so that it was never quite clear on what basis Jews were to be put forward for office.

At Reichstag elections a Jewish candidate appeared as more of a liability than an asset, though the election of someone like Felix Waldstein in deepest Schleswig-Holstein suggests that party managers' fears may have been exaggerated. The fears nevertheless existed. The National Liberal constituency chairman in Wetzlar-Altenkirchen expressed surprise in 1912 at being asked to support, as a joint Liberal candidate, a Progressive 'who, on top of everything, is a Jew' ('der noch dazu Jude ist'),[92] though the candidate concerned, Professor Schloßmann, was in fact baptized. All parties needed non-Jewish votes more than Jewish ones and places where Jewish votes were worth competing for were few. If one assumes that between 60 and 65 per cent of Jews regularly voted for the Left-Liberal parties, this amounts to 7–10 per cent of their total, but it was not necessarily concentrated where it was most useful.

It was all the less necessary for the Liberal parties to court the Jewish vote systematically, since it was obvious that the C.V.'s instructions to oppose anti-Semitism at the cost of all other considerations were frequently ignored. One of the few indubitable successes the C.V. could claim was the defeat of the anti-Semite Ludwig Werner by 13 votes in the Hersfeld constituency in the 1908 Prussian Landtag elections.[93] In general, threats such as that support

91 *ISFAM* 1898/31, p. 3, cit. Toury, *Orientierungen*, p. 243.
92 Bertram, *Die Wahlen zum deutschen Reichstag*, p. 76.
93 *IdR* XIV/7–8, July–August 1908, pp. 453–5.

by the FVp for 'dyed-in-the-wool anti-Semites would bring down a heavy penalty on the party',[94] proved empty. Nor did the C.V.'s injunction that the Jewish elector should '*ceteris paribus* ... give unconditional support for members of his faith'[95] carry much weight. The C.V. was particularly troubled by the candidature of the convert Dr Otto Mugdan, first for the Berlin city council and then for the much-coveted Berlin I seat in the Landtag. The C.V., having moved from a position of merely defending equality before the law to one of actively cultivating Jewish consciousness, viewed baptism with increasing hostility; it also pointed out, with considerable justice, that in so far as the motives for baptism were mostly opportunist, it constituted an encouragement to popular and official anti-Semitism. The FVp had caused special annoyance by emphasizing Mugdan's Christian allegiance when he was first Reichstag candidate for Görlitz.[96] On the other hand, words like 'renegade' and 'deserter' with which the C.V. leaders denounced him[97] were inappropriate, since Mugdan, unlike some other baptized Jews, remained a vocal opponent of anti-Semitism and discrimination. They were also ineffectual, since the leadership of the Berlin FVp turned down the C.V.'s request for a less embarrassing candidate[98] and the Jewish electors of the constituency experienced little compunction in voting for him.

Intervention in elections was not the sole nor, as time went on, the main pre-occupation of the C.V. and there were compensations in other fields for its frustrations in electoral politics. Stories of Liberal connivance at anti-Semitism excited few beside addicts of political manoeuvering. Most Jews had other worries and regarded the Liberal parties as imperfect instruments in an imperfect world. Nevertheless disillusionment was growing within the Jewish community, not so much with the Liberal parties as such as with the ideology that had promised, with the attainment of free and equal citizenship, a solution to the question of the Jew's relationship with his fellow-men. There were several alternatives. A handful were attracted to Zionism and a rather larger handful to the idea of Jewish cultural separation within Germany. But more and more were drawn towards an ideal that had magnetized some German Jews from the very beginning and at whose origins, indeed, more than one Jew had been present, namely Socialism.

---

94 *AZJ*, 26 June 1908, p. 302.
95 *IdR* IV/5, May 1898, pp. 239–40.
96 Hamburger, *Juden im öffentlichen Leben Deutschlands*, p. 366; 'Nach den Wahlen', *AZJ*, 26 June 1903, p. 301.
97 'Falsche Auffassungen', *IdR* XVII/5, May 1911, pp. 253–6; ibid., 'Der Fall Mugdan-Rickert'. *IdR* XV/1, January 1909, pp. 1–7. See also 'Getaufte Juden', *AZJ*, 25 February 1898, p. 86.
98 Paucker, 'Zur Problematik', *WD*, pp. 515–6.

7   JEWS AND THE SOCIALIST MOVEMENT

Few Jews were active in radical politics during the consensus decades. The achievement of the *kleindeutsch* nation-state, with its promise, ultimately unfulfilled, of bourgeois liberties and bourgeois political structures, converted many ex-revolutionaries, whether Jewish (Ludwig Bamberger) or not (Johannes Miquel). Ferdinand Lassalle, the father of the infant labour movement, had died in Byronic circumstances in 1864; one can only speculate in which direction he would have moved when faced with the triumph of a Bismarck whom he had always regarded as a potential ally. Marx preferred to live in London, Moses Hess in Paris. Their successors, who built up the fragmented movement to its unification at Gotha in 1875 – Wilhelm Liebknecht, August Bebel, Johann Baptist von Schweitzer – included no Jews. Some Jews, up to then on the left wing of the Liberal movement, prophetically detected in the nationalist hysteria and incipient repressions of the 1870s the fatal defects of the later Empire. Johann Jacoby, jailed for a protest meeting against the annexation of Alsace-Lorraine, and appalled by the treason trial against those other anti-annexationists, Bebel and Liebknecht, joined the Social Democrats in 1872. Elected for the Leipzig-Land constituency in 1874, he declined to take his seat in a Reichstag that he regarded with contempt. Eduard Bernstein, too, found 'the evil by-products of the war ... especially repulsive. ... I simply could not tolerate ... the violent abuse of [the French] as a nation',[1] and joined the party in the same year as Jacoby. Paul Singer, later to be joint chairman of the party with Bebel, and originally a follower of Jacoby, was stung by the Anti-Socialist Law into active participation in and, above all, financial generosity to the party.

Of the earliest Jewish SPD deputies in the Reichstag neither Adolf Sabor (Frankfurt, 1884–90) nor Max Kayser (Freiberg 1878–84, Reichenberg, 1884–8) reached great eminence; Singer, who joined them in 1884, was of a different calibre. Jews were, however, prominent from the beginning in a party activity that they made peculiarly their own, that of journalism. Samuel Kokosky edited the *Braunschweiger Volksfreund* in the 1870s, Gabriel Löwenstein edited the *Fränkische Tagespost*, which he helped to found, and Eduard Bernstein edited from exile, first in Switzerland then in London, the weekly *Sozialdemokrat*, the sole journal which helped to keep the party going during the years of illegality. Among the financial patrons of the *Sozial-*

---

1   Eduard Bernstein, *Von 1850 bis 1872. Kindheit und Jugendjahre*. Berlin: E. Reiss, 1926, p. 216.

demokrat was Karl Höchberg, an idiosyncratic Jewish idealist who never overcame his distrust of Marx and Engels.[2]

It was from the 1890s onwards, as the party expanded rapidly after regaining its full legality, that Jewish association with it became a significant factor both in the public life of the *Reich* and in the internal politics of the labour movement. There was, however, a disparity between the large number of Jews prominent in the party's leadership and debates and the slower growth of its electoral following among Jews, a situation that mirrored the relationship between Jews and radicalism before 1848.

What attracted Jews, whether as activists or as passive voters, to the party of revolution is a complex question. As far as voting for the Social Democrats is concerned, changing social structure provides at least a clue. The Jewish population still differed from the total population in that virtually no-one was engaged in agriculture, but in other respects it was not immune from the trends of the time. In Prussia the proportion of the self-employed in trade declined from 74.5 per cent in 1861 to 58.6 per cent in 1907 and the proportion in industry and handicrafts from 72.3 per cent to 44.7 per cent over the same period. Moreover, whereas three times as many Jews had been occupied in trade as in industry (58.2 per cent, 19.5 per cent) in 1861, there were only twice as many (48.6 per cent, 25.1 per cent) in 1907 – there was, in other words, a shift towards those branches of the economy in which the trend towards paid employment was fastest. Of these employees, only a small minority were proletarians, but many of the others, especially in so far as they lived in large cities or worked in large enterprises, would have reasons for left-wing allegiances quite independently of their being Jews.

But one clearly cannot ignore in this analysis the attitude of the Social Democratic Party to anti-Semitism and Judaism. Given no less an authority than Marx for equating Jews with money and capitalism, it would be surprising if the SPD's general opposition to anti-Semitism had been unanimous or unambiguous. Through most of the nineteenth century there had been strong currents of anti-Semitism in the European revolutionary movement; a catalogue of tasteless or hateful remarks about Jews by Proudhon, Bakunin, Marx and Lassalle, not to mention their epigones, would be long and varied. Nothing did more to cure Social Democracy of lingering anti-Semitic ingredients than the growth of a right-wing anti-Semitic movement, allied with, or at least not unwelcome to, the state. Even Eduard Bernstein confessed

---

2 Peter Gay, *The Dilemma of Democratic Socialism. Eduard Bernstein's Challenge to Marx*, New York: Collier, 1962, pp. 42–5; Vernon L. Lidtke, *The Outlawed Party. Social Democracy in Germany, 1878–1890*, Princeton, NJ: Princeton University Press, 1966, pp. 89–92.

in retrospect: 'Only when anti-Semitism turned from an accusing movement into a persecuting one, did I change my attitude.'[3]

Indeed the relationship between Jews and Socialism was circular. Though some Jewish recruits to the Socialist movement grated on Gentile nerves, their numbers were, in the main, taken as evidence of Jewish altruism and political insight. Wilhelm Liebknecht attributed to Jews 'a much greater sum of idealism than among non-Jews'.[4] Bebel wrote to Engels: 'Curiously enough, or perhaps not, ... it is the Jews who are moving towards us. I have already often said that if you want to be in decent company here, you can only mix with the Jews.' Engels, who could see disadvantages in this development, agreed that this was 'because they have more sense than the other bourgeois'.[5]

Anti-Semitism was explained either in terms of surviving mediaeval prejudice[6] or as a response to a particular phase in the development of capitalism,[7] in either event as a doomed phenomenon. There was also a temptation to see it, in so far as it imbued hitherto apolitical strata with anti-capitalist consciousness, as hastening the collapse of capitalism and the coming of Socialism, however unintentionally. The conclusion of *Vorwärts*, 'the discontented, the oppressed, the anti-Semitic mass will have to follow us, because conditions will lead them to our flag', was typical of many.[8]

Yet these exegeses, important and interesting though they were, did not reach a very wide public. Much more important was the general impression that the Social Democrats, by virtue of being the enemy of the Right, must be the ally of the Right's victims; that, by virtue of being in favour of human equality, they must be the enemy of discrimination. These considerations gradually came to balance the originally unfavourable image of Social Democracy inside the Jewish community, as enemies of both property and religion, an image especially strong in the 1870s and 1880s when Jews were at their

3 Eduard Bernstein, 'Wie ich als Jude in der Diaspora aufwuchs', *Der Jude* II/3, June 1917, p. 194.
4 Wilhelm Liebknecht, *Rede über den Kölner Parteitag mit besonderer Berücksichtigung der Gewerkschaftsbewegung*, Bielefeld: 'Volkswacht', 1893, p. 33.
5 Werner Blumenberg (ed.), *August Bebels Briefwechsel mit Friedrich Engels*, The Hague: Mouton, 1965, pp. 478, 487.
6 E.g. Karl Kautsky, 'Das Massaker von Kischineff und die Judenfrage', *NZ* XXI/2, no. 36, 3 June 1903.
7 E.g. August Bebel, *Sozialdemokratie und Antisemitismus*, Berlin: Buchhandlung Vorwärts, 1906, esp. pp. 27–8.
8 *Vorwärts*, 5 June 1891; also ibid., 8 December 1892, 21 June 1893, 29 August 1893; see also Robert S. Wistrich, *Socialism and the Jews. The Dilemmas of Assimilation in Germany and Austria-Hungary*, London and Toronto: Associated University Presses, 1982.

most anxious to display their loyalty to the new order. The *Allgemeine Zeitung des Judentums* categorically asserted that 'Judaism is ... opposed to Socialism in all its components' and lumped the SPD together with the 'no less dangerous Christian Social Party of Pastor Stoecker and the academic social reformers known as *Kathedersozialisten*'.[9] Among the more Bismarckian Jews in public life, Levin Goldschmidt and Bleichröder were emphatic supporters of repressive measures against Socialism;[10] Lasker and Bamberger opposed the renewal of the Anti-Socialist Law only after they had broken with the National Liberal Party.

The *Abwehr-Verein* argued in its early years that Jewish sympathy for Socialism was to be explained only by anti-Semitism[11] and Emil Lehmann of the DIGB compared the alleged ties of Jews and Social Democracy with mediaeval accusations of well-poisoning.[12] Well-poisoning or not, a good many governmental authorities in Wilhelmine Germany regarded the link as a fact. The *Regierungspräsident* of Westphalia thought it deplorable that the 'dangerous weapon' of the Social Democratic press 'is kept on a viable footing only by the support given it through advertising by Jewish businesses'.[13] He was also relieved in 1907 that agitation among Polish miners in the Ruhr 'had quietened down ... since the Polish-Jewish agitator Haase had left Dortmund'.[14] The Chancellor and his ministers were not exempt from this conviction: Bülow and Count Posadowsky agreed at a meeting of the Prussian cabinet after the 1907 Reichstag election that 'students of Austro-Hungarian and Russian nationality had campaigned in an unheard of way for the Social Democrats' and that this 'alien invasion' applied as much to the press as to the universities.[15]

From the turn of the century onwards, following the growing disillusionment with the opportunism of the Left Liberals, the defence organizations began to take more seriously the possibility of allying with the SPD. The

9   *AZJ*, 25 June 1878, p. 403; also 16 July 1878, p. 455.
10   Goldschmidt: to Professor Stobbe, 25 June 1878, Adele Goldschmidt (ed.), *Levin Goldschmidt. Ein Lebensbild in Briefen*, Berlin: E. Goldschmidt, 1898, p. 410; Bleichröder: to King Leopold II of Belgium, 24 April 1883, cit. Stern, *Gold and Iron*, p. 415 fn.
11   'Judenthum und Sozialdemokratie', *MVA* III/46, 12 November 1893, p. 418.
12   Emil Lehmann, 'Judentum und Sozialdemokratie', *AZJ*, 30 April 1897, pp. 210–1.
13   Alan Hall, *Scandal, Sensation and Social Democracy. The SPD Press and Wilhelmine Germany, 1890–1914*, Cambridge: Cambridge University Press, 1977, p. 45, fn. 111.
14   'Jahresbericht betr. den Stand der sozialdemokratischen und anarchistischen Bewegung,' ZStM, Rep. 120 BB, VIII 1, no. 18, vol. 6 (25).
15   G St Dahlem, Rep. 90, 307.

Abwehr-Verein, under the more aggressive leadership of Theodor Barth, advocated the withholding of financial support to candidates who would not unconditionally endorse opponents of anti-Semitism at a run-off election, even if these were Social Democrats.[16] The C.V., too, began acknowledging that the SPD was a reliable ally[17] in the maintenance of equality before the law and in 1907 specified the Social Democrats as one of the parties to be supported at run-offs against anti-Semites.[18] These instructions evoked only a limited response, and are more convincing as a symptom of the SPD's growing respectability than of growing revolutionary enthusiasm among Jews or opponents of anti-Semitism. Jewish leaders had moved a long way from fearing, as they had done only nine years earlier, that Social Democratic advocacy of Jewish civil rights would prove an embarrassment.[19]

The most impressive evidence of the SPD's indifference to the pressures of fashion was its willingness to put up Jews as parliamentary candidates. The number of its Jewish Reichstag deputies rose steadily as the party's overall strength increased, reaching eight in 1898 and twelve in 1912, rising to an all-time high of thirteen after a by-election. From the 1880s onwards at least 10 per cent of the party group were Jewish. Although the majority of them represented metropolitan constituencies – these being, after all, the party's strongholds – they also sat for areas dominated by medium and small towns, e.g. Reichenberg in Saxony (Kayser, 1884–8), Grünberg in Silesia (Davidsohn, 1912–18) and the two principalities of Reuß (Emanuel Wurm, 1890–1907, 1912–18; Max Cohen, 1912–18). They were frequently put up for marginal seats, irrespective of whether this was tactically prudent. In part, this arose out of the party's proclaimed pre-occupation with votes rather than seats as a barometer of popularity, in part out of the relatively low valuation it put on the individual personality of the candidate, and in part out of the educational function it attributed to election campaigns. But it arose equally out of a determination not to be diverted by concessions to popular prejudice.

However, the conditions under which a Jew could rise in the party also

16   Speech by Theodor Barth at General Meeting of *Verein zur Abwehr des Antisemitismus*, 16 April 1904, *MVA* XIV/16, 19 April 1904, p. 122; also 'Die Reichstagsstichwahl in Eschwege-Schmalkalden', ibid., XIV/9, 3 March 1904, pp. 60–9; speech by Theodor Barth at General Meeting of *Verein zur Abwehr des Antisemitismus*, 2 March 1907, ibid., XVII/10, 6 March 1907, pp. 74–5.

17   Sonnenfeld, *IdR* IX/11, pp. 628, 632; ibid., IX/8, August 1903, p. 457; XII/6, June 1906, p. 561; 'Nach den Wahlen', *AZJ*, 8 February 1907, p. 62; Paucker, 'Zur Problematik', *WD* pp. 501–4.

18   'Zu den Stichwahlen', *IdR* XIII/2, February 1907, p. 105; also *AZJ*, 8 February 1907, p. 62.

19   *AZJ*, 25 February 1898, p. 87.

indicated the limits of the SPD's attractiveness. One could be a Jewish Socialist, but not a Socialist Jew. An SPD Reichstag seat was for long incompatible with the representation of special interests, such as those of the C.V. Opposition to anti-Semitism was the function of the whole party, not of its Jewish members, some of whom, like Paul Singer, were not at all keen to lay great stress on it.[20] When Bernstein intervened in a debate on reserve officers, he spoke out of turn and in breach of party discipline.[21] The great majority of Jewish Social Democrats, including the great majority of Revisionists, accepted the party line that with the coming of Socialism the Jewish Question would be solved by making 'the complete absorption of Judaism' possible[22] and accepted above all the doctrine, which caused more trouble in Austria-Hungary and Russia than in Germany, that the Jews were not a separate nation. As support for the SPD grew among the Jewish population, so SPD adherents began playing a part in the C.V. At least one SPD deputy, Georg Davidsohn, a journalist with the *Berliner Börsen-Courier*, elected in 1912, identified with it.[23] Kurt Eisner was briefly a salaried employee of the *Abwehr-Verein*.[24] It was only with the coming of the war, bringing greater contact with Eastern Jewry and Zionism, and the disillusioning revival of anti-Semitism after 1918, that an increasing number of Socialists began re-identifying with Jewish nationality, notably Eduard Bernstein and Oskar Cohn.[25] Thus in 1907 the C.V. could correctly observe that side by side with the SPD's steadfastness in anti-Semitic matters:

Take a look at the way official Social Democracy warms towards Judaism, and you will find that the temperature is below zero.[26]

As far as Jewish Socialists are concerned – these who were born as members of our faith have not stood up for us as Jews, even where our religious community was exposed to the worst slanders from anti-Semites.[27]

20   Above all at the Brussels congress of the Socialist International in 1891. Edmund Silberner, *Sozialisten zur Judenfrage*, Berlin: Colloquium-Verlag, 1962, pp. 180, 182.
21   *StBR*, 19 and 20 June 1913, vol. 290, pp. 5638, 5656–7; Angress, *LBYB* XVII, (1972), p. 39; Erich Matthias and Eberhard Pikart (eds), *Die Reichstagsfraktion der deutschen Sozialdemokratie*, Düsseldorf: Droste, 1966, vol. I, p. 298. Bernstein had been selected to speak on behalf of the party in the debate on the military budget, but not on this topic.
22   Karl Kautsky, *Rasse and Judentum*, 2nd edn, Stuttgart: J. H. W. Dietz, 1921, p. 73.
23   Paucker, 'Zur Problematik', *WD*, p. 502.
24   Suchy, *LBYB* (1983), p. 225.
25   See below, p. 248.
26   Sonnenfeld, *IdR* IX/11, p. 629.
27   'Das Resultat', *AZJ*, 15 February 1907, p. 73.

Few Social Democrats would have dissented from this verdict. Some went further, and condemned the one-sided struggle against anti-Semitism, as if it were the sole or most important evil in Imperial Germany. Franz Mehring, for instance, regarded the campaign as a disguised defence of capitalism and proclaimed even-handed contempt for anti-Semitism and 'philo-Semitism',[28] an attitude much more common in the Austrian party. Social Democrats were also apt to complain of selective indignation in the Jewish-edited bourgeois press, which gave great prominence to the Dreyfus Case but ignored the frequent incidence of 'class justice' from which German workers or their functionaries suffered.[29] On the other hand, by the turn of the century the SPD was no longer monolithic and some of its spokesmen were prepared to appeal directly for Jewish votes. After the 1898 Reichstag election the *Schwäbische Tagwacht* found the 'indifferent, indolent attitude of our Jewish fellow-citizens ... incomprehensible' in the light of the failure of the bourgeois parties to fight anti-Semitism effectively: 'We would almost wish things might get even worse, so that the Jews' eyes would be opened by the force of circumstances.'[30] At a meeting during the campaign for the following Reichstag election in 1903, Georg Davidsohn and Wolfgang Heine argued similarly: 'Social Democracy does not want to flatter the Jews in order to catch votes – every Jew needs to have enough sense to vote for Social Democracy out of his own motivation.'[31] In the 1907 Reichstag election the SPD urged Jewish voters not to support the Jewish Progressive candidate Oskar Cassel, since his party had allied itself with the Right.[32] In all, even if class considerations are left out of account, the appeal that Socialism could make to Jews was limited. The number who were beginning to feel some sort of heightened communal identity were least likely to find the Social Democratic prescription attractive and even those whose Zionism had a Socialist emphasis felt little in common with the SPD. Those, on the other hand, who saw in a new social order, secular and egalitarian, the solvent of Jewish–Gentile conflicts that liberalism and nationalism had failed to provide, also saw in the SPD the vehicle of their salvation. They joined the party, not because of its day-to-day opposition to prejudice and discrimination, but because of its vision of a future in which the grounds for this prejudice and discrimination would have ceased to exist. Viktor Adler's perceptive comment that most

28 Anon. (i.e. Franz Mehring), 'Anti- und Philosemitisches', *NZ*, IX/2, no. 45, 27 July 1891, pp. 586–7.
29 'Das Dresdner Urteil', ibid., XVII/1, no. 21, 8 February 1899, p. 643; 'Nochmals das Dresdner Urteil', no. 23, 22 February 1899, p. 705.
30 *Schwäbische Tagwacht*, no. 144, 1898.
31 *Vorwärts*, 27 May 1903.
32 Lamberti, *Jewish Activism*, p. 80.

workers yearned 'to live one day like everybody else',[33] could equally have applied to many Jews.

Nevertheless a surprisingly large number of Socialist Jews did not disown their Judaism, even though the purely religious links must have snapped long ago. Some publicly derived their adherence to Socialism from Jewish ethical teaching, others emphasized, often in controversy with right-wing Jews, that the originators of anti-Semitism were identical with those of anti-Socialism. Typical of these was Samuel Kokosky of the *Braunschweiger Volksfreund* who reminded Adolph Aronheim, the president of the Braunschweig Jewish community and, through the local employers' association, a leading advocate of an employment boycott against Social Democrats in the 1870s, that: 'The hep-hep cry against the Jews has not been silent for all that long, that they might be the first to raise the hep-hep cry against Social Democracy.'[34]

Of the eighteen Social Democrats of Jewish descent who were elected to the Reichstag between 1874 and 1914, eight remained members of their religious community, a far higher proportion than among Protestants and Catholics. Kurt Eisner spoke for many when he declared that he 'would not forsake a persecuted and despised community'; indeed a survey of Social Democratic deputies conducted by the *Allgemeine Zeitung* elicited very similar replies from Oskar Cohn, Georg Davidsohn and Emanuel Wurm.[35] Ludwig Frank, commenting on the number of Jews at an election meeting he had addressed in Cologne, wrote, 'the feeling within me of identifying with members of my nation [*Stammesgenossen*] becomes stronger and deeper with the passage of the years, rather than weaker'.[36]

Strictly speaking, the search for a society without Jew or Gentile was an argument for Socialism as an idea rather than for the SPD as an organization. In the Weimar Republic there was indeed a large class of left-wing publicists, independent of any party, more often than not Jewish – Kurt Tucholsky, Stefan Großmann, Kurt Hiller. But in Wilhelmine Germany ideology and organization overlapped almost completely. Outside the party only Gustav Landauer, who considered himself an anarchist, was of significance and this

33 To August Bebel, 8 September 1903. Friedrich Adler (ed.), *Viktor Adler, Briefwechsel mit Friedrich Engels und Karl Kautsky*, Vienna: Braumüller, 1954, pp. 421–2.
34 Georg Eckert, *Die Braunschweiger Arbeiterbewegung unter dem Sozialistengesetz*, Braunschweig: Waisenhaus-Buchdruckerei, 1961, vol. I, pp. 24, 28.
35 Franz Schade, *Kurt Eisner und die bayerische Sozialdemokratie*, Hanover: Verlag für Literatur und Zeitgeschehen, 1961, p. 105, fn. 209; *AZJ*, 5 April 1912, p. 160; 26 July 1912, p. 353.
36 Werner T. Angress, ' "Between Baden and Luxemburg" – Jewish Socialists on the Eve of World War I', *LBYB* XXII (1977), p. 16, fn. 14.

was chiefly literary.[37] His direct political commitment dates from the years of Revolution, when he was instrumental in proclaiming the first Bavarian Soviet Republic in April 1919. His principal colleague in this, Erich Mühsam, tried retrospectively to construct a career of subversive achievements for himself, but was in this period a complete unknown.[38] Finally there was Julian Borchardt who, after a brief period as Prussian Landtag deputy, went on to form the anti-war *Internationale Sozialisten Deutschlands* and its journal, *Lichtstrahlen*. He was the only German delegate at the Zimmerwald conference in September 1915 to support Lenin's proposal for revolutionary action against the war and a split in the International. However, within Germany he remained unacceptable to the other radical opponents of the war, such as Rosa Luxemburg and Georg Ledebour.[39] He may serve as an example of the sectarianism that is so often a part of the pilgrim's progress from ghetto to utopia.

The Jew in the SPD was significant in a number of ways. Firstly, by 1914 in sheer numbers, out of proportion not only to the Jewish population but to Jewish voting support for the party in the country; secondly, in the type of recruit that predominated. In one way or another, most of the Jews in the SPD could be described as intellectuals. This does not necessarily mean they were bourgeois in origin: quite a few of them came from poor (though not, in the main, proletarian) families. Nor that they were all academically trained: we are, after all, in the golden age of the autodidact. What it did mean was that Jews had a considerable influence on debate and communication within the party, as opposed to organizational control or long-term strategy, and this, much more than any identifiable ideological stance, characterized their contribution. That applied in particular to the triangular debate between the 'Revisionists', whose challenge to Marxist orthodoxy was launched in 1899 by Eduard Bernstein's *Voraussetzungen des Sozialismus*, the orthodox party centre, represented by Karl Kautsky's theoretical journal *Neue Zeit*, and the 'Radicals' grouped round Rosa Luxemburg and Rudolf Hilferding, who advocated a more revolutionary strategy.

In party journalism, Jews amply fulfilled Adler's early remark 'We Jews

37 Eugene Lunn, *Prophet of Community. The Romantic Socialism of Gustav Landauer*, Berkeley and Los Angeles: University of California Press, 1973; Charles B. Maurer, *Call To Revolution. The Mystical Anarchism of Gustav Landauer*, Detroit: Wayne State University Press, 1971.
38 Werner T. Angress, 'Juden im politischen Leben der Revolutionszeit', *KuR*, p. 267.
39 Francis L. Carsten, *War Against War. British and German Radical Movements in the First World War*, Berkeley and Los Angeles: University of California Press, 1972, pp. 37, 40.

are nothing less than destined for news-hawking [*Colportage*]'.[40] The most important figure in this respect after the lapse of the Anti-Socialist Law was Bruno Schoenlank. After a promising career on the *Süddeutsche Post* and the *Fränkische Tagespost*, of which he became chief editor at the age of twenty-five, he was appointed chief editor of the *Leipziger Volkszeitung* in 1894. With this appointment came the specific instruction of turning the paper into a popular journal that would rival the commercial press and spread propaganda beyond the confines of functionaries who were the main body of the party papers' readership up to then. He accepted this brief on condition that he had a free hand in appointing his own collaborators, and on this basis raised the paper's circulation to 90,000, second only to that of the Berlin *Vorwärts*.[41]

In doing so he bequeathed a problem as well as a service to the party, for the improved quality of the press made it an independent force within the labour movement, one whose relationship with the party leadership and local party authorities was never satisfactorily clarified.[42] It was within the pages of these barely controllable papers and journals that many of the ideological conflicts that the party leadership would have liked to dampen down flourished, and that the Jewish predilection for controversy found a welcoming opening.

Many of those journalists who later became famous found an early opportunity in Schoenlank's *Leipziger Volkszeitung*. His editorial colleagues in the seven years between appointment and death were Simon Katzenstein, Albert Südekum, Gustav Morgenstern and Friedrich Stampfer, of whom only Südekum was not Jewish. Schoenlank was also instrumental in inviting two of the leading revolutionary ideologues of the party to contribute, Alexander Israel Helphand (Parvus) and Rosa Luxemburg, who wrote twenty-eight articles between them in 1898 and 1899: it was here rather than in her other main outlet, the semi-official *Neue Zeit*, that Luxemburg published her series in refutation of Bernstein's *Voraussetzungen des Sozialismus*. Katzenstein went on to work with Eduard David in the *Mitteldeutsche Sonntagszeitung* of Gießen, which aimed to be similarly popular, and then to the *Mainzer Volkszeitung*, of which he became *de facto* editor in 1897.

Schoenlank's ideological eclecticism and volatility – he moved from

40 To Kautsky, 21 August 1886. Adler, *Briefwechsel*, p. 15.

41 Paul Mayer, *Bruno Schoenlank (1859–1901). Reformer der sozialdemokratischen Tagespresse*, Hanover: Verlag für Literatur und Zeitgeschehen, 1972, p. 69.

42 Carl E. Schorske, *German Social Democracy 1905–1917. The Development of the Great Schism*, Cambridge, Mass: Harvard University Press, 1965, pp. 182, 201–4; Gerhard A. Ritter, *Die Arbeiterbewegung im wilhelminischen Reich*, 2nd edn, Berlin: Colloquium-Verlag, 1963, pp. 65–6.

revisionism, a term he himself had coined, to brief admiration of Rosa Luxemburg's position – caused the paper some difficulty. Parvus had quickly quarrelled with Schoenlank, and in 1896 succeeded the moderate Georg Gradnauer as chief editor of the Dresden *Sächsische Arbeiterzeitung*, recruiting another famous Jewish Radical, Julian Marchlewski ('Karski'), as co-editor. The Viennese-born Friedrich Stampfer, who had been acting editor during Schoenlank's illness and who belonged to the moderate wing of the party, disapproved of Rosa Luxemburg's continuing contributions and resigned from the paper when Franz Mehring, who was moving closer to her position, gained the editorship. Mehring was very much in a minority in this milieu in not being a Jew.

Stampfer himself moved to Berlin to join the staff of the party's central organ, *Vorwärts*. Here he worked with Gradnauer, who had moved to the paper after leaving the *Sächsische Arbeiterzeitung*, as well as Kurt Eisner. Between them they gave the paper a distinctly revisionist tone, in contrast with the increasingly radical character of the Social Democratic press of Saxony. Though Eisner's principal claim to fame is the first Bavarian revolutionary government of 1918–19, which he proclaimed and headed, he was at this time a moderate and scarcely a Marxist. His first journalistic job had been with the *Frankfurter Zeitung*, which he left for the Social Democratic *Hessische Landespost*, whose political editor he became. It was at this period of his life (1893–8) that he was befriended by the neo-Kantian Hermann Cohen of Marburg, who strongly influenced his ethical cast of thought and tried to persuade him to take up an academic career.[43] However, through Philipp Scheidemann's influence he moved to *Vorwärts*. Having been political editor under Wilhelm Liebknecht (and *de facto* acting editor), he continued in this post on Liebknecht's death in 1900.

Though many in the party objected to the revisionist tone of *Vorwärts* during these years, the great row that resulted in the dismissal of the editorial board had more to do with their independence and insubordination than with their ideological stance. In any case, the disappearance of Eisner, Gradnauer and Julius Kaliski did not diminish Jewish participation. They were replaced by, among others, Georg Davidsohn and Arthur Stadthagen from the party's Left.[44] Gradnauer returned to his old paper, now renamed *Dresdner Volkszeitung*, while Eisner went to the *Fränkische Tagespost* of Nuremberg, thus beginning his connection with Bavaria, and in 1910 to the *Münchener Post*, where his principal contribution was an *Arbeiterfeuilleton*, a literary and cultural column that was used by many other Social Democratic papers.[45]

43   Schade, *Kurt Eisner*, pp. 27, 105.
44   *Vorwärts*, 24 October 1905, 7 November 1905.
45   Schade, *Kurt Eisner*, p. 29.

Eisner's interest in cultural journalism and in generally popularizing the Social Democratic press was in the tradition of Schoenlank and typical of Jewish work for the party's media. The greatest contribution of this kind was made by Friedrich Stampfer, who founded and became editor of the *Parteikorrespondenz* with the intention of providing a Social Democratic news agency. By the outbreak of the war it had 40,000 subscribers. Its material naturally reflected Stampfer's own right-wing stance within the party and was accordingly denounced by Rosa Luxemburg as the 'Groß-Lichterfeld opinion factory for gumming up the brains of proletarians'.[46] To counter-act this gumming up she herself, with the aid of Marchlewski and Mehring, founded the *Sozialdemokratische Korrespondenz*. Eisner, Stampfer and the heterodox Joseph Bloch were also artistic governors of the avant-garde theatre, the *Freie Volksbühne*, but non-Jewish participation was strong here, in the persons of the chairman, Dr Conrad Schmidt (the brother of Käthe Kollwitz), and his deputy, Kurt Baake.[47]

The party's principal theoretical journal, *Neue Zeit*, was edited throughout this period by Karl Kautsky, but Jews were to be found among his principal collaborators: Eduard Bernstein until 1901, when doctrinal disputes no longer made this possible, and from 1902 onwards Emanuel Wurm as the principal member of the editorial staff. Jews were also instrumental in founding a number of less official theoretical journals. Heinrich Braun, the brother-in-law of Viktor Adler, founded both *Neue Gesellschaft* and the *Jahrbuch für Politik und Arbeiterbewegung*, which sought to employ economics and sociology in discussing the problems of the labour movement, in contrast to the more philosophical approach of *Neue Zeit*. The *Sozialistische Monatshefte* of Joseph Bloch was more specifically devoted to propagating the views of the revisionist wing of the party, but its role needs to be discussed in the general context of the relationship of Jews to the theoretical disputes within the party.[48]

As in journalism, so in the elaboration of party theory, the principal characteristic of Jewish participation was in its quantity rather than its content. Popular stereotypes notwithstanding, Jews were not more strongly identified with the party's left wing than with its right wing. For instance in

46 'Groß-Lichterfelder Meinungsfabrik zur Verkleisterung der Proletariergehirne.' Friedrich Stampfer, *Erfahrungen und Erkenntnisse. Aufzeichnungen aus meinem Leben*, Cologne: Verlag für Politik und Wirtschaft, 1957, pp. 92–4; Kurt Koszyk, *Anfänge und frühe Entwicklung der sozialdemokratischen Presse im Ruhrgebiet, 1875–1908*, Dortmund: Ruhfus, 1953, p. 141.
47 Stampfer, *Erfahrungen und Erkenntnisse*, pp. 96–7.
48 See Roger Fletcher, *Revisionism and Empire. Socialist Imperialism in Germany, 1897–1914*, London: Allen & Unwin, 1984, pp. 43–122.

160   *Jews in German Politics*

the crucial debate at the 1913 Jena congress on the party's support for the progressive taxation that financed the military budget, thirteen Jewish delegates, including Bernstein, supported the party line and only five voted for Rosa Luxemburg's opposition.[49] What can be said is that relatively few of the party's prominent Jewish members were content with the *attentiste* outlook of the party's centre and of the majority of the party officials and Reichstag deputies. Their disproportionately bourgeois origins, and their tendency to derive their views from first principles rather than empirical experience, led them into a dominating position in the party's debates. The party would not have been what it was without Bernstein and Luxemburg, and the Socialist movement throughout the world still resounds to the questions they first raised.

The Revisionists' challenge to the orthodoxy of party doctrine was greater than that of the Radicals. While the Radicals urged the party to resist all colonialism and imperialism and emphasized the primacy of the class struggle in all political action, the Revisionists challenged the basic premises of dialectical materialism. Bernstein denied that capitalism was moving towards crisis and catastrophe, that class conflict would exacerbate itself more and more, that 'immiseration' would proceed unchecked. His objection to capitalism was ethical, for its destruction of the quality of life. His objection to the Marxism of the party was based on its aridity, its cant, 'the untrue idle phrases, either thoughtlessly babbled, or exploited for some purpose in full knowledge of their untruthfulness',[50] a category from which he did not exempt the idea of the dictatorship of the proletariat. It belonged, in his view, 'to a less advanced culture'; its use would be 'a relapse' and 'political atavism'.[51]

Yet the gradualist programme that he proposed for the achievements of the labour movement's aims was closer to the habits of thought and everyday practice of the majority of party members and functionaries than the appeals to violence and general strike that came from Rosa Luxemburg, however logically she might derive them from the party's declared principles. This may be one reason why, although he was crushingly defeated at party conferences, he never aroused the personal animosity that the Radicals succeeded in attracting. The other reason, which may also be connected with his and his rivals' intellectual positions, is that he was personally a humble and likeable man: even the party's chief theoreticians and patriarchs responded to his heresy more in sorrow than in anger. Viktor Adler wrote to him *in camera caritatis*: 'that I am painfully surprised ... by the total lack of any political

49 Angress, *LBYB* (1977), p. 24.
50 Eduard Bernstein, *Die Voraussetzungen des Sozialismus und die Aufgaben der Sozialdemokratie*, Stuttgart: J. H. W. Dietz, 1902, p. 169.
51 Ibid., p. 127.

instinct that ought to have taught you that one must not talk like this *now*, even if one were *completely* right',[52] and Kautsky, asking Adler to review *Die Voraussetzungen des Sozialismus* for *Vorwärts*, reinforced his request with the words: 'For the sake of Ede [i.e. Eduard] I should have wished you had volunteered, and not some Parvus or Luxemburg.'[53]

The last phrase gave away the tension that the Radicals introduced into the party by the superiority and intolerance of their intellects. The Radicals' Jewish origins were frequently alluded to, admittedly more in private than in public, those of the Revisionists never. The former were apparently 'typically Jewish', the latter not. Many memoirs, including those of Jewish party veterans, agree that Rosa Luxemburg grated on her comrades' nerves. Friedrich Stampfer records that 'I disliked her arrogant way of treating people' and Viktor Adler referred to her as 'hysterical materialism'.[54] Gustav Noske, in memoirs published after the Second World War, records 'that the Marxists of East European origin had a special predisposition for turning Marxism into a dogma – they hatched a secret lore which has always been incomprehensible to German workers'.[55] A number of the party's right-wingers, including Richard Fischer and Karl Grillenberger, often privately disparaged the Left in anti-Semitic terms. Grillenberger felt no embarrassment in his letters to Schoenlank in referring to Parvus as 'the Russian buffalo-jew' and to the party's Berlin section as the 'Judaean district office',[56] while Richard Fischer, who strongly sympathized with the Revisionists in the *Vorwärts* row,[57] was in no way disturbed by the fact that the majority of them, too, were Jewish. In the SPD, as elsewhere, it was open to everyone to decide who was a Jew.

Two other men, prominent in the party, may be taken to typify the Jewish contribution to the reformist and radical wings, Ludwig Frank and Hugo Haase. In contrast with the Bernstein and Luxemburg circles, their main activity was in the Reichstag itself. Unlike Bernstein, Frank was not a revisionist theorist. He had no eschatology. He was simply concerned to secure the material and cultural improvement of the working class; he

---

52 17 March 1899, Adler, *Briefwechsel*, p. 297.

53 'Und nicht irgend ein Parvus oder eine Luxemburg.' 7 March 1899, ibid., p. 294.

54 Stampfer, *Erfahrungen und Erkenntnisse*, pp. 75, 175; Adler: oral information from the late Julius Braunthal.

55 Gustav Noske, *Aufstieg und Niedergang der deutschen Sozialdemokratie. Erlebtes aus Aufstieg und Untergang einer Demokratie*, Zürich and Offenbach: Aeroverlag, 1947, p. 27.

56 Paul Mayer, *Bruno Schoenlank*, pp. 123, 119.

57 Benedikt Kautsky (ed.), *August Bebels Briefwechsel mit Karl Kautsky*, Assen: van Gorcum, 1971, p. 379; Noske, *Aufstieg und Niedergang*, pp. 147–8.

considered it both possible and desirable to achieve this by working through existing institutions. In this he was typical of the party line of the Southern states and, in particular, a product of the tolerant political climate of Baden, where the Social Democrats were in alliance with the two Liberal parties and aroused the anger of Berlin headquarters by approving the state budget. He was floor leader of the Social Democrats in the Baden Landtag and in this capacity defended his followers' deviationism at the Magdeburg party conference in 1910, not by disputing scriptural texts, but by pointing to his group's solid achievements in fiscal and social policy.[58]

This pragmatic reformism was not typically Jewish. His principal colleagues, Georg von Vollmar and Ignaz Auer from Bavaria, Wilhelm Keil from Württemberg and Eduard David from Hesse, not to mention the principal trade union leaders, were not Jews. What singled him out from them was his interest in foreign policy, his humanitarian internationalism, which he shared with his principal antagonist at the Magdeburg conference, Hugo Haase. Haase's devotion to the party's revolutionary impetus did not rest, as did that of Rosa Luxemburg, on special interest in, or understanding of, Marxism. His inspiration, as befitted a native of Königsberg, came from Kant, whose first editions he collected.[59] In this respect he was closer to Bernstein and Eisner than to the leaders of the party's radical wing. This idealism led him, as a lawyer, to take up the defence, free of charge, of workers and party members whom he saw as the victims of class justice. It also made him the major authority in the party on legal reform, which he justified, characteristically, by saying that 'modern penal law must be filled with the spirit of humanity'.[60] But it was his devotion to party unity and the principles of the party programme that made him the Radicals' candidate for the post of deputy party chairman on the death of Singer in 1911, and his hard-fought victory opened the way to his election as co-chairman of the party (with Friedrich Ebert) on the death of Bebel in 1913. It was during this period also that his interest in foreign affairs became more prominent. It was Haase who had formulated the German delegation's statement at the 1907 meeting of the

58   *Protokoll über die Verhandlungen des Parteitages der Sozialdemokratischen Partei Deutschlands, abgehalten in Magdeburg* (1910), Berlin: Buchhandlung Vorwärts, 1910, pp. 259–76, esp. 264–7.
59   Schorske, *German Social Democracy 1905–1917*, p. 209; Kenneth R. Calkins, *Hugo Haase, Democrat and Revolutionary*, Chapel Hill: University of North Carolina Press, 1979, pp. 11, 201, 208.
60   *Protokoll über die Verhandlungen des Parteitages der Sozialdemokratischen Partei Deutschlands, abgehalten zu Mannheim* (1906), Berlin: Buchhandlung Vorwärts, 1906, p. 141.

Socialist International, denouncing militarism but disavowing the mass strike as illusory. In the light of his pacifist humanism he saw himself and his fellow-Socialists, in words that sound strangely modern, as 'citizens of the impending great European cultural community'.[61] He was also co-chairman of the Franco-German inter-parliamentary committee that first met in Berne in 1913 to avert the danger of war between the two states, an event also notable for a passionate speech by Ludwig Frank.[62] Other Jewish Socialists who attended were Bernstein and Georges Weill; the six Progressive delegates included Ludwig Haas.

With the coming of the war the ideals of all Social Democrats, whether inspired by Marx or Kant, were put to their severest test by the pressures of the political situation, their mental and emotional unpreparedness and the ambiguous dictates of the principle of defence of the fatherland (*Landesverteidigung*). The crisis confused Jews and non-Jews alike; though the division in the party bore recognizable resemblances to earlier and later splits, one cannot detect a characteristically Jewish role during the days of July and August 1914. The immediate response to the Austrian ultimatum of 23 July, denouncing Austrian 'war mongering', expressed the whole range of party opinion, though the text itself was mainly drafted by Haase, who saw, earlier than most of his colleagues, how serious the danger of war now was.[63] Men on the far Right of the party took part enthusiastically in anti-war demonstrations.[64] The divisions arose once it was clear that war was probable, thus presenting the need to make a decision, not merely on whether to support the principle of defence of the fatherland (which was perfectly consistent with party policy) but on the practical question of whether to vote the war credits in the Reichstag.

Some of the Jewish activists on the Right of the party responded with the instinctive emotionalism of Friedrich Stampfer, whose *Parteikorrespondenz* distributed, on 31 July, a leading article that proclaimed: 'We do not want our women and children to become the victims of Cossack bestialities ... The "scoundrels without a country" will do their duty.' It was widely printed,

---

61 *StBR*, 9 April, 1913, p. 4600.

62 Hamburger, *Juden im öffentlichen Leben Deutschlands*, pp. 430–1, 452; Matthias and Pikart, *Die Reichstagsfraktion*, vol. I, p. 307. Seven of the participants were Jews.

63 Hamburger, *Juden im öffentlichen Leben Deutschlands*, p. 286; Susanne Miller, *Burgfrieden und Klassenkampf. Die deutsche Sozialdemokratie im Weltkrieg*, Düsseldorf: Droste, 1974, p. 39.

64 Susanne Miller (ed.) *Das Kriegstagebuch des Reichstagsabgeordneten Eduard David, 1914 bis 1918*, Düsseldorf: Droste, 1966, p. 3 (30 July 1914); Carl Severing, *Mein Lebensweg*. vol. I: *Vom Schlosser zum Minister*, Cologne: Greven-Verlag, 1950, p. 196.

though Stampfer himself withdrew it at Haase's insistence.[65] Ludwig Frank, in contrast, had appreciated at an early stage that war would require Social Democratic acquiescence: anything else would contradict the position the party had acquired in the Empire and would destroy the possibilities of further development. To this end he had secured the written agreement of about a quarter of the Reichstag group to vote for the credits, if necessary in breach of discipline.[66] Frank, peace-lover that he had been, carried this logic further than any other member of the party group. Though aged forty, he volunteered for service and was killed a month later.

In the event, opponents of the credits were in a small minority. Of the Jewish deputies, only two, Haase and Joseph Herzfeld, were against. The spirit of the national truce, the *Burgfrieden*, had entered into the labour movement, and the differences between Orthodox and Revisionists, intellectuals and trade unionists, Jewish and non-Jewish members, were for the moment bridged. Only a minority of the Radicals were isolated. But the truce could last only as long as there was wide agreement that Germany's war was defensive, and as long as there was a prospect of quick military success without burdening the social and political structure of the *Reich*. Once it became evident that there was no prospect of this, the truce began to disintegrate, within the Social Democratic Party as well as in the country as a whole. The minority that opposed further war credits grew with each meeting of the Reichstag group. By June 1915 the leaders of the formerly hostile wings, Bernstein, Haase and Kautsky, had joined forces in *Das Gebot der Stunde* ('The Demands of the Hour'): in a text largely drafted by Bernstein, the party was urged to seek a peace of reconciliation, in contrast with the evident trend of the policies of the government.[67] By December 1915 the party could no longer conceal its disunity in a divergent vote in the Reichstag on war credits. The twenty deputies who opposed included six of the grouping's eleven Jews (see table 3.10);[68] the twenty-two who abstained included one further Jew, the trade unionist Gustav Hoch. By March 1916 the twenty dissidents of December had formed themselves into a separate *Fraktion*, the *Sozialdemokratische Arbeitsgemeinschaft* (SAG) under the chairmanship of Hugo Haase; they were the nucleus of the later Independent Social Democratic Party (USPD). Even before the fateful Reichstag vote, Haase and Hoch had resigned from the executive of the parliamentary group. One of their

---

65   Miller, *Burgfrieden*, p. 54.
66   *Idem, Eduard David*, p. 13 (5 August 1914).
67   *Leipziger Volkszeitung*, 19 June 1915.
68   Matthias and Pikart, *Die Reichstagsfraktion*, vol. I, pp. clxxxviii–clxxxix. Of the originally thirteen members of the parliamentary group, Ludwig Frank had been killed and Georges Weill, who represented the Lorraine constituency of Metz, had remained in France on the outbreak of the war.

replacements, however, was also Jewish: Georg Gradnauer, 'the last of the Jews', Eduard David noted, 'in whom I still have confidence'.[69]

Gradnauer's position showed how over-simplified stereotypes about political Jews were, within the SPD as well as – much more commonly – outside. There were other party loyalists, like Otto Landsberg, who became celebrated for their patriotic oratory;[70] there was that wing of the Revisionists, including the editor of *Sozialistische Monatshefte*, Joseph Bloch, who had been anglophobe and colonialist before the war and now experienced no difficulty in supporting government policy. Max Cohen-Reuß, a close associate of Bloch, even supported unrestricted U-boat warfare.[71]

What facilitated the association of Jews with the opposition was that among them the old Left (from Haase to Luxemburg) was joined by the Revisionist Kantians. Kurt Eisner, though convinced in 1914 of the Tsar's aggressiveness, was merely being consistent when he wrote in 1915 that for any student of German foreign policy from the Kruger telegram and the Morocco crises onwards 'there could be no disputing that what we have is a *German* world war'.[72] Already in 1906 he had contributed a prophetic pamphlet on the first Moroccan crisis[73] which, ironically, was not circulated by the party because of his role in the *Vorwärts* dispute.[74] Similarly Bernstein did not share the anglophobia of the *Sozialistische Monatshefte*. He not only identified with British political institutions, no doubt because of his long and happy stay in London, but was convinced that the anti-British propaganda of the German Right was a manipulation of public opinion.[75] So, too, he had vigorously opposed German intervention in China in 1900 and, perhaps more surprisingly, voted against the military budget of 1913, in opposition to the majority of the party group, which was willing to accept the attendant wealth tax. Like Eisner, he felt in 1914 that Germany was the victim of Russian aggression; in retrospect he regarded the party's vote on 4 August as a 'catastrophe'.[76] A further factor was the development of Bernstein's thought in the direction of a specifically Jewish mission to bring about international

69 Miller, *Eduard David*, p. 165 (14 March 1916).
70 *Idem, Burgfrieden*, pp. 122, 185.
71 Matthias and Pikart, *Die Reichstagsfraktion*, vol. II, p. 244.
72 To Wolfgang Heine, 11 February 1915, cit. Miller, *Burgfrieden*, p. 184.
73 Kurt Eisner, *Der Sultan des Weltkrieges. Ein marokkanisches Sittenbild deutscher Diplomaten-Politik*, Dresden: Kaden & Co., 1906. *Gesammelte Schriften*, Berlin: Paul Cassirer, 1919, vol. I, pp. 326–41.
74 Schorske, *German Social Democracy 1905–1917*, p. 72.
75 Eduard Bernstein, *Die englische Gefahr und das deutsche Volk*, Berlin: Buchhandlung Vorwärts, 1911.
76 Gay, *The Dilemma of Democratic Socialism*, pp. 277, 296; Eduard Bernstein, 'Der Krieg, sein Urheber und sein erstes Opfer', *Sozialistische Monatshefte* XX/2, 13 August 1914.

Table 3.10 Evolution of oppositional attitudes among Jewish SPD deputies, 1914–1917

	Against war credits. Fraktion meeting 3 August 1914	Against war credits. Fraktion meeting 18 March 1915	Against war credits or abstention. Reichstag vote 21 Dec. 1915	Member of SAG/USPD
Bernstein		×	×	×
Cohen-Reuß				
Cohn			×	×
Davidsohn				
Frank				
Gradnauer				
Haase	×	×	×	×
Herzfeld	×	×	×	×
Hoch		×	×	
Landsberg				
Stadthagen		×	×	×
Wurm			×	×

Source: Erich Matthias and Eberhard Pikart (eds), *Die Reichstagsfraktion der deutschen Sozialdemokratie*, Düsseldorf: Droste, 1966, vol. I, pp. cliii, clxxxviii–ix

understanding,[77] a view he tried to direct at even such unsympathetic ears as Friedrich Stampfer's.[78] Yet, as before the war, a Jew was more conspicuous in the party on the Left than on the Right. Eduard David might complain, 'all my critics are Austrian Jews',[79] yet he collaborated without friction with supporters of expansionism like Joseph Bloch and Max Cohen-Reuß.[80] Reactions like those of David, and of Engelbert Pernerstorfer in the Austrian party, are symptoms of the irritations introduced by bitter disputes, and of the sensitivity that all parties of the Left show towards displays of intellectual and moral superiority. The Jew as leftist caused a much stronger reaction outside the party than inside.

To summarize the importance of Jews for the party one must stress in the first place their numbers, in the second place their professional distribution

77 Eduard Bernstein, *Von den Aufgaben der Juden im Weltkriege*, Berlin: E. Reiss, 1917.
78 Miller, *Eduard David*, p. 112 (12 July 1915).
79 Ibid., pp. 136–7 (4 July, 12 July 1915). Kautsky was promoted to honorary membership of this undesirable group.
80 Ibid., pp. 92 (5 January 1915), 155 (25 January 1916), 164 (9 March 1916).

and only in the third place the question of a particular ideological posture. Their crucial role in party journalism has already been mentioned. Within parliamentary delegations they played an equally specific role: what distinguished them from their colleagues was their much higher level of education. In 1898, 7 out of the 8 Jewish SPD deputies were graduates, compared with 8 out of the 48 non-Jews; in 1912, 11 out of 12 Jews and 8 out of 98 non-Jews.[81] In the Prussian Landtag the party was led by the economist Paul Hirsch, in the Baden Landtag by the lawyer Ludwig Frank. Given that much parliamentary business was technical, the expertise brought by these middle-class idealists was indispensable. It meant, in return, however, that in many areas of party work Jews were only sparsely represented. Though Emanuel Wurm was one of the founders of the workers' co-operative movement, few other Jews were active here. Gustav Hoch's trade union activity, which was journalistic rather than organizational, has already been mentioned and to it should be added the work of Adolf Cohen in the Metal Workers' Union and of Siegfried Aufhäuser in the white-collar *Arbeitsgemeinschaft freier Angestelltenverbänd*. Although it was the anomalous position of Jews in German society that may have led an increasing number of them into the Socialist movement, this nevertheless did nothing to reduce the scale of that anomaly, either inside the party or in society as a whole.

8 JEWS AND PUBLIC OPINION, INTEREST GROUPS AND GOVERNMENT POLICY

Important, even historic, though the contribution of the Jews to the German labour movement may have been, it had little direct influence on the government of the Empire. Bernstein and Frank could not change the party structure and the powers of the Reichstag, nor could Haase prevent the outbreak of the war; and, contrary to myths long accepted and widely believed, the collapse of Germany in 1918 was not due to Rosa Luxemburg and Kurt Eisner. The Jewish members of the Liberal parties in the various legislatures after 1890 achieved a few limited objectives, e.g. in the appointment to judgeships in Prussia, but on matters of broad policy they had no collective impact and, indeed, no common line. Who, then, did have influence? Against whom was the *Verband gegen die Überhebung des Judentums* ('League against Jewish Arrogance'), founded in 1912, directed? No doubt against phantoms. But the belief in these phantoms tells us much about the nature of public opinion in Imperial Germany, about the available means of directing it, of who tried to do so, and with what aims.

81 Hamburger, *Juden im öffentlichen Leben Deutschlands*, p. 409.

In a state with universal suffrage and some freedom of the press, but a constitutional system that gave the executive considerable prerogatives, the means of access to the central policy-makers were limited. One possibility was the use of the press, another the personal relationship between a private individual and one of the Empire's rulers – the Emperor, the Chancellor or the Chief of the Civil Cabinet. Among Gentile industrialists Friedrich Alfred Krupp and Carl Freiherr von Stumm enjoyed this status; among Jews there were the so-called 'Kaiserjuden',[1] who included Albert Ballin, Max Warburg, Walther Rathenau, Carl Fürstenberg and James Simon. Despite his well-documented and sometimes vitriolic anti-Semitic outbursts,[2] the Emperor evidently enjoyed the company of these cultured and well-informed men, who compared favourably in these respects with his own court circle. There is, however, no evidence that they tried to influence the Emperor or his ministers on questions affecting the Jews or that their social intercourse had any political or practical significance.[3] A third possibility, and the one most easily checked by research, is the formation of interest groups to defend and advance the interests of different branches of the economy and to organize propaganda for ideologically or economically motivated policies. This was a form of political organization particularly developed in Wilhelminian Germany, with its mixture of public liberties and parliamentary weakness.[4] The first and the third possibilities will in the main be investigated here.

1 The expression was coined by Chaim Weizmann in his memoirs *Trial and Error*, London: East and West Library, 1949, p. 183. He gravely misinterpreted the aims, cohesiveness and influence of this group. See also Hans Tramer, 'Die Hamburger Kaiserjuden', *BLBI* 11 (1969), pp. 177–89; Werner E. Mosse, 'Wilhelm II and the Kaiserjuden: A Problematical Encounter', in Jehuda Reinharz and Walter Schatzberg (eds), *The Jewish Response to German Culture*, Hanover, NH: New England University Press, 1986, pp. 164–94.

2 See Lamar Cecil, 'Wilhelm II und die Juden', *WD*, pp. 313–47; John Roehl, *Kaiser, Hof und Staat. Wilhelm II und die deutsche Politik*, Munich: C. H. Beck, 1987.

3 Mosse, 'Wilhelm II and the Kaiserjuden', p. 190, 194.

4 See Thomas Nipperdey, 'Interessenverbände und Parteien in Deutschland vor dem ersten Weltkrieg', *Politische Vierteljahresschrift* II, 1961, pp. 262–80; Hans-Jürgen Puhle, 'Parlament, Parteien und Interessenverbände 1890–1914', in Michael Stürmer (ed.), *Das Kaiserliche Deutschland. Politik und Gesellschaft, 1870–1914*, Düsseldorf: Droste, 1970, pp. 340–77; Hartmut Kaelble, 'Industrielle Interessenverbände vor 1914', in Walter Rüegg and Otto Neuloh (eds), *Zur soziologischen Theorie und Analyse des 19. Jahrhunderts*, Göttingen: Vandenhoeck & Ruprecht, 1971, pp. 180–92; Wolfram Fischer, 'Staatsverwaltung und Interssenverbände im Deutschen Reich', in *idem, Wirtschaft und Gesellschaft im Zeitalter der Industrialisierung*, Göttingen: Vandenhoeck & Ruprecht, 1972, pp. 194–214.

It was taken for granted, not only by all anti-Semites but probably also by many Jews, that there was such a thing as a 'jüdische Presse'[5] or 'Judenpresse' – a number of newspaper chains, owned, edited and largely written by Jews, devoted, with massive resources, to spreading the propaganda of Liberalism and even democracy. This is a picture that needs serious modification. That journalism as a profession, and newspaper publishing as a form of enterprise, were especially attractive to Jews is undeniable. It had been observed, in general unfavourably, long before 1848.[6] Nor can it be denied that in the first two-thirds of the nineteenth century that section of the press which favoured liberal or radical causes, of whatever kind, was the more active and more substantial. Nevertheless, there was a large and, as the century progressed, increasing sector that was neither Liberal nor Jewish.

Most Germans, if they lived outside large cities, tended to read a *Kreisblatt*, locally owned and printed, dependent on agency despatches and, if not ideologically conservative, at least loyal to the government. Since much of its revenue came from public announcements, it was also under the thumb of the local political official, who could therefore influence it in any matters of controversy, particularly at election time. Among metropolitan papers there were those which stood close to the Conservative parties (*Kreuz-Zeitung, Norddeutsche Allgemeine Zeitung*), the *Zentrum* (*Germania* and *Kölnische Volkszeitung*, to name the most important) and, from the 1890s onwards, an increasing number financed by pressure groups of the Right, principally heavy industry (*Berliner Neueste Nachrichten, Die Post*) and the Agrarian League (*Deutsche Tageszeitung, Berliner Blatt*). With the exception of the *Zentrum* papers these had relatively small circulations.[7] Even when they were not overtly anti-Semitic, they tended not to employ Jews. The one major exception to this rule was Victor Schweinburg, a baptized Jew from Moravia and protégé of Krupp, who, after an unhappy start as the propagandist of the Navy League in 1898,[8] became editor of Krupp's *Berliner Neueste Nachrichten* as well as of the *Neue Reichskorrespondenz*, an agency service subsidized by the *Central-Verband der Deutschen Industrie* (CVDI), which was

5 Heinrich von Treitschke, 'Eine Erwiderung', 19 October 1880, in *idem, Deutsche Kämpfe, Neue Folge. Schriften zur Tagespolitik*, Leipzig: S. Hirzel, 1896, p. 125.
6 See above, p. 81.
7 Around 1914 between 8,500 for the *Kreuz-Zeitung* and 60,000 for the *Tägliche Rundschau*, compared with 235,000 for the *Berliner Tageblatt* and 405,000 for the *Berliner Morgenpost*. Klaus Wernecke, *Der Wille zur Weltgeltung. Außenpolitik und Öffentlichkeit im Kaiserreich am Vorabend des Ersten Weltkrieges*, Düsseldorf: Droste, 1970, pp. 318–24.
8 See below pp. 179–80.

compulsory reading for all *Prussian Landräte* (rural mayors) and *Ober-präsidenten* (provincial governors) and circulated to 800 *Kreisblätter*.[9] In 1907 Schweinburg was appointed to co-ordinate all the CVDI's propaganda material.[10] However, Schweinburg's manifold activities did not count as part of the 'Jew press', unless it was propagandistically convenient to do so.

Nor was the Liberal press itself predominantly Jewish in its composition. The *Kölnische Zeitung* and the *Münchener Neueste Nachrichten*, which tended towards the National Liberals, had virtually no Jewish collaborators, though this had not been true in the 1870s (e.g. the brothers Gumbinner of the *Kölnische Zeitung*). Bismarck's remark of the *National-Zeitung*, that it had always been a Jew paper ('das war immer ein Judenblatt'),[11] perhaps a reference to its foundation by Bernhard Wolff, scarcely applied by the time he made it in the late 1870s.

In effect, the *Judenpresse* meant the papers owned by Mosse, Ullstein and Sonnemann, centred on Berlin and Frankfurt. The most respected of these was undoubtedly the *Frankfurter Zeitung*. Its unique status dates from 1866 when the banker Leopold Sonnemann, its co-founder, became sole owner and editor until his death in 1909. The paper had numerous eminent Jewish contributors during the Wilhelmine period, including August Stein, its Berlin correspondent, Bernhard Guthmann, its London correspondent, Gustav Stolper, its Vienna correspondent, Arthur Feiler, who became its political editor in 1910, and its American correspondent Wilhelm Cohnstaedt, son of Ludwig Cohnstaedt, first head of the commerce section and then the paper's managing director. But, its Semitic reputation notwithstanding, it never failed to attract non-Jews to leading editorial and business posts.[12]

The *Berliner Tageblatt*, reflecting the post-unification shift of political power to the new capital, was founded in 1872 by Rudolf Mosse, already the proprietor of a successful advertising agency. To this he added in the 1880s the less intellectual *Berliner Volkszeitung* and *Berliner Morgenzeitung*. He also took over the publication of the *Allgemeine Zeitung des Judentums* and the printing of the C.V.'s journal, though without ever influencing the editorial line of either, which occasionally differed from that of the *Berliner Tageblatt*, especially during the 1907 Block elections. The *Berliner Tageblatt*, like the

9   Willi Boelcke, *Krupp und die Hohenzollern. Aus der Korrespondenz der Familie Krupp, 1850–1916*, Berlin: Rütten & Loening, 1956, pp. 67, 90; Hartmut Kaelble, *Industrielle Interessenpolitik in der Wilhelminischen Gesellschaft (CVDI 1895–1914)*, Berlin: de Gruyter, 1967, p. 17.
10   Kaelble, *Industrielle Interessenpolitik*, p. 19.
11   Busch, *Tagebuchblätter*, vol. III, p. 44.
12   Werner Becker, 'Die Rolle der liberalen Presse', *KuR*, pp. 76–8; Ernst Kahn, 'The Frankfurter Zeitung', *LBYB* II (1957), pp. 228–35.

Frankfurter Zeitung, acquired the services of eminent non-Jews; they were, however, overshadowed by Mosse's nephew, Theodor Wolff, who became its editor-in-chief in 1906 and combined journalism with direct political activity in a way not rivalled since Sonnemann's heyday.[13] But his direct impact on Imperial politics did not come until the war years.

The house of Ullstein, established by Leopold and directed after his death in 1899 by his sons, bought rather than founded new papers, beginning in 1877 with the *Berliner Zeitung* and culminating in the *Vossische Zeitung*, Berlin's oldest paper, acquired in 1914. The company also launched the *Berliner Morgenpost*, which had the highest circulation of any in the capital, as well as the *Berliner Zeitung am Mittag* and the very popular *Berliner Illustrierte Zeitung*. It was, however, only with the acquisition of the *Vossische* that Ullstein could compete with the *Berliner Tageblatt* and the *Frankfurter Zeitung* in addressing a politically serious public. It did so not through its nominal editor Hermann Bachmann, but through a man who stood second only to Theodor Wolff among Liberal Jewish journalists, Georg Bernhard. Bernhard had already been editor of the commerce section of the *Berliner Morgenpost* when he left Ullstein in 1903, but returned to the business side of the publishing house in 1908, having meanwhile founded his own publications and freelanced for, among others, Maximilian Harden's *Zukunft*. He had originally belonged to the right wing of the SPD, but considered himself a Liberal by the time he gained command of the *Vossische Zeitung*. He also drew closer to Jewish organizational life, in a way that Wolff never did, and became a member of the C.V. executive.[14]

In important ways all these papers had common features that identified them to their enemies if not always to their readers. They were liberal in the broad sense that they addressed, and spoke for, the urban bourgeoisie, that they favoured trade and industry over agriculture and an extension of parliamentary against executive power. They carried a business section, dedicated to the workings of a free-market economy, that made them the principal forum for the interests of trade and finance in the Empire. On a number of important issues, however, the *Berliner Tageblatt* and the *Frankfurter Zeitung* diverged: on the question of colonies, the navy, social reform and relationships with the SPD the *Berliner Tageblatt* tended to take a more right-wing line than its rival. It was only under Wolff that an evolution towards a more democratic outlook began, and the convergence of the two papers' views on

13 Becker, 'Die Rolle der liberalen Presse', *KuR*, pp. 83–86; Werner E. Mosse, 'Rudolf Mosse and the House of Mosse, 1867–1920', *LBYB* IV (1959), pp. 237–9; Theodor Wolff, *Vollendete Tatsachen*, Berlin: R. Mosse, 1918.
14 Becker, 'Die Rolle der liberalen Presse', *KuR*, pp. 93–4; Hermann Ullstein, *The Rise and Fall of the House of Ullstein*, New York: Simon & Schuster, [1943].

war aims and internal political development climaxed in November 1918 in their joint support for the foundation of the *Deutsche Demokratische Partei*, in which Wolff had taken the initiative.

Compared with these men, whose activities stood at the centre of high politics, there were others whose journalistic enterprises were more of interest for their symptomatic character. The most important was no doubt the baptized Maximilian Harden, of whose idiosyncratic journal *Die Zukunft* it would be easier to say what it opposed than what it favoured. Though it became increasingly critical of the Emperor's personal rule and achieved its hour of glory in exposing the decadence of the court 'camarilla' in 1907, it cannot be classified as Liberal and it disapproved deeply of Jewish involvement with finance capital, often in terms that were indistinguishable from those of the anti-Semitic Right.[15]

Further still to the Right was Paul Nikolaus Cossmann, a convert to Catholicism, whose *Süddeutsche Monatshefte*, founded in 1903, achieved notoriety during and after the war for its support of pan-German and *völkisch* causes. At the other ideological extreme was Siegfried Jacobsohn's *Schaubühne*, in which Kurt Tucholsky's contributions began to appear in 1913, but it, too, was a marginal phenomenon before 1914 and achieved fame only through its transformation into the *Weltbühne* in 1918.[16]

If one wants to trace significant Jewish impact on the policies of the Empire, one must leave self-indulgent sectors of the media and return to the world of Sonnemann and Wolff, bearing in mind Wilhelm Treue's conclusion 'that the overwhelming part of German ... Jews supported private-enterprise capitalism, as it existed in Germany. ... It can be assumed, leaving aside only the Jews active as Social Democrats, that the great mass of the Jews of Germany were, until 1918, state-supporting in economic and social policy and to that extent "conservative".'[17] But, given the structural peculiarity of capitalism 'as it existed in Germany', and its far from secure social and political implantation, we cannot be surprised either that this degree of 'state affirmation' was greeted with rejection or scepticism by those who regarded themselves as the true pillars of state and society; or that that rejection led men in

15   See B. Uwe Weller, *Maximilian Harden und die 'Zukunft'*, Bremen: Schönemann, 1970; Harry F. Young, *Censor Germaniae. The Critic in Opposition from Bismarck to the Rise of Nazism*, The Hague: Nijhoff, 1959.
16   See Wolfram Selig, *Paul Nikolaus Cossmann und die Süddeutschen Monatshefte von 1914–1918. Ein Beitrag zur Geschichte der nationalen Publizistik im ersten Weltkrieg*, Osnabrück: Fromm, 1967; Alf Enseling, *Die Weltbühne. Organ der intellektuellen Linken*, Münster: Fahle, 1962.
17   Wilhelm Treue, 'Zur Frage der wirtschaftlichen Motive im deutschen Antisemitismus', *KuR*, pp. 388–9.

the economic activities in which Jews predominated into political paths that were not conservative in the context of the Wilhelminian *Reich*.

From 1878 onwards the major forces in German economic life could be divided into three groups. The first was dominated by the East Elbian landowners, protectionist in tariff policy, monarchist and autocratic in politics. It was close to the *Deutschkonservative Partei* and from 1893 onwards was organized in the Agrarian League (*Bund der Landwirte*, BdL). The second was dominated by heavy industry, also protectionist, paternalistic in its managerial attitudes, organised through the *Central verband der Deutschen Industrie*, linked politically with the *Reichspartei* and the right wing of the National Liberals. The third was dominated by manufacturing industry, especially chemical and electrical, and by trade and finance, export-conscious and free-trading. Its principal representative was the *Bund der Industriellen* (BdI); politically it was linked with the left wing of the National Liberals and the various parties of Left Liberalism. The relationship of these three was characterized by shifting alliances. The first two shared an interest in tariffs and firm government, the last two in an expansion of Germany's industrial base and export potential. More than once – in 1897, in 1909 and in 1913 – there were attempts to unite all three into a concentration (*Sammlung*) of employers and producers.

Interest group politics in Imperial Germany was dominated by a mixture of rational policy considerations and ideology. Thus the place of Jews in any given organization depended not only on its policy demands but on its *Weltanschauung*. Typical of the misunderstandings that could arise out of these dual criteria was the contretemps between Bismarck and Franz Mendelssohn in 1884 over the stock exchange tax.[18] Thus there were political as well as professional reasons why there should be virtually no Jews in the Agrarian League. Ideology, not economic interest, demanded that it restrict membership to anyone who 'belongs to a Christian denomination'.[19] One of the few men of Jewish descent who rose in the League's hierarchy, Count Limburg-Stirum, was not allowed to forget his ancestry. As leader of the Prussian Conservatives he had opposed the government's Canal Bill, which landowners feared would lower grain prices and raise wages, and found himself denounced by the Kaiser as 'Judenabkömmling' and 'Judenjunge'.[20]

On the other hand, it was economic interest rather than ideology that kept Jews out of the CVDI. There were few Jews in heavy industry and the

18 See above, p. 104.
19 Article 4 of the constitution of the Agrarian League. Hans-Jürgen Puhle, *Agrarische Interessenpolitik und preußischer Konservatismus im wilhelminischen Reich (1893–1914)*, Hanover: Verlag für Literatur und Zeitgeschehen, 1966, p. 35.
20 Bülow, *Denkwürdigkeiten*, vol. I, p. 296.

CVDI's leaders were in frequent alliance with the anti-Semitic BdL and, through the *Reichspartei*, with the anti-Semitic *Deutschkonservative*. On the other hand, even the largest firms of Rhine, Ruhr and Silesia were dependent on bank capital, and representatives of the banks, sometimes Jewish, sat on their boards: Louis Hagen (formerly Levy) of Cologne, 'the king of the supervisory boards', sat on almost every Rhenish-Westphalian board, in nineteen cases as chairman or deputy chairman;[21] Eugen Gutmann (baptized, like Hagen), founder of the Dresdner Bank, was a director of Kirdorf's *Gelsenkirchener Bergwerks AG*;[22] Eduard Arnhold, who had risen from the family bank of *Gebrüder Arnhold* to becoming a director of the Dresdner Bank and a member of the Prussian Upper House, held a total of 119 directorships, mainly in brewing and the electrical industry.[23] Moreover it was characteristic of the political climate of the Empire that almost any industrialist, however *bien-pensant*, was suspect as an associate of Jews. During the First World War the naval command saw 'the whole of Jewish finance' behind Vice-Chancellor Karl Helfferich's opposition to the planned U-boat offensive.[24] (Helfferich, formerly Director of the Deutsche Bank, was in every other respect an unimpeachable hawk.) Thus, though the leading industrialists, however right wing in domestic political matters, steered scrupulously clear of personal involvement in anti-Semitism, their narrow and authoritarian outlook repelled the majority of Jewish financiers and industrialists. The major exception was Louis Hagen, with his exceptionally close links in the world of coal and iron, who became one of the directors of the *Deutscher Verlagsverein*, founded in 1914, largely to save the mass-circulation Scherl publishing house from falling into the hands of the 'repulsive and repugnant ... Mosse publishers',[25] and creating the basis for Alfred Hugenberg's control of a popular right-wing press during the Weimar Republic. Ironically the main financiers of this

21   *Neue Deutsche Biographie*, vol. VII, pp. 479–80; W. E. Mosse, *German Economy*, pp. 250–2.
22   *Neue Deutsche Biographie*, vol. VII, p. 347, Mosse, *German Economy*, pp. 224–6.
23   *Universal Jewish Encyclopaedia*, New York: The Universal Jewish Encyclopaedia, Inc., 1939, vol. I, p. 484; Mosse, *German Economy*, pp. 155–6, 254.
24   Herwig, *The German Naval Officer Corps*, p. 97; similar accusation in Westarp, *Konservative Politik*, vol. II, p. 36. See also Fritz Fischer, *Griff nach der Weltmacht. Die Kriegszielpolitik des kaiserlichen Deutschland, 1914–1918*, 3rd edn, Düsseldorf: Droste, 1964, p. 377, fn. 49; John G. Williamson, *Karl Helfferich. Economist, Financier, Politician*, Princeton, NJ: Princeton University Press, 1971, pp. 155–62.
25   'abstoßenden und widerwärtigen ... Mosse'schen Verlag', Paul Reusch to Franz Haniel, July 1913, cit. Dirk Stegmann, *Die Erben Bismarcks. Parteien und Verbände in der Spätphase des wilhelminischen Deutschlands*, Cologne and Berlin: Kiepenheuer & Wietsch, 1970, p. 174.

transaction were the Oppenheim bank.[26] There was a precedent for this episode in 1880, when Bleichröder offered Bismarck his help in buying the National Liberal *Kölnische Zeitung*, to save it 'from the well-known Socialist Sonnemann'.[27]

The same instincts kept Jews from large-scale support of other organizations which might be thought to further the interests of finance and industry, but which were infiltrated with varying degrees of right-wing ideology, namely the Pan-German League, the Colonial Society (*Kolonialgesellschaft*) and the Army League (*Wehrverein*). These and other bodies may be loosely called imperialist, in that they favoured the expansion of German diplomatic and commercial power, a course of action that was favoured by a near-consensus of public opinion, including sizeable sections of Social Democracy. This consensus also included the greater part of Jewish opinion – especially, though not only, the opinion of those with financial and industrial interests. Within this wide and vague consensus, however, there were frequent, sometimes bitter, conflicts between those who saw German expansion in territorial terms, risking, if necessary, military confrontation, and those who favoured peaceful penetration of spheres of interest, a division of opinion that can be traced from the 1880s to the war aims debate after 1914. Since these policy options had internal political implications – the first requiring a more authoritarian regime than the second – it is all the less surprising that the majority of Jewish opinion was on the side of free-trade imperialism; in Marx's words, the replacement 'of the feudal method of warfare by the commercial ..., guns by capital'.[28]

Thus Jews did not find the Pan-German League attractive. Although it did not adopt a formally anti-Semitic and racialist programme until 1920,[29] it grew increasingly hospitable to anti-Semitism after *Justizrat* Heinrich Claß became chairman in 1908. Claß himself was the author of the imperialist-dictatorial manifesto, *Wenn ich der Kaiser wär'*, in which he advocated the exclusion of all Jews – racially defined – from German citizenship,[30] and most leading anti-Semitic parliamentarians were members of the League. Professing Jews were not to be found in its ranks, but prominent baptized deputies who belonged included Otto Arendt and Robert Friedberg, as well as the

26 Stürmer, Teichmann and Treue, *Wägen und Wagen*, pp. 304–7.
27 Stern, *Gold and Iron*, pp. 274–5.
28 Cit. Eckhart Kehr, *Schlachtflottenbau und Parteipolitik, 1894–1901*, Berlin: E. Ebering, 1930 (Historische Studien 197), p. 339.
29 Alfred Kruck, *Geschichte des Alldeutschen Verbandes, 1890–1939*, Wiesbaden: Franz Steiner, 1954, p. 130.
30 Daniel Frymann (i.e. Heinrich Claß), *Wenn ich der Kaiser wär. Politische Wahrheiten und Notwendigkeiten*, Leipzig: Dieterich, 1912, esp. pp. 74–8.

National Liberal leaders Bassermann and Stresemann who had Jewish wives.[31] But in the eyes of most otherwise conformist Jews, it did not compensate for its far-Right associations with its advocacy of overseas expansion.

A closely-related organization which was often explicit in its anti-Semitism was the Army League, given the temptation to identify all pacifism as Jewish-inspired. When the German Peace Society (*Deutsche Friedensgesellschaft*) pointed to the small armies of Britain and the USA as an example to follow, the League claimed that this would 'convince only adherents of Mammon-ism'.[32] Bernstein was pointedly referred to as 'konfessionslos' (i.e. without religious affiliation).[33] The overlap in membership and leadership positions of ultra-nationalist bodies and journals was considerable. Rudolf Lebius, a journalist with and later editor of the anti-Semitic *Staatsbürger-Zeitung*, was also active in the League Against Social Democrary (*Reichsverband gegen die Sozialdemokratie*).[34] The League's founder, General Georg von Liebert, was also a member of the Pan-German League and of the executive of the Navy League (*Flottenverein*).[35] The founder of the Army League, General August Keim, had been a controversial chairman of the Navy League in 1907 and on the executive of the Pan-German League as a close supporter of Claß.[36] Indeed there was a hard core of full-time and even professional activists in the radical Right of the late Wilhelmine period who were to be found, often in leading positions, in almost every one of the increasing number of ultra-nationalist 'leagues' – in addition to Keim and Liebert, they included the Munich publisher J. F. Lehmann, the academic and publicist Dietrich Schäfer, Dr Heinrich Rippler, the editor of the leading right-wing daily, *Tägliche Rundschau*, the aristocratic demagogues Kurd von Strantz and Count Ernst zu Reventlow, and General Karl Litzmann. All of these were committed, in some cases fanatical, anti-Semites. Nor were their organizations' pretensions to non-partisanship very convincing. Keim's membership of the *Antiultramontaner Reichsverband* caused problems in the Navy League, since

31   Kruck, *Geschichte des Alldeutschen Verbandes*, p. 19; Hamburger, *Juden im öffentlichen Leben Deutschlands*, p. 130; Roger Chickering, *We Men Who Feel Most German. A Cultural Study of the Pan-German League 1886–1914*, London: Allen & Unwin, 1984, pp. 46, 134, 160, 249 fn. 118.

32   *Tägliche Rundschau*, 30 May 1914.

33   *Die Friedensbewegung und ihre Gefahr für das deutsche Volk*, Deutscher Wehrverein e.V., Schrift 10, Berlin, 1914, p. 10. ZStP Rk 1415. See also *MVA*, XXII/12, 5 June 1912, p. 93.

34   Stegmann, *Die Erben Bismarcks*, p. 277.

35   Dieter Fricke, 'Der Reichsverband gegen die Sozialdemokratie von seiner Gründung bis zu den Reichstagswahlen von 1907', *ZfG* VII, 1959, pp. 246–7, 249.

36   Marilyn Shevin Coetzee, *The German Army League. Popular Nationalism in Imperial Germany*, New York: Oxford University Press, 1990, p. 23.

it inhibited co-operation with the *Zentrum*. Keim's ally, Dr Gerhard, became Secretary of the Pan-German League after the fall of his mentor, besides joining the Berlin-Brandenburg regional executive of the *Antiultramontaner Reichsverband*.[37] And though National Liberals, including the party leader, Ernst Bassermann, joined the Army League, they soon found that they were not welcome. The National Liberal deputy Hermann Paasche was obliged to resign the vice-presidency of the Army League on the grounds that he was 'a friend of both Jews and Socialists'.[38] The war merely exacerbated the latent anti-Semitism in these various leagues; by 1920 the Army League's journal *Die Wehr* was printing excerpts from *The Protocols of the Elders of Zion*.[39] But it was the implied as much as the explicit anti-Semitism of these leagues that had warned most Jews off; and even though most German Jews held the Catholic Church at arm's length, the 'anti-ultramontanism' of Keim and others conveyed a degree of fanaticism that was alien to their secular world-view.

The Navy League's journal also gave an enthusiastic reception to Claß's *Wenn ich der Kaiser wär'*.[40] In general, however, both the Colonial Society and the Navy League avoided anti-Semitism in their public statements. With their more explicitly mercantile appeal they might have been thought more attractive to Jewish membership. Initially this was indeed so. In the pessimistic economic climate of the early 1880s overseas possessions seemed to many the answer to the apparent crisis of overproduction. The membership list of the provisional committee for 'opening up Central East Africa for commercial purposes' (1882) reads like a list of the National Liberal *Sezession* – it included the Lord Mayor of Berlin, Max von Forckenbeck, Rudolf Mosse, the industrialist Isidor Loewe and the banker Eugen Landau.[41] The bigger and much more important Colonial Society, founded in the same year, expressed what the historian Hans-Ulrich Wehler has called an 'embracing bourgeois consensus' and contained almost every name in industry and shipping; almost every notable intellectual and politician from Right of centre to far Right, from the National Liberals Rudolf von Bennigsen and Heinrich von Sybel through Karl Rudolf Friedenthal to the anti-Semites Adolf Wagner and Adolf Stoecker; and a generous sprinkling of Jewish bankers, including Franz von Mendelssohn, Arthur Salomonsohn of the

---

37 Geoff Eley, *Reshaping the German Right. Radical Nationalism and Political Change After Bismarck*, New Haven, Conn., and London: Yale University Press, pp. 171–5, 114. See also Chickering, *We Men*, p. 139.
38 Coetzee, *The German Army League*, p. 49.
39 Ibid., p. 120.
40 Angress, *LBYB* (1983), p. 397, fn. 105.
41 Wehler, *Bismarck und der Imperialismus*, p. 368.

Disconto-Gesellschaft, Hermann Wallich and Max Steinthal of the Deutsche Bank, Paul Schwabach, Carl Fürstenberg, and the Cologne bank of Sal. Oppenheim & Cie.[42]

But, equally significantly, the principal spokesman of dogmatic free-trade, of 'trade and not dominion',[43] was Ludwig Bamberger, denounced by the *Preußische Jahrbücher* as having 'the point of view of the haggling Jew … for whom it is the greatest honour to push his way in everywhere and to be thrown out through every door, who attaches himself to production and trade sometimes as a useful go-between, often as a parasite, with self-interest and without independence'.[44]

Great as was the initial enthusiasm for colonies, it waned as the colonial movement became more and more part of the programme of *Weltpolitik*, a development that led to a split in 1896, the year in which the Kaiser sent a telegram to the Boer President Kruger, congratulating him on repulsing the British-backed Jameson raid. As the probable price for territorial expansion, namely the hostility of Britain, became more evident, its following came to resemble that of the Pan-German League (of which it became a corporate affiliate). Those who did not welcome British political antagonism or commercial retaliation had seceded. Even a banker like Carl Fürstenberg of the *Berliner Handelsgesellschaft*, who virtually controlled the export trade of German South-West Africa through the diamond monopoly which he had founded, opposed the colonial programme on general diplomatic grounds.[45] Arnhold, however, with his closer links with heavy industry, remained on the executive.[46]

The same development, from enthusiasm to doubt, characterized the attitudes of Jewish bankers and businessmen to a German navy. The navy was, as we have seen, intended to be a middle-class pendant to the aristocratic army, and indeed evoked the strong hostility of agrarian interests. There was no greater initial enthusiast for the navy than the managing director of the HAPAG shipping line, Albert Ballin, who telegraphed his pleasure to the Kaiser at the Reichstag's acceptance of the Naval Bill and had indeed submitted a memorandum in favour of naval expansion.[47] In company with a

42   Ibid., pp. 165–6, 176.
43   *StBR*, 26 June 1884, col. 1066.
44   *PJ* LIV/1, July 1884, p. 97.
45   Carl Fürstenberg, *Die Lebensgeschichte eines deutschen Bankiers, niedergeschrieben von Hans Fürstenberg*, Wiesbaden: Rheinische Verlags-Anstalt, 1961, p. 339.
46   Jäger, *Unternehmer*, p. 142.
47   'Eine Abhandlung über die Notwendigkeit der schnelleren Verstärkung unserer Kriegsmarine' (1899), in Volker Berghahn, *Der Tirpitz-Plan. Genesis und Verfall einer innenpolitischen Krisenstrategie*, Düsseldorf: Droste, 1971, p. 141.

large number of other Hamburg notables, many of them Jewish (Siegmund Hinrichsen, Eduard Isaakson, R. L. Oppenheimer, Hermann Robinow), he signed the invitation for the opening meeting of the Navy League in Hamburg.[48] He remained a vice-chairman of the League; in 1907 he signed an appeal for funds that raised 60,000 RM and as late as 1912 he was still in the executive of the Hamburg branch.[49] The Silesian magnate Fritz Friedländer even offered to underwrite the League's entire budget in 1900.[50] But much of their colleagues' enthusiasm was waning and Ballin's own public political actions implied profound dislike and fear of the most probable outcome of the Empire's naval policy: a breach with the Anglo-Saxon world. He demonstrated this in his dialogue with Sir Ernest Cassel, which led to the Haldane Mission of 1912 with the aim of ending the naval race; his approaches to Churchill in 1912 to bring about a meeting with Tirpitz; and his visit to London in July 1914 at the request of the State Secretary for Foreign Affairs, Gottlieb von Jagow.[51] As the war approached, it was pan-German industrialists – Ernst von Borsig, Alfred Hugenberg, Adolf and Emil Kirdorf – who outnumbered financiers, whether Jewish or not, among the League's backers and office-holders.[52] It would in any case be misleading to suggest that there was predominant Jewish-Liberal support for the navy from the beginning. In contrast with the *Berliner Tageblatt*, the *Frankfurter Zeitung* was hostile.[53]

Two men of Jewish descent were, however, crucial to the success of Grand Admiral Tirpitz's publicity drive. The first was Victor Schweinburg, already mentioned. His career as the first general secretary of the Navy League, which he owed to Krupp, lasted only a year. Tirpitz himself did not like the 'air of business interest' that he gave to the agitation, and his unsavoury reputation made it easy for Agrarian and anti-Semitic opponents of the navy to sneer at 'Jewish naval enthusiasm'.[54] However, Schweinburg's continued

48 Kehr, *Schlachtflottenbau*, p. 240, fn. 50; Ekkehard Böhm, *Überseehandel und Flottenbau. Hanseatische Kaufmannschaft und deutsche Seerüstung, 1879–1902*, Düsseldorf: Bertelsmann, 1972, pp. 92, 100, 174–5, 177, 182–3, 223.
49 Jäger, *Unternehmer*, pp. 145, 210; Cecil, *Albert Ballin. Business and Politics in Imperial Germany, 1888–1918*, Princeton: Princeton University Press, 1967, pp. 152–9.
50 Eley, *Reshaping the German Right*, p. 137.
51 Bernhard Huldermann, *Albert Ballin*, 2nd edn, Oldenburg and Berlin: Stalling, 1922, pp. 247–8, 275; Cecil, *Ballin*, pp. 161–2, 189–95, 204–9.
52 Jäger, *Unternehmer*, pp. 144–5.
53 *BT*, 11 January 1898; *FZ*, 25 March 1898; *Geschichte der Frankfurter Zeitung, 1856–1906*, Frankfurt: Verlag der Frankfurter Zeitung, 1906, pp. 677–82.
54 'jüdische Marine-Begeisterung', *Deutsche Reform*, 22 October 1899; Kehr, *Schlachtflottenbau*, pp. 175, 184–7. See also the National Liberal *Münchener Neueste Nachrichten*, 7 November 1899.

command of the Krupp and CVDI press in no way diminished his propaganda role.

Tirpitz's propaganda chief, 'the crown of the pro-Navy Jews',[55] was Ernst Hermann Levy von Halle, the son of a Hamburg lawyer, Dr Heymann Levy, who had been a member of the Bürgerschaft, one of the few Jews in the anti-Prussian *Reformverein* and a close collaborator of Isaak Wolffson. The son changed his name to Levy von Halle in 1894, by which time he had also converted to Protestantism. In 1897 he joined the Imperial Navy Office on the recommendation of Gustav von Schmoller, and also became Associate Professor at the University of Berlin and honorary Professor at the Berlin Technical University. He was a voluminous author on naval matters;[56] his principal achievements as official propagandist were to edit, under the pseudonym Nauticus, the *Jahrbuch für Deutschlands Seeinteressen*, which was sponsored by the Navy Office, and to organize the petition of academics on behalf of the Naval Bill.[57]

Von Halle could best be described as a conservative technocrat, who was principally concerned with establishing Germany securely as a world power and with establishing a domestic basis for this against the parliamentary opposition of the Left and the economic opposition of the far Right. This predestined him for a crucial role in one of the most critical episodes of the later Wilhelminian Empire, that of the attempted financial reform. This proposal had a fiscal purpose: to produce the increased revenue demanded by *Weltpolitik*, in particular the naval programme; and a political programme: to conciliate the middle classes and the Liberal parties by placing the main burden on the landed classes by means of an inheritance tax. Tirpitz strongly supported the proposal, as did almost the whole range of middle-class opinion from the Pan-German League to the major bankers and merchant shipping directors – Ballin, Friedrich Hallgarten, the Mendelssohns and the (non-Jewish) head of the biggest of all banks, Arthur von Gwinner of the Deutsche Bank – and almost all economists of repute.[58] Tirpitz released von Halle to join the Imperial Treasury, where he became director of the Econ-omic Policy Office (*Leiter des volkswirtschaftlichen Büros*) and supervised the

55 'die Krone der flottenfreundlichen Juden', Kehr, *Schlachtflottenbau*, p. 185.

56 Tjard Schwarz and Ernst von Halle, *Die Schiffbauindustrie in Deutschland und im Auslande*, Berlin: E. S. Mittler, 1902; Ernst Levy von Halle, *Volks- und Seewirthschaft. Reden und Aufsätze*, 2 vols., Berlin: E. S. Mittler, 1902.

57 Biographical details kindly supplied by Professor Peter-Christian Witt, University of Bielefeld. See also Kehr, *Schlachtflottenbau*, pp. 101–3.

58 Peter-Christian Witt, *Die Finanzpolitik des Deutschen Reiches von 1903 bis 1911*, Lübeck and Hamburg: Matthiesen, 1970, pp. 224–5, 276.

compilation of the two-volume *Denkschrift zur Reichsreform*, a formidably-argued documentation in favour of the government's proposal.[59] The proposal was defeated in the Reichstag by the combined forces of the Right and the *Zentrum*; not the least of the Right's objections to the proposal, frequently voiced in the BdL's *Deutsche Tageszeitung* and the *Kreuz-Zeitung*, was its alleged Jewish inspiration: 'The *spiritus rector* is Herr Levy von Halle', wrote Gustav Roesicke, the editor of the *Deutsche Tageszeitung* to Conrad von Wangenheim, the BdL's chairman: 'You can recognize the nature of the efforts by these origins.'[60]

The defeat of the reform led to the resignation of Chancellor Bülow and the end of the 'Bülow Block', an attempt to base the government on a coalition of the Liberal and Conservative parties and to include the Left-Liberal deputies in the government majority. To appreciate the importance of the end of this experiment, it is necessary to go back ten years and trace the fluctuating relationships between the three principal interest-groupings in the German economy. For most of the time between 1897, when Johannes Miquel first proclaimed the desirability of a *Sammlung* (concentration) of the 'producing classes',[61] and 1907 the main dividing line was that of tariffs. The occasion of Miquel's initiative was the expiry of the trade treaties of Caprivi's chancellorship which, by liberalizing trade and thus giving Germany's export industries an unprecedented fillip, also earned the opposition of the Agrarians. To underline the difficulty inherent in Miquel's enterprise, a rival body to the CVDI, the *Bund der Industriellen*, had been founded two years earlier to represent manufacturing and exporting industry, but also a rather less authoritarian posture in industrial relations. The Miquel plan failed: the 'economic election programme' for the 1898 Reichstag elections, intended to gain support from the entire range of entrepreneurs for higher tariffs, was in the end signed only by the BdL, the CVDI, the two Conservative parties and some National Liberals. Anyone seeking Jewish names would have had to look in the counter-manifesto of those who preferred a renewal of the treaties and opposed the much higher tariffs proposed by Chancellor Bülow. The list included, among many names from the major banks and the sea-ports, those of the founder of the *Berliner Handelsgesellschaft*, Ludwig Max Goldberger, the presiding senior member (*Präsident des Ältestenkollegiums*) of the Berlin merchant corporation, *Geheimer Kommerzienrat* Wilhelm Herz, Emil Rathenau

59 Ibid., pp. 217–19.
60 1 April 1909, ZStP, Nachlaß Wangenheim 4. Information provided by Professor Witt.
61 John C. G. Roehl, *Germany Without Bismarck. The Crisis of Government in the Second Reich, 1890–1900*, London: Batsford, 1967, pp. 246–51.

of the AEG and leading Berlin industrialists, including Ernst Simon and Isidor Loewe.[62]

On Ballin's initiative this anti-tariff lobby took firmer form and the *Handelsvertragsverein* was founded in 1900. Its initial meeting was impressively attended: those present included Carl Fürstenberg, Jakob Riesser, Aby S. Warburg, Ludwig Max Goldberger and Eduard Arnhold (bankers); Franz Oppenheim, James Simon, Emil Rathenau and Julius Loewe (manufacturers); and Ballin and Hinrichsen (shipping). On the death of the first chairman, Georg von Siemens of the Deutsche Bank, GKR Wilhelm Herz succeeded to that post. The executive included Arnhold, Goldberger, Rathenau, Hinrichsen and GKR Michael Herz of the Posen Chamber of Commerce. The vice-chairman was Georg Gothein, a later president of the *Abwehr-Verein*.[63] The cleavage between the two branches of industry went beyond questions of tariff interest. The free-trading wing tended also to be less interested in the constant plans to undermine the powers of the Reichstag through some form of corporatist representation, and they were less hostile to trade unionism. For instance, the League against Social Democracy, founded in the aftermath of the SPD's huge gains in the 1903 Reichstag elections, was largely coterminous with the CVDI, the Pan-German League and the *Reichspartei*.

Nevertheless, as the episode of the Bülow Block showed, the cleavage was not unbridgeable. Those sections of the German middle class who felt excluded from power or favour did not, in the main, respond with negative resentment but with redoubled attempts at integration, and the so-called 'Hottentot elections' of 1907 provided an opportunity for this. The proximate cause of the premature election was the Reichstag's rejection of the colonial budget after the rising in German South-West Africa. The *Zentrum*'s opposition to the government on this issue gave the Left Liberals their chance to replace them in the government's favour; the joint enmity of Social Democracy and clericalism towards German national honour cemented the alliance. The new Director of Colonies, soon to be State Secretary for Colonies, Bernhard Dernburg, was director of the Darmstädter Bank and had a Liberal background. He was also of Jewish descent, though his father, the National Liberal Friedrich Dernburg, had already been baptized. Nevertheless, this daring innovation, unique in peace-time Wilhelminian Germany, evoked one of the *Zentrum*'s rare public anti-Semitic outbursts, when its spokesman, Hermann Roeren, who belonged to its Right 'integralist' wing, complained of the 'stock jobber and counting-house tone' of the colonial administration.[64]

62   Stegmann, *Die Erben Bismarcks*, pp. 74–6.
63   Ibid., pp. 79–81; Walther Borgius, *Der Handelsvertragsverein. Ein Rückblick auf die ersten drei Jahre seiner Tätigkeit*, Berlin: F. Siemenroth, 1903, pp. 12–21, 67–8.
64   Bülow, *Denkwürdigkeiten*, vol. II, p. 267.

The Dernburg episode showed how even a second-generation Protestant in public life could not lose his Jewish image. His appointment, according to the *Staatsbürger-Zeitung*, 'will not allow the Jews' ecstasy of joy to come to an end'; it was the climax of an 'undermining operation' to open the state service to Jews.[65] The mere mention of his name sufficed to reduce a congress of the Agrarian League to laughter.[66] The *Allgemeine Zeitung des Judentums* took the hint. It responded by welcoming the appointment of someone 'whom *we* have ceased to regard as a Jew for a long time, but in whom the anti-Semites, and not only they, see only the descendant of Jews [*Judenstämmling*].'[67]

Even before the colonial episode, the government had taken steps to secure funds for an all-out election campaign against the Social Democrats. A *Komitee Patria* had been founded under the aegis of the head of the Imperial Chancellery, Freiherr von Loebell, and the industrialist and leader of the *Reichspartei*, Freiherr von Zedlitz-Neukirch,[68] aided by the inevitable Victor Schweinburg, much to Bülow's disapproval.[69] The re-alignment of parties made fund-raising much easier. Among the signatories of the appeal were Ballin, Paul von Schwabach, by now the proprietor of the Bleichröder bank, and Robert von Mendelssohn. Out of a total of nearly 600,000 RM Schwabach and Mendelssohn donated 30,000 RM each, Franz von Mendelssohn 25,000 and the HAPAG 15,000.[70] The Emperor personally expressed to Robert von Mendelssohn his recognition of the contributors' generosity.[71]

The failure of the finance reform demonstrated the obstacles to complete equality for the middle class in Imperial Germany. But the break-up of the short-lived Bülow Block did not bring about an immediate reversion to the older alignment. Hence, though the government's Reichstag majority was once more 'black and blue', the CVDI, the BdI and the world of finance joined in the biggest attempt yet at a united front for industry – the *Hansa-Bund für Gewerbe, Handel und Industrie.*

The immediate occasion for the foundation of the *Hansa-Bund* in 1909 was

65 *Staatsbürger-Zeitung*, 16 September 1906 a.m.; similarly *Das Reich*, 17 September 1906, *Deutsche Zeitung*, 18 September 1906.
66 *Korrespondenz des Bundes der Landwirte*, 1907/12, 11 February 1907.
67 'Nach den Wahlen', *AZJ*, 8 February 1907, p. 61.
68 Dieter Fricke, 'Der deutsche Imperialismus und die Reichstagswahlen von 1907', *ZfG* IX (1961), pp. 554–5.
69 'Unverläßlich', 'ein übler Stänkerer', Bülow, *Denkwürdigkeiten*, vol. I, pp. 295, 390.
70 Fricke, *ZfG* IX, pp. 557–8, 560–561.
71 Ludwig Elm, *Zwischen Fortschritt und Reaktion. Geschichte der Parteien der liberalen Bourgeoisie in Deutschland 1893–1918*, Berlin: Akademie-Verlag, 1968, p. 192.

the imminence of the finance reform debate in the Reichstag, which united not merely the traditionally hostile wings of industry and the banks, but representatives of white-collar workers and artisans – veterans of the *Handelsvertragsverein* and of its opponents. The fact that numerous well-known Jewish names were to be found among the signatories of the founding appeal and in the directorate and executive of the new organization therefore signified little. For beside Warburg, Emil Rathenau, Fürstenberg and Schwabach there were industrial magnates of the Ruhr (Emil Kirdorf and Hugo Stinnes), the Saar (Carl Röchling) and Silesia (Ewald Hilger).[72] Nevertheless, conservative and liberal forces were not entirely equal. The president was Jakob Riesser of the Darmstädter Bank, the baptized nephew of Gabriel Riesser, and banking and manufacturing industry predominated in its counsels. In contrast with the proclaimed principles of the Agrarian League, the *Hansa-Bund* opened its ranks, 'as is to be most strongly emphasized, without distinction of religious or confessional conviction'.[73] The context of this statement, made in Cologne, suggests that it was aimed at least as much at welcoming Catholics as Jews. It was also consistent with the *Hansa-Bund*'s general insistence on equality of rights (Gleichberechtigung); which it demanded for German small businesses, trade and industry 'on the basis of their economic importance', and for the filling of all public positions 'solely on the basis of personal competence and qualifications'.[74] Indeed, in the heavily-ideologized atmosphere of Imperial Germany, it was inevitable that both the *Handelsvertragsverein* and the *Hansa-Bund* should acquire an ideological identity. The official historian of the *Handelsvertragsverein* confirmed that by the 1903 election its 'specifically liberal character had become stabilised'.[75] The ideological character of the *Hansa-Bund* was even more explicit. Agrarian and anti-Semitic newspapers knew exactly what to make of its programme: 'What his uncle, Gabriel Riesser, the well-known pioneer of Jewish emancipation aimed at, but did not quite achieve, the president of the *Hansa-Bund* seeks to complete. All that is now missing is the unrestricted admission of the Jews to the officer and diplomatic corps.'[76] Jewish organizations and the Jewish media reciprocated. The DIGB saw the *Hansa-Bund* as a 'great movement, which also applies itself indirectly against anti-Semitism. ... Therefore all our co-religionists are advised to join the

72 Stegmann, *Die Erben Bismarcks*, pp. 178–81.
73 Jacob Riesser, *Der Hansabund*. Staatsbürgerliche Flugschriften 6, Jena: Eugen Diederichs, 1912, p. 22.
74 'Die Richtlinien des Hansabundes', Felix Salomon, *Die deutschen Parteiprogramme*, Heft 2, 2nd edn, Leipzig: Teubner, 1912, p. 162.
75 Borgius, *Der Handelsvertragsverein*, p. 33.
76 'Der Hansabund ohne Maske', *Reichsbote*, 25 July 1913.

Hansa-Bund'.[77] The *Allgemeine Zeitung des Judentums* was equally explicit: 'The *Hansa-Bund* inscribes on its colours: justice. That also is what we German Jews want, justice that regulates the degree of effort and reciprocal obligations of citizens and the state. ... We do not want to play our part there as Jews, but as citizens of the Jewish faith. We do not want to proclaim denominational differences there, but to find justice.'[78] As in 1878, what affected German-Jewish opinion was not that it had a collective interest in free trade, but that it had a collective stake in a more liberal Empire.

The over-arching alliance within the *Hansa-Bund* did not last long. To the inherent divergences of interest there were added the strains of foreign policy and the threat of war during the second Morocco crisis of 1911, as well as a gradual evolution in the direction of party politics. The re-unification of the Left Liberals in 1910 and the cautious leftward shift of the National Liberal Party's Reichstag grouping under Bassermann's guidance suggested a trend in the direction the *Hansa-Bund*'s majority desired. What finally became intolerable to the CVDI wing was Riesser's refusal to issue an unconditionally anti-SPD instruction for the run-offs in the 1912 Reichstag elections. In June 1911 the representatives of heavy industry walked out, leaving Riesser in the presidency, surrounded in the directorate by Arthur Salomonsohn, Franz von Mendelssohn, Schwabach, Warburg and, perhaps more surprisingly, Louis Hagen, all duly denounced by the secessionists as the 'stock exchange mob'.[79]

Riesser's flirtation with the Left split the forces of industry and torpedoed Ballin's plans to arrange a meeting between him and the Kaiser; Ballin was obliged to reconsider his intention of inviting Riesser to the Kiel regatta.[80] But it was not the first occasion on which the bourgeois Left saw the SPD as a potential ally. In 1903 the *Handelsvertragsverein* had deplored the failure of Liberal electors to support the SPD in run-off elections, with the result that many constituencies in which there was an anti-Agrarian majority were lost.[81] The growing intensity of electoral confrontation in the last three Reichstag elections of the Empire, the increasing role that well-financed and ideologically-directed interest groups played in electoral politics, meant that Jewish involvement with the Liberal parties required harder choices and presented sizeable dilemmas. The main reasons for this were the fluctuating alliance policy of the Left Liberals and the division of the National Liberals into a heavy-industrial-protectionist-authoritarian wing and a more oppositional one associated with manufacturing industry, banking and free trade. In

77 Cit. *DT*, 6 July 1909.
78 'Neue Fronten', *AZJ*, 20 August 1909, p. 6.
79 Jäger, *Unternehmer*, p. 156.
80 Treutler to Bethmann-Hollweg, ZStP, Rk 1422/4, 62–3.
81 Borgius, *Der Handelsvertragsverein*, pp. 22–3.

1903 and 1912 there was a fairly clear-cut antagonism between conservative protectionism and liberal free trade. The *Handelvertragsverein* may have deplored in 1903 that 'the multi-coloured character of political life in Germany prevented the grouping of two great blocs on the basis of specific platforms',[82] but the bi-polarity of the contest was fairly easily recognizable. As 1912 approached this was even clearer, so that the *Allgemeine Zeitung des Judentums* could assert well before the election that 'in the political combination that the organization of the two great economic groups, the *Hansa-Bund* and the Agrarian League, has brought about, we German Jews cannot avoid taking sides in view of our civic interests'.[83]

In 1907, however, the Bülow Block saw the various Liberal parties allied with the Conservatives – including anti-Semites – and this provided both an opportunity and a risk. Bülow's aim was to incorporate the middle classes more closely into support for the regime and to do so on the question that most readily lent itself to such an alliance: foreign and colonial policy, 'a place in the sun'. The widespread support that this strategy secured from the moneyed Jewish bourgeoisie through the *Komitee Patria* has already been mentioned. The *Allgemeine Zeitung* saw nothing but good in the victory of the Block, with the 'unmistakeable turn for the better for Liberalism' that had begun with the appointment of Dernburg. Above all it hoped for a general liberalization of political life, so that every Jew 'can choose his political affiliation in his own way, and is not to a certain extent obliged to belong to the opposition, obliged to sit on the Left'.[84] The C.V., however, saw the outcome as far from favourable[85] and the President of the *Abwehr–Verein*, Theodor Barth, was so disgusted by his party's alliance with reaction that he resigned from it. With his fellow-secessionists he went on to found the *Demokratische Vereinigung*.[86] (Barth himself died in 1909.)

One problem arising out of the creation of the Block was that of Jewish parliamentary candidates. The Progressive parties had nominated Jews in a number of winnable seats in 1903, in particular in Frankfurt and Breslau West, though these had in the event gone to Social Democrats. In 1907 these and similar seats could be won for the Block only with right-wing votes, for whom a Progressive Jew would have been anathema. A memorandum by Ludwig Asch, a Jewish member of the FVp, therefore recommended 'a common Democratic Christian candidate' for Frankfurt;[87] his advice was

82   Borgius, *Der Handelsvertragsverein*, p. 128.
83   'Neue Fronten', *AZJ*, 20 August 1909, p. 6.
84   'Nach den Wahlen', *AZJ*, 8 February 1907, p. 61; similarly 'Die Blockpolitik und der Antisemitismus', ibid., 13 December 1907, p. 589.
85   *IdR*, XIII/2, February 1907, p. 101; ibid., XIII/3, March 1907, p. 143.
86   On Barth see above, pp. 139, 145.
87   ZStP, Rk 1794(67).

followed there and in Breslau, in both cases with success. Of the various components of the Block the FVg, which stood closest to the *Abwehr-Verein*, was least happy about this alliance with the Right. It asked its supporters to vote only for those candidates in the run-off who would respect all established civic rights.[88] In practice this meant preferring a Social Democrat to a Conservative.

These Liberal concessions to anti-Semitism no doubt accounted for the increased support that Jews gave to the *Zentrum* at this election. Both the *Deutsche Israelitische Zeitung* and the *Israelitisches Familienblatt* recommended their (respectively) Orthodox and Liberal readers to vote for the *Zentrum*, not only on grounds of religious affinity, but as a more reliable guardian of Jewish civil rights than the National Liberals.[89] The C.V., too, in its election statement, acknowledged that the *Zentrum* was, with certain exceptions, a reliable defender of constitutional rights[90] and the Zionist Carl Kassel warned Jews against becoming involved in another *Kulturkampf*.[91]

Once the *Zentrum* reverted to its alliance with the Conservative parties after 1909, relations between it and Jewish organizations cooled off again, while their alliance with Liberalism resumed its former strength. The 1912 election, above all, was dominated by the battle between 'modern' and 'traditional' Germany, in which the *Zentrum* and the Catholic Church generally were part of the traditional coalition and the great majority of Jews sided with modernity. A crucial combatant in this battle was the *Hansa-Bund*, with its impressive organizational and financial resources.

While it would still have been a caricature to describe the *Hansa-Bund*, even after the secession of heavy industry, as Jewish, it did now represent a coherent political and economic policy that could, within the stereotypes of German politics, be recognized as such. Men like Ballin may have had doubts about Riesser's flirtation with radicalism; on the other hand, few Jewish businessmen were openly identified with the industrial Right: Baron Simon Alfred von Oppenheim sat with Louis Hagen in the *Deutscher Verlagsverein*,[92] and Leopold Levy (Hohensalza) was one of the eleven National Liberals in the Prussian Landtag who joined the *Altnationalliberaler Verein*, dissociating themselves from the leftward course of Bassermann,[93] but there were not many others.

The manner of the *Hansa-Bund*'s intervention in the 1912 election

---

88 Lamberti, Activism, p. 64.
89 *DIZ*, 31 January 1907; *ISFAM*, 10 January 1907; *KVZ*, 2 February 1907.
90 *IdR*, XIII/1 January 1907, p. 1.
91 *Die Welt*, 1906/46, pp. 6–7, cit. Toury, *Orientierungen*, p. 255.
92 See above, pp. 174–5.
93 Reiss, *Von Bassermann zu Stresemann*, pp. 166–7.

presented a striking contrast to that of the *Komitee Patria* of 1907, to which so many of its members had belonged. It worked hard to ensure that Progressives and National Liberals did not oppose each other in the first round, and refused campaign funds (which could amount to 10,000 RM) where there was not a united Liberal candidate.[94] 'We have nothing. The *Hansa-Bund* has everything', one member of the FVP executive, Otto Fischbeck, complained at a joint conference of the two parties.[95] The total amount at the disposal of the *Hansa-Bund* for campaign finance has been estimated at between 1.5 and 2.5 million RM.[96] Some of the meetings called to avert conflicting candidatures took place on *Hansa-Bund* premises and in several instances *Hansa-Bund* officials acted as mediators.[97] By directing its propaganda against 'agrarian demagogy', it approved, by implication, the run-off agreement between Progressives and Social Democrats[98] and helped to bring about the unprecedented Left victory at the polls that reflected the unpopularity of the 'blue–black' bloc's tariffs and taxes.

Following its defeat, the Right was in no doubt what the issue had been: 'On our side, German Imperial and royal monarchy, against Republicanism and the Jewish international! On our side, fear of God and Christianity against faithlessness and materialism. On our side, love of one's neighbour and honest labour against communism and mammonism.'[99] Since the election the Jews 'regard themselves as our leaders', wrote the *Kreuz-Zeitung*, having already remarked on the power of 'the world of banking and the stock market, which likes to give itself the euphemistic name of ' "deutsches Bürgertum" '.[100] The Agrarian League, which had borne the brunt of the *Hansa-Bund*'s campaign, was even more vehement: it had experienced an unprecedented 'attack ... by the Jewish spirit on our national and *völkisch* life'.[101] For Elard von Oldenburg-Januschau the campaign had been 'a battle by international Jewry against the Christian-monarchical state'.[102] Before long the 1912

94　Elm, *Zwischen Forschritt und Reaktion*, p. 213; Bertram, *Die Wahlen zum deutschen Reichstag*, pp. 79, 106, 155; Nipperdey, *Organisation*, p. 157.
95　ZStP 60 Vo3, 32 (113–17).
96　Siegfried Mielke, *Der Hansa-Bund für Handel, Gewerbe und Industrie, 1909–1914*, Göttingen: Vandenhoeck & Ruprecht, 1975, pp. 151–2.
97　*Ibid.*, p. 150; ZStP 60 Vo3, 32(107).
98　Mielke, *Der Hansa-Bund*, pp. 163–4.
99　*KZ*, 27 January 1912.
100　*KZ*, 4 January 1912, 14 January 1912; similarly *ibid.*, 19, 20, 28 January 1912.
101　'Das Judentum im Wahlkampf', *DT*, 25 January 1912.
102　19. General-Versammlung des Bundes der Landwirte. *Korrespondenz des Bundes der Landwirte*, 20 February 1912.

election entered into anti-Semitic mythology as the 'Jew elections' (*Judenwahlen*).[103]

Given this thickening of the atmosphere, it was not surprising that Jewish opinion-leaders saw the election in equally simple terms. Three days before polling the *Allgemeine Zeitung* called for a 'front against the Right'.[104] The journal of the Jewish student fraternities saw the fight as one between democracy and feudalism, in which Jews 'stand in the democratic camp'.[105] In terms of party affiliation the tone of the campaign brought about clarification after the ambiguities of 1907. The close relationship between the bulk of Jewish voters and the Progressives was restored. The Social Democrats, now more closely allied with the Progressives, were viewed more favourably than ever before.[106] The *Zentrum*, which had withdrawn its candidates in 87 constituencies in order to give a clear run to a Conservative or anti-Semite, was once more viewed with suspicion. Though some Jewish papers, especially the Orthodox, continued to speak kindly of it,[107] most comment was unfavourable. The *Zentrum* was criticized not only for its alliance with the frequently anti-Semitic Right, but for an increase in its own anti-Semitic rhetoric.[108] Indeed the *Kölnische Volkszeitung* had the last word, complaining of 'various newspapers, with huge circulations, which serve free-thinking and progressive propaganda [and] are financed by Jewish capital'.[109]

It is therefore not surprising that though Jewish spokesmen welcomed the strengthening of the Left and, above all, the defeat of many Conservatives and anti-Semites, they were also impressed by the intensity of the right-wing backlash.[110] It is in this context that the initially secret 'League against Jewish Arrogance' was founded on 11 February, 1912. It belonged to the lunatic fringe, if only because for its members the 'Jewish Question' was the dominant political issue, in contrast with most Conservatives, pan-Germans or even followers of the parliamentary anti-Semitic parties, for whom it was a

103 Werner Jochmann, 'Struktur und Funktion des deutschen Antisemitismus', *WD*, p. 464, fn. 255.
104 'Die Front nach rechts', *AZJ*, 9 January 1912, p. 14; similarly *IGB*, 1912, p. 298.
105 *K.C.-Blätter*, 1 January 1912, p. 60, cit. Angress, *LBYB* (1983), p. 374.
106 Lamberti, *Activism*, pp. 114, 117; Angress, *LBYB* (1983), p. 374, 376.
107 Angress, *LBYB* (1983), pp. 374, 385–6.
108 *IdR* XVII/12, December 1911, pp. 678–9; XVIII/2, February 1912, pp. 85–6; XVIII/3, March 1912, p. 150; XVIII/4, April 1912, p. 165.
109 *KVZ*, 4 March 1912.
110 *IdR* XVIII/2, February 1912, pp. 81–2; XVIII/3, March 1912, pp. 121–8; *AZJ*, 19 January 1912, pp. 26–7; 2 February 1912, pp. 50–1; 9 February 1912, pp. 62–3.

subordinate component of a generally anti-liberal and anti-democratic set of fears and instincts. But within that fringe its founders were prominent. They included Theodor Fritsch, Germany's leading publicist of racial anti-Semitism, editor of the *Hammer-Blätter* and compiler of the *Antisemiten-Katechismus*; Count Ernst zu Reventlow of the Pan-German League; and Alfred Roth of the Commercial Employees' Union, a founder of the post-war right-wing terrorist group, the *Deutschvölkischer Schutz- und Trutzbund*.[111] Had the war not broken out two years later, leading to defeat and revolution, they might have gone down as yet another quixotic sect; as it turned out, they formed a direct link with the early National Socialist Party.

In the short run, the anti-Semitic reaction seemed exaggerated and Jewish scepticism justified. The new Reichstag had a narrow pro-*Hansa-Bund* majority, but this was not very cohesive and in any case Reichstag majorities did not govern the *Reich*. Apart from a modest inheritance tax nothing happened to qualify Riesser's assertion that 'we are immensely far removed from the practical implementation of the equal rights of all classes and professions and all citizens.'[112] The constitutional reforms necessary to bring this about – the abolition of the graded Prussian franchise and ministerial responsibility in the Reichstag – were as distant as ever.

The Position in 1914

Within the political structure of the *Reich* four main party camps could be identified, their character stable from 1867 onwards, when universal suffrage was first introduced, though their relative strengths had shifted. These were an Agrarian-Conservative camp, concentrated in, but not restricted to, Prussia, which was aristocratic, bureaucratic and military and with an addition of heavy industry; a Catholic-Conservative camp, embracing a wide social spectrum; a bourgeois-Liberal camp, subject to fragmentation and strained by the divergent attractions of nationalism and imperialism on the one hand and domestic reform on the other; and a working-class Socialist camp. Within this alignment Jews had a recognized place. While individual predilections could account for all sorts of idiosyncratic positions, most Jews were, for the whole of this period, in the Liberal camp. Up to the Liberal split of 1879 that meant predominant support for the National Liberals, thereafter for the Left Liberals or Progressives in their various guises. Most authorities agree that

111   Willi Buch, *50 Jahre antisemitische Bewegung, Beiträge zu ihrer Geschichte*, Munich: Deutscher Volksverlag, 1937, p. 27; Pulzer, *The Rise of Political Anti-Semitism*, p. 283; Jochmann, 'Struktur und Funktion', *WD*, p. 477.
112   Jakob Riesser, 'Der deutsche Handel im letzten Vierteljahrhundert', *Nord und Süd*, 37. Jg., Heft 465, cit. Stegmann, *Die Erben Bismarcks*, p. 351.

towards the end of the Imperial period about two-thirds of Jews voted Progressive,[113] which meant that about one Progressive vote in ten came from a Jewish elector. Of the rest about half voted Social Democrat;[114] the remainder were scattered among the *Zentrum*, National Liberals and minor parties, preferences that were sometimes influenced by local or regional factors.

This political concentration, widely recognized and commented on at the time, reveals much about German society and the Jewish minority's place in it. For by 1914 none of the three aspects of the Jewish Question, as outlined in the Introduction,[115] had been satisfactorily answered.

The formal answer of the Germans to the Jews was: assimilate. Yet the policies of the *Reich* and state governments in refusing or restricting career opportunities made this condition unfulfillable, even if we ignore the anti-Semitism of the parties and press of the Right. But official action and unofficial propaganda were intertwined, logically as well as politically. As Rathenau observed: 'The extinction of this aversion is hardly to be hoped for, as long as the state permits, recommends and justifies it by acting in the opposite direction', with the consequence that: 'In the days of every German Jew's youth there is a painful moment which he remembers for the whole of his life: when he becomes fully conscious for the first time that he has entered the world as a second-class citizen and that no skill or merit can ever free him from this situation.'[116]

But the Jewish answer to the Germans was also ambiguous. To aim at being a 'German citizen of the Jewish faith' was a formula, not a solution. As early as 1835 that ardent prophet of emancipation, Abraham Geiger, made it clear that he was not one of those who wanted 'to abandon everything willingly in order to achieve only one gain'.[117] The 'religious autonomy' that Geiger wanted to retain was bound to have social, and therefore political, implications.

Nor was there unanimity in the answer Jews gave to themselves. Much remained of the liberal-enlightened view that civic equality was to be achieved through the good works of Christians. 'On motions of this kind',

113 Hamburger, *Juden im öffentlichen Leben Deutschlands*, p. 163; Toury, *Orientierungen*, p. 275.

114 Hamburger, *Juden im öffentlichen Leben Deutschlands*, pp. 145–8; Toury, *Orientierungen*, p. 275.

115 See above, p. 1.

116 Walther Rathenau, 'Staat und Judentum', *Gesammelte Werke*, vol. I, pp. 186, 189.

117 Abraham Geiger, 'Das Judentum unserer Zeit und die Bestrebungen in ihm', in Ludwig Geiger (ed.), *Abraham Geigers Nachgelassene Schriften*, Breslau: Jacobsohn 1875–8, vol. I, pp. 453–4.

Lasker told the Reichstag of the North German Confederation, 'that affect me and my co-religionists so closely, it is my principle not to ask to speak.'[118] In this he echoed Moses Mendelssohn's view that nothing furthered a cause more than disinterestedness: 'Jews should not get in the least involved. ... As soon as that happens, [the involvement] is bound to be misconstrued and maliciously interpreted.'[119] The very existence of the C.V., the *Verband der Deutschen Juden* and other representative institutions, with their growing membership, illustrated the decline of this viewpoint, but it was far from dead, since many Jews continued to regard these organizations with indifference, embarrassment or hostility. Nevertheless, the overlap between public office and Jewish activism, no longer unusual in 1914, shows how the notion had become again accepted that on certain issues Jews, *qua* Jews, had an interest to represent.

But it is also evident that Jews as a group had recognizable political outlooks that distinguished them from their fellow-citizens, even if the details must be impressionistic. One can deduce this from the kinds of newspapers that Jews were known to read, from their concentration in major cities and their occupational structure, from the decline of the politically indifferent rural and itinerant Jew. One can generalize more confidently about those Jews who became active in public life. There are very few points of view that did not at some time or another have a prominent Jewish advocate, especially if one includes the baptized. Against Otto Arendt, the principal non-Agrarian defender of bimetallism, one can put Ludwig Bamberger, the principal defender of the gold standard; against Leopold Levy, uncritical supporter of an anti-Polish *Ostmarkenpolitik*, his colleague Moritz Baerwald, who favoured conciliation; against the National Liberals Friedberg and Schiffer, opponents of any political reform in Prussia, its National Liberal supporters Schwabach and Riesser; against Victor Schweinburg and Georg Bernhard, journalists of free trade and international peace like August Stein and Theodor Wolff; and among Social Democrats, against ethically inspired internationalists like Bernstein and Eisner one can put conformist patriots like Landsberg and Stampfer, and against the revolutionary critics of imperialism, Luxemburg and Hilferding, imperialists like Bloch and Cohen-Reuß. Yet such a list, ranging from pan-Germans to pacifists and from bankers to anarchists, would be misleading.

More Jews were politically active to the left-of-centre than to the right. Within the National Liberal Party, the furthest right that most Jews were prepared to consider, more Jews were active on behalf of the left wing than

118　*StBRNB*, 16 June 1868, vol. I, p. 496.
119　Moses Mendelssohn, 'An den Baron Hirschen in Dresen', 18 October 1775, *Gesammelte Schriften*, vol. V, p. 640.

of the right. Especially among its non-parliamentary supporters, who were mainly bankers (Fürstenberg, Riesser, Dernburg, Witting, Warburg, Speyer), the balance was towards the *Hansa-Bund* and co-operation with the Progressives rather than in favour of a producers' concentration (*Sammlung*). Among the few parliamentarians and candidates, Felix Schwabach and Bernhard Falk were well to the left of their colleagues, Paul Liepmann more cautiously so. What they favoured was a coalition from Bassermann to (almost) Bebel. It is significant that after 1918 a high proportion of Jewish National Liberals joined the *Deutsche Demokratische Partei*, including Bernhard Dernburg, Carl Melchior (of Warburg & Co.), Falk, Schiffer, the Jena jurist Eduard Rosenthal and even Friedberg.

Among Progressives Jews were numerous in trying to interest their party in labour and social questions: Max Hirsch was no doubt the most eminent, but others included Leopold Rosenow, Siegfried Heckscher, Otto Mugdan and Otto Münsterberg. Enterprises of social research relied disproportionately on Jewish charity. Heckscher, a director of HAPAG, sat on the executive of the *Verein für Sozialpolitik* and the Liberal banker Charles Hallgarten subsidized it.[120]

Perhaps more understandably, Jewish politicians were readier than others to resist encroachments on the rule of law and support law reform. Friedenthal of the *Reichspartei* was the only Jewish deputy to vote for the death penalty in 1876; even he, alone in his party, opposed the Anti-Jesuit Law, for which no Jewish votes were cast.[121] Two other causes dear to many liberal Jews were those of female emancipation and world peace.[122] The founders of the *Deutsche Friedensgesellschaft* included Alfred Fried (the winner of the Nobel Peace Prize in 1911) and Max Hirsch. Its prominent supporters included Professor Moritz Lazarus, Theodor Lessing and Alfred Nossig. The otherwise rather conservative banker Eduard Arnhold managed to combine his interests in the *Deutsche Waffen- und Munitionsgesellschaft* with enthusiasm for the World Peace Conference of 1906. The concern with peace was what united many Socialist and bourgeois Jews. It is this, not revolutionary enthusiasm, that brought so many Jews in the Socialist movement, whether they had been Revisionist or Radical before 1914, into the dissenting minority in the course of the war and finally into the USPD.

All generalizations are risky; all need to be qualified. Not all Radicals, pacifists and liberal social reformers were Jews; by no means all Jews embraced these beliefs. But if one examines the centre of gravity of the political

---

120 Hamburger, *Juden im öffentlichen Leben Deutschlands*, p. 367; *Neue Deutsche Biographie*, vol. VII, pp. 562–3.
121 Hamburger, *Juden im öffentlichen Leben Deutschlands*, p. 553.
122 Toury, *Orientierungen*, p. 238, fn. 39; p. 239, fn. 40.

commitment of individual Jews, one finds it to be in favour of the rule of law, the furthering of education, the reform of society and international understanding. One can further say that Jews were proportionately more in evidence in these movements than non-Jews, and that in founding and furthering some of them the Jewish contribution was decisive.

This is not to say that the Jewish population as a whole, or its spokesmen, were inclined towards democracy or radicalism, let alone revolution. They thought of themselves as patriotic citizens, as 1914 showed; few of them wore their subversive hearts on their sleeves like Kurt Tucholsky. They were critically loyal; excluded from the full embrace of the glory of the Empire (*die Herrlichkeit des Reiches*), they could see its blemishes more easily. They wanted to remove the blemishes, not the *Reich*; hence, many of them saw the Bülow Block as a hope, not a trap. But it does not follow that because they rose to wealth, were flattered with titles and tea-time visits by the Emperor, the *haute bourgeoisie* had become, as Helmut Böhme claims, 'national conservative' as a group.[123] As long as Paul von Schwabach (cited by Böhme as typical of this genre) could say of the Navy League that 'I regard its very existence as pernicious'[124] and Ballin could emphasize his 'marked aversion' towards the Pan-German League,[125] the distance from the unthinking consensus of the court was maintained. 'Jewry', wrote the liberal Protestant theologian Martin Rade in 1912, 'should neither be despised nor driven to unhealthy self-consciousness through passionate Pro and Contra'.[126] To follow this advice in Wilhelmine Germany was perhaps not totally impossible, but it proved too difficult. As a result, there was little Jewish separatism, not much of a Jewish lobby, but instead a way of looking at public affairs that distinguished many Jews from non-Jews of their class.

9   THE FIRST WORLD WAR

Like most of their fellow-citizens, German Jews responded to the outbreak of war in August 1914 with electrified enthusiasm. The Kaiser's words of 5 August, 'I see no parties any longer, I see only Germans', had a particular significance for them, as did the proclamation of a 'civic truce' (*Burgfrieden*) for the duration of the war. The hopes of 1869 now seemed closer than ever to realization, as did the prospects that an 'inner Sedan' would embrace Jews

123   Böhme, *Deutschlands Weg zur Großmacht*, pp. 352–3.
124   Schwabach to Sir Eyre Crowe, 4 September 1912. Paul von Schwabach, *Aus meinen Akten*, Berlin: Flemming & Wiskott, 1927, p. 249.
125   Huldermann, *Albert Ballin*, pp. 201, 333.
126   Cit. Kluke, *Die Stiftungsuniversität Frankfurt-am-Main*, p. 117.

too. The patriotic consensus covered almost the entire spectrum of Jewish opinion. A joint appeal by the C.V. and the *Verband der deutschen Juden* called on all Jews to sacrifice their property and lives ('Gut and Blut'): 'Co-religionists! We call on you to devote your resources to the fatherland above and beyond the call of duty! Hasten voluntarily to the colours! All of you – men and women – place yourselves in the service of the fatherland through personal help of every kind and through donating money and property.'[1] Zionists echoed this call in almost identical words. Out of 'our self-evident loyalty to the German fatherland, we shall, as German citizens, gladly fulfil all demands on our possessions, on life and blood [*Hab und Gut, ... Leben und Blut*].'[2] Even Jews who had emigrated to Palestine volunteered for military service 'out of love for the land of our birth'.[3] As for the Orthodox, all the evidence is that they were as committed in their patriotism as Liberals or Zionists.[4]

There were a number of reasons for this reaction. There is no reason to doubt that in the great majority of cases the sentiments were sincere. But there was also a strong incentive to re-emphasize the patriotism which had been a consistent component of Jewish defensive strategy for the previous two decades. The C.V.'s commitment to the 'cultivation of German sentiment' had been repeated on every conceivable occasion. A few weeks after the outbreak of war Eugen Fuchs ended a patriotic speech to the C.V. with the call, 'Deutschland, Deutschland über alles!'[5] One factor that weighed powerfully with Jews, as with many Gentile Liberals and Socialists, was that the enemy was Tsarist Russia;[6] and any sympathy that Liberal Jews might otherwise have had with Britain and France was neutralized by their perfidy in allying with the Tsar. In an appeal to the Jews of America, the neo-Kantian philosopher Hermann Cohen asked rhetorically whether neutral Jews were to desire victory for 'this Russia' over a 'Germany in whose states the Jew may freely hold his head upright'.[7]

1 *IdR* XX/9, September 1914, p. 339.
2 *JR*, 7 August 1914, p. 343.
3 Egmont Zechlin, *Die deutsche Politik und die Juden im ersten Weltkrieg*, Göttingen: Vandenhoeck & Ruprecht, 1969, p. 91, n. 34.
4 Breuer, *Jüdische Orthodoxie im deutschen Reich*, p. 342.
5 Eugen Fuchs, *Um Deutschtum und Judentum. Reden und Aufsätze (1894–1919)* (ed. Leo Hirschfeld), Frankfurt: Kauffmann, 1919, p. 155.
6 Zionists: 'Feinde ringsum!', *JR*, 7 August 1914, pp. 343–4; 'Der Zar und seine Juden', *JR*, 14 August 1914, p. 345; Liberals: Eugen Fuchs, 'Der Krieg', *IdR* XXI/1–2, January–February 1915, p. 14; *idem*, 'Unter den Waffen', *IdR* XXI/9, September 1915, p. 342.
7 Hermann Cohen, 'Du sollst nicht einhergehen als ein Verleumder. Ein Appell an die Juden Amerikas', in *idem*, *Jüdische Schriften*, vol. II, p. 232.

Many Jews who had been critical of aspects of German public life before the war entered into the spirit of the *Burgfrieden*. Hermann Cohen was convinced that 'the believing Jew … loves his fatherland like his religion and his religion like his fatherland'.[8] Maximilian Harden 'did everything in my power, since the outbreak of the war, to raise and maintain public morale'.[9] Nor was the call for financial sacrifice ignored. Jews, as individuals and as bankers, were prominent subscribers to war loans, sometimes to an extent that caused resentment. In Nuremberg the Lord Mayor, Otto Geßler, appointed six prominent Jewish lawyers to run war relief agencies (*Kriegs-fürsorgeämter*); a quarter of the directors of the *Kriegskreditbank*, formed to relieve economic distress, were Jews, causing Fritsch's *Der Hammer* to claim that war charity was becoming a Jewish monopoly.[10] Nor were Jewish hopes for more conciliatory government policies illusory. The more extreme pan-German and anti-Semitic publications, which were often also critical of the government's failure to prosecute the war more aggressively, were regularly banned by the censors.[11] Rudolf Lebius, the editor of the *Staatsbürger-Zeitung*, was warned that if he did not want his paper to be banned 'it would have to commit itself to a different attitude towards the Jews for peace-time as well'.[12] Kurd von Strantz, a leading member of the Army League, who claimed that the *Berliner Tageblatt* had been created 'for the special interests of a foreign tribe in the German Empire'[13] was banned from speaking in public.[14]

Jews were recruited to a quite unprecedented extent into responsible public positions. The Jewish expert called in to advise governments on technical questions of public finance, commercial or company law or international trade had been a familiar figure in nineteenth- and twentieth-century Germany, a modern descendant of the court Jew and, like his predecessor, subject to the caprices of his ruler. To some extent such votes of confidence could compensate eminent and successful Jews for their exclusion from conventional political careers.[15] The war provided increased scope for them, not only because of the requirements of the war effort, but because the spirit of the *Burgfrieden*

8   Hermann Cohen, 'Religion und Zionismus', *K.C.-Blätter*, May–June 1916, pp. 643–6. *Jüdische Schriften*, vol. II, p. 326.
9   Young, *Censor Germaniae*, pp. 178–9.
10   *AZJ*, *Der Gemeindebote* Nr. 42, 16 October 1914, p. 2; Müller, *Geschichte der Juden in Nürnberg*, p. 168.
11   Jochmann, 'Struktur und Funktion', *WD*, p. 416.
12   Verhandlungsbericht über die Sitzung des Alldeutschen Verbandes am Sonntag, den 24. Oktober 1915, ZStP, Rk 1416 (199), pp. 177–200.
13   Kurd von Strantz, *Ein starkes Volk – ein starkes Heer*, Berlin: Politik, 1914, p. 30.
14   Minister of War to Chancellor Bethmann-Hollweg, 2 February 1916, ZStP, Rk 1417, pp. 8–9.
15   Mosse, *Economic Elite*, pp. 216–17, 294–5.

temporarily removed some taboos. Albert Ballin created a central purchasing agency, *Reichseinkauf*, at the end of August 1914 to ensure essential supplies for the civilian population, initially largely staffed by HAPAG employees. At the beginning of 1915 it moved to Berlin as the *Zentraleinkaufsgesellschaft* (ZEG); Carl Melchior of the Warburg bank joined it after being invalided out of the army. The economist Julius Hirsch was responsible for the regulation of food prices and Eduard Arnhold organized coal supplies through the *Reichskohlenamt*. The Tietz department stores played a crucial role in supplying foodstuffs. The most spectacular administrative achievement of all was that of Walther Rathenau. Sceptical from the start of the chances of a quick victory, he persuaded the government to create a special procurement department in the War Ministry, the *Kriegsrohstoffabteilung* (KRA). If, as has been claimed, Rathenau's organizational skill enabled Germany to prolong its war effort by two years, 'it may well have been a truly fateful contribution by a member of the Jewish economic elite to the course of German, and indeed world, history. ... The organization of the German war-economy was, possibly, the climax of the public achievement of the German-Jewish economic elite.'[16] This sudden elevation of Jews into political prominence was not uncontroversial; under the pressure of anti-Semitism both Rathenau and Melchior vacated their positions within a fairly short period.[17] There nevertheless remained a qualitative difference in the public status of Jews before and during the war.

If members of the economic elite were recruited in their individual capacities, Jewish dignitaries served the government in a representative capacity in matters of foreign policy. This was an even greater step forward. The German government hoped to enlist Jewish bodies in support of their aims of reconstructing Eastern Europe at the expense of Russia. Representative Jews seized the opportunity to get a foot into the front door; in so far as they were Zionists they hoped to advance the claims of Eastern Jewry to be recognized as a nationality. As early as August 1914 the 'German Committee for the Liberation of the Russian Jews' (*Deutsches Komitee zur Befreiung der russischen Juden*), largely Zionist in composition, came into being. In November this transformed itself into the more broadly based *Komitee für den Osten* (KfdO), which was joined, in their individual capacities, by Eugen Fuchs of the C.V., his colleague Maximilian Horwitz, who was also president of the *Verein der deutschen Juden*, Berthold Timendorfer, president of *B'nai B'rith*, Professor Moritz Sobernheim of the DIGB and (briefly) the SPD Reichstag deputy Oscar Cohn.[18]

Although the German government welcomed any help that Jewish

16   Ibid., p. 278.
17   See below, p. 205.
18   Zechlin, *Die deutsche Politik und die Juden*, pp. 132–3.

personalities might give to its own efforts to subvert the national minorities of the Tsarist Empire, the KfdO did not get very far. It did not speak for a consensus of German Jewry. Jewish businessmen and bankers in general steered clear of it. It had a rival in Paul Nathan's *Interkonfessionelles Komitee zur Linderung der Not in den besetzten Gebieten* which, like his *Hilfsverein*, was concerned with much-needed philanthropy rather than utopian cartography. But above all the KfdO's aims did not coincide sufficiently with those of the other parties involved. The German government was unwilling to embark on changes in the civil law in the occupied territories as long as the war lasted. Moreover, it was anxious to secure the collaboration of Polish nationalists who uniformly opposed any Jewish claims to autonomy, whether political or cultural. The response of Polish Jews was also lukewarm. Most of them were not willing, as long as the outcome of the war was uncertain, to appear as collaborators with the Germans and expose themselves to Russian reprisals.

As the star of the KfdO waned, a large number of prominent German Jews, including James Simon, Albert Ballin and leading members of the C.V., the *Verein der Deutschen Juden*, the *Hilfsverein* and *B'nai B'rith*, formed the *Deutsche Vereinigung für die Interessen der osteuropäischen Juden*. This body accepted that pressing for political solutions was premature and largely concentrated on the advancement and protection of the civic rights of East European Jewry.[19] The German authorities, meanwhile, had taken their own initiative in an attempt to satisfy the Jews without antagonizing the Poles and had set up a Jewish Department (*jüdisches Referat*) under the military governor in Warsaw, General Hans von Beseler. The Progressive Reichstag deputy Ludwig Haas was put at its head. One of his many ideas for mobilizing Jews in the German cause was the creation of a Jewish legion to fight Russia under Turkish command, following Turkey's entry into the war on the German side. It foundered on Turkish opposition. Turkey's emergence as an ally of Germany gave the German Zionists a final chance to reconcile their aims with Germany's strategic interests, by pressing the German government to support the establishment of a Jewish national home in Palestine. This strategy was defeated not only by German indifference and Turkish opposition, but by the entry of a sympathetic United States into the war on the Allied side and the publication of the Balfour Declaration by Britain in November 1917.

The last attempt on the part of the various factions within German Jewry to present a united front to the German government was the *Vereinigung jüdischer Organisationen Deutschlands zur Wahrung der Rechte der Juden des Ostens* ('Union of Jewish Organizations of Germany for the Protection of the Jews of the East' – VIOD), founded in January 1918. It embraced both the

19   Ibid., pp. 167–72.

C.V. and Zionists and in that sense was as much an exercise in intra-Jewish reconciliation as in pressure politics. It not only sought to defend the civic rights of the Jews in the German-occupied territories – much extended, following the Russian Revolution and the Russian military collapse – but demanded free immigration, and cultural autonomy for Jews in Palestine and all parts of the Ottoman Empire.[20] Anglo-American support for Zionism had convinced the C.V. that it was now in Germany's interests to compete for Zionist sympathies. One of the issues dividing Zionists from 'patriotic' C.V. supporters, that of appearing to harbour dual loyalties, therefore diminished in importance. In the end the VIOD was no more effective than its predecessors; not only did its leaders over-simplify the problem of integrating Jewish aspirations into German war aims, all their schemes assumed military victory, or at least lasting political influence for Germany and its allies in Eastern Europe and the Middle East. Practical failure should not, however, disguise a change of status. A precedent had been set by the German government in mobilizing Jews *qua* Jews to represent German interests abroad, a precedent that was to be followed in the period following the armistice.

If the spokesmen for German Jews were frustrated in their foreign policy endeavours, they were doubly disillusioned at home. The *Burgfrieden* did not last. The initial response of the Jewish leadership had been to hope that in the newly-found national unity the last relics of anti-Semitism would be buried. For Eugen Fuchs the war would bring 'internal peace, the strongest force for unification' and would demonstrate to all Germans 'what a faithful and genuine component of the whole German people the Jewish population constitutes'.[21] As late as 1916 some Jews continued to share this hope.[22] The reasons why these expectations were a miscalculation are not far to seek. The first is simply that all wars, like all national crises, put an enormous premium on cohesion and conformity. They encourage domestic intolerance and authoritarianism, xenophobia and a search for the 'enemy within'. If these effects were not felt immediately, this was because there was a widespread expectation of a short campaign and a quick victory. Once neither of these materialized, other factors encouraged the re-emergence of anti-Semitism. The rigours of war demanded increasing sacrifices, whether from those on active service or from civilians, and hardships breed resentments. These in

20 Jürgen Matthäus, 'Deutschtum and Judentum under Fire: The Impact of the First World War on the Strategies of the Centralverein and the Zionistische Vereinigung', *LBYB* XXXIII (1988), p. 144; Isaiah Friedman, *Germany, Turkey and Zionism 1897–1918*, Oxford: Oxford University Press, 1977, p. 394.
21 *IdR* XXI/1–2, January–February 1915, pp. 5, 19.
22 E.g. Max Simon, *Der Weltkrieg und die Judenfrage*, Leipzig and Berlin: Teubner, 1916.

turn could be matched with the inherited stereotypes of Jews as cosmopolitans, cowards, exploiters, racketeers and wielders of undue and illegitimate influence. The activists of the extreme Right – the 'national opposition' – had in any case never accepted the *Burgfrieden*, which to them meant appeasing Social Democrats, Liberals, Jews and advocates of a compromise peace. For them domestic politics continued as before the war, in accordance with the agenda of the 1912 elections. Their chief villain among the politicians was Theobald von Bethmann-Hollweg, 'this Chancellor who, helped by the golden and red international, is now doing everything to harm the firm structure of the *Reich* and its dynasties and to undermine its roots',[23] as the pan-German publisher J. F. Lehmann put it to the Gießen chemistry professor Hans von Liebig. Liebig himself coined the term 'B-System' for Bethmann-Hollweg's system of government, in a book that was banned by the censorship on the day that it appeared. For him the dispute about war aims was 'a battle between the objectives of German Jewry and those of the Germanic Germans'.[24]

The debate about war aims genuinely divided German elite opinion; it reflected the debate about imperialism before 1914. While there had been widespread support pre-war for a greater German role in world affairs, there was no agreement on how this should be pursued, and this conflict had considerable implications for domestic as well as foreign policy. In foreign politics, on the one hand there was a predominantly military, territorial and, as time went on, racial imperialism; on the other there was a primary concern with commercial penetration and therefore the maintenance of peace. In domestic politics the first impulse was authoritarian and anti-parliamentary, whereas the other was liberal. The categorizations of Lehmann and Liebig became common currency after 1918, when scapegoats had to be found for the defeat. For the pan-German historian Otto Bonhard there were three main sources of enfeeblement ('Flaumacherei'): Bethmann-Hollweg, Social Democracy and 'certain inter-racially interpenetrated circles of high commerce'.[25] Not all German bankers and financiers were Jews; they never had been. Indeed from the 1860s to 1914 the growth of the composite banks led to the relative and absolute decline of the main category of Jewish commercial activity, the private bank. The largest bank, the Deutsche Bank, had relatively low Jewish participation but had indirect links with the Jewish banking sector. Its president, Georg von Siemens, had been one of the inspirers of the

---

23   J. F. Lehmann to Freiherr Hans von Liebig, 10 April 1916, ZStP, Rk, 1416 (235).
24   Hans von Liebig, *Die Politik von Bethmann-Hollwegs*, repr. Munich: J. F. Lehmann, 1918, p. 278; Zechlin, *Die deutsche Politik und die Juden*, p. 519.
25   'gewisse zwischenvölkisch verfilzte Großhandelskreise', Otto Bonhard, *Geschichte des Alldeutschen Verbandes*, Leipzig and Berlin: Theodor Weicher, 1922, p. 35.

Handelsvertragsverein; his successor Arthur von Gwinner (married to a Speyer) led the warnings against 'annexationism' in the summer of 1914.[26] Heinrich Claß, more specific than Bonhard, names him as the principal villain among the 'so-called German high finance'.[27] One had only to be a banker to become an honorary Jew. Alfred Roth blamed defeat on 'das System Ballin-Rathenau' that allowed Jews to run the war-time planning apparatus[28] and Ludendorff took it for granted that Jews formed part of the 'swamp of international-pacifist defeatist thinking'.[29] They had a point. Both political instinct and commercial interest predisposed the majority of the Jewish economic elite against Armageddon. There is a common strand to Walther Rathenau's mission in 1909 to secure agreement between the rival claims of Krupp and Mannesmann to Moroccan ores, which he tried to solve in a way that would respect French susceptibilities;[30] Ballin's mission to London in July 1914 in a last-minute attempt to mediate; and Paul von Schwabach's letter to Alfred Lord Rothschild on 1 August: 'Only a miracle could now avert the outbreak of war. What depresses me most about that is the certain expectation that England will also draw the sword against us. ... You and I are conscious of having tried, with all our might, to improve relations between our countries.'[31]

When the war did break out Jewish opinion divided, as might have been anticipated from pre-war attitudes. Outright opponents were few, apart from the minority of Jewish revolutionaries and pacifists in the Socialist movement. Among them was Albert Einstein, who had become a Swiss citizen but was working in Berlin at the time. During the war he became acquainted with Romain Rolland, who recorded: 'it is noteworthy that Einstein is Jewish, which explains the internationalism of his position and the caustic character of his criticism.'[32] Kurt Tucholsky, who served in the army for three years, regretted in retrospect that he had not, 'like the great Karl Liebknecht,

26 Fischer, *Griff nach der Weltmacht*, p. 333.

27 Heinrich Claß, *Wider den Strom. Vom Werden und Wachsen der nationalen Opposition im alten Reich*, Leipzig: Koehler, 1932, pp. 321, 343.

28 Otto Armin (i.e. Alfred Roth), *Die Juden in den Kriegs-Gesellschaften und in der Kriegs-Wirtschaft*, Munich: E. Boepple, 1921, p. 14.

29 Erich Ludendorff, *Kriegführung und Politik*, Berlin: E. S. Mittler, 1923, p. 141; see also pp. 322, 330.

30 Hartmut Pogge von Strandmann, 'Rathenau, die Gebrüder Mannesmann und die zweite Marokkokrise', in Immanuel Geiss and Bernd-Jürgen Wendt (eds), *Deutschland und die Weltpolitik im 19. und 20. Jahrhundert. Fritz Fischer zum 65. Geburtstag*, Düsseldorf: Bertelsmann, 1973, pp. 257–67.

31 Schwabach, *Aus meinen Akten*, p. 268.

32 Rivka Horwitz, 'Voices of Opposition to the First World War Among Jewish Thinkers', *LBYB* XXXIII (1988), p. 239.

summoned the courage to say no and resist the draft'.[33] The great majority were divided into enthusiastic patriots and critical patriots. The 'Manifesto of the Ninety-three', issued in support of the justice of Germany's cause, contained the signatures of numerous Jewish academics and artists, including Paul Ehrlich, Fritz Haber, Paul Laband, Max Liebermann and Max Reinhardt.[34] Of Ernst Lissauer's immensely popular *Haßgesang gegen England* (*Hate-Song against England*) the less said the better. But at the time many Jews, and even the *Allgemeine Zeitung*, claimed credit for him[35] and the Emperor decorated him with the Order of the Red Eagle, second class. It would also be misleading to say that all the leading Jewish figures in commerce were necessarily anglophile: it was not true of Riesser, still less of Georg Solmssen or of Georg Bernhard, the editor of the *Vossische Zeitung*.[36] Solmssen and Louis Hagen, both baptized, were among the few persons of Jewish descent who joined the ultra-nationalist *Deutsche Vaterlandspartei* in 1917.

What can be said is that if Jews were not exempt from the war euphoria of 1914, they recovered from it more quickly. When Ballin wrote to Rathenau in December 1917 that they had always been opposed to unrestricted U-boat warfare, they were deceiving themselves.[37] But they could claim that by 1916 they, unlike Kirdorf, Hugenberg and Stinnes, had seen through the slogans and faced reality rationally: they, in company with Dernburg, Schwabach and Warburg, could see not only that the campaign would not defeat Britain, but that it would antagonize the USA.[38]

---

33 Cit. Saul Friedländer, 'Die politischen Veränderungen der Kriegszeit und ihre Auswirkungen auf die Judenfrage', *KuR*, p. 37.

34 Ibid., p. 30, fn. 7.

35 Ludwig Geiger, *Die deutschen Juden und der Krieg. Kriegspolitische Einzelschriften*, 3. Heft, Berlin: C. A. Schwetschke, 1915, p. 74.

36 Jakob Riesser, *England und wir. Finanzielle und wirtschaftliche Kriegswirkungen in England und Deutschland*, Leipzig: S. Hirzel, 1914; Georg Solmssen, 'England und Wir!' (13 November 1916), *Beiträge zur deutschen Politik und Wirtschaft, 1900–1933*, Munich and Leipzig: Duncker & Humblot, 1934, p. 16; Georg Bernhard, *Die Kriegspolitik der 'Vossischen Zeitung'*, Berlin: Vossische Zeitung, 1919.

37 Ballin to Rathenau, December 1917, cit. Jäger, *Unternehmer*, p. 247. On Ballin's hesitations, see Eduard Rosenbaum, 'Albert Ballin. A Note on the Style of his Economic and Political Activities', *LBYB* III (1958), pp. 295–6; also Huldermann, *Albert Ballin*, pp. 326, 328, 329, 334.

38 Ballin to Ludendorff, 19 October 1916. Margarete von Eynern (ed.), *Walther Rathenau. Ein preußischer Europäer. Briefe mit bibliographischen Hinweisen*, Berlin: Vogt, 1955, p. 160; Huldermann, *Albert Ballin*, pp. 334, 359; Fischer, *Griff nach der Weltmacht*, p. 292; Max M. Warburg, *Aus meinen Aufzeichnungen*, New York, 1952, p. 43.

The same division of opinion applied to the question of war aims in general. The 'Memorandum of the Six Federations' of spring 1915 – which united, among others, the Agrarians and both industrial groups, the CVDI and the BdI, in extreme annexationist demands – came up against the *Freie Vaterländische Vereinigung* (later *Deutscher Nationalausschuß*) and its familiar liberal-Jewish membership: Schiffer, Schwabach, the Mendelssohns, Franz Oppenheim, Wilhelm Merton and Riesser, but also Gentile Liberals from the banking and exporting sectors: Gwinner, Carl Duisberg of the chemical industry and the Erzberger wing of the *Zentrum*.[39] It was Schwabach who first took up the possibility of a counter-petition, but it was the by no means racially alien Lujo Brentano who summarized the Memorandum to Hans Delbrück, the editor of the *Preußische Jahrbücher*: 'It signifies a justification for all the reproaches that our enemies abroad have hitherto made against us.'[40] In the drafting of the counter-petition, Theodor Wolff, the editor of the *Berliner Tageblatt*, who shared the task with Delbrück, entered the war aims debate as a major participant. It is tempting to agree with Delbrück that it was precisely because they were outsiders in Wilhelminian society that Jews (and workers) 'had shown a sound political instinct during the war'.[41] What else enabled Ballin to denounce 'the foolish mood of victory, based on nothing but anticipation';[42] Schwabach to appreciate that 'the demands of the [six] Federations presuppose more than the defeat of our enemies – their total destruction';[43] Rathenau to warn Bethmann-Hollweg against 'contemplating the map rather than the globe'?[44]

Certainly many good Protestant patriots, Troeltsch and Harnack, Brentano and Weber, were equally appalled at the pan-German dreams; yet one finds Jewish names again and again in organizations not merely to moderate government policy, but to bring about an end to the war: Hermann Tietz in one circle, along with Felix Pinner, the editor of the *Berliner Tageblatt*'s business supplement, the Social Democrat Paul Hirsch, as well as civil servants and the Catholic social theorist Carl von Sonnenschein;[45] Richard Witting in

39 Stegmann, *Die Erben Bismarcks*, pp. 464, 472.
40 Brentano to Delbrück, 28 June 1915, cit. Anneliese Thimme, *Hans Delbrück als Kritiker der wilhelminischen Epoche*, Düsseldorf: Droste, 1955, p. 121.
41 Hans Delbrück, 'Juden und Proleten', in *idem., Vor und nach dem Weltkriege. Politische und Historische Aufsätze, 1902–1925*, Berlin: Verlag für Politik und Wissenschaft, 1927, p. 437.
42 Cit. Stegmann, *Die Erben Bismarcks*, p. 455.
43 'Zur Eingabe der fünf [*sic*] Verbände', Schwabach, *Aus meinen Akten*, p. 274.
44 Rathenau to Bethmann-Hollweg, 7 September 1914, in *idem., Politische Briefe*, Dresden: Reissner, 1929, p. 10.
45 Georg Tietz, *Hermann Tietz. Geschichte einer Familie und ihrer Warenhäuser* (ed. J. Hirsch and E. Hirsch), Stuttgart: Deutsche Verlags-Anstalt, 1955, p. 182.

another;[46] *Generalkonsul* Eugen Landau in a third, along with Professor Julius Hirsch, later to be State Secretary in the Ministry of Economic Affairs, Rudolf Mosse and Gentile industrialists as mediators between the 'peace circles' and annexationists;[47] and Warburg, Dernburg and Gothein proposing that the *Handelsvertragsverein* should initiate a scheme for post-war international arbitration.[48] Of the principal Jewish-owned newspapers, both the *Berliner Tageblatt* and the *Frankfurter Zeitung* supported the 1917 Peace Resolution of the Reichstag, whereas the *Vossische Zeitung* persisted in its anti-Western, annexationist line.[49] Indeed, as the war dragged on and the war aims debate intensified, the *Berliner Tageblatt* became the principal organ favouring a compromise peace and domestic democratization, a line that did not harm its circulation.[50] Its editor Wolff became a symbol of Jewish-liberal 'defeatism', so that even Gustav Stresemann, not normally given to anti-Semitic outbursts, could point to him to distinguish between 'cosmopolitan' and 'German' feeling.[51] The pan-German Right felt justified in their distrust of the *Burgfrieden* and Bethmann-Hollweg's appeasement of parliament. The 'Reichstag of the Jew-elections', General von Gebsattel claimed, would bring about a 'Jew peace'.[52]

As before, there was no consensus among Jews either on war aims or on domestic reform. Some, but fewer and fewer, could still be found beating the drum: Arthur Salomonsohn was in Tirpitz's expert commission on U-boat warfare, the Prussian Landtag deputy Leopold Levy in the annexationist 'Independent Committee for a German Peace'.[53] Nor should one ignore the element of self-interest contained in the alternative policies. The idea of a Central European Customs Union that the men of the *Mittwochabendgesellschaft* – led by Rathenau and the Deutsche Bank – presented at the beginning of the war was certainly not self-denying. But its contrast with the aims of the peace-through-victory party showed a profoundly different approach to the map of Europe and Germany's internal order.

These activities, and the reactions to them, affected only members of the

46   Jäger, *Unternehmer*, p. 236.
47   Tietz, *Hermann Tietz*, pp. 182–3.
48   Dernburg to Gothein, 25 July 1917, cit. Jäger, *Unternehmer*, p. 238.
49   Becker, 'Die Rolle der liberalen Presse', *KuR*, pp. 79, 87, 95–7, 108–9.
50   Its circulation rose from 235,000 at the beginning of the war to 300,000 at the end. Wernecke, *Der Wille zum Weltgeltung*, p. 319; Becker, 'Die Rolle der liberalen Presse', *KuR*, p. 87.
51   Wolfgang Hartenstein, *Die Anfänge der Deutschen Volkspartei, 1918–1920*, Düsseldorf: Droste, 1962, p. 44.
52   'Judenwahlen – Judenfriede?' *Deutsche Zeitung*, 21 September 1917.
53   Stegmann, *Die Erben Bismarcks*, pp. 471, 465.

Jewish elite. What hit the Jewish population at large like a hammer-blow was the demand for a so-called Jewish census (*Judenzählung*). The proclaimed purpose of this was to investigate whether Jews were making their fair share of sacrifices in the war effort. Its true intention was both demagogic and conspiratorial. From the beginning of the war Theodor Fritsch's *Reichshammerbund* began collecting material on Jewish participation in military service and philanthropic bodies.[54] As we have seen, the members of this 'national opposition' were as hostile to the moderate government of Bethmann-Hollweg as to Jews; what they were assembling was ammunition for the nationalist dictatorship they advocated. They also feared that the war would permanently ease Jewish access to the public service and officer corps. But it was only as the war dragged on and its hardships increased that they found a ready audience for their insinuations that Jews were shirking military service, that those in uniform served disproportionately behind the front and that Jews were excessively prominent in the war-time supply corporations. And it was only with the rise of their sympathizers in the military command, in particular the appointment of Ludendorff as Quartermaster-General of the army, that they could hope for success among the Empire's rulers.

While the War Ministry's plans for a comprehensive enquiry into the military status of Jews were being drawn up, a number of Reichstag deputies, led by Erzberger of the *Zentrum*, demanded a survey of employees in the supply corporations, broken down by sex, age, pay and religion. Sensing the damage this would do to what remained of the *Burgfrieden*, the government vigorously opposed it, but it was unable to stop the army from going ahead with its own survey in October 1916.[55] The census caused offence at various levels. Jewish soldiers resented being singled out for a humiliating questionnaire. Some commanding officers arbitrarily transferred Jewish soldiers from staff to front-line duties. The Jewish population as a whole sensed a charge of collective guilt, 'as if the yellow patch had been sewn back on'.[56] Not much remained of the Emperor's assurance that he saw only Germans.

Stung by Erzberger's innuendo, Carl Melchior resigned from the *Zentraleinkaufsgesellschaft*. Rathenau had already left the KRA in 1915, sensing anti-Semitic pressures.[57] But the *Judenzählung* had a broader effect. The Police President of Frankfurt, Rieß von Scheuernschloß, reported in December 1916 that contributions to war charities had fallen by two-thirds,

54 Jochmann, 'Struktur und Funktion', *WD*, p. 411.
55 Werner T. Angress, 'The German Army's "Judenzählung" of 1916 – Genesis–Consequences–Significance', *LBYB* XXIII (1978), p. 131.
56 Adolf Eckstein, 'Aus der Seele unserer jüdischen Kriegsteilnehmer', *IdR* XXIII/2, February 1917, pp. 68–9.
57 Mosse, *Economic Elite*, p. 278.

and feared the impact on the impending sixth war loan.[58] Beyond annoying the Jews and satisfying the anti-Semites, the census achieved nothing. Its findings were never published. Pressed by *Justizrat* Oskar Cassel for the *Verband der Deutschen Juden*, the War Minister, General Hermann von Stein, acknowledged that 'the conduct of the Jewish soldiers and fellow-citizens during the war' was unconnected with the decision to undertake the survey.[59] Selective statistics leaked to the pan-German agitator Alfred Roth after the end of the war implied the opposite of Stein's assurance.[60] More thorough and scholarly studies by Franz Oppenheimer and the sociologist Jakob Segall, based on the number of Jews killed or wounded, promoted or decorated between 1914 and 1918, suggest that the Jewish contribution was, if anything, disproportionately high.[61]

The *Judenzählung* was the most spectacular, though not the only, symptom of growing anti-Semitism and discrimination in the final years of the war. In April 1918 the Eastern frontier of Prussia was closed to all Polish-Jewish immigrants, under the pretext of a typhus epidemic. All Jewish organizations protested, to no avail. It was a further example of growing intra-Jewish co-operation imposed by the exigencies of the war, though the Jews of Germany were not unanimously sympathetic to their Eastern co-religionists.[62]

The high hopes that the war had raised among the German Jewish community were largely disappointed. True, Jews moved, individually and collectively, nearer the centre of the political stage, but this move evoked more resentment than reward. In public, at least, some of their spokesmen refused to be downhearted. At the time of the *Judenzählung* Eugen Fuchs, now chairman of the C.V., insisted that 'Jews must remain silent ... for the sake of the fatherland';[63] as late as the summer of 1918 he had not abandoned the aspiration that Jews become 'not only German citizens, but members of the people'.[64] But, as the war lengthened, the old eirenic, internationalist, anti-militarist instinct of Jews re-emerged. Until the turn of the military tide

58 Zechlin, *Die deutsche Politik und die Juden*, p. 536; Angress, *LBYB* (1978), p. 131.
59 Angress, *LBYB* (1978), p. 133.
60 Otto Armin [i.e. Alfred Roth], *Die Juden im Heere. Eine statistische Untersuchung*, Munich: E. Boepple, 1919.
61 Franz Oppenheimer, *Die Judenstatistik des preußischen Kriegsministeriums*, Munich: Verlag für Kulturpolitik, 1922; Jacob Segall, *Die deutschen Juden als Soldaten im Kriege 1914–1918. Eine statistische Studie*, Berlin: Philo, 1922.
62 See Jack Wertheimer, *Unwelcome Stangers. Eastern European Jews in Imperial Germany*, New York: Oxford University Press, 1987.
63 *JR*, 9 February 1917, p. 54.
64 Eugen Fuchs, 'Deutschtum und Christentum', *IdR* XXIV/7–8, July–August 1918, p. 280.

against Germany on 8 August 1918, the views of these men had no more impact on the conduct of the war than the *Handelsvertragsverein* and *Hansa-Bund* on Germany's peace-time politics. When they were proved right, when it emerged that the enmity of the Western powers had been irresponsibly provoked, and that the enemy's parliamentary institutions had stood the strain, they were blamed for the failure. But however we may interpret Ballin's suicide on 9 November 1918,[65] it scarcely bears out the pan-German claim that 'every Jew was a voluntary agent of the Entente'.[66] Finally disillusioned with the old regime, the Liberal Jewish leadership welcomed the democratic revolution that ended the war. They saw the events of November 1918 as a step towards 'the self-emancipation of mankind' and a victory for 'the spirit [of] freedom and justice';[67] they were confident that 'a relationship of friendship and sympathy would very soon develop between the new Germany and Jewry.'[68] But at the very moment that these hopes were being voiced General von Gebsattel told the leadership of the Pan-German League 'to take advantage of the situation for fanfares against the Jews and to use the Jews as lightning-rods for all injustice'.[69] That was the view that was to prevail in the end. No more did it follow in 1918 than in 1848 that the cause of the people was identical with that of its Jewish minority. If there was a golden age for the Jews of modern Germany, it came to an end in 1914.

10 THE REVOLUTION OF 1918–1919

The Great War, having begun with a patriotic consensus, ended with a population polarized between out-and-out chauvinists and their critics. Just as the great majority of Jews had been reassured by the civic truce of 1914, so they were disillusioned by its collapse and the resurgence of official and unofficial anti-Semitism in the closing years of the war. While many regretted the passing of the old monarchical order,[1] few believed that it could be restored. The

---

65 Cecil, *Ballin*, p. 345.
66 Friedländer, 'Die politischen Veränderungen der Kriegszeit', *KuR*, p. 53.
67 Jochmann, 'Struktur und Funktion', *WD*, pp. 445–6.
68 'Die Revolution' *NJM* 3, 1918–19, p. 49.
69 Meeting of Pan-German League leadership, 19–20 October 1918. Uwe Lohalm, *Völkischer Radikalismus. Die Geschichte des Deutschvölkischen Schutz- und Trutzbundes 1919–1923*, Hamburg: Leibniz, 1970, p. 53.

1 Donald L. Niewyk, 'The German Jews in Revolution and Revolt, 1918–1919', in Jonathan Frankel et al. (eds), *Studies in Contemporary Jewry IV*, New York: Oxford University Press, 1988, pp. 43–5.

political developments of the war years had re-awakened in many of them the attractions of democracy and internationalism that had been latent in their political mentality in the previous decades. In addition the abdication of the Emperor and the end of the Imperial regime opened the political door to hitherto excluded strata and to oppositional individuals – workers, peasants, left-wing Liberals, Socialists, pacifists and sectarian revolutionaries of many kinds. The majority of these were not Jews, but there was clearly a place for Jews in these categories when war-time radicalization was added to pre-war frustrations.

In the November days two forms of political authority appeared. The first, emerging out of the military and civilian grass-roots revolts, was the Workers' and Soldiers' Councils, varying from moderate to revolutionary in their political orientation, which came together in the Berlin executive (*Vollzugsrat*) and, in December, in the National Council (*Zentralrat*), also sitting in Berlin. Only one Jew sat on these two executives, the moderate Social Democrat Max Cohen-Reuß. The only other Jew prominent in the Council movement was the white-collar trade unionist Julius Kaliski.

The other authorities were the provisional governments of the *Reich* and the various states. The SPD was represented in all of them, in most cases in a dominant position, and shared power either with the USPD, the newly-formed Liberal *Deutsche Demokratische Partei* (DDP) or the *Zentrum*. The extent of Jewish participation in them reflected the trends noted before and during the war: the growing tendency of politically active Jews to join the SPD; the tendency of Jews within the SPD to move to the anti-war USPD when the party split in 1917;[2] and the tendency of most of those of Jewish descent who were in the pre-war Progressive or National Liberal parties to join the DDP. The country's general shift to the Left under the impact of military collapse and the shift to the Left among Jewish politicians both reinforced the opportunities for Jews.

From 10 November onwards the government of the *Reich* was in the hands of a Council of People's Commissars, consisting of three SPD members, of whom one, Otto Landsberg, was a Jew, and three from the USPD, of whom Hugo Haase was a Jew. Three of the state secretaries (*de facto* departmental heads) were also Jews: Hugo Preuß (DDP, Interior), Eugen Schiffer (DDP, Finance; baptized and formerly National Liberal), and Emanuel Wurm (USPD, Food Supplies), as were three of the deputy state secretaries: Joseph Herzfeld (USPD, Interior), Eduard Bernstein (USPD, Finance) and Oskar Cohn (USPD, Food Supplies). Following the elections to the National Assembly of 19 January 1919, a coalition government was formed under Philipp Scheidemann, in which Landsberg, Preuß and Schiffer held cabinet

2   See above, pp. 164–6.

posts, with Bernhard Dernburg (DDP), who was half-Jewish, replacing Schiffer after his resignation and Georg Gothein (DDP), who was also half-Jewish and President of the *Abwehr-Verein*, briefly at the head of the newly-created Treasury Office.

The prominence of Jews in revolutionary Berlin was further illustrated by the new Prussian cabinet, which had a Jewish Prime Minister, Paul Hirsch (SPD), Finance Minister, Hugo Simon (USPD), and Minister of Justice, Kurt Rosenfeld (USPD). Of the four People's Commissars who governed the city of Berlin, three were Jews: Rosenfeld, Hermann Weyl (USPD) and Hugo Heimann (SPD), who became chairman of the city council.

No doubt the most spectacular and controversial example of Jewish revolutionary participation took place in Munich. The first revolutionary government, headed by Kurt Eisner, also contained Edgar Jaffé (USPD) as Minister of Finance. Following the assassination of Eisner and the first constitutional government of Johannes Hoffmann, which contained no Jews, the first (mainly anarchist) Soviet Republic was proclaimed on 7 April, headed by Ernst Toller, Gustav Landauer and Erich Mühsam (non-party) and Arnold Wadler (USPD). Mühsam, Toller and Wadler were all members of the Revolutionary Workers' Council (RAR) of Munich. It was succeeded by the second (Communist) Soviet Republic, the leading members of which included Eugen Leviné, Tovia Axelrod and Ernst Toller. Elsewhere, Jews were thinner on the ground. In Saxony, Richard Lipinski (USPD), who was partly Jewish, was Minister of the Interior. Georg Gradnauer (SPD) became Minister of Justice, then succeeded Lipinski as Minister of the Interior and in March 1919 headed the first constitutional government of Saxony. In Baden Ludwig Marum (SPD) became Minister of Justice and Ludwig Haas (DDP) Minister of the Interior. In Württemberg Berthold Heymann (SPD) became Minister of Education, then of the Interior. In the small state of Anhalt Hermann Cohn (DDP), already prominent in state politics and the C.V. before 1918, was one of the seven members of the provisional government.

The Weimar National Assembly contained fifteen Jews of whom seven belonged to the SPD, four to the USPD and four to the DDP. There were also four baptized Jews (one SPD, two DDP and one DVP) and five others of Jewish descent, four in the DDP and one in the newly-formed right-wing Nationalist Party (DNVP).[3] One new party that did not initially take part in the constitutional life of the new Germany, but at whose foundation Jews were present in great numbers, was the re-named Spartakus League, which became the German Communist Party. It will be discussed below.

In addition to these active politicians a number of other Jews served in influential administrative or advisory positions. Dr Hugo Sinzheimer was

3 See below, p. 237.

briefly Police President of Frankfurt-on-Main. Eduard Rosenthal, Professor of Constitutional Law at Jena, played a leading part in drafting the new constitution of the former Grand Duchy of Sachsen-Weimar and then of the newly-created state of Thuringia, in which Sachsen-Weimar was absorbed. The Viennese economist Otto Neurath headed the socialization commission in Bavaria under Hoffmann's SPD government. The greatest direct influence on the politics of the Weimar Republic was that of Hugo Preuß, who was responsible for the original draft of the republican constitution. Though this was much amended before its final adoption, particularly in the rejection of Preuß's proposal for a unitary state, his remained a powerful inspiration.[4]

This escalation in political activity by Jews met with extreme hostility by the Right, some misgivings in the political centre[5] and great ambivalence within the Jewish community itself. There is little support for the proposition, common in anti-Semitic propaganda, that Jews thrust themselves on to the German body politic in the crisis of 1918–19. With the exception of the leaders of the Bavarian revolution and the Spartacists, none seized power or tried to seize it. The great majority were deputed to their positions by their parties, or even appointed to them by departing monarchs, e.g. Ludwig Haas by the Grand Duke of Baden. Indeed Max Warburg declined the invitation to join Prince Max of Baden's government in September 1918 as Finance Minister on the grounds that a Jew would not be acceptable in that post.[6] Five of the revolutionary Jewish politicians paid with their lives for their activities: Eisner, assassinated in February 1919, Haase, assassinated in October 1919, Leviné executed, and Landauer and Rosa Luxemburg murdered by counter-revolutionary soldiers.

The reaction of German Jews to this sudden invasion of the political stage by Jewish actors was, as might be expected, mixed. As in 1848, the most articulate were not necessarily the most representative. Some Jews certainly welcomed the role that their co-religionists had played in what they saw as a great emancipatory movement, not only in Germany but above all in Russia. In one way or another Arnold Zweig, Martin Buber and Rudolf Kayser, the editor of *Neue Rundschau*, belonged to this group.[7] They were, however, a minority. Most Liberals and Zionists as well as Orthodox, for different reasons, disapproved. Zionists, because many of them felt that Jews had no business

4 Ernest Hamburger, 'Hugo Preuß: Scholar and Statesman', *LBYB* XX (1975), esp. pp. 190–7.
5 See below, pp. 221–3.
6 Alfred Vagts, 'M. M. Warburg & Co.: Ein Bankhaus in der deutschen Weltpolitik', *Vierteljahresschrift für Sozial- und Wirtschaftsgeschichte* 45, 1958, p. 366.
7 Eva Reichmann, 'Der Bewußtseinswandel der deutschen Juden', *KuR*, pp. 555–8; Angress, 'Juden im politischen Leben der Revolutionszeit', in ibid., p. 147.

dictating the politics of their host nations, especially if this meant neglecting the claims of the Jewish people. Indeed, according to Nathan Birnbaum, all they did was to 'endanger ... the Jewish people through their lack of restraint'.[8] Other Zionists, while ready to acknowledge that Jews should play a full part as German citizens, disapproved of the revolutionary extremism. Their calls for 'restraint' and 'tact' were echoed even more emphatically by the principal Liberal organs. The *Allgemeine Zeitung* warned against the 'arrogant and dominant manner' of some young Jewish revolutionaries and regretted that among the leaders of the revolution 'in Northern and Central Germany so many Jews are to be found'.[9] The C.V. also hoped 'that Jews would at this moment avoid leading positions in the state',[10] while the Orthodox *Jüdische Monatshefte* warned that it was not for Jews to exploit the collapse of the monarchy 'to attain power and positions that the old regime had denied them'.[11]

The *Abwehr-Verein* was, if anything, even more censorious of the excessive number of radical Jews in the Revolution: 'It is not the conspicuous Jewish activity in politics that is a matter for reproach ... but the manner in which a number of individuals fail to show the tact that the general political situation of the Jew ... demands, and for which the entirety of their co-religionists have to atone, that causes bitterness.'[12] But the *Abwehr-Verein* objected not only to the way Jewish revolutionaries fuelled anti-Semitism, but to the actions of 'Spartacist scribblers' and 'defamers of the bourgeoisie'.[13] In part this peculiar form of opposition to anti-Semitism may be attributed to the *Abwehr-Verein*'s close association with political Liberalism and its pre-war defence tactic of emphasizing its anti-Socialism. In part the anti-Socialism was a peculiar obsession of the editor of the *Abwehr-Verein*'s journal, Curt Bürger.[14] It was not shared by the *Verein*'s President, Gothein, who was anxious to broaden the political base of his organization.

The presence of so many Jews in the ranks of revolution and even liberal democracy was certainly a heaven-sent opportunity to the propagandists of the Right and no doubt helped it to mobilize support in the moment of the

---

8   Reichmann, 'Der Bewußtseinswandel', *KuR*, p. 555.

9   *AZJ*, 22 November, 6 December 1918.

10   'Der Jude als Ministerpräsident', *IdR* XXIV/12, December 1918, pp. 459–60.

11   'Zur Lage', *JM* V/10–11, October–November 1918, p. 334.

12   *MVA* XXVIII/24–5, 17 December 1918, pp. 120–1; also 'Die Juden und die Revolution', ibid., XXVIII/22–3, 30 November 1918, pp. 111–12.

13   'Die Zweite Revolution, Bolschewismus und Judentum', *MVA* XXIX/6, 19 March 1919, p. 44.

14   Barbara Suchy, 'The Verein zur Abwehr des Antisemitismus (II) – From the First World War to its Dissolution in 1933', *LBYB* XXX (1985), pp. 76–7.

old regime's defeat. But it was a bonus, not a necessary condition. As we have seen, anti-Semitic organizations were preparing to name Jews as scapegoats for the deteriorating war situation long before Eisner, Toller or Mühsam had become a household name.[15] Otto Landsberg, one of the Social Democrats recruited by Gothein to the *Abwehr-Verein*, made this point in possibly exaggerated form:

Political abstinence is of absolutely no help to the Jews. If there were no Jews to be found among the Spartacists and the Independent Social Democrats, that would make absolutely no difference to anti-Semitism; it is designed to be a means to an end, to divert responsibility from those who are supposed to carry it, but do not want to carry it, to others who are innocent.[16]

While most Jews viewed revolutionary activity with suspicion or fear, some actively supported counter-revolution. Two Berlin businessmen, Consul Salomon Marx and GKR Hermann Frenkel, the head of the private bank Jacquier and Securius, helped to finance armed resistance against the Revolution through the *Bürgerwehr*. Anti-revolutionary sentiment was particularly strong in Bavaria, partly because of the anxiety to dissociate Jews from 'red terror', but also because of the generally more conservative and monarchical inclinations of the Jewish community there. For the Nobel laureate Richard Willstätter the Munich revolutionaries were a mere 'rabble'. The Orthodox Sigmund Fraenkel, a leading Munich industrialist, publicly declared that 'our hands are unsullied with the horrible chaos, ... misery and pain' that the revolutionaries had created.[17] The Eisner government's decree ending compulsory religious education in state schools no doubt alienated the Orthodox further. Eisner was not impressed with these Jewish anxieties. 'I am the creator and representative of this most marvellous of all freedom movements. ... I have greater concerns than to consider for only a moment such "questions of tact" that date from a vanquished time', he wrote to *Kommerzienrat* J. Mayer.[18] The assassin of Eisner, Anton Count Arco-Valley, was partly of Jewish ancestry, his mother being a von Oppenheim. So was Captain Fritz Rothenheim, the operations chief of the *Freikorps* that crushed

15 See above, p. 207.
16 Ordentliche Generalversammlung des Vereins zur Abwehr des Antisemitismus, *MVA* XXIX/24, 24 November 1919, p. 182; Suchy, *LBYB* (1985), p. 81.
17 *DIZ*, 31 October, 28 November 1918, cit. Reichmann, 'Der Bewußtseinswandel', *KuR*, p. 554; Niewyk, 'The German Jews in Revolution and Revolt', pp. 43, 47; Sigmund Fraenkel, 'Ein Brief aus der Räterepublik und ein Aufsatz aus der Frühzeit des Nationalsozialismus', in Hans Lamm (ed.), *Von Juden in München*, Munich: Ner-Tamid, 1958, pp. 304–6.
18 12 November 1918, cit. Toury, *Orientierungen*, p. 344.

the second Bavarian Soviet Republic. Similarly along Germany's Eastern frontier there were numerous Jewish volunteers for the *Freikorps*, mainly to fight Polish insurgents. The pogroms that accompanied the establishment of an independent Polish state merely reinforced the general desire of most Jews in Posen and Silesia to identify with Germans rather than Poles.[19]

There was one further part that Jews played in the events of 1918–20 that emphasized continuity with their pre-war roles, that of expert advisers to governments of the *Reich*. Max Warburg, having declined the office of Finance Minister in September 1918, became adviser to the Provisional government in November. His partner Carl Melchior and the economist Moritz Julius Bonn were among the delegation to Versailles to negotiate the peace treaty. With four others of Jewish origin (Dernburg, Rathenau, Arnhold, Hagen), Warburg and Bonn were included in the delegation to the coal reparations conference at Spa in Belgium, at which the French threatened to occupy the Ruhr unless their demands were met. In the face of this ultimatum the German representatives were split. The industrialist Hugo Stinnes, who urged rejection, was opposed by Bonn, Dernburg and Rathenau, which led him to blame their 'alien psyche' and 'soul of a foreign race'[20] for their 'defeatism' and went so far as to speak of a 'vote on racial lines' (*Rasseabstimmung*).[21] One might well be tempted to accept the stereotypes on which this outburst was based. Had not Jewish business leaders, before and during the war, shown a more realistic and far-sighted understanding of the complexities of the world economy than many of their Gentile colleagues and a greater desire to maintain it on a stable, pacific basis? Warburg's own retro-spective verdict on the episode, that it was one of a 'clash of mentalities', might seem to confirm this.[22] Yet of the Jewish delegates Arnhold certainly and Hagen probably supported Stinnes, and in the previous year the experts at Versailles had been unanimous in favouring rejection of the Allied terms – Melchior, Warburg and Hagen included.[23] Among the 'revolutionary' politicians Landsberg and Hirsch (SPD) as well as Schiffer, Preuß, Gothein and Haas (DDP) opposed acceptance of the treaty by the National Assembly, as did Friedrich Stampfer, editor of the SPD daily *Vorwärts*.[24] The *Berliner*

19 Ulrich Dunker, *Der Reichsbund jüdischer Frontsoldaten 1919–1938. Geschichte eines jüdischen Abwehrvereins*, Düsseldorf: Droste, 1977, pp. 45, 251.
20 Warburg, *Aus meinen Aufzeichnungen*, pp. 90ff.
21 Wilhelm Treue, 'Zur Frage der wirtschaftlichen Motive im deutschen Anti-semitismus', *KuR*, p. 392; Joseph Wirth, 'Die Festigung der Republik', in *Friedrich Ebert und seine Zeit*, Charlottenburg: Dr Wilhelm Glass, 1927, pp. 314–16; W. E. Mosse, *Economic Elite*, p. 263.
22 Warburg, *Aus meinen Aufzeichnungen*, p. 90.
23 Mosse, *Economic Elite*, p. 263, fn. 30.
24 Angress, 'Juden im politischen Leben der Revolutionszeit', p. 306.

Tageblatt and *Frankfurter Zeitung* vigorously opposed acceptance until almost the last moment; the *Vossische Zeitung*, on the other hand, no doubt atoning for its war-time expansionism, advocated acceptance from the start.[25] In their fluctuating and often agonized decisions, the Jewish experts and opinion leaders displayed no clear line, which at times of crisis helped them to react pragmatically.

Neither the Spartacists nor the Berlin businessmen who bankrolled the *Bürgerwehr* were typical of Jewish attitudes during these confused and harrowing months, though there were precedents for both, especially in 1848. The majority welcomed the coming of democracy, even if they regretted that it took a republican form. They recognized that once the war was over and the Hohenzollerns had abdicated, those who wanted either a monarchical restoration or some other authoritarian alternative were, almost by definition, ill-disposed towards their civil rights. The ex-Emperor, who had been happy enough to enjoy Jewish society and generosity when it suited him, spoke for these circles when he blamed the collapse on 'the hated tribe of Juda': 'Let no German ever forget this, or rest until these parasites have been extirpated and exterminated from German soil. This toadstool on the German oak!'[26] At the same time such Jews did not want the prospect of parliamentary government and bourgeois civil liberties negated by radical revolution. Though it was the anarchists, Spartacists and People's Commissars who dominated the popular image of the Jew in politics, the less spectacular acts of those who fought in civilian militias against the far Left in order to defend the recent democratic gains were probably closest to the epicentre of Jewish opinion.[27] These were indeed the positions of the SPD and DDP, the parties that dominated politics in the months after the collapse and gained nearly 60 per cent of the vote in the elections to the National Assembly. The constant evocation of 'restraint' and 'tact' in Jewish publications, more reflective of the mentality of 'protected Jews' than of self-confident citizens, indicated how narrow the room for manoeuvre was for Jewish representative organizations.

11 JEWS AND THE WEIMAR PARTIES

The German party system underwent considerable changes in the years 1917–19, but the predominant features of the ideological spectrum showed

25 Becker, 'Die Rolle de liberalen Presse', *KuR*, pp. 110–11.
26 John Roehl, *Kaiser, Hof und Staat. Wilhelm II und die deutsche Politik*, Munich: C. H. Beck, 1987, p. 87.
27 Robert M. W. Kempner, *Ankläger einer Epoche. Lebenserinnerungen*, Frankfurt: Ullstein, 1983, pp. 25–6; Immanuel Birnbaum, 'Juden in der Münchener Räterepublik', in Lamm, *Von Juden*, pp. 302–3; Niewyk, 'The German Jews in Revolution and Revolt', p. 44.

continuity with the Imperial period. Indeed the biggest change was in the electoral system and the franchise. The voting age was reduced from 25 years to 20 and women got the vote on the same basis as men. The first change did not make a major difference, though it may have marginally helped the radical parties of the Left and the Right during the Depression. Voting rights for women had a more substantial impact in that they helped the parties of the centre-right with a religious base, especially the *Zentrum* and the Nationalists, both of whom got some 60 per cent of their support from female voters. The electoral system was changed completely. All elections, at whatever level, were henceforth by proportional representation. Both reforms, introduced by the Provisional government in 1918, were enshrined in the Weimar constitution.[1] Their effect was two-fold. The first was a genuine nationalization of party campaigning. Compared with the Empire, all parties now faced stiffer competition in their former strongholds and improved their performance where they had been weakest.[2] Secondly, all votes were now of equal value and tactical considerations counted for less in electoral choice. This meant that Jewish votes were now less influential than they had been in municipal politics, but gained in influence in national politics, given that under the Empire few Jewish voters had lived in marginal seats.

The changes in party structure were more notable in the Centre and on the Right than on the Left. Among the non-Socialist parties it was the defeat that caused the re-alignment; among the Socialists it was the war itself that was the cause. Social Democracy embarked on the post-war period divided into three. Beside the SPD itself, at that time generally referred to as the Majority Social Democrats, were the Independent Social Democrats (USPD), who had split off in 1917. The Spartacist wing of the USPD in turn established itself as the German Communist Party (KPD) at the turn of the year 1918/19. It, however, boycotted the elections for the National Assembly of 19 January 1919.

The names and organizations of the non-Socialist parties were discredited by association with a departed world; their membership and leadership, however, showed considerable continuity. The process of reorganization began with the foundation of a new middle-class democratic party, the *Deutsche Demokratische Partei* (DDP), which absorbed the pre-war Progressives and some National Liberals. Gustav Stresemann, the chairman of the Reichstag National Liberal group, was, however, too controversial a figure to be included in the new formation, having been a war-time annexationist. He,

---

1 Peter Pulzer, 'Germany', in Vernon Bogdanor and David Butler (eds), *Democracy and Elections. Electoral Systems and their Political Consequences*, Cambridge: Cambridge University Press, 1983, pp. 84–109.
2 Gerhard A. Ritter, *Arbeiterbewegung, Parteien und Parlamentarismus*, Göttingen: Vandenhoeck & Ruprecht, 1976, pp. 147–53.

in turn, founded the *Deutsche Volkspartei* (DVP), which gradually established itself as the successor to the old National Liberal Party. The Protestant Right began with a concentration of forces that had been anticipated by the creation of the *Deutsche Vaterlandspartei* during the war.[3] The pre-war Conservatives, *Reichspartei*, Christian Socials and other anti-Semitic splinter parties joined in the German National People's Party (DNVP). This unity did not, however, last long. As early as 1922 some of the more extreme nationalists and racialists broke away to form the *Deutschvölkische Freiheitspartei*, which established close links with the NSDAP, in existence since 1920. In 1930 the more moderate elements in the party broke away in protest against the extreme course advocated by Alfred Hugenberg, party leader since 1928.

The *Zentrum* also toyed with the fashion for 'people's parties' by adopting the name *Christliche Volkspartei*, but soon reverted to the old label. Following the Revolution the Bavarian *Zentrum* severed its connections with the rest of the party, and established itself as the *Bayerische Volkspartei* (BVP), in order to be in a better position to defend its federalist claims and the more conservative ideas of its peasant and lower-middle-class clientele. Initially it maintained a joint grouping with the *Zentrum* in the Reichstag, but this, too, came to an end in 1920 when the BVP disapproved of the *Zentrum*'s decision to enter into a coalition with the SPD.

The elections for the National Assembly showed a general swing to the Left thanks to the discredit into which the old regime had been thrown. This applied not only between parties, but also within them. The new leader of the DNVP in the Weimar National Assembly was Count Arthur von Posadowsky-Wehner, a former Secretary of State for Internal Affairs and Vice-Chancellor, an independent personality who was averse to all demagogy and found anti-Semitism distasteful. Other leading DNVP members such as Oskar Hergt, the party's first chairman and former Prussian Minister of Finance, Clemens von Delbrück, Secretary of State for Internal Affairs under Chancellor Bethmann-Hollweg, and Adalbert von Düringer, the last Minister of Justice in the Grand Duchy of Baden, were typical civil servants, pragmatists rather than ideologues. In the *Zentrum* the growing influence of Matthias Erzberger demonstrated the increasing strength of the left wing. Liberalism showed a similar picture. In the thirteen Reichstag elections in the course of the Empire the National Liberals had emerged the stronger of the two Liberal formations on ten occasions. Now the DDP had almost four times as many seats as the DVP.

As during the Empire, persons of Jewish descent were to be found in all political parties from the DNVP to the Communists. Heinrich Brüning, Chancellor from 1930 to 1932, recalled in his memoirs: 'Anyone who lived

3   See above, p. 202.

through the first post-war years in Berlin could never draw the conclusion that the German Jews constituted a spiritual or political unit.'[4] That statement, though true, needs qualifying. Not many Jews were to be found on the Right; a more sizeable minority supported the parties of the Left. The majority saw their political home in the new German Democratic Party.

The German Democratic Party

The DDP was the meeting point of those committed Republicans who were not Socialists and of the so-called *Vernunftsrepublikaner* – 'rational Republicans' who appreciated, however regretfully, that the old order had passed for good. It also offered shelter to the large number of undecided voters who saw it as the most effective force for moderation and the defence of middle-class interests. The list of those who signed the appeal for its launch in the *Berliner Tageblatt* of 10 November 1918 was illustrious, representing various shades of Liberalism among German Jews. They included Albert Einstein; the newspaper publisher and owner of the *Berliner Tageblatt* and Rudolf Mosse, the paper's editor-in-chief, Theodor Wolff, who was the driving force behind the appeal; academics like the economist Moritz Julius Bonn and the newly-appointed Rector of the Commercial Academy of Berlin, Hugo Preuß; and industrialists like Consul Sally Segall, the director general of the Rütgers factories. Other persons of Jewish descent who signed included the banker Richard Witting (the brother of Maximilian Harden), the academic Max Theodor Vogelstein, in whose home the party was founded, the director of the *Hansa-Bund*, Kurt von Kleefeld (the brother-in-law of Gustav Stresemann), Paul Nathan, Otto Richard Frankfurter and the Progressive Reichstag deputy and President of the *Abwehr-Verein*, Georg Gothein.

The party's founders aimed at creating something more than a successor to the old Progressives. Indeed the founding group was drawn overwhelmingly from the intelligentsia – 40 per cent of the signatories held doctoral degrees and three were Nobel Prize winners[5] – and included only four former Reichstag deputies. In important respects they succeeded in transcending the old Progressive electoral base and recruited the support of the civil servants' union (*Deutscher Beamtenbund*), one of the main shop assistants' unions (*Verein deutscher Handlungsgehilfen*) and the *Deutscher Bauernbund*, formerly

---

4 Heinrich Brüning, *Memoiren 1918–1934*, Stuttgart: Deutsche Verlags-Anstalt, 1970, p. 48. See also Ernest Hamburger, 'Betrachtungen über Heinrich Brünings Memoiren', *Internationale Wissenschaftliche Korrespondenz*, 15 April 1972, p. 34.
5 Bruce B. Frye, *Liberal Democrats in the Weimar Republic. The History of the German Democratic Party and the German State Party*, Carbondale and Edwardsville: Southern Illinois University Press, 1985, p. 48.

affiliated to the National Liberal Party.[6] They also succeeded in breaking into the ranks of the National Liberals by recruiting prominent members of the *Jungliberalen*. Significantly most of the National Liberal politicans of Jewish descent joined the DDP, even though some of them had been well to the right within that party. They included Eugen Schiffer, a member of both the Reichstag and the Prussian Landtag, who openly declared himself to be 'rational Republican';[7] Robert Friedberg, chairman of the Prussian Landtag grouping and member of the Pan-German League, who joined after considerable hesitation[8] and whose final decision was a great boost to the DDP's fortunes; and Bernhard Falk, a Cologne city councillor who had been a National Liberal parliamentary candidate.[9] Like other middle-class Jews, he had longed for a military career, but was frustrated by the army's discriminatory practices.[10] He held a reserve commission in the Bavarian army, remained on active service until 1917 and retired in 1918, at the age of fifty, with the rank of Captain in the Territorial Army. Like many in the middle classes, Jewish or not, he was a monarchist until disillusioned by the Emperor's flight.

All three of the ex-National Liberals played a prominent role in the DDP. Friedberg served as chairman of the party executive (*Vorstand* or *Hauptvorstand*), making him the second most important figure in the party, until his death in 1920. Schiffer, following his brief tenure of office as a minister in 1919, became chairman of the Reichstag party grouping and Falk became chairman of the Prussian Landtag party grouping from 1925 to 1933.[11] Not all of this group were equally happy in their new political home. Schiffer was one of the founders of the *Liberale Vereinigung* in 1924, with the aim of bringing about a reconciliation with Stresemann and the DVP, but he found few followers.

At the beginning of the Weimar period Jews were prominent in the DDP at all levels, including some twenty of the 150-strong provisional executive.[12] Of the seventy-five DDP deputies in the National Assembly, four were

6   Larry Eugene Jones, *German Liberalism and the Dissolution of the Weimar Party System, 1918–1933*, Chapel Hill, NC: University of North Carolina Press, 1988, pp. 23–4.

7   Eugen Schiffer, *Ein Leben für den Liberalismus*, Berlin: Herbig, 1951, p. 211.

8   Frye, *Liberal Democrats*, pp. 53–4.

9   See above, p. 127.

10   Hamburger, *Juden im öffentlichen Leben Deutschlands*, p. 141. Comments by Bernhard Falk in BAK, Kl. Erw. p. 385. Concerning his family home, his childhood and his inclination to military life, ibid., pp. 3–8.

11   Horst Möller, *Parlamentarismus in Preußen 1919–1932*, Düsseldorf: Droste, 1985, pp. 603–4.

12   Becker, 'Die Rolle der liberalen Presse', *KuR*, p. 119, fn. 133.

professing Jews – Moritz Baerwald, Bernhard Falk, Ludwig Haas and Felix Waldstein, the last two having been Progressive members of the Imperial Reichstag –, two were baptized Jews – Julius Lippmann and Eugen Schiffer – and four more were of Jewish descent – Bernhard Dernburg, Georg Gothein, Carl Petersen (later to be Lord Mayor of Hamburg, 1924–1933) and Erich Koch-Weser, a future party leader. Haas became head of the party group in the Reichstag in 1929, a year before his death; he was succeeded by the baptized Oscar Meyer. The Prussian Constitutent Assembly contained, in addition to Robert Friedberg, five professing Jews – Oskar Cassel, Bernhard Falk, Hugo Preuß, Arthur Kochmann and Leon Zeitlin. Prominent politicians in other states included Hermann Cohn in Dessau, Norbert Regensburger in Braunschweig, and Carl Melchior of the banking house M. M. Warburg in Hamburg. Two Jewish Democrats in particularly exposed positions were Walther Rathenau, who, following his conspicuous role in the reparations negotiations, served as Minister for Reconstruction in 1921 and as Foreign Minister in 1922 until his assassination; and Bernhard Weiß, Vice-President of the Berlin police, who earned the (no doubt reciprocated) undying hatred of Joseph Goebbels.

Numerous Democratic politicians combined their party activity with offices in Jewish organizations. Oskar Cassel and Ludwig Haas were members of the Executive of the C.V., and Cassel became chairman of the *Verband der Deutschen Juden* in 1917. Kochmann in Silesia, Cohn in Dessau and Regensburger in Braunschweig all held prominent positions in the C.V.; Regensburger was also one of the founders of the *Verband der jüdischen Jugendvereine Deutschlands.*[13] Some eminent Jewish academics also participated in DDP politics, e.g. the pioneer of social policy, Frida Wunderlich, who served both on the Berlin City Council and, briefly, in the Prussian Landtag.[14]

The example of these and many other individuals no doubt helped to recruit Jewish voters for the DDP. But most of them would in any case need no persuading. Their broad political ideals were not greatly changed by the upheavals of 1918. They wanted a society in which the individual was judged by his merits and in which all groups had equal access to the decision-making of a neutral, impartial state; a political system that rested, in the words of the

13 Information about Regensburger kindly supplied by the city archive of Braunschweig and Mrs Resi Regensburger in London [H]. See also Ernst-August Roloff, *Braunschweig und der Staat von Weimar. Politik, Wirtschaft und Gesellschaft 1918–1933*, Braunschweig: Waisenhaus, 1964, p. 50. On Kochmann, see below, p. 286.
14 Frida Wunderlich's literary estate is in the archive of the Leo Baeck Institute, New York. After her emigration she held a Chair at the New School for Social Research, New York.

constitutional lawyer Hans Kelsen, 'on the compromises between competing social forces'.[15] Such a state the Weimar Republic promised to be, and the DDP the nearest embodiment of its principles. The DDP rejected both revolution and counter-revolution. In its first manifesto of 16 November it declared itself to be 'bourgeois', its programme of 15 December emphasized its allegiance to private enterprise. It entered the election campaign for the National Assembly with the declared aim of preventing a Socialist majority, for this reason turning down proposals for joint lists with the SPD, but also with 'reactionary' parties (which were, however, not specified).[16]

The close association of Jews and the new party was the cause of difficulties that were never resolved. Two factors, in particular, aggravated these. The first was the party's dependence on a relatively small number of financial benefactors. These included, especially in the early years, Carl Fürstenberg, Walther Rathenau, the Arnhold brothers and the Tietz family, as well as some lesser-known Jewish industrialists. There were non-Jews, too: Robert Bosch, Hugo Stinnes and Carl Friedrich von Siemens. Hjalmar Schacht, the later President of the Reichsbank, was a formidable fund-raiser.[17] But in so far as Jewish money flowed in any direction, it was towards the DDP. The other factor was the controversial status of the three leading newspaper publishing houses of Mosse (*Berliner Tageblatt, Berliner Volkszeitung*), Ullstein (*Vossische Zeitung, Berliner Morgenpost, BZ am Mittag*), and Simons-Sonnemann (*Frankfurter Zeitung*). These supported the DDP editorially and many of their employees, led by Theodor Wolff, editor-in-chief of the *Berliner Tageblatt*, were prominent party members.[18]

This made the DDP even more vulnerable to the charge, which was probably in any case unavoidable, of being a *Judenpartei*. At a time when it was easy to associate Jews with defeatism, internationalism, Bolshevism and cultural decadence, the parties and newspapers of the Right made full use of the opportunity to denounce the DDP on these grounds. Even Stresemann and the DVP succumbed to this temptation, given the intense competition

15   Hans Kelsen, *Vom Wesen und Wert der Demokratie*, 2nd edn, Tübingen: J. C. B. Mohr, 1929, p. 58.
16   Lothar Albertin, *Liberalismus und Demokratie am Anfang der Weimarer Republik*, Düsseldorf: Droste, 1972, pp. 57, 73, 85–8; Treue, *Deutsche Parteiprogramme*, pp. 135–40.
17   Frye, *Liberal Democrats*, p. 57.
18   Gotthart Schwarz, *Theodor Wolff und das 'Berliner Tageblatt'. Eine liberale Stimme in der deutschen Politik, 1906–1933*, Tübingen: J. C. B. Mohr, 1968; Werner Becker, *Demokratie des sozialen Rechts. Die politische Haltung der Frankfurter Zeitung, der Vossischen Zeitung und des Berliner Tageblatts, 1918 bis 1924*, Göttingen: Musterschmidt, 1971.

between the two parties for the National Liberal constituency and for money from industry, though in later years Stresemann disavowed, and indeed opposed, this kind of campaigning.[19]

The DDP was committed by its programme and, indeed, by its whole pre-history, to opposing anti-Semitism, and the close links that had existed before 1914 between left-wing Liberalism and the *Abwehr-Verein* continued throughout the 1920s. Nevertheless, it was a fact of life that there were few votes to be had in Weimar Germany by posing as a friend of Jews. Otto Fischbeck was anxious, in December 1919, 'not to encourage anything that might once more label us as a *Judenschutztruppe*'; the signatures on the party's manifesto gave him the impression that this was 'a Jewish-capitalist creation'.[20] A number of Jewish members of the DDP, including Felix Waldstein and Ludwig Haas, shared these anxieties.[21]

But it was not only tactical considerations that led many members of the DDP to resent or oppose the leading role of Jews in the party. Many provincial dignitaries and the representatives of farmers and small business were genuinely disturbed by the influence of the radical, metropolitan group that propagated views out of keeping with their own more traditionalist outlook on politics. It was these men and women who had the last say in drawing up the lists of candidates at elections, and it was thanks to them that a number of prominent intellectuals failed to get attractive placings. Nor were all the victims Jewish: Max Weber and Hellmut von Gerlach were as unlucky as Georg Bernhard, editor-in-chief of the *Vossische Zeitung*, and Hugo Preuß.[22] Public anti-Semitic utterances by DDP personalities were rare; private ones less so.[23] Generally they were veiled in coded references to 'Berlin influence', 'the Berlin clique', 'big city degeneracy'[24] or 'the pompous relativism of big city dwellers'.[25] The 'Jewish' association divided the party in two ways. Those,

---

19 Hartenstein, *Die Anfänge der Deutschen Volkspartei, 1918–1920*, pp. 44–50; Frye, *Liberal Democrats*, p. 58; Jones, *German Liberalism*, pp. 61–9.
20 Albertin, *Liberalismus und Demokratie*, p. 80.
21 Ibid., p. 80, n. 264; Ernest Hamburger, *LBYB* (1975), p. 200; Donald L. Niewyk, *The Jews in Weimar Germany*, Baton Rouge: Louisiana State University Press, 1980, p. 72, fn. 114.
22 Albertin, *Liberalismus und Demokratie*, p. 78.
23 Robert Pois, *The Bourgeois Democrats of Weimar Germany*, Philadelphia, 1976, Transactions of the American Philosophical Society, N.S., vol. 66, Pt. 4, pp. 79–87; Jürgen Hess, *'Das Ganze Deutschland soll es sein.' Demokratischer Nationalismus in der Weimarer Republik am Beispiel der Deutschen Demokratischen Partei*, Stuttgart: Klett-Cotta, 1978, pp. 353–4, takes a more charitable line.
24 Otto Geßler, *Reichswehrpolitik in der Weimarer Zeit*, Stuttgart: Deutsche Verlags-Anstalt, 1958, pp. 173–4.
25 Gertrud Bäumer, cit. Pois, *The Bourgeois Democrats of Weimar Germany*, p. 72.

drawn in the main from the provinces and from the old-guard Progressives, who wished to see the DDP as a broad, patriotic social coalition, a kind of democratic *Volksgemeinschaft*, resented the pressures of the industrial wing in favour of a strictly market economy. This applied particularly to the *Hansa-Bund*, one of the party's biggest financial supporters. The employers' lobby, Erich Koch-Weser complained in 1925, 'want to turn us into a party of Jewish entrepreneurs'.[26] The ex-National Liberal Hartmann von Richthofen echoed this sentiment within the executive: 'There is no getting round the fact that we are perceived as the party of Jewish capitalism.'[27] These tensions were exacerbated during the Depression, and were one of the main obstacles to the fusion with the *Jungdeutscher Orden* that led to the creation of the *Deutsche Staatspartei* in 1930.[28]

Parallel with this division, the cultural cleavage continued, increasingly isolating the '*Berliner Tageblatt* faction' that had briefly dominated the new party in 1918–19. The DDP had at that time not been exempt from internal resentment at 'Jewish radicalism'. Ernst Müller-Meiningen, writing about the events in Munich, blamed 'alien elements' with their 'literary and rhetorical skills' for the ensuing anti-Semitic reaction.[29] Müller-Meiningen left the party in 1925 in order to support the candidacy of Field-Marshal Hindenburg in the presidential election. Two factors in particular helped to perpetuate this conflict. One was the personality of Otto Geßler, the DDP War Minister in numerous Weimar governments, who was considered too friendly to the army by the 'Berliner Judenjungen', as Theodor Heuss's brother Ludwig called them.[30] The other was the anti-pornography bill, introduced in 1926 by the DDP Minister of the Interior, Wilhelm Külz, and strongly supported by such DDP Protestants as Theodor Heuss and Gertrud Bäumer. Theodor Wolff resigned from the party in protest against this measure and the incident led to a long-standing feud between Bäumer, the principal advocate of political romanticism in the party, and the *Berliner Tageblatt*. One scholar has concluded from these varied episodes that: 'Theirs was not a systematic racial anti-Semitism, but a somewhat gentlemanly *Biedermeier* variety which saw the Jews as being an occasionally obnoxious, often loud group of people, who

---

26 Diary, 3 February 1925, cit. Michael Stürmer, *Koalition und Opposition in der Weimarer Republik, 1924–1928*, Düsseldorf: Droste, 1967, p. 88, n. 22.

27 15 June 1928, Konstanze Wegner (ed.), *Linksliberalismus in der Weimarer Republik. Die Führungsgremien der Deutschen Demokratischen Partei und der Deutschen Staatspartei, 1918–1933*, Düsseldorf: Droste, 1980, p. 465.

28 See below, pp. 290–1.

29 Ernst Müller-Meiningen, *Aus Bayerns schwersten Tagen. Erinnerungen und Betrachtungen aus der Revolutionszeit*, Berlin and Leipzig: de Gruyter, 1924, p. 206.

30 Frye, *Liberal Democrats*, p. 263, fn. 73.

somehow did not really fit into German life.'[31] Yet that judgement, too, though containing much truth, needs qualifying. Gertrud Bäumer was a member of the executive of the *Abwehr-Verein*; Heuss had a Jewish son-in-law and in his influential book on Hitler drew particular attention to his anti-Semitism.[32] What we are faced with here is what the Austrian sociologist Bernd Marin has called 'anti-Semitism without anti-Semites' – the often unconscious acceptance of stereotypical thinking, without the desire to discriminate or persecute.[33]

These tensions within the DDP became all the more damaging since its electoral success was short-lived. From 18.6 per cent of the vote in 1919 it dropped to 8.3 per cent in the first Reichstag election of 1920, and to 5.7 per cent in May 1924. Thereafter it stabilized until it suffered the fate of the other middle-class parties in the wake of the Depression, its followers having drifted to the Right, to the DVP and even the DNVP, or towards such special interest parties as the *Wirtschaftspartei*. One consequence of this development was that the Jewish component in its electorate rose as time went on. One DDP organizer calculated that if 60 per cent of the Jewish electorate voted DDP that would have amounted to 3 per cent of the party's vote in 1919 and 6 per cent in 1920.[34] If one further assumes that Jewish support for the DDP declined more slowly than non-Jewish – since the alternatives were much less attractive for the Jewish voter – so that at least 50 per cent of Jews continued to support the DDP, then by the mid-1920s one DDP vote in ten would have been Jewish. In its fissiparous development the DDP resembled its pre-war predecessors.

The party never reached a consensus on whether it wanted to be a middle-class *rassemblement* or to spearhead a democratic and social reformist movement. Schiffer, as we have seen, left in 1924, aiming at closer co-operation with the DVP. Four years earlier Otto Mugdan, a baptized Jew who had been a Left-Liberal member of the Prussian Landtag, had switched over to the DVP. Among non-Jews Hjalmar Schacht, whose work in connection with the creation of the 'Rentenmark' during the inflation of 1923 had been made the focal point of the DDP's election propaganda only two years previously, moved to the Right in 1925. His reason was the party's attitude to

31 Pois, *The Bourgeois Democrats of Weimar Germany*, p. 86.
32 Theodor Heuss, *Hitlers Weg. Eine historisch-politische Studie über den National-sozialismus*, Stuttgart and Berlin: Union, 1932, pp. 31–46, 105–6, 148–149.
33 Bernd Marin, 'Antisemitism Before and After the Holocaust: The Austrian Case', in Ivar Oxaal, Michael Pollack and Gerhard Botz (eds), *Jews, Antisemitism and Culture in Vienna*, London: Routledge, 1987, pp. 216–33.
34 Reinhold Issberner, *Demokratisches ABC-Buch*, Berlin: Demokratischer Verlag, 1920, p. 43, cit. Frye, *Liberal Democrats*, p. 147, note 22.

the dispossession of members of the former royal families and he took with him a number of other Democrats, including the publicist Paul Rohrbach.[35] It was the beginning of a political transformation which in the end was to lead him to collaboration with Hitler. Bernhard Dernburg, who as State Secretary for Colonies had been a notable imperialist but was now a loyal Republican, confessed to Gothein in 1927 that 'he no longer felt the same bonds towards the party as previously'.[36] On the left wing of the party Theodor Wolff was not alone in suffering disillusionment. In January 1930 one of the party veterans, Friedrich von Payer, resigned his membership along with his family in protest at the participation of the Württemberg DDP in a state government which was dominated by the DNVP.[37] In the eyes of the extreme Right Payer had long counted as an honorary Jew: 'Herr von Payer is indeed typical of the democratic state-workers of our day: in so far as they are not Jews, they are South Germans', Conrad von Wangenheim had told the annual conference of the Agrarian League in 1919.[38]

This survey of the withdrawals of leaders or important members of the DDP reveals that Jews did not represent any particular trend. Paul Nathan[39] and Wolff left the party because it was not Liberal enough in its social or cultural policies. Schiffer and Mugdan resigned because it tended politically too far to the Left. Among non-Jews Payer and Schacht paralleled these trends. Similarly disparate tendencies were apparent among the electorate. These defections should not disguise the fact that a great many Jews could not conceive of a political home other than the DDP, especially if they were associated with Jewish representative organizations, such as the C.V., or with the *Hansa-Bund*. Ludwig Haas, Otto Richard Frankfurter, Bernhard Falk, Georg Bernhard and Wilhelm Cohnstaedt remained loyal to the party, despite regular disputes and occasional misgivings.

Notwithstanding all these personal and doctrinal tensions, the DDP

35   Ulrich Schüren, *Der Volksentscheid zur Fürstenenteignung*, Düsseldorf: Droste, 1978, pp. 224–6.
36   Werner Schiefel, *Bernhard Dernburg, 1865–1937. Kolonialpolitiker und Bankier im Wilhelminischen Deutschland*, Zürich: Atlantis, 1974, p. 168.
37   Werner Stephan, *Aufstieg und Verfall des Linksliberalismus, 1918–1933*, Göttingen: Vandenhoeck & Ruprecht, 1973, p. 454; Erich Matthias and Rudolf Morsey (eds), *Das Ende der Parteien 1933*, Düsseldorf: Droste, 1960, p. 38.
38   *Deutsche Tageszeitung*, 17 February 1919; Hans Freiherr von Wangenheim (ed.), *Conrad Freiherr von Wangenheim Klein-Spiegel. Lebensbild. Briefe und Reden*, Berlin: Deutsche Verlags-Gesellschaft, 1935, p. 145.
39   For the circumstances of Nathan's breach with the DDP, see Hartmut Schustereit, *Linksliberalismus und Sozialdemokratie in der Weimarer Republik. Eine vergleichende Betrachtung der Politik der DDP und SPD, 1919–1930*, Düsseldorf: Pädagogischer Verlag Schwann, 1975, pp. 267–8.

continued to adopt Jews as election candidates, in contrast with the general reluctance of the left-wing Liberals to do so during much of the Wilhelminian period. In the 1920 *Reichstag* 8 out of 44 DDP members were Jews or of Jewish descent; in May 1924, 4 out of 28; in December 1924, 4 out of 32; in 1928, 5 out of 25; in 1930, 3 out of 15; in July 1932, 1 out of 4; in November 1932, neither of 2.[40] Individual candidatures were, however, sometimes controversial. At the height of the anti-Semitic wave in May 1924 Ludwig Haas found himself demoted on the party list in Baden.[41]

The German People's Party

For most of the Weimar period there were two main parties to the Right of the DDP: the *Deutsche Volkspartei* (DVP) and the *Deutschnationale Volkspartei* (DNVP). At times these two parties were allied in their battle against the Republic or against the parties of the 'Weimar Coalition'. They frequently formed electoral pacts or coalition governments in the various states or in municipalities. However, there were also manifest differences between them, above all in foreign policy. The DVP retained some of the Liberal characteristics of the National Liberals, in particular in cultural matters, and its hesitations over loyalty to the Republic ended after the failure of the Kapp putsch in 1920. They could therefore rely on a certain share of Jewish voters, though the number was not great.

There was an old tradition of Jewish support for the National Liberals. This party was strongest in the non-Prussian states and the new Prussian provinces – Hanover, Schleswig-Holstein and Hesse-Nassau – that had been incorporated after 1866. Of the 119 seats that the National Liberals won in the first Reichstag election of 1871, 91 came from outside old Prussia. However, most of the Jews lived in the old Prussian provinces. There the political awareness in the middle classes was mainly influenced by the constitutional conflict of the 1860s between Bismarck and the Progressive Party. In contrast in some of the new Prussian areas, such as Hanover, as well as in parts of the Rhineland and Baden, many Jews remained loyal to the old party even after it split in 1879 and allied with the political Right. These were areas where anti-Semitism was less widespread than elsewhere in the *Reich*.

With Stresemann unacceptable to the founders of the DDP, the dreams of a single, united liberal force were shattered. The *Deutsche Volkspartei*, which he founded in December 1918, gained the support of other former National Liberals to whom the DDP seemed too Republican. However, some former

---

40 Bruce B. Frye, 'The German Democratic Party and the "Jewish Problem"', *LBYB* XXI (1976), p. 149, fn. 30.
41 *Idem., Liberal Democrats*, p. 139.

National Liberals, who saw no future for another splinter party of the Right, joined the more promising-looking DNVP, especially in Silesia, Baden and Württemberg.

In the elections for the National Assembly, however, the votes of even those Jews whose views were on the Right probably went, with few exceptions, to the DDP. The general trend to the Left of that time would have also caused former National Liberal Jewish voters to follow leaders like Friedberg and Schiffer into the ranks of the Democrats. From 1920 onwards the DVP and DDP frequently collaborated in the same government coalition. Gradually Stresemann made the DVP into the right wing of the political centre and his efforts were crowned when he headed the Great Coalition in 1923, which ranged from Social Democrats to the DVP.

In its attitude to the Jewish Question the DVP was not consistent. Its programme on the one hand proclaimed its belief in 'freedom of conscience and individual responsibility in all religious and ecclesiastical affairs', but on the other saw 'in Christianity a mainstay of German culture and of the people's life'.[42] In reply to a question from the *Centralverein* in March 1919 Rudolf Heinze, a member of the Reichstag, replied on behalf of the party's executive that 'the German People's Party abhors and fights anti-Semitism in every form and rejects as irrelevant and unjust every generalization of reproaches (which may possibly be justified in individual cases) against German citizens of the Jewish faith'.[43] At the elections for the Prussian Landtag in 1921 the DNVP did not fail to accuse the People's Party of being unable to sever its links with Jewry.[44] Stresemann also campaigned against anti-Semitism after he had turned away from his war-time aberrations and the temptation to campaign against the DDP with anti-Semitic innuendoes.[45] As early as October 1919 he went out of his way to assert that 'a liberal party cannot champion anti-Semitic principles', sentiments that he repeated after the murder of Rathenau.[46] The responsibility of office gave him insights into the foreign policy implications of domestic events. As Chancellor at the end of October 1923 he drew the attention of the Bavarian government to the unwelcome consequences for foreign policy of the ruthless policy of extraditing East European and in particular Polish Jews. The next month the Prussian Premier Otto Braun pointed out to him the possible consequences for Prussia of

42 Treue, *Deutsche Parteiprogramme*, p. 131.
43 *IdR* XXVI/6, June 1919, p. 283.
44 Helmut Lange, *Julius Curtius, 1877–1948. Aspekte einer Politikbiographie* (Diss.), Kiel, 1970, p. 163.
45 See above, pp. 204, 220–1.
46 Niewyk, *The Jews in Weimar Germany*, p. 74; Harold A. Turner, *Stresemann and the Politics of the Weimar Republic*, Princeton, NJ: Princeton University Press, 1963, p. 97.

the Bavarian extradition orders and the possibility of reprisals by the Polish government against Germans living in the Western Polish provinces. Stresemann took up the warning with good effect. The Bavarian Landtag, which had accepted a resolution of its Constitutional Committee to ascertain where and in what numbers 'members of the Jewish race were employed by the Bavarian state', rescinded this decision in response to pressure from Berlin. In 1924 Stresemann once more commented on anti-Semitism in Bavaria – this time as Foreign Minister. Supported by a report from the German Embassy in Washington, he drew the attention of the Bavarian government to the irritation in the international world of finance at the anti-Semitism prevalent in the Bavarian Landtag, in particular within the Bavarian People's Party.[47]

The activity of the party at the lower levels shows a rather different picture. The DVP never once put up an unbaptized Jew as a candidate in elections to either the Reichstag or any Landtag. In this respect it was even more restrictive than its National Liberal predecessor.[48] However, the anti-pathy went deeper than was apparent in the attitude taken to Jews as parliamentarians. Stresemann had to keep up a permanent struggle against anti-Semitic tendencies in the party all over the country. The Reichstag deputy Fritz Mittelmann put forward a proposal to reduce the economic influence of Jews in proportion to their share of the population. The district organization of Chemnitz did not want to admit Jews as party members. Jakob Riesser, a DVP deputy who enjoyed high esteem within his party, repeatedly appealed to Stresemann in connection with these and other cases and asked him to intervene.[49] A city councillor and lawyer in Dresden, Nathanson, was equally disturbed by the anti-Semitism in the party in Saxony. Heinrich Frenzel, a salaried official of the DVP in Dresden, distributed an anti-Semitic leaflet which he himself had written. After the murder of Rathenau he called for a collective effort by members since the murder of the 'uncrowned king of international Jewry' would most certainly cause the champions of Jewish world dominion to come together in a unified

---

47   BAK Reichskanzlei, R 431/2193, pp. 86ff; p. 109 (Poland); letter from Otto Braun of 5 November 1923; letter from the Secretary of State in the *Reich* Chancellery of 11 November 1923; telegram from Stresemann of 20 November 1923, in which he presses for cessation of all extraditions – ibid., p. 140; international world of finance, p. 153. For a treatment of these events based on Polish sources, see Józef Adelson, 'The Expulsion of Jews with Polish Citizenship from Bavaria in 1923', *Polin: A Journal of Polish-Jewish Studies* V (1991), pp. 57–73.
48   See above, pp. 125, 127.
49   Felix Hirsch, *Stresemann. Ein Lebensbild*, Göttingen: Musterschmidt, 1978, p. 103.

red front. Frenzel (originally called Fränkel), who made anti-Semitic speeches within the DVP in and near Berlin, was a baptized Jew.[50] Stresemann was obliged to reassure Nathanson that his own opposition to anti-Semitism was based on *Weltanschauung*, not merely on concern for party finances.[51] Indeed Stresemann himself was not immune from attacks from Saxony on the grounds of his Jewish family connections.[52]

The efforts of subsidiary organizations of the People's Party which sought unity on the Right tended to move in the same direction. In the Prussian State Council, which represented the provinces in legislation and administration, the DVP and DNVP formed one parliamentary group. In the spring of 1928 the DVP in Frankfurt-on-Main joined with the entire Right, including the National Socialists, in order to bring about the election of a right-wing ticket of city aldermen against that of the Left. This was made possible by the influence of Richard Merton, a member of the city council from 1928 to 1930, the son of baptized Jewish parents, whose father had been one of the founders of the University of Frankfurt. The Lord Mayor of Frankfurt, Ludwig Landmann, considered him a man of alert but restless intelligence and the initiator of the early swing to the Right in the DVP.[53] In Hamburg, on the other hand, Jews were prominent and well-received in the DVP. The general secretary of the Hamburg party branch, W. O. Rose, maintained close contact with Max Warburg, who had joined the DVP 'not least out of admiration for Stresemann'.[54] Rose even suggested to Stresemann in 1922 that Carl Melchior be appointed Finance Minister, which both Melchior and Warburg considered 'impossible under present circumstances'.[55]

The voters of the DVP included small property owners and artisans, civil servants and school teachers. There were only very few Jews in the last two categories. Rich Jews of the upper bourgeoisie were not numerous, but they played a more important role because of their influence and their financial

50   See 'Dr. Frenzel, alias Fränkel, und die Deutsche Volkspartei in Sachsen', *CVZ*, 3 August 1922, p. 163; also ibid., 4 May 1922.

51   Stresemann to Nathanson, 27 February 1922. Cit. Alfred Vagts, 'M. M. Warburg & Co.', p. 379, fn. 259.

52   Ibid., p. 379.

53   Dieter Rebentisch, *Ludwig Landmann, Frankfurter Oberbürgermeister der Weimarer Republik*, Wiesbaden: Steiner, 1975, p. 230. See below, p. 229–30, 308, for his election to the Reichstag in November 1932. In 1938 he was sent to the concentration camp of Buchenwald and released after three weeks in return for his promise to emigrate. He spent the years 1939–47 in England and then returned to Frankfurt. See his memoirs, Richard Merton, *Erinnernswertes aus meinem Leben*, Frankfurt: Knapp, 1955.

54   Warburg, *Aus meinen Aufzeichnungen*, p. 134.

55   Vagts, 'M. M. Warburg & Co.', p. 380.

potential. This is the reason why some baptized Jews held parliamentary seats for the DVP, thereby, too, maintaining continuity with the Wilhelminian period. The presence of these men among DVP deputies also demonstrates that racial concepts did not dominate the party, even if at times they gained ground within it during the Weimar Republic.

The best-known DVP deputy of Jewish extraction was Jakob Riesser (1853–1932), the baptized nephew of Gabriel Riesser, vice-president of the Frankfurt Parliament and pioneer of Jewish emancipation. He was elected to the Reichstag in an uncontested by-election in Heidelberg in 1916, at the time of the party truce. Riesser was a member of the Weimar National Assembly, having headed the DVP list for Frankfurt, and remained a member of the Reichstag until 1928, when he retired on grounds of age. He was one of its vice-presidents. He had all the qualities that made his candidacy appear promising: Captain in the *Landwehr* (militia), director of the Darmstädter Bank and, after resigning this post, Professor of Commercial Law at Berlin University and first president of the *Hansa-Bund*.[56] Within the party his main role was as a director of the ailing daily newspaper, *Die Zeit*. In his campaign against anti-Semitic currents within the party Stresemann frequently referred to Riesser and his influence and work.

Riesser's attitude to his Jewish extraction was ambivalent. He was the only Reichstag deputy in any of the non-Socialist parties who did not state his religion in the official handbook. By declaring himself as a Protestant he could of course have concealed his origins to those outside his own intimate circle. He may have avoided doing this to prevent controversy, as well as allusions from Jewish organizations to his relationship to Gabriel Riesser. He did not care to advertise this relationship too widely; for instance, he would not allow the C.V. to name its publishing house 'Gabriel Riesser Verlag'.[57] On the other hand his campaign within his party against anti-Semitism showed the limits of his discretion. He was not prepared to tolerate open attacks on the community to which his uncle had dedicated intense political and literary activity. It was Jakob Riesser who proposed a paragraph against anti-Semitism in the National Liberal Party programme. He suggested it in 1916 – the year of the census of Jews in the war effort. Stresemann rejected Riesser's proposal on the grounds that it would attach too much significance to anti-Semitism; this was a mere pretext for the Stresemann of the war years.

Apart from Riesser only one other DVP member of the Reichstag was of Jewish extraction. Richard Merton (1881–1960), who has already been mentioned, was one of the seven DVP deputies in the Reichstag which was

---

56 Short (auto)biography of Jakob Riesser in *Reichstags-Handbuch, III. Wahlperiode*, 1924, p. 335; also above, p. 184.
57 *CVZ*, 13 May 1932, p. 199, which erroneously states that Riesser died a Jew.

elected in November 1932 and dissolved on 4 February 1933, five days after the appointment of Hitler as Chancellor. Like Riesser he was a typical representative of the bourgeoisie: a lieutenant in the First World War, chairman of the supervisory board of the Metallgesellschaft AG which his father had founded in Frankfurt. Also, like Riesser's, his attitude to his Jewish origins was complex. He made no secret of them, but thought that Jewishness was a matter of culture, not race, and therefore capable of being 'overcome'.[58] Though this hardly coincided with National Socialist views on the subject, he and they succeeded in collaborating in Frankfurt municipal politics, as we have seen. However, it is worth noting that the DVP in Frankfurt had no misgivings about nominating a baptized Jew for the Reichstag at the head of the party list, even in November 1932.

A number of other persons of Jewish origin were prominent in DVP state or municipal politics. Lotte Garnich (1881–1939) was a DVP member of the Prussian Constituent Assembly and of the first Prussian Landtag. She was the daughter of Robert Friedberg, DDP leader in the National Assembly, and had been baptized as a child. She was married to the lawyer Hugo Garnich, also of the DVP, who was one of the Vice-Presidents of the Landtag from 1921 to 1928. In Königsberg Paul Stettiner (1862–1941) was elected as delegate to the Prussian State Council by the provincial Landtag of East Prussia. His father had been converted to the Protestant faith before the birth of his son. Stettiner was a philologist who in 1910 became chairman of the city's Education Committee. From 1914 onwards he was a member of the *Fortschrittliche Volkspartei*. During the Weimar Republic he was chairman of the DVP in the province of East Prussia until 1933. He took his life in September 1941 when forced to wear the Star of David.[59]

DVP politicians of Jewish origins were most common in Baden. A highly respected member of the Landtag was Florian Waldeck (1886–1960).[60] From

58   Merton, *Erinnernswertes*, p. 83; Mosse, *Economic Elite*, pp. 61–4.
59   Stettiner retired on reaching the age-limit in 1928 and received the honorary title of City Elder. Information on Stettiner from Ministerialrat a.D. Wilhelm Matull [H], who wrote a commemorative volume on Stettiner for Fritz Gause (ed.), *Acta Borussica 1968*, Beiheft XXIX, *Jahrbuch der Albertus-Universität Königsberg i. Pr.*, Würzburg, 1968.
60   Information about Florian Waldeck, Marie Bernays and Richard Lenel kindly supplied by the City Archive of Mannheim [H]. The City Archive has assembled a list of the names of Jewish citizens who had worked as Reichstag deputies, members of the Baden Landtag, in the City of Mannheim or as local government officials, on the initiative of the retired Lord Mayor, Dr K. O. Watzinger, and the Director of the City Archive, Dr Bleich. See F. Waldeck, 'Erzählungs-Stufen des Lebens', in *Mannheimer Hefte*, 3/1954, pp. 11–16 and Karl Otto Watzinger, *Geschichte der Juden in Mannheim, 1650–1945*, Stuttgart: Kohlhammer, 1987, pp. 43, 56, 105–9.

1919 onwards he was a member of the law practice founded by Ernst Bassermann, chairman of the National Liberal Party in the Reichstag, who had died in 1917. In 1925 Waldeck was elected deputy-chairman of the Mannheim branch of the DVP and later became its chairman. He was a DVP city councillor and the party leader on the city executive. He was also his party's leader in the Landtag from 1927 until 1933, and Vice-President of the Landtag from 1929 onwards. He returned to Mannheim after spending the years 1939–1947 in exile in the Netherlands. There he joined the CDU and was again active as a city councillor from 1947 until 1953.

The example of Waldeck and others may have persuaded Jewish voters to remain loyal to the DVP. However, Jewish politicians of other parties were equally active in the municipal politics of Baden, especially in its largest city, Mannheim, with its Jewish population of over 6,000. Throughout the Weimar period the city council contained between five and seven members of Jewish origin, at least half of them from the SPD. The merchant Julius Dreyfuß, a councillor since 1908, served as leader of the SPD grouping from 1919 to 1926, when he became chairman of the city council executive (*Stadtverordnetenvorstand*). He was succeeded as group leader by Franz Hirschler, also Jewish. Max Jeselson, who had been FVP group leader before 1918, took over the leadership of the DDP group in the Weimar Republic, until he was made an alderman in 1931. As late as 1930 there were five city council members of Jewish descent, three of the SPD, including one alderman, and one each of the DDP and DVP.

Marie Bernays (1883–1939) was also a member of the Baden Landtag from 1921 until 1925. She was a versatile woman, the daughter of a Professor of the History of Literature at the University of Munich, himself a baptized Jew. In 1920 she appeared on the DVP's national list, albeit in fourteenth place, i.e. a hopeless position. In the second half of April 1919 she launched sociological discussion evenings in Heidelberg together with Eugen Leviné, the founder and leader of the second (i.e. Communist) Soviet Republic in Munich. Together with Elisabeth Altmann-Gottheimer, Marie Bernays founded the Women's Social School in Mannheim and from 1919 until 1932 was its director. She wrote widely-read documents on the women's movement, on the care of the young and on social welfare. In 1933 she sought refuge in a convent and was converted there from the Protestant to the Catholic faith.

Richard Lenel (1869–1950) played an important role in the municipal politics of Mannheim. He came from an old-established Jewish family of industrialists and was one of the founders of the Rheinische Gummi- und Zelluloidfabrik. He had served as a National Liberal member of the city executive. From 1923 until 1931 he represented the DVP. He was the third member of his family in three generations to be president of the Mannheim Chamber of Commerce. Along with the rest of his family he had left the

Jewish faith in 1902, but without converting to Christianity. None of the DVP deputies and city councillors of Jewish origin in Mannheim had remained in the Jewish community, in contrast with the Democrats.

Hermann Reincke-Bloch, Professor of Mediaeval History at Rostock and a pre-war National Liberal, became leader of the DVP in Mecklenburg-Schwerin. He was briefly Prime Minister after the 1918 Revolution, thereafter Minister of Education.[61] Moritz Neumark (born in 1866), managing director of a large industrial concern, was a member of the Lübeck Bürgerschaft. He did not become politically active until after the Revolution, at first in the DDP and then, after 1921, in the DVP; this party formed an alliance with the *Vereinigte Politische Parteien*, later on with the *Hanseatischer Volksbund*, a middle-class coalition formed to oppose Social Democracy. Neumark resigned from politics in 1929. In 1936 he moved from Lübeck to Berlin.[62]

Jewish voters and supporters of the DVP included Ernst Schwerin, the owner of the textile factory I. Schwerin and Sons in Breslau; *Justizrat* Emil Josephthal, a member of the communal council and chairman of the C.V. in Nuremberg, who came from a long-established National Liberal family;[63] the lawyer Nathanson in Dresden, already mentioned; Fritz Rathenau, a cousin of Emil Rathenau, and a senior civil servant, an extremely capable administrator in the Prussian Ministry of the Interior who was responsible for frontier questions and overseas Germans and who resigned from the DVP in protest against its drift to the Right;[64] Richard Salomon, a baptized Jew, who was Professor of History at Hamburg University; and Kurt Alexander, a lawyer and DVP councillor in Krefeld, a member of the executive of the C.V. After 1933 Alexander was a member of the *Reichsvereinigung der deutschen Juden* in Berlin, and later of Jewish organizations in London and New York.

After Jakob Riesser, the most important Jewish personality in the party was Max Moritz Warburg. A number of other Jewish directors of the large banks shared his political affiliation. They included Eugen Gutmann, the founder of the Dresdner Bank, who was encouraged by Stresemann to join the party; his son Herbert, who was also on good personal terms with Stresemann; Arthur

---

61   Siegmund Kaznelson (ed.), *Juden im deutschen Kulturbereich. Ein Sammelwerk*, 2nd edn, Berlin: Jüdischer Verlag, 1959, p. 573; Friedrich Meinecke, *Straßburg, Freiburg, Berlin 1901–1919. Erinnerungen*, Stuttgart: Koehler, 1949, pp. 28–9.

62   Information about Moritz Neumark kindly supplied by the Lübeck City Archive [H].

63   Freudenthal, *Die israelitische Kultusgemeinde Nürnberg*, pp. 58ff., 124.

64   Fritz Rathenau left behind a typescript memoir which is deposited in the Leo Baeck Institute, New York (no. 317). See Arnold Paucker, *Der jüdische Abwehrkampf gegen Antisemitismus und Nationalsozialismus in den letzten Jahren der Weimarer Republik*, 2nd edn, Hamburg: Leibniz, 1969, p. 167, fn. 34.

Salomonsohn, owner of the Diskonto-Gesellschaft and, after its amalgamation with the Deutsche Bank, chairman of the supervisory board of the D-D Bank; Paul von Schwabach, who belonged to the party's executive; and Jakob Goldschmidt of the Danat Bank.[65] Goldschmidt served on the executive of the C.V., but resigned in 1927 in protest against that body's closer relations with the SPD.[66] Warburg did not serve on the Hamburg Bürgerschaft, to which he had belonged from 1903 to 1919, after the end of the Empire. He was, however, on the Board of the *Zentralwohlfahrtsstelle der deutschen Juden* and other Jewish organizations.[67] Warburg was filled with passionate German nationalism. To what extent it gripped him can be seen in a letter that he wrote to Georg Gothein after the Nazis' electoral triumph in 1932:

There cannot be many who feel as strongly about the Nazi movement as I do and yet I regard it without a feeling of bitterness. It is the natural consequence of an insane policy by Germany's enemies. In a way one must rejoice that after all these years of suffering there are still such strong forces within the German people as have joined together in this movement. It is deeply regrettable that it is also sowing so much hatred which will take many years to eliminate. But this is a necessary reaction. You are too great a historian and philosopher not to feel as I do. One must never lose the hope that hereafter sound and just conditions will be restored once more.[68]

Given the position of the DVP in the German party spectrum, it could not hope for a substantial electoral following from Jews. There were, however, two organizations which, while nominally neutral in party terms, tended more towards the DVP than towards any other Weimar party. The more substantial of these was the League of Jewish Veterans, the *Reichsbund jüdischer Frontsoldaten*. It was founded in 1919 to combat anti-Semitism by drawing attention to the patriotic sacrifices Jews had made during the war. Its initial membership of 15,000 had doubled by 1932.[69] The RjF collaborated with the C.V. in election campaigns and in general shared the C.V.'s premise that its members were public Germans and private Jews. This suggests that many, perhaps even the majority, of its adherents were DDP supporters.

On the other hand the RjF's public statements show concessions to the Right. It protested at being accused of a lack of patriotic feeling 'because

65 The Gutmanns: Hirsch, *Stresemann*, p. 115; *ADB* VII, p. 347; Schwabach: Jäger, *Unternehmer*, p. 121.
66 Mosse, *Economic Elite*, p. 326.
67 Hamburger, *Juden im öffentlichen Leben Deutschlands*, p. 391.
68 Warburg to Gothein, 21 August 1932. BAK, Nachlaß Gothein, Politischer und privater Briefwechsel, No. 33, p. 134.
69 Dunker, *Der Reichsbund jüdischer Frontsoldaten* p. 32; Niewyk, *The Jews in Weimar Germany*, p. 90.

internal political movements within our circles have caused some confusion'. The chairman of the RjF, Leo Löwenstein, tended to the German People's Party and could well have had a DVP parliamentary candidature, had he been willing to stand.[70] After the Nazi seizure of power Löwenstein and his followers lost no time in declaring their readiness to take an active part in the creation of a National Socialist state. The RjF co-operated relatively well with *Stahlhelm*, the veterans' organization that accepted no Jews and was closely associated with the DNVP. This indicates that some members of the RjF, though probably a minority, held political views to the Right of the parties of the Weimar coalition.[71]

A smaller and more explicitly right-wing body was the *Verband national-deutscher Juden* (V.n.J.). It was founded in 1921 by Max Naumann, a former reserve officer of the Bavarian army who had served with distinction in the war. He had been active in the National Liberal Party before 1918 and then joined the DVP.[72] He was strongly opposed to Zionism and all manifestations of Jewish nationalism and to the tendency of German-Jewish organizations, especially the C.V., to collaborate with the parties of the Left. He strongly denied any identity between the Jews of Germany and those of Eastern Europe.[73] Naumann's quarrel with the C.V. rested not only on the question of Jewish identity – he accused the C.V. of constituting an 'intermediate stratum' (*Zwischenschicht*) between German patriotism and Zionism – but also on the question of partisanship. The dispute between him and Ludwig Holländer, the Executive Secretary of the C.V., began when Holländer turned down an article of Naumann's for the C.V.'s journal *Im deutschen Reich* which advocated voting for the DVP; Naumann's reply, which became, in effect, the V.n.J.'s manifesto, was then published in the *Kölner Zeitung*, a DVP organ.[74]

How many of the V.n.J.'s 3,000 members[75] followed Naumann's party affiliation is difficult to establish. A handful belonged to parties of the Left,

70　Information from Prof. Klaus J. Herrmann, Montreal [H].
71　Dunker, *Der Reichsbund jüdischer Frontsoldaten* pp. 132, 135, 152. Asch, Memoirs No. 13, Yad Vashem, Callmann Manuscript, Reichsbund jüdischer Frontsoldaten, 61/142.
72　Carl J. Rheins, 'The Verband nationaldeutscher Juden, 1921–1933', *LBYB* XXV (1980), pp. 243–5.
73　Niewyk, *The Jews in Weimar Germany*, pp. 165–77; Rheins, *LBYB* (1980), pp. 255–64; Steven E. Aschheim, *Brothers and Strangers. The East European Jew in German and German Jewish Consciousness*, Madison, Wis.: University of Wisconsin Press, 1982, pp. 220–4.
74　Niewyk, *The Jews in Weimar Germany*, pp. 165–8.
75　Rheins, *LBYB* (1980), p. 246, fn. 24.

including the SPD.[76] The vice-chairman of the V.n.J., Dr Siegfried Breslauer, was chief political editor of the *Berliner Lokalanzeiger*, which belonged to Hugenberg's right-wing Scherl chain. There was limited reciprocation from the DVP and its press to Naumann's overtures, but this grew rarer as the 1920s wore on.[77] The choice of the word *nationaldeutsch* did not mean German Nationalist in the party political sense, but was still significant in view of the V.n.J.'s proclaimed party political neutrality. In the coded language of German politics, the word 'national' appeared in the titles of nationalistic organizations such as *Deutschnationaler Handlungsgehilfenverband* or *Nationalverband deutscher Offiziere*.

Naumann insisted both on an open avowal of Jewish extraction and an indissoluble bond between German Jews and German character and consciousness. The V.n.J.'s task was, in his words, to fight

all statements and activity of an un-German nature, regardless of whether they emanate from Jews or non-Jews, which could prejudice the revival of the German nation's strength, of German integrity and German self-respect and thus endanger Germany's rise to a respected position in the world once more. Its aim is co-operation between all Germans whether of Jewish or non-Jewish extraction based on understanding and mutual respect. They should meet together on the common ground of German patriotism and love for their German fatherland and regardless of their personal positions, to discuss questions of party politics.[78]

The similarity of this phraseology with that of the nationalistic Right is striking. It suggests that many members of the V.n.J. inclined towards a right-wing party. That would mean the DVP; the open declaration of anti-Semitism by the DNVP will have deterred most Jewish voters from voting for it.

The German National People's Party

Until the National Socialist breakthrough of 1930, the DNVP was the main German party of the Right. The history of the DNVP explains why Jews, even baptized Jews, only very rarely gave it their support.

---

76   Disputes about the role of the V.n.J. became the stuff of exile politics. In the New York German-language weekly *Aufbau* of 6 October 1972 Professor Klaus J. Herrmann emphasized the party political neutrality of the *Verband*. In reply Hans Sahl pointed out that the V.n.J. openly attacked left-wing Jews and challenged Herrmann to name left-wingers who belonged (*Aufbau*, 22 December 1972). Niewyk names two SPD members: *The Jews in Weimar Germany*, p. 172, fn. 25.
77   Rheins, *LBYB* (1980), pp. 263–4.
78   Cit. Hans-Helmut Knütter, *Die Juden und die deutsche Linke in der Weimarer Republik*, Düsseldorf: Droste, 1971, pp. 101ff.

The situation in the weeks after the Revolution led the founders of the party to believe that it was inadvisable to make an open declaration of anti-Semitism. They thought this despite the anti-Semitic antecedents of most of the new party's components – Conservatives, Christian Socials and the racialist splinter groups – and the rising tide of anti-Semitism as the war situation deteriorated. Defeat, despite the opportunities it offered for scapegoat-hunting, had also discredited the ultra-Right. For the moment, therefore, the moderate, Christian-Conservative wing of the party was dominant; it preferred, in the words of one of its spokesmen, Professor Otto Hoetzsch, to protect conservative values by embarking on parliamentary democracy rather than relying on 'extreme-nationalist radicalism' and 'the anti-Semitic wave'.[79] The founding manifesto of the party, issued on 24 November 1918, merely affirmed its support of the vital strength of Christianity and its support for a strong German nationhood free of foreign influence. The declaration of the party's executive committee of 27 December 1918 on the occasion of the election for the National Assembly was couched in similar terms.[80] Up to the elections for the National Assembly there was no party that made anti-Semitism a central point of its programme.

However, this restraint did not last for long. Though some regional organizations of the DNVP in the Eastern provinces rejected anti-Semitic material, in the hope of gaining 'national' (i.e. anti-Polish) Jewish votes, elsewhere the reactions of audiences at meetings suggested that anti-Semitism was a more popular cry than the leadership had suspected.[81] Some of the party's leaflets and newspaper articles were quite vehemently anti-Semitic, especially in their attacks on the DDP, so much so that the party's chairman, Oskar Hergt, was obliged to disavow them.[82] But the party's moderate leadership was soon outmanoeuvred. Extreme *völkisch* groupings organized outside and inside the DNVP. The chief patron of these was the Pan-German League and its terroristic offspring, the *Deutschvölkischer Schutz- und Trutzbund*. Reinhard Wulle, editor of the *Deutsche Zeitung* and at that stage still a member of the DNVP, urged his followers in the spring of 1919 'to rouse the depths of the people' and denounce the revolution as 'the star of Judah'.[83] By October 1919 the party executive signalled a partial surrender to *völkisch*

79   Otto Hoetzsch to Count Westarp, 5 December 1918. Cit. Jochmann, *KuR*, p. 444.
80   Werner Liebe, *Die deutschnationale Volkspartei 1918–1924* Düsseldorf: Droste, 1956, p. 8 (founding manifesto); pp. 109ff. (appeal by Executive Committee).
81   Lewis Hertzmann, *DNVP. Right-wing Opposition in the Weimar Republic 1918–1924*, Lincoln: Nebraska University Press, 1963, pp. 51, 46.
82   *VZ*, 4 February 1919 (a.m.), p. 3.
83   *DZ*, 13 March 1919, cit. Jochmann, *WD*, p. 451.

pressures by declaring: 'Based on this principle we fight against any corrosive, un-German spirit whether it emanates from Jewish or any other circles. We oppose most expressly the increasing predominance of Jewish participation in the Government and in public life. The flow of alien stock over our frontiers is to be stopped.'

The party's manifesto for the Reichstag election of June 1920 contained the same passage.[84] The manifesto for the Reichstag election of December 1924 was even more explicit, maintaining that the DDP was led by Jews and dependent on Marxism. It no longer referred to Jewish and other circles, nor just to predominance of Jews in government and public life, nor to the infiltration of alien stock. It stated point-blank: 'In the same way that we demand a German nationalistic spirit and measures against Jewish predominance for the German people as a whole, so also do we demand for East Prussia in particular that the infiltration of East European Jews be stemmed. Germany for the Germans.'[85]

Needless to say, there were no political candidates of the Jewish faith in the DNVP and few of Jewish ancestry. The only DNVP member of the National Assembly who was of Jewish descent was Anna von Gierke, the daughter of the eminent legal historian. Through her mother she was a cousin of the banker and DDP politician Bernhard Dernburg. She was not re-nominated in 1920, whereupon she and her father resigned from the party. An unsuccessful candidate for the National Assembly was the industrialist Richard Friedländer, who was nominated in Silesia.[86] Thereafter the only person of Jewish ancestry to play a prominent part in the DNVP was Reinhold Quaatz, a Reichstag deputy from 1920 to 1933. He was a close associate of Alfred Hugenberg, who secured his nomination for him (with some difficulty) in 1928. Indeed the Scherl newspaper chain and Ufa film company, both run by Hugenberg and employing numerous Jews, were probably a main source of Jewish votes for the DNVP.[87] A few other well-known Jewish personalities were supporters of the party. One of them was the industrialist Consul Salomon Marx, a member of the Executive Committee and Chairman of the anti-revolutionary Berlin *Bürgerrat*. He was obliged to resign from the party executive committee as anti-Semitism increased within the DNVP. Otto Arendt, the only baptized Jew to be a Free Conservative/*Reichspartei* deputy

84 Liebe, *Die deutschnationale Volkspartei 1918–1924*, pp. 115, 120.
85 Declaration and election manifesto in *Reichstags-Handbuch, III. Wahlperiode*, 1924, pp. 129–33. Democrats: p. 129; measures against Jewish predominance: p. 132.
86 Hertzmann, *DNVP*, p. 128.
87 John A. Leopold, *Alfred Hugenberg. The Radical Nationalist Campaign Against the Weimar Republic*, New Haven: Yale University Press, 1977, pp. 44, 196, fn. 101, p. 185, fn. 138.

in the Wilhelmine period, also joined the DNVP. After the Kapp putsch he changed to the DVP along with a number of prominent non-Jews, including the industrialist Siegfried von Kardorff, Otto von Dewitz and the former Baden Minister of Justice, Adalbert von Düringer, in protest against 'the increasing prominence of extreme right-wing personalities' in the DNVP.[88]

Otto Lubarsch (1860–1933) also joined the DNVP immediately after its foundation. Like Arendt he was baptized. Lubarsch, who was a prominent scholar and Professor of Pathology at Berlin University, dedicated a chapter of his memoirs to his political activities and his attitude to Judaism. He took the view that Judaism should disappear. For this reason he married a Christian wife and he wished his sons to marry Christians also. Together with three like-minded men Lubarsch had called for the founding of the Pan-German League in 1890. During the war he was active as one of the campaigners for the *Deutsche Vaterlandspartei* and became the first vice-chairman and later chairman of the *Reichsausschuß deutschnationaler Hochschullehrer*. He was 'passionately opposed' to the state which had been created after the Revolution. At a time when the National Socialists had become the strongest party he supported the referendum for the dissolution of the Prussian Landtag in which the parties forming the Weimar coalition still had a majority. Lubarsch saw in the National Socialist movement an attempt to throw off a yoke and oppose excessive foreign elements and declared that one could condemn National Socialism from a partisan, but not a patriotic, point of view.

In the DNVP Lubarsch fought the exclusion of Jews and persons of Jewish extraction from membership, though ultimately without success. He rejected racial anti-Semitism, observing that the Germans were one of the most racially-mixed nations in the world. Lubarsch not only deplored the way he was attacked by Jewish circles as a 'renegade', but also regretted the attitude of the Protestant section of the population that could not overcome its antipathy even to baptized Jews or persons of partly Jewish extraction. He said of himself that he owed his strongest influences to the German-Prussian-Christian spirit.[89]

Reflecting both its own historical legacy and the climate of opinion in the Weimar Republic, the DNVP fluctuated between varying degrees of anti-Semitism. In part this was a function of factional disputes within the party, in part a response to competition from further Right, as in the National

88 Jones, *German Liberalism*, pp. 88, 70.

89 Otto Lubarsch, *Ein bewegtes Gelehrtenleben, Erinnerungen und Erlebnisse, Kämpfe und Gedanken*, Berlin: Julius Springer, 1931, p. 540 (German-Prussian-Christian spirit); p. 563 (Jews in DNVP); p. 566 (marriage to a Christian wife); p. 577 (National Socialism).

Socialist surge of 1923–4. But it was also inherent in its own ideological premises. Otto Hoetzsch recognized this: 'With "national" thinking and work on its behalf, anti-Semitism is, the way things are, intimately connected ... The battle in the anti-Semitic sense may only be fought with decent means, with clean weapons – not forgetting common sense.'[90] How difficult it was to draw the line he was himself to experience when in 1925, at a time when the DNVP was a partner in the government, he attended an official dinner for Chaim Weizmann and found himself under strong attack from his own party.[91] There were undoubtedly conservatively-inclined Jews in the Weimar period, monarchists nostalgic for the old order, distrustful of democracy and of the increased bargaining power of organized labour. Lone voices inside the DNVP, such as Friedrich von Oppeln-Bronikowski, hoped to persuade their party to welcome them and thereby increase their number.[92] They failed; the number of Jews who supported the DNVP was at all times insignificant.

The Zentrum *and the Bavarian People's Party*

While the DNVP and Germany's Jews regarded each other with either indifference or hostility, the relationship between Jews and political Catholicism was more complex. Their interests did not coincide strongly, but there was some overlap, just as there had been before 1914. The statement by Georg Schreiber at the *Zentrum*'s first post-war conference that the party had 'always rejected' anti-Semitism[93] needs to be qualified. The political atmosphere immediately after the collapse re-awakened the latent anti-Semitism of both church and party. The association of Jews with Liberalism, capitalism and secularism, and now with subversion and anarchy, evoked renewed hostility towards a minority with whom German Catholics had at other times achieved a satisfactory *modus vivendi*. Both during the Revolution and later we have to distinguish between statements by theologians, the press and the clergy and those made by politicians, and by Catholic politicians outside the *Zentrum* as opposed to those within it, though whether these distinctions made much difference to Catholic voters, or to the Jewish assessment of the *Zentrum*, is difficult to establish.

90 Hoetzsch to Professor Karl Pflug, 24 July 1922, cit. Jochmann, *WD*, pp. 490–1, fn. 300.

91 Manfred Dörr, *Die deutschnationale Volkspartei* [Diss.], Marburg, 1964, p. 257, fn. 18.

92 Friedrich von Oppeln-Bronikowski, *Antisemitismus? Eine unparteiische Prüfung des Problems*, Charlottenburg: Verlagsgesellschaft für Politik und Geschichte, 1920; *idem*, 'Gerechtigkeit'. *Zur Lösung der Judenfrage*, Berlin: 1932.

93 Rudolf Morsey, *Die deutsche Zentrumspartei 1917–1923*, Düsseldorf: Droste, 1966, p. 135, fn. 7.

Two concerns, in particular, irritated Catholic sensitivities. One was the fear that the Revolution would bring about a totally centralized political authority in Germany, as advocated, for instance, in Hugo Preuß's constitutional draft, and with it an irreligious educational system; the other was the spectre of Bolshevism, as evoked by the short-lived Soviet Republics in the Catholic heartland of Bavaria. Secularization was also threatened by the educational policies of the new Prussian government. In Prussia, as in the *Reich*, the people's delegates of the USPD resigned from the government at the end of 1918. Thus the period of office of the militant atheist Adolph Hoffmann at the head of the Ministry of Education came to an early end. But his appearance at this particular point, together with memories of decades of his polemics against 'clericalism', sufficed to kindle storms of indignation in ecclesiastically-minded circles. The historian Rudolf Morsey sees his tenure of office as a main reason why the *Zentrum* could make the threat of a new *Kulturkampf* plausible.[94] Though Hoffmann had originally been a Protestant, anti-Semitism seemed an appropriate means of reviving opposition to 'godless Berlin'. The *Kölnische Volkszeitung* found 'the racially alien masters of Prussia' as repellent as 'the rough dictatorship of the alien intruder Kurt Eisner in the good land of the Bavarians',[95] while *Germania* muttered darkly that pogroms were in the offing:

For the time being the Jews themselves are called upon to look after their own interests and the best way to achieve that is to dissociate themselves from the subversives in their own ranks, as they are at the moment doing in Budapest. Then, once the Spartacists have been toppled, there need be no fears of persecutions of the Jews or pogroms. Should things go on in the present manner, however, then no human being will be able to avert what must come.[96]

In Bavaria the experience of the revolutionary governments in which numerous Jews were prominent led to even greater polarization. The Bavarian People's Party (BVP), which had separated itself from the more liberal-minded *Zentrum* in the rest of Germany, was vehement in its opposition to these developments, whether in Munich or Berlin. Its initial pronouncement was relatively moderate: 'The Bavarian People's Party knows no differences between Bavarians of the Jewish faith and Germans and Bavarians of the Christian faith ... for the Bavarian People's Party membership of a race plays no role either. ... What must be fought are the numerous

94   Ibid., p. 119.
95   *KVZ*, 4 December 1918.
96   *Germania*, 1 July 1919; see also *MVA*, 10 July 1919; *IdR* XXI/7, July–August 1919, pp. 300–1.

atheistic elements of a certain international Jewry with predominantly Russian colouring.'[97] By the following April it stated that 'the Bavarian People's Party decisively rejects all violations of the entity of the people by a terroristic minority, led by elements alien in origin and race, and demands that there should at last be an end to the agitation among wide circles of the population on the part of foreign, politicizing Jews.'[98] Georg Heim, one of the leading proponents of the BVP's breach with the *Zentrum*, thundered against the 'centralizing Jews' Preuß and Landsberg. Georg Strang, in contrast, wanted to 'bring together the entire religiously observant people, including the Jews, against the red peril'.[99] Though these polemics subsided as time went on, they illustrated the divided political emotions of German Catholics. Though many of them were no doubt monarchists at heart, the *Zentrum* was pragmatic in the choice of constitutional forms: it existed to defend an interest, not a principle. Once a democratic republic seemed unstoppable, accommodation was feasible. What *Zentrum* leaders like Karl Bachem feared was that 'our democracy is ... in religious matters "free-thinking" and "social democratic"'.[100] The Hoffmann and Eisner episodes, with their 'godless' school policies, confirmed the worst fears. Similarly the trend of cultural developments in the Weimar Republic drove many in the *Zentrum* to tactical alliances with the conservative and anti-democratic Right, whether in the 1926 controversy over the pornography laws or the public agitation against performances of Schnitzler's *Reigen*.[101]

However, as the Republic stabilized, there was a growing contrast between the official policies of the *Zentrum* and Catholic publicists not formally connected with it, or indeed opposed to it. With the secession of the BVP, the overwhelming part of *Zentrum* support came from the Rhineland, Baden and Württemberg, regions in which democratic traditions were strong. The December 1918 programme of the *Zentrum* demanded 'equal consideration for the members and institutions of the various religious denominations in all areas of public life'; one of the *Zentrum*'s Protestant supporters, Professor Karl Dunkmann, saw it as 'a collective name for all religious forces,

---

97   'BVP und Judentum', *Bayerischer Kurier*, 6 December 1918, cit. Allan Mitchell, *Revolution in Bavaria 1918–1919. The Eisner Regime and the Soviet Republic*, Princeton: Princeton University Press, 1965, p. 192.
98   Rudolf Kanzler, *Bayerns Kampf gegen den Bolschewismus. Geschichte der bayerischen Einwohnerwehren*, Munich: Park-Verlag, 1931, p. 14.
99   Ernest Hamburger, *LBYB* (1975), p. 194; Roland Flade, *Juden in Würzburg 1918–1933*, Würzburg: Freunde mainfränkischer Kunst und Geschichte, 1986, p. 79.
100   Bachem to *Reichsrat* Franz von Buhl, 25 August 1917, cit. Morsey, *Die deutsche Zentrumspartei*, p. 64.
101   Jochmann, 'Struktur und Funktion', *WD*, p. 495.

including Jewry'.[102] By 1922, however, the *Zentrum* stressed the cultivation of 'Christian-German spiritual heritage [*christlich-deutsches Geisteserbe*]'.[103] An increasing number of *Zentrum* politicians were prepared to take public stands against anti-Semitism or express solidarity with Jews in some other respect. Prominent *Zentrum* politicians to become associated with the *Abwehr-Verein* included the former Chancellor Konstantin Fehrenbach (from Baden), Prelate Carl Ulitzka (from Silesia) and the secretary of the *Zentrum* youth wing, the *Windthorst-Bünde*, Heinrich Krone.[104] Krone became the last chairman of the *Abwehr-Verein* after Gothein's resignation in the spring of 1933 and had the painful duty of winding up its affairs. He was one of the founders of the CDU after the Second World War and chairman of its Bundestag grouping from 1956 to 1961. Joseph Wirth (also from Baden), who was Chancellor at the time of the murder of Rathenau, was an explicit opponent of those behind that crime: 'There stands the enemy, where Mephisto drips his poison into a people's wounds. ... That enemy stands on the Right.'[105] Wilhelm Marx, party chairman from 1922 to 1928 and himself a four-time Chancellor, denounced the murder in similar terms. He regarded anti-Semitism as inherently anti-Christian and something that 'Catholics fundamentally and consciously reject'. In a letter to the C.V., written shortly before the appointment of Hitler as Chancellor, he found it 'simply inconceivable that a nation like the Germans that was otherwise so sensible and restrained could be taken in by so much nonsense in such large numbers'.[106] On one occasion he went so far as to refer to himself as a spokesman for the Jews.[107] Since he was also president of the Catholic mass organization, the *Volksverein für das katholische Deutschland*, these views were presumably of some influence. In general, the further to the Left a *Zentrum* politician stood, the more closely he was associated with the Republican defence league, *Reichsbanner Schwarz–Rot–Gold*, or other indicators of loyalty to the Weimar constitution, the more likely he was to be actively opposed to anti-Semitism. The outstanding instance of this was the Frankfurt-on-Main branch of the party, the leading figure of which was the bio-physicist Friedrich Dessauer, editor from 1923 onwards of the *Rhein-Mainische Volkszeitung*. He and his

102   Morsey, *Die deutsche Zentrumspartei*, pp. 129–30, 134.
103   Karl Bachem, *Vorgeschichte, Geschichte und Politik der deutschen Zentrumspartei*, Cologne: Bachem, 1927–32, vol. VIII, pp. 369ff.
104   Suchy, *LBYB* (1985), pp. 90, 91.
105   *StBR*, 25 June 1922, vol. 354, p. 8055A.
106   'Das Zentrum und die Völkischen. Ein Brief des Senatspräsidenten Marx', *CVZ*, 31 August 1922, p. 211; 'Reichskanzler Marx an den Centralverein', ibid., 15 January 1933, p. 14; BAK, Reichskanzlei R 431/2193.
107   Paucker, *Abwehrkampf*, p. 231.

managing director, Dr Josef Knecht, were both members of the *Reichsbanner*, Dessauer of the *Abwehr-Verein* and his literary editor Walter Dirks of the pacifist *Friedensbund Deutscher Katholiken*. Dessauer and Krone were sympathetic to the *Friedensbund*, even if not members, a view that correlated strongly with support for the Republic and opposition to anti-Semitism.[108] Dessauer's was virtually the only Catholic paper to protest against the 1933 Nazi boycott of Jewish businesses and invited Martin Buber to contribute articles.[109] He was repeatedly attacked as a 'Jew-lout' by the Nazi press for his pains.[110] His stance may well have accounted for the exceptional swing of Frankfurt Jewish voters to the *Zentrum* after the collapse of the Liberal parties in 1932.[111]

A number of Jewish religious leaders urged their flocks to support the *Zentrum*. These included Rabbi Isidor Scheftelowitz of Cologne[112] and, most prominent of all, Rabbi Esra Munk, chairman of the Orthodox *Bund gesetzestreuer jüdischer Gemeinden Deutschland* and the *Landesverband gesetzestreuer Synagogengemeinden* of Prussia. In these capacities he was an adviser to the Prussian government on Jewish religious affairs. The congregations affiliated to Munk's organization were, however, small. There was a more consistent Jewish electorate for the *Zentrum* in Silesia, dating from before 1914. The leader of the *Zentrum* in Silesia, Prelate Carl Ulitzka, who became a member of the executive of the *Abwehr-Verein*, was instrumental in maintaining this. While he may have had a political motive in cultivating Jewish support in his campaign to establish Upper Silesia as a separate province in Prussia, it was apparent that he also saw a convergence of Christian and Jewish religious values: 'Why cannot our political axioms of respect for authority, of tolerance, of social conscience, of charitable activity, of culture conditioned by positive faith, not also be the ideals of a German Jew?',[113] he wrote to the C.V. Zionists fluctuated in their support for the

---

108 Bruno Lowitsch, *Der Kreis um die Rhein-Mainische Volkszeitung*, Wiesbaden: Franz Steiner, 1980, pp. 6, 12, 14, 25; Dieter Riesenberger, 'Der "Friedensbund Deutscher Katholiken" und der politische Katholizismus in der Weimarer Republik', in Karl Holl and Wolfram Wette (eds), *Pazifismus in der Weimarer Republik*, Paderborn: Schöning, 1981, pp. 107–8. Dirks was one of the founders of the CDU in Frankfurt in 1945 and, with Eugen Kogon, spoke for its left wing through the *Frankfurter Hefte*.

109 Boycott: *Rhein-Mainische Volkszeitung*, 4 April 1933, Buber: ibid., 13 April, 4 May 1933. Lowitsch, *Der Kreis*, p. 127.

110 Lowitsch, *Der Kreis*, p. 22; Heinz Blankenberg, *Politischer Katholizismus in Frankfurt am Main 1918–1933*, Mainz: Matthias Grünewald Verlag, 1981, p. 247.

111 See below, pp. 305–8.

112 *KVZ*, 18 January 1919.

113 'Oberschlesien und die deutschen Juden', *CVZ*, 15 June 1922, pp. 86ff.

Zentrum. At the time of the Reichstag elections of May 1924 the *Jüdische Rundschau* recommended a vote for the SPD, the only party faithful to 'the great ideal claims of equal rights and liberating humanity.' Of the *Zentrum* it warned that it 'contained not very many Wirths but a great many curates and country priests who pass judgments about Jews and Jewish matters with frivolous ignorance'.[114]

In Bavaria the situation was somewhat different. The BVP was anxious to establish itself as more than the successor to the old *Zentrum*. It proclaimed itself to be a 'general collective Christian party of all citizens of positive non-Socialist views',[115] though it did not succeed in recruiting all pre-war Protestant Conservatives or Liberals under this banner. The *Zentrum*'s commitment to religious tolerance had never been uniformly accepted in Bavaria under the Empire. This reflected the conflict between the Catholic small and medium farmers and artisans, who were under-represented by the limited franchise that lasted until 1906, and a Liberal or secular-minded civil service. The Liberal attitude of the administration continued into the war, when the Bavarian War Minister opposed the census of Jews ordered by the Berlin military authorities. Anti-Semitism was a useful weapon in the hands of populists like Georg Heim and those of the clergy that supported him in his battle against this oligarchy. The reaction to the revolutionary governments in Munich therefore intensified an already widespread predisposition and anti-Semitism survived the 1918 upheavals for longer than in the *Zentrum*. The Württemberg ambassador, who was no admirer of the political culture of Bavaria, spoke of 'anti-Semitism [which is] so popular in these parts'. In 1922 Heinrich Held, one of the moderate members of the BVP and later Prime Minister of Bavaria, having first assured his Landtag audience that he was neither a racial nor any other kind of anti-Semite, went on to ask: 'Is it not perhaps correct after all that for over a hundred years the German nation has been led into a morass, principally under Jewish influence, mainly by philosophers, poets, writers, at least in a spiritual and moral sense?'[116] There was therefore little deterrence to continued agitation against Jews and

114 'Wahlmerkzettel', *JR* 29 April 1924, p. 245.
115 Klaus Schönhoven, *Die bayerische Volkspartei 1924–1932*, Düsseldorf: Droste, 1972, p. 21.
116 'Den hier so beliebten Antisemitismus', 20 April 1920. *Politik in Bayern, 1919–1933. Berichte des württembergischen Gesandten Carl Moser von Filseck* (ed. Wolfgang Benz), Stuttgart: Deutsche Verlags-Anstalt, 1971, p. 58; Held: *Stenographische Berichte der Verhandlungen des Bayerischen Landtags*, IV. Tagung 1922/3, vol. II, p. 79; reprinted in *Ursachen und Folgen. Vom deutschen Zusammenbruch 1918 und 1945 bis zur staatlichen Neuordnung Deutschlands in der Gegenwart*. Urkunden- und Dokumentensammlung zur Zeitgeschichte, vol. VII (ed. Herbert Michaelis, Ernst Schraepler and Günter Scheel), Berlin: Wendler, 1961, pp. 199ff.

those from Eastern Europe in particular. This applied especially to the Bavarian government's actions under State Commissioner Gustav von Kahr in 1923 and 1924, where the opposition came from the *Reich* and Prussian governments.[117]

The anti-Semitic tendencies of the BVP did not stop Jewish citizens from voting for it. Among them were rabbis in Munich and Regensburg, where Rabbi S. Mayer saw the BVP as the protector of 'the religion of all confessions',[118] members of the Schweinfurt branch of the *Bund gesetzestreuer jüdischer Gemeinden*, as well as other Orthodox and Conservative Jews, who were more numerous in Bavaria than in other parts of Germany. In addition the weakness of the SPD and DDP in Bavaria and the strength of National Socialism there made the BVP more attractive as the lesser evil. The C.V. treated the BVP with understandable circumspection,[119] but was anxious not to break off contact with the party that dominated the government of Bavaria throughout the Weimar Republic.[120] Its advice to members was neutral: they were never warned not to vote for the BVP, a stance of which it became more confident in the later stages of the Republic.[121]

Just as the BVP was more hospitable to anti-Semitic currents than the less conservative *Zentrum*, so conservatively-minded Catholics outside those two parties showed even greater hostility to Jewish rights and Jewish claims. That applied in particular to important segments of the Catholic intelligentsia. Many Catholic publications continued to show hostility to Jews, or at least indifference to their interests, e.g. in encyclopaedias, such as the *Staatslexikon der Görresgesellschaft* (1927 edition), the *Lexikon für Theologie und Kirche* (1930 edition) and the more popular *Der große Herder* (1931 edition).[122] The same applied to some priests and even bishops, including Buchberger of

117 See above, p. 227.

118 Flade, *Juden in Würzburg*, p. 79.

119 Cf. the report on the 1928 Reichstag election campaign in Bavaria, 'Aus dem Wahlkampf! Für den Wahlkampf', *CVZ*, 27 April 1928, p. 228. Among the leading BVP papers containing anti-Semitic remarks, the article mentions the *Bayerischer Kurier* and *Regensburger Anzeiger*.

120 Werner J. Cahnman, 'The Nazi Threat and the Centralverein – A Recollection', in Herbert A. Strauss (ed.), *Conference on Anti-Semitism 1969*, New York: American Federation of Jews from Central Europe, 1969, pp. 33–4.

121 See below, pp. 313–14.

122 Hermann Greive, *Theologie und Ideologie. Katholizismus und Judentum in Deutschland und Österreich 1918–1935*, Heidelberg: Lambert Schneider, 1969, pp. 95–116; Karl Thieme, 'Deutsche Katholiken', in *Entscheidungsjahr 1932*, pp. 247–284; Rudolf Lill, 'Die deutschen Katholiken und die Juden in der Zeit von 1850 bis zur Machtübernahme Hitlers', *KuS*, vol. II, pp. 400–5.

Regensburg and Ow-Felldorf of Passau.[123] The *Verein katholischer Edelleute* (Union of Catholic Noblemen), which included some *Zentrum* members, committed itself in 1920 to 'excluding, as far as possible, from the public life of Germany the influence of racially alien elements as the main agents of the pernicious spirit of usury, corruption, the desire for profit without work'.[124] The most prominent Catholic politician to express his move to the anti-Republican Right in anti-Semitic terms was Martin Spahn, the son of Peter Spahn, one of the founders of the *Zentrum* who, as the last pre-revolutionary Minister of Justice in Prussia, had been instrumental in accelerating the promotion of Jews in the judiciary. Before 1914 the younger Spahn had belonged to the 'Cologne' wing of the party, which favoured a less explicitly confessional stance and greater collaboration with Protestant conservatives. After the Revolution he became increasingly alienated from the *Zentrum*'s accommodation with democracy and the surrender, as he saw it, to the political values of the West. He joined the DNVP in 1920 and was prominent in the *Nationale Arbeitsgemeinschaft deutscher Katholiken*, with the aim of winning Catholic voters for the Nationalist Right. This group gained the support of the old-established *Görres-Korrespondenz*, edited by his brother-in-law Karl Görres, as well as the *Historisch-Politische Blätter* (later *Gelbe Blätter*), which occasionally spiced their polemics with anti-Semitism.[125] His own *Katholische Wochenzeitung* pursued a similar line. Having denounced the Weimar constitution as the work of 'the Jew Preuß, who lives and operates exclusively in the concepts of Western constitutionalism',[126] he moved towards an increasingly racial interpretation of politics. The concept of 'spiritual' racialism enabled him to identify all liberals and democrats as 'spiritual Jews',[127] to define a people as 'a community of blood, labour and culture'[128] and to denounce capitalism as 'racially and spatially alien' to Germans.[129] These thoughts were a direct development of his pre-war position in which he had diagnosed Jews as a mobile element 'with a preference for tending to the Left and engaging in radical activity'. It was they who, through the 'root-

123   Gunther Lewy, *The Catholic Church and Nazi Germany*, London: Weidenfeld & Nicolson, 1964, pp. 268–74, Lill, *KuS*, vol. II, p. 404.

124   Morsey, *Die deutsche Zentrumspartei*, p. 314, fn. 21.

125   Ibid., pp. 312–15; Trude Maurer, *Ostjuden in Deutschland, 1918–1933*, Hamburg: Christians, 1986, pp. 206–9.

126   *Das neue Reich*, 9 May 1920, p. 512, cit. Morsey, *Die deutsche Zentrumspartei*, p. 314, fn. 16.

127   Gabriele Clemens, *Martin Spahn und der Rechtskatholizismus in der Weimarer Republik*, Mainz: Matthias Grünewald Verlag, 1983, p. 109.

128   *StBR*, 10 June 1929, vol. 452, p. 2255.

129   Martin Spahn, 'Volk im Raum I', in *idem, Für den Reichsgedanken. Historisch-politische Aufsätze, 1915–1934*, Berlin and Bonn: Dümmler, 1934, p. 111.

less metropolitan press', had been disproportionately responsible for the defeat of the Right in the 1912 election.[130] It is not surprising that these views led him to join the Nazi Party in 1933.

The smaller right-of-centre parties

Splinter parties like the *Wirtschaftspartei*, the various regional agricultural groups and the *Christlich-Sozialer Volksdienst* (CSVD) had little appeal for Jews at Reichstag elections. The CSVD, which gained a following among Pietists and Protestant trade unionists in the early 1930s and therefore appeared as a barrier against the rise of Nazism, may have got some campaign funds from the C.V.; at any rate the Nazis accused them of this.[131] Only the *Wirtschaftspartei*, which represented small businessmen and property owners, made any efforts to attract Jewish voters, including – up to 1930 – advertisements in the *C.V.-Zeitung* and the *Jüdisch-Liberale Zeitung*.[132] The party's founder, Professor Johann Victor Bredt, recorded in his memoirs: 'Jews and dissidents could also become members of our party, provided they did not oppose its Christian character. All we did was to avoid Jews in any way becoming prominent within the party.'[133] Like other parties of the centre-right, the *Wirtschaftspartei* was torn between the anti-Semitic pressures of some local organizations and campaigners, and a national leadership that sought to maintain more enlightened policies.[134] Jews were perhaps more likely to vote for parties of this type at the local than at the national level. In Berlin Hermann Perl led the *Wirtschaftspartei* in the city council.[135] In the years after the Revolution two deputies of the *Hamburger Wirtschaftliche Partei*, Max Moses Isaac (1865–1940), who owned a ladies' clothing firm, and Franz Viktor Liebermann (1870–1938), who owned an import and export trading firm, sat in the Bürgerschaft.[136] In Mannheim Max Moses (1884–1951), a baptized Jew, founded a branch of the *Evangelisch-Soziale Partei*

---

130 *Idem*, 'Die radikale Krise im Reich', *Hochland* IX, March 1912, p. 705. See also Introduction, p. 000.

131 Günther Opitz, *Der Christlich-soziale Volksdienst*, Düsseldorf: Droste, 1969, p. 176, fn. 63.

132 Paucker, *Abwehrkampf*, pp. 92, 272, fn. 92.

133 Martin Schumacher (ed.), *Erinnerungen und Dokumente von Joh. Victor Bredt*, Düsseldorf: Droste, 1970, p. 36, fn. 48.

134 Martin Schumacher, *Mittelstandsfront und Republik. Wirtschaftspartei – Die Reichspartei des deutschen Mittelstandes, 1919–1933*, Düsseldorf: Droste, 1972, pp. 49, 55.

135 Information from Professor Donna Harsch, Carnegie University, Pittsburgh.

136 Information from the Hamburg State Archive (letter of 19 May 1970) and Dr Arnold Herzfeld of New York [H].

immediately after the Revolution and became its chairman at the beginning of 1919. At the city council election in May 1919 his name appeared on the joint list of his party and the Tenants' Association. In the city council Moses then became chairman of the *Deutschliberale Partei*, in which these parties had amalgamated, and remained in this position until 1926. In his personal record he noted that he had tried to oppose 'heathen-Jewish materialism' with the Christian spirit. After the war he refused an offer to take charge of compensation claims of Jews who had been in concentration camps on the grounds that, though he was racially a Jew, he was by religion a Protestant.[137]

The Socialist parties

Jews were prominent in the leadership of both the majority Social Democratic Party (SPD) and the Independent Social Democratic Party (USPD), as well as the newly-founded Communist Party, discussed in the next section. This was true particularly in the months following the Revolution; thereafter Jewish participation receded. Of the pre-war Jewish Socialist leaders Hugo Haase and Emanuel Wurm died before the re-unification of the two parties; Gustav Hoch and Eduard Bernstein fell into the background and retired on grounds of age in 1928. Oskar Cohn devoted his attention to the Zionist Labour Party *Poale Zion*, which he led in the Berlin community council and represented in the *Preußischen Landesverband* after 1925. The successor generation of Jewish Socialists were more active outside the parliamentary parties than within them.

As before 1914, Jewish prominence among the Social Democratic leadership was not necessarily reflected in Jewish voting support. The social structure of the Jewish population did not favour identification with the Left. The move into paid or manual work that had begun before 1914 continued, but did not accelerate. The percentage of Jews who were self-employed was 50 in 1907 and 46 in 1933; among non-Jews the figures were 22 and 16.[138] Many Jews were willing to endure hardship rather than relinquish economic independence. It was often easier to obtain credit or support from within the family network than to compete in a hostile labour market. Those Jews who were employed in manual work in the Rhenish-Westphalian industrial area or in Hesse and Saxony had been almost exclusively recruited from Eastern

137 Information on Max Moses is deposited in the Archive of the City of Mannheim (see also above, p. 230, fn. 60).

138 Esra Bennathan, 'Die demographische und wirtschaftliche Struktur der Juden', *Entscheidungsjahr 1932*, pp. 103, 123–4.

Europe during the war or had immigrated immediately afterwards.[139] As foreigners they had no franchise. However, *Poale Zion* was active in the Rhineland and Westphalia and urged Jewish workers to support the SPD and its trade unions.[140] The main change in the Jewish social structure was the increase in white-collar employment, which rose from 12.5 per cent to 33.5 per cent between 1907 and 1933.[141]

There were nevertheless other factors that led Jews in the direction of Social Democracy. One was continuing urbanization, which diminished the ties of traditionalism characteristic of the smaller communities and in general encouraged political radicalization. Another was economic pressure. A substantial proportion of white-collar trade union organization was directly or indirectly anti-Semitic. The *Deutschnationaler Handlungsgehilfenverband* (DNHV) was openly anti-Semitic; it was one of a number of non-Socialist unions, generally nationalist or denominational in character, who came together in the *Deutscher Gewerkschaftsbund* in 1920, whose chairman and secretary were the *Zentrum* politicians Adam Stegerwald and Heinrich Brüning.[142] Employers, including Jewish ones, sought to avoid conflict with white-collar unions, thereby diminishing the employment chances of Jews. It could be easier for a Jew to become the director of a bank than a bank clerk. The SPD, on the other hand, which had repelled many white-collar workers before 1914 by its aggressively proletarian outlook, became more reformist in the course of the Weimar Republic.

The leader of the left-wing white-collar workers' organizations, which came together in the *Arbeitsgemeinschaft freier Angestelltenverbände* (AfA), was the Jewish Reichstag deputy Siegfried Aufhäuser. Aufhäuser, who was born in Augsburg in 1884, had been active in the white-collar employees' movement from 1903 onwards. He became secretary of the *Bund der technisch-industriellen Beamten* in 1913 and in 1919 general secretary of the *Bund der technischen Angestellten und Beamten*. In 1921 he was elected full-time chairman of the AfA. Like a number of middle-class inter-war Social Democrats, he began his political career before 1914 in the *Demokratische Vereinigung*.

139   S. Adler-Rudel, *Ostjuden in Deutschland. Zugleich eine Geschichte der Organisationen, die sie betreuten*, Tübingen: J. C. B. Mohr, 1959, esp. tables on pp. 163–6; Maurer, *Ostjuden in Deutschland 1918–1933*, pp. 63–100.
140   'An die jüdische Arbeiterschaft in Rheinland und Westfalen', cit. Adler-Rudel, *Ostjuden in Deutschland*, pp. 161–2.
141   Bennathan, 'Die demographische und wirrschaftliche Struktur der Juden', p. 123.
142   Heinrich Brüning, *Memoiren 1918–1934*, Stuttgart: Deutsche Verlags-Anstalt, 1970, p. 76. For a detailed account of the party connections of Christian and nationalist trade union officials, see Michael Schneider, *Die christlichen Gewerkschaften, 1894–1933*, Bonn and Bad Godesberg: Neue Gesellschaft 1982, pp. 486–96, 624–51.

During the war he joined the USPD and in 1920 he was appointed to the National Economic Council (*Reichswirtschaftsrat*). He became a member of the Reichstag in 1921. After the amalgamation of the two Socialist parties in 1922 he became a respected but critical member of the SPD and its Reichstag delegation;[143] his radicalism was less fundamental than verbal and tactical. His political example may well have influenced Jewish employees to vote SPD or, until 1922, USPD.

Despite the general broadening of its appeal after 1918, the SPD made only limited progress among the business and professional bourgeoisie, whether Jewish or not. As before 1914, there was a handful of Jewish merchants and industrialists, whose social idealism or pacifist convictions led them to the SPD. Louis Cohn, a factory-owner in Görlitz, was elected to the Silesian provincial Landtag and was also an active member of the Prussian Staatsrat. Hugo Frey, a merchant, became an SPD Breslau city councillor and his brother Georg was elected an honorary alderman. In Halberstadt Willy Cohn, who owned the largest department store, supported the SPD and the Republican defence league, *Reichsbanner Schwarz–Rot–Gold*, both in spirit and materially, as did his cousin Hugo Rosenbaum. Hugo Simon, the joint owner of a banking house in Berlin, was a Socialist whose pacifist conviction had led him to join the USPD during the war; at the time of the Revolution he was briefly Prussian Minister of Finance. However, these were all isolated cases.[144]

Whereas Socialist sympathies were fairly rare among Jewish businessmen, academics had more influence, sometimes gathering small circles of intellectuals about them. Before 1918 left-wing students, many of them Jews, had been in the habit of meeting at the academic courses for workers; those studying in Berlin met at the houses of Socialist leaders like Hugo Haase or Karl Kautsky, often motivated by a desire to improve the social lot of both the German nation and mankind in general. They were joined by sympathizers who were inspired by the life-style and example of these men. One of them was Georg Flatow, a senior civil servant in the Prussian Ministry of Trade and the author of the standard commentary on the law on works' councils. Among those who frequented his house was Otto Kahn-Freund (1900–74), an industrial judge in Berlin, whom Flatow recruited as joint author of the last editions of his commentary. Kahn-Freund made a name for himself as a lawyer well beyond the subject of industrial legislation. After his emigration he became Professor of Comparative Law at the University of

143   *Reichstags-Handbuch, III. Wahlperiode*, 1924, pp. 193ff; Siegfried Aufhäuser, *An der Schwelle des Zeitalters der Angestellten*, Berlin: Heenemann, 1963.
144   See also Ernest Hamburger and Peter Pulzer, 'Jews as Voters in the Weimar Republic', *LBYB* XXX (1985), p. 36.

Oxford and was knighted for his services. Fritz Wittelshöfer's main sphere of work in the Prussian Ministry of Social Welfare was the whole subject of public relief and assistance. He also figured prominently in the legal re-organization of the social welfare system in the *Reich* and in Prussia. Under his influence his assistant, Ernst Herrnstadt, became a Social Democrat; both worked for the monthly journal *Arbeiterwohlfahrt*. Alfred Oborniker, a criminal lawyer, frequently wrote for the journal of Republican lawyers, *Die Justiz*. Hilde Oppenheimer, a trained social worker, became a senior civil servant in the *Reich* Ministry of Labour. Ministers who headed this department, including Rudolf Wissell of the SPD and Heinrich Brauns of the *Zentrum*, held her in high esteem.

Leading Jewish personalities in another group, whose members were mostly pacifists and supporters of the USPD, were Rudolf Hilferding, Hugo Simon and Leo Kestenberg. Hilferding, who had already made a name for himself before the war as the author of *Finanzkapital* (1910) and as a prominent member of the party's radical faction, replaced Kautsky as the party's leading theoretician during the Weimar period. He was also the most influential Jewish member of the SPD leadership after the re-unification of the two Socialist parties, a member of the party executive and the only Jew to hold cabinet office on behalf of the SPD in the post-revolutionary period. He did so twice as Minister of Finance, in 1923 when he played a leading role in the stabilization of the currency, and in the Great Coalition from 1928 to 1929. Kestenberg, a professor of music, was in time promoted to a senior civil service post in the Prussian Ministry of Education.[145]

Professional contacts often led to wider social connections. The aura that emanated from these circles could be more attractive for young people than the customary mass meetings. Thus groups and circles were formed of Republican, mainly Socialist, civil servants and professionals that were also a meeting-place for Jews and non-Jews. Politics in general was by no means always the main subject of the discussions; instead, interest was shown in detailed topics such as welfare, industrial legislation and education. In this way a student's special interests could be developed. Examples of this are Richard Joachim, who later had responsibility for industrial law in the *Reich* Ministry of Labour; Georg Flatow, already referred to, of the Prussian Ministry of Trade; and Otto Brahn, an industrial arbitrator in Upper Silesia and later in Rhineland-Westphalia. All of them were Socialists.

These developments were most apparent in Berlin. The major Social Democratic journals were published here. After the theoretical journal of the party, *Neue Zeit*, had ceased publication, *Die Gesellschaft* was launched in

---

145 See Leo Kestenberg, *Bewegte Zeiten. Musischmusikantische Lebenserrinerungen*, Wolfenbüttel and Zürich: Möseler, 1961.

1924. It was edited by Hilferding who was replaced, during his periods of office as a cabinet minister, by the sociologist Albert Salomon. Before the re-unification of the two Socialist parties Hilferding had edited the USPD's journal, *Die Freiheit*; in exile after 1933 he edited the *Zeitschrift für Sozialismus*, published in Karlsbad. During and after the Third Reich Salomon taught at the New School for Social Research in New York. The rather less theoretical weekly *Das freie Wort* was edited by Ernst Heilmann. The revisionist *Sozialistische Monatshefte*, edited, as before 1918, by Joseph Bloch, and the radical *Glocke*, edited by Parvus, continued to exist. The journal *Der Klassenkampf*, the mouthpiece of the left wing of the party, was first published in 1927 with a five-man editorial staff of whom three were Jews: the Austrian Max Adler, as well as Paul Levi and Kurt Rosenfeld. In the later years of the Weimar Republic the *Neue Blätter für den Sozialismus* appeared, designed to improve the election prospects of Social Democracy. Jews were the principal editors of most of these publications and provided between 20 per cent and 40 per cent of the staff.

In the main these journals influenced the allegiance of intellectual, often Jewish, circles in the capital. Their circulation was small. One exception was *Weltbühne* which in its prime had a circulation of approximately 20,000. After the death of its founder Siegfried Jacobsohn in 1927, this was taken over by Carl von Ossietzky, a non-Jew. He died in a Nazi concentration camp in 1938, two years after having been awarded the Nobel Peace Prize. Of the 68 contributors to *Weltbühne* whose religious origins could be established, only 24 were non-Jewish; of these, three had Jewish wives.[146] The purely party journals were well satisfied with a print run of about one thousand and had few individual subscribers beyond Berlin. As far as the daily press was concerned, Stampfer of *Vorwärts* was joined by Victor Schiff, a well-informed foreign affairs editor, and Erich Kuttner, a clever and humorous permanent contributor. Of the more important provincial Socialist dailies Hermann Liebmann edited the *Leipziger Volksblatt* and Gustav Warburg was assistant editor of the *Hamburger Echo*. Lower down the scale Walter Fabian edited the *Chemnitzer Volksstimme* until his breach with the party and Immanuel Birnbaum the *Volkswacht für Schlesien*. Both Fabian and Birnbaum resumed their journalistic careers in the Federal Republic, Fabian as editor of the *Gewerkschaftliche Monatshefte*, Birnbaum as one of the editors-in-chief and the foreign affairs editor of the Munich *Süddeutsche Zeitung*. Hans Marckwald, an SPD member of the Hesse Landtag, edited the Frankfurt

146 Istvan Déak, *Weimar's Left-Wing Intellectuals. A Political History of the 'Weltbühne' and its Circle*, Berkeley and Los Angeles: University of California Press, 1968, p. 24; Elke Suhr, *Carl von Ossietzky. Eine Biografie*, Cologne: Kiepenheuer & Wietsch, 1988, pp. 141–61, 226–51.

Volksstimme, generally representing the views of the more radical urban party members. Before the First World War he had served a two-year prison sentence for *lèse-majesté*. However, his line met with strong opposition from Social Democrats in the rural areas of Hesse. A man of integrity, this doctrinaire and one-sided journalist failed to attract Jewish readers; they remained loyal to the superior *Frankfurter Zeitung*.[147] With the onset of the Depression the circulation of these papers declined sharply, and with it their influence within the party and on public opinion generally.[148]

Jewish Socialists were not numerous in the liberal professions or academia, except in Berlin for the reasons already given. These were in any case relatively small occupational groups, even in the centres of greatest Jewish population, such as Frankfurt, Breslau or Hamburg. Nor is there any evidence that the existence of such individuals, however distinguished, exercised any influence beyond their own immediate circle. Prominent Jewish academics associated with the SPD included Hermann Heller, a lecturer in Constitutional Law first at Berlin and then Frankfurt. He belonged to the 'Hofgeismar Circle', a reformist group of young Socialists that aimed at the integration of the working classes into the state and the nation's cultural life.[149] Siegfried Marck, who in the later years of the Weimar Republic was a Professor in the philosophical faculty of Breslau University, had a following among the Young Socialists and working-class youth. Jewish intellectuals regarded him with more scepticism. In contrast to these two men, the eminent legal theorist Hans Kelsen was not a political activist. He was Professor at Cologne, the creator of the 'pure theory of law'[150] and father of the Austrian constitution of 1920. He had a large following in legal circles, but he remained aloof politically. He voted for the SPD, but did not join the party.

In any Jewish population centre one could name lawyers and doctors who were party members; but they represented a small minority everywhere. The lawyers involved tended to be politicians or civil servants with a legal training, rather than in private practice. Most of the Jewish Reichstag members

147   See E. G. Lowenthal, 'Die Juden im öffentlichen Leben', in *Entscheidungsjahr 1932*, pp. 63–4; also Friedrich Stampfer, *Erfahrungen und Erkenntnisse*; Immanuel Birnbaum, *Achtzig Jahre debeigewesen. Erinnerungen eines Journalisten*, Munich: Süddeutscher Verlag, 1974.

148   Kurt Koszyk, *Zwischen Kaiserreich und Diktatur. Die sozialdemokratische Presse von 1914 bis 1933*, Heidelberg: Quelle und Mayer, 1958, p. 188.

149   For Heller's political stance see his *Rechtsstaat oder Diktatur?* Tübingen: J. C. B. Mohr, 1930; *Europa und der Fascismus*, Berlin: de Gruyter, 1931; *Staatslehre* (ed. Gerhart Niemeyer), Leiden: Sijthoff, 1934; also *Gesammelte Schriften* (eds Martin Draht, Otto Stammer, Gerhart Niemeyer and Fritz Borinski), Tübingen: J. C. B. Mohr, 1971.

150   See above, pp. 119–20.

during the Weimar Republic fall into this category. Others include persons who, despite their qualifications, had been denied entry into the legal profession under the Empire because of their political activities. Among them were Ernst Heilmann, Erich Kuttner and Simon Katzenstein, all prominent in the SPD during the Weimar Republic. Jews were prominent in the organization of pro-Republican judges, the *Republikanischer Richterbund*, but the predominant tendency of this was towards the DDP rather than the SPD. However, Hugo Sinzheimer, a Jewish Social Democrat, was co-editor of the *Richterbund's* journal, *Die Justiz*, along with Gustav Radbruch. Among its regular contributors was Robert Kempner, later to gain fame as chief prosecutor at Nuremberg.[151] A particular interest in industrial legislation led some Jewish lawyers into the SPD, or at least to voting for it. Sinzheimer, elected to the National Assembly in 1919, was notable in instigating new legislation on industrial questions. However, even before his time local government officials had opened up new ground in social policy without being active Social Democrats. One of them was Adolf Neumann, chairman of the Berlin commercial tribunal. He had helped prepare a new code of labour law and, as an official of the Berlin municipality, had rendered outstanding services before this branch of the law had gained a clearly defined outline. The collection of labour law verdicts pronounced by the Berlin industrial and commercial courts that he and other lawyers published was exemplary. Neumann was an Orthodox Jew who made no concessions in the observance of Jewish laws for himself but was tolerant towards others. In Breslau Ernst Eckstein was party leader in the city council from 1928 onwards. He had originally been a follower of Ludwig Frank but moved to the extreme left wing of the party and joined the *Sozialistische Arbeiterpartei* (SAP), which split away from the SPD in 1931. The population of Breslau provided him with an impressive cortège in May 1933 after he had been tortured to death in the concentration camp of Oels.[152] One of Eckstein's supporters was the lawyer Kurt Oppler who worked for the Foreign Ministry of the German Federal Republic after the Second World War and for a while was Ambassador in Brussels. Josef Neuberger, who began his career in Düsseldorf, also became better known in the Federal Republic, having been SPD Minister of Justice in North-Rhine Westphalia for a number of years.

151　Birger Schulz, *Der Republikanische Richterbund (1921–1933)*, Frankfurt and Berne: Lang, 1982, pp. 125, 128, 145–6, 175. See also Hugo Sinzheimer and Ernst Fraenkel, *Die Justiz in der Weimarer Republik. Eine Chronik*, Berlin: Luchterhand, 1968, esp. pp. 7–15.

152　Hanno Drechsler, *Die Sozialistische Arbeiterpartei Deutschlands (SAPD). Ein Beitrag zur Geschichte der deutschen Arbeiterbewegung am Ende der Weimarer Republik*, Meisenheim am Glan: Anton Hain, 1965, p. 363.

The number of doctors who declared their allegiance to Socialism was also small. In 1932 approximately 50,000 doctors were in practice in Germany, of whom 18 per cent were Jews.[153] This was a somewhat lower proportion than among lawyers, of whom 23.4 per cent were Jewish.[154] The *Verein sozialistischer Ärzte* had just over 1,500 members, representing about 3 per cent of all German doctors; 150–200 of them lived in Berlin. Even if one were to assume that a relatively high percentage of these Socialist doctors was Jewish, one must conclude that there was only a small minority of Socialists among the approximately 9,000 Jewish doctors. Some of them, however, reached political eminence: both Viktor Adler, founder and leader of the Austrian Social Democratic movement, who died in November 1918, and Rudolf Hilferding were originally doctors by profession. They were shaken by their confrontation with the health and living conditions in the working-class tenements of Vienna. Despite their small number, Jewish Socialist doctors played a prominent part in policy-making in social and industrial health, in setting up out-patient clinics, regarded by some as a prelude to the socialization of medicine, and in acting as advisers or administrators of the social and health insurance service. Often they combined these activities with SPD membership and political office-holding.[155] They were also active in the SPD-affiliated first-aid service, the *Arbeiter-Samariterbund*. Jewish hospitals pioneered treatment for the poor, for instance through Professor Siegfried Korach, medical director of the Israelitisches Krankenhaus in the Hamburg working-class area of St Pauli.[156]

Politically the most prominent was Julius Moses. He was a doctor from Berlin who had followed Theodor Barth from the FVg into the *Demokratische Vereinigung*. He then joined the USPD during the war and returned in 1922 to the re-united SPD. He belonged to the executive of the USPD from 1919 to 1922, thereafter to the executive of the SPD. From 1920 until 1932 Moses was an extremely active and combative Reichstag deputy. His life's work was devoted to working out the principles of a health policy based on social responsibility and the need for a programme of preventive medical care and welfare. He gathered about himself those doctors who were committed to the

153 Stephan Leibfried, 'Stationen der Abwehr. Berufsverbote für Ärzte im deutschen Reich 1933–1938 und die Zerstörung des sozialen Asyls durch die organisierten Ärzteschaften des Auslands', *BLBI* 62 (1982), p. 11.
154 Udo Beer, *Die Juden, das Recht und die Republik. Verbandswesen und Rechtsschutz, 1919–1933*, Frankfurt: Lang, 1986, p. 196.
155 Florian Tennstedt, *Sozialgeschichte der Sozialversicherung*, Göttingen: Vandenhoeck & Ruprecht, pp. 407, 458.
156 Werner Jochmann and Hans-Dieter Loose, *Hamburg. Geschichte der Stadt und ihre Bewohner*, Hamburg: Hoffmann & Campe, 1986, vol. II, pp. 55–6.

principle of social health insurance, which he publicized in the journal *Der Kassenarzt*. He was one of the few members of the SPD who was particularly interested in the Jewish Question and was a frequent contributor to the Jewish press, though most of this activity dates from before 1914. His son and biographer has concluded that Moses' transition from left-wing Liberalism to Social Democracy can be explained by his conclusion that the cause of Judaism should be incorporated into the great crusading body of the working-class movement for the liberation of the human personality.[157] He declined to leave Germany after Hitler came to power and died in Theresienstadt concentration camp in 1942 at the age of seventy-four.

The doyen of Jewish medical Socialists was Ignaz Zadek, the brother-in-law of Eduard Bernstein and allegedly the first medical practitioner in Berlin to join the SPD, which he represented from 1892 onwards in the city council.[158] He was instrumental in founding the *Sozialdemokratischer Ärzteverein* (Association of Social Democratic Doctors) in 1913, aiming particularly at doctors who served the self-governing social insurance funds (*Krankenkassen*), in which the SPD was strongly represented. In 1926 the association combined with others to form the *Arbeitsgemeinschaft sozialdemokratischer Ärzte*, though the more radical *Verein sozialistischer Ärzte*, to which Zadek now belonged, remained independent. Most of the doctors involved had engaged in campaigns for improving the conditions of health of the urban poor before 1918, generally known by the term *Sozialhygiene*.[159] Its main spokesman was Alfred Grotjahn, who was not a Jew and kept aloof from the SPD until 1918, but was a crucial figure in the party's health policy thereafter. He held the newly-created Chair of Social Hygiene at Berlin from 1920 onwards. A demand common to all the *Sozialhygieniker* was the creation of a *Reich* Ministry of Health; when this did not come about after the creation of the Weimar Republic, their efforts were concentrated on states and cities dominated by the SPD, which meant above all Prussia and Berlin.

Berlin was predictably the centre of their activities. Alfred Korach, who became president of the *Arbeitsgemeinschaft* in 1929, worked in the Prussian Ministry of Social Welfare from 1921 to 1922 and then joined the Berlin

157   Kurt Nemitz, 'Julius Moses' Weg zur Sozialdemokratie', *JIDG*, Beiheft 2: *Juden und jüdische Aspekte der deutschen Arbeiterbewegung*, 1977, pp. 178; Daniel S. Nadav, *Julius Moses und die Politik der Sozialhygiene in Deutschland*, Gerlingen: Bleicher, 1985, pp. 120–36, 259–92. Also Hamburger and Pulzer, *LBYB* (1985), p. 41, fn. 122.
158   Nadav, *Julius Moses*, pp. 73–4.
159   Ibid., pp. 55–115; Paul Weindling, *Health, Race and German Politics between National Unification and Nazism, 1870–1945*, Cambridge: Cambridge University Press, 1989, pp. 155–289.

municipal medical service. He served on the executive of the Wilmersdorf branch of the SPD and on the city council. He had been one of the founders of the Socialist students' union, the *Verband der Deutschen Sozialistischen Studentenorganisationen*. His deputies as *Arbeitsgemeinschaft* president were both Jews: Ludwig Jaffé, like Korach a member of the Berlin city council, and Franz-Karl Meyer-Brodnitz, head of the industrial medicine unit of the *Allgemeiner Deutscher Gewerkschaftsbund* (ADGB), the Socialist trade union federation.[160] Benno Chajes, a Social Democratic member of Schöneberg borough council before its incorporation in Greater Berlin and a member of the Prussian Landtag, who taught industrial and social medicine at the Technical University in Charlottenburg, became Grotjahn's successor at Berlin University in 1932, though only with the rank of Associate Professor and only until dismissed in 1933 by the Nazi regime. With the reform of Berlin local government in 1920 a medical officer (*Stadtarzt*) was appointed to each of the twenty constituent districts. These positions were largely staffed by Jews, including Korach in Prenzlauer Berg; Raphael Silberstein, a nephew of Eduard Bernstein, in Neukölln, where he was a member of the district council; Käthe Frankenthal, a member of the city council and the city SPD executive until she switched to the *Sozialistische Arbeiterpartei Deutschlands* (SAP) in 1931, and Silberstein's successor in Neukölln;[161] Richard Roeder in Treptow; and Walter Dettinger in Charlottenburg, where he was also an SPD alderman. Further to the Left was the dentist Ewald Fabian. Like Moses he came to the SPD via the *Demokratische Vereinigung*, joined the USPD and then – unlike Moses – the KPD. He was expelled from this in 1926, joined the dissident *Kommunistische Partei Deutschlands-Opposition* (KPO) and, with a number of his fellow-members, the SAP in 1931. He was editor of *Der Sozialistische Arzt*, the journal of the *Verein sozialistischer Ärzte*.[162]

Better known than any of these to the general public was Magnus Hirschfeld who came to occupy positions close to those of the Socialists. From the late 1890s onwards he had been involved in promoting a more rational understanding of unorthodox sexual phenomena, especially homosexuality. Politically he fluctuated between pacifism and ultra-patriotism and in 1915 published a patriotic pamphlet, *Warum hassen uns die Völker?* The

160 Leibfried, *BLBI* 62, pp. 25–6; Stephan Leibfried and Florian Tennstedt, *Berufsverbote und Sozialpolitik 1933. Die Auswirkungen der nationalsozialistischen Machtergreifung auf die Krankenkassenverwaltung und die Kassenärzte*, 2nd edn, Bremen: Universität Bremen, 1980, p. 116, fn. 47.
161 Käthe Frankenthal, *Der dreifache Fluch: Jüdin, Intellektuelle, Sozialistin*, Frankfurt: Campus, 1981, pp. 120–1; Leibfried, *BLBI* 62, pp. 24–6.
162 Leibfried, *BLBI* 62, p. 24.

events of 1918 moved him to the Left, though he did not join the SPD until 1923.[163] At the end of the war he was instrumental, along with Julius Moses and Grotjahn, in drawing up the petition for a *Reich* Ministry of Health and the nationalization of the medical service.[164] In the more favourable post-war atmosphere he was able to found an Institute for Sexual Science (*Institut für Sexualwissenschaft*) in 1919, which became the nucleus for the World League for Sexual Reform, whose first congress took place in Berlin in 1921. Nothing could be more calculated to enrage the political Right: his lectures were broken up by the *Deutschvölkischer Schutz- und Trutzbund* and in 1920 he was so badly beaten up that his life was in danger.[165] Though there was no consensus within the SPD, or the Left in general, on such issues as contraception, homosexuality and abortion, Hirschfeld was one of many who urged a liberalization of the law on these questions – with little success, especially on the last two. The notoriety of Hirschfeld's institute, the prominence of Jewish 'social hygenists' in the public medical service and the commercialization of 'daring' entertainments all helped to give Berlin its reputation for 'sexual Bolshevism'.[166]

Less sensational than Hirschfeld's crusade and more widely spread through Germany than the politically-committed city medical officers of Berlin were the doctors who served the social insurance funds. In Berlin 52 per cent of insurance fund doctors (*Kassenärzte*) were Jews, in Hamburg 30 per cent, in the Wiesbaden district, which included Frankfurt, 29 per cent and in Silesia 22 per cent.[167] Albert Kohn presided over the Berlin federation of insurance funds from 1911 to 1925; the journal *Der Kassenarzt* was edited by Julius Moses from its beginning in 1924 until 1933.

Apart from the leading representatives of social medicine and their followers, not many other doctors openly supported the SPD. In Cologne Benjamin Auerbach, one of the city's senior medical officers and director of the Jewish Hospital, was known to be a Social Democrat. Georg Landsberg, brother of the People's Commissar in the Provisional government, became city medical officer of Breslau during the Weimar Republic. In Königsberg Alfred Gottschalk of the USPD, who had previously led the SPD on the city

163   Charlotte Wolff, *Magnus Hirschfeld*, London: Quartet Books, 1986, pp. 161, 217.

164   Magnus Hirschfeld, *Verstaatlichung des Gesundheitswesens. Flugschriften des Bundes Neues Vaterland 10*, Berlin: E. Berger, 1919; Kurt Nemitz, 'Die Bemühungen zur Schaffung eines Reichsgesundheitsministeriums in der ersten Phase der Weimarer Republik 1918–1922', *Medizinhistorisches Journal* XVI, 1981, pp. 424ff.

165   Weindling, *Health, Race and German Politics*, p. 374; Wolff, *Magnus Hirschfeld*, pp. 197–200.

166   Weindling, *Health, Race and German Politics*, pp. 368–70.

167   Leibfried and Tennstedt, *Berufsverbote und Sozialpolitik 1933*, p. vi.

council, was briefly chairman of the city council after the Revolution. Kurt Glaser, a city councillor in Chemnitz, was also closely associated with the left wing of the party. After his return to the Federal Republic from exile he became director of the Public Health Department in Hamburg. One consequence of the comparatively large number of politically-inspired Jewish doctors in the public and social insurance medical service was that these branches of medical care suffered particularly drastically from the political and racial purges instigated by the Nazis after 1933.[168]

While Jews were highly involved in elaborating and implementing the SDP's social policies, few of them were to be found in the trade union movement, either as organizers or advisers. Apart from Aufhäuser and Meyer-Brodnitz, who have already been mentioned, the most important was Fritz Naphtali, director of the SPD's Research Office for Economic Policy (*Forschungsstelle für Wirtschaftspolitik*). In 1928 the ADGB commissioned from him a set of proposals on 'economic democracy', which it duly accepted. It was designed not so much to replace Socialism, which remained the movement's long-term (though increasingly distant) aim, but to be an intermediate step in counter-acting the autocratic character of capitalist management. At the time it made little impact, but there were echoes of it after the war in the nationalization laws of various West German *Länder*, in the speech by the trade union leader Victor Agartz at the SPD's first post-war congress at Hanover in 1946 and even in the 1947 Ahlen programme of the CDU. It has been twice reprinted, the second time as recently as 1977.[169]

Though the SPD's Jews ceased to hold leading positions in *Reich* and state cabinets in the post-revolutionary period, with the exception of Hilferding, they remained prominent in the organization of the parliamentary parties and of parliamentary business. This was true particularly of Prussia. Ernst Heilmann, who was a member of the Prussian Landtag throughout the Weimar period, was chairman of the parliamentary group from 1921 to 1933. Along with *Oberregierungsrat* Ernst Hamburger, who became his deputy chairman, he played a crucial role in negotiations with Joseph Heß, who led the *Zentrum* group. The Heß–Heilmann link was widely regarded as the

168 Ibid., *passim*.
169 Fritz Naphtali, *Wirtschaftsdemokratie. Ihr Wesen, Weg und Ziel*, Berlin: Verlagsgesellschaft des ADGB, 1928; Jehuda Riemer, 'Konzeptionen der Wirtschaftsdemokratie. Vergleich oder Zerstörung', *JIDG* XIV (1985), pp. 349–58; Rudolf Kuda, 'Das Konzept der Wirtschaftsdemokratie', in Heinz Oskar Vetter (ed.), *Vom Sozialistengesetz zur Mitbestimmung. Zum 100. Geburtstag von Hans Böckler*, pp. 253–74, esp. pp. 265–74, Cologne: Bund-Verlag, 1975; Heinrich Potthoff, *Freie Gewerkschaften, 1918–1933. Der Allgemeine Deutsche Gewerkschaftsbund in der Weimarer Republik*, Düsseldorf: Droste, 1988, pp. 182–4.

mainstay of the Prussian coalition government, one of the stablest of the Weimar period.[170] Another leading official of the Prussian government was *Ministerialrat* Herbert Weichmann, who acted as personal assistant to the Prime Minister, Otto Braun, from 1928 to 1933. Unlike Heilmann, who was murdered at Buchenwald in 1940, and Hamburger, who emigrated to the USA via France, Weichmann returned to the Federal Republic after the war and became Lord Mayor of Hamburg.

Of those Jews who neither held nor sought office in the SPD, Paul Levi was the most significant. A South German lawyer who belonged to the radical Left of the party, he had first made a name for himself as defence counsel for Rosa Luxemburg in 1914. He spent much of 1917 and 1918 in Switzerland, having 'starved' himself out of the army, and there made the acquaintance of Lenin and Radek. He returned to Germany at the end of the war and was one of the founders of the Spartacus League and the KPD. He served on its executive from the beginning, and after the deaths of Liebknecht, Luxemburg and Leo Jogiches became its leader. Yet within the party that he led he was, as in all parties that he belonged to, in a minority. He favoured participation in the elections to the National Assembly and was defeated. He opposed the growing domination of Comintern influence, found himself excluded from the party and formed the *Kommunistische Arbeitsgemeinschaft* (KAG), which he led into the USPD and, when the USPD dissolved itself, into the SPD. Within the re-united party he quickly became the main spokesman against a policy of coalition with the non-Socialist parties and for maintaining the SPD as an instrument of working-class unity: the basis of this was 'class solidarity against the capitalist parties, expressed in parliamentary terms as opposition parties'.[171] He preached this gospel first in the weekly *Sozialistische Politik und Wirtschaft* (*SPW*) and then, from 1927 onwards, in *Der Klassenkampf*, which he co-edited and which absorbed the *SPW* in 1928.

He needed the SPD because, for all its bureaucratic authoritarianism, it gave him a platform that the KPD had denied him. He needed it also because the political struggle he envisaged could be carried on only by a large party. A

---

170   Horst Möller, *Parlamentarismus in Preußen, 1919–1932*, Düsseldorf: Droste, 1985, pp. 384–7; *idem*, 'Ernst Heilmann. Ein Sozialdemokrat in der Weimarer Republik', *JIDG* XI (1982), p. 270; Ernst Feder, *Heute sprach ich mit … Tagebücher eines Berliner Publizisten, 1926–1932* (ed. Cécile Lowenthal-Hensel and Arnold Paucker), Stuttgart: Deutsche Verlags-Anstalt, 1971, p. 157; Hagen Schulze, *Otto Braun oder Preußens demokratische Sendung*, Frankfurt: Ullstein, 1977, p. 391.

171   Paul Levi, *Zwischen Spartakus und Sozialdemokratie. Schriften, Aufsätze, Reden und Briefe* (ed. and introduction by Charlotte Beradt), Frankfurt: Europäische Verlagsanstalt, 1969, p. 166.

sectarian by instinct, he was anxious not to be associated with sects. Having changed parties five times, he could not afford to lose credibility with yet another switch of allegiance. Many of those associated with him in *Der Klassenkampf* were among the founders of the *Sozialistische Arbeiterpartei* in 1931 (considered in section 14), though it is doubtful whether he would have approved of this move and might well, had he not died in 1930, have prevented it. He was sensitive to the charge: 'You have destroyed two parties, leave the third one alone.'[172] He thought in moral absolutes, a position that was difficult to maintain under the conditions of parliamentary multi-partism, and thus turned the best into the enemy of the fairly good. He wished to avoid both 'the relapse into a sect and the collapse into a bourgeois reform movement',[173] but the world did not grant him this luxury. His finest hour came not in parliament (where he spoke increasingly rarely) or at party conferences, but in a court of law, where he defended one of the editors of *Das Tagebuch* who had exposed the role of the investigating judge in the Liebknecht–Luxemburg murder trial. It enabled him to live up to one of his role-models, Georges Clemenceau, and earned him the encomium from Albert Einstein: 'In the noblest among us Jews there still lives something of the social justice of the Old Testament.'[174]

One of the many factors that drew a slowly increasing number of Jews to the SPD was its attitude towards anti-Semitism. As before 1914, this was far from homogeneous and the question did not as a rule occupy a very high place in the party's order of priorities. Since the stereotyping of Jews was so widely diffused in the German population, however, it would have been surprising if this had been absent from the thinking of rank-and-file SPD members or from the party press and other publications. Anti-Semitic innuendoes had certainly entered ideological disputes within the party involving the intellectuals of the radical Left.[175] At the same time the party emerged as a committed opponent of organized anti-Semitism, a tendency that was, if anything, strengthened by the prevalence of anti-Semitism among the counter-revolutionary forces of 1918–1923 and in attacks on the Republic.[176] When rioting and looting took place against East European Jews in Berlin in 1923, the SPD and Socialist trade unions organized a protest meeting.

172 Charlotte Beradt, *Paul Levi. Ein demokratischer Sozialist in der Weimarer Republik*, Frankfurt: Europäische Verlagsanstalt, 1969, p. 85.
173 Levi, *Zwischen Spartakus und Sozialdemokratie*, p. 90.
174 Beradt, *Paul Levi*, p. 126. Text of summing-up speech in Levi, *Zwischen Spartakus und Sozialdemokratie*, pp. 267–8.
175 See above, pp. 161, 166.
176 Donald L. Niewyk, *Socialist, Anti-Semite and Jew. German Social Democracy Confronts the Problem of Anti-Semitism*, Baton Rouge: Louisiana State University Press, 1971, chap. III.

Indeed, it was not on the question of Socialism or Jewish interests that the two sides converged, but more generally on loyalty to the Weimar constitution. More than any other denominational group in inter-war Germany, Jews had an incentive to support the Republic; more than any other major party the SPD was the Republic's pillar. Along with sections of the *Zentrum* and the DDP it was the main source of support for the Republican defence league, the *Reichsbanner Schwarz–Rot–Gold*. The more Weimar was denounced as the *Judenrepublik*, the more Jews and Socialists were drawn together. This was clearly recognized by many in the SPD, such as the bright young moderate Carlo Mierendorff, who responded to the murder of Rathenau while still a student at Heidelberg with the words: 'The racially-pure black-white-and-red slogan-mongers beat the Jew, but mean the Republican.'[177] However, the recognition that anti-Semitism was often merely instrumentalized anti-Republicanism could lead Social Democrats to downgrade the importance of anti-Semitism as such; and their rationalist mind-sets could be a barrier to comprehending the appeal of Nazi racial doctrine. Too many were tempted, like Ferdinand Tönnies, to dismiss it as 'so grotesque ... that it exceeds by far the bounds of the ridiculous'.[178] There was therefore a temptation to regard the Nazis as either just another anti-Semitic party or just another anti-working-class party, since 'a small pogrom is, after all, better than a great confiscation of wealth'.[179] A realization of the full extent of the Nazi threat came only slowly: more sophisticated analyses of its appeal can be seen in the articles by Carlo Mierendorff and Theodor Haubach in *Neue Blätter für den Sozialismus* and Alexander Schifrin and Georg Decker in *Die Gesellschaft*.[180] Few had the insight that Paul Levi had shown at the time of the Munich Beer Hall putsch of 1923:

Here is the first movement that, however grotesque it might appear, grows out of a deep social movement and that needs to be looked at eye-to-eye. ... The hungry bodies and souls begin to wander ... they wander back to old dreams: this great

177 Carlo Mierendorff, *Arisches Kaisertum oder Juden-Republik*, Berlin: Vorwärts, 1922, p. 14.

178 Ferdinand Tönnies, 'Parteipolitische Prognose', *Die Arbeit*, 1931, p. 79.

179 Cit. Wolfram Pyta, *Gegen Hitler und für die Republik. Die Auseinandersetzung der deutschen Sozialdemokratie mit der NSDAP in der Weimarer Republik*, Düsseldorf: Droste, 1989, p. 64.

180 Carl Mierendorff, 'Was ist der Nationalsozialismus? Zur Topographie des Faschismus in Deutschland', *Neue Blätter für den Sozialismus*, April 1931, pp. 149–54; Theodor Haubach, 'Die militante Partei', ibid., pp. 208–13; Alexander Schifrin, 'Parteiprobleme nach den Wahlen', *Die Gesellschaft*, November 1930, pp. 395–412; Georg Decker, 'Faschistische Gefahr und Sozialdemokratie', ibid., June 1931.

stratum of the desperate and the recently disinherited are the social foundation, ... that provides the social acceptability for the putsch named after Hitler that that named after Kapp lacked.[181]

While the SPD's attitude to anti-Semitism was clear-cut, that towards Jews as a community was less so. The party was hostile to organized religion, and though this hostility was directed primarily at the Christian churches, it did cause numerous Jews to regard the SPD with suspicion. Above all, the party had little sympathy with the Jewish desire to survive as a community with a separate identity. For most Socialists the solution to the Jewish Question remained complete assimilation. One symptom of this was the tension between the party and East European immigrants, who were either war-time labourers or refugees from pogroms in post-war Poland.[182] They were frequently collectively stigmatized as 'those elements who have immigrated from the East who are suspected ... of profiteering in foodstuffs or any black market',[183] or as persons whose unclean habits and morals were almost ineradicable.[184] This tension reached a climax in March 1920 when the Social Democratic police chief of Brandenburg, Eugen Ernst, a man of strong nationalist sentiments, organized a *razzia* against East European Jews. His immediate superior, the SPD Minister of the Interior Wolfgang Heine, was suspect in the eyes of Jewish activists for his past membership of the anti-Semitic *Verein deutscher Studenten*; however, his decree of November 1919, containing guide-lines for the treatment of Eastern Jews, was drawn up in consultation with representative Jewish bodies[185] and earned him the title of 'the protecting hand of Eastern Jewish blood-suckers'.[186]

On the other hand, the experience of personal friendship and political co-operation between Jew and non-Jew in the Socialist movement led to a softening of these attitudes under Weimar. An increasing number of SPD leaders became interested in Zionism and sympathetic towards it. There was a degree of public and private co-operation between the SPD and the C.V. that would have been unthinkable before 1918. There were two Socialists, Oskar Cohn and Ernst Behrendt, on the executive of the C.V. and the SPD

181   *SPW*, 19 November 1923, cit. Beradt, *Paul Levi*, p. 87.

182   Aschheim, *Brothers and Strangers*, pp. 237–40; Niewyk, *Socialist, Anti-Semite and Jew*, pp. 100–1.

183   Prussian Interior Minister Wolfgang Heine to Police President of Berlin, 20 February 1920, cit. Maurer, *Ostjuden in Deutschland, 1918–1933*, p. 362.

184   Theodor Müller, 'Die Einwanderung der Ostjuden', NZ XXXIX, 24 June, 1 August 1921.

185   Adler-Rudel, *Ostjuden in Deutschland*, pp. 158–61.

186   *Der Hammer*, 15 January 1920, cit. Maurer, *Ostjuden in Deutschland, 1918–1933*, p. 283.

solicited Jewish votes by advertising in the *C.V.-Zeitung*.[187] Behind-the-scenes contacts were much closer, inspired as they were by the shared need to defend the Republic, but since secrecy was the essence of such operations they would obviously have had no impact on the political attitudes of individual Jews. In any case, all such exchanges were on a small scale before 1928 and became significant only with the rise of Nazism.

The Communist Party

Of the 99 participants at the founding party convention whom we can identify – in all 117 delegates took part – seven were Jews.[188] Four of them, all university-educated, were elected to the eleven member Central Committee; Rosa Luxemburg, Leo Jogiches, Paul Levi and August Thalheimer were all Spartacists of the first hour. Jews were strongly represented in the leadership of the KPD. However, as with the SPD, this fact is not a reliable guide to the number of Jews within the membership of the party or of those who voted for it. Those Jews of the Socialist Left who rejected the policies of the SPD before, and especially during, the war gathered mainly around Hugo Haase. In the Socialism proclaimed by Haase and his followers there was a mixture of humanism, political ethics, pacifism and Marxism with a differing and individual dosage in each member.[189] The Jews of the radical Left were more attracted by this mixture than by the extremism and fanaticism of Rosa Luxemburg. The transformation of the World War into an international civil war, driving the Revolution further towards Western Europe, and erecting the dictatorship of the proletariat on the ruins of capitalist Europe could attract, at most, only a tiny number of young, left-wing intellectuals and white-collar workers. Because the intellectuals of the KPD were articulate and productive in their writings and therefore in the public eye, the insignificance of the number of Jews among Communist Party members has frequently not been recognized. It was also habitually exaggerated by their anti-Semitic opponents. Even at the elections for the first

---

187 Niewyk, *Socialist, Anti-Semite and Jew*, pp. 105–6, 194; Paucker, *Abwehrkampf*, p. 29.

188 For information on the 99 identifiable participants of the founding convention and the Central Committee see Hermann Weber (ed.), *Der Gründungsparteitag der KPD. Protokoll und Materialien*, Frankfurt: Europäische Verlagsanstalt, 1969, pp. 310–12. The minutes allow 62 persons to be identified quite clearly. Others are added on the basis of other publications or recollections of participants. Members of the Central Committee: ibid., p. 319. Among those named by Weber three appear as representatives of the USSR (among them Karl Radek) and seven as guests.

189 See Calkins, *Hugo Haase*.

Reichstag on 6 June 1920 it was not the Communists but the USPD who benefited from the sharp swing to the Left that had occurred since the election to the National Assembly. The Communists received 2.1 per cent of the votes – one-twentieth of the share of the two Social Democratic parties.

The turning-point came only when the USPD split at the Halle conference in October 1920 and the majority of its members went over to the Communists. A successor generation also appeared among the leaders. Among the delegates who went over to the Communists were Iwan Katz and Werner Scholem. They constituted the 'ultra-left' wing and under Ruth Fischer's leadership took over the previously 'right-wing' executive of Brandler and Thalheimer. Among Communist academics the most prominent was Arthur Rosenberg, a pupil of Eduard Meyer, the eminent Professor of Ancient History at Berlin University. Rosenberg became a University Lecturer in Ancient History and had published a considerable number of essays before becoming known to a wider circle of readers through his later works on the Weimar Republic and Bolshevism. Thus by the mid-1920s Jews were present in large numbers in the leadership of the party and among the deputies of the Communist parliamentary parties. Rosenberg and Ernst Schwarz, a teacher from Berlin-Lichtenberg, were deputies in the Reichstag; so were two members of the party's editorial staff – Katz and Scholem; so were Kurt Rosenbaum and Eugen Eppstein who had been active in the white-collar workers' movement. Katz, Scholem and Eppstein together with Rosi Wolfstein, an old Spartacist who had also been active in the white-collar workers' movement, also sat in the Prussian Landtag for a number of years.[190] In Lübeck Ismar Heilbronn, editor of the local party paper, and in Hamburg Alfred Levy, who was severely handicapped and worked first in Hamburg's Labour Exchange and then in the Welfare Centre, were members of the Bürgerschaft. Stefan Heymann, a clerical worker, was briefly a Reichstag member. In the last phase of the Weimar Republic he worked as a journalist for *Rote Fahne* in Berlin and then for the *Schlesische Arbeiterzeitung* in Breslau. During the war he had set off for the front as a glowing patriot, but

---

190   For short biographies see *Reichstags-Handbuch, Wahlperiode III*, 1924, p. 279 (Katz), p. 337 (Rosenbaum), pp. 337ff (Rosenberg), p. 351 (Scholem), p. 362 (Schwarz), p. 248 (Elfriede Golke, i.e. Ruth Fischer, daughter of a Jewish father), p. 405 (Eppstein). More detailed biographies in Hermann Weber, *Die Wandlung des deutschen Kommunismus. Die Stalinisierung der KPD in der Weimarer Republik*, vol. II, Frankfurt: Europäische Verlagsanstalt, 1969, pp. 177–9 (Katz), pp. 261ff. (Rosenbaum), pp. 262ff (Rosenberg), pp. 282ff (Scholem), pp. 299ff (Schwarz), pp. 117–20 (Golke), p. 140 (Eppstein). More biographical information on Rosenberg can be found on microfilm in Brooklyn College, Brooklyn, New York: Personal Records, Office of the President.

later on became an anarchist and entered into correspondence with Erich Mühsam in Munich. During the Revolution he proclaimed a 'Soviet Republic' in the Palatinate but did not join the KPD until June 1919.[191]

Intimately involved in the various factional conflicts, these pioneers were unable to hold their ground either in the party or in leading positions. As intellectuals they were vulnerable once Stalin gained control of the CPSU and Comintern. In a blunt speech in 1926, which was directed against the intellectuals, Stalin gave his blessing to the change of power when Ernst Thälmann had taken over the leadership of the KPD in the previous autumn by ousting Katz, Scholem and Rosenberg. He exhorted Thälmann to drive out the intellectuals if they wanted to be in command and praised the new composition of the committee, in which the workers now predominated.[192] Katz, Scholem, Rosenberg, as well as Ruth Fischer and Arkady Maslow, soon found themselves outside the party and gathered in a number of Left-Communist groupings; in 1928 the 'right wingers' in the party, including Wolfstein, were expelled and formed the rather more significant 'Opposition Communist Party', KPO.[193]

The question arises whether and to what extent the anti-intellectual tendencies of the Stalinized party had an anti-Semitic tinge, and whether this frightened off Jewish voters in general and intellectuals in particular. Each time the German nation was roused to particularly passionate nationalism, as during the Ruhr occupation in 1923 and the economic crisis from 1929 onwards, the Communists tried to recruit voters from the Right by the use of nationalist slogans. To this end they did not hesitate to use anti-Semitism. Even Communists with some Jewish blood felt no restraint in this matter. Ruth Fischer, whose father was Jewish, was quite prepared to agitate against 'capitalist Jews' in 1923: anyone who exhorted others to join the conflict against Jewish capitalism was participating in the class war, even if he did not know it.[194] Many in the KPD were shocked by this line. Clara Zetkin complained that the 'Left' majority included 'fascist anti-Semites'.[195] Heinz

191 Information on Alfred Levy from the State Archive of Hamburg (letter of 19th May 1970); on Stefan Heymann from the City Archive of Mannheim [H].
192 Speech by Stalin in the German Commission of the Sixth extended plenum of the Executive Committee of the Communist International, 8 March 1926. Text in E. H. Carr, *Foundations of a Planned Economy 1926–1929*, vol. III–2, London: Macmillan, 1976, p. 404. Bukharin and Zinoviev (himself a Jew) used similar language.
193 Theodor Bergmann, *'Gegen den Strom'. Die Geschichte der Kommunistischen-Partei-Opposition*, Hamburg: VSA, 1987, pp. 402–3, 405, 430–1, 443.
194 Werner T. Angress, *Stillborn Revolution. The Communist Bid for Power in Germany, 1921–1923*, Princeton, NJ: Princeton University Press, 1963, pp. 339–41; Knütter, *Deutsche Linke*, pp. 179–80.
195 Edmund Silberner, *Kommunisten zur Judenfrage. Zur Geschichte von Theorie und Praxis des Kommunismus*, Opladen: Westdeutscher Verlag, 1983, p. 267.

Neumann, the last Jewish Communist to be nominated and elected to the Reichstag, formulated the party's 1930 programme which called for the 'national and social liberation of the German people'.[196] Thus class-war slogans were supplemented by and subordinated to an appeal to nationalism. Werner Scholem pointed out that in the battle for the party line only Jews were attacked for being intellectuals, while other academics were assiduously spared.[197]

The number of Jews in the Central Committee sank considerably after 1925, so that by the end of the Weimar Republic it had dropped to zero. In the Communist parliamentary party in the second Reichstag, elected in May 1924, there were 6 Jews among the 62 members; in the third Reichstag, elected in December of the same year, there were 5 out of 54, in each case approximately 10 per cent. However, in the Reichstag of November 1932 the Communist parliamentary party had 89 members, not one of whom was Jewish. Heinz Neumann's 'national' course had been condemned at the party conference in October and Neumann was not re-nominated. In the Prussian Landtag elected in April 1932 the Communist grouping numbered 57 members, not one of whom was Jewish. Fritz Ausländer, a grammar-school teacher who had been a member of the previous Landtag, was eliminated. The only graduate Communist deputy in that Landtag was a lawyer, Gerhard Obuch, who was not Jewish. In the party's lists of candidates, with a total of over 500 names, there were no Jews, even in positions with hopeless prospects.[198] In the later years of the Weimar Republic all Jews disappeared from Communist parliamentary parties in other Landtag assemblies, including the Bürgerschaften of the Free Cities.

However, it would not be reasonable on the basis of this evidence to classify the KPD as anti-Semitic. Jews were still in official positions and often active on the editorial staff of the party papers. Their names changed as the party line changed. The *Rote Fahne* in Berlin nearly always had Jewish editors-in-chief. Heinrich Süßkind followed Rosa Luxemburg and August Thalheimer as editor-in-chief; after that Stefan Heymann, already mentioned,

196 Knütter, *Deutsche Linke*, p. 187. See also Lothar Berthold (ed.), *Das Programm der KPD zur nationalen und sozialen Befreiung Deutschlands vom August 1930*, E. Berlin: Dietz, 1956. The role of Neumann, who was later purged, is not mentioned by Berthold.

197 Weber, *Der Gründungsparteitag der KPD*, vol. I, pp. 327ff; p. 305, fn. 50.

198 Constituency and state lists of candidates in *Handbuch für den Preußischen Landtag*, 1932, list no. 4, pp. 252–371. The Communist deputies always described themselves as 'dissidents', of no religious affiliation, atheists or free-thinkers. That there were no Jewish members of the Communist parliamentary party in either the Reichstag of November 1932 or the Prussian Landtag of April 1932 is beyond dispute. One cannot quite guarantee this of the lists of candidates, but there is a high degree of probability.

held the position. Peter Maslowski, a Communist of the very early days who had taken part in the founding party convention, could not recall 'that in the long years of his activity within the party from 1918 onwards action was taken against any one person only because he was a Jew'.[199] In this form the information is no doubt correct, as is Maslowski's observation that in National Socialist propaganda Marxists, Bolsheviks and Jews were given more or less identical treatment and that it would have been useless for the non-Jewish leadership to have protested against this generalization. He himself had always been represented as a Jew, a stock-exchange jobber and a man who was selling out the German nation, and he would 'only have made a fool of himself if he had tried to explain to the Nazis that he was an Aryan, came from a Catholic family and had never set foot in the stock exchange'.[200]

However, Maslowski's statement does need to be supplemented. In the conflicts for setting the course of the party anti-Semitic sentiments were not disdained. It is obvious that the party took anti-Semitic tendencies into account through the elimination of Jews from important bodies such as the Central Committee and legislatures. The party was anxious not to give the National Socialists any reason for an attack on this front, or to deter radical voters with strong nationalist feelings. Even more than the SPD, the KPD was indifferent to the 'Jewish Question' and as such to anti-Semitism. In the later years of the Weimar Republic only two books by party members appeared on these topics: Otto Heller's *Der Untergang des Judentums* (1931), which commented favourably on the Soviet Jewish autonomous region of Birobidjan, and *Der Jud' ist schuld ... ?* (1932), which interpreted anti-Semitism as a diversionary device of the Right.[201] However, the relatively few Jewish voters who were determined to vote for a Communist candidate will hardly have been dissuaded by the ambivalent attitudes or conduct of the KPD.

Conclusion

Despite the upheavals of the Great War and the Revolution, there was considerable continuity in the social structure of Germany, and the party systems of the Empire and of the first ten years of the Republic shared similarly recognizable continuities. The biggest difference was in the role of the Social Democratic Party. The events of 1918–19 prepared a way for equal

199   Letter from Mr Peter Maslowski, Coburg, 6 July 1970 [H].
200   Ibid., p. 3.
201   Silberner, *Kommunisten zur Judenfrage*, pp. 274–80; Otto Heller, *Der Untergang des Judentums. Die Judenfrage, ihre Kritik, ihre Lösung durch den Sozialismus*, Vienna: Verlag für Literatur und Politik, 1931.

citizenship for all. The SPD's position was also changed; it moved into a position where it could command events, rather than react to them. But the SPD not only faced a number of external obstacles to the achievement of this task – the odium of defeat and of the Versailles settlement and the constant accusation that its leaders were the 'November criminals', responsible for the disaster – but also lacked administrative experience and skills, and many of its leaders and members doubted whether genuine equality of the classes could be achieved under capitalism. They were therefore tempted to prefer opposition to the responsibilities of being a pillar of the new state and to the risks of losing even more supporters to the new rivals on the Left.[202]

The same dilemma was experienced by the forces of Liberalism, the chief home ground of Jewish voters. Having also been an oppositional force in the Empire, albeit a moderate one, they, too, were pitched by the Revolution into a position of having to make national political decisions. The DDP regarded it as its principal mission to maintain co-operation between the middle and working classes, one to which the Jewish population was especially receptive. The Jewish middle classes could expect only adverse consequences from a breakdown of social peace or from a political or economic reaction within the Republic. On the other hand the material interests of the majority of Jewish citizens were opposed to any socialization measures. They felt more affinity with the parties of the centre than with the Social Democrats, but felt politically most secure if they could be active with the DDP along the boundary between the middle and working classes.

Jewish citizens felt elated by the splendour of the names of those who signed the first appeals for the formation of the DDP – Jews like Albert Einstein and Hugo Preuß, non-Jews like Friedrich Naumann, Walter Schücking (a teacher of international law) and Ludwig Quidde (a pacifist) – and were not repelled when the DDP took over the old apparatus of the Progressive People's Party. Realistic politics based on democratic and republican principles appeared to guarantee the safeguarding of the interests of the middle classes in commerce, industry and banking. In this respect the Jews did not differ from other citizens. They were, however, aware of the special nature of the situation in which they found themselves, showing more consistent loyalty to the DDP, as can be seen from the results of the elections in the middle and late 1920s. This continuity can also be seen among the Jewish voters who did not give their vote to the DDP. There was some move towards the SPD. Small groups of voters, particularly in Western and Southern Germany, moved over to the DVP, reverting to a tradition of

---

202 Richard Breitman, *German Socialism and Weimar Democracy*, Chapel Hill, NC: University of North Carolina Press, 1981, pp. 9–21.

pre-1914 support for the National Liberals. The *Zentrum* and the Bavarian People's Party gained a few new supporters from among Orthodox Jews.

Exactly in what proportions Jews cast their votes for the various parties cannot, of course, now be established. Even authoritative estimates vary quite widely. One knowledgeable contemporary Catholic observer suggested an average in 1924 of 42 per cent for the SPD, 40 per cent for the DDP, 8 per cent for the KPD, 5 per cent for the DVP and 2 per cent for the *Wirtschaftspartei*, curiously enough allowing nothing for the Catholic parties.[203] A much later estimate by Arnold Paucker, based on interviews but of necessity not on a scientific sample, suggests an average for the 1920s of DDP 64 per cent, SPD 28 per cent, DVP 4 per cent, KPD 4 per cent.[204] Paucker's sample, being biased in the direction of Berlin, probably underestimates the Right and the Catholic parties. Where both estimates agree is in giving the lion's share to the DDP and SPD – with the latter probably gaining as the decade wore on – a pattern quite unusual in Germany for a predominantly middle-class section of the population.

The reasons for the trend, however gradual, in favour of the SPD are not particularly mysterious. Some have already been suggested: the continuing migration into metropolitan areas, the move from self-employment to wage-earning, a generational change and the appeal of idealism and utopianism to a marginalized and insecure minority. The split in the Socialist Left offered different options to Jewish Socialists. The USPD had attracted quite a number of them during its short life through its rejection of force and brutality, its affirmation of the purity of Socialist idealism and its emphasis on the concept of justice without concessions to *Realpolitik*. The Communists also had a few supporters, particularly among the younger intellectuals. But there was also a perfectly realistic motivation for the Jews to support the SPD. They had a vested interest in the democratic Republic. With the decline of the DDP a vote for the SPD might seem the only effective way of defending a polity on whose survival so much depended.

The Reichstag elections of 1928, when the 'Weimar' parties did better than at any time since 1919, marked the end of republican stability and of the continuities in party loyalty that went back to the 1890s and even beyond. In the four years that followed German party politics were revolutionized and the Jewish voter – and anyone who sought to speak on his behalf – was confronted with an existential crisis.

---

203   Johannes Schauff, *Die deutschen Katholiken und die Zentrumspartei*, Cologne: Bachem, 1928, p. 131.
204   Arnold Paucker, 'Jewish Defence Against Nazism in the Weimar Republic', *Wiener Library Bulletin*, New Series 26/7, 1972, p. 27.

12 JEWS AND THE STATE, 1918–1933

The first German Republic in many ways promised to be a Jewish Elysium. Much as individual Jews had flourished in the second half of the nineteenth century, much as they had succeeded in rising into, and with, the German bourgeoisie, they remained half inside and half outside German society. Political anti-Semitism, though frequently shrill and sometimes violent, had not been their main worry. It was containable and had in the main been contained. What prevented Jews from being full citizens was the semi-authoritarian character of the *Reich* and, even more, of some of the individual states, as well as the continuing privileges of many of its central organs, such as the military and the bureaucracy. Even in those branches of the public service to which they were admitted, as in the judiciary and academia, it was on an unequal footing.

All of this the coming of the Republic promised to change, both formally and informally. Formally Article 136 of the Weimar constitution enshrined the principle of the law of 1869, that the exercise of public rights and duties was not affected by religious affiliation. Article 137 guaranteed the autonomy and equality of religious bodies. Some doors that had been closed to Jews before 1918 were undoubtedly now opened, even if not completely or consistently. But there were a number of reasons why Jewish expectations were ultimately disappointed. Some of these were organizational, to be found in German federalism and in the fragmentation of Jewish political and religious loyalties. These two factors between them ensured that at no stage between 1918 and 1933 could a mutually acceptable framework of state–synagogue relations be established.

These organizational hurdles were, however, not the main obstacle to the completion of Jewish equality. The greatest was the resurgence of anti-Semitism both in the aftermath of defeat and revolution and with the coming of the slump and the rise of National Socialism. In this atmosphere, which pervaded not only public polemics in general, but academia and parts of the bureaucracy and judiciary in particular, any Jew in public life was in an exposed and vulnerable position, as the toll of assassinations testified. Any attempt to secure even-handedness from public authorities involved a battle whose outcome was uncertain. This, in turn, underlined the incompleteness of the political change of 1918–19. To the popular saying, 'The kings depart, the generals remain', one could add that much of the civilian administrative apparatus also stayed as it was. For all the complaints that the left-wing parties were swamping the public service with their nominees (which may have been true of some municipalities), recruitment to the higher ranks remained the prerogative of the Protestant upper middle class. This caused as

much resentment among Catholics as among Jews. The *Zentrum* politician
Leo Schwering complained in 1922 that 90 per cent of the higher reaches of
the Prussian bureaucracy were supporters of the DNVP[1] and his colleague
Joseph Heß demanded steps to prevent the 'continuing German Nationalist
incursion into the ministries'.[2] Only in the judiciary and, to a lesser extent,
academia was some progress towards Catholic–Protestant parity noticeable.[3]

The brief glory of Jewish politicians at the time of the Revolution has
served to conceal how few of them held public office in the last ten years of
the Weimar Republic. After the murder of Rathenau only Rudolf Hilferding
of the SPD twice held the *Reich* finance portfolio and two persons of Jewish
descent the *Reich* justice portfolio: Erich Koch-Weser (DDP) from 1928 to
1929 in the last Great Coalition and the non-partisan Curt Joël from 1931 to
1932 under Brüning. Similarly the number of Jews in state governments was
negligible after 1922, with Ludwig Marum (SPD) in Baden the only notable
exception.[4] There were, however, Jewish members of the Senate in Hamburg,
an honour that had been denied even to Max Warburg before 1918, including
Max Mendel (SPD) and Carl Cohn (DDP). In the often highly-charged
political atmosphere of the Weimar Republic Jewish politicians were sometimes more reluctant to accept high political office than their Gentile
colleagues were to offer it. In 1920 Ludwig Haas was proposed as DDP
Minister of War. Haas, however, 'in view of the anti-Semitic wave',[5]
declined the office, which instead went to Otto Geßler.[6] Two years later
Rathenau, by then Foreign Minister, urged Max Warburg to join him as
Finance Minister. Warburg, who was always reluctant to occupy public
positions and who felt that Rathenau had crossed the invisible line of the
acceptable by going to the Foreign Ministry, pointed out that two Jews in one
cabinet was too much of a risk.[7] Later that year, after the assassination of
Rathenau, his partner Carl Melchior declined an offer to become Finance
Minister, a decision supported by Warburg.[8] In 1930 Brüning wanted to
bring the baptized Paul Silverberg into the cabinet: 'I had very great
confidence in [him], but his inclusion in the cabinet would only have

1 *KVZ*, 31 June 1922.
2 *StPrA*, 21 June 1922.
3 Morsey, *Die deutsche Zentrumspartei*, pp. 614–15.
4 Heinrich Stern, *Angriff und Abwehr. Ein Handbuch über die Judenfrage*, 2nd edn,
Berlin: Philo, 1924, p. 136; *Anti-Anti. Tatsachen zur Judenfrage* (ed. Centralverein
deutscher Staatsbürger jüdischen Glaubens), 7th edn, Berlin: Philo, 1932.
5 Albertin, *Liberalismus und Demokratie*, p. 383.
6 See above, p. 222.
7 Vagts, 'M. M. Warburg & Co.', p. 377.
8 Ibid., p. 380; Mosse, *Economic Elite*, p. 287.

strengthened the increase in anti-Semitism'.[9] In 1931 Brüning changed his mind and approached Silverberg with a cabinet post, but without success.

This public diffidence was not universal. Shortly before his death Hugo Preuß argued that anyone 'equal to the task would be wrong to back out in order to avoid the charge of self-promotion'.[10] Jews were also involved in the leadership of parliamentary delegations, as Ernst Heilmann and Bernhard Falk in Prussia illustrated. However, among parliamentarians generally, Jews, broadly defined, were a small minority. In the first Reichstag, that of 1920, there were four professing Jews and nine deputies of Jewish descent, in that of 1930 two professing Jews and fourteen of Jewish descent, in each case 2.8 per cent of the total. The Reichstag of July 1932 had one professing Jew (Hugo Heimann, SPD, as in 1930) and thirteen of Jewish descent, all SPD except one DStP and one Communist, who made up 2.3 per cent of the total. In the last Prussian Landtag, that elected in April 1932, there were two professing Jews and two of Jewish descent, all SPD.[11] The trend away from professing Jews confirms the decline of the DDP and the growing inclination of the younger SPD members to accept the party's norm of severing links with any religious body. In the Landtage the proportion of Jewish deputies was no higher; two states, Prussia and Hamburg, accounted for almost three-quarters of them.[12]

One branch of government in which Jews did make a breakthrough was the state administration, including its higher reaches, in both the *Reich* and the states. Some of these appointments, such as those of *Ministerialräte* Herbert Weichmann and Hans Goslar in the Prussian State Ministry (i.e. Prime Minister's department) and Ernst Hamburger in the Interior Ministry, they owed to their party affiliation. Others, like *Legationsrat* Moritz Sobernheim in the *Reich* Foreign Ministry, were appointed specifically to advise on Jewish affairs.[13] But there were also those who climbed the regular career ladder, especially in the *Reich* and in Prussia. The most eminent of these was Hans Schäffer, who rose to the rank of State Secretary in the *Reich* Finance Ministry. He was the son-in-law of the Breslau politician Adolf Heilberg and a cousin of the SPD's house economist Fritz Naphtali. He was recruited into

9   Brüning, *Memoiren 1918–1934*, p. 370.

10   22 June 1925, *Jüdisch-Liberale Zeitung*, 1.Beilage 26 June 1925, cit. Hamburger, *LBYB* (1975), p. 190.

11   'Juden in der Regierung', *CVZ*, 11 May 1922, p. 26; *Anti-Anti*, 6th edn, p. 61; ibid., 7th edn, p. 59.

12   'Juden in der Regierung', p. 25.

13   Francis R. Nicosia, 'Jewish Affairs and German Foreign Policy during the Weimar Republic – Moritz Sobernheim and the Referat für jüdische Angelegenheiten', *LBYB* XXIII (1988), pp. 261–83.

the newly-created *Reich* Economic Ministry in 1919. At that time he was a member of the DDP, but this affiliation was short-lived; thereafter his posture was 'to the left of the DDP and the right of the SPD'.[14] He played a leading role in the negotiations for both the Dawes and Young Plans, which laid down the conditions for German reparations, and became *Staatssekretär* in 1930. Though he continued to live in Sweden, where he had emigrated, after the Second World War, he was a close adviser of Chancellor Adenauer on the Schuman Plan for a European Coal and Steel Community, the forerunner of the EEC.[15] The only other civil servant of Jewish descent to reach the same rank – the highest in the German public service – was Curt Joël, already mentioned as Brüning's Minister of Justice. He was a convert who kept his Jewish origins quiet; he had entered the *Reich* civil service under the Empire and had reached the rank of *Ministerialdirektor* in the Justice Department by 1918.[16] In contrast with the central administrations, by 1932 there were no Jews in the provincial administrations of the states, whether among the governors (*Oberpräsidenten*) of the 12 Prussian provinces or the *Regierungspräsidenten* of the 35 administrative districts, or their equivalents in the other states, or among the rural mayors (*Landräte*) of the 400 rural local government units. There were, however, three *Regierungsvizepräsidenten* in Prussia[17] and the baptized Liberal Julius Lippmann had been Governor of Pomerania from 1919 to 1929. Outside Berlin few Jews held important positions in local government. Ludwig Landmann, who had resigned from the Jewish community during the First World War, served as Lord Mayor of Frankfurt from 1920 onwards[18] and Carl Petersen, who had one Jewish parent, became Lord Mayor of Hamburg in 1924, having been national chairman of the DDP for the previous five years.

In the two branches of the public service where Jews most coveted opportunities and which had been the subject of the greatest controversy before the war, the judiciary and academia, the widening of career chances was limited. There is no analysis for the Weimar period as detailed as that of Bernhard Breslauer for the Empire;[19] we therefore have to rely on various

14 Ekkehard Wandel, *Hans Schäffer. Steuermann in wirtschaftlichen und politischen Krisen, 1886–1937*, Stuttgart: Deutsche Verlags-Anstalt, 1974, p. 29.
15 Ibid., pp. 281–2.
16 Klaus-Detlev Godau-Schüttke, *Rechtsverwalter des Reiches. Staatssekretär Dr Curt Joël*, Frankfurt: Lang, 1981; Beer, *Die Juden, Das Recht und die Republik*, p. 167.
17 *Anti-Anti*, 7th edn, p. 44.
18 Dieter Rebentisch, *Ludwig Landmann. Frankfurter Oberbürgermeister der Weimarer Republik*, Wiesbaden: Steiner, 1975, pp. 63, 65ff; *Bürgermeister Carl Petersen 1868–1933*, Hamburg: Verein für Hamburgische Geschichte, 1971.
19 Bernhard Breslauer, *Die Zurücksetzung der Juden an den Universitäten Deutschlands. Denkschrift im Auftrage des Verbandes der Deutschen Juden*, Berlin: Verband der Deutschen Juden 1911. See also p. 44, fn. 1.

individual studies. In some instances they differ quite widely in their estimates; in all cases, except post-1933 Nazi sources, they identify professing Jews only, ignoring converts and the non-denominational ('Dissidenten'). According to the Prussian occupational census of 1925 of the 8,187 lawyers in private practice 2,208, or 27 per cent, were professing Jews; Nazi statistics for 1933 give 3,370 'non-Aryans' out of 11,815, or 28.5 per cent for Prussia and 23.4 per cent for Germany as a whole.[20] Jews were prominent in the lawyers' professional organisation, the *Deutscher Anwaltsverein*, accounting for eleven of the twenty-five members of the executive, including Eugen Fuchs, the vice-chairman of the C.V., who was vice-chairman in the last years of his life.[21] Another, Max Hachenburg, was invited to become chairman, but declined, feeling a Jew should not occupy such a position. Hachenburg was also a regular contributor to *Die Justiz*, the journal of the *Republikanischer Richterbund*.[22] The 'non-Aryan' share among notaries was somewhat higher, 2,051 out of 6,226, or 33 per cent. In the Berlin court district 56 per cent of notaries were 'non-Aryan', compared with 48 per cent of lawyers; in the Frankfurt court district 49 per cent compared with 45 per cent.[23] The frequently-aired grievance that Jewish lawyers were passed over in the nomination of notaries before 1918 seems therefore to have been remedied. As far as judicial office was concerned, the number of Jewish incumbents did not increase dramatically, and there were indeed signs of decline towards the end of the Weimar Republic, but the higher grades, including those of public prosecutors, were now open to them. The overall total rose slowly but steadily, peaking in 1933. The increase was greatest in the lowest grade, that of magistrates, but the next two grades (presiding magistrates, associate high court judges, presiding high court judges) also showed a considerable improvement on the pre-war period. There had been only one presiding high court judge in monarchical Prussia, appointed in 1918, and no state attorneys of any rank. Similarly membership of the Imperial Supreme Court (*Reichsgericht*) had been a rarity.[24] Even so, it is notable that after 1918 only one Jew became a chief justice and few became senior

---

20 Beer, *Die Juden, das Recht und die Republik*, pp. 196–7.
21 Udo Beer, 'The Protection of Jewish Civil Rights in the Weimar Republic. Jewish Self-Defence through Legal Action', *LBYB* XXIII (1988), p. 158; Max Hachenburg, *Lebenserinnerungen eines Rechtsanwalts und Briefe aus der Emigration* (ed. Jörg Schadt), Stuttgart: Kohlhammer, 1978, p. 265.
22 Hachenburg, *Lebenserinnerungen eines Rechtsanwalts*, p. 75, cit. Beer, *LBYB* (1988), p. 159; Sinzheimer and Fraenkel, *Die Justiz in der Weimarer Republik*, p. 12.
23 Beer, *Die Juden, das Recht und die Republik*, pp. 196, 198–9; Sievert Lorenzen, 'Das Eindringen der Juden in die Justiz. Ein historischer Rückblick-III', *Deutsche Justiz*, 6 February 1939, p. 966. See also below, p. 278.
24 See above p. 91.

state or *Reich* attorneys. Time might have remedied that, though as long as Curt Joël was State Secretary at the Ministry of Justice there was a virtual ban on the appointment of members of the *Republikanischer Richterbund*, which counted many Jews among its members. Equally significant was the trend among court clerks (*Gerichtsassessoren*), from among whom future judges would be recruited. Their numbers peaked in 1924 (in Prussia in 1926), and by 1933, before the Nazi purge began, there were fewer than at the end of the First World War (see table 3.11). The great majority of Jewish judicial officials were to be found in Prussia – 77 per cent by 1933, well above the Prussian share of the total population. In the non-Prussian states Jewish career patterns reflected those of the *Reich* in general, with two significant exceptions. In Saxony, which had rigorously excluded Jews from the judicial service before 1914, numbers rose to 13 by 1933. In Bavaria, by contrast, where a relatively liberal policy had prevailed, the post-1918 political atmosphere was distinctly less tolerant. After peaking at 69 in 1921, the number of Jewish judges declined to 58 by 1933. Franz Gürtner of the DNVP, Minister of Justice from 1922 to 1932, was particularly hostile to the appointment of Jews.[25] In 1932 he became *Reich* Minister of Justice, serving the Third Reich until his death in 1941. In this, as in other respects, it looks as if the Nazi seizure of power did not initiate the departure of Jews from the centre stage of German public life, but gave it a radical acceleration.

This was true even more of academia than of the judiciary, for two reasons. Jewish entry into academic life had come earlier and progressed faster than in the judiciary and therefore benefited more from the opportunities offered by the Liberal decades. Though Jews certainly suffered from discrimination and complained of it, they were better placed in higher education by, say, 1890 than in any other part of the public service. After 1918 the situation was reversed. While the democratization of political life and the entry of Liberal and Socialist parties into government liberalized civil service recruitment patterns, the atmosphere in universities became more reactionary and anti-Semitic, with the student body an early stronghold of the radical Right. Though the number of Jewish professors increased in absolute numbers during the Weimar period, it did not do so relatively. In the academic year 1909/10, the year of Bernhard Breslauer's detailed analysis, there were 69 full professors (*Ordinarien*) of Jewish descent (professing or baptized),[26] or 6.9 per cent of the total. In the academic year 1931/2 there were 114 or 5.6 per cent.[27]

25 Lorenzen, *Deutsche Justiz*, 6 February 1939, p. 964; *idem*, *Die Juden in der Justiz*, 2nd edn, Berlin: Deckert, 1943, p. 164; Schulz, *Der Republikanische Richterbund*, p. 159.
26 Breslauer, *Die Zurüchsertzung der Juden an den Universitäten Deutschlands*, p. 12.
27 Lowenthal, 'Die Juden im öffentlichen Leben', pp. 76–9.

Table 3.11 Professing Jews in judicial posts, 1919–1933

	Court clerks	Grade V	Grade IV	Grade III	Grade II	Reichs Gericht	State attorneys	Senior state attorneys	Reich attorneys	Total
1919	187	327	50	10		9	24	5	–	612
1920	190	344	57	12		9	26	6	–	644
1921	207	347	67	13		10	36	5	–	685
1922	224	343	65	16		12	40	6	2	708
1923	241	356	76	16	1	12	41	5	2	750
1924	278	343	91	15	1	11	44	4	2	789
1925	219	307	95	9	1	10	42	4	2	689
1926	211	326	90	11	1	9	35	4	2	689
1927	209	336	99	8	1	8	35	4	2	702
1928	192	365	105	9	1	11	36	4	2	725
1929	183	390	108	15	1	11	36	6	2	752
1930	170	392	117	17	1	11	39	6	2	755
1931	175	398	126	20		10	26	7	2	764
1932	192	402	124	21		10	40	6	2	797
1933	184	405	127	29		10	37	5	1	798

Note: For explanation of grades see table 2.1, p. 45.
Source: Deutsche Justiz, vol. CI/1, p. 964

If one further considers that of the 114, 14 taught at the University of Frankfurt, which was not in existence in 1909 and which was characterized by specifically liberal statutes and atmosphere,[28] and therefore deducts them from the total, the Jewish share for 1931/2 drops to 5.1 per cent.[29] This decreasingly favourable position of Jews was illustrated even more starkly by the steady decline of the Jewish share in the student body, from 10.1 per cent in 1879/80 to 8.3 per cent in 1891/2 and 4.3 per cent in 1930. In the academic profession, even more than in the judicial service, the decline in German-Jewish fortunes had set in well before 1933.

Another favoured form of Jewish public activity that survived in an attenuated form in the Weimar years was that of the policy adviser. It was a substitute for formal political office or permanent administrative appointment and, as such, convenient and welcome to both Jews and Gentiles. It helped to perpetuate the status of many of the German-Jewish economic elite as privileged outsiders. Like direct political activity it reached a brief heyday immediately after the war, in Jewish participation in the armistice and reparations delegations. But even here there were inhibitions, as much on the Jewish as on the Gentile side, especially on the part of Max Warburg and his partner Carl Melchior, a posture that was consistent with Warburg's reluctance to serve in the governments of Prince Max of Baden and Joseph Wirth.[30] However, Melchior continued to play a prominent advisory role and in 1925 became the only German member of the finance committee of the League of Nations.[31] Warburg himself was a central figure in the counsels of the Reichsbank, serving on its executive (*Zentralausschuß*) from 1919 to 1924 and thereafter, until 1933, on its general council (*Generalrat*), where he joined the banker Oskar Wassermann. He was instrumental in securing the appointment of Hjalmar Schacht as president of the Reichsbank in 1923 and in his dismissal in 1930.[32] More surprisingly he was as influential as ever when Schacht's successor, Hans Luther, resigned after Hitler had become Chancellor and supported the re-appointment of Schacht.[33] In both 1924 and 1930 he opposed the candidature of Melchior, considering a Jew unsuitable for such an exposed position.[34] In 1930 he supported Luther for the post, who was also the nominee of Franz von Mendelssohn, the chairman of the general council. Melchior, who was undoubtedly well qualified, enjoyed considerable

28   See above, pp. 112–13.
29   *Statistisches Jahrbuch für das Deutsche Reich 1931*, p. 432.
30   See above, p. 210.
31   Vagts, 'M. M. Warburg & Co.', p. 172; Mosse, *Economic Elite*, p. 288.
32   Warburg, *Aus meinen Aufzeichnungen*, p. 141; Mosse, *Economic Elite*.
33   Mosse, *Economic Elite*, p. 289.
34   Warburg, *Aus meinen Aufzeichnungen*, p. 122.

cabinet support, including that of General Groener and Joseph Wirth, but the SPD Minister Carl Severing, who also had a personal preference for him, pointed out that 'in present-day circumstances the successor of Schacht could be neither a Jew nor a Social Democrat'.[35]

Second only to Warburg as a confidant of politicians was the baptized industrialist Paul Silverberg, a leading figure in the *Reichsverband der deutschen Industrie*, who was close to both the Lord Mayor of Cologne, Konrad Adenauer, and Brüning during his Chancellorship. Though he declined Brüning's offer of a cabinet post, he urged a more expansionist, counter-cyclical economic strategy on him[36] and was the principal organizer of the so-called *Osthilfe*, a scheme to relieve the debts of agriculture in the Eastern provinces. This was not an inspired initiative and soon degenerated into a virtually limitless subsidy to large landowners.

Rather less influential than the Reichsbank was the National Economic Council (*Reichswirtschaftsrat*) which was required to comment on social and economic legislation. This was a large body with up to 326 members, which enjoyed only provisional status (*Vorläufiger Wirtschaftsrat*) until 1928. Those who served on it included Walther Rathenau, Rudolf Hilferding, Maximilian Kempner, a leading figure in the potash industry, Arthur Feiler, the economics editor of the *Frankfurter Zeitung*, Fritz Naphtali and Max Cohen-Reuß (all nominated by the government); Arthur Salomonsohn, Georg Solmssen, Louis Hagen, Franz von Mendelssohn, Fritz Demuth, the executive secretary of the Berlin Chamber of Commerce, and Heinrich Grünfeld (nominated by the employers); Siegfried Aufhäuser and Adolf Cohen (nominated by the trade unions); and Max Hachenburg, Leon Zeitlin and Georg Bernhard (representing the professions).[37]

In contrast with the gradual departure of Jews from the public political stage in the middle and final years of the Weimar Republic, efforts increased to put the relationship of the Jewish community with the *Reich* and state authorities on a more regular basis. Parallel with that came an increase in the polarization and partisanship of intra-Jewish politics. Up to 1918 the structure of Jewish representative bodies and their relationships with governments had reflected the fragmentation of both the Jewish community and the political system of the *Reich*, as well as the absence of democratic legitimacy in the

---

35 *Akten der Reichskanzlei, Weimarer Republik. Kabinett Müller II* (ed. Martin Vogt), Boppard: Harald Boldt, pp. 1551–3.
36 Reinhard Neebe, *Großindustrie, Staat und NSDAP 1930–1933. Paul Silverberg und der Reichsverband der Deutschen Industrie in der Krise der Weimarer Republik*, Göttingen: Vandenhoeck & Ruprecht, 1981, pp. 111–16.
37 Lowenthal, 'Die Juden im öffentlichen Leben', p. 59; Hachenburg, *Lebenserinnerungen eines Rechtsanwalts*, pp. 327–8, 344–5.

one as in the other. Of the two principal Jewish bodies in existence at the turn
of the century the DIGB represented the interests of the religious communities, though this inevitably gave it, or at least some of its officials, a political
role, while the C.V. began as a defence league against discrimination and
anti-Semitism but developed in time into a broadly-based lay organization.
Though the DIGB had in 1899 acquired the status of legal incorporation,
there was no one body that could speak for the Jews of Germany, or even
Prussia, in their entirety.

Formal relations between the Jewish community and state authorities
varied from state to state. In some, notably Baden and Württemberg, there
were over-arching communal organizations with official standing and an
entitlement to public subsidy. Conditions in Prussia, in contrast, were
governed by the 1847 law (*Gesetz über die Verhältnisse der Juden*), which
recognized only the individual parishes (*Gemeinden*) as the basis of Jewish
religious life. Though intended to bring uniformity into Jewish affairs, this
law was not extended to the territories acquired during the wars of unification, so that within twenty years the same confusion reigned as before 1847.

It was this state of affairs that the *Verband der Deutschen Juden* (VdDJ),
created in 1904, was designed to remedy. Yet the difficulties that attended its
formation reflected the divisions within German Jewry. The initiative came
from a group of notables already prominent in Jewish organizations under the
impulse of a number of short-term factors – the split in the Left-Liberal
parties, which further weakened the political voice closest to Jewish interests;
the proposed school legislation of the Prussian government; and the informal
contacts between those Jewish notables and Prussian bureaucrats who
favoured a rationalization of their relationships.[38] The VdDJ as it emerged
was neither the mass-based organization that some had advocated, nor one
with plenipotentiary powers. It was broadly representative, but not accountable – or rather, it was accountable to an annual meeting whose members
were themselves local oligarchs. Jewish executives 'swarmed with *Justizräte,
Sanitätsräte and Kommerzienräte*'[39] – titles that governments were happy
to shower on Jewish professionals and businessmen as compensation for
exclusion from positions of power. The VdDJ's executive contained delegates
of the C.V., the DIGB, the association of rabbis (*Rabbinerverband*),
educational bodies, theological colleges and the larger communities. Unlike
the C.V., it managed to recruit the active support of a number of Zionists,

38 Walter Breslauer, 'Der Verband der Deutschen Juden (1904–1922)', *BLBI* 28
(1964), p. 347.
39 Ibid., p. 351; also Marjorie Lamberti, 'The Attempt to Form a Jewish Bloc:
Jewish Notables and Politics in Wilhelminian Germany', *CEH* III, May–July 1970,
p. 84.

including Max Bodenheimer, Alfred Klee and Arthur Handtke. Like the DIGB, it failed to encompass all the Orthodox. The ultra-Orthodox 'secessionists' grouped themselves in the Frankfurt-based *Freie Vereinigung für die Interessen des orthodoxen Judentums* and gained government recognition as a separate representative body.

A loose federation of Prussian-Jewish notables was the type of structure that divided Jews least. The established Liberal leadership distrusted the mass organization that some advocated, because it feared the more activist Zionists would benefit from it. The communities of the Southern states feared that a centralized organization would mean Prussian dominance, the Orthodox that it would mean Reformist dominance, the rabbis that it would undermine their autonomy. The success of German Catholics in building up an effective mass base and electoral machine was viewed with mixed feelings: there was no consensus among the Jewish leadership on how high a profile was desirable, or how 'separate' it was prudent for German Jews to appear. What kept the Wilhelmine 'Jewish lobby' – such as it was – together was not organization but personalities and overlapping office-holding. The same names – Martin Philippson, Maximilian Horwitz, Eugen Fuchs, Oskar Cassel – occur in the leading positions of the C.V., the DIGB and the VdDJ. The success of the VdDJ in affecting official policy before 1918 was limited. It gave more effective publicity to discrimination in the public service and Bernhard Breslauer's pamphlet on the judiciary did lead to some liberalization in Prussia. Equally it was successful, in concert with the DIGB, in securing a small annual subsidy of 40,000 RM for Jewish rural schools in Prussia from 1908 onwards, though the complex conditions attached to this meant that only a fraction of it was ever paid out.[40]

The public representation of Jewish interests by these semi-formal networks could not survive the end of the Empire. The war had brought about closer and more structured contacts with the Imperial government. The accelerated immigration of Eastern Jews had altered the composition of the Jewish population. These, and the revival of anti-Semitism, especially as exemplified by the military census, heightened the political awareness of Jews. Zionism in particular was strengthened, partly by the Balfour Declaration, but also in response to the general stimulus that the war gave to the movement for national self-determination. The Weimar constitution promised greater equality of treatment for the Jewish community compared with the Christian churches; it also, by establishing universal suffrage, proportional representation and equality of the sexes, affected the internal structure of Jewish associational life, undermining the power base of the middle-class

---

40 Max P. Birnbaum, 'On the Struggle for Jewish Religious Equality in Prussia, 1897–1914', *LBYB* XXV (1980), pp. 165–6.

oligarchs. The democratization of communal life, however, proceeded unevenly and was by no means complete by 1933. The death or retirement of most of the first-generation leadership, including Philippson and Horwitz, also removed an important element of cohesion. The first result of this was that the *Verband der Deutschen Juden* ceased to exist in 1922, though there is no record of its having been formally wound up, and the DIGB was once more the sole nation-wide body capable of speaking on behalf of Jewish interests. The practical obstacles to achieving a single voice were the same as before 1918. Religious matters remained the responsibility of the individual states, requiring a whole range of parallel negotiations; and minorities within the Jewish communities continued to distrust any move towards all-embracing, centralized structures. Those Orthodox congregations not already organized in the Frankfurt *Freie Vereinigung* joined in the *Reichsbund gesetzestreuer jüdischer Gemeinden Deutschlands*, known as the *Halberstädter Verein* after its headquarters.

As before 1918, it was state–synagogue relations in Prussia that were crucial.[41] To comply with Article 137(5) of the Weimar constitution, which gave only legally-constituted religious bodies ('Körperschaften des öffentlichen Rechtes') the right to raise taxes, and the known wish of the Prussian government to deal only with a properly representative body, the *Preußischer Landesverband jüdischer Gemeinden* (PLV) was founded in 1922. It did not become fully operational until 1925, by which time 646 Jewish communities were affiliated, compared with about 140 to the *Halberstädter Verein*; many, however, had dual membership.[42] The PLV's main achievement was in securing a regular subsidy from the Prussian government from 1925 onwards: 200,000 RM for the salaries and pensions of rabbis and an additional sum that peaked at 400,000 RM in 1929 and 1930 for religious instruction,[43] which was distributed through the two *Vereine*. That was rather less *per capita* than the Christian churches got, though the disproportion was not as great as in Bavaria, where the grant was 50,000 RM in 1924, 60,000 RM from 1925 to 1928 and 70,000 RM thereafter, about one-third of the level for the Catholic Church.[44] That subvention was, however, the limit of the PLV's success. It would have liked a 'concordat', similar to that achieved by the Catholic Church, but the Prussian government was not interested. What the government preferred was a new statute to regulate Jewish religious organization, to

---

41   See Ismar Freund, *Synagogengemeinden in Preußen und die Reichsverfassung*, Berlin: Philo, 1926.
42   Max P. Birnbaum, *Staat und Synagoge 1918–1938. Eine Geschichte des preußischen Landesverbandes jüdischer Gemeinden*, Tübingen: J. C. B. Mohr, 1981, pp. 88–9.
43   Ibid., p. 139.
44   Niewyk, *The Jews in Weimar Germany*, p. 187.

replace the outdated 1847 law. This was duly drafted, largely by the PLV, and tabled on 12 March 1932 in the Landtag. But the dissolution of the Prussian government by Chancellor Papen in July ended the career of that particular project. Progress towards setting up a national representative body had been equally limited by the time the Weimar Republic came to an end. An attempt in 1926 at creating a *Reichsverband* on the lines of the Prussian *Landesverband* foundered on the same obstacles as previous attempts. An eleventh-hour meeting of the *Landesverbände* with the same aim in 1932 was equally fruitless.[45] What did come about in 1928 was a loose confederation in the form of the *Reichsarbeitsgemeinschaft der jüdischen Landesverbände*, which acquired some standing in the crisis of 1932–3.

A further task that faced Jewish bodies was the legal defence of individual Jews against discrimination and harassment, and the defence of Jews collectively against abuse and incitement to hatred. This raised tactical as well as jurisprudential problems. It was by no means self-evident that it was a good idea to seek the protection of the state or the courts to inhibit extremist propaganda, even though the constitution now specifically laid down the equal protection of all religions, Article 136 of the Criminal Code forbade incitement of one class of the population against another and Article 160 protected religious bodies against defamation. A related problem was how far it was possible to trust the appropriate authorities to act effectively against anti-Semitic agitation. After some hesitation the C.V. had decided before 1914 to take advantage of the Code's provisions, with modest but increasing success.[46] After 1918 the greater aggressiveness of anti-Semitism made the question more urgent and the coming to power of Republican politicians improved the chances of success. The central authorities certainly seemed more sympathetic. In November 1919 the Berlin Public Prosecutor circulated an enquiry on anti-Semitic agitation to all police directorates; in September 1922 a directive from the Prussian Minister of Justice instructed Senior Public Prosecutors to take action whenever an anti-Semitically-inspired insult was brought to their attention.[47] Such solicitude did not guarantee compliance on the ground. It nevertheless encouraged the C.V. to pursue legal redress, along with other bodies, such as the *Reichsbund jüdischer Frontsoldaten*, the student corporation *Kartell–Convent* (KC) and the *B'nai B'rith*. In particular the C.V. offered a free legal service to any Jew who had reason to complain of discrimination, which it was professionally well qualified to do.[48]

45 Kurt Loewenstein, 'Die innerjüdische Reaktion auf die Krise der deutschen Demokratie', *Entscheidungsjahr 1932*, pp. 402–3.
46 See above, p. 120.
47 'Die Staatsanwaltschaft gegen den Antisemitismus', *MVA* XXIX/46, 24 December 1919, p. 198; Beer, *LBYB* (1988), p. 152.
48 Beer, *LBYB* (1988), p. 150.

Its services, however, tended to exclude those who did not accept the leadership claims of the C.V., in particular the poorer Eastern European Jews.

As time went on and the C.V. gained experience, its legal activities became more effective. Though the Weimar judiciary was certainly not politically impartial and tended to be more indulgent towards crimes originating from the Right than from the Left, an analysis of their record in cases involving anti-Semitism shows no systematic bias.[49] Resort to the civil law, which in any case the lawyers of the C.V. were more conversant with, was more promising than to the criminal law. It was particularly effective in securing injunctions against boycotts of Jewish businesses.[50] Increasingly the C.V. came round to the view of Bruno Weil that the publicity attending its litigation did more good than harm, provided the political nature of the litigation was clearly appreciated. In any case there was something to be said for a strategy that resulted in the convictions of Theodor Fritsch and Julius Streicher and led Gregor Strasser to instruct party orators to tone down their language.[51]

The effect of the political constellation on Jewish rights was not always predictable. In general relations were best in Prussia and in particular with the Berlin Police Directorate.[52] On the other hand few politicians were anxious to be known primarily as friends or protectors of the Jews. The *Zentrum*, though not free from anti-Semitism, generally supported religious equality. The parties of the Left, in contrast, though reliable opponents of anti-Semitism, were less well-disposed towards organized religion. Just as the Eisner government in Bavaria had ended compulsory school prayers, so in 1922 the USPD Minister of Education in Saxony, Hermann Fleißner, allowed absence from school only on public holidays, which Jewish feast-days were not. In Hesse-Darmstadt the left-inclined SPD opposed all subsidies to religious bodies, whether Christian or Jewish.[53] In some states the Left also favoured the prohibition of ritual slaughter; the ban in Bavaria was approved with the votes of the Communist and Social Democratic parties.[54] Similarly during the debates on the reform of the Criminal Code in 1928 the SPD

---

49   Donald L. Niewyk, 'Jews and the Courts and Weimar Germany', *JSS* XXXVII (1975), pp. 99–113.
50   Beer, *LBYB* (1988), pp. 167–9.
51   'Fritsch zu drei Monaten Gefängnis verurteilt', *CVZ*, 19 December 1924, p. 815; 'Zwei Monate Gefängnis für Streicher', *CVZ*, 24 December 1925, p. 808; Arnold Paucker, 'Documents on the Fight of Jewish Organisations against Right-Wing Extremism', *Michael* II, 1973, pp. 216–46.
52   Beer, *LBYB* (1988), p. 168.
53   Niewyk, *The Jews in Weimar Germany*, p. 187.
54   Beer, *LBYB* (1988), p. 171.

favoured dropping the law against blasphemy, which had been a useful instrument in the C.V.'s litigation, though nothing came of the new draft.[55]

A final aspect of the increased formalization of politics in the Weimar Republic was the partisan polarization inside the Jewish community. The initiative for this came from the *Jüdische Volkspartei*, founded in 1919 and designed to represent all those who felt excluded by the 'liberal establishment' that had governed Jewish affairs under the Empire. Its following was therefore among the Orthodox, Zionists and East European immigrants. To keep together this heterogeneous constituency the party's programme needed to be general: in essence it amounted to a rejection of the purely religious definition of post-emancipation Jewry favoured by the Liberal majority and aimed to restore the Jewish community's consciousness as a *Volksgemeinde*,[56] especially by fostering Jewish education. The JVP did not have a national organization and its coalition tactics varied from locality to locality. But it did provide a focus of opposition to the Liberals. In the nearest thing to a nation-wide test of Jewish political preferences, the first and only election to the PLV in 1925 in which almost half of those eligible turned out to vote, the Liberal lists gained 55 per cent and the JVP 26 per cent. In the Berlin communal elections of 1926 the JVP challenge was sufficient to deprive the Liberals of an overall majority, though they regained this in 1930.[57]

The JVP was a purely intra-Jewish party and had no links with the German parliamentary party system. But it was significant that few of its members were associated with the DDP, the natural home of the German-Jewish leadership. A number of them were supporters of the *Zentrum*, a few stood even further to the Right.[58] But it also contained members of the SPD, including the high-ranking Prussian civil servants Hans Goslar and Hermann Badt.[59]

Just as Weimar political developments led to increasing partisanship in communal affairs, so they led to the professionalization of Jewish political life. Those who sought election to the PLV and the major communal councils tended to be functionaries rather than prominent citizens or persons who

---

55   Ibid., pp. 166–7.
56   Michael Brenner, 'The Jüdische Volkspartei. National-Jewish Communal Politics during the Weimar Republic', *LBYB* XXXV (1990), pp. 221–6. Text of the JVP manifesto, 'An die Juden in Preussen!', *JR*, 7 November 1924, p. 629.
57   Birnbaum, *Staat und Synagoge*, pp. 273–87.
58   Brenner, *LBYB* (1990), p. 228.
59   On Goslar's politics see Trude Maurer, 'Auch ein Weg als Deutscher und Jude: Hans Goslar (1889–1945)', in Julius H. Schoeps (ed.), *Juden als Träger bürgerlicher Kultur in Deutschland*, Stuttgart and Bonn: Burg-Verlag, 1989, pp. 193–239, esp. pp. 222, 236 fn. 130.

straddled the boundary between communal concerns and public life. Klee, Badt and Goslar were exceptions in this respect, as were the luminaries whom the Berlin JVP included in its 1930 list – Simon Dubnow, Arnold Zweig, Lesser Ury. Before 1918 a figure like *Justizrat* Arthur Kochmann, an alderman of Gleiwitz, member of the executive of the Prussian DDP and chairman of the synagogue federation of Upper Silesia, would have been an easily recognized type. Now the decline of political Liberalism and the professionalization of intra-Jewish politics made him an example of a dying breed. To a lesser extent this applied even to the C.V. Those of its leaders who had already been active in Left-Liberal politics under the Empire – Bruno Weil, Ludwig Haas and Georg Bernhard – continued to be so. But the C.V. made few new recruits among the eminent, an exception being the banker Jakob Goldschmidt, who served on the organization's executive until he resigned in 1927 out of disapproval of its growing intimacy with the SPD.[60]

Many commentators have thought it ironical that a single Jewish representative body, the *Reichsvereinigung der deutschen Juden*, emerged only in 1933 under the pressure of National Socialism. Retrospective criticism of Jewish disunity has tended to assume that bureaucratic uniformity is a virtue. The lack of a single organization was undoubtedly an inconvenience in dealings with governments and the courts of law. But it also reflected genuine divergences of interest and opinion, ones that could be accommodated within a civilized pluralism, the promise of which the Weimar Republic had originally held out.

13   THE REVOLUTION IN THE PARTY STRUCTURE, 1928–1930

Three characteristics stand out from the Reichstag elections of 1928. The first is the recovery of the Left, both Socialist and Communist. The SPD achieved its best vote since 1919 and together with the KPD scored 40.4 per cent. The second was the extremely poor showing of the National Socialists, with only 2.6 per cent of the vote, though this national average disguised some much higher percentages in certain areas of agricultural depression. The third was the fragmentation of the non-Catholic political middle. All the historically established parties within this spectrum, the DDP, the DVP and the DNVP, lost votes; the benefit of this instability went to a variety of denominational, regional and economic special-interest formations. These developments by themselves stimulated various attempts to re-organize right-wing and middle-class politics. When the onset of the Depression and the concomitant rise of the Nazi Party added to the confusion and panic among the bourgeois party

60   Paucker, *Abwehrkampf*, p. 91.

leaders, this process was accelerated. It is no exaggeration to say that between 1928 and 1930 the electoral landscape of Germany was transformed.

The radicalization of the Right

The first stages of this radicalization were to be observed in the DNVP and the *Zentrum*. In the DNVP, which had lost over a quarter of its seats in 1928, the intransigently anti-democratic wing made its long-prepared take-over at the expense of the more conservative elements. Its leader, Alfred Hugenberg, replaced Count Westarp as party chairman in October 1928, which led in the next two years to two major secessions from the party.[1] The *Zentrum*, too, shifted to the Right, electing Prelate Ludwig Kaas in December 1928 to succeed the more conciliatory and democratically inclined Wilhelm Marx as chairman. The next year Heinrich Brüning became leader of the *Zentrum* in the Reichstag. His period as Chancellor, from 1930–2, when he governed largely by presidential decree and with little reference to the Reichstag, illustrated the new preference for a more authoritarian style of government.

Though the new Kaas–Brüning leadership succeeded in stabilizing the *Zentrum*'s vote, neither Hugenberg's hard line, nor his opponents' attempt to rally their middle-class constituents into new party coalitions (*Sammlungsparteien*), had any effect on the non-Catholic bourgeoisie. They deserted in increasing numbers to the National Socialists even before the full impact of the Depression hit them. In the Landtag elections in Thuringia at the end of 1929 the Nazis rose to 11.3 per cent, compared with 3.7 per cent at the Reichstag election, and were able to enter the state government. Municipal elections in Prussia and Bavaria in November and December of the same year also showed Nazi advances, even if on a lesser scale. This disintegration of the political middle left those Jews who had, until 1929, remained faithful to the DDP even more isolated and threatened. As the Liberal parties moved towards their terminal crisis they, too, were faced with unprecedently hard choices.

The collapse of the Liberal parties

Faced with the radicalization of the other middle-class parties, and even more of their own electorate, the DVP and DDP also turned to the Right in the hope of staging a last rally. Following the death of Gustav Stresemann in 1929, Ernst Scholz briefly tried to maintain the DVP as a party of moderation in domestic and foreign policy. His successor, Eduard Dingeldey, elected

---

1 Leopold, *Alfred Hugenberg*, pp. 45–54; Erasmus Jonas, *Die Volkskonservativen 1928–1933*, Düsseldorf: Droste, 1965, pp. 33–79.

after the débâcle of the 1930 elections, led the party further to the Right, partly out of inclination, even more in response to pressure from below. The DVP attempted to join the 'Harzburg Front' formed by the veterans' association *Stahlhelm*, the DNVP and the Nazis; they participated in the popular initiative to have the Prussian Landtag dissolved, instigated by *Stahlhelm* and supported by the parties of the Right as well as the Communists; the last of the prominent Liberals within the party, Julius Curtius and Siegfried von Kardorff, were excluded from membership – all to no avail. None of this – not to mention the increasing tolerance of anti-Semitism within its own ranks[2] – would have made the DVP more attractive to Jewish voters than before, though as late as 1930 the DVP still solicited Jewish votes in the *C.V.-Zeitung*.[3]

Much more traumatic for the middle-class Jewish voter were the developments within the DDP. Anxious to broaden the DDP's electoral base and to compete more effectively with the nationalist-authoritarian wave that the rise of Nazism had stimulated, the party's leader Erich Koch-Weser (whose mother was Jewish)[4] launched a number of initiatives to amalgamate the Centre-Right. One was the old dream of a single Liberal party, consisting of the DDP and DVP. This came to nothing, since the gap between the two had, if anything, widened after the death of Stresemann. In the DVP the Right was in the ascendant; within the DDP there was strong opposition to such a union from the Left, collected around the Hirsch–Duncker trade unions and the youth wing, the *Jungdemokraten*. The effect that such an amalgamation would have had on Jewish support for the DDP is not easy to evaluate. Some Jews on the party's business wing, including Carl Melchior and the baptized Oscar Meyer, the executive secretary of the Berlin Chamber of Commerce and acting leader of the Reichstag grouping, favoured it; those primarily concerned with the party's Republican credentials would have been less happy. A similar dilemma arose out of the amalgamation that did take place, that with the *Volksnationale Reichsvereinigung* (VNR), the political wing of the *Jungdeutscher Orden* (*Jungdo*). Koch-Weser hoped that the *Jungdo*'s charismatic leader, Arthur Mahraun, would provide a 'Hitler of the Centre', especially as the VNR had achieved a modest success in its first electoral foray when it contested the Landtag elections in Saxony in the spring of 1930. Like most of the youth leagues of the Weimar Republic, the *Jungdo* had a

2   P. B. Wiener, 'Die Parteien der Mitte', *Entscheidungsjahr 1932*, pp. 315–20.
3   Paucker, *Abwehrkampf*, p. 91.
4   Koch-Weser, a grandson of a master-carpenter in Jever who came from a farming family in Hesel (Kreis Wittmund), East Friesland, was descended through his mother from one of the oldest Jewish families in Oldenburg, the Loewensteins. *Genealogie* 1975, Heft 5, pp. 518 ff.

neo-romantic, anti-capitalist, anti-democratic and ultra-nationalist ideology. In its early years it, and its leaders, had certainly been anti-Semitic. As the 1920s wore on, it became more conciliatory towards the Republic and ceased to be overtly anti-Semitic, though continuing to exclude Jews from membership.[5] Despite the large majority with which merger of these two disparate bodies into the *Deutsche Staatspartei* (DStP) was accepted by the DDP executive, the move caused major defections in which the Jewish Question was by no means the only or even the primary issue.

The principal incompatibility was between the new party and the DDP's pacifist wing, led by Professor Ludwig Quidde and Erich Lüth. They objected to the way the word 'democratic' had been dropped from the party's name, the new emphasis on a 'strong foreign policy' and what they saw as the 'open and covert anti-Semitism'.[6] They were joined by other pacifist Liberals, like Hellmut von Gerlach and General Paul von Schoeniach, who had already severed links with the DDP.[7] They formed the *Vereinigung Unabhängiger Demokraten*, re-named the *Radikaldemokratische Partei*. Its chairman was Willy Braubach, an executive member of the *Abwehr-Verein*; its most prominent Jewish member was Georg Bernhard of the *Vossische Zeitung*. Electorally it got nowhere. The DDP's trade union wing was divided. While its leader, Anton Erkelenz, went over to the SPD, others, such as Ernst Lemmer, who was also chairman of the *Jungdemokraten* and who had in the past bewailed the party's rightward drift, were more sympathetic to the *Jungdo's* anti-plutocratic rhetoric and its evocation of war-time comradeship.[8] The VNR's success in bringing over a number of nationalist trade unionists formerly affiliated to the DNVP was no doubt an added attraction.

The Jews in the DDP were also divided. Some, including Oscar Meyer, played an active part in the fusion, though he regretted in retrospect that he had accepted nomination as a parliamentary candidate.[9] Carl Melchior and Gustav Stolper gave their support to the DStP; Otto Richard Frankfurter, a

---

5 Pois, *The Bourgeois Democrats*, pp. 74–5; Klaus Hornung, *Der Jungdeutsche Orden*, Düsseldorf: Droste, 1958, pp. 87–90.

6 Ludwig Quidde, 'Absage an die deutsche Staatspartei', *Das Tagebuch* 1930, pp. 1255–60, cit. Burkhard Gutleben, 'Volksgemeinschaft oder Zweite Republik? Die Reaktionen des deutschen Linksliberalismus auf die Krise der 30er Jahre', *JIDG* XVII (1988), p. 268.

7 Ursula S. Gilbert, *Hellmut von Gerlach (1866–1935). Stationen eines deutschen Liberalen zwischen Kaiserreich und Drittem Reich*, Frankfurt: Lang, 1984, pp. 114–15.

8 Feder, *Heute sprach ich mit ...*, pp. 254, 260, 268; Werner Schneider, *Die Deutsche Demokratische Partei in der Weimarer Republik, 1924–1930*, Munich: Fink, 1978, pp. 258–9; Frye, *Liberal Democrats*, p. 169; Matthias and Morsey, *Das Ende der Parteien 1933*, p. 36.

9 Meyer, *Von Bismarck zu Hitler*, p. 151.

former Reichstag deputy, opposed the fusion, but remained loyal to the party. The Liberal press also gave its blessing. This was true of the *Frankfurter Zeitung*, admittedly now under new management and less committed to Liberalism, and of the *Vossische Zeitung*, now no longer edited by Georg Bernhard. The *Berliner Tageblatt* was more detached and Wolff was privately contemptuous of the new party, likening Mahraun to Parsifal. His children voted for the SPD; so, for that matter, did Koch-Weser's.[10] By the autumn of 1932 Wolff, too, was recommending a vote for the SPD.[11] One prominent member of the *Tageblatt*'s staff, Ernst Feder, chairman of the Berlin-Mitte DDP organization, refused to lead his branch into the new party.[12] Other Jewish Democrats elsewhere acted similarly, e.g. Dr Hans Robinsohn in Hamburg.[13]

The role of Jews in the new party turned out to be a major divisive factor. Mahraun gave repeated public assurances that he opposed anti-Semitism, and the VNR, unlike the *Jungdo*, was open to Jewish members.[14] Nevertheless there was widespread trouble about Jewish parliamentary candidatures. Two prominent officials of the C.V., Bruno Weil and Ludwig Holländer, were nominated, Weil with a reasonable chance of being elected, despite his judgment that 'large circles of Jews ... were suffering from a feeling of having been abandoned'.[15] The most controversial nomination, however, was that of Gustav Stolper in Hamburg, which illustrated all the Democrats' problems of identity. Stolper, a leading economist, had caused a stir at the DDP's Mannheim congress in 1929 by urging a stronger commitment to a free-market economy and a lowering of direct taxes, which alone, he argued, were capable of creating wealth.[16] Though he was careful to show sympathy with the claims of the *Mittelstand*, including peasants and white-collar workers,[17]

---

10 Frye, *Liberal Democrats*, pp. 167, 270–1, fn. 39.

11 *BT*, 10 September 1932; Bernd Sösemann, 'Liberaler Journalismus in der politischen Kultur der Weimarer Republik. Der Beitrag des jüdischen Publizisten und Politikers Theodor Wolff' in Schoeps, *Juden als Träger bürgerlicher Kultur in Deutschland*, p. 265, fn. 61.

12 Frye, *Liberal Democrats*, p. 161.

13 Ursula Büttner, *Hamburg in der Staats- und Wirtschaftskrise, 1928–1931*, Hamburg: Christians, 1982, p. 468.

14 Hornung, *Der Jungdeutsche Orden*, p. 101; Stephan, *Aufstieg und Verfall des Linksliberalismus, 1918–1933*, p. 466; Koch-Weser at Party Executive, 30 July 1930, Wegner, *Linksliberalismus in der Weimarer Republik*, p. 565; Hans Mühle, ibid., p. 569.

15 Wegner, *Linksliberalismus in der Weimarer Republik*, p. 570.

16 Gustav Stolper, *Die wirtschaftlich-soziale Weltanschauung der Demokratie. Programmrede auf dem Mannheimer Parteitag der Deutschen Demokratischen Partei am 5. Oktober 1929*, Berlin: Stilke, 1930.

17 Ibid., pp. 27–30.

this stance identified him with the right wing of the party and earned him the enmity of the DDP's trade unionists. That was of some importance in Hamburg, a stronghold of the liberal *Zentralverband der Angestellten*, which had more members there than the right-wing DNHV and the Socialist AfA combined.[18] The irony of this situation was that Stolper was also a strong Republican and favoured co-operation with the SPD on political grounds, despite his pro-capitalist economic outlook – a combination of attitudes that probably reflected that of a good many middle-class Jews. In the end Stolper was nominated to head the DStP's list in Hamburg (and was subsequently elected), a decision that was made partly out of consideration for the city's sizeable Jewish electorate. What effect this had on the various sources of the DStP's support is difficult to evaluate, since the DStP vote held up fairly well all over Hamburg, compared with the 1928 DDP vote. Ursula Büttner's assertion that the DStP lost disproportionately and the NSDAP gained disproportionately in white-collar districts as a result of Stolper's nomination is misleading.[19] There was little correlation between DStP losses and Nazi gains, which came mainly at the expense of the DNVP and DVP. Nazi gains correlated less with the *Angestellten* population than with those who were self-employed, which explains the above-average Nazi gains even in the most heavily Jewish districts, Rotherbaum and Harvestehude, which also had the highest proportion of self-employed.[20]

Koch-Weser's device to save German Liberalism by allying with nationalist illiberalism came to nothing. The DStP did not escape the fate of the other middle-class parties in 1930. Its vote fell from 4.9 per cent to 3.8 per cent, though this was a less severe loss than that suffered by the DVP and DNVP. Three weeks later the six deputies elected for the VNR left the DStP. Mahraun was in no doubt where the fault lay: 'The Jews [*das Judentum*] did not observe the necessary restraint. Everywhere they pushed themselves into the foreground. ... They were the same pushy Jews who destroyed the Democratic Party.'[21] Koch-Weser retired from politics. Liberalism, the political home of German Jewry since 1848, had all but ceased to exist.

14 THE ELECTORAL STANCE OF THE JEWS, 1930–1933

The great mass of German Jews remained loyal to the Weimar Republic even after 1930 and until it came to an end. This reflected their inner convictions

18 Büttner, *Hamburg in der Staats- und Wirtschaftskrise*, p. 297.
19 Ibid., p. 654, fn. 148.
20 See below, pp. 299–304.
21 *Der Orden*, 21 October 1930, cit. P. B. Wiener, 'Die Parteien der Mitte', *Entscheidungsjahr 1932*, p. 296.

but also, of course, their objective interests. The National Socialists aimed at the destruction of their economic and social existence; the policy of the DNVP, their allies, did not differ greatly from that. On the extreme Left the Communists threatened the life-style of the Jewish community in both its religious and its economic aspects and occasionally coquetted with anti-Semitism. From 1928 onwards the Communists made gains at every election, recruiting first-time voters, previous non-voters and former Social Democrats. Thus Jews remained a mainstay of the parties of the Weimar Coalition even at a time when the left-of-centre middle class was undergoing an unparalleled shrinking process.

The transformation of the DDP into the DStP before the Reichstag election of 1930 enhanced the dilemma for Jewish voters, who received conflicting advice from their opinion leaders. The C.V. was more concerned with defending the Republic and defeating Nazism than with favouring any particular Republican party, though its historic links with left-wing Liberalism no doubt helped it in pronouncing the DStP electable.[1] When the radical literary and political weekly *Weltbühne*, on the strength of this advice, disputed the C.V.'s continuing right to present itself as an opponent of anti-Semitism, Ludwig Holländer summoned his ablest assistant, Eva Reichmann, to mount a defence. She did not deny Mahraun's nationalistic past but drew attention to the positive developments inside the *Jungdo*, the declarations of the DStP on the Jewish Question and the nomination of Bruno Weil, one of the C.V.'s vice-chairmen, as a DStP candidate. Furthermore, the *C.V.-Zeitung* regarded the experiment with the DStP as a last attempt to preserve a middle-class Left: otherwise middle-class Jews would be politically homeless between the anti-Semitic parties on the Right and the Socialists on the Left. The example of Austria, where this situation had arisen, was frightening.[2]

Opinions, in fact, diverged widely. The attitudes of Georg Bernhard, Theodor Wolff and Ernst Feder, who edited the two newspapers most widely read by Berlin Jews, have already been mentioned. But a substantial number of Jewish voters remained loyal to tradition. Casting one's vote for the DStP appeared to strengthen Brüning's government, which in turn was regarded as a bulwark against the National Socialist wave. The DStP still offered personalities whom these voters could respect. Hermann Dietrich, a member of the DDP in Baden since 1918, was Vice-Chancellor and Minister of

---

1 Paucker, *Abwehrkampf*, p. 95.
2 Carl Ossietzky, 'Wahlkampf, C.V. und Staatspartei', *Weltbühne*, 26 August 1930; Eva Reichmann-Jungmann, 'Zum Verständnis unseres politischen Seins', *CVZ*, 5 September 1930, pp. 465–6. On Weil's candidature, see *CVZ*, 22 August 1930, p. 442; also Paucker, *Abwehrkampf*, p. 283.

Finance in Brüning's Cabinet. Hermann Höpker-Aschoff continued as Prussian Minister of Finance in Otto Braun's Cabinet. Falk, a leading Jewish figure in the Rhineland and chairman of the Prussian Landtag DDP, stayed with the DStP. The position of Oscar Meyer and Gustav Stolper, both well respected in commercial circles, has already been mentioned. Optimists concluded from all this that one could get along with Mahraun. He was, after all, the only leader of nationalist-minded youth who believed in the Republic and the black–red–gold flag. That the alliance would be quite so short-lived was not immediately obvious.

Though the majority of Jewish DDP supporters remained loyal to the DStP at this stage, they did so with a growing sense of disillusionment. As the Nobel Prize winner Fritz Haber wrote to Finance Minister Dietrich: 'The new generation ... no longer believes in the Liberalism of our grandfathers and the long evolutionary path of trade-union Social Democracy.'[3] Haber was responding to the rise of National Socialism and Communism, but among Jews, too, the defection from old political habits was generationally determined. Liberal veterans like Max Lichtenstein in Königsberg might bring themselves to vote for the DStP; his son Erwin switched to the SPD,[4] like Rudolf Mosse's sons and nephew.

Among Jewish white-collar workers the deterioration of the economic situation was an important factor. They were affected by the considerable decrease in the number of Jewish firms. Those private banks that had not perished in the inflation were later absorbed by the large banks, with consequences for Jewish employees which have already been outlined. Anti-capitalist ideas, largely undefined, were increasingly held among white-collar workers and exploited by the National Socialists. This in turn drove Jewish white-collar workers to the Left. Before 1914 only non-German Jews living in Germany had applied for assistance from the *Jüdische Wander-fürsorge*. After the war, however, German Jews represented one-third of those receiving Jewish welfare assistance. During the Great Depression, Jewish employees, whether industrial or white-collar, were harder hit by unemployment than were the general population.[5]

---

3 Haber to Dietrich, 18 May 1931, cit. Rudolf Stern, *LBYB* (1963), p. 97.
4 Information contained in a letter dated 12 June 1976 from Dr Erwin Lichtenstein, Tel-Aviv [H]. On Max Lichtenstein see Hamburger, *Juden im öffentlichen Leben Deutschlands*, pp. 376ff., and above, p. 134.
5 Leo Baeck, *Die Rechtsstellung der jüdischen Gemeinde*, New York: Leo Baeck Institute, p. 440; Alfred Marcus, *Die wirtschaftliche Krise des deutschen Juden: Eine soziologische Untersuchung*, Berlin: Georg Stilke, 1931; Jakob Lestschinsky, *Das wirtschaftliche Schicksal des deutschen Judentums. Aufstieg, Wandlung, Krise, Ausblick*. Berlin: Zentralwohlfahrtsstelle der deutschen Juden, 1932, pp. 3–14, 140–169.

One important aspect of the Jewish response to the threat to the Republic was an increase in co-operation with the democratic parties and with sympathetic officials. The principal, though not the sole, instrument of this was the C.V. While it retained its close personal and ideological links with the Left Liberals, contacts with the SPD increased in the course of the Republic, though not without misgivings on both sides. There was considerable collaboration with *Reichsbanner Schwarz–Rot–Gold*, in which the SPD played a preponderant role. Much of this work was directed at the non-Jewish rather than the Jewish public: to alert the moderate parties to the danger of Nazism, to supply them with material for counter-propaganda and to provide some help with campaign funds. To be effective, these efforts had to be confidential; any impact on voters was therefore indirect.[6]

Appeals to Jewish voters were directed more and more towards simple defence of Republican institutions, less and less in favour of particular parties and candidates. The year 1930 saw the unprecedented collaboration of the C.V., *B'nai B'rith*, the veterans' organization RjF and Zionists in the form of the *Reichstagswahlausschuß* to maximize opposition to the Nazi threat.[7]

The continuing electoral advance of the Nazi Party after 1930, and the intensifying squeeze on the parties of the centre-right, aggravated the dilemma both of individual Jews and of those organizations that sought to provide them with a political lead. Voters abandoned the DStP at an increasing rate. This became most apparent in the Prussian Landtag election of April 1932 and the two Reichstag elections in July and November of the same year, when it received respectively 1.5 per cent, 1.0 per cent and 1.0 per cent of the total vote. But, as we shall see, a significant proportion of Jews clung to the DStP until a very late stage.

There were only two directions – other than total resignation and abstention – in which liberal-minded Jews could go: towards the SPD or to the *Zentrum*. Of the two the SPD was the greater beneficiary. Those who moved to the SPD ignored its economic programme – the preservation of the Republic was now of primary importance. Others, more concerned with the protection of their property or professional rights, or suspicious of the SPD's attitude to religion, preferred the *Zentrum*. It and the BVP were the only parties, apart from the Nazis and Communists, to register gains at the Reichstag election of July 1932, thus reversing a long trend. The two parties' support had steadily declined from 19.7 per cent in 1919 to 14.8 per cent in 1930. Now it stood at 15.7 per cent. In part this was no doubt due to improved mobilization of traditional Catholic voters through identification with the two-year chancellorship of Brüning and in response to the Nazi

6   Paucker, *Abwehrkampf*, pp. 95–9.
7   Ibid., pp. 42–4, 180–1.

threat. But sizeable gains in areas where Catholics were thin on the ground suggested that the *Zentrum* had also become the last refuge of a significant number of Protestants and Jews.[8] It was no doubt a gross exaggeration for the Conservative publicist Hans Zehrer to claim that, with the collapse of Liberalism, Jews had become the 'protected citizens' (*Schutzbürger*) of the *Zentrum*,[9] though this interpretation has been echoed by some post-war historians. Arnold Paucker's estimate that most Jews turned to the SPD, with a leap of support from 28 per cent before 1930 to 62 per cent afterwards,[10] probably also exaggerates the extent of that move.

To reconstruct the electoral behaviour of a small minority sixty years after the event is not easy. It is possible to make sense of the data only for those large cities where the Jewish population was sufficiently concentrated. That means Berlin, Hamburg and Frankfurt, which between them contained over 40 per cent of the Jewish population of Germany. Even then, the best one can manage is to establish certain correlations, subject to the usual caution that these fall short of ideal standards of statistical rigour. These three cities show a number of significant parallels in the evolution of the vote, but also some interesting differences.

Berlin Table 3.12 shows what happened to the DDP/DStP and *Zentrum* votes in two groups of districts. The first has high Jewish populations, all of them with an above-average share of middle-class residents. The second has a similar social composition, but few Jews. The only predominantly working-class district with a high Jewish population, Prenzlauer Berg, also had a high proportion of non-citizens and is therefore not suitable for analysis.[11] The figures show firstly that at the last 'normal' Reichstag election of the Weimar Republic, that of 1928, the DDP did better in those districts that were most heavily Jewish and middle class than in those where the middle class was overwhelmingly Gentile. In Wilmersdorf, which had the highest Jewish concentration, the DDP polled more than twice the city average. They demonstrate secondly the collapse of the Jewish support of the DDP/DStP,

8 See Werner Stephan, 'Grenzen des nationalsozialistischen Vormarsches. Eine Analyse der Wahlziffern seit der Reichstagswahl 1930', *ZfP* XXI (1931–2), pp. 570–8; *idem*, 'Die Parteien nach den großen Frühjahrswahlkämpfen', ibid., XXII (1932), pp. 110–18; *idem*, 'Die Reichstagswahlen vom 31. Juli 1932. Eine Analyse der Wahlziffern', ibid., pp. 353–60. Stephan makes the point that the greater part of the Catholic parties' gains took place in Catholic regions (*ZfP* XXII, pp. 114, 358). For our purposes, however, it is the exceptions to this rule that are significant.

9 Paucker, *Abwehrkampf*, p. 273, fn. 96; Knütter, *Deutsche Linke*, p. 119.

10 Paucker, 'Jewish Defence Against Nazism in the Weimar Republic', p. 27.

11 Steven M. Lowenstein, 'Jewish Residential Concentration in Post-Emancipation Germany', *LBYB* XXVIII (1983), pp. 490–2.

Table 3.12 Evolution of DDP and *Zentrum* votes in selected Berlin districts, 1928–1932

District	% of population (1925)			DDP/DStP vote (%)				Zentrum vote %			
	Jewish	*Catholic*	*Middle class**	*1928*	*1930*	*April 1932*	*July 1932*	*1928*	*1930*	*April 1932*	*July 1932*
Wilmersdorf	13.0	10.0	59.5	15.4	12.0	7.1	3.5	3.5	4.3	5.5	8.1
Mitte	10.5	11.4	46.0	8.7	5.3	2.5	1.3	3.7	3.9	4.1	5.0
Charlottenburg	8.9	10.8	51.5	12.6	8.8	5.2	2.4	3.7	4.2	4.9	6.7
Schöneberg	7.7	8.2	57.3	11.9	8.3	5.0	2.4	3.7	4.1	4.6	6.2
Steglitz	1.5	8.8	57.8	8.9	7.1	4.4	2.4	3.4	3.6	4.0	5.4
Zehlendorf	3.4	8.3	56.3	10.4	9.8	5.7	3.2	3.7	4.0	5.3	7.4
Berlin average	4.3	10.0	44.4	7.3	5.3	3.1	1.6	3.3	3.6	4.0	4.9

*Self-employed *plus* civil servants *plus* white-collar workers.

Sources: Statistisches Jahrbuch der Stadt Berlin, 1927, p. 9; 1928, p. 308; 1931, pp. 339–40; 1932, pp. 259–60, 262–5

especially in Berlin-Mitte (10.5 per cent Jews, 1.3 per cent DStP in July 1932). They show lastly an above-average rise in the *Zentrum* vote in almost all middle-class districts (city-wide average from 1928 to July 1932: +1.6 per cent), but especially in Jewish-populated Wilmersdorf (+4.6 per cent), Charlottenburg (+3.0 per cent), Schöneberg (+2.5 per cent) and Tiergarten (+2.4 per cent). It was, however, low in Mitte (+1.3 per cent) and high in upper-middle-class but Gentile Zehlendorf (+3.7 per cent), while fairly low in less select but equally Gentile Steglitz (+2.0 per cent), where the Nazis got their highest vote (42.1 per cent; city average 28.7 per cent).

The SPD vote is more difficult to analyse for two reasons. Unlike the DDP, it had an overwhelmingly non-Jewish constituency. And, while gaining votes from the middle, it also lost them to the Communists. Changes for the SPD have therefore to be calculated in the context of votes for the Left as a whole. Table 3.13 shows that between 1928 and 1930 the Left dropped by 2.9 per cent in Berlin, with the KPD gaining (+2.7 per cent) at the expense of the SPD (−5.6 per cent). From 1930 to July 1932 there was virtually no change for either of the two parties of the Left. (The Prussian Landtag elections of April 1932, included in table 3.12, are here omitted, as the results were exceptionally favourable for the SPD and exceptionally bad for the KPD.) But while the Left did not move overall in Berlin between 1930 and July 1932, individual districts showed considerable movements. All middle-class districts except Mitte showed an improvement for the Left, the highest being Wilmersdorf (+4.1 per cent), Charlottenburg (+2.8 per cent), Zehlendorf (+2.6 per cent), Schöneberg (+1.9 per cent) and Tiergarten (+1.6 per cent). As before, Mitte behaved averagely for the city (0.0 per cent) and Steglitz almost so (+0.7 per cent). More interestingly still, the gains for the Left were attributable almost exclusively to the SPD in Wilmersdorf (+3.3 per cent), Zehlendorf (+1.5 per cent), Schöneberg (+1.4 per cent), though less so in Charlottenburg (+0.6 per cent) and Tiergarten (+0.6 per cent).

A further common feature of these shifts is that the gains for the two Weimar parties, *Zentrum* and SPD, occurred at a very late stage, being most noticeable in July 1932. The crisis in the DDP in 1930 appears to have affected the activists more than the rank-and-file voter. The surge of the *Zentrum* and, to a lesser extent, the SPD came only as a response to the doubling of the Nazi vote in the presidential and various Landtag elections in the spring of 1932. Since the Jews of Berlin were concentrated in middle-class areas, it is difficult to separate their electoral behaviour from that section of the Gentile middle class that did not succumb to National Socialism. The *Zentrum* and SPD gains in Zehlendorf suggest that voters of the former democratic middle moved in parallel directions, irrespective of religion. However, the exceptional surge of these two parties in Wilmersdorf (+7.1 per cent) and Schöneberg (+3.5 per cent) between 1930 and July 1932 also suggests that the trend was more pronounced among Jews.

Table 3.13 Evolution of left-wing vote (%) in selected Berlin districts, 1928–1932

District	% of population (1925)		1928			1930			July 1932			Change in Left vote		
	Jewish	Middle class	SPD	KPD	Total Left	SPD	KPD	Total Left	SPD	KPD	Total Left	1928–30	1930–2	1928–32
Wilmersdorf	13.0	59.5	23.6	7.0	30.6	22.1	9.4	31.5	25.4	10.2	35.6	+0.9	+4.1	+5.0
Mitte	10.5	46.0	31.3	25.9	57.1	26.5	29.8	56.3	26.1	30.2	56.3	−0.8	0	−0.8
Charlottenburg	8.9	51.5	28.7	15.5	44.2	24.5	18.1	42.6	26.0	19.5	45.4	−1.6	+2.8	+1.2
Schöneberg	7.7	57.3	27.6	12.8	40.4	23.7	14.9	38.6	25.1	15.4	40.5	−1.8	+1.9	+0.1
Steglitz	1.5	57.8	22.9	11.2	34.1	18.8	11.8	30.6	19.0	12.3	31.3	−3.5	+0.7	−2.8
Zehlendorf	3.4	56.3	23.2	5.8	29.0	19.7	7.4	27.1	21.2	8.4	29.7	−1.9	+2.6	+0.7
Berlin average	4.3	44.4	32.9	24.6	57.5	27.3	27.3	54.6	27.3	27.3	54.7	−2.9	+0.1	−2.8

Sources: As table 3.11

What happened between July and November 1932, when the Nazis suffered their first electoral setback, is more difficult to establish (table 3.14). In all the Jewish districts examined the DStP vote stayed within 0.2 per cent of its July low. It neither recovered nor dissolved further. The *Zentrum* vote went down slightly, between 0.5 per cent and 1.6 per cent, which was close to the city-wide average. Nor did the evolution of the Left vote show a more clear-cut pattern. City-wide it declined by 0.2 per cent (KPD: +3.8 per cent, SPD: −4.0 per cent). It rose by 0.7 per cent in Wilmersdorf, declined by 0.6 per cent in Schöneberg and Charlottenburg and rose by 0.3 per cent in Mitte. Within the Left the SPD maintained its relatively good performance, with below-average losses: 1.5 per cent in Wilmersdorf, 3.2 per cent in Schöneberg and 3.5 per cent in Charlottenburg. But the same trend applied to Gentile middle-class districts. In Steglitz and Zehlendorf the decline of the combined Left was close to the average (−0.9 per cent and −0.8 per cent respectively) and that of the SPD below average (−2.8 per cent in Zehlendorf, −3.0 per cent in Steglitz). Apart from the Communists the principal victor in the November 1932 Reichstag election − the last that was genuinely free − was the DNVP, re-establishing itself as the only viable force of the non-Nazi Right. In Berlin its vote rose from 8.3 per cent to 11.4 per cent. Most of its gains no doubt came from those who had voted National Socialist in July, but it also offered some hope, however fleeting, to non-Nazis of providing a bulwark against a Nazi government. However, nothing in the voting figures suggests that it succeeded in attracting a significant number of Jews: if anything, the DNVP (and DVP) results were slightly more favourable in Gentile districts.

Over the entire period from 1928 to November 1932 what stands out in the Jewish middle-class areas is the above-average performance of the *Zentrum* and the SPD. In the whole of Berlin the *Zentrum* went up by 1.1 per cent, while the SPD declined by 9.6 per cent. In Wilmersdorf, the district with proportionately the highest Jewish population and at all times the highest DDP/DStP vote, the *Zentrum* vote rose by 3.0 per cent, the highest in the city, the SPD vote rose by 0.3 per cent, by far the best in the city, and the total Left vote went up by 5.7 per cent, the only district, other than Charlottenburg (+0.7 per cent), to show a Left improvement.

Hamburg The social structure and political behaviour of the Jewish population of Hamburg showed some similarities with, and some differences from, those of Berlin. Like that of Berlin it was predominantly middle-class. The two heaviest concentrations, accounting for almost half the Jewish population, were in the districts of Harvestehude and Rotherbaum, which were also the most bourgeois of the city, with only 11 per cent and 17 per cent workers respectively, and 29 per cent and 15 per cent domestic servants. There is

Table 3.14   Evolution of party shares (%) in selected Berlin districts,
July–November 1932

District	NSDAP July Nov.			DNVP July Nov.			DVP July Nov.			Zentrum July Nov.		
Wilmersdorf	35.1	29.3	−5.8	15.2	21.4	+6.2	1.7	2.6	+0.9	8.1	6.5	−1.6
Mitte	28.4	25.9	−2.5	7.4	9.9	+2.5	0.4	0.6	+0.2	5.0	4.5	−0.5
Charlottenburg	33.1	29.4	−3.7	10.3	14.5	+4.2	1.1	1.7	+0.6	6.7	5.7	−1.0
Schöneberg	35.7	31.7	−4.0	12.2	17.8	+5.6	1.1	1.8	+0.7	6.3	5.3	−1.0
Steglitz	42.1	36.1	−6.0	15.6	22.0	+6.4	2.1	3.1	+1.0	5.4	4.7	−0.7
Zehlendorf	36.4	29.4	−7.0	19.4	26.7	+7.3	3.4	4.8	+1.4	7.4	5.9	−1.5
Berlin average	28.7	26.0	−2.7	8.3	11.4	+3.1	0.7	1.1	+0.4	4.9	4.4	−0.5

Sources: *Statistisches Jahrbuch der Stadt Berlin 1932*, pp. 262–5

therefore the same difficulty in separating the Jewish vote from the general
middle-class vote. The Catholic population of Hamburg was even smaller
than that of Berlin (5 per cent compared with 10 per cent), so that major
fluctuations in the *Zentrum* vote can be attributed even more safely to
non-Catholics. The greatest difference between the two cities, and one indeed
that distinguished Hamburg from almost all the rest of Germany, was the
firm implantation of the DDP. Since the *Jungdo* had few followers in
Hamburg the DStP was, from 1930 onwards, the continuation of the DDP
under another name. In the 1928 Reichstag election the DDP obtained 11.7
per cent of the vote and in the simultaneous Bürgerschaft election 12.9
per cent, compared with a national average of 4.9 per cent. As late as the
Bürgerschaft election of April 1932 the DStP secured 11.5 per cent, although
its share had been lower in the intervening elections and dropped again in the
two Reichstag elections of 1932: 6.1 per cent in July and 5.5 per cent in
November. Part of the answer to the question how Hamburg Jews voted
between 1928 and 1932 is therefore that they stayed with the DDP/DStP.
    As in Berlin, the districts with the highest Jewish populations were those
with the highest DDP vote (table 3.15): 21.0 per cent in Harvestehude and
19.9 per cent in Rotherbaum in the 1928 Reichstag election, though it was
substantial in some other middle-class districts too. The stability of the DStP
can therefore be only partly attributed to the Jewish vote. However the DStP
vote held up somewhat better in the more Jewish districts than elsewhere in
the city. Between the Bürgerschaft elections of 1928 and 1932 the city-wide
DDP/DStP vote declined by 1.4 per cent. In Harvestehude it actually rose
fractionally (by 0.1 per cent), in Rotherbaum it dropped (by 2.0 per cent). In
Eppendorf, which had the third-largest Jewish concentration in absolute terms,

DStP July Nov.			SPD July Nov.			KPD July Nov.			Changes 1928–Nov. 1932 DDP/ DStP	Zen- trum	SPD	KPD	Total Left
3.5	3.3	−0.2	25.4	23.9	−1.5	10.2	12.4	+2.2	−12.1	+3.0	+0.3	+5.4	+5.7
1.3	1.2	−0.1	26.1	22.2	−3.9	30.2	34.4	+4.2	−7.5	+0.8	−9.1	+8.5	−0.6
2.4	2.2	−0.2	26.0	22.5	−3.5	19.5	22.4	+2.9	−10.4	+2.0	−6.2	+6.9	+0.7
2.4	2.2	−0.2	25.1	21.9	−3.2	15.4	18.0	+2.6	−9.7	+1.6	−5.7	+5.2	−0.7
2.4	1.9	−0.5	19.0	16.0	−3.0	12.3	14.4	+2.1	−7.0	+1.3	−6.9	+3.2	−3.7
3.2	2.8	−0.4	21.2	18.4	−2.8	8.4	10.4	+2.0	−7.6	+2.2	−4.8	+4.6	−0.2
1.6	1.4	−0.2	27.3	23.3	−4.0	27.3	31.1	+3.8	−5.9	+1.1	−9.6	+6.5	−3.1

the DDP/DStP vote dropped by 0.5 per cent. In DDP strongholds with no Jewish population it dropped rather more: Fuhlsbüttel, −2.6 per cent, Kleinborstel, −3.2 per cent, Ohlsdorf, −4.2 per cent. But even in this latter group the DStP vote remained substantial.

It is evident that the DStP did less well in national than in local elections in Hamburg after 1928. If we want to know in which directions the Jewish ex-DDP vote defected we therefore need to look at the Reichstag elections of 1930 and 1932. But here, too, the decline of the DStP vote was moderate compared with Berlin (and, as we shall see, Frankfurt). In July 1932 the DStP still got 12.5 per cent in Harvestehude and 10.5 per cent in Rotherbaum; it also got 11.5 per cent in non-Jewish Fuhlsbüttel and 8.7 per cent in non-Jewish Ohlsdorf. There is, however, some difference in who benefited from the DStP losses between the two categories of districts, and here the fortunes of the *Zentrum* and the SPD run parallel to those in Berlin. For most of the Weimar Republic the *Zentrum* vote in Hamburg was negligible. Between 1928 and July 1932 it rose by 0.5 per cent from 1.6 per cent to 2.1 per cent. However, in Rotherbaum it rose by 1.8 per cent, in Harvestehude by 2.9 per cent. In the non-Jewish middle-class district of Fuhlsbüttel it rose only by the city average of 0.5 per cent, in Hohenfelde by 1.1 per cent, in Ohlsdorf by 0.1 per cent. The divergent fortunes of the Left are rather more significant (see table 3.16). City-wide the Left declined by 4.3 per cent between 1928 and July 1932 (SPD: −5.3 per cent, KPD: +1.0 per cent). In Harvestehude the Left went up by 1.5 per cent, in Rotherbaum it rose by only 0.6 per cent. In Fuhlsbüttel and Hohenfelde the Left lost, but also below the city average: 1.6 per cent and 1.9 per cent respectively; so also in Eppendorf (−3.2 per cent). As in Berlin, it is the performance of the SPD

Table 3.15 Evolution of DDP and Zentrum votes (%) in selected Hamburg districts, 1928–July 1932

District	% of population			DDP/DStP vote					Zentrum vote				
	Jewish	Middle class	(Civil servants)	1928	1930	April 1932	July 1932	1928– July 1932	1928	1930	April 1932	July 1932	1928– July 1932
Harvestehude	15.9	55.4	(6.6)	21.0	17.6	22.5	12.5	−8.5	1.5	2.4	1.2	4.4	+2.9
Rotherbaum	15.2	64.3	(11.2)	19.9	13.0	20.0	10.5	−9.4	1.6	2.5	1.4	3.4	+1.8
Eppendorf	3.4	55.7	(6.6)	14.0	11.1	15.8	8.0	−6.0	1.3	1.3	1.2	2.2	+0.9
Hohenfelde	0.9	63.2	(6.8)	11.4	9.2	11.5	5.9	−5.5	2.8	3.2	3.2	3.9	+1.1
Fuhlsbüttel	0.3	65.8	(11.4)	18.7	14.6	17.7	11.5	−7.2	1.0	1.0	0.8	1.5	+0.5
Ohlsdorf	0.4	55.9	(11.2)	17.2	12.7	14.6	8.7	−8.5	1.6	1.1	1.0	1.7	+0.1
Hamburg average	1.8	48.2	(5.6)	11.7	8.6	11.5	6.1	−5.6	1.6	1.5	1.0	2.1	+0.5

Sources: Statistisches Mitteilungen über den Hamburgischen Staat, Heft 23, pp. 47–51; Heft 25, pp. 95–104; Heft 28, pp. 113–15; Heft 29, pp. 24–7, 39; Heft 30, pp. 21–39, 51–3; Heft 33, pp. 78–9.

that is most striking. It rose by 0.9 per cent in Harvestehude and fell by only 0.9 per cent in Rotherbaum. Its losses were higher in Fuhlsbüttel (−2.1 per cent) and Hohenfelde (−3.9 per cent), but still below the city average. As in Berlin, Jewish DDP voters moved in the same direction as DDP voters generally, but more decisively so.

Just as the good performance of the DStP in the 1932 Bürgerschaft election was not repeated in the Reichstag elections, so the *Zentrum* and SPD improvements in middle-class districts in the Reichstag elections had not been in evidence in the Bürgerschaft election. It therefore seems highly probable that there was an interchange of votes between the various 'Weimar' parties in 1931−2. This can be illustrated in greater detail from individual polling districts that were DDP strongholds (table 3.17).

It is evident from this sample that the DDP/DStP withstood its débâcle better here than almost anywhere else in the *Reich* − almost spectacularly so − and that in so far as its vote went down, this led to *Zentrum* and SPD gains that were clearly against the national trend. By no means all ex-DDP votes went to the other Weimar parties; all one can establish is that the transfer was more clear-cut in areas of heavy Jewish population, but was not restricted to them.

Between July and November 1932 Hamburg followed the trends of Berlin (table 3.18). The DStP fell back slightly, but still managed to poll around 10 per cent in its strongholds, both Jewish and non-Jewish. The *Zentrum* also fell back, but stayed above its 1928 level. The Nazis lost 6.3 percentage points, well above their national average loss of 4.2. There was a major recovery by the DNVP (up 4.0) and a minor one by the DVP (up 1.3), but much higher for both parties in the middle-class districts. No doubt most of their gains came at the expense of the Nazis, but in both Harvestehude and Rotherbaum the combined DNVP and DVP gains exceeded the Nazi losses; some cross-pressured Left-wing Liberals may also have been attracted to them, especially as the Left also stagnated. In Germany as a whole the Left advanced 1.4 per cent (KPD: +2.6 per cent, SPD: −1.2 per cent), in Hamburg 0.9 per cent (KPD: +4.1 per cent, SPD: −3.2 per cent). In Harvestehude, Rotherbaum and non-Jewish Fuhlsbüttel the total Left vote was virtually unchanged and SPD losses were below the city average (1.5 per cent, 1.8 per cent and 1.8 per cent respectively). In Ohlsdorf the SPD lost 1.0 per cent, but the Left as a whole gained 1.7 per cent. It is therefore slightly more possible in Hamburg than Berlin that some Jewish voters sought their last refuge with the DNVP or DVP; but in each case we are talking about a very small sample. For the period from 1928 to November 1932 clear patterns can be ascertained. In contrast with almost all other parts of Germany the DDP/DStP held about half of its vote in both Jewish and non-Jewish districts. However, the destination of the ex-DDP vote varied according the

Table 3.16   Evolution of left-wing vote (%) in selected Hamburg districts,
1928–July 1932

District	% of population			1928			1930		
	Jewish	*Middle class*	*(Civil servants)*	*SPD*	*KPD*	*Total*	*SPD*	*KPD*	*Total*
Harvestehude	15.9	55.4	(6.6)	17.6	4.4	28.0	16.2	5.0	21.2
Rotherbaum	15.2	64.3	(11.2)	23.2	5.6	28.8	21.8	6.6	28.4
Eppendorf	3.4	55.7	(6.6)	33.0	11.6	44.6	29.1	12.7	41.8
Hohenfelde	0.9	63.2	(6.8)	28.4	6.3	28.7	17.9	7.6	25.5
Fuhlsbüttel	0.3	65.8	(11.4)	25.1	4.0	29.1	23.1	4.7	27.8
Ohlsdorf	0.4	55.9	(11.2)	30.1	5.8	35.9	25.4	8.6	34.0
Hamburg average	1.8	48.2	(5.6)	36.4	17.2	53.6	31.5	18.5	50.0

Source: As table 3.15

religious composition of the district concerned. Rotherbaum and Harvestehude were the only two districts in which the *Zentrum* vote rose significantly
and the only two districts in which the Left improved (see table 3.16). They
were also the two districts in which the SPD had the lowest losses (2.7 and
0.6 per cent, compared with 8.5 per cent city-wide). In all the other middle-
class districts the Left performance was also above average, but less conspicuously so.

Frankfurt   Frankfurt differed from Berlin and Hamburg in two important
respects. The first was that the Jewish population was divided into two
clusters: in the affluent Western districts (Westliche Außenstadt, Nordwestliche Außenstadt, Nördliche Außenstadt) accounting for 37.6 per cent of the
total, and the less affluent Eastern districts (Östliche Neustadt, Östliche
Außenstadt, Nordöstliche Außenstadt) accounting for 43.7 per cent. The
Orthodox population, more numerous than in Berlin and Hamburg, lived
predominantly in the Eastern districts.[12] The second was that one-third of the
population (33.1 per cent) was Catholic, so that the *Zentrum* vote was both
more substantial and more difficult to evaluate.
  Up to 1928 the voting behaviour of the two Western districts with the
highest Jewish density followed the pattern we might expect. They had by far
the highest DDP votes in the city. Since they were also the most affluent
districts in the city, we have the familiar difficulty of separating Jewish votes

12   Ibid., pp. 484–5, 492.

April 1932			July 1932			Change in Left vote			Change in SPD vote
SPD	KPD	Total	SPD	KPD	Total	1928–1930	1930–July 1932	1928–July 1932	1928–July 1932
14.1	4.3	18.4	18.5	5.0	23.5	−0.8	+2.3	+1.5	+0.9
18.9	6.2	25.1	28.3	7.1	29.4	−0.4	+1.0	+0.6	−0.9
26.6	11.0	37.6	29.1	12.3	41.4	−2.8	−0.4	−3.2	−3.9
16.6	7.4	24.0	18.5	8.3	26.8	−3.2	+1.3	−1.9	−3.9
21.5	3.9	25.4	23.0	4.5	27.5	−1.3	−0.3	−1.6	−2.1
23.5	6.8	30.3	24.8	6.7	31.5	−1.9	−2.5	−4.4	−5.3
29.7	16.4	46.1	31.1	18.2	49.3	−3.6	−0.7	−4.3	−5.3

from middle-class votes generally. Two factors help, however. In the city as a whole, the DDP and the more right-wing DVP were of approximately equal strength. The W. and NW. Außenstädte were the only two districts in which the DDP outvoted the DVP by a substantial margin in 1928. Moreover, the DDP had maintained its level of support here during the 1920s, while there was city-wide decline. Between May 1924 and 1928 there was a 1.0 per cent gain by the DDP in W. Außenstadt and a 0.6 per cent loss in NW. Außenstadt, compared with a loss of 2.0 per cent throughout the city. All of this suggests a positive correlation between the Jewish middle class and DDP voting.

Between 1928 and July 1932 these two districts deviated sharply in their political development from similar areas elsewhere in Germany (table 3.19). In the first place the DDP vote collapsed almost entirely, though, as in Berlin, this happened late, i.e. after the Prussian Landtag election of April 1932. The Left gained 4.3 and 4.5 per cent in these districts, almost all of it attributable to the SPD. While this gain was on a scale similar to that observed in Berlin and Hamburg, it was impressive against a much larger city-wide decline, namely 6.9 per cent. Even more striking, however, were the gains of the *Zentrum*, from 8.1 per cent to 22.6 per cent in NW. Außenstadt and from 11.5 per cent to 28.0 per cent in W. Außenstadt. Over the city as a whole the *Zentrum* gain was 2.7 per cent; in middle-class areas with few Jews it was slightly above average: 4.4 per cent in Äußeres Sachsenhausen and 3.0 per cent in W. Neustadt; and rather higher in middle-class areas with a moderate Jewish population – e.g. 6 per cent in N. Außenstadt. In the most

Table 3.17 Evolution of DDP/DStP, SPD and *Zentrum* votes (%) in selected Hamburg precincts, 1928–July 1932

	1928			July 1932			Change		
	DDP	Zentrum	SPD	DStP	Zentrum	SPD	DDP/DStP	Zentrum	SPD
Rotherbaum 212/216	26.1	1.8	21.5	17.2	2.3	25.4	−8.9	+0.5	+3.9
Rotherbaum 213/215	34.0	1.5	18.4	10.5	5.9	22.0	−23.5	+4.4	+3.6
Rotherbaum average	19.9	1.6	23.2	10.5	3.4	22.3	−9.4	+1.8	−0.9
Harvestehude 231/229	24.6	1.8	12.9	17.7	5.9	16.2	−6.9	+4.1	+3.3
Harvestehude 233/230	24.9	1.3	10.9	15.0	5.1	16.2	−9.9	+3.8	+5.3
Harvestehude average	21.0	1.5	17.6	12.5	4.4	18.5	−8.5	+2.9	+0.9
Eppendorf 273/272	28.7	0.8	13.2	18.6	5.3	19.3	−10.1	+4.5	+6.1
Eppendorf 274/273	24.2	0.8	12.6	12.7	5.2	14.1	−11.5	+4.4	+1.5
Eppendorf average	14.0	1.3	33.0	8.0	2.2	29.1	−6.0	+0.9	−4.0

Source: Statistische Mitteilungen über den Hamburgischen Staat, Heft 23, pp. 47–51; Heft 29, pp. 24–6

strongly Catholic working-class areas the *Zentrum* change was erratic, with gains of 6.7 per cent in Sindlingen and 0.6 per cent in Alt-Hoechst, and drops of between 1.2 per cent and 1.4 per cent in Schwanheim, Zeilsheim and Sossenheim. There is therefore a good case for following the hypothesis of Richard Hamilton that only half the 1932 *Zentrum* vote in the Western suburbs was attributable to hitherto unmobilised Catholic voters, and for accepting Heinz Blankenberg's conclusion that the left-wing stance of the Frankfurt *Zentrum* failed to make it particularly attractive to Catholic working-class voters.[13] If the peculiar character of the Frankfurt *Zentrum*, with its strong commitment to the Weimar Republic and its opposition to anti-Semitism, achieved anything, it was to attract Jewish middle-class voters.

In the poorer, Eastern areas of the city the Jewish vote is more difficult to disentangle. In none of the three districts with high Jewish concentrations was the DDP vote ever significantly above the city average, or higher than in purely non-Jewish districts with a similar social structure. All one can observe is that even in 1928 the DDP just outvoted the DVP in Östliche Neustadt and Östliche Außenstadt, the only districts where this happened other than the two Western Jewish middle-class districts, and was only narrowly behind in the Nordöstliche Außenstadt. Between 1928 and July 1932 the DDP vote collapsed here, as in the rest of the city, and fell below 1 per cent. None of this benefited the *Zentrum*, which gained 3 per cent in Ö. Außenstadt, very close to the city average, and actually lost 1.4 per cent in Ö. Neustadt. The development of the Left vote was in sharp contrast (table 3.20). In the Ö. Neustadt, which had the densest Jewish population of the Eastern districts (19.4 per cent), the Left lost only 0.7 per cent, compared with the city-wide average of 6.9 per cent, with KPD gains (+4.3 per cent) almost compensating for the SPD losses (−5.0 per cent). Moreover the loss was restricted to the period 1928–30: between 1930 and July 1932 the Left recovered (+2.1 per cent), the gain being attributable solely to the SPD. The only other districts to show SPD gains between these two elections were the middle-class Jewish districts of the W., NW. and N. Außenstädte. It is therefore tempting to conclude that the poorer Jews of the Eastern districts, though not drawn to the *Zentrum*, swung to the SPD during this period, even if not to the same degree as their more affluent co-religionists. This thesis is, however, undermined by the behaviour of the Ö. Außenstadt, which had an only slightly lower Jewish population (16.7 per cent). Here the fall of the Left vote between 1928 and July 1932 followed the city-wide average closely, a slight Communist gain (+0.7 per cent) failing to make good a substantial SPD loss (−6.0 per cent). It is therefore easier to arrive at negative than at positive

13   Richard F. Hamilton, *Who Voted for Hitler?*, Princeton, NJ: Princeton University Press, 1982, p. 202; Blankenberg, *Politischer Katholizismus*, pp. 273–4, 283.

Table 3.18 Evolution of party shares (%) in selected Hamburg districts, July–November 1932

District	NSDAP July Nov.		DNVP July Nov.		DVP July Nov.		Zentrum July Nov.	
Harvestejude	40.6 30.4 −10.2		12.8 21.3 +8.5		4.5 8.4 +3.9		4.2 2.7 −1.5	
Rotherbaum	43.0 35.9 −7.1		8.5 14.1 +5.6		2.9 5.1 +2.2		3.5 2.8 −0.7	
Eppendorf	36.4 28.9 −7.5		6.3 11.4 +5.1		2.7 4.7 +2.0		2.2 1.8 −0.4	
Hohenfelde	47.4 37.6 −9.8		10.3 17.7 +7.4		3.2 5.8 +2.6		3.9 3.5 −0.4	
Fuhlsbüttel	45.3 35.9 −9.4		8.0 14.8 +6.8		3.5 5.7 +2.2		1.5 1.3 −0.2	
Ohlsdorf	44.1 32.7 −11.4		7.1 14.7 +7.6		3.7 5.5 +1.8		1.7 1.4 −0.3	
Hamburg average	32.9 26.6 −6.3		4.9 8.9 +4.0		1.9 3.2 +1.3		2.1 1.8 −0.3	

Source: *Statistische Mitteilungen über den Hamburgischen Staat*, Heft 29, p. 39; Heft 30, pp. 50–3

conclusions about the voting behaviour of Jews in the Eastern districts of Frankfurt. Any propensity to vote DDP was much lower than in the Western districts. The *Zentrum* appeared to hold out no attraction, in contrast with the response of Liberals in the Western districts and some Orthodox in rural areas. If they were drawn to the Left, whether SPD or KPD, this does not show up consistently. Perhaps they had already moved to the Left in the early 1920s, a hypothesis to be investigated below.

Between July and November 1932 the Eastern and Western districts also behaved divergently (table 3.21). In the W. and NW. Außenstädte the DStP made a moderate recovery, the only two districts where this movement was at all substantial. The *Zentrum* fell back, but remained well above its 1930 level. The combined Left gained, as it did city-wide (+1.5 per cent). In W. Außenstadt this gain was near the city average (+0.9 per cent), but in NW. Außenstadt it was higher (+2.6 per cent). More remarkably, the SPD went up again here (+0.5 per cent), against a city-wide loss of 2.9 per cent. The Nazis, whose strength was above the national average in Frankfurt, showed an above-average decline (−4.5 per cent). In contrast with Berlin and Hamburg the main beneficiary of this movement was not the DNVP, always weak in this city, but the DVP. In W. Außenstadt it recovered from 4.8 per cent to 14.8 per cent, in NW. Außenstadt from 4.3 per cent to 12.3 per cent. If conservatively-inclined Jews were looking for a last-chance barrier to Hitler here, it would have been to the DVP rather than the DNVP that they would have turned. In both these districts the DVP gains were well in excess of Nazi losses, so the DVP must also have recruited voters who had supported the *Zentrum* in July. The fact that Richard Merton headed the DVP list could

DStP July	DStP Nov.	SPD July	SPD Nov.	KPD July	KPD Nov.	DDP/DstP	Zen-trum	SPD	KPD	Total Left
12.5	10.8 −1.7	18.5	17.0 −1.5	5.0	6.3 +1.3	−10.2	+1.2	−0.6	+1.9	+1.3
10.5	9.0 −1.5	22.3	20.5 −1.8	7.1	9.1 +2.0	−10.9	+1.2	−2.7	+3.5	+0.8
8.0	7.1 −0.9	29.1	26.0 −3.1	12.3	16.0 +3.7	−6.9	+0.5	−7.0	+4.4	−2.6
5.9	5.3 −0.6	18.5	16.0 −2.5	8.3	10.5 +2.2	−6.1	+0.6	−6.4	+4.2	−2.2
11.5	9.9 −1.6	28.0	21.2 −1.8	4.5	6.2 +1.7	−8.8	+0.3	−3.9	+2.2	−1.7
8.7	6.9 −1.8	24.8	28.8 −1.0	6.7	9.4 +2.7	−10.3	−0.2	−6.3	+3.6	−2.7
6.1	5.5 −0.6	31.1	27.9 −3.2	18.2	22.3 +4.1	−6.2	+0.2	−8.5	+5.1	−3.4

The header reads: DStP (July Nov.) | SPD (July Nov.) | KPD (July Nov.) | Changes 1928–Nov. 1932: DDP/DstP, Zentrum, SPD, KPD, Total Left.

have been an attraction for some Jewish voters. But since the DStP vote also went up, there is no foolproof way of distinguishing Jewish from Gentile vote-switchers. In the Eastern districts the DStP recovery was negligible and the *Zentrum* decline smaller. The Left improvement was slightly above the city average (+2.1 per cent in Ö. Neustadt, +2.5 per cent in Ö. Außenstadt). In Ö. Außenstadt the SPD loss was low; in Ö. Neustadt, in contrast, where the KPD gained 7.4 per cent, its loss was correspondingly high: 5.3 per cent.

If we look at the whole period from 1928 to November 1932 we find that city-wide the Left lost 5.4 per cent (KPD +5.5 per cent, SPD −10.9 per cent). Against this trend the Left gained in three districts (NW. Außenstadt: +7.1 per cent, W. Außenstadt: +5.4 per cent, Ö. Neustadt: +1.4 per cent), more or less held its own in N. Außenstadt (−0.2 per cent) and lost well below average in Ö. Außenstadt (−2.8 per cent). These were the districts with the highest Jewish populations. These relatively good performances by the Left cannot be attributed exclusively to the middle- or lower-middle-class character of these districts. Admittedly there were no districts as affluent as W. and NW. Außenstädte that had few Jews, but others like Äußeres Sachsenhausen and W. Neustadt had a social composition similar to the remaining Jewish districts and showed losses for the Left that were either average or above. It should be added that in Frankfurt, in contrast with many other cities in Germany, the losses of the Left were greatest in the most working-class districts: −9.8 per cent in Altstadt, −10.8 per cent in Inneres Sachsenhausen. Within the Left, the SPD vote went up in both W. and NW. Außenstädte (+2.6 per cent, +4.7 per cent) and suffered a below-average loss in N. Außenstadt (−3.8 per cent). But the SPD did not benefit from the

Table 3-19   Evolution of DDP and *Zentrum* votes (%) in selected Frankfurt districts, May 1924–July 1932

District	% of population		% of dwellings with 6 or more rooms	DDP/DStP vote				
	Jewish	*Catholic*		*May 1924*	*1928*	*1930*	*April 1932*	*July 1932*
Middle-class Jewish								
NW. Außenstadt	22.9	23.2	28.5	27.2	26.6	20.2	11.8	1.3
W. Außenstadt	21.9	25.2	40.4	25.7	26.7	23.0	12.5	1.5
N. Außenstadt	9.1	29.6	9.3	14.5	13.0	9.9	5.5	0.9
Middle-class non-Jewish								
W. Neustadt	4.7	32.9	8.1	11.9	8.5	6.3	3.3	0.6
Äuß. Sachsenhausen	2.1	30.3	5.9	9.9	9.6	7.0	4.2	1.1
Lower-class Jewish								
Ö. Neustadt	19.4	33.1	4.7	9.1	8.2	4.3	2.5	0.6
Ö. Außenstadt	16.7	28.8	5.2	13.6	11.5	7.3	3.2	0.7
Frankfurt average	6.3	31.1	5.8	10.2	8.2	5.8	3.0	0.7

Sources: *Statistische Jahresubersichten der Stadt Frankfurt a. Main* 1927/8, pp. 15, 162–3; ibid., 1931/2, p. 19; *Statistisches Handbuch der Stadt Frankfurt a. M.*, 2. Ausgabe, Frankfurt, 1928, pp. 34–5, 68, 447–8; *FZ*, 9 December 1924, 26 April 1932, 2 August 1932, 8 November 1932, *Stadtblatt*, in each case

better-than-average performances of the Left in the Eastern districts. Evidently two conditions needed to be satisfied for a good SPD performance during the Depression: a high middle-class population *and* a high Jewish population.

A survey over a longer period still (May 1924 to November 1932) gives some clue whether the Jews of the Eastern districts moved Left earlier, so that their predilections could not be picked up so easily once the Depression had set in. Over this longer period the Left went up by 0.5 per cent in Frankfurt. All the Jewish districts went up by substantially more, ranging from 3.7 per cent in Ö. Außenstadt to 11.8 per cent in NW. Außenstadt. In the Western districts that was due entirely to the rise after 1928. In the Eastern districts the same applied to Ö. Neustadt, which had a Left performance similar to the Western districts, but a poor SPD performance; but in Ö. Außenstadt the greater part of the Left's improvement, especially for the SPD, came before 1928. In this respect it resembled the working-class

Change		Zentrum vote					Change	
1924–8	*1928–32*	*May 1924*	*1928*	*1930*	*April 1932*	*July 1932*	*1924–8*	*1928– July 1932*
−0.6	−25.3	11.6	8.1	10.5	16.3	22.6	−3.5	+14.5
+1.0	−25.2	15.5	11.5	13.4	22.9	28.0	−4.0	+16.5
−1.5	−12.1	13.6	11.8	11.4	14.3	17.8	−1.8	+6.0
−3.4	−7.9	12.1	9.3	9.7	11.2	12.3	−2.8	+3.0
−0.3	−8.5	12.1	10.8	10.4	12.4	15.2	−1.3	+4.4
−0.9	−7.6	13.8	12.6	11.6	9.5	11.2	−1.2	−1.4
−2.1	−10.8	13.1	10.0	10.5	12.2	13.0	−3.1	+3.0
−2.0	−7.5	12.2	11.1	10.8	12.4	13.8	−1.1	+2.7

districts, with the difference that it retained the greater part of the Left's gains during the Depression.

What can we conclude about Jewish voting decisions during this critical period from the evidence of these three cities? The first factor to bear in mind is that the Jewish population was disproportionately middle-class and lived disproportionately in middle-class areas. Voting movements in these areas are therefore likely to tell us as much about middle-class behaviour as about Jewish behaviour. With few exceptions these areas, being predominantly Protestant as well, show above-average Nazi gains, a trend from which Jews were presumably exempt. Up to 1928 there are good reasons to suppose that Jews supported the DDP more heavily than non-Jews of equivalent social status. Jürgen Falter's regression analysis shows Jewish population to correlate more positively with DDP strength from 1924 to 1933 than with that of any other party[14] (which does not, of course, tell us how any individual voted). Because the DDP vote was small it is relatively easy to trace what happened to it as the DDP declined. In contrast there is no way of

14 Jürgen Falter, Thomas Lindenberger and Siegfried Schumann, *Wahlen und Abstimmungen in der Weimarer Republik. Materialien zum Wahlverhalten, 1919–1933*, Munich: C. H. Beck, 1986, pp. 163–70.

Table 3.20   Evolution of left-wing vote (%) in selected Frankfurt districts, 1924–1932

District	% of population		% of dwellings with 6 or more rooms	May 1924			1928		
	Jewish	*Catholic*		*SPD*	*KPD*	*Total**	*SPD*	*KPD*	*Total*
NW. Außenstadt	22.9	28.2	23.5	13.5	3.7	18.0	19.5	3.4	22.9
W. Außenstadt	21.9	25.2	40.4	13.4	2.7	17.1	17.9	3.0	20.9
N. Außenstadt	9.1	29.6	9.3	19.4	5.1	25.7	24.4	6.2	30.6
W. Neustadt	4.7	32.9	8.1	24.8	6.8	32.9	29.3	9.3	38.6
Äuß. Sachsenhausen	2.1	30.3	5.9	22.9	6.2	29.9	27.1	6.4	33.5
Ö. Neustadt	19.4	33.1	4.7	31.8	12.7	46.3	33.8	16.5	50.3
Ö. Außenstadt	16.7	28.8	5.2	26.9	10.7	39.0	34.0	11.5	45.5
Frankfurt average	6.3	31.1	5.8	27.7	11.4	40.5	33.9	12.5	46.4

* incl. USPD
Source: As table 3.19

determining whether those who voted SPD, DVP or *Zentrum* in the 1920s changed after 1928 and, if so, in what direction, except on the basis of individual testimony.

What happened to the Jewish DDP vote varied in detail from place to place, but the underlying tendency was consistent. In Hamburg, where the DDP had a firm base, it remained impressively intact. In Berlin and Frankfurt it largely disappeared, but did so very late. Up to and including the Landtag elections of spring 1932 the DDP/DStP held about half its 1928 support there; the rout began after that. In July 1932 the ex-DDP vote seems to have divided evenly between *Zentrum* and SPD; in November 1932 rather less went to the *Zentrum* and rather more to the Left. How much of the Communist gain in that election was due to Jewish votes is impossible to gauge, nor how far Jews voted for the DVP and DNVP, steps that were certainly contemplated, as will be seen below. Some, especially in Frankfurt, returned to the DStP, even at this late stage. Perhaps the clearest indication of how metropolitan Jews voted can be gained from the districts with the highest Jewish concentrations in Berlin (Wilmersdorf), Hamburg (Harvestehude) and Frankfurt (NW. Außenstadt). All had high DDP votes up to 1928, all had high *Zentrum* gains in 1930 and July 1932, all showed gains by the Left at a time when the Left was in decline nationally, and particularly for the SPD at a time when that party lost a third of its voting share nationally. How typical these metropolitan Jews were of the Jewish population as a whole is a matter that needs further investigation. There were size-

1930			July 1932			Changes in total Left July					Changes in SPD		
SPD	KPD	Total	SPD	KPD	Total	1924–8	1928–30	1930–July 1932	1932–Nov 1932	1928–Nov 1932	1924–Nov 1932	1928–July 1932	1924–Nov 1932
17.3	3.7	21.0	23.7	3.5	27.2	+6.2	−1.7	+6.2	+2.6	+7.1	+11.8	+4.2	+10.7
16.7	3.5	20.2	21.9	3.5	25.4	+4.8	−0.7	+5.2	+0.9	+5.4	+9.3	+4.0	+7.1
20.7	7.5	28.2	21.4	6.6	28.0	+6.1	−2.4	−0.2	+2.4	−0.2	+4.7	−3.0	+1.2
24.0	10.9	34.9	21.6	10.7	32.3	+7.0	−3.7	−2.6	+2.0	−4.3	+1.5	−7.7	−5.1
21.2	7.1	28.3	21.1	6.1	27.2	+5.1	−5.2	−1.1	+0.2	−6.1	−2.5	−6.0	−3.6
26.3	21.2	47.5	28.8	20.8	49.6	+5.8	−2.8	+2.1	+2.1	+1.4	+5.4	−5.0	−8.3
29.0	13.3	42.3	28.0	12.2	40.2	+7.9	−3.2	−2.1	+2.5	−2.8	+3.7	−6.0	−5.8
27.2	15.0	42.2	25.9	13.6	39.5	+7.3	−4.2	−2.7	+1.5	−5.4	+0.5	−8.0	−4.7

able Jewish communities in Breslau, Cologne, Mannheim and Nuremberg where the DDP was weaker. And there was the Jewish population scattered in small towns and villages that had even fewer political resources.

How Jews should respond to the crisis of Weimar democracy was a matter of much debate. Local and national leaders gave conflicting advice. The chairman of the Jewish *Landesverband* in Hesse, the businessman Bernhard Albert Meyer, recommended a vote for the *Zentrum*[15] in 1932. In Franconia the Democrat Julie Meyer, an active member of the C.V., advised support for the SPD, which she later joined.[16] In Munich the executive director of the Bavarian C.V., Werner Cahnman, sought help where he could. Given the weakness of the SPD, its trade unions and the DDP in Bavaria, Cahnman 'reckoned that the powerful Catholic party was the only hitching-post to which the Jewish wagon could be hitched'.[17] Cahnman collaborated closely with the BVP deputies Josef Baumgartner, Sebastian Schlittenbauer and Alois Hundhammer, the general secretary of the *Bayerischer Christlicher Bauernverein*. Cahnman and Hundhammer jointly compiled a pamphlet, *Nationalsozialismus und Landwirtschaft*, of which 200,000 copies were distributed in rural areas. Cahnman also took up closer contact with Karl Simbeck of the *Bayerischer Bauernbund* (BBB), a small party not noted for its sympathy for Jews. In 1932 there was an informal anti-Nazi electoral committee that included the BVP, the BBB, the Socialist trade unions and

15　Feder, *Heute sprach ich mit ...*, p. 306.
16　Information from Dr Ernest Hamburger.
17　Cahnman, 'The Nazi Threat and the Centralverein – A Recollection', p. 32.

Table 3.21   Evolution of party shares (%) in selected Frankfurt districts, July–November 1932

District	NSDAP July Nov.			DNVP July Nov.			DVP July Nov.			Zentrum July Nov.		
N.W. Außenstadt	35.9	29.5	−6.4	6.5	7.6	+1.1	4.3	12.3	+8.0	22.6	14.6	−8.0
W. Außenstadt	30.7	26.1	−4.6	5.9	8.0	+2.1	4.8	14.8	+10.0	28.0	17.0	−11.0
N. Außenstadt	42.7	38.6	−4.1	4.4	6.1	+1.7	3.5	8.4	+4.9	17.8	14.1	−3.7
W. Neustadt	46.4	39.7	−6.7	2.9	4.6	+1.7	3.6	7.8	+4.2	12.3	10.7	−1.6
Äuß. Sachsen-hausen	48.2	40.9	−7.3	4.3	6.4	+2.1	3.6	9.6	+6.0	15.2	12.0	−3.2
Ö. Neustadt	34.0	31.8	−2.2	1.6	2.6	+1.0	1.1	2.7	+1.6	11.2	9.1	−2.1
Ö. Außenstadt	38.4	35.9	−2.5	2.2	3.4	+1.2	1.9	3.8	+1.9	13.0	11.2	−1.8
Frankfurt average	38.7	34.2	−4.5	2.6	3.7	+1.1	2.2	5.3	+3.1	13.8	11.8	−2.0

Source: *FZ*, 2 August, 8 November 1932

Reichsbanner – the last two represented by Alois Dichtl – and Cahnman.[18] In Prussia a formal organization of Jewish *Zentrum* voters was established for the Landtag elections;[19] the *Zentrum* reciprocated by nominating the Zionist functionary Georg Zareski on their list, though he did not get elected.

The DStP reacted with some indignation to these developments. Adam Barteld complained at a meeting of the party's executive committee that 'in spite of the efforts of those Jews loyal to this party, the majority of Jewish voters went to the *Zentrum* and to the Social Democrats'. Bernhard Falk added that it was impossible to prevail against the belief that votes cast for the *Staatspartei* were wasted: that was a view not restricted to Jews. Falk, like Barteld, had failed to get re-elected to the Landtag. The Reichstag deputy Heinrich Rönneburg charged Jewish voters with having deserted the *Staatspartei* in the shabbiest fashion: 'They whipped up feelings against us from mouth to mouth, through letters and leaflets.'[20] Though Oscar Meyer and Leon Zeitlin remained on the executive of the DStP and persons of

18   Donald L. Niewyk, 'Das Selbstverständnis der Juden und ihre Beteiligung am politischen Leben des Kaiserreiches und der Weimarer Republik', in Manfred Treml and Wolf Weigand (eds), *Geschichte und Kultur der Juden in Bayern*, Munich: Haus der bayerischen Geschichte, 1988, pp. 382–3.

19   Paucker, *Abwehrkampf*, p. 102.

20   Wegner, *Linksliberalismus in der Weimarer Republik*, pp. 704–9.

DStP July Nov.			SPD July Nov.			KPD July Nov.			DDP/ DStP	Zen- trum	SPD	KPD	Total Left
									\multicolumn{5}{c}{*Changes 1928–Nov. 1932*}				
1.3	5.0	+3.7	23.7	24.2	+0.5	3.5	5.6	+2.1	−21.6	+6.5	+4.9	+2.2	+7.1
1.5	5.7	+4.2	21.9	20.5	−1.4	3.5	5.8	+2.3	−21.0	+5.5	+2.6	+2.8	+5.4
0.9	2.3	+1.4	21.4	20.6	−0.8	6.6	9.8	+3.2	−10.7	+2.3	−3.8	+3.6	−0.2
0.6	1.2	+0.6	21.6	19.7	−1.9	10.7	14.6	+3.9	−7.3	+1.4	−9.6	+5.3	−4.3
1.1	1.8	+0.7	21.1	18.6	−2.5	6.1	8.8	+2.7	−7.8	+1.2	−8.5	+2.4	−6.1
0.6	0.8	+0.2	28.8	23.5	−5.3	20.8	28.2	+7.4	−7.4	−3.5	−10.3	+11.7	+1.4
0.7	1.4	+0.7	28.0	26.0	−2.0	12.2	16.7	+4.5	−10.1	+1.2	−8.0	+5.2	−2.8
0.7	1.4	+0.7	25.9	23.0	−2.9	13.6	18.0	+4.4	−6.8	+0.7	−10.9	+5.5	−5.4

Jewish descent featured on its lists of candidates, there is no doubt that the party was on the point of losing its Jewish constituency. There is no dissenting from the judgment of the DStP leader in Saxony, Wilhelm Külz, that Jewish party members, more than any others, had succumbed to 'a psychosis of fear'.[21] The only remaining question was where to turn instead.

From 1930 to 1932, during Brüning's chancellorship, leaders of Jewish organizations pressed him to take an open stand against the anti-Jewish propaganda and offences, either by receiving a Jewish delegation or by including a denunciation of anti-Semitism in one of his speeches. The initiative for this came both from the C.V., through its director, Ludwig Holländer, and from the *Zionistische Vereinigung für Deutschland*. The former Secretary of State, Julius Hirsch, also intervened at the instigation of the C.V. Leading members of the DStP supported the C.V.'s request, including August Weber and Oscar Meyer, as well as the former *Zentrum* chancellor Wilhelm Marx. A statement by the Chancellor, at a time when the Reichstag was in eclipse, would have carried weight both within the country and overseas. These efforts were unsuccessful. Brüning expressed his readiness in principle, to accede to their wishes, but in fact did nothing. Hermann Pünder, the head of the Chancellor's office, attributed this to pressure of work. A more probable explanation is Brüning's readiness to form a coalition between the *Zentrum*

21 Ibid., p. 732.

and the National Socialists, provided the conditions for his own party were favourable. He was not prepared to jeopardize such a possibility by committing himself on a question that was of secondary importance. A few days after Brüning's dismissal, the *Jüdische Rundschau* observed with resignation that 'under Brüning's government one had with deep regret waited in vain for those in responsible positions in the *Reich* to speak out clearly against the anti-Semitic excesses' and 'that the *Reich* government had preferred to remain silent and to let the Prussian government of Braun-Severing energetically repudiate excesses against Jews'.[22]

At the last free elections on 6 November 1932 the C.V. received more requests for advice than ever before. Brüning's successor as Chancellor, Franz von Papen, had called an election for 31 July, the outcome of which had shown that a democratic government based on a parliamentary majority was no longer possible. In November 1932, therefore, many Jewish voters were tempted by the same considerations that had caused some Jewish voters in Bavaria to vote for the BVP, and above all to support President Hindenburg in his re-election fight against Hitler in March–April 1932.[23] Under the circumstances it might be wiser to support Papen's government in the fight against the National Socialists than to vote for one of the Weimar parties. These were without power; von Papen was in power. The *C.V.-Zeitung* took refuge in the neutral statement that 'Papen's government has won popularity in wider middle-class circles',[24] which turned out not to be the case.

But the C.V.'s contention throws much light on the mood of its leaders. They were anxious not to rule out support for the government from Jewish voters, but such support was only possible by voting for the DNVP. Hence the C.V.'s dilemma. While Papen considered himself the grave-digger of the Republic, he did not want to entrust this duty to the National Socialists. Since the C.V. was guided only by the Jewish Question and took no other political stance, it looked on Papen's government as a bulwark against the National Socialists. Moreover, Papen had acted more positively towards the Jewish community than his predecessor. Soon after taking office as Chancellor, he had appointed Heinrich von Kaufmann-Asser as a leading government official and *Reichspressechef*, having first acquired the consent both of the cabinet and of the President. Kaufmann-Asser was born into the Christian faith though both his parents were Jewish. His father, a well-known economist and art collector, was Professor at the Technical University in Charlottenburg. His mother was descended from the Eltzbacher and Kaulla families

---

22   Paucker, *Abwehrkampf*, pp. 133, 284; detailed account of negotiations, ibid., pp. 130–3; documents, ibid., pp. 217–33.
23   Ibid., pp. 102–3.
24   Alfred Wiener, 'Rat' uns, C.V.', *CVZ*, 21 October 1932.

– banking and commercial dynasties in the Rhineland and in Southern Germany. Prior to this appointment, Kaufmann-Asser had been a senior diplomat and deputy chief of the Government Press office.[25]

Kaufmann-Asser's appointment to such a prominent position had symbolic importance. It was designed to differentiate Papen from the National Socialists. Inspired by Professor Moritz Sobernheim, who was responsible for Jewish affairs in the Foreign Ministry, the Jewish Telegraph Agency issued a statement the next day that:

We have received reassurances from a well-informed personality that there is no reason at all for concern. Up till now all statements by the Chancellor von Papen as well as the official government declaration have made it clear that the new government is determined to adhere strictly to the terms of the constitution in accordance with the spirit in which the President von Hindenburg entrusted this assignment to them. They will not allow the equality of rights of any one or other section of society to be encroached upon, nor for the state to be prejudiced against any one class or religion. Further proof of this is seen in the new appointment of high officials in the past few days.[26]

Sobernheim cleared this notice with the newly-appointed State Secretary of the Chancellery, Erwin Planck. In his written reply Planck emphasized that the government was in no position to restrict by extra-parliamentary means, to the detriment of any one section of the population, any of the rights which the constitution guaranteed to all citizens and asked Sobernheim to continue with his work of enlightenment.[27]

Since there was no change in this attitude during Papen's chancellorship, the C.V. did not feel constrained in its friendly attitude towards the government. On the other hand, the *C.V.-Zeitung* had always warned its readers against voting for the DNVP and did not move away from its traditional position now. It reminded its readers of the anti-Semitic content of the party programme and of the paragraph of the party charter adopted in 1929 that barred Jews from membership. It pointed out that in the Landtage of Prussia, Braunschweig and Anhalt the anti-Jewish resolutions proposed by the National Socialists had been carried with the help of the DNVP: 'If the question arises "German National or not" for even the most minimal section of German Jewry, then we must repeat here that we can under no circumstances at all recommend voting for the German National People's Party.' The words

25 Information on Kaufmann-Asser from the Political Archive of the Foreign Ministry in Bonn. Kaufmann-Asser, whose wife was not Jewish, survived the Third Reich, in Berlin.

26 BAK, Reichskanzlei R. 431/2192, p. 164.

27 Ibid., p. 165.

were carefully chosen. Before the elections of July 1932 the *C.V.-Zeitung* had asserted that no honourable Jew could vote for the DNVP;[28] now it no longer tried to dissuade, but restricted itself to refusing responsibility for such a decision. The exchange of views in its correspondence columns makes it clear that a number of Jews who had previously voted for middle-of-the-road parties were now contemplating a vote for the DNVP.

On the other hand the C.V. still adhered to its conviction that Jewish voters could safely vote for the German People's Party. In a letter signed by all the members of the Breslau branch of the C.V., the organization's leadership was pressed to declare its opposition to votes being cast for the DVP. This branch of the party (like the National Liberal Party in Silesia before 1918) had often entered election campaigns with anti-Semitic slogans. But the C.V.'s own newspaper refused to generalize from this and insisted that the party's programme contained nothing that should frighten away Jewish voters. Furthermore at a recent conference one of the party's leading members, Professor Paul Moldenhauer, a former *Reich* Finance Minister, had refused to join the 'anti-Semitic war cries'. But the same article expressed its misgivings over the electoral alliance between the DNVP and DVP list. 'Every single Jewish voter must make his own judgement in his own private conscience about the significance of this fact.'[29] The C.V., it was evident, was as much at a loss as some of its members. Though the voting figures do not suggest that many Jews voted for the parties of the Right, the debate was symptomatic of the political crisis of German Jewry.

Though the C.V. remained the biggest single representative organization of German Jewry, it did not speak for the whole community. Some Jews were, of course, indifferent to all attempts to organize them. Those on the Left regarded the C.V. as too bourgeois and too inclined to look for friends on the moderate Right, particularly the DVP. Others, however, dissented from the C.V.'s position on the national question. There were those, like the *Verband nationaldeutscher Juden*, who thought the C.V. insufficiently 'German', whereas the Zionists thought it too much so.

Max Naumann, the President of the V.n.J, was almost alone in thinking the question posed no problem. Even before the elections of 31 July in an article for the *Deutsche Allgemeine Zeitung* he had referred to National Socialism as the most visible indication of a national movement that was embracing by far the greatest part of the German nation, in spite of all its distasteful secondary features. Many Jews did not dare to understand that this was a 'renunciation of the mania of freedom and brotherhood of the period of revolution and

28   *CVZ*, 8 July 1932, p. 285.
29   *CVZ*, 28 October 1932, pp. 437ff. Moldenhauer deserted to the National Socialists soon after Hitler was appointed Chancellor.

fulfilment' and 'that here and only here a way was being prepared which should and, one hoped, would prepare for a rebirth of the German way of life and the restoration of German prestige'.[30]

These words ran counter to his proclamations of political neutrality. But he had always felt deeply at variance with the protagonists of the 'policy of fulfilment' – the Weimar Coalition in general and the Social Democrats in particular. The article evoked such an outcry that after the elections Naumann maintained that his words had not referred to the National Socialists but to the entire nationalist movement. But the text leaves no doubt that he wanted to recommend the election of all representatives of the nationalist movement without discrimination, including the National Socialists. After the nomination of Hitler as chancellor, Naumann appears to have had second thoughts and in February 1933, before the last Reichstag elections, he recommended support for the right-wing coalition of DNVP, *Stahlhelm* and smaller reactionary groups.[31] It is not possible to ascertain whether members of the V.n.J. followed the advice of their chairman or whether any of them did in fact vote for the National Socialists. But Naumann's attitude may have helped a certain number of Jewish voters to conquer their doubts and to vote for one of the right-wing parties even after these had been caught by the flood-tide of anti-Semitism.

While the developments of 1930–3 merely drew attention to the V.n.J.'s isolation, the Zionists gained support during this period: events seemed, after all, to be confirming their contention that anti-Semitism was inherent in Gentile society and that the policy of assimilation was based on a set of delusions. But German Zionism also moved further into the mainstream of German-Jewish political life and the bitter rivalries between liberal assimilationism and Jewish nationalism diminished somewhat. The *Reichstagswahlausschuß* of 1930, though short-lived, was one symptom of that. Some convergence of aims and methods nevertheless continued. While the C.V. preached a commitment to German politics, the Zionists restricted themselves to defending the civic rights of all Jews. The main newspaper of the Zionist movement, the *Jüdische Rundschau*, refused to regard the German Jews as one political unit and instead emphasized the political and economic distinctions within the Jewish population. Jews, including Zionists, 'may vote for any one of the political parties participating in the election campaign according to their political inclinations or their expectations of the future direction of German politics', but should review the attitudes of the party which they wished to support towards Jews and Jewry. With the rise of Nazism in 1930, the Zionist paper urged most strongly that all Jews should exercise their right

30 Ludwig Holländer, 'Hitler und Max Naumann', *CVZ*, 19 August 1932, pp. 350ff.
31 Rheins, *LBYB* (1980), p. 266.

to vote. Everyone was to decide quite freely which party he wished to support, provided its programme was not anti-Semitic.[32] It also reported that some of its correspondents had recommended support for the DVP and the *Wirtschaftspartei* on the grounds that neither of these was committed to anti-Semitism. To the *Jüdische Rundschau* this was further proof of the diversity of political opinions among German Jews.

There were also specific appeals on behalf of the 'Weimar' parties from prominent Zionists. Georg Kareski, having been nominated as a *Zentrum* candidate, circulated an essay through the Jewish Telegraph Agency in which he declared that Jews could vote for the *Zentrum*, the 'champion of religious minorities', without 'sacrificing their intellects'.[33] A number of high-ranking Prussian civil servants, including Hermann Badt and Hans Goslar as well as Alfred Klee, urged support for the SPD.

The rise of Nazism created a crisis not only for German Liberalism but also for the Left. A number of smaller groupings arose to accommodate those who felt that both the SPD and the KPD were trapped in culs-de-sac. One of these, which dated back to the 1920s, was particularly associated with its Jewish founder. The *Internationaler Sozialistischer Kampfbund* (ISK) was the creation of the Göttingen philosopher Leonard Nelson, descended on his mother's side from the Mendelssohn family. It was the successor of the *Internationaler Jugendbund* (IJB) which he had helped to found in 1917. The ideology of the IJB and ISK, which in the end made them incompatible with affiliation to the SPD, was a mixture of libertarianism and authoritarianism. Nelson rejected parliamentary democracy, regarding majority decisions as too imperfect an instrument, and imposed a hierarchical organization on the ISK. But he also rejected Marxist historical materialism and the nationalization of the means of production. Socialism was for him an ethically-based life-style, derived from the philosophy of Kant. These imperatives and his encouragement of critical thought gave the ISK a long-term influence out of all proportion to its sectarian appearance before 1933.[34]

---

32 *JR*, 12 September 1930.
33 'ohne "Opfer des Intellekts"', *JR*, 12 September 1930. During the Third Reich Kareski was excluded from the *Zionistische Vereinigung*. See Herbert S. Levine, 'A Jewish Collaborator in Nazi Germany: The Strange Career of Georg Kareski 1923–1937', *CEH*, September 1975, pp. 251–81.
34 Werner Link, *Die Geschichte des Internationalen Jugendbundes (IJB) und des Internationalen Sozialistischen Kampfbundes (ISK). Ein Beitrag zur Geschichte der Arbeiterbewegung in der Weimarer Republik und im 'Dritten Reich'*, Meisenheim-am-Glan: Althenäum, 1964; Susanne Miller, 'Leonard Nelson und die sozialistische Arbeiterbewegung', in Grab and Schoeps, *Juden in der Weimarer Republik*, pp. 263–75; *idem*, 'Der Internationale Sozialistische Kampfbund (ISK)', in Helga Haas-Rietschel

A body rather more in the political mainstream was the Socialist Workers' Party (SAP), founded in 1931 by a group of SPD left-wingers and a substantial minority of the KPO. Those who came from the SPD were in the main followers of Paul Levi, grouped round the journal *Der Klassenkampf* and in many cases veterans of the USPD. What caused the final breach between them and the main body of the party was the SPD's parliamentary support for Chancellor Brüning's government by emergency decree. Whether Levi himself would have approved of the breach must remain in doubt, but a number of his faithful lieutenants took this fateful step, led by two USPD veterans, Max Seydewitz and Kurt Rosenfeld, who became the new party's co-chairmen. Apart from Rosenfeld the main Jewish members in the ex-SPD wing were the journalist Walter Fabian, for some time editor of the Chemnitz *Volksstimme*, and Ernst Eckstein, chairman of the Breslau SPD. Those who came from the dissident Communist KPO also included a sizeable Jewish contingent, among them Rosi Wolfstein and Josef Lang. The purpose of the SAP was to fight Fascism with a united proletariat and through the trade union movement.[35] Since this required criticism of the existing working-class parties as well as attempts to co-operate with them, it is not surprising that it failed to make an impact. Its membership reached a maximum of some 27,000, with a bias towards youth. Its idealism and anti-Fascism attracted some Jewish adherents,[36] but its only significant electoral successes were in remote industrial areas of Saxony and Hesse, where there were few Jewish voters.[37]

While neither the ISK nor the SAP had any impact on Weimar politics, their role in exile politics and their legacy to post-war Germany were considerable. The most prominent SAP members in post-1945 Germany were Willy Brandt (who rose to prominence in exile) and Max Seydewitz, who joined the Socialist Unity Party (SED) in the Soviet zone and was Prime Minister of Saxony from 1947 to 1952. But Seydewitz's deviationist past caught up with him and he ended his career as director of the Dresden art

and Sabine Hering, *Nora Platiel, Sozialistin, Emigrantin, Politikerin. Eine Biographie*, Cologne: Bund-Verlag, 1990, pp. 195–206. For an assessment of Nelson's philosophy see Thomas Meyer, 'Die Aktualität Leonard Nelsons. Zum 100. Geburtstag des Philosophen und Sozialisten', in Detlef Horster and Dieter Krohn (eds), *Vernunft, Ethik, Politik. Gustav Heckmann zum 85. Geburtstag*, Hanover: SOAK-Verlag, 1983, pp. 35–53. I am greatly indebted to Dr Susanne Miller, Bonn, for guidance on both the ISK and the SAP.
35 For the SAP's programmatic debates, see Drechsler, *Die Sozialistische Arbeiterpartei Deutschlands*, pp. 203–51.
36 Paucker, *Abwehrkampf*, p. 273, n. 95.
37 Drechsler, *Die Sozialistische Arbeiterpartei: Deutschlands*, pp. 268–74.

collections. Of the Jewish SAP members who returned to the Federal Republic Rosi Wolfstein became an active member of the SPD in Frankfurt and
died in 1987 in her hundredth year; Josef Lang also joined the SPD in
Frankfurt, where he belonged to its left wing and became secretary of the
city party; Walter Fabian settled in Cologne, where he became editor of the
Gewerkschaftliche Monatshefte.

The ISK had an even more notable impact on the post-war SPD. The
most important figure was Willi Eichler, who took over the political direction
of the ISK after Nelson's death in 1927. He was – like many ISK members –
active in German Socialist exile politics in London and provided the principal
inspiration for the SPD's Bad Godesberg programme of 1959. This marked
the party's final abandonment of orthodox Marxism and acceptance of ideological pluralism. However remote this might at first sight seem from
Nelson's own outlook, the connection is there. The failure of Weimar democracy and the experience of exile cured many in the ISK of sectarianism. What
they retained was Nelson's Socratic questioning and his insistence on an
ethically-founded libertarianism.[38] Minna Specht, who had been co-founder
with Nelson of the IJB, returned to her pedagogic work, directing the
progressive Odenwaldschule, worked for UNESCO and then became an
educational adviser to the German Federal Government. Alfred Kubel
became Prime Minister of the briefly reconstituted *Land* of Braunschweig in
1945 and finally of Lower Saxony, in which Braunschweig was absorbed.
None of these was Jewish. Of those who were, Arthur Levi also settled in
Lower Saxony where he became Lord Mayor of Göttingen; Nora Bloch-
Platiel became vice-chairman of the SPD grouping in the Hesse Landtag and
narrowly missed becoming its president in 1962.[39] In their different and
unexpected ways the spirits of Paul Levi and Leonard Nelson helped to form
the political culture of the Federal Republic.

Conclusion

Jewish voting behaviour, stable for much of the period between 1880 and
1930, became fragmented and disorientated in the years of Hitler's rise to
power. In the first ten years of the Weimar Republic the pattern differed little
from that of the late Imperial epoch. The majority of Jews supported
left-wing Liberalism in the shape of the DDP, a substantial minority the
SPD. Smaller minorities supported parties further to the Left or the Right. A
few committed Zionists deliberately abstained.

38   Meyer, 'Die Aktualität Leonard Nelsons', p. 52; Miller in Haas-Rietschel and
Hering, *Nora Platiel*, p. 205.
39   Haas-Rietschel and Hering, *Nora Platiel*, p. 160.

What changed thereafter was the disintegration of German Liberalism. Jews deserted the DDP not only because it ceased to be an effective force, but because, with the creation of the *Staatspartei*, it changed its character. Of these ex-Liberals, some will have withdrawn into resigned abstention, the rest, in about equal proportions, went over to the *Zentrum* and the SPD as the last remaining bastions of parliamentary institutions. Some may have decided to support the DNVP in November 1932, despite its anti-Semitic past and present, in the hope that Papen might be a barrier to Hitler. Similarly the Communists benefited to some extent from the Jewish search for an effective antidote to the extreme Right, despite their unsympathetic attitude to Jewish concerns, and some younger Jews went over to the *Sozialistische Arbeiterpartei*.

During the period under review a little over a quarter of a million adult Jews participated in the average national election, equivalent to the votes needed to elect four members of the Reichstag. Given that the Jewish population was fairly heavily concentrated in a few major cities, these votes would have been used quite effectively. It is reasonable to assume that up to and including 1928 Jewish votes were responsible for electing one SPD and two DDP deputies; after 1930 two SPD and one *Zentrum* deputy: not enough to save those parties – or the Jews.

4
Jews and the Crisis of German Liberalism

It is difficult to think of a time when German Liberalism was not in crisis – whether before 1848 in the unequal fight against absolutism; in 1848 and 1849 in the attempt to create a constitutional united Germany; between 1849 and 1871 over the role of Bismarck and Prussia as propellors of German unity; during the Empire over the rule of law and the rights of the individual; or in the Weimar Republic in the defence of free institutions against a variety of enemies: indifference, malice and totalitarian challenge. For much of this time German Liberalism was divided, both organizationally and ideologically; for very little of this time was it capable of providing national political leadership through a viable party. But though crisis was rarely absent, it varied in intensity. There were times of stability and hope as well years of impending or actual disaster. The relevance of such fluctuations to the Jews of Germany are too obvious to need underlining. Jewish prosperity and survival in modern conditions needed liberal institutions and an open civil society. But a simple equation between Jews and Liberalism would ignore the varieties within both Jews and Liberals: not all Jews were Liberals or sympathetic to liberalism in the century before 1933; by no means all Liberals were sympathetic to the claims and interests of Jews. It is these varieties that are to be addressed here.

The crucial year for the convergence was 1848, when the Jewish Question for the first time featured as an issue in a national political forum and when the Frankfurt Parliament, largely through the efforts of its second Vice-President, Gabriel Riesser, included the full civic and political equality of

Jews in the Basic Rights of the German People. The disappointment that many Germans, and many German Liberals, felt at the failure of the Revolution, and the disillusionment with parliamentary methods that was a lasting legacy of this failure, were not shared by articulate and politically conscious Jews. What mattered to them was the declaratory and normative effect of 1848; the proclamation that Jews were equal citizens was more important than the absence of an immediate and total implementation of this principle. These collective memories were one of the main reasons for the heightened expectations that Jews had of German Liberalism and their disproportionately strong commitment to it.

But 1848 did not remove all conflicts. Jews remembered the reluctance with which many noteworthy Liberals had embraced the cause of emancipation in the pre-March era. The 1844 *Brockhaus* encyclopaedia commented with some justice: 'Liberals who are concerned with maintaining popular support, have for most of the time had reservations about declaring themselves openly and without qualifications in favour of the Jews; for the cause of the Jews is not popular.'[1] Equally, the cause of Liberalism, constitutionalism and German national unity was more popular with Jewish political activists, like Johann Jacoby, Leopold Zunz or Moritz Veit – not to mention the many radicals of Jewish origins who no longer identified with Judaism –, than it was among the bulk of the Jewish population. Among the Orthodox there was a fear that emancipation would lead to total assimilation and therefore to the disappearance of a Jewish community. The Orthodox *Der Treue Zionswächter* welcomed the Prussian *Judengesetz* of 1847, which had disappointed the out-and-out emancipationists by continuing to recognize the corporate character of the Jewish community: 'We live in the firm conviction that even the possession of political rights is something that can and must be partially dispensed with and sacrificed, as long as the dominant authority demands such a sacrifice or at least makes it necessary.'[2] Among many humbler Jews there was a respect for established authority and a fear of the mob, a fear reinforced by the rural pogroms that accompanied the outbreak of

---

1 'Emanzipation der Juden', *Allgemeine deutsche Real-Encyklopädie für die gebildeteten Stände*, 9th edn, Leipzig: Brockhaus, 1844, vol. IV, p. 688. Cit. Reinhard Rürup, 'Die Emanzipation der Juden in Baden', *Emanzipation und Antisemitismus. Studien zur 'Judenfrage' der bürgerlichen Gesellschaft*, Göttingen: Vandenhoeck & Ruprecht, 1975, p. 62.

2 *Der Treue Zionswächter*, 1847, p. 181. Quoted by Jacob Toury, 'Die Revolution von 1848 als innerjüdischer Wendepunkt' in Hans Liebeschütz and Arnold Paucker (eds), *Das Judentum in der deutschen Umwelt 1800–1850. Studien zur Frühgeschichte der Emanzipation*, Tübingen: J. C. B. Mohr, 1977, p. 363.

the Revolution in 1848.[3] Among rich and established merchants there was no love of social upheaval. Nevertheless, in spite of all these qualifications, 1848 played a crucial role in raising the consciousness of German Jewry: from that time onwards, civic equality and national unity were the goal of the great majority. The traditionalist monarchical loyalism of the silent majority evaporated.

But the decision to support liberalism raised as many problems as it solved. Most Liberals between 1849 and 1866 preferred a *kleindeutsch* to a *großdeutsch* solution to the national question, i.e. a Germany under the leadership of Prussia and excluding Austria. But most Liberals also opposed the administration of Bismarck in Prussia, given its hostility to constitutionalism and to parliamentary control over the military budget. Jewish political commitments reflected this dilemma. Thirteen Jews were among the 190 signatories of the manifesto of the *kleindeutsch Deutscher Nationalverein* in 1859; Gabriel Riesser and Moritz Veit, as well as the baptized August Metz, served on its executive. The fifteen Jews who supported the rival *Deutscher Reformverein*, with *großdeutsch* sympathies, were a smaller proportion of the participants, and played a less prominent role.[4] When, after the battle of Königgrätz and the formation of the North German Confederation, Liberals divided into supporters and opponents of Bismarck, Jewish opinion also split. Of the sixteen Jews who were elected to the Reichstag from 1867 to 1878, thirteen were Liberals: six of them Progressives and seven National Liberals. The latter included two of the most prominent parliamentarians of the day, Eduard Lasker and Ludwig Bamberger.[5] It is reasonable to assume that this distribution reflected the opinions of ordinary Jews.

If 1848 marked the first crisis of German liberalism, 1866 marked the second, presenting a dilemma that was to repeat itself more than once: whether to remain an opposition of principle, with potentially little influence on policy, or to make the best of a *fait accompli*. In any case, not all National Liberals regarded the Empire of 1871 as the lesser evil; they saw a powerful nation-state as a geopolitical necessity, a pre-condition for domestic constitutional development, not an obstacle to it. It was under the aegis of Bismarck,

---

3   Michael Riff, 'The Anti-Jewish Aspect of Revolutionary Unrest of 1848 in Baden and its Impact on Emancipation', *LBYB* XXI (1976), pp. 27–40; Eleonore Sterling, *Judenhaß. Die Anfänge des politischen Antisemitismus in Deutschland 1815–1850*, Frankfurt: Europäische Verlagsanstalt 1969, pp. 162–6, 171–4; Adolf Lewin, *Geschichte der badischen Juden seit der Regierung Karl Friedrichs (1738–1909)*, Karlsruhe, 1909, pp. 277–81.

4   See above, p. 86.

5   See above, pp. 93–4.

as he never tired of telling his Jewish acquaintances, that the final emancipation law, that of 1869, was passed.[6]

Above all, given the record of relations between Jews and the Catholic Church, at least some Jewish opinion-leaders supported aspects of one of Bismarck's least liberal policies, the *Kulturkampf*. Within a few months of the creation of the Empire, Levin Goldschmidt, by then a member of the Federal Supreme Commercial Court, wrote: 'Nor could the new German Empire have celebrated its joyful resurrection better and more significantly than with the double and triple defeat of the Ultramontanes. I, too, see in these the only dangerous enemies of our future.'[7] The *Allgemeine Zeitung des Judentums* spelt the issue out even more clearly: 'In general our existence is tied to the liberal state, and if reaction in general and Ultramontanism in particular were to gain dominance, we should immediately suffer the saddest consequences.'[8] Yet though every Liberal Jew was by definition a supporter of the subordination of church to state, he was also likely to be an opponent of discriminatory legislation. Some Jewish-owned papers, in particular the Left-Liberal *Frankfurter Zeitung*, opposed the *Kulturkampf* on principle, but all Jewish members of the Reichstag, irrespective of party, drew the line at the openly discriminatory Anti-Jesuit Law. Lasker and Bamberger were the only National Liberals to vote against it. In this respect the development of anti-Catholic legislation provided a test of the Jewish Liberal's liberalism.

But for most Jews Liberalism did not primarily mean constitutional details, but a particular form of society – an open, individualistic society that favoured merit and equal opportunity over status and protectionist corporatism. The attainment of that would rest on attitudes as much as on institutions and legislation. Because the aspirations of Jews and of the Liberal middle class generally converged in this period, because Jews were the almost incidental beneficiaries of the legal and commercial reforms of the 1860s and 1870s, the identification of Jews with the advance of Liberalism, first demonstrated in 1848, was further confirmed.

The third crisis of German Liberalism came in 1878, with Bismarck's turn to protectionist tariffs and his reconciliation with the Catholic *Zentrum* and the Conservatives. For most Jews the question was now not *whether* to support Liberalism, but *how*. The dilemma was all the greater since Bismarck's switch coincided with the revival of anti-Semitism, a development which,

---

6 Bismarck, *Die gesammelten Werke*, Berlin: Stollberg, 1926, vol. VII, pp. 424–4, 434; Otto Jöhlinger, *Bismarck und die Juden*, Berlin: Reimer, 1921, pp. 22–3.
7 To Professor Stobbe, 23 April 1871. *Levin Goldschmidt. Ein Lebensbild in Briefen* (ed. Adele Goldschmidt), Berlin: E. Goldschmidt, 1898, p. 347.
8 'Der ultramontane Bau', *AZJ*, 24 July 1877, p. 469.

while not initiated by Bismarck, was not discouraged by him.[9] This new configuration in German politics had two consequences for the political stance of Jews.

The first arose out of the split in the National Liberal Party, with the free-traders, led by Lasker and Bamberger, forming a new grouping that amalgamated in 1884 with the old Progressives. What remained of the National Liberal Party was now predominantly reconciled to the semi-Liberalism of the Bismarckian constitution and to sharing power with agrarian lobbyists. The National Liberals were not a homogeneous or centrally organized grouping and their character varied from region to region. In the Rhineland and in the Grand Duchies of Hesse and Baden, where the Progressives were weak, they retained a more Liberal character and considerable Jewish support. Jews continued to sit as National Liberal parliamentarians in state parliaments. But at the national level they lost their role in the party; from 1881 onwards no unbaptized Jew sat in the Reichstag as a National Liberal or as a member of the party's executive.[10] It would be an exaggeration to say that these developments drove Jews back into a political ghetto. But from then on until the end of the Empire the identification of the Jewish community with Left-Liberalism, its press and its institutions was taken for granted; it contributed to the revival of the image and reputation of the Jew as oppositional and subversive, an attribution that was, needless to say, self-fulfilling.

The second consequence was associated with the revival of conservative values in German society. However hesitant and uncertain the moves towards an open, meritocratic society may have been until 1878, they were, after that date, slowed down and even reversed. Jews had little difficulty in recognizing renewed anti-Semitism as an assault on Liberalism generally: 'The way things are we are the pioneers of progress', Bamberger commented.[11] They had equally little difficulty in recognizing Bismarck's shift to the right as diminishing their chances of further integration. For Bamberger, Bismarck's pro-tariff speech in the Reichstag symbolized 'the war of the agrarians against

---

9   Fritz Stern, *Gold and Iron. Bismarck, Bleichröder and the Building of the German Empire*, London: Allen & Unwin, 1977, pp. 511–24; Walter Frank, *Hofprediger Adolf Stoecker und die christlichsoziale Bewegung*, 2nd edn, Hamburg: Hanseatische Verlagsanstalt, 1935, pp. 86–7, 305; Günther Brakelmann, Martin Greschat and Werner Jochmann, *Protestantismus und Politik. Werk und Wirkung Adolf Stoeckers*, Hamburg: Christians, 1982, pp. 154–5.
10   See above, p. 101.
11   To his mother-in-law, 19 December 1879, Nachlaß, Ludwig Bamberger G St Dahlem.

modern civilization'.[12] With the return of the Conservatives to the governing majority, fewer Jews were appointed to university professorships and judicial posts. From the early 1880s onwards no Jew could become a reserve officer in the Prussian army.

The assumption that with the achievement of national unity progress towards the liberalization and secularization of society would continue was now undermined. That was more decisive in re-orientating Jewish political strategies than was the revival of anti-Semitism. Political anti-Semitism could be dismissed as a marginal phenomenon that periodically flared up and then subsided. Wilhelm Marr, Otto Böckel, even the Court Preacher Adolf Stoecker, could be dismissed as fringe figures. The more widespread tendency to treat the Jew as not quite a first-class citizen, as the step-child of the nation, was a more serious problem and a long-term one. Bismarck's change of course, through which liberalism ceased to be the dominant force in German politics, was the most serious of the three crises I have so far discussed for the Jewish community. The first two were setbacks for the cause of constitutional development but not for Jewish hopes; the third underlined that progress was not inevitable.

A long-term result of this third crisis was a re-alignment of the Jewish relationship with Liberalism. It emerged in the early 1890s, as left-wing liberalism became stabilized as a predominantly oppositional but not anti-system force, with some legislative influence and considerable power in local government, chambers of commerce and sectors of the banking and mercantile community. Side by side with this there emerged, in the post-Bismarckian Empire, a change in political style, a trend towards greater activism and mass organization. One obvious example of this is the Social Democratic Party, as it emerged from illegality after 1890. Another, specifically relevant to Jewish political calculations, was the second phase of anti-Semitism: rural, populist and with an altogether more secure base than the paternalistic demagogy of Stoecker. A third example was the spread of pressure groups to middle and upper-class strata who had previously relied on personal ties or status to influence opinion and policies. The Agrarian League and Pan-German League are the best-known instances of this development. Two organizations also founded at roughly the same time reflected the Liberal and Jewish consciences, the *Verein zur Abwehr des Antisemitismus (Abwehr-Verein)* and the *Centralverein deutscher Staatsbürger jüdischen Glaubens* (C.V.), both of 1893.

12 To Franz Schenk von Stauffenberg, 21 May 1897. Quoted by Stanley Zucker, *Ludwig Bamberger. German Liberal Politician and Social Critic, 1823–1899*, Pittsburgh, PA: University of Pittsburgh Press 1975, p. 152.

Their aims and composition were complementary, but not identical. The *Abwehr-Verein* was specifically a single-issue lobby. Its leadership was Gentile and its early membership largely so, though it was partly dependent, even from the start, on Jewish encouragement and financial generosity.[13] The C.V., on the other hand, was, as its name implied, a specifically Jewish organization. Though it, too, sought to combat anti-Semitism it had wider aims as well, above all to turn the nominal emancipation of the 1869 law into social and political reality by exposing and agitating against continuing discrimination.

The growth of these organizations raised two problems for the relationship between Jews and Liberals. The first was organizational, the second had to do with Jewish identity, especially the German identity of German Jews. As far as political affiliation was concerned, Jewish representative institutions were at pains to emphasize their neutrality. The C.V.'s statutes echoed this principle: 'As Jews we belong to no political party',[14] while the *Abwehr-Verein* declared: 'The Jew as such can be a Conservative, Liberal or Social Democrat. He is this as a citizen, not as a Jew'.[15] In fact, for the reasons already given, the fight against anti-Semitism and discrimination could take place only within the framework of Liberal politics, and Left-Liberal politics at that. Although the first president of the *Abwehr-Verein*, the eminent constitutional lawyer Rudolf von Gneist, was a National Liberal and a number of other prominent supporters came from that party, the bulk of the *Abwehr-Verein's* officials and dignitaries were Progressives.[16] That included all its later presidents, Heinrich Rickert, Theodor Barth and Georg Gothein. The first two presidents of the C.V., Maximilian Horwitz and Eugen Fuchs, were both members of the *Freisinnige Volkspartei*. The founder generation of the *Abwehr-Verein*, in contrast, were drawn more from the *Freisinnige Vereinigung*, a party closer to the old left wing of the pre-1878 National Liberals. It was more upper middle class in its composition than the *Freisinnige Volkspartei*, from which it had split in 1893 in order to support Caprivi's military budget. But too much should not be read into this distinction between the two groups of founders. The differences between the parties soon diminished and in 1910 they amalgamated into the *Fortschrittliche Volkspartei*.

13   Ismar Schorsch, *Jewish Reactions to German Anti-Semitism, 1870–1914*, New York: Columbia University Press 1972, pp. 93–5; Barbara Suchy, 'The Verein zur Abwehr des Antisemitismus (I) – From Its Beginnings to the First World War', LBYB XXVIII (1983), pp. 206–8.
14   Arnold Paucker, 'Zur Problematik einer jüdischen Abwehrstrategie in der deutschen Gesellschaft', *WD*, p. 488.
15   *MVA* (1896), p. 128.
16   Suchy, *LBYB* (1983), pp. 209, 233.

One matter on which the *Abwehr-Verein* and the C.V. gradually diverged, at least in emphasis, was the question of a Jewish identity. Jewish support for emancipation within the nation-state had originally accepted, perhaps rather unthinkingly, the idea of reciprocity or *Gegenleistung*. Emancipation, according to this thesis, implied assimilation, the abandonment of all cultural peculiarities. Theodor Mommsen, the great opponent of anti-Semitism, had spelled this out quite brutally:

Entry into a great nation exacts its price. ... Even the Jews will not be led back to the promised land by a Moses. ... It is their duty, in so far as they are able and without acting contrary to their conscience on their part, to divest themselves to the best of their ability of their pecularities and to knock down all barriers between themselves and the other German fellow-citizens with a determined hand.[17]

This position was largely upheld by the *Abwehr-Verein*. It deplored the tendency towards the creation of a specifically Jewish associational life, as instanced by the creation of a *Verein jüdischer Studenten* and the *Verband national-jüdischer Turnvereine* which it regarded as 'Jewish exclusionist games';[18] it supported Jews as 'Germans with equal rights' (Rickert) and expected them to behave accordingly.[19] Even Georg Gothein, one of the most liberal Liberals of the Wilhelmine era, proclaimed his continued faith in 'a united people': 'That is why we want a process of complete amalgamation [*vollkommenen Verschmelzungsprozeß*] and no segregated culture.'[20]

The C.V., dedicated to the proposition that Jews did have a special interest to defend, could not go so far. While it was representative of Liberal Jewry rather than of the German Jewish community in its entirety, unsympathetic to Orthodoxy and hostile to Zionism, its very existence was evidence of a revival of Jewish consciousness. While the founders of the C.V. belonged to the generation of integrated Jews, its later notables, such as Ludwig Holländer, Ludwig Haas and Bruno Weil, tended to be old members of Jewish student corporations, organized in the *Kartell Convent jüdischer Corporationen*, founded in 1896.[21] From a position of defence the C.V. slowly moved to one of affirmation.

Though both the C.V. and the *Abwehr-Verein* had close personal links with the parties of Left Liberalism, their support for these was not uncritical. One

17 Theodor Mommsen, 'Auch ein Wort über unser Judentum', in Walter Boehlich (ed.), *Der Berliner Antisemitismusstreit*, Frankfurt: Insel-Verlag, 1964, p. 227.
18 *MVA* (1897), p. 123; 1903, pp. 176ff., 281ff.
19 *MVA* (1902), p. 404.
20 *MVA* (1912), p. 184.
21 Jehuda Reinharz, *Fatherland or Promised Land. The Dilemma of the German Jew, 1893–1914*, Ann Arbor, Mich: University of Michigan Press, 1975, pp. 50–1.

of the C.V.'s objectives was the election of Jewish legislators to the Reichstag and state parliaments at a time when parties other than the Social Democrats were reluctant to adopt practising Jews as candidates. There were frequent criticisms of Liberal 'cowardice' in this respect.[22] Both organizations gave absolute priority to the defeat of anti-Semitic candidates in all elections, whereas tactical considerations sometimes gave Liberal candidates other priorities. That applied particularly in the 'Hottentot elections' of 1907, when the Liberal parties formed a bloc with the Conservatives against the SPD and *Zentrum*, an arrangement that required Liberal supporters in some cases to give their votes to candidates of the Right in the run-off ballot.[23] Indeed, the creation of this 'Bülow Block' seemed to Theodor Barth, the president of the *Abwehr-Verein*, to be a betrayal of the Liberal parties' mission and led to his resignation from the *Freisinnige Vereinigung*.[24]

The Jewish–Liberal collaboration was, it will be seen, fruitful, but it had its limits. The Liberal assimilationism of the *Abwehr-Verein* and, with qualifications, of the C.V. represented the views of the majority of German Jews, as the growing membership of the C.V. showed.[25] But it did not speak for the religiously Orthodox, for Jewish nationalists or Zionists, or for recent Eastern immigrants, who tended not to be German citizens, and only to a very limited extent for the growing number of Socialists. Given the limited electoral appeal of left Liberalism after 1893, it is fair to calculate that about one Left-Liberal vote in ten came from Jews,[26] and more than one *Reichsmark* in ten for the coffers of the Left-Liberal parties. On the other hand, while the C.V. and *Abwehr-Verein* were, by definition, single-issue bodies, the Left-Liberal parties had, by definition, to aggregate a number of interests. They made frequent public denunciations of anti-Semitism. From the turn of the century onwards they became more willing to countenance Jews as parliamentary candidates, especially for the Prussian Landtag. They took the initiative in protesting against continuing discrimination against Jews in public appointments and in the army, in the latter case with some help from National Liberals, *Zentrum* and SPD.[27] They did so because now, as a half a century

---

22 Eugen Fuchs, 'Konfessionelle Kandidaturen', *IdR*, December 1898, pp. 612–23; also ibid., May 1898, p. 239; September 1898, p. 424.

23 *IdR*, March 1907, p. 141; also *AZJ*, 8 February 1907, p. 62.

24 Theodor Barth, *Der Freisinn im Block*, Berlin: Concordia, 1908.

25 Reinharz, *Fatherland or Promised Land*, p. 53.

26 See above, pp. 145, 191.

27 Werner T. Angress, 'Prussia's Army and the Jewish Reserve Officer Controversy Before World War I', *LBYB* XVII (1972), pp. 19–42; Marjorie Lamberti, 'Liberals, Socialists and the Defence against Anti-Semitism in the Wilhelminian Period', *LBYB* XXV (1980), pp. 147–62; and above, pp. 44–66, 142, 144.

earlier, the advancement of Jews went hand in hand with the advancement of the *Rechtsstaat* and the battle against aristocratic privilege. But the exigencies of the Reichstag electoral system also put a premium on opportunism and compromise. There was not much profit in being a *Judenschutztruppe* (a 'Jewish protective guard') and no guarantee that the lower middle-class, often provincial, electorate of the Left-Liberal parties shared the values of the leadership. There was therefore a limit to what Jews and Liberals could offer each other.

What we witness in the Wilhelmine epoch is the changing character of German Liberalism. The era in which it was possible to believe in the rational individual as citizen and the independent notable as legislator was over. The conflict between sectional interests was now open and organized. To these changed conditions Jews adapted. Their Liberalism was always defined as much in societal as in constitutional or party political terms. Hence, as the parliamentary weakness of the Liberal parties became more evident, they placed more faith in the lobbies whose existence had once been thought inconsistent with classical Liberalism. These included not only the ones we have already mentioned, but such bodies dedicated to free trade and mercantile interests in general as the *Handelsvertragsverein* of 1900 and the *Hansa-Bund für Gewerbe, Handel und Industrie* of 1909. The opponents of these organizations were not slow to denounce them as run 'by people with crooked noses and crooked legs' and the 'stock exchange mob'.[28]

A further feature of the evolution of German Liberalism was the emerging role of Social Democracy. In the last ten years of the peace the SPD was decreasingly the party of class war and materialism that its rhetoric proclaimed it to be. It was also an increasingly effective defender of existing constitutional liberties, as much a reinforcer of Liberalism as its enemy. This was slowly recognized by the *Abwehr-Verein* and the C.V., both of which had initially been anxious not be associated with the cause of revolution. Though unsympathetic towards special Jewish interests, the SPD was a stout bulwark against anti-Semitism.[29] Liberals increasingly realized that some co-operation with it was necessary, even desirable, a realization that culminated in the pact for the second round of the 1912 Reichstag elections. But close collaboration had already been advocated by Theodor Barth, and Ludwig Bamberger had, before his death, been converted to the view that Liberals and Social

28 'Leute mit krummen Nasen und krummen Beinen', Prussian Landtag deputy Pastor Ludwig Heckenroth (Conservative), quoted in *AZJ*, 3 September 1909; 'Mob der Börse', *Rheinisch-Westfälische Zeitung*, 13 May 1909; also *KZ*, 25 June 1909; *Der Hammer*, 1 October 1909; *Staatsbürger-Zeitung*, 1 November 1911.
29 As acknowledged in *AZJ*, 8 February 1907, p. 62; *IdR*, August 1903, p. 457; September 1903, p. 459, November 1903, pp. 628–32.

Democrats would have to fuse.[30] The growing attractiveness of the SPD to Jews is therefore readily understood. In part it was simply a reflection of the change in the Jewish social structure towards urbanization and paid employment. In part it was no doubt an idealistic reaction against the self-satisfied and ineffectual Liberalism of the older generation. But it was also a recognition of the extent to which the SPD was more and more becoming an extension – an indispensable extension – of German Liberalism.

The last and the greatest test of German liberalism came with the Weimar Republic. Most German Liberals and probably most German Jews were not Republicans by conviction and remained 'emotional monarchists' (*Herzensmonarchisten*) after 1918. Most German Liberals and most German Jews were patriots who deplored the defeat of 1918 and resented the peace terms of Versailles. But in the main they adapted, for a variety of reasons. Liberals in general and Jews in particular were disillusioned with the *Burgfrieden* (civic truce) of the war years. The Emperor's promise that he knew no parties any longer, only Germans, turned out to be empty. Progress towards domestic reform was slow; government became more authoritarian, not less, under the guise of patriotic endeavour; and anti-Semitism revived in the later years of the war under the stress of military frustration. The special Jewish census in the armed forces reminded any Jews who might have been tempted to forget to what extent they remained step-children.[31] Their monarchism was therefore under strain.

Perhaps more important was the impact of the Revolution. All revolutions are polarizing events, and that in Germany reinforced already existing polarities. More than ever Germany was divided into 'patriots' and 'traitors'; those who formed the Reichstag majority after the 'Jew elections' of 1912 and passed the peace resolution of 1917 (Progressives, *Zentrum* and SPD) were the back-stabbers of 1918. Those who had been in opposition under the Empire, whether loyal or disloyal, now had the political initiative and that meant that Jews were prominent participants in the provisional governments of the *Reich* and numerous states. The Jewish reaction to this surge of activism was ambivalent. Jewish newspapers and journals were aware of the

---

30 Theodor Barth, *Liberalismus und Sozialdemokratie*, Berlin: Concordia, [1908], pp. 23, 32–3; Ludwig Bamberger, 'Die Krisis in Deutschland und der deutsche Kaiser', *Gesammelte Schriften*, Berlin, 1894–8, vol. V, pp. 419–39; Lujo Brentano, *Mein Leben im Kampf um die soziale Entwicklung in Deutschland*, Jena: Diederichs, 1931, pp. 206–7, 239.
31 Werner T. Angress, 'The German Army's "Judenzählung" of 1916 – Genesis – Consequences – Significance', *LBYB* XXIII (1978), pp. 117–37.

anti-Semitic backlash that it risked.[32] Some displayed the Pavlovian reaction of the *Schutzjude* in times of crisis: self-restraint ('Zurückhaltung').[33] But the surging anti-Semitism of the defeated Right and the growing violence of such bodies as the *Deutschvölkischer Schutz- und Trutzbund* left most Jews little choice. If the new republic was to be a 'Judenrepublik', then Jews might as well identify with it.

In any case there was a position waiting to be occupied between monarchical nostalgia and the dictatorship of the workers' and soldiers' councils. It was in the offices of the great Liberal newspaper, the *Berliner Tageblatt*, Jewish-owned and Jewish-edited, that the appeal for 'a great democratic party for the united *Reich*' was drafted, under the guidance of its editor-in-chief, Theodor Wolff. The signatures of Albert Einstein, Moritz Julius Bonn, Paul Nathan and Kurt von Kleefeld (director of the *Hansa-Bund* and Gustav Stresemann's brother-in-law), as well as those of such eminent Gentiles as Alfred Weber, Franz von Liszt, Hjalmar Schacht and Hellmut von Gerlach, must have been reassuring, perhaps even inspiring. This party, the *Deutsche Demokratische Partei*, won 18.5 per cent of the votes for the Weimar National Assembly, a better share for Left-Liberalism than at any time since 1881. The constitution that the National Assembly promulgated satisfied the most stringent demands a religious or ethnic minority could make. Article 109 proclaimed: 'All Germans are equal before the law.' Article 136 declared: 'The enjoyment of the right of citizenship and nationality, as well as access to public positions, are not dependent on religious denomination.' The constitution itself was based on a draft by the constitutional lawyer Hugo Preuß, rector of the Commercial Academy of Berlin and a prominent member of the C.V. If anything, the Liberalism of the Republic seemed designed to serve Jewish aspirations for an open society better than did the Liberalism of the Empire. That was its strength; it was also its weakness.

The weaknesses, indeed, were manifold. The first was that the electoral strength of the DDP proved to be deceptive. In 1919 it had become the repository of all those who had unrealistic hopes for democracy and panic-stricken fears of Socialism. The 'normal' DDP vote, it turned out, was much lower, lower even than that of Progressive parties in the Empire. True, some of the lost votes went to the *Deutsche Volkspartei*, which, after some early temptations, was a fairly consistent opponent of anti-Semitism, at least

32 *Deutsche Israelitische Zeitung* (Munich), 28 November 1918, *Der Israelit*, 14 November 1918; *MVA* (1918), pp. 111–12, 120–1. See Werner T. Angress, 'Juden im politischen Leben der Revolutionszeit', p. 148 and Eva G. Reichmann, 'Der Bewußtseinswandel der deutschen Juden', *KuR*, p. 554.

33 *Der Israelit*, 14 November 1918, quoted by Angress, *LBYB* (1978), p. 148.

336 Jews and the Crisis of Liberalism

until the death of Gustav Stresemann in 1929.[34] Similarly the two other parties that formed the 'Weimar coalition' along with the DDP, i.e. the SPD and the *Zentrum*, now lent greater support to such bodies as the *Abwehr-Verein*[35] and collaborated in the *Reichsbanner Schwarz–Rot–Gold*, the militant Republican defence league.

But even if one defines the Liberalism of the Weimar Republic not by the narrow party boundaries of the DDP but by all those willing to support – or accept – the Republican constitution, one still finds that it formed a minority, and that was its second and even greater weakness. To be Jewish was, if anything, more controversial in the Republic than in the Empire, because the Republic itself was more controversial. Its legitimacy was a constant political issue. But the fact that some greater career opportunities now existed for Jews, in particular in political and cultural life, meant that Jewry as a whole was more conspicuous and vulnerable. After 1920 very few Jews served in high political office, either in the *Reich* or in individual states, but they gained some high administrative appointments, especially in Prussia.[36] Their contribution to the avant-garde culture and left-wing intellectual scene has been often recorded. That, too, was offensive to the silent majority that did not care for *Kulturbolschewismus*. But most Jews, it need hardly be stressed, were not Berlin cabaret artists or bankers or Nobel Prize-winners; nor were they brothel-keepers, black-marketeers or currency smugglers. They were, in the main, ordinary people, trying to earn an honest living, who suffered at least as much from the inflation and the Depression as their Christian fellow-citizens. What made their situation different was that they also suffered from the old and new stereotypes that abounded in the post-1918 political labyrinth.

That meant that, though they had good friends and allies, few were prepared to put the defence of Jewish rights above all other priorities. The broader range of Jewish political activity opened more doors, but rather cautiously. The C.V. continued to be the principal organization of German Jewry, but it became less exclusive towards Zionists, Eastern Jews or the Orthodox. Its main party links, and those of the *Abwehr-Verein*, were still with

34 Wolfgang Hartenstein, *Die Anfänge der Deutschen Volkspartei, 1918–1920*, Düsseldorf: Droste 1962, pp. 44–50, 127; Henry A. Turner, *Stresemann and the Politics of the Weimar Republic*, Princeton, NJ: Princeton University Press, 1963, p. 97; for the limits of this commitment see Barbara Suchy, 'The Verein zur Abwehr des Antisemitismus', (II) – From the First World War to its Dissolution in 1933', *LBYB* XXX (1985), p. 85.

35 Suchy, *LBYB* (1985), pp. 90–2.

36 E. G. Lowenthal, 'Die Juden im öffentlichen Leben', *Entscheidungsjahr 1932*, pp. 59–85; and above, pp. 273–4.

the DDP, but again less exclusively so.[37] In any case, as in the Empire, none of the parties was totally welcoming to the representation of Jewish interests. The tensions within the DDP, between the secular, cosmopolitan and intellectual tendency of Berlin and the more traditionally-minded branches in the provinces, often resulted in an implied resentment of Jewish influence within the party. The 1926 debate on the anti-pornography bill of the DDP Minister of the Interior Wilhelm Külz was a good illustration of this ill-feeling.[38]

The extent of the one-sided dependence of Jews on Liberalism was revealed during the terminal crisis of Liberalism from 1929 to 1932. The disintegration of the DDP and its fusion with the *Jungdeutscher Orden* to form the *Deutsche Staatspartei* confronted middle-class Jews with an acute dilemma. Many remained faithful for a surprisingly long time – in many instances until July 1932[39] – to the party that had been their traditional home. It was only then that they joined those who had attached themselves to the other parties of the Republic, the SPD and *Zentrum*. But the fact that the DDP was a visibly sinking ship was only a symbol of the wider collapse of the Liberal civilization of Germany. Those who first burn books will soon burn people. The burnt included indiscriminately those who retained their faith in the Liberalism of their neighbours and those who had lost it, those who had been Weimar loyalists to the end and those who had found some alternative allegiance in Communism, Zionism or even German ultra-nationalism, as in the *Verband nationaldeutscher Juden*.

The human need for Liberalism is universal; the anti-Liberal needs Liberalism as much as does the Liberal. The Jew's need of it may be more immediate or more obvious, but he was not the only victim of its failure.

---

37   Donald L. Niewyk, *The Jews in Weimar Germany*, Baton Rouge: Louisiana State University Press, 1980, pp. 82–124; Arnold Paucker, *Der jüdische Abwehrkampf gegen Antisemitismus und Nationalsozialismus in den letzten Jahren der Weimarer Republik*, 2nd edn, Hamburg: Leibniz, 1969, pp. 57, 87–92, 120–4.
38   Bruce B. Frye, *Liberal Democrats in the Weimar Republic. The History of the German Democratic Party and the German State Party*, Carbondale and Edwardsville: Southern Illinois University Press, 1985, pp. 129–131.
39   See above, pp. 291–313.

5

The Beginning of the End

Dates are essential for an understanding of history: the idea that the past is a seamless web, in which epochs, movements, institutions and ideas have no significant starting or terminal point is difficult to grasp, whether for the professional or the layman. Dates impose order on the chaos of the past and, like all impositions of order, they over-simplify. They also have great symbolic power and, in extreme cases, signalize great destructive events or new expectations. 1789, 1848, 1917 and 1945 are not merely points in the calendar, they are expressions of profound upheavals in human affairs. They can be mentioned to a professional, even a lay, audience without further explanation. Most people would put 1933 in this category; few would dispute that Hitler's coming to power was the most fateful event in Jewish history since the destruction of the Second Temple.

But we also know that every present has its roots in the past. 1933 did not come out of the blue, any more than 1917 or 1848 or 1789. It is this knowledge that makes us stake out the ground between the extreme poles of pure chance and inevitability; and ask how perceptive men and women should have surveyed the rise and fall of Jewish emancipation in Germany. Those who witness or remember historic events have no need to be told that these events do not, by themselves, produce a total change in the conditions of their lives. Events are milestones and signposts, not the road itself. That consideration applies pre-eminently to the long, gradual and never complete process of emancipation. It also applies to the much faster process of disemancipation.

Let us consider emancipation first. In terms of legal enactments we can trace its development over nearly a century, beginning with Joseph II's *Toleranzedikte* of 1781–2 in the Habsburg lands and the Hardenberg edict of

1812 in Prussia, and continuing with partial alleviations of the conditions of Jews in a number of states, in particular Hesse-Cassel in 1833. That phase culminated in the proclamation of the Basic Rights of the German People by the Frankfurt Parliament in 1848. It in turn led to the adoption of constitutions guaranteeing equal rights in most states, and these generally survived, in the letter if not in the spirit, the decade of reaction that followed the defeat of the Revolution. Final and juridically complete emancipation came with the North German Law of 3 July 1869 which was applied, after the formation of the *Reich*, to all those constituent states that had not already enacted an end to religious discrimination.

Yet anyone at all familiar with the history of equal rights for Jews will recognize at once that a survey of legislation tells only a small part of the story. True, enabling legislation is a necessary condition for the enjoyment of rights. But much else has to happen before sufficient conditions operate. The first proviso is that the law should be comprehensive. The *Toleranzedikte* opened certain occupations and careers to Jews, in return for some control over their communal activities, but it did not grant them rights of citizenship. The Prussian edict of 1812 did not extend to the whole of the territory of the kingdom. That did not make these enactments worthless. Laws have normative and declaratory functions, as well as purely positivistic ones. They register which way opinion is moving, they indicate to citizens and authorities what attitudes they should adopt to particular categories of people. Above all they influence the expectations, and therefore the behaviour, of those who are the objects of the laws. No-one understood this more clearly than Wilhelm von Humboldt, in outlining the duties of the state in this respect in 1809:

The state should not simply teach respect for the Jews, but it should abandon the inhuman and prejudiced ways of thought that judge a man not by his particular qualities, but according to his descent and religion. ... The state can do this only if it proclaims, loudly and clearly, that it no longer recognizes any distinction between Jews and Christians.[1]

Given this normative element, the governments' own failure to live up to their precepts not only retarded the *de facto* move of Jews towards equal civic status, but affected Christian-Jewish attitudes and relations in general. One of the best-known examples of this policy was the refusal of the Prussian government to appoint the jurist Eduard Gans to a professorship at Berlin in

---

1 Ismar Freund, *Die Emanzipation der Juden in Preußen unter besonderer Berücksichtigung des Gesetzes vom 11. März 1812. Ein Beitrag zur Rechtsgeschichte der Juden in Preußen*, Berlin: M. Poppelauer, 1912, vol. II, p. 410.

1822 solely on the grounds of his religion, an objection that no longer applied six years later, when he was appointed, having first accepted baptism.[2]

In a similar way the law of 1869, though formulated in quite categorical terms, making the rights of citizenship 'independent of religious adherence', was applied very unevenly. There was, firstly, the problem that it co-existed with older state constitutions; these were in many cases ambiguous on the question of Jewish rights. For instance, Article 4 of the Prussian constitution of 1850 – valid until 1918 – prescribed the equality of all citizens before the law and Article 12 gave equal civic rights to citizens of all religions. However, Article 14 reserved all public institutions 'connected with the exercise of religious functions' to the Christian religion.[3] What these institutions were was never specified. But until 1869 the Prussian government used it to debar Jews from all judicial appointments, since they would have to administer Christian oaths. Even thereafter the Christian basis of the state meant that virtually no unbaptized Jews were employed as teachers in state schools or in the state bureaucracy or diplomatic service, and there was considerable discrimination against them in judicial and academic appointments.[4] The well-known controversy caused by the inability of Jews to become reserve officers in Prussia was central to the problem of emancipation, not merely because it raised a principle or because of the intrinsic desirability of this honour, but because the possession of a reserve commission was the key to a great many other public and private appointments.[5] Prussian practice was in this respect fairly typical of the Imperial period. Some states, like Hamburg and Baden, gradually became more liberal in their public appointments policy; others, like Saxony and Hesse-Darmstadt, remained almost completely intolerant.

This mismatch between legal provision and administrative practice, between constitutional norm and social reality, remained part of the German Jew's folk-memory. But there was another, compensatory, part that enabled him to see his experience in a more encouraging light. Legal equality is, as we have seen, a necessary condition of complete emancipation, but it is not the sole or sufficient one. Social acceptance and professional integration are

---

2   Hans Günther Reissner, *Eduard Gans. Ein Leben im Vormärz*, Tübingen: J. C. B. Mohr, 1965, pp. 91–3, 113, 117.

3   E. R. Huber, *Dokumente zur deutschen Verfassungsgeschichte*, Stuttgart: Kohlhammer, 1961, vol. I, p. 402.

4   Ernest Hamburger, *Juden im öffentlichen Leben Deutschlands. Regierungsmitglieder, Beamte und Parlamentarier in der monarchischen Zeit, 1848–1918*, Tübingen: J. C. B. Mohr, 1968, pp. 21–119.

5   Werner T. Angress, 'Prussia's Army and the Jewish Reserve Officer Controversy Before World War I', *LB YB* XVII (1972), pp. 19–42.

equally important. But which comes first? Advocates of Jewish emancipation argued that it was discrimination and segregation that were to blame for the undesirable characteristics of Jews: moral improvement could come only if there was legal improvement. Opponents argued the opposite: Jews must show that they deserved emancipation by first dropping their peculiarities.

On balance the second argument proved the more powerful. Social emancipation preceded political; indeed social emancipation made its political corollary acceptable to many who had previously been sceptical towards it. The move from the ghetto into bourgeois occupations, the abandonment of Yiddish, of special clothing and of at least some Orthodox practices, the impact of the Enlightenment on a small but significant commercial and intellectual Jewish elite – all these developments signalled to Jews and non-Jews alike a cultural *rapprochement* that made common citizenship not merely desirable but possible. The salons of Henriette Herz and Rahel Varnhagen in early nineteenth-century Berlin may have been the tip of a pyramid that still reached very far down; but if one adds to them the increasing number of Jews who served in municipal authorities and chambers of commerce a picture of Jews as an increasingly integral part of German public life begins to emerge.[6] It did not take Jewish spokesmen long to appreciate that there was more than legal reform to the change in status they were experiencing. What, Ludwig Philippson asked Christian legislators in 1850, did emancipation consist of?

You do not emancipate the Jews, they have long ago emancipated themselves, you merely complete the externals of emancipation. From the time onwards that Jews step out of the ghetto, that they participate in all the industrial and intellectual endeavours of mankind, that their children attend schools, *gymnasien* and universities, that their men participate in scholarship, art, industry and crafts, that their women immerse themselves in general education – from that moment onwards they are emancipated and do not need to wait for a few words in the constitution.[7]

The legislators had in the meantime got the message. Some, indeed, regarded Jewish success in the absence of formal emancipation as an argument against adding legal rights to economic power and social influence. But such voices became less and less characteristic in the course of the century. By 1860 the Conservative deputy F. T. Schaaff, a long-time opponent of emancipation, could say in the Baden Chamber:

6 Jacob Toury, *Die politischen Orientierungen der Juden in Deutschland. Von Jena bis Weimar*, Tübingen: J. C. B. Mohr, 1966, p. 101; Stefi Wenzel, *Jüdische Bürger und kommunale Selbstverwaltung in preußischen Städten 1808–1848*, Berlin: Colloquium-Verlag, 1967, *passim*.
7 'Das Judenthum und die Emanzipation', *AZJ*, 14 January 1850, pp. 29–30.

Those who are not precisely acquainted with the matter always conceive of the Jew with a pack on his back, a goat on the lead and a stove-pipe hat perched on the back of his neck, of how he has wormed something out of a peasant by outsmarting him, exactly as one imagines the haggling Jew. But there are now few such persons in our land.[8]

Germany's Jews could draw a number of conclusions from this experience. The first was that there was a parallelism between legal, social and economic emancipation, but not an exact identity. On the one hand, neither the 1812 edict, nor the Basic Rights of 1848, nor the law of 1869 guaranteed an end to discrimination, whether by individuals, private associations or public authorities; either it had to be fought for separately or one had grudgingly to accept the imperfection of the world. On the other hand it was possible to achieve commercial and professional success, at least within a limited range of callings, even in the absence of complete legal equality. There was more than one way of being emancipated, and if one chose one's way carefully one could do quite well.

The second conclusion was that while emancipatory laws did not guarantee an end to anti-Semitism – indeed, for some anti-Semites they were an incentive for redoubled efforts – it was at least reduced to manageable proportions. Some relief, however half-hearted, was forthcoming from the courts and from governments against the worst excesses, and the anti-Semitic agitator in general found himself excluded from polite society. That, too, though less than perfect, was a substantial gain.

These experiences and conclusions informed the attitudes of Jews towards the Weimar Republic, the appointment of Hitler as Chancellor, the early years of the Third Reich and what Reinhard Rürup has called the end of emancipation.[9] These attitudes were a mixture of illusion and realism.

Some of the illusions have featured prominently in the retrospective controversy about German Jewry. There was the illusion, or the alleged illusion, about the German–Jewish symbiosis, the fusion of two great cultures to create a yet higher achievement.[10] No doubt many Jews idealized their

8 Quoted by Reinhard Rürup, 'Die Emanzipation der Juden in Baden', in *Emanzipation und Antisemitismus. Studien zur 'Judenfrage' der bürgerlichen Gesellschaft*, in *idem*, Göttingen: Vandenhoeck & Ruprecht, 1975, p. 69.

9 Reinhard Rürup, 'Das Ende der Emanzipation: Die antijüdische Politik in Deutschland von der "Machtergreifung" bis zum zweiten Weltkrieg', Arnold Paucker (ed.), *The Jews in Nazi Germany, 1933–1943*, Tübingen: J. C. B. Mohr, 1987, pp. 97–114.

10 See, for instance, Gershom Scholem, *On Jews and Judaism in Crisis. Selected Essays*, New York: Schocken, 1977, pp. 61–92. For a more balanced assessment see Jehuda Reinharz and Walter Schatzberg (eds), *The Jewish Response to German Culture. From the Enlightenment to the Second World War*, Hanover, NH: New England University Press, 1986.

Deutschtum and exaggerated the extent to which Germany had clasped them to its bosom. Those who proclaimed it in a pathological form, like the *Verband nationaldeutscher Juden* of Max Naumann, were a small minority. Others who wore their German heart on their sleeves, like the *Reichsbund jüdischer Frontsoldaten*, were concerned with emphasizing their patriotism rather than their *Deutschtum*. In any case, *Deutschtum* made sense as an identity for Germany's Jews. Germans had been a cultural nation before they became a political nation; a shared language and literary and philosophical tradition is what united Prussians and Bavarians, Saxons and Hamburgers, Protestants and Catholics – and Jews. The very imperfection of the union of 1871, the survival of particularism, localism and social segmentation made *Deutschtum* an invaluable and indispensable ideological device for many categories of citizens and publicists.

In any case, *Deutschtum* was not the only illusion, if that is what it was. An increasing number of idealistic Jews turned to Socialism and even Communism in the hope that a society without classes would also be a society without other inherited distinctions. This idealism rested on beliefs about the ability of human beings, including Germans, to overcome prejudice and jealousies. But its starting point was the recognition of how unsatisfactory human relations still were. Zionism, to which an increasing minority of German Jews were drawn, also had its illusory element. It, too, was there to provide German Jews with an identity; it, too, had a thesis about German–Jewish co-existence. German Zionists did not, in the main, accept Theodor Herzl's political programme before 1933. Theirs was not an ideology of emigration; unlike their fellow-Zionists in Eastern Europe they did not consider themselves strangers in their own land. This anti-emigration Zionism was best expressed by Franz Oppenheimer:

I am not an assimilationist, but I am assimilated. I am German and at the same time proud of being a Jew, proud of descent from seventy generations of proud men. ... I am just as proud, however, of having grown up in the land of Walther and Wolfram, Goethe, Kant and Fichte and to have immersed myself in their culture. My *Deutschtum* is sacred to me.[11]

But in addition to his *Deutschtum* and his sense of territorial belonging (*Heimatbewußtsein*), he insisted on his clan consciousness (*Stammesbewußtsein*).

Divided loyalties such as these led to divided counsels on how far Jews should participate in public life. Zionism certainly insisted that Jews should have, and use, full civic rights and had, in 1914, emphasized the Zionist's

---

11 *JR*, 19 June 1914; see also Franz Oppenheimer, 'Stammesbewußtsein und Volksbewußtsein', *Die Welt*, 18 February 1910.

duty to fight for his German fatherland.[12] How far this formula of the 'German citizen of the Jewish *Volk*'[13] met the political and emotional needs of German Jews is highly questionable. But until 1933 Zionists – like Liberal assimilationist, German nationalist and Socialist Jews – were, in their own way, in Peter Gay's phrase, at home in Germany.[14]

The Jewish experience of the Weimar Republic was as ambiguous as that of the Empire and the pre-unification period. On the one hand the political framework was a great deal more favourable to Jewish aspirations. Most Jews may not have wanted to overthrow the monarchy, but few wanted to restore it once it was gone. The liberal egalitarianism of the Republic, its constitution drafted by 'one of us', seemed, to quote Peter Gay again, the realization of an authentic political dream.[15] For the first time Jews could participate in public life as ministers, mayors and senior civil servants, a development that was not an unmixed blessing. Perhaps even more important was the enormous influx of Jewish talent into both high and popular culture – another mixed blessing.

The obvious conclusion to draw was that a society in which Walther Rathenau and Rudolf Hilferding, Max Reinhardt and Ernst Lubitsch, Lion Feuchtwanger and Emil Ludwig reached such recognition could not be all bad. Perhaps such recognition induced a sense of false confidence. Other symptoms of integration, such as the increasing rate of inter-marriage, led some observers to fear that a separate Jewish community in Germany was doomed to disappear. Yet there were plenty of danger signals. Active, even terroristic, anti-Semitism reached a pre-1933 peak in 1918 to 1923, the years between the defeat and the stabilization of the mark. The activities of the *Deutschvölkischer Schutz- und Trutzbund*, the assassination of Rathenau, Hitler's first bid for power in Munich and the pogrom-like agitation against Eastern Jews were only the most obvious examples. After 1923 only one Jew, Rudolf Hilferding, served as a *Reich* cabinet minister (1928–9) and none in the cabinets of Prussia and the smaller states. When Heinrich Brüning wanted to offer a ministerial post to Paul Silverberg in 1930 he concluded that the political obstacles to this step were too great.[16] In large areas of public and private life Jews flourished as never before. But it is difficult to

12 *JR*, 7 August 1914, quoted by Jehuda Reinharz, *Fatherland or Promised Land. The Dilemma of the German Jew, 1893–1914*, Ann Arbor, Mich.: University of Michigan Press, 1975, pp. 222–3.
13 *JR*, 31 January 1919, quoted by Stephen M. Poppel, *Zionism in Germany 1897–1933. The Shaping of a Jewish Identity*, Philadelphia: Jewish Publication Society of America, 1977, p. 121.
14 Peter Gay, 'In Deutschland zu Hause ... Die Juden der Weimarer Zeit', in Paucker, *The Jews in Nazi Germany*, pp. 31–44.
15 Ibid., p. 37.
16 Heinrich Brüning, *Memoiren 1918–1934*, Stuttgart: Deutsche Verlags-Anstalt, 1970, p. 370.

believe those who avowed retrospectively that only Hitler had reminded them of their Jewishness. There was a case for believing that anti-Semitism was a relic of primitive politics and would decline, however slowly and unevenly; there was a case for believing that anti-Semitism was a cyclical phenomenon that flared during crises but would normally lie fairly dormant; but none for believing that it did not exist. The retrospective comment of the nuclear physicist Sir Rudolf Peierls that 'in pre-Hitler Germany, being Jewish was a bearable handicap' is close to the mark.[17]

Indeed I would argue that a principal reason why German Jews under-estimated the significance of Hitler's coming to power was not their delusions of symbiosis or utopian belief in German Idealism, but their familiarity with prejudice and discrimination. It was there, they had coped with it before and they could cope with it again. It was unfortunate, but it was not the end of the world. It is this consideration that should make us question, even if only as a working hypothesis, whether 1933 was such an unmistakable and absolute caesura. Three considerations could guide Jews on 30 January.

The first was that they had been there before. There had been several waves of anti-Semitism, even of mob violence, in the years since final emancipation: the wave of the late 1870s associated with Adolf Stoecker, that of the early 1890s associated with Otto Böckel and Hermann Ahlwardt, that of the First World War which culminated in the 'Jewish census' of the armed forces, and that of 1919–23 in the wake of defeat and the Revolution. Another was to be deplored, but it seemed, in the light of its predecessors, to be survivable.

The second consideration was that Jews had gained some experience of combating anti-Semitism, whether at the individual or collective level. Sir Rudolf Peierls recalled that learning to cope with anti-Semitism had been 'a good education'.[18] The *Verein zur Abwehr des Antisemitismus* and the *Centralverein deutscher Staatsbürger jüdischen Glaubens* had all remained active during the Weimar period. They had at least some friends in high places, mainly in the SPD, the DDP and the Republican defence league, *Reichsbanner Schwarz–Rot–Gold*, but also within the Catholic *Zentrum* and the National-Liberal DVP. Nor were they unaware of the rising tide of anti-Semitism after 1929, which caused them to collaborate more closely than before and even to include Zionist organizations in their joint efforts.[19] If they

17 Rudolf Peierls, *Bird of Passage. Recollections of A Physicist*, Princeton, NJ: Princeton University Press, 1985, p. 6.
18 Ibid., p. 6.
19 Arnold Paucker, *Der jüdische Abwehrkampf gegen Antisemitismus und National-sozialismus in den letzten Jahren der Weimarer Republik*, 2nd edn, Hamburg: Leibniz, 1969, pp. 42–4; Barbara Suchy, 'The Verein zur Abwehr des Antisemitismus (II) – From the First World War to its Dissolution in 1933', *LBYB* XXX (1985), esp. pp. 85–100.

were fairly late in reacting to Nazism as a special enemy, it was because they had, not unreasonably, identified the classical Right of the DNVP and the *Stahlhelm* as more dangerous.[20] What Jews did appreciate was that anti-Semitism was also anti-liberal and anti-democratic. The assault on the Jews was also, perhaps primarily, an assault on the Republic. It was therefore more important to defend the Republic than to identify specific enemies.

These two considerations could lead to a third, an under-estimate of Hitler and the Nazi movement, a fault that was not, after all, restricted to Jews and to be found across the political spectrum from Franz von Papen to Stalin. Wild threats were the stock-in-trade of the demagogue on the make. George Clare gives an excellent account of how these defence-mechanisms worked from afar, but not that afar, in Vienna.

We knew about his anti-Semitic tirades, of course; we knew about the 1933 anti-Jewish boycott, but ... having used anti-Semitism to help him achieve power, like so many demagogues before him, did Hitler have any choice but to allow his storm-troopers their field-day? Had we not been there before? What about Lueger's anti-Semitic speeches? They had sounded just like Hitler's. ... Had one Jew ever been physically harmed under Lueger? Hitler was a rabble-rouser, just like the young Lueger. Would he, now that he had achieved his ambition, behave any differently? In any case, Germany's powerful and traditional conservative forces were bound to make him toe the line. How servilely Hitler bows before the ramrod old field marshal. How disdainfully that old soldier looks down on that little man – the Bohemian lance-corporal, he calls him privately. ... The sound and fury of the early days could not last for ever. Even Hitler would have to mellow in the end. Political realities, last but not least the great powers, would see to it.[21]

The expectation was not so much that Germans would behave decently, but that they would behave in accordance with rational self-interest.

If that was a reasonable expectation in the immediate aftermath of Hitler's appointment as Chancellor, it became less and less so as time went on. It was clear that 1933 was not a *pogromchik* spasm, but the reversal of emancipation. True, it did not happen at once and at no stage did it happen systematically. That would have been contrary to the haphazard and arbitrary way policy evolved in the Third Reich. But, beginning with the proclamation of the *Gesetz zur Wiederherstellung des Berufsbeamtentums* (the 'Law for the Restoration of Professionalism in the Public Service') in April 1933, there was now a statutory basis for discrimination, as opposed to the informal one that had survived the 1869 law.

20   George L. Mosse, 'Die deutsche Rechte und die Juden', *Entscheidungsjahr 1932*, p. 233.
21   George Clare, *Last Waltz in Vienna. The Destruction of a Family 1842–1942*, London: Pan, 1982, pp. 121–2.

That was a major act of discontinuity. But the relative smoothness with which Jews were eased out of one sector after another of professional and economic life, the lack of protest against and opposition to discrimination in general, as opposed to specific instances of it, was evidence of continuity. It suggested all too convincingly that there had always been a widespread right-wing anti-Semitic consensus, that the emancipation of 1869 had never been whole-heartedly embraced by the German nation, that large sectors of German society would adapt painlessly to a 'post-liberal apartheid'.[22] There is little evidence of positive German support for persecution, let alone anti-Semitic violence, outside the ranks of Nazi activists. There is ample evidence of a relatively easy acceptance of pariah status for a significant section of German citizens.[23]

The effect of these painful events on the Jewish community was not uniform. Those who had most to lose from the end of the assimilationist process found the adjustment most difficult, and took longest to decide whether the coming of the Third Reich was a temporary setback to their aspirations or the final reversal of a liberal trend. It is therefore not surprising that Zionists, who had never believed in the dream of symbiosis, adapted more promptly to the new environment and found it easier to formulate a basis for co-existence with the Nazi authorities. Emigration to Palestine, which had not been a main policy plank of the majority faction in German Zionism before 1933, suddenly appeared an attractive option; as time went on even leading functionaries of the Liberal, anti-Zionist *Centralverein* became enthusiastic advocates of it. Partly because they offered emigration as a solution, partly because the Nazi authorities preferred dealing with them, partly simply because the turn of events seemed to have proved them right, Zionists gradually increased their influence in the unitary Jewish representative body, the *Reichsvereinigung der deutschen Juden* (later *der Juden in Deutschland, Reichsverband* after 1938, *Reichsvertretung* after 1939). Indeed, the very creation of such a body, voluntary in the first instance, was a victory for some and a defeat for others. All previous attempts at such unification had failed, thanks to the fragmentation of interests and ideology among German Jews. Up to half the Jewish population had no formal organizational affiliation, except to their congregation. For many others it was by no means self-evident that a single lobby was necessary or desirable; they had a 'liberal

---

22   Werner Mosse, 'German Jews: Citizens of the Republic', in Paucker, *The Jews in Nazi Germany*, p. 52.

23   See, e.g., Ian Kershaw, *Popular Opinion and Political Dissent in the Third Reich. Bavaria 1933–1945*, Oxford: Oxford University Press, 1983, pp. 224–77; Martin Broszat, 'Resistenz und Widerstand', in M. Broszat et al. (eds), *Bayern in der NS-Zeit*, vol. IV, Munich and Vienna: Oldenbourg, 1981.

distrust of uniformity', reinforcing their claim that they were private Jews and public Germans. 'It had required the full force of the totalitarian state to overcome the outward manifestations of German Jewry's internal differences.'[24]

Here, too, there was a tension between continuity and upheaval. The fact of a single representative body was new; the often bitter factional and personal disputes within it were not. Nor was the continuing autonomy of Jewish social organizations, whether in welfare, education or culture, which continued well beyond the constitution of the Nazi-imposed *Reichsvereinigung*.[25] The coming of the Third Reich resulted in a revival of Jewish communal activity in almost every sphere. A renewed emphasis on Jewish education and the learning of Hebrew, on participation in Jewish theatrical or sporting groups had a two-fold function. It was a rational response to increasing exclusion from German society, but it was also a rediscovery of identity, a form of perseverance and spiritual resistance. Most 'resistance' movements are not concerned with military heroics or physical sabotage, but with preserving, on an unofficial basis, a form of society or polity that is threatened by an imposed regime or alien occupier.[26] It is in this sense that Jews engaged in resistance to National Socialism rather than through any political conspiracy, doomed as that was by definition.

But this process was also gradual and incomplete. The strength of the impulse to resist depended on the degree of exclusion suffered. Where, as in rural areas, traditional anti-Semitism had never died down and the Jewish population was predominantly Orthodox, relatively little adjustment was needed. The limited contacts between Jews and Christians and the strong internal cohesion of the Jewish community meant that for much of the 1930s the conditions of life did not change radically. The Jewish population of Treuchtlingen, south of Nuremberg, declined very little between *Machtergreifung* and *Kristallnacht* – from 115 to 93. For the first five years of the Third Reich the cattle trade continued much as before.[27]

But even in urban areas disemancipation and the Aryanization of life

24   Donald L. Niewyk, *The Jews in Weimar Germany*, Baton Rouge: Louisiana State University Press, 1980, pp. 186, 194.

25   See Herbert A. Strauss, 'Jewish Autonomy Within the Limits of National Socialist Policy – The Communities and the Reichsvertretung', in Paucker, *The Jews in Nazi Germany*, pp. 125–52; on education, see Julius Carlebach, 'Orthodox Jewry in Germany: The Final Stages', in ibid., pp. 75–96.

26   There is an excellent discussion of this function of resistance in Jan T. Gross, *Polish Society Under German Occupation. The Generalgouvernement, 1939–1944*, Princeton, NJ: Princeton University Press, 1979.

27   Steven M. Lowenstein, 'The Struggle for Survival of Rural Jews 1933–38. The Case of Bezirksamt Weißenburg, Mittelfranken', in Paucker, *The Jews in Nazi Germany*, pp. 115–24.

proceeded fitfully and unsystematically. Pressures of one kind or another steadily reduced Jewish business activity even before legal discrimination was intensified at the end of 1937. By then over 60 per cent of Jewish enterprises had ceased to exist and large numbers of Jews were unemployed or in receipt of charity. On the other hand three Jewish-owned banks, including M. M. Warburg & Co, remained a member of the *Reichsanleihe-Konsortium* until 1938; medical and legal practice was open to Jews until that year – no doubt increasingly serving Jewish clients[28] – and a quarter of Jewish children still attended ordinary state schools.[29] George Clare, arriving in Berlin from the pogrom-like atmosphere of Vienna in the summer of 1938, was amazed to find Jews driving cars and frequenting cinemas and cafés. Only one shop in the whole of the Kurfürstendamm displayed the anti-Jewish sign that was almost universal in the Führer's native country.[30] The process of disemancipation and dissimilation was a mirror-image of that of emancipation and assimilation, even if telescoped. It was rarely consonant with the proclamation of the law. Sometimes economic or social exclusion preceded legislation, sometimes it lagged behind. It varied from place to place according to local traditions or the arbitrary behaviour of particular individuals.

'History', Tolstoy wrote to Nikolai Nikolaievich Gusev, 'would be an excellent thing, if only it were true.'[31] Need we face the years following the *Machtergreifung*, the beginning of the end of German Jewry, with the same incomprehension with which he – or at least his characters as portrayed by him – faced Ulm, Austerlitz or Borodino? Events have their causes, which does not mean that chains of events have only one possible outcome. Life for Jews was tolerable in the Empire and the Republic – for many it was distinctly good. They were, for better or worse, at home. It was the very imperfection of their existence that made them initially complacent about surviving even under Hitler. Here was another bout of hep! hep! that would come and go. That the only sane thing to do was to get out dawned on only a few after the April boycott of 1933 and the setting-up of the first concentration camps. That the new regime meant to make Germany *judenrein* was increasingly obvious once the Nuremberg Laws were in force. That a

---

28   A. Barkai, *Vom Boykott zur 'Entjudung'. Der wirtschaftliche Existenzkampf der Juden im Dritten Reich 1933–1943*, Frankfurt: Fischer, 1988, pp. 70–1, 87, 123, 133; E. Rosenbaum and A. J. Sherman, *M. M. Warburg & Co., 1798–1938, Merchant Bankers of Hamburg*, London: Hurst, 1979, p. 167.

29   Jacob Boas, 'German-Jewish Internal Politics under Hitler 1933–1939', *LBYB* XXIX (1984), p. 3.

30   Clare, *Last Waltz in Vienna*, p. 209.

31   Quoted by Isaiah Berlin, *The Hedgehog and the Fox. An Essay on Tolstoy's view of History*, New York: Mentor, 1957, p. 25.

physical holocaust was intended, even in Hitler's own mind at that stage, was far from evident.[32]

It was at that point that the encouragement of emigration became the official policy of Jewish representative bodies. This was a momentous decision. Up to and even beyond 1933 the primary function of all Jewish bodies in Germany had been the defence of the Jew in Germany, whether by emphasizing German patriotism, like the *Reichsbund jüdischer Frontsoldaten*, or engaging in counter-propaganda, like the *Centralverein*, or strengthening the inner consciousness of Jews, like the Zionists. But even the irrevocable change of climate affected Jews unevenly. Many made the final decision to emigrate only in 1938 or 1939. Not all of them found the re-entry into Jewish culture easy. A survey of Jewish youth in 1936 revealed that one of their favourite authors was Hermann Hesse.[33] Max Born, the Nobel Prize-winning physicist, was not alone in his desire to re-visit Germany after 1945 because of his 'inextinguishable homesickness for the German language and landscape'.[34] The 'fourth Reich' that established itself in Hampstead and Washington Heights, in Hollywood and Nahariya, with battered tomes of Lessing, Kant and Goethe and scratched records of Furtwängler and the Threepenny Opera, bore witness to the tenacity of roots in the German *Kulturnation*. But one way or another it was the end. The German-Jewish community survived, scattered and diminished; a community of Jews in Germany did not.

32   On the as yet unsettled question when a decision was made to implement a policy of genocide, see Martin Broszat, 'Hitler und die Genesis der "Endlösung"', *VfZ* (1977/4), pp. 739–75; Eberhard Jäckel and Jürgen Rohwer (eds), *Der Mord an den Juden im Zweiten Weltkrieg*, Stuttgart: Deutsche Verlags-Anstalt, 1985; Gerald Fleming, *Hitler and the Final Solution*, London: Oxford University Press, 1985; Christopher Browning, *Fateful Months. Essays on the Emergence of the Final Solution*, New York: Holmes & Meier, 1985; Michael Marrus, *The Holocaust in History*, Hanover, NH: University Press of New England, 1987.

33   Paucker, *The Jews in Nazi Germany*, p. 304.

34   Max Born, *My Life. Recollections of a Nobel Laureate*, London: Taylor & Francis, 1978, p. 281.

Bibliography

ARCHIVES

Bundesarchiv Koblenz
   P. 135/11 Justiz-Ministerium
   Kleine Erwerbungen (Bernhard Falk)
   Reichskanzlei
Nachlaß Gothein Geheimes Staatsarchiv, Dahlem
   Rep. 84a Justiz-Ministerium
   Rep. 90 Königliches Staatsministerium
   Nachlaß Ludwig Bamberger
Staatsarchiv Potsdam-Orangerie [since 1991: Brandenburgisches Landesarchiv]
   Pr. Br. Rep. 30, Polizeipräsident Brandenburg
Zentrales Staatsarchiv Merseburg [since 1991: Geheimes Staatsarchiv Kulturbesitz Merseburg]
   Rep. 77 Innenministerium
   Rep. 92 Rodbertus-Jagetzow
   Rep. 120 Handelsministerium
   2.2.1.   Geheimes Zivilkabinett
Zentrales Staatsarchiv Potsdam [since 1991: Bundesarchiv Potsdam]
   07.01 Reichskanzlei
   09.01 Auswärtiges Amt
   15.01 Reichsministerium des Inneren
   60 Re1 Deutschsoziale Reformpartei
   60 Ve1 Alldeutscher Verband
   60 Vo3 Fortschrittliche Volkspartei
   61 Re1 Reichslandbund

Central Archives of the History of the Jewish People, Jerusalem
  M1/9   Deutsch-Israelitischer Gemeindebund
  M1/15   do.
  M1/16   do.

NEWSPAPERS AND JOURNALS

Allgemeine Zeitung des Judentums
Berliner Revue
Berliner Tageblatt
Bulletin des Leo Baeck Instituts
Central European History
C.V. – Zeitung
Deutsche Israelitische Zeitung
Deutsche Justiz
Deutsche Reform
Deutsche Tageszeitung
Deutsche Zeitung
Frankfurter Zeitung
Germania
Die Gesellschaft
Hochland
Im deutschen Reich
Im Neuen Reich
Israelitisches Familienblatt
Israelitisches Gemeindeblatt
Jahrbuch des Instituts für Deutsche Geschichte/Jahrbuch für Deutsche Geschichte
Jewish Social Studies
Der Jude
Jüdische Rundschau
Kölnische Volkszeitung
Kölnische Zeitung
Kreuz-Zeitung
Der Kunstwart
Mitteilungen des Vereins zur Abwehr des Antisemitismus
Münchener Neueste Nachrichten
National-Zeitung
Neue Jüdische Monatshefte
Die Neue Zeit
Norddeutsche Allgemeine Zeitung
Der Orient
Die Post
Polin
Preußische Jahrbücher

Das Reich
Reichsbote
Rheinisch-Westfälische Zeitung
Sozialistische Monatshefte
Sozialistische Politik und Wirtschaft
Staatsbürger-Zeitung
Tägliche Rundschau
Der Treue Zionswächter
Vierteljahrshefte für Zeitgeschichte
Vorwärts
Vossische Zeitung
Year Book of the Leo Baeck Institute
Die Zeit
Die Zeitschrift
Zeitschrift für Geschichtswissenschaft
Zeitschrift für Politik
Die Zukunft

WORKS FREQUENTLY CITED

Adler, Friedrich (ed.), *Victor Adler. Briefwechsel mit Friedrich Engels und Karl Kautsky*, Vienna: Braumüller, 1954.
Albertin, Lothar, *Liberalismus und Demokratie am Anfang der Weimarer Republik*, Düsseldorf: Droste, 1972.
Angress, Werner T., 'Prussia's Army and the Reserve Officer Controversy Before World War I', *LBYB* XVII (1972).
Angress, Werner T., '"Between Baden and Luxemburg" – Jewish Socialists on the Eve of World War I', *LBYB* XXII (1977).
Angress, Werner T., 'The German Army's "Judenzählung" of 1916 – Genesis – Consequences – Significance', *LBYB* XXIII (1978).
Angress Werner T., 'The Impact of the "Judenwahlen" of 1912 on the Jewish Question – A Synthesis', *LBYB* XXVIII (1983).
Anti-Anti. Tatsachen zur Judenfrage (ed. Centralverein deutscher Staatsbürger jüdischen Glaubens), Berlin: Philo, 6th edn, 1932; 7th edn., 1932.
Aschheim, Steven E., *Brothers and Strangers. The East European Jew in German and German Jewish Consciousness, 1800–1923*, Madison, Wis.: University of Wisconsin Press, 1982.
Bachem, Karl, *Vorgeschichte, Geschichte und Politik der deutschen Zentrumspartei*, Cologne: J. P. Bachem, 1927–32.
Bamberger, Ludwig, *Erinnerungen*, (ed. Paul Nathan), Berlin: Georg Reimer, 1899.
Beer, Udo, *Die Juden, das Recht und die Republik. Verbandswesen und Rechtsschutz, 1919–1933*, Frankfurt: Lang, 1986.
Beer, Udo, 'The Protection of Jewish Civil Rights in the Weimar Republic. Jewish Self-Defence through Legal Action', *LBYB* XXXIII (1988).

Beradt, Charlotte, *Paul Levi. Ein demokratischer Sozialist in der Weimarer Republik*, Frankfurt: Europäische Verlagsanstalt, 1969.

Bertram, Jürgen, *Die Wahlen zum deutschen Reichstag vom Jahre 1912*, Düsseldorf: Droste, 1964.

Bismarck, Otto von, *Die gesammelten Werke*, Berlin: Stollberg, 1924ff.

Blankenberg, Heinz, *Politischer Katholizismus in Frankfurt am Main 1918–1933*, Mainz: Matthias Grünewald Verlag, 1981.

Boehlich, Walter (ed.), *Der Berliner Antisemitismusstreit*, Frankfurt: Insel-Verlag, 1964.

Böhme, Helmut, *Deutschlands Weg zur Großmacht. Studien zum Verhältnis von Wirtschaft und Staat während der Reichsgründungszeit*, Cologne: Kiepenheuer & Wietsch, 1966.

Borgius, Walther, *Der Handelsvertragsverein. Ein Rückblick auf die ersten drei Jahre seiner Tätigkeit*, Berlin: F. Siemenroth, 1903.

Breslauer, Walter, 'Der Verband der Deutschen Juden 1904–1922', *BLBI* 28 (1964).

Breuer, Mordechai, *Jüdische Orthodoxie im deutschen Reich, 1871–1918. Sozialgeschichte einer religiösen Minderheit*, Frankfurt: Athenäum-Jüdischer Verlag, 1986.

Brüning, Heinrich, *Memoiren 1918–1934*, Stuttgart: Deutsche Verlags-Anstalt, 1970.

Bülow, Bernhard Fürst von, *Denkwürdigkeiten*, Berlin: Ullstein, 1930.

Busch, Moritz, *Tagebuchblätter*, Leipzig: Grunow, 1888–9.

Cecil, Lamar, *Albert Ballin. Business and Politics in Imperial Germany, 1888–1918*, Princeton, NJ: Princeton University Press, 1967.

Chickering, Roger, *We Men Who Feel Most German. A Cultural Study of the Pan-German League, 1886–1914*, London: Allen & Unwin, 1984.

Cohen, Hermann, *Jüdische Schriften* (ed. Bruno Strauss), Berlin: C. A. Schwetschke, 1924.

Dubnow, Simon, *Die neueste Geschichte des jüdischen Volkes*, Berlin: Jüdischer Verlag, 1920.

Dunker, Ulrich, *Der Reichsbund jüdischer Frontsoldaten 1919–1938. Geschichte eines jüdischen Abwehrvereins*, Düsseldorf: Droste, 1977.

Erb, Rainer, and Michael Schmidt (eds), *Antisemitismus und jüdische Geschichte. Studien zu Ehren von Herbert A. Strauss*, Berlin: Wissenschaftlicher Autoren-Verlag, 1987.

Feder, Ernst (ed.), *Bismarcks großes Spiel. Die geheimen Tagebücher Ludwig Bambergers*, Frankfurt: Societäts-Verlag, 1933.

Feder, Ernst, *Heute sprach ich mit... Tagebücher eines Berliner Publizisten 1926–1932* (ed. Cécile Lowenthal-Hensel and Arnold Paucker), Stuttgart: Deutsche Verlags-Anstalt, 1971.

Fischer, Fritz, *Griff nach der Weltmacht. Die Kriegszielpolitik des kaiserlichen Deutschland 1914–1918*, 3rd edn, Düsseldorf: Droste, 1964.

Frank, Walter, *Hofprediger Adolf Stoecker und die christlichsoziale Bewegung*, 2nd edn, Hamburg: Hanseatische Verlagsanstalt, 1935.

Frankel, Jonathan et al. (eds), *Studies in Contemporary Jewry IV*, New York: Oxford University Press, 1988.

Freund, Ismar, *Die Emanzipation der Juden in Preußen unter besonderer Berück-*

sichtigung des Gesetzes vom 11. März 1812. Ein Beitrag zur Rechtsgeschichte der Juden in Preußen, Berlin: M. Poppelauer, 1912.

Frye, Bruce B., *Liberal Democrats in the Weimar Republic. The History of the German Democratic Party and the German State Party*, Carbondale and Edwardsville: Southern Illinois University Press, 1985.

Gilbert, Felix (ed.), *Bankiers, Fürsten und Gelehrte. Unveröffentlichte Briefe der Familie Mendelssohn aus dem 19. Jahrhundert*, Tübingen: J. C. B. Mohr, 1975.

Goldschmidt, Adele (ed.), *Levin Goldschmidt. Ein Lebensbild in Briefen*, Berlin: E. Goldschmidt, 1898.

Grab, Walter, and Julius H. Schoeps (eds), *Juden in der Weimarer Republik*, Stuttgart and Bonn: Burg Verlag, 1986.

Hachenburg, Max, *Lebenserinnerungen eines Rechtsanwalts und Briefe aus der Emigration* (ed. Jörg Schadt), Stuttgart: Kohlhammer, 1978.

Hagen, William H., *Germans, Poles and Jews. The Nationality Conflict in the Prussian East, 1772–1914*, Chicago: University of Chicago Press, 1980.

Hallgarten, George W. F., *Imperialismus vor 1914. Die soziologischen Grundlagen der Außenpolitik europäischer Großmächte vor dem ersten Weltkrieg*, 2nd edn, Munich: C. H. Beck, 1963.

Hamburger, Ernest, *Juden im öffentlichen Leben Deutschlands. Regierungsmitglieder, Beamte und Parlamentarier in der monarchischen Zeit, 1848–1918*, Tübingen: J. C. B. Mohr, 1968.

Hamburger, Ernest, 'Hugo Preuß. Scholar and Statesman', *LBYB* XX (1975).

Harris, James F., *A Study in the Theory and Practice of German Liberalism. Eduard Lasker, 1829–1884*, Lanham, MD: University Press of America, 1984.

Hartenstein, Wolfgang, *Die Anfänge der Deutschen Volkspartei, 1918–1920*, Düsseldorf: Droste, 1962.

Heppner, Aaron, *Jüdische Persönlichkeiten in und aus Breslau*, Breslau: Schatzky, 1931.

Heppner, Aron, and Isaak Herzberg, *Aus Vergangenheit und Gegenwart der Juden und der jüdischen Gemeinden in den Posener Landen*, Koschmin and Breslau: J. Tuch, 1904–29.

Heppner, Aron, and Isaak Herzberg, *Aus Vergangenheit und Gegenwart der Juden in Posen (Stadt)*, Koschmin: J. Tuch, 1914.

Heyderhoff, Julius, and Paul Wentzke (eds), *Deutscher Liberalismus im Zeitalter Bismarcks. Eine politische Briefsammlung*, Bonn: K. Schroeder, 1925–6.

Hornung, Klaus, *Der Jungdeutsche Orden*, Düsseldorf: Droste, 1958.

Huldermann, Bernhard, *Albert Ballin*, 2nd edn, Oldenburg and Berlin: Stalling, 1922.

Jäger, Hans, *Unternehmer in der deutschen Politik (1890–1918)*, Bonn: Röhrscheid, 1967.

Kaelble, Hartmut, *Industrielle Interessenpolitik in der Wilhelminischen Gesellschaft (CVDI 1895–1914)*, Berlin: de Gruyter, 1967.

Kampe, Norbert, *Studenten und 'Judenfrage' im Deutschen Kaiserrech. Die Entstehung einer akademischen Trägerschicht des Antisemitismus*, Göttingen: Vandenhoeck & Ruprecht, 1988.

Kaznelson, Siegmund (ed.), *Juden im deutschen Kulturbereich. Ein Sammelwerk*, 2nd edn, Berlin: Jüdischer Verlag, 1959.

356 *Bibliography*

159Kehr, Eckhart, *Der Primat der Innenpolitik. Gesammelte Aufsätze zur preußisch-deutschen Sozialgeschichte im 19. und 20. Jahrhundert* (ed. Hans-Ulrich Wehler), Berlin: de Gruyter, 1965.

Knütter, Hans-Helmut, *Die Juden und die deutsche Linke in der Weimarer Republik*, Düsseldorf: Droste, 1971.

Krohn, Helga, *Die Juden in Hamburg. Die politische, soziale und kulturelle Entwicklung einer jüdischen Großstadtgemeinde*, Hamburg: Christians, 1974.

Lamberti, Marjorie, 'The Prussian Government and the Jews: Official Behaviour and Policy-Making in the Wilhelminian Era', *LB YB* XVII (1972).

Lamberti, Marjorie, *Jewish Activism in Imperial Germany. The Struggle for Civil Equality*, New Haven, Conn., and London: Yale University Press, 1978.

Lamberti, Marjorie, 'Liberals, Socialists and the Defence Against Anti-Semitism in the Wilhelmine Period', *LB YB* XXV (1980).

Lamm, Hans (ed.), *Von Juden in München*, Munich: Ner-Tamid, 1958.

Lehmann, Emil, *Gesammelte Schriften*, Dresden: C. Weiske, 1899.

Lestschinsky, Jakob, *Das wirtschaftliche Schicksal des deutschen Judentums: Aufstieg, Wandlung, Krise, Ausblick*, Berlin: Zentralwohlfahrtsstelle der deutschen Juden, 1932.

Lohalm, Uwe, *Völkischer Radikalismus. Die Geschichte des Deutschvölkischen Schutz- und Trutzbundes, 1919–1923*, Hamburg: Leibniz, 1970.

Lorenzen, Sievert, *Die Juden in der Justiz*, 2nd edn, Berlin: Deckert, 1943.

Matthias, Erich, and Rudolf Morsey (eds), *Das Ende der Parteien 1933*, Düsseldorf: Droste, 1960.

Matthias, Erich, and Eberhard Pikart (eds), *Die Reichstagsfraktion der deutschen Sozialdemokratie*, Düsseldorf: Droste, 1966.

Maurer, Trude, *Ostjuden in Deutschland 1918–1933*, Hamburg: Christians, 1986.

Mendelssohn, Moses, *Moses Mendelssohn's Gesammelte Schriften. Nach den Originaldrucken und Handschriften* (ed. G. B. Mendelssohn), Leipzig: Brockhaus, 1843–5.

Miller, Susanne (ed.), *Das Kriegstagebuch des Reichstagsabgeordneten Eduard David*, Düsseldorf: Droste, 1966.

Miller, Susanne, *Burgfrieden und Klassenkampf. Die deutsche Sozialdemokratie im Weltkrieg*, Düsseldorf: Droste, 1974.

Morsey, Rudolf, *Die deutsche Zentrumspartei 1917–1923*, Düsseldorf: Droste, 1966.

Mosse, Werner E., *Jews in the German Economy. The German-Jewish Economic Elite, 1820–1935*, Oxford: Oxford University Press, 1987.

Mosse, Werner E., *The German-Jewish Economic Elite, 1820–1935. A Socio-Cultural Profile*, Oxford: Oxford University Press, 1989.

Mosse, Werner, and Arnold Paucker (eds), *Entscheidungsjahr 1932. Zur Judenfrage in der Endphase der Weimarer Republik*, Tübingen: J. C. B. Mohr, 1965.

Mosse, Werner, and Arnold Paucker (eds), *Deutsches Judentum in Krieg und Revolution, 1916–1923*, Tübingen: J. C. B. Mohr, 1971.

Mosse, Werner, and Arnold Paucker (eds), *Juden im wilhelminischen Deutschland 1890–1914*, Tübingen: J. C. B. Mohr, 1976.

Mosse, Werner, Arnold Paucker and Reinhard Rürup (eds), *Revolution and Evolution. 1848 in German-Jewish History*, Tübingen: J. C. B. Mohr, 1981.

Niewyk, Donald L., *Socialist, Anti-Semite and Jews. German Social Democracy Confronts the Problem of Anti-Semitism*, Baton Rouge: Louisiana State University Press, 1971.

Niewyk, Donald L., *The Jews in Weimar Germany*, Baton Rouge: Louisiana State University Press, 1980.

Nipperdey, Thomas, *Die Organisation der deutschen Parteien vor 1918*, Düsseldorf: Droste, 1961.

Noske, Gustav, *Aufstieg und Niedergang der deutschen Sozialdemokratie. Erlebtes aus Aufstieg und Untergang einer Demokratie*, Zürich and Offenbach: Aeroverlag, 1947.

Paucker, Arnold, *Der jüdische Abwehrkampf gegen Antisemitismus und Nationalsozialismus in den letzten Jahren der Weimarer Republik*, 2nd edn, Hamburg: Leibniz, 1969.

Paucker, Arnold (ed.), *The Jews in Nazi Germany, 1933–1943*, Tübingen: J. C. B. Mohr, 1987.

Philippson, Martin, *Neueste Geschichte des jüdischen Volkes*, 2nd edn, Frankfurt: J. Kauffmann, 1922–30.

Pogge von Strandmann, Hartmut, and Immanuel Geiss, *Die Erforderlichkeit des Unmöglichen. Deutschland am Vorabend des ersten Weltkrieges*, Frankfurt: Europäische Verlags-Anstalt, 1965.

Pois, Robert, *The Bourgeois Democrats of Weimar Germany*, Philadelphia: The American Philosophical Society, 1976.

Pulzer, Peter, *The Rise of Political Anti-Semitism in Germany and Austria*, rev. edn, London: Peter Halban, 1988.

Rathenau, Walther, *Gesammelte Schriften*, 6 vols, Berlin: S. Fischer, 1918.

Reinharz, Jehuda, *Fatherland or Promised Land. The Dilemma of the German Jew, 1893–1914*, Ann Arbor, Mich.: University of Michigan Press, 1975.

Reinharz, Jehuda, and Walter Schatzberg (eds), *The Jewish Response to German Culture. From the Enlightenment to the Second World War*, Hanover NH: New England University Press, 1986.

Rengstorf, Karl Heinrich, and Siegfried von Kortzfleisch (eds), *Kirche und Synagoge. Handbuch zur Geschichte von Christen und Juden*, Stuttgart: Ernst Klett, 1970.

Richarz, Monika, *Der Eintritt der Juden in die akademischen Berufe. Jüdische Studenten und Akademiker in Deutschland, 1678–1848*, Tübingen, J. C. B. Mohr, 1974.

Richarz, Monika (ed.), *Jüdisches Leben in Deutschland. Selbstzeugnisse zur Sozialgeschichte des Kaiserreichs*, Stuttgart: Deutsche Verlags-Anstalt, 1979–82.

Riesser, Gabriel, *Gesammelte Schriften*, 4 vols, Frankfurt: Riesser-Stiftung, 1867–8.

Riff, Michael, 'The Government of Baden against Antisemitism. Political Expediency or Principle?', *LBYB* XXXII (1987).

Rosenbaum, Eduard, and A. J. Sherman, *M. M. Warburg & Co., 1798–1938. Merchant Bankers of Hamburg*, London: Hurst, 1979.

Rürup, Reinhard, *Emanzipation und Antisemitismus. Studien zur 'Judenfrage' der bürgerlichen Gesellschaft*, Göttingen: Vandenhoeck & Ruprecht, 1975.

Schmoller, Gustav, *Zwanzig Jahre deutscher Politik, 1897–1917*, Munich and Leipzig: Duncker & Humblot, 1920.

Schorsch, Ismar, *Jewish Reactions to German Anti-Semitism, 1870–1914*, New York, London and Philadelphia: Columbia University Press, 1972.

Schulz, Birger, *Der Republikanische Richterbund (1921–1933)*, Frankfurt and Berne: Lang, 1982.

Schwabach, Paul von, *Aus meinen Akten*, Berlin: Flemming & Wiskott, 1927.

Schwerin, Kurt, 'Die Juden in Schlesien. Aus ihrer Geschichte und ihrem Beitrag zu Wirtschaft und Kultur', *BLBI* 56/7 (1980).

Sombart, Werner, *Die Juden und das Wirtschaftsleben*, Leipzig: Duncker & Humblot, 1911.

Sorkin, David, *The Transformation of German Jewry, 1780–1840*, Oxford: Oxford University Press, 1987.

Stampfer, Friedrich, *Erfahrungen und Erkenntnisse. Aufzeichnungen aus meinem Leben*, Cologne: Verlag für Politik und Wirtschaft, 1957.

Stegmann, Dirk, *Die Erben Bismarcks. Parteien und Verbände in der Spätphase des wilhelminischen Deutschlands*, Cologne and Berlin: Kiepenheuer & Wietsch, 1970.

Stephan, Werner, *Aufstieg und Verfall des Linksliberalismus, 1918–1933*, Göttingen: Vandenhoeck & Ruprecht, 1973.

Stern, Fritz, *Gold and Iron. Bismarck, Bleichröder and the Building of the German Empire*, London: Allen & Unwin, 1977.

Stern, Rudolf A., 'Fritz Haber. Personal Recollections', *LBYB* VIII (1963).

Strauss, Herbert A. (ed.), *Conference on Anti-Semitism 1969*, New York: American Federation of Jews from Central Europe, 1969.

Stürmer, Michael, Gabriele Teichmann and Wilhelm Treue, *Wägen und Wagen. Sal. Oppenheim jr. & Cie. Geschichte einer Bank und einer Familie*, Munich: Piper, 1989.

Suchy, Barbara, 'The Verein zur Abwehr des Antisemitismus (I) – From its Beginnings to the First World War', *LBYB* XXVIII (1983).

Suchy, Barbara, 'The Verein zur Abwehr des Antisemitismus (II) – From the First World War to its Dissolution in 1933' *LBYB* XXX (1985).

Toury, Jacob, 'Der Anteil der Juden an der städtischen Selbstverwaltung im vormärzlichen Deutschland', *BLBI* 23 (1963).

Toury, Jacob, *Die politischen Orientierungen der Juden in Deutschland. Von Jena bis Weimar*, Tübingen: J. C. B. Mohr, 1966.

Toury, Jacob, *Soziale und politische Geschichte der Juden in Deutschland 1847–1871. Zwischen Revolution, Reaktion und Emanzipation*, Düsseldorf: Droste, 1977.

Treitschke, Heinrich von, *Deutsche Geschichte im Neunzehnten Jahrhundert*, Leipzig: S. Hirzel, 1878–94.

Treue, Wolfgang (ed.), *Deutsche Parteiprogramme seit 1861*, 4th edn, Göttingen: Musterschmidt, 1968.

Vagts, Alfred, 'M. M. Warburg & Co. Ein Bankhaus in der deutschen Weltpolitik', *Vierteljahresschrift für Sozial- und Wirtschaftsgeschichte*, 45 (1958).

Vierhaus, Rudolf (ed.), *Das Tagebuch der Baronin Spitzemberg*, Göttingen: Vandenhoeck & Ruprecht, 1961.

Vierhaus, Rudolf, *Deutschland im 18. Jahrhundert. Politische Verfassung, soziales Gefüge, geistige Bewegungen*, Göttingen, Vandenhoeck & Ruprecht, 1987.

Warburg, Max M., *Aus meinen Aufzeichnungen*, New York, 1952.

Weber, Max, *Economy and Society. An Outline of Interpretive Sociology* (ed. Guenther Roth and Claus Wittich), New York: Bedminster Press, 1968.

Wegner, Konstanze (ed.), *Linksliberalismus in der Weimarer Republik. Die Führungsgremien der Deutschen Demokratischen Partei und der Deutschen Staatspartei 1918–1933*, Düsseldorf: Droste, 1980.

Wehler, Hans-Ulrich, *Bismarck und der Imperialismus*, Cologne: Westdeutscher Verlag, 1969.

Wenzel, Stefi, *Jüdische Bürger und kommunale Selbstverwaltung in preußischen Städten, 1808–1848*, Berlin: Colloquium-Verlag, 1967.

Wernecke, Klaus, *Der Wille zur Weltgeltung. Außenpolitik und Öffentlichkeit im Kaiserreich am Vorabend des Ersten Weltkrieges*, Düsseldorf: Droste, 1970.

Wertheimer, Jack, *Unwelcome Strangers. East European Jews in Imperial Germany*, New York: Oxford University Press, 1987.

Young, Harry F., *Censor Germaniae. The Critic in Opposition from Bismarck to the Rise of Nazism*, The Hague: Nijhoff, 1959.

Zechlin, Egmont, *Die deutsche Politik und die Juden im ersten Weltkrieg*, Göttingen: Vandenhoeck & Ruprecht, 1969.

Zucker, Stanley, *Ludwig Bamberger. German Liberal Politician and Social Critic, 1823–1899*, Pittsburgh, PA: University of Pittsburgh Press, 1975.

Index